On the Edge

ON THE EDGE

Baptists and Other Free Church Evangelicals
in Tsarist Russia, 1855–1917

ALBERT W. WARDIN JR.

WIPF & STOCK · Eugene, Oregon

ON THE EDGE
Baptists and Other Free Church Evangelicals in Tsarist Russia, 1855–1917

Copyright © 2013 Albert W. Wardin Jr. All rights reserved. Except for brief quotations in critical publications or reviews, no part of this book may be reproduced in any manner without prior written permission from the publisher. Write: Permissions, Wipf and Stock Publishers, 199 W. 8th Ave., Suite 3, Eugene, OR 97401.

Wipf & Stock
An Imprint of Wipf and Stock Publishers
199 W. 8th Ave., Suite 3
Eugene, OR 97401

www.wipfandstock.com

ISBN 13: 978-1-62032-962-7

Manufactured in the U.S.A.

Contents

Foreword by Gregory L. Nichols | *vii*
Preface | *ix*

PART ONE: Prologue

1. The Russian Empire at Mid-Century | 3
2. The Protestant Presence | 9
3. The German Baptist Movement | 19

PART TWO: Prospects: German and Baltic Beginnings, 1855–1884

4. Baptists Beginnings in the Baltic | 29
5. German Baptists in Russian Poland and Volhynia | 47
6. Emergence of the Mennonite Brethren | 55
7. Mennonite Brethren and German Baptist Relations | 68
8. Mennonite Brethren and German Baptists: Identity and Stability | 78

PART THREE: Prospects: Ukrainian and Russian Beginnings, 1860–1884

9. The Stundist Movement: Preparation and Obstacles | 93
10. Ukrainian Stundism | 101
11. Stundo-Baptism, Mladostundism, and State Relations | 111
12. The Stundist/Stundo-Baptist Community | 132
13. Baptists from the Caucasus | 151

PART FOUR: Prospects: The Aristocratic Impulse, 1874–1884

14. The Radstock Phenomenon | 169
15. Pashkovite Ascendancy | 177
16. Pashkovite Denouement | 187

Contents

PART FIVE: Peril, 1884–1905

17 The Attack | 203
18 The Suppression | 215
19 Evangelical Substratum | 232
20 Survival | 249
21 Tolerated Confession: Mennonite Brethren, 1885–1905 | 286
22 Tolerated Confession: German and Baltic Baptists, 1885–1905 | 295

PART SIX: Possibilities and Uncertainties, 1905–1917

23 The Russian Baptist Union: The New Era, 1905–1908 | 325
24 The Russian Baptist Union: The Era of Reaction, 1909–1914 | 334
25 The Rivals: Baptists and Evangelical Christians | 364
26 Theological Education: The Problems | 389
27 Mennonite Brethren: Prosperous and Challenged, 1905–1914 | 406
28 German and Baltic Baptists: Growth and Stability, 1905–1914 | 424
29 Evangelical Agencies and Other Religious Bodies | 448
30 War and Revolution, 1914–1917 | 475

Images | 495
Maps | 499
Bibliography | 501
Periodicals | 517
Index | 521

Foreword

ON THE EDGE PROVIDES a comprehensive view into the history of the free-church movement in the Slavic cultures from 1855 through 1917. The book not only presents the facts in a logical order but offers unique backgrounds into many of the events as well as unrecorded biographical snippets on the lives of the people involved. Other writers have taken pieces of the story, such as a geographical location or a denominational history, and explored its part in light of the whole. Few could do what Dr. Albert Wardin Jr. has done in this book by weaving all the researchable individuals, groups, and locations into one cohesive story.

Albert W. Wardin, professor emeritus of history at Belmont University, is one who is deeply acquainted with the material. His bibliographic guide *Evangelical Sectarianism in the Russian Empire and the USSR* and his numerous books and articles have provided many with foundational research in this area. You will find as you read this book that he takes a fresh opportunity to expand and detail events in a way that he has not previously felt the freedom to do. *On the Edge* teases out the fine details of many of the events, denominations, and personalities of the evangelical movement in the Slavic culture. He brings in the role of the state churches such as the Lutheran Church as German immigrants moved into a Slavic context. He fills in the story by presenting often-unrecognized participants such as the Moravians and the Armenians. He traces worship patterns and activities of communities showing distinctions and similarities to counterparts in non-Slavic contexts. There is a passion in Wardin as he tells the story. This passion was kindled at an early age as he explored the life of a distant relative of his, Gottfried Alf. His original research revealed that Alf was actually the founder of Baptist work in Poland and the first German Baptist minister in the Russian Empire. From that early research, Wardin has been relentless in his pursuit of the story of evangelicals in the Slavic countries. He has a unique ability to keep a vast number of facts and details in their historic perspective, easily moving present day geographic boundaries to previous locations, accurately conveying the twist and turns of history. He is able to communicate the historic political situations well as he explains the effects of the changing laws and powers on the lives of immigrants, peasants, and nobility.

For those looking to gain an understanding of the free-church movement in the Slavic context, you will find this book to be comprehensive and all inclusive. For those that know this area well, you will be surprised and intrigued by Wardin's coverage of well rehearsed topics such as theological education, for example his explanation of the role played by the Alliance Bible School in Berlin. You will read of the inner tensions of the first Baptist church in Tiflis. You will find remarkable details of the lives of well known people such as Wieler, Pashkov and Kargel but you will also learn of events behind often overlooked people such as Skvortsov, Urshan and Wüst. You may also discover new areas for further research in the section which highlights mission efforts to Muslims, tracing the lives of Plymouth Brethren, German Mennonites and Lutherans in Turkestan.

One of the most remarkable points of this book will be the work that Wardin has done with his comprehensive explanation of the Stundist movement. This book explores the critical question regarding the indigenous nature of the evangelical movement in the Slavic culture. This question has been tossed back and forth by those either trying to prove that evangelicals have no legitimate claim to a Slavic heritage or that an evangelical expression of Christianity sprang from Slavic stock. Many have taken bits and pieces of this story to highlight or downplay the indigenous nature of the Stundist movement. Wardin gathers them all together, organizes them and logically places them into the story. He gives attention to the details and the background stories of well-known Stundists like Ryaboshapka and Ratushnyï as well as drawing into the story unknown events and personalities. Wardin goes to great length to show the subtle differences between Stundism and Stundo-Baptism and the distinct history of German Stundism, Russian Stundism and Ukrainian Stundism. Wardin brings conclusive research to the table which will shape the research of the indigenous nature of evangelicals in the Slavic context for years to come.

Many researchers have used the impressive collection of the Southern Baptist Historical Library and Archives in Nashville as they have researched various aspects of this and similar movements. Some have identified useful material and been told that they would have to wait a few hours until it was collected from Dr. Wardin. Others have had the pleasure to be invited to his house to collect it personally. Those of us who have had the memorable experience of climbing the stairs into his attic office will always remember the mind-boggling experience of seeing the immense amount of archives, books and original papers that he keeps at his finger tips. There is now an Albert W. Wardin Jr. Research Room at the Southern Baptist Convention's Historical Library and Archives commemorating Dr. Wardin's passionate desire to uncover accurately the stories of evangelicals. I am deeply grateful to God for the blessing He has provided as this book and others by Dr Wardin have helped many to trace God's footprints in history.

Gregory L. Nichols, PhD
International Baptist Theological Seminary
Prague, 2013

Preface

THE VOLUME IS AN account of the penetration and development of a Protestant Free Church movement in the Russian Empire. In Russian historiography, it is considered a sectarian movement. It was a revival movement that stressed personal conversion and believer's baptism, whose mode in most cases was immersion. Its leaders rejected state established churches with their infant baptism and membership that included both converted and unconverted. It was anti-sacerdotal and anti-sacramental, rejecting sacraments as conduits of grace.

The movement looked upon Russia as a mission field. With its aggressive evangelism, it found itself on the edge of Russian society. It sought members from bodies with inclusive memberships whether Russian Orthodox, Russian sectarians, or Protestants, such as Lutherans or Old Mennonites. The Russian government and the Russian Orthodox Church regarded the movement as heretical and a threat to the unity of the state. The regime attempted to suppress it or place it under strict regulation. The movement also met strong resistance from other Protestants or Russian sectarians who felt threatened by it.

Because of cultural differences the movement was divided between its German and Slavic members. Germans were either members of the German Baptist Union (or the Union of Baptist Churches of Russia) or the Mennonite Brethren. The Slavic members, who were at first Ukrainian stundists, or Baptist converts from the Molokans or Orthodox, or Pashkovites, became in time members of the Russian Baptist Union or the Evangelical Christian Union. The four groups were one in doctrine and polity except that Mennonite Brethren continued to maintain certain Mennonite distinctives. The four bodies interacted among each other and at times found opportunities of mutual support. Much smaller evangelical groups also appeared among the German and more likely the Slavic population. They were primarily imports from the West, which were either cooperative or competitive with Baptists or Mennonite Brethren.

The work raises numerous issues that have not been adequately explored in general histories. To what extent was the Slavic part of the movement indigenous or simply a foreign import? German Baptists and Mennonite Brethren recognized, of course, their German or Dutch antecedents, but Slavic evangelicals have wrestled with the problem.

Another issue is the aggressive evangelism of the Free Church evangelicals. Were their attacks counter productive and brought on them unnecessary opposition? What factors enabled the Slavic Stundo-Baptists and Pashkovites to survive and even grow during the period of intense oppression from 1884 to 1905? To what extent did evangelical agencies and churches in the West further the Free Church movement? What role did liberals within Russia advance its cause?

To what extent were the two German bodies indigenous to Russia itself? What were their relations to the Russian state? What were their relations with other evangelicals? Even though both gained toleration rather early, how did they fare in a growing environment of anti-German sentiment? What were the tensions among Mennonite Brethren who adopted Baptist principles and were one in communion with Baptists but at the same time tried to maintain Mennonite distinctives while refusing to commune with other Mennonites?

What were the factors that produced such intense rivalry between the Russian Baptist Union and Evangelical Christian Union? What were the relations among their leaders?

Although Russian Orthodox researchers regarded the Free Church evangelical movement as a whole, today authors both West and East tend to write on separate entities within the movement, failing to recognize the links with the other bodies. Western and Russian authors tend to write only on the Russian Baptist Union, Evangelical Christians only on Evangelical Christians, and Mennonites only on Mennonites. In addition, the minor evangelical bodies are overlooked.

Much of the work is based on primary sources, such as official documents, articles and reports in periodicals, and the memoirs, letters, and speeches of church leaders. It uses not only evangelical sources but also material from their Orthodox and German Lutheran opponents. The sources are primarily in English, Russian, and German but also include in translation Swedish, Latvian, and Estonian.

The work is more than a recital of administrative development and the relationships of church and state. It seeks to set the Free Church movement in the context of the times. It includes theology, congregational life, internal tensions, pastoral leadership, theological education, state relations, and statistical data. The work is divided into six section, each a self-contained entity.

Much of the work is based on documents that I gathered since 1970. I published this material in my earlier work, *Evangelical Sectarianism in the Russian Empire and the USSR: A Bibliographic Guide*. With periodical references, this work included around 11,000 entries. I had gained a special interest in Russian Baptist history since the maternal branch of my family migrated in 1893 to America from Ukraine and included a great-great grand uncle, Gottfried Alf, who was founder of the Baptists in Russian Poland in 1858.

The author is indebted to Johannes Dyck, one of the three authors of the Russian Baptist work in 1989, *Istoriya Evangel'skikh khristian-baptistov v SSSR*, who read the manuscript and provided helpful corrections and endorsed the effort. I am also grateful to Bill Sumners, director and archivist, Taffey Hall, archivist, and Michelle Herr, archival assistant, at the Southern Baptist Historical Library and Archives in Nashville for their technical assistance.

PART ONE

Prologue

1

The Russian Empire At Mid-Century

IN THE MIDDLE OF the nineteenth century, Russia was a leading world power. The empire incorporated Russian Poland and the Baltic in the west, Bessarabia and Ukraine in the south, crossed the Caucasus Mountains toward Turkey and Persia, and traversed the Ural Mountains into Siberia and on to the Far East on the Pacific Ocean. At this time it also included Alaska on the North American continent. Although selling Alaska to the USA in 1867, its expansion continued into Central Asia during the latter half of the nineteenth century. By the turn of the century, it incorporated 8,600,000 square miles, while Europe to the west had less than half the area.

Much of its terrritory was a vast plain, lacking the geographical variety of Western Europe. Distances were vast. Its climate was continental, beset with extremes—cold winters and hot summers. Rainfall was adequate in northern regions but decreased farther south, becoming desert in Central Asia. The tundra, a treeless area, prevailed in the north, followed farther south by a forest region and then to steppes with its excellent black earth. In contrast to the rest of Europe with its maritime climate and variety of soil and vegetation, Russia was monolithic, separate in its own distinct Eurasian world. In spite of its vast size, its limited access to the Atlantic Ocean and lack of ice-free ports isolated it from much of the world.[1]

---

1. For a description of Russia's distinct geographical features, see Parker, *An Historical Geography of Russia*, 13–29.

PART ONE—Prologue

THE PEOPLE

The population of the Empire in 1850 was about sixty-seven million but its density was only twelve persons per square kilometer, an eighth of Great Britain and a sixth of France. Population was concentrated in the central provinces of European Russia. Over ninety percent of the population was rural. Its largest city was St. Petersburg, the capital, with over half a million.

The population was multi-national. About three-fourths of its people were Slavic—Russian, Belorussian, and Ukrainian. Another Slavic people were the Poles in the west who numbered five million. Baltic peoples (Lithuanians and Latvians) lived in the west; Finno-Ugrians (including Estonians and Finns), lived in the north with Finnish tribal peoples to the east; and Romanians in Bessarabia. The Caucasus included a medley of people including Armenians, Georgians, and Turkish peoples, while Turkish and Mongolian peoples inhabited central Asia. Many tribal peoples lived in Siberia.

A leading nationality, which will be an important bridge in the movement of evangelical free churches, were the Germans, which numbered around one million, growing to around 1,800,000 by the end of the century. As early as the sixteenth century under Ivan the Terrible, Germans settled in Moscow, some as captives in the Livonian Wars, but many came as officers, craftsmen, merchants, and technicians. With Russia's incorporation of Baltic territories under Peter the Great in the eighteenth century, Baltic Germans were added and in turn found high places of service in the Russian state. Under Catherine the Great in the last half of the eighteenth century and her grandson Alexander I in the early nineteenth, large numbers of Germans settled on agricultural lands in the Volga region and Ukraine. Later in the century, other Germans migrated from Russian Poland and Germany into Volhynia in Ukraine.

The diverse populations produced a variety of cultural differences. While the Slavic peoples were Orthodox, other peoples such as Poles and Baltic peoples looked to the West and were primarily either Roman Catholic or Lutheran. Germans were predominantly Protestant but with a significant Roman Catholic minority. Jews were a large minority in Russian Poland and the western provinces. Moslems were well represented in the Caucasus and Central Asia. Schismatics were found in various parts of the empire but were particularly important in the Caucasus. Pagan tribes and Buddhists lived in Siberia and the Far East.

Racial, linguistic, religious, and social differences produced diverse lifestyles and perceptions. This was particularly noticeable between German and Slav. Germans were commonly regarded as people of self-discipline, order, hard work, frugality, and energy. They in turn regarded the Slavs as more relaxed, punctuated with sudden bursts of energy, even disorderly and squanderers of time. Although the regime drew on the skills of the Germans in government, trade, and agriculture, numbers of Russians began to resent the predominance of Germans in government and their cultural influence and economic strength in society in the last decades of the nineteenth century. They also became increasingly concerned about German power on the world scene.

Although the aristocracy was less than 1.5 percent of the population, they appropriated much of the nation's wealth. The upper ranks of the nobility, numbers of them living in extreme luxury, were strongly westernized, speaking French or other languages as well as Russian. Some of the population was in manufacture, mining, trade, and the military, but the masses toiled on the land with possibly around forty-five percent of the population serfs. Serfdom was a backward economic system that hindered innovation and mobility. The serf owned the feudal lord either payments in money or kind or labor services. The land holdings of the serf were part of a village commune. Serfs were unskilled, unmotivated, generally illiterate, and poor workers.[2]

Government and the Economy

At mid-century the Tsar was Nicholas I (1825–1855), who was an absolute monarch. Nicholas admired the patriarchal Prussian regime and sought to govern by militaristic principles. The Third Department of the Chancery employed political police who guarded against subversion. Rigid censorship prevailed, and travel abroad was curtailed. The minister of education, S. S. Uvarov, enunciated the doctrine of "Official Nationality"—Autocracy, Orthodoxy, and Nationality. Autocracy was the principle of governance, the Orthodox Church was arbiter in religious values, and Nationality reflected the role of the Russian people. Legal rights for the masses were few.

Socially and economically a great chasm existed between the nobility and gentry on the top and the serfs at the bottom. Although manufacturing increased in the first half of the nineteenth century, Russia was far behind in economic development and education. Russia was farther behind the West in 1850 than in 1800. Russia possessed some hard-surfaced roads but most roads were poor and distances were great. In 1855 it possessed only 1,000 kilometers of railroad, only a sixth of Germany's mileage. Russia, however, improved shipping on its waterways. Schooling was limited with unqualified teachers and low standards. Nevertheless Russia produced notable figures in literature, music, and art. Beginning in the sixteenth century, Russia borrowed from the West and welcomed foreign technicians, merchants, and military figures who would enhance its strength. Both Peter the Great and Catherine the Great widely adopted western standards and encouraged western migrants. But Russia with its own eastern traditions was also xenophobic and sought to preserve its own unique heritage. The Slavophiles romanticized Russia's past, extolling its social harmony and Slavic institutions, including the commune and the Orthodox Church. Westerners, on

---

2. See. Riasnovksy, 278–384, for a description of social and economic conditions. Also see Parker, 215–19.

the other hand, looked upon Russia as backward and looked to the West, some advocating liberal constitutionalism, others socialism, and still others radical revolution.

For an outside observer, Russia with its vast territory and military establishment looked formidable. In comparison with Western Europe, it was different. The Crimean War (1854–1856) that began at the close of Nicholas's reign and lasting after his death clearly showed Russia's internal weaknesses that will lead to significant changes. New currents will arise that will provide opportunities for new initiatives.

The Russian Orthodox Church

The Russian Orthodox Church was the established church that had existed for over eight hundred years since its establishment by Prince Vladimir of Kiev in 988.[3] He led his people in a mass immersion in the Dnieper River. The church brought the Russian/Ukrainian people into the orbit of Greek Orthodoxy, significantly shaping their culture. Old Russian traditions and pagan superstitions, however, continued to persist.

The church was a formidable institution, incorporating the eastern Slavic population. In 1840 it had 31,000 churches, almost 117,000 secular clergy, and over 500 monasteries and convents.[4] The church also sustained its own system of parish schools. Peter the Great abolished the office of patriarch and, following Protestant example, established in 1721 a Holy Synod, headed by a lay procurator, to govern the church. Although the church continued with bishops who appointed the clergy, the church lost its independence and was a support to the autocratic regime. During Nicholas's reign the church incorporated the Uniate Church (Orthodox who recognized the Pope), fought schismatics, converted Protestants in the Baltic area, and sought to convert pagans in the east. It was illegal to proselyte an Orthodox. Both the government and the church fought against schismatics and sectarians. Bishops and priests were controlled from above in a church that became increasingly centralized. The priesthood became a special class with members in the priesthood often devolving from father to son or son-in-law. The church, of course, included faithful priests but numbers of them were notably lacking in righteous conduct and noted for drunken behavior. Too often a priest's sacramental role overshadowed his pastoral role due in part to the large size of the parish and his numerous liturgical duties. The priest was also a civil servant, compelled to compile vital statistics that often took much time. He was also required to report on schismatics.

In the eighteenth century the government confiscated the church's lands, but its compensation for clergy was inadequate. The priest had to depend on gratuities from parishioners who were already taxed for support of the church. Although educational

---

3. A valuable study of the Russian Orthodox church, studying particularly its clergy, is the work by Freeze, *The Parish Clergy in Nineteenth-Century Russia*.

4. Miliukov, in Karpovich, ed., *Religion and the Church*, 147.

standards for priests had significantly risen, other clergy, such as deacons and sacristans, were often poorly educated.

The ritual and beauty of the liturgy, chanted in the old Slavonic that few understood, brought to the worshiper a sense of the divine. The Russian soul sought spiritual union. Icons of the saints in the church and home were representatives of the spiritual world. Although anticlericalism and secularism were beginning to affect the educated classes, the masses of people were pious. Their piety, mixed with superstition, however, followed traditional forms and was based on feeling rather than Scriptural knowledge or reason. Church leaders complained how little the peasant knew of church dogma or even ordinary prayers.

Even though outwardly the Russian Church exhibited strength and unlike the West a more faithful constituency but yet manifested serious weaknesses. During the time of Nicholas, attempts at reform were largely unfruitful. As other institutions, it was subordinate to state policy, limiting its spiritual potential. Changing times will bring new challenges.

SCHISMATICS AND DISSENTERS

Over the years schismatic and dissenting movements beset the Russian Orthodox Church.[5] The Great Russian Schism or *Raskol* centered on the liturgical reforms of Patriarch Nikon, a powerful cleric of strong will who aroused strong opposition. In 1667 a church council, although formally deposing Nikon, affirmed his reforms and excommunicated those who opposed them. The excommunicated became known as the Old Believers. The Old Believers rejected the legitimacy of the Orthodox Church and split into a priestist faction, recognizing priests and sacraments, and a priestless faction that believed the priesthood and the sacraments (except baptism) were lost. The regime imposed stiff penal penalties against both factions. In 1863 the regime acknowledged the existence of 8,000,000 Old Believers.

Numerous indigenous religious sects and their subdivisions, bodies that exhibited dissatisfaction with the sacramental ritualism of the Orthodox Church, also assailed Russia. The government discovered in the 1730s the Khlysty or People of God, a sect that probably began much earlier. They rejected Jesus as a unique incarnation. God, who was immanent, dwelt as a divine incarnation in those who have been illuminated. The Khlysty produced the Skoptsy, a movement that advocated castration to overcome lustful desire. Another sect was the Dukhobors who arose in the eighteenth century. Although less extreme than the Khlysty and Skoptsy, the Dukhobors also taught a divine indwelling of the soul. These three sects denied the authority of Scripture and the sacrificial death and resurrection of Christ.

---

5. Bolshakoff, *Russian Nonconformity*, provides an excellent survey of schismatic and dissenting bodies in Russia. For the statistics in 1863 of these bodies, see p. 15.

PART ONE—Prologue

The Molokans or Milk Drinkers, so-called for drinking milk during Lent, appeared in the middle of the eighteenth century. Their leader, Simeon Uklein, left the Dukhobors and accepted the Bible as authoritative. He rejected all rites and sacraments and as the Quakers spiritualized them. Molokans also rejected military service and the taking of oaths. The Molokans came closest to western Protestantism than any other Russian sect.

In its efforts to protect national unity and prevent heresy, the Russian regime made strenuous efforts to restrict if not destroy the dissenting bodies. Nicholas I undertook special measures in persecuting both Old Believers and sectarians. In legislation in 1837 classifying "the most pernicious sects," the regime signaled out the Khlysty, Skoptsy, Dukhobors, and Molokans. In 1863 the government recognized 220,000 as the total for the four bodies. Measures against dissenters included removal of civil rights, closing centers of worship, and deportation.[6]

OTHER RELIGIONS

In its expansion the Russian Empire included populations with other religions. In its spread down the Volga and into the Caucasus and Central Asia, it gained many Moslems, which at mid-century numbered around 2,300,000. In spreading across Siberia to the Pacific, it added pagan tribal peoples and Buddhists, who numbered a quarter million. In its acquisition of territory of the Polish-Lithuanian Commonwealth in the eighteenth and early nineteenth centuries, it gained both Roman Catholics and Uniates, Orthodox in faith and practice who acknowledged the pope. Roman Catholics numbered over 1,700,000, a figure that also included Roman Catholic colonists who settled in southern Russia. Before the end of the reign of Nicholas, most Uniates, however, were forced to join the Orthodox Church. With their center in the Caucasus, Armenian Christians included over 350,000. Many Jews also resided in the western territories and numbered around 1,190,000. In addition to this complex of religious faiths, Protestantism numbered around 1,800,000.[7]

---

6. For measures against schismatic and dissenting bodies during the reign of Nicholas I, see Florinsky, *Russia: A History and an Interpretation*, 2:798.

7. Figures for bodies in the section of other religions were based primarily on the report of a corespondent on Russia in *EC*, 1848, 93.

2

The Protestant Presence

IN THE MID-NINETEENTH CENTURY, Protestants, although a minority of around 1,800,00, were a prominent feature of religious life of the Russian Empire. In coming from the West, Protestantism did not arise as a reform movement within the Russian Orthodox Church nor was it an indigenous movement among the Slavic population. Within Russia, its adherents generally immigrated into the country for economic opportunity, either as individuals or as colonists. As Russia expanded to the Baltic in the eighteenth and early nineteenth centuries, it incorporated traditional Protestant territory with roots in the Protestant Reformation of the sixteenth century.[1]

For a nation that often resisted western invasion, either militarily or ideationally, protective of its own culture, it is rather remarkable that Russia incorporated such a significant Protestant presence. Monarchs who sought development of the nation and some under the influence of the Enlightenment or even western mysticism helped to open the door. Russia needed western technicians and western colonists. To insure loyalty to the crown, the regime also granted religious rights to inhabitants of newly acquired territory.

In contrast to Western Europe with its conflict between Roman Catholics and Protestants, Russia was a haven of toleration. In the latter years of the seventeenth century and into the eighteenth century, Catholic regimes expelled Huguenots in France, Salzburgers in Austria, and Waldensians in Italy with the Huguenots finding refuge

---

1. For a general history of Protestantism in Russia, see Amburger, *Geschichte des Protestantismus in Russland*. For a more poplar work, see Hebly, *Protestants in Russia*. Also see Delius, *Der Protestantismus und der russisch-orthodoxe Kirche*.

PART ONE—Prologue

in both America and Russia. At this time England extended no toleration to Roman Catholics.

Other factors helped to nurture a Protestant presence. Russians feared more from Roman Catholic encroachment than from Protestantism. The Orthodox Church, unlike the Roman Catholic Church at the time, was more open to the distribution of the Bible among the laity. In addition, pietism arising from Protestantism with its stress on personal evangelical commitment had an impact in Russian Orthodox circles, especially on Alexander I (1801–1825), that helped to open the door to several Protestant initiatives. Pietism will also be influential among the German colonists.

Protestant Bodies

Lutherans

The first Protestants in Russia were Lutherans, a denomination that from the sixteenth century to the collapse of the Tsarist regime in 1917 was by far the largest Protestant body in the country.[2] Strangely its first adherents in 1558 were prisoners of war as a result of the Livonian Wars in the Baltic fought by Tsar Ivan the Terrible (1533–1584). Among the hostages was Timan Brakel who became the first Lutheran minister in Moscow, serving families of the dispossessed. In 1575–1576 the regime permitted the erection of a wooden prayer house in Moscow. Although destroyed after four years, the influx of Germans who settled in their own section of the city led to the construction of another building in 1601. Ivan himself engaged in theological discussions and became knowledgeable of Protestant beliefs. During most of his reign Protestants received toleration, only forbidden to proselyte the native population.

Under Peter the Great (1682–1725), who welcomed foreigners and granted them religious toleration in 1702, a great influx of Protestants entered the country with Lutherans present at the establishment in 1703 of St. Petersburg, the new capital. His annexation of Baltic territories, granting them religious freedom, incorporated more Lutherans. The manifestos of Catherine the Great in 1762–1763 with freedom of religion brought in Protestant colonists to the Volga Region and later in the century Mennonite colonists into Ukrainian territory in southern Russia. In the early nineteenth Century under Alexander I, additional Mennonites and other Germans settled in Ukraine.

In a Church Ordinance of 1832, the Russian regime granted the Lutheran Church an administrative structure that lasted during the remainder of the regime's life to 1917.[3] It covered Lutherans in the entire empire except the Duchy of Finland and the Kingdom of Poland. The doctrinal standards were the Book of Concord. The

---

2. For a standard history of Lutherans in Russia, see Duin, *Lutheranism under the Tsars and the Soviets*.

3. For a discussion of the Church Ordinance of 1832, see Duin, 1:287–33.

structure itself was somewhat like the Holy Synod of the Russian Orthodox Church with a General Consistory at St. Petersburg composed of six members, including a lay chairman, a clerical deputy, two other lay members, and two other clerical members. Eight lower consistories (reduced to five in 1890), were St. Petersburg with parishes in the north and Ukraine; Moscow, including the rest of Russia proper, Trans-Caucasus, Central Asia, and Siberia; and six others in the Baltic. No general synod was ever held but synods convened in the lower consistories. The Tsar appointed the top two officials and approved the other officials.

The Lutheran Church in Russia, although independent in doctrine and liturgy, was an established church under state administrative control. Although the ordinance brought consolidation, it, however, increased dependence on the state and thus circumscribed its independence. Unlike the Orthodox Church, it received no support from the government. As other religious groups, it was forbidden to proselyte among the Orthodox nor use Russian for such a purpose. On the other hand, the St. Petersburg Consistory moved in the late 1840s to supply material in Russian for Lutherans who were becoming conversant in Russian, to provide instruction in Russian in the seminary, and to encourage pastors to acquire the use of Russian.[4]

In 1848 the journal, *Evangelical Christendom*, published an article from a correspondent whose statistics allegedly came from a report of the Minister of the Interior for 1846, listing 1,756,763 Lutherans with 927 places of worship and 440 clergy. In 1862, E. H. Busch, a Lutheran clergyman, published his statistical analysis of the eight consistories as well as parishes in Georgia, listing 1,922,777 members, 469 clergy, 992 churches and prayer houses, 2,100 schools, 3,051 teachers, and 110,059 students. If one added 2,500,000 Lutherans in Finland and 300,000 in Russian Poland, the Lutheran Church in the empire probably numbered in mid-century over four and a half million.[5]

Besides a large parochial school system, including gymnasiums or high schools attended by the Russian elite, it maintained a seminary at the University of Dorpat. Its institutions also included an Evangelical Hospital in St. Petersburg, founded in 1859, in addition to other hospitals, deaconess institutions, orphanages, homes for the aged, and other benevolent organizations. It helped to establish in 1831 an Evangelical Bible Society, restricted to work among Protestants, and in 1860 a Lutheran Home Mission Society, besides numerous city missions. St. Petersburg became a strong Protestant center, conducting services here in six different languages. In Sunday school work Lutherans, however, lagged behind; only fifty existed in Russia itself in the 1890s and only three of them organized before 1878. In population centers, Lutherans built impressive church structures.[6] They were well established in the larger population

---

4. *EC*, 1848, 94.

5. For statistics, see *EC*, 1848, 93; Busch, *Materialen zur Geschichte und Statistik*, 49–50; and Lenker, *Lutherans in All Lands*, 8, for Lutherans in Poland and Finland.

6. For institutional development, see Lenker, 438–57.

centers but elsewhere were scattered over large territories and inadequately served by clergy. Lutheran clergy were particularly lacking in broad areas of the Crimea, Arctic North, Siberia, or even in Volhynia in Ukraine.[7]

The Lutheran Church in Russia was impacted by a strong pietistic movement from Germany that was influential during the time of Alexander I in St. Petersburg and the Baltic. In the south among the German peasant population, pietism flourished among the stundists, individuals who gathered in a Bible hour or *Stunde* (German for hour) for Bible study and prayer. Stundists opposed the rationalistic influences in the church and were indifferent if not opposed to scholastic theology and ritual. For them religion included conversion, a heart-warming experience, a personal devotional life, and a separation from worldly activities that hindered one's spiritual life. Many stundists also participated in waves of revivalism and supported mission efforts.

The greatest number of pietists remained in the Lutheran Church, but others were separatists. In the early nineteenth century during the reign of Alexander I, numbers of Swabians in Württemberg, influenced by pietism and rejecting the changes in liturgy and rationalism of the Lutheran Church, immigrated into the Russian Empire. One group in 1816–1817 settled in Georgia. Another pietist group, influenced by millennial ideas, left in 1817 with a portion of them going to Georgia in 1818, forming seven villages, but others remained in Ukraine, settling north of Odessa in Kherson Province. A third group left for Russia in 1822 and established four colonies near Berdyansk in Taurida Province in southern Ukraine. In 1822 in Bessarabia, Ignaz Lindl, a Roman Catholic priest, influenced by evangelical revivalism, founded a place of refuge for his followers at Sarata. Although expelled from Russia in the following year, Lindl began a revival among the German colonists with some becoming separatists.[8]

Although separatism did not produce great numbers, it was an irritant to Lutheran officials, who opposed not only its schismatic character but also signs of religious fanaticism that might appear within it. On the other hand, it helped to produce evangelical if not revivalistic currents in the German community. In 1862 Busch recorded five separatist congregations in Georgia, not part of the General Consistory, with a membership of 3,716. In Kherson he recorded one congregation of 1,187

---

7. See Lenker, 45–51, and Kiploks, "The Lutheran Church in Russia," *LQ* 3/1 (Feb. 1951), 52, on the difficulty of serving large parishes with scattered populations.

8. For an extensive listing of bibliographic sources on German pietism/stundism in the Black Sea and Volga regions, including migration of Swabian separatists and Ignaz Lindl and Bessarabian separatists, see Wardin, *Evangelical Sectarianism in the Russian Empire and the USSR*, 23–26. See Duin, 2:202–21, for material on separatists, especially those who settled in Georgia. For material on Schwabian colonies in Russia, see Stroelin, *Die Schwaben in Ausland*, 26–32. For separatism in Bessarabia, see "Der Bessarabische Separatismus," in Busch, *Ergänzungen der Materialen zur Geschichte und Statistik* (1867), 1:231–37.

and in Taurida five congregations with 1,799 members. In Bessarabia separatists had declined to 300.⁹

Moravians

The Moravian Brethren (or Herrnhut), founded by Count Nikolas Ludwig von Zinzendorf, was a pietistic movement. Its adherents were nominally Lutheran, but the Moravians maintained their own assemblies or "classes," erected prayer houses, and followed separate worship practices. In the eighteenth century they were very active in the Baltic region, but in 1743 the Russian government banned their activity. In 1764 Catherine the Great gave them full liberty, and as a consequence they established in the following year a colony at Sarepta near the Volga River. They attempted to reach the Buddhist Kalmucks but with little success. Nevertheless Sarepta was an influential religious center for German settlers, providing ministerial services to the Lutheran congregations in Sarepta and the Lower Volga. In the 1860s Sarepta numbered around 860 of whom 455 were Moravians. In St. Petersburg Moravians had around thirty members.[10]

Reformed

The Evangelical Reformed Church in Russia was a small minority, acting practically as an adjunct to the large Lutheran constituency. Reformed came from Dutch, German, and French immigrants. A Reformed Church opened in Moscow in 1629. In St. Petersburg Dutch formed their own congregation in 1717, and the French with a German segment in 1723 with the latter acquiring its own pastor in 1773. The French and Germans completely separated in 1858. From 1858 to 1889 Hermann Dalton (1813–1913) served the German Reformed Church in St. Petersburg. Dalton was a prolific and scholarly writer who was an astute observer of religious life in Russia. In the 1860s in St. Petersburg, Reformed supported Dutch, French, and German parishes with 3,722 members, and six others in Russia proper and the Baltic with 4,060 members that included Rohrbach-Worms in Ukraine with 1,480 parishioners. In addition, the Reformed in Lithuania included almost 9,000. Reformed were also in Russian Poland, the Lutheran colonies in the Volga and Black Sea regions, and in the military. In 1817 Reformed and Lutherans in Archangel formed a united church.[11]

In doctrine they were aligned with Lutherans and rejected extreme predestinarian views. For them Christ was present spiritually in the sacrament and not, as

---

9. For statistics, see Busch (1862), 49, 67–71, and Busch (1867), 1:237.

10. For bibliographic sources on Sarepta, see Wardin, *Evangelical Sectarianism*, 6. For Lutheran congregations served by Moravian Brethren from Sarepta in the 1860s, see Busch (1867), 1:336–37. For statistics, see Busch (1862), 670.

11. Amburger, 125–30. Busch (1862), 660–67.

with Lutheranism, present with it. They differed as well in communion practices with Reformed using broken bread rather than wafers and taking the cup themselves. In southern Russia intermixed with fellow Lutherans, Reformed found it difficult to adopt the more rigid Lutheran order and adjustments were made; by and large, they conformed to the new standards. In Russia proper the Reformed maintained independent "sessions" (*Sitzungen*), coordinated with the Lutheran consistories. In Russian Poland Reformed maintained their own consistory and synod and in Lithuania a synod.[12]

Protestant Missions

With the support of Alexander I and Prince Alexander N. Golitsyn, minister of education and president of the Russian Bible Society, a window of opportunity opened in the early nineteenth century for several Protestant missions.[13] In 1802 the Edinburgh Missionary Society established Karass, a colony near Pyatigorsk in the Caucasus to work among Moslems. The colony with a growing German population was a successful economic enterprise but practically a failure as a mission—only nine confirmed converts before the regime terminated the mission in 1835. The local church, which dedicated a building in 1854, continued as an independent "Free Scottish Church" with a Reformed ritual. It was predominately German but in mid-century still included some English speakers and mission converts.[14]

Felician Zaremba and Heinrich Dietrich, missionaries of the Evangelical Mission Society in Basel, Switzerland, non-denominational but with pietistic roots, settled in Shusha in the Caucasus in 1823. Their goal of reaching Moslems was unsuccessful, but they found a field among Armenians, members of the Gregorian Armenian Church with roots in the fourth century. Although the mission was terminated in 1835 by the government, one of the Armenian converts, after study abroad returned to the area. As a result of his ministry, the government permitted in 1866 the establishment of an Armenian Lutheran church at Shemakha under the jurisdiction of the Moscow Consistory.[15]

Beginning in 1810 the London Missionary Society began a Mongolian mission among the Buryats, southeast of Lake Baikal in Siberia. In spite of heroic efforts, converts were few. The regime of Nicholas I, following its policy of terminating the work of Protestant missionaries, ended this last mission outpost in 1840.[16]

---

12. Duin, 1:385–86. Hebly, 28–29. *The New Schaff-Herzog Encyclopedia*, 10:121–22.

13. For bibliographic materials on Protestant missions, see Wardin, *Evangelical Sectarianism*, 19–23.

14. Jones, "The Sad and Curious Story of Karass, 1802–35," *OSP* 8 (1975): 53–81. Amburger, 138–39. Busch (1862), 667.

15. Duin, 1:460–64. Smith and Dwight, *Missionary Researches in Armenia*, 194–216.

16. For an exhaustive and well-written history of the Buryat mission, see Bawden, *Shamans, Lamas and Evangelicals*.

Mennonites

Mennonites were descendants of the Anabaptists, a radical sectarian movement during the Protestant Reformation of the sixteenth century.[17] State and church authorities considered them a serious threat to the social order for both church and state. As the later Baptists, they were a believer's church, rejecting infant baptism and practiced believer's baptism but by pouring or sprinkling. In politics the Anabaptists rejected the existing political order, refusing public office, serving in the military, or taking the oath. Although numbers of them were pacifists, others, however, favored revolutionary action. As a persecuted minority, they advocated religious liberty.

Anabaptists gained supporters in The Netherlands, Germany, and Switzerland but were seriously divided among different parties. A significant number of nonresistant Dutch Anabaptists, called Mennonites after their leader Menno Simons, gained refuge in the Vistula Valley then under Polish control. After Prussia acquired the area, they were threatened with serving in the military and also faced restriction in purchase of land. Thereupon many of them accepted the invitation of the Russian government to settle in Ukraine as colonists with the promise of self-government, religious freedom, exemption from military service and the oath, and for a period of time exemption from taxes. Beginning in 1789 Mennonites established Chortitza, (the old colony) in Yekaterinoslav Province on the Dnieper River, a settlement that came to include nineteen villages. A second and much larger colony was Molochna (or Molotschna), begun in 1804 on the Molochnaya River in Taurida Province north of the port city of Berdyansk, that came to include sixty villages. Mennonites also settled in Russian Poland and Volhynia as well as establishing colonies in other parts of the Russian Empire.[18]

Mennonites, now speaking German, developed self-contained communities. Their relationship with the surrounding Russian population was minimal; comparatively few learned Russian. Both Russians and foreigners recognized Mennonites for their economic achievements as model farmers, neat villages, honesty, and hard work. Although responsible to a Bureau of Guardianship and then later to a Guardian's Committee, the colonists were autonomous. Each village had an assembly of four members, including the mayor (*Schulze*), who exercised police powers. A group of villages made up a district with its own assembly and mayor.[19]

All colonists must be members of the Mennonite Church, which one joined when a teenager. Baptism became perfunctory, and congregations included both dedicated and nominal members. Pastors were untrained and read their sermons; attendance

---

17. A standard history of Mennonites worldwide is Smith, *Smith's Story of the Mennonites*.
18. For the settlement and development of Mennonites in Russia up to 1874, see Epp, *Der Geschichte der Mennoniten in Russland*. Also see Krahn, "Russia," *ME* 4, 381–93. "Molochna," based on the Russian, is preferred rather than the German "Molotschna."
19. Krahn, "Government of Mennonites in Russia," *ME* 2, 556–57.

at services was low. In a report in 1843 on the Mennonites in Chortitza, John Melville, a distributor of Scripture, found a lack of religious instruction for youth but in Molochna found a few who maintained "spiritual worship," held missionary meetings, and supported a temperance society. Church leaders of a settlement formed a *Kirchenconvent*, a conference of ministers and elders that came to dominate the churches and at times came in conflict with civil authority. As the Orthodox and Lutherans, Mennonites also formed their own schools, but at this time lacked standards and often even religious instruction.[20]

By 1860 Mennonites in the Black Sea colonies, Volga, and Volhynia numbered around 34,000. But they were no longer a believer's church separate from the government but a parish church with special privileges as the Orthodox and other Protestants. Church and state were intertwined. The constituency of each congregation included the general population, bringing a decline of discipline and moral standards. As a self-governing community, in spite of their principles of non-participation in secular government, ironically they were forced by necessity to form their own governmental units and use force in the exercise of governmental power.[21]

Embassy and Independent Churches

The British merchants (or British Factory) in Russia and the Russian Company in London provided chaplains of the Church of England for British factors in St. Petersburg where a church was built in 1754. The church served the British population and also served as an embassy church. By the mid-nineteenth century, the Church of England also had congregations in Moscow, Kronstadt, Archangelsk, and Riga. Busch claimed in 1862 that the Anglican congregation in St. Petersburg numbered 2,700. The Dutch also formed an independent embassy church in St. Petersburg.[22]

In 1816 a Congregational Church or the English and American Chapel was formed around John Paterson, agent of the British and Foreign Bible Society who also served with the Russian Bible Society.

The church was an important evangelical center, distributing Scripture and engaged in social ministry, including the support of boys' and girls' schools. In 1840 it dedicated its own small building, worshipping up to that time in the chapel of the Moravian Brethren. The Russian government licensed its building as the chapel of the American Legation. Busch reported the congregation had around 110 adherents.[23]

---

20. For Melville's report, see BFBS, *Monthly Extracts*, March 1843, 404–6.
21. For Mennonite statistics, see Busch (1862), 672–76.
22. For congregations of the Church of England, see Cross, "Chaplains to the British Factory in St. Petersburg, 1723–1813," *ESR* 2/2 (Apr. 1972): 125–42. Also see Amburger, 136–38, and Busch (1862), 667.
23. Amburger, 136–38. Birrell, *Rev. Richard Knill*, 87. Busch (1862), 667.

Bible and Tract Societies

Bible and tract societies were organizations that provided entry for Protestantism to penetrate Russia.[24] With their stress on knowledge of the Bible and personal acceptance of its teachings, Protestants found such societies as natural vehicles for their ideals. As with the entry of Protestant missionaries during the reign of Alexander I, conditions opened for the formation of a Russian Bible Society in 1812 but nationalistic forces forced its closure in 1826. The Holy Synod of the Orthodox Church now held a monopoly of publishing Scripture for the Russian populace, which until 1862 consisted primarily of producing the Slavonic text, difficult for most Russians to comprehend.

The parent body of the Russian Bible Society was the British and Foreign Bible Society (BFBS), organized in 1804, that, however, after the termination of the Russian Bible Society continued its activities in the Russian Empire, officially and unofficially, in distribution of Scripture and translation work. The regime greatly hampered its work by forbidding the importation of Russian Scripture from abroad. John Melville (1802–1886), a Scot who settled in Odessa in 1837, engaged in a notable ministry, although working unofficially as an independent agent, distributing Bibles from the BFBS and tracts from the Religious Tract Society. He traveled over much of southern Russia, including the Caucasus, and continued at least into the 1880s.[25]

With the closing of the Russian Bible Society, the Protestant section of the Bible Society formed in 1827 under Prince Karl Lieven a committee to continue its work. In 1831 the government approved the Evangelical Bible Society to serve Protestants and receiving support from Lutherans, Reformed, and Mennonites.[26]

The Religious Tract Society (RTS), formed in England in 1799, to publish tracts and other evangelical materials, also found its way into Russia. Richard Knill, missionary of the London Missionary Society and pastor of the Congregational church in SPB from 1820 to 1833, engaged in an extensive ministry in distributing both Bibles and tracts. Earlier Princess Sophia Meshcherskiĭ heard Robert Pinkerton, an agent of the BFBS but also the tutor of her children, read to her children the tract, "The Dairyman's Daughter." This moved her to translate by 1814 fourteen tracts of the RTS; she provided a large sum of money for their publication. By 1850 the RTS supplied around £4,500 for the tract ministry. Although distribution of Russian Bibles had more or less stopped, tract distribution continued with the approval, by and large, from the

---

24. For bibliographic materials on Bible and tract societies, see Wardin, *Evangelical Sectarianism*, 13–19.

25. For Melville's career, see Urry, "John Melville and the Mennonites," *MQR* 54/4 (Oct. 1980), 305–22, as well as in the *Reports* of the BFBS and the RTS. Also see Wardin, *Evangelical Sectarianism*, 19.

26. For the origins and development of the Evangelical Bible Society, see Benford, "Hermann Dalton and Protestantism in Russia," 180–84, and also bibliographic entries in Wardin, *Evangelical Sectarianism*, 17–18.

authorities. By the middle of the century, Dalton, the Reformed pastor in SPB, however, claimed it was difficult to obtain any tract.[27]

Conclusion

With rights as tolerated bodies, Protestants in Russia, as the Orthodox Church, were part of a state church system. Even the Mennonites, descendants of a free church movement, were treated as a state church that enjoyed special privileges. Rights and privileges for all of them depended on the approbation of an autocratic government.

The regime prohibited Protestants to evangelize the Orthodox population. It was very intolerant of any schismatic group that left Orthodoxy or threatened its monopoly over the Eastern Slavic population. It terminated Protestant missions among non-Orthodox peoples. Although not entirely successful, the government also attempted to restrict the Bible work of Protestants.

From an evangelical perspective, Protestantism, by and large, was devoid of religious vitality. It was beset with bureaucratic control, rationalistic influences, formalism, lack of sufficient clergy, and a contentment simply to baptize the natural increase from the births of their own children. As already noted, a visitor to the Mennonite colonies in the 1840s noted with one exception a serious lack of religious commitment. After listing the statistics of the non-Orthodox bodies in Russia, a correspondent to the periodical, *Evangelical Christendom*, declared that "lamentably few" in 1848 "are instructed to place their hopes of salvation on the finished work of Christ." But he, too, found "some stars of light" in the Lutheran Church in the Baltic, in the missionaries of the Basel Missionary Society serving in the German colonies, and in the attempted reforms of the St. Petersburg Synod of the Lutheran Church.[28] German stundism among both Lutherans and Reformed also nurtured a more personal and active Christian life.

As a new competing body, Baptists will find on entry into Russia a hostile reception from the established Protestant bodies, particularly from the Lutheran Church and Mennonite leadership. On the other hand, some Protestants in Russia, however, will prove to be a bridge for a Baptist advance, especially from Lutherans and Mennonites under pietistic influence. But even in these circles, Baptists will find a mixed reception—some open and receiving but others with reservations if not outright opposition.

---

27. See Wardin, *Evangelical Sectarianism*, 18, for bibliographic sources for the RTS.
28. *EC*, 1848, 93–96.

3

The German Baptist Movement

THE FOREMOST INSTRUMENT IN introducing the evangelical free church movement into the Russian Empire was the Baptist movement in Germany. Baptists established themselves on the Continent of Europe in Germany in the 1830s two centuries after they had first appeared in the seventeenth century in England and the American colonies. In less than two decades, German Baptists spread across northern Europe and were soon knocking on Russia's door.

The progenitor of the German Baptist Union was Johann Gerhard Oncken (1800–1884), born in Varel, Oldenburg, in northwest Germany.[1] His beginnings were inauspicious. His mother was unwed, he never saw his father who left for England before his birth, and was reared in his grandmother's home. During the French occupation a relief fund provided assistance, and he found work in an inn. He was baptized as an infant in the Lutheran Church and confirmed at the age of fourteen. In a sudden turn of events, John Walker Anderson, a Scottish merchant, who had known Oncken's father, took him at age fourteen to Leith, Scotland, to serve with him in his business. Before leaving Germany, Anderson bought Oncken a Bible. Oncken not only gained business experience, an opportunity of travel to neighboring countries, and acquired an excellent command of English but was also profoundly influenced in his spiritual development. With Anderson's mother he attended in Glasgow a Reformed Presbyterian Church and was exposed to a strict Sabbath. Later in England he resided in the home of a deacon of an Independent Church, where at family worship prayer

---

1. For biographies of Oncken, see Luckey, *Johann Gerhard Oncken*, and Balders, *Theure Bruder Oncken*. For a description of the Oncken movement, see Wardin, "The Oncken Movement," *ABQ* 28/4 (Winter 2009): 396–406.

was lifted up for his conversion, and attended a Methodist congregatgion. At the age of twenty in the Great Queen Street Methodist Church in London, upon hearing the preaching from the text in Romans 8:1, "There is therefore now no condemnation to them which are in Christ Jesus, who walk not after the flesh, but after the Spirit," he had a spiritual experience that changed his life. He was in a line of other religious figures in which Romans played a decisive impact, such as Augustine of Hippo, Martin Luther, and John Wesley. As an enthusiastic convert he began to distribute tracts and soon led a mulatto to the Christian faith, who soon returned to Jamaica.

In 1823 he severed his relation with Anderson and settled in Hamburg where he served as an agent of the Continental Society for the Diffusion of Religious Knowledge, preaching and distributing Christian literature. He joined the English Reformed Church in the city. With a pastor of the State Lutheran Church he opened in 1825 the first permanent Sunday school in Germany that taught children Scripture as well as reading and writing. In 1828 he became an agent of the Edinburgh Bible Society and opened a small depository and publishing house. In the same year he became a citizen of Hamburg and married in England.

Through study of Scripture with a small group of believers, Oncken concluded that a true apostolic church was composed only of believers baptized on the confession of their faith. But who would baptize him? Oncken rejected Robert Haldane's suggestion that he immerse himself, finding no scriptural warrant for it. He found the suggestion of a British pastor to come to England for baptism as impractical for the time it would take from his ministry. After waiting some years, an American Baptist professor from America, Bernas Sears who arrived for a sabbatical in Germany and had heard of Oncken, came to Hamburg to investigate. On April 22, 1834, Sears immersed Oncken, his wife, and five others in the Elbe River. On the following day he formed the first Baptist church in Germany as well as ordaining Oncken for the Christian ministry.

Oncken proved to be the right man in the right place. In first meeting him, Sears wrote, "Though not a man of liberal education, has a very strong, acute mind, has read much, a man of immense practical knowledge, and is very winning in his personal appearance and manners."[2] A contemporary described Oncken as "A strong person of medium height, black hair, . . . fiery eyes, quick movements, an intimate tone in his voice, a deep warm-heartedness, and an outstanding gift to speak."[3] Through his vision, energy, organizational talents, doctrinal convictions, and mission strategy, he came to embody German Baptists. Because of the movement's spread to other countries, he became known as "the father of Continental Baptists."

From the beginning Oncken enlisted co-workers. One was Julius Köbner (1806–1884), a Danish Jew, son of a rabbi, and a member of the Lutheran Church who was

2. *American Baptist Magazine*, July 1834, 290.

3. Balders, "Johann Gerhard Oncken—Aspect of His Life and Work," paper at the General Council of the Baptist World Alliance, Dresden, 1999, 1.

noted for his impassioned preaching and a writer of hymns. A second was Gottfried Wilhelm Lehmann (1799–1882), notable for his organizational skills and first pastor of the church in Berlin, the second German Baptist church in the country. Oncken with Köbner and Lehmann became known as the "*Kleeblatt*" or "cloverleaf" of the German Baptist movement.

Denominational Characteristics

The German Baptist movement took root during a time of religious revival. Mission and publication societies within Germany and abroad, the rise of a new pietistic movement, the appearance of training schools, and the example of Methodism in England all helped to bring a wave of religious interest.[4] As an agent of a mission society and then a Bible society, Oncken was part of this movement, but now unlike others, who were primarily devoted to one major mission object, he became the leader of a new denomination. Oncken was not only an evangelist but also desired to form churches of believers under scriptural discipline. Unlike pietists in the state church or continental Methodists who at first only established Methodist classes but not independent churches, Oncken separated himself completely from the state church and confronted it on biblical grounds. For Oncken there was, "One Lord, one faith, one baptism," a baptism distinct in candidate (believer) in mode (immersion) and in design (non-sacramental), far removed from the sacramental infant baptism of Protestant and Catholic bodies. The Lord's Supper, rejecting both Catholic and Lutheran views of Christ's presence in or with the sacrament, was a memorial and a divine pledge. It was also close—i.e., restricted to immersed believers.[5]

After reconciling some differences among themselves, the German Baptists printed a Confession of Faith of fifteen articles in 1847.[6] It became the doctrinal basis for the General Conference or *Bund* that was formed two years later and the doctrinal standard for Baptists in Eastern Europe. The confession footnoted in detail its statements with biblical references. It carried Oncken's imprint although it also included contributions from Köbner and Lehmann. Although it incorporated Baptist principles of church order, it was a uniquely German Baptist composition. As other Reformed/Puritan confessions, the first article declared the books of the Old and New Testaments as the sole authority for faith and practice. In article five on election to salvation it was Calvinistic, based on God's initiative. Article twelve on the divine law outlined Puritan views of the role of the moral law with emphasis on the Sabbath. But

---

4. See Scharpff, *History of Evangelism*, 110–68, 198–214, for revival and mission efforts in Germany in the nineteenth century.

5. See Köbner, "The Baptist Missionary Society," *EC*, 1851, 495–96, for a statement on the rationale and purpose of the German Baptist movement. The proper term is "close communion," not "closed," as often written today.

6. For an English translation, see McGlothlin, *Baptist Confessions of Faith*, 330–54.

the confession was far more than a scholastic treatise. In article six on the means of grace and article seven on conversion of the sinner, it was also an evangelistic tract.

The confession declared that all members were of equal standing and had "equal voices" in voting. The church elected its own officers—elders (who led the church), preachers, and deacons who assisted the elders and preachers and looked after temporal affairs. Elders and preachers were ordained and were of equal standing with the possibility of one person holding simultaneously the two positions. Members were responsible for "active participation," including regular attendance at all services. Article eleven on sanctification enjoined the believer to a life of holiness. Members were subject to church discipline and possible exclusion. In article fourteen on Civil Order, the confession recognized the authority of government except in limiting the practice of one's Christian faith. As over against Mennonites, the confession recognized the legitimacy of oaths (not, however, their misuse), military service, and participation in civil office. At the same time, it made it clear that its members could still unite with those who differed on such issues. In any case, it tried to convey to the world that it was not a revolutionary body threatening the social order.

Although German Baptists possessed an elected leadership and only the ordained or those authorized by the church administered the ordinances of baptism and the Lord's Supper, the German Baptist movement was primarily a layperson's movement. It engaged the entire membership in its life. Its churches provided not only worship and nurture but also served as missionary entities that sought to win souls through ardent preaching, distribution of Christian literature, mission stations, and the establishment of Sunday schools as well as women's and youth organizations. In 1836 Oncken formed the Hamburg Tract Society, and the movement kept careful records as to the number of Scriptures and tracts distributed. It was understood that every Baptist carried a tract. In 1844 he started *Missionsblatt*, a paper for mission reports and promotion. In 1849 Köbner published *Glaubensstimme*, a very successful hymnal, which was another evangelistic tool. The movement began with young leadership—its first leaders were in their thirties—and attracted young men who as *Handwerker* or artisans supported themselves in establishing new work. Although desirable, theological training was not mandatory. Before the establishment of a seminary in 1880, German Baptists conducted nine short-term mission schools. On one occasion when asked how many missionaries German Baptists were supporting, Oncken replied with the figures of the total membership. For Onken it was "*Jeder Baptist—ein Missionar*" or "Every Baptist a missionary." Both men and women were incorporated in the work.

Although churches were self-governing, they were part of a General Convention or *Bund*, formed in 1849, as well as local associations, the first formed in 1848. As the General Missionary Convention or Triennial Convention in the USA, it met every three years. The *Bund* provided a strong sense of corporate unity, unlike bodies in England or America, and in Oncken's mind was in a sense an extension of the first church in Hamburg. The *Bund* not only helped to preserve doctrinal unity but also furthered the missionary purposes of the movement. Oncken was able to dominate the *Bund* until the 1870s, when controversy over centralization in the last years of his life brought more church independence.

Opposition

Oncken's new position had serious consequences for him in both church and state. First, his personal ties changed. He lost friends, including members of the English Reformed Church. He lost his ties with the Netherlands Tract Society. Two years earlier Oncken lost his position with the Sunday school he helped to found.[7]

But worse was to come from the opposition of both the Lutheran Church and the Hamburg city government. As a small group, his church remained unmolested for its first three years, but in 1837 a public baptism brought complaint and investigation. The Lutheran Church demanded punishment against the "sectarians" who were members of an independent and thus illegal conventicle. In its opposition, it was more than ready to tar Baptists with the term, "Anabaptist," a term of great reproach bringing memories of the revolutionary Anabaptists of the sixteenth century. Although an evangelical party existed in the Lutheran Church, many of its members were affected by rationalism and thus hostile toward any movement of religious enthusiasm. The state, supporting social cohesion and good order and fearful of social disturbance, was more than ready to support the established church.[8]

Lutherans also accused Baptists of proselyting other Christians. A Lutheran supporter of the Evangelical Alliance, "W. G.," wrote a report on Germany for *Evangelical Christendom* in 1862, commending Baptists for their zeal. But, on the other hand, he pointed out that some Baptist missionaries were intolerant toward the established churches and charged them "with attacking, in unmeasured terms, the Establishment, calling it Babel, and accusing of infidelity Christians who remain members in it, in order to draw them over to themselves." He also noted that Baptists had recently signed a Declaration defending themselves from unjust accusations and declared their main purpose was to preach the gospel. They rejected the suggestion that they drew "living members" of the National Churches instead of attempting to convert the "dead members."[9]

In May 1840, Oncken was imprisoned and held for a month. Köbner and J. C. F. Lange were imprisoned for a shorter time. After his release, Oncken refused

---

7. Donat, *Wie das Werk begann*, 42.

8. For early German Baptist conflict with church and state, see Donat, *Wie das Werk begann*, 46–53; Donat, *Das wachsende Werk*, 234–53; Luckey, 144–66; and Balders, "Kurze Geschichte des deutschen Baptisten," Balders, ed., *Ein Herr, ein Glaube, eine Taufe*, 28–34. An early appraisal of Oncken and the opposition he faced is "Rev. J. G. Oncken," *American Baptist Memorial*, May 1854, 129–36. A very excellent article on Oncken's struggle is Detzler, "Johann Gerhard Oncken's Long Road to Toleration," *JETS* 36/2 (June 1993), 229–40.

9. *EC*, Sep. 1, 1862, 47–48.

on principle to pay his fine and court costs that led the state to sell all his household goods. The Hamburg fire of 1842 gave Baptists the opportunity to provide shelter for many of the homeless, which brought sympathy to the Baptist cause. Oncken, however, was imprisoned again for four days in 1843. With the revolutions in 1848 in Germany and elsewhere in Europe, German Baptists hoped for religious freedom. In that year Köbner penned his "Manifesto of the Free Primitive Christianity to the German People," patterned somewhat after the famous *Communist Manifesto* of Karl Marx that appeared a few months before. Köbner called for religious freedom for all and separation of church and state.[10] Although reaction set in after the revolutions, at least in Prussia, the largest state, Baptists received general toleration. But in some other areas of Germany, especially in the first half of the 1850s, Baptists faced fines, imprisonment, and expulsion for assembling, baptizing, Bible distribution, and refusal to participate in the practices of the Lutheran Church. Oncken and his supporters also faced mob violence.

Even after Baptists gained the right to assemble, they still faced discrimination. At first Baptists were not allowed to perform marriages or in many cases be buried in the main section of public cemeteries, which were controlled by the state church. The acquisition and legal security of church property were often difficult. Prussia did not grant the right of incorporation until the 1870s.

German Baptists received support from the wider Baptist community in Great Britain and America. With Oncken's imprisonment of 1840, petitions and personal representatives were sent from there. Petitions also came from the Scottish Bible Society, the mayor of Leith, and even from people of different confessions in Hamburg. By joining the Evangelical Alliance, German Baptists also received additional support from abroad even though some state church representatives in the Alliance did not appreciate the Baptist presence.[11] Oncken, Köbner, and Lehmann were present at the first meeting of the Alliance in London in 1846, and Lehmann was a co-founder of the German branch of the Alliance in 1852. Even though they differed with other Protestants on church order, German Baptists were not exclusive but were willing to fellowship with others whom they considered sound in the evangelical faith.

Expansion

The German Baptist movement received financial assistance from England and Scotland as well as America. As early as 1835 the Triennial Convention in the U.S.A. appointed Oncken as one of its missionaries. The new movement, however, was indigenous, not a result of the work of foreign missionaries, and sustained itself. By

---

10. For a discussion of Köbner's *Manifesto* and its translation into English, see McGlashan and Brackney, "German Baptists and the Manifesto of 1848," *ABQ* 33/3 (Sep. 2004): 258–80.

11. See Geldbach, "The Religious Situation in Germany: Past and Present," *ABQ* 33/3 (Sep. 2004), 248–49, for early German Baptist relations with the Evangelical Alliance.

1849 it had a denominational structure that included a general convention, regional associations, a corps of mission workers, dedicated laypersons, a tract society and other publishing interests, Sunday schools for children, and its own periodical and hymnbook. It was a movement that had been tested by opposition and persecution with more to come.

Baptist growth was among the poorer classes of the population. The Hamburg church experienced steady growth, numbering 380 in 1845, and constructed its first chapel in 1847. Oncken was a tireless missionary, establishing with coworkers Baptist churches and missions in other parts of Germany. In 1849 the German Baptist *Bund* included twenty-five churches in Germany and an additional five in Denmark. Membership was 2,849.[12] The work in Denmark had been started by Oncken and Köbner in Copenhagen in 1839. Small beginnings had also been made outside of Germany in The Netherlands (1845), Switzerland (1847), and Sweden (1848). Baptists experienced strong opposition in Denmark and Sweden.

German Baptist work was somewhat successful across northern Germany but very unsuccessful in the south where Roman Catholicism prevailed. It found a fruitful field in East Prussia where a church was established in Memel as early as 1841 (reestablished in 1843). East Prussia adjoined the territory of the Russian Empire, touching the Baltic region to the north and Russian Poland to the east and south. In addition, Sweden adjoined Finland, another Russian territory. It is not surprising that the dynamic German Baptist movement, even with its small numbers, would come lapping up to the Russian border. But could Baptists penetrate such a huge empire as Russia with its alien culture, its autocratic government, and its established churches utterly opposed to a Baptist penetration? The challenge was great.

---

12. For statistics, see Wagner, *New Move Forward in Europe*, 12, 16, and Donat, *Wie das Werk begann*, 468–70.

PART TWO

Prospects

German and Baltic Beginnings, 1855–1884

4

Baptist Beginnings in the Baltic

IN THE GERMAN CONFEDERATION, the Kingdom of Prussia was the largest entity of the thirty-nine states, extending from the Rhineland in the West to the province of East Prussia in the East. Except for its coastal area on the Baltic Sea in the northwest and its boundary with West Prussia in the West, East Prussia bordered the Russian Empire. Its northern trip was adjacent to the Province of Kovno and practically extended to the Province of Courland (today part of Latvia). In the east and south it bordered the Kingdom of Poland (Congress Poland), which was under the Russian Tsar.

In October 1841, Oncken formed at Memel on the very northeastern tip of Germany (today Klaipeda, Lithuania) the first Baptist church in East Prussia and the tenth in all Germany. At the time it was the only Baptist church east of Berlin, far from any other, and on the Russian border. Oncken baptized twenty-five individuals, including Eduard Wilhelm Grimm (1808–1873), who was ordained as pastor. While in Switzerland, Grimm had been converted by attending meetings of a separatist group led by Samuel Frölich and was baptized by sprinkling. After his return to Memel, Grimm began his own group but upon hearing of Baptists sought believer's baptism by immersion.[1]

The first years of the Memel Church were difficult. Grimm was aggressive and faced strong opposition, including imprisonment and threat from mob violence. He fled on an English ship, disguised as a sailor, that took him to England. His church divided into two parties with Oncken recognizing the anti-Grimm group as the rightful church. After three months, Grimm returned to Memel but in 1846 turned over

---

1. For historical data on the first years of the church in Memel, see Donat, *Wie das Werk begann*, 309–22, and Ekelmann, *Gnadenwunder*, 1–41, 131–43.

his leadership to his son-in-law, F. W. Licht. Grimm then led a company of fourteen to America where, after a short stay in New York, he settled in Milwaukee, Wisconsin, where he continued his work as a German Baptist missionary.

The congregation that received Oncken's support was reconstituted in 1843 and also received legal recognition. The congregation continued to grow in spite of short pastorates, reaching 181 members in 1850. In January 1851, Ferdinand Niemetz (1814–1873) began a very fruitful ministry of twenty-three years that continued until his death. In October the church opened a large chapel with seating for 800. The church extended its outreach in establishing numerous mission stations in what today is Kaliningrad Oblast of Russia. The church baptized its first Lithuanian in 1851; in 1854 Karl Albrecht, who spoke Lithuanian, began a very successful mission among Lithuanians in East Prussia. Other early congregations were Elbing (today Elblag, Poland) in 1844 in West Prussia and Stolzenberg in 1849 in East Prussia south of Königsberg (today Kaliningrad).

At the beginning of the 1850s, German Baptists were showing increasing vigor. In 1851 Julius Köbner in Hamburg published an article in *Evangelical Christendom* on the German Baptist mission work that by that time had spread from Germany into Denmark and Sweden to the north, The Netherlands in the west, Switzerland in the south, and to Vienna, Austria, and Pest, Hungary. Membership had increased from seven in 1834 to 3,746 in Germany and Denmark, figures that did not include those who only attended divine worship. Köbner claimed around eighty percent of the members were first time converts. He stressed "that every member may be considered a missionary, each one looking on the mission-work as the grand end and aim of his life; even the women taking an active part in the circulation of the Scriptures and religious tracts." Köbner stated that within the last two years 50,000 copies of the Bible were distributed and each year from 700,000 to 800,000 tracts.[2]

In 1851 Ferdinand Niemetz, the new pastor in Memel, wrote that police constantly watched the services. Complaints were lodged against him at the court of justice for administering the Lord' Supper, and orders issued against conducting a Sunday school. He sent to the Baptist press a strong critique of Baptists printed in the *Königsberger Zeitung*, published in November 1851. The article condemned Baptists for their fanatical separatism, confused interpretation of Scripture, administration of sacraments by those without proper ordination, and even immorality (a common charge against any new group). On the other hand, the article admitted that Baptist services were very attractive with "very melodious singing" and with sermons that stressed conversion rather than burdened by theological doctrine.[3]

In 1850 Köbner joined Gottfried Lehmann for a preaching tour, including distribution of tracts, in Prussia. They attended the Prussian Association at Elbing and visited work in East Prussia, going to Stolzenberg, Tilsit, and Memel. They then

2. *EC*, 1851, 495–96.
3. *MM*, Mar. 1852, 78–80.

attempted to cross into Russia, whose border was near but guarded by Cossacks and soldiers. Without visas they could proceed no further, but then on Russian ground they with other members of their company sang a missionary hymn and fervently prayed "that day might at length spring up in these dark regions."[4]

It is not surprising that with the proximity of Baptist work in East Prussia to the Russian Empire German Baptists would consider Russia a prime mission field. For most Westerners, Russia with its autocracy and Eastern Orthodox culture was a forbidding if not barbaric region. It was no wonder that German Baptists looked on Russia as a "dark region" that needed the gospel. The urgency was there, but how realistic was the prospect of a Baptist penetration? Russia carefully guarded her borders not only militarily but also culturally. Russia was huge and complex, already filled with numerous religious bodies that were more than ready to oppose any western religious incursions. Religious resistance would not only come, as expected, from the Orthodox state church, a guardian of Russian values, but even vociferously from Protestants already in the country, protecting their own interests. In addition, the Russian government prohibited any proselyting of its Orthodox population and forbade, except for work among Jews, Protestant missions.

Even with their great mission enthusiasm supported with financial support from the West, German Baptists were an extremely small group, widely dispersed with great needs at home. Although they had cultural affinity with Germans in the Russian Empire, they were culturally alienated from the general population, the great majority of whom were illiterate. Except for German, their members, by and large, were not conversant with other languages in the Empire. Both Orthodox and most Protestants considered Baptists heretical. From a human standpoint, it appeared an almost impossible situation.

Tilsit

One of the productive mission stations of the Memel church was at Tilsit, a city on the Niemen River on the border of Russia where meetings were begun around 1850. The Tilsit mission expanded to include eleven additional preaching points. It was reported in 1853 that the Tilsit mission was beginning to attract converts in Russia. One was a young man converted through a letter written by a female member of the mission. In addition, two brothers who were government inspectors in Russia became converts. After receiving a tract, the younger brother purchased a Bible and became a convert. The older brother became a convert after his younger brother wrote him. *Missionsblatt* reported in 1859 that in the Tilsit orbit four individuals from the Russian border were baptized and a frail woman had come many miles from behind the Russian border to hear the preaching. But these cases as yet led to no Baptist church on Russian soil.[5]

4. *MM*, Nov. 1850, 337–41.
5. *MM*, July 1853, 307. *Missionsblatt*, Aug. 1859, 130. For an account of the Tiflis mission, see Ekelmann, 34–35.

PART TWO—Prospects: German and Baltic Beginnings, 1855–1884

Åland Islands/Finnish Mainland

The Crimean War that broke out between the Ottoman Empire and Russia in 1853 led in the following year to the involvement of Great Britain and France on the side of the Ottomans. This development unexpectedly gave Baptists a small foothold on Russian soil. In its offensive against Russia in the summer of 1854, the British navy occupied the Åland Islands, inhabited by a Swedish population but part of Russia, which lay between Sweden and Finland in the Baltic Sea. The Swedish branch of the Evangelical Alliance, recently organized in 1853, received a letter from individuals on the islands, including a Lutheran clergyman, requesting the Alliance to send preaching for a revival.

The Swedish Alliance included some Baptists, including David Forssell, a merchant in Stockholm, who in 1854 had just been baptized in Hamburg. Not long afterwards, authorities entered Forssell's home and forcibly baptized his six-month-old daughter into the Lutheran Church. With a trip to the Åland Islands, Forssell himself became acquainted with conditions there. The Alliance decided to send Carl Möllersvärd (1832–1901), who in 1853 had been baptized in the Baptist Mariners' Church in New York City. He soon returned to Sweden and was active as a preacher in Stockholm. Forssell arranged for Möllersvärd and a second Baptist to go as businessmen to sell goods to the British Navy, thereby assisting in their support.[6]

Möllersvärd, only twenty-one years of age, began his evangelistic work in the islands, apparently in October 1854, ministering for two weeks. He returned in November after the British naval forces had left but received some protection from a British ship captain. He preached in a hall and many flocked to hear him; numbers were converted. He came as a revivalist and did not preach Baptist doctrine nor establish any church. Nevertheless the Lutheran clergy opposed him. The Russian authorities threatened his arrest and deportation to Russia. He fled across several islands and found a place of safety where he could preach for three weeks more. But after a ministry of two and a half months, he finally left, rescued by a Swedish fishing boat.

In the meantime Baptists on the mainland in Sweden, still a very young denominational body, only begun in 1848, were making great strides. Anders Wiberg, a pastor of the Lutheran Church who had become a Baptist, went to America where the American Baptist Publication Society commissioned him as a colporteur. Wiberg returned to Stockholm in November 1854. He became the major leader of the Swedish Baptist work and wrote an influential book on baptism that spread Baptist principles. The Baptists in Stockholm completed their church organization with Wiberg and Möllersvärd as co-elders.

In the spring of 1856, Erik Östling, a farmer from Föglö, an island where Möllersvärd had worked, and influenced by Wiberg's writing, came to the Stockholm church

---

6. For the activity of Carl Möllersvärd in the Åland Islands and his background, see Alwar Sundell, *De Började—Vi Fortsätter*, 7–12. Also see *MM*, Sep. 1854, 388.

for baptism. Although Lutheran authorities tried to change his views, he held to his convictions and meetings were held in his home. In the fall, two others were also baptized in Stockholm—Gustav Fägerström and August Lindblom. Soon after their return, Fägerström, appointed to head the congregation, baptized the wives of the three men already baptized. The group now operated as a church and observed the Lord's Supper, the first Baptist congregation on Russian soil. Fägerström soon baptized Alexander Selenius, a blacksmith.[7]

The members of the small Baptist group faced interrogations, underwent pressure to have their children baptized, and were placed under watch.[8] The neighboring population was hostile. The group also had its own internal problems—it excluded Fägerström from its fellowship for lack of Christian dedication. In 1860 the Föglö congregation numbered only ten, while a second congregation had six and will later die out. Even though the Baptist movement in the Åland Islands was only a trickle, it provided a stepping stone to the Russian mainland in Finland.

In 1859 the Lutheran Consistory summoned Baptists from Föglö to the Finnish mainland at Turku for interrogation. Henrik Heikel, a member of the Consistory and a vicar of a Lutheran Church, invited the Baptists to his home to know them better. This initial contact with Baptists will bear fruit. In 1861 Heikel moved to another parish near Jakobstad (Pietarsaari) in Österbotten (Pohjanmaa) in western Finland. After his death in 1867, the family moved to Jakobstad. In 1868 Wiberg baptized two of the Heikel children—Victor in the Stockholm church and Anna in the Örebro church, followed in the following year by two other Heikel children. In the summer of 1869 Adolph Herman Walén, pastor from Föglö, preached in Jakobstad and baptized two candidates, the first on Finland's mainland. On August 14, 1870, thirteen persons, including four from the Heikel family, formed at Jacobstad a Baptist church, a Swedish-speaking congregation.[9]

At the same time Swedish Baptist work was established on the mainland of Finland, work among the national Finns also began. J. Henriksson, a sailor converted in the Baptist Mariners' Church in New York City, returned in 1870 to Pori (Björneborg), his birthplace. As a result of his preaching, a church was formed nearby at Luvia that in the following year numbered twelve members. Another center among national Finns began in southeastern Finland. John Hymander, dean of the parish of Parikkala but

---

7. Sundell, 13–14. Also see Anderson, *The Baptists in Sweden*, 163–64. No exact date has been recorded for the organization of the church on Föglö. Anderson is incorrect in dating it in 1857 (see p. 191). She is incorrect in claiming Fägerström was ordained. Magnus Lindvall, archivist and assistant mission secretary of the Swedish Baptist Union, wrote to the author on October 8, 2002, that Fägerström, although given authority to baptize, was not ordained.

8. See Sundell, 13–22, for measures against the Baptists.

9. For beginnings of Baptists on the Finnish mainland, see Aaltio, "A History of the National Baptists in Finland," 8. Also see Sundell, 26. For Wiberg's letter recounting the baptisms of Victor and Anna Heikel and for letters from Victor and Anna, see *BMM*, June 1869, 175–79. For the account by Anna Heikel of the first baptism on the mainland of Finland, see *BMM*, Feb. 1870, 55–56.

PART TWO—Prospects: German and Baltic Beginnings, 1855–1884

influenced by Baptist literature, resigned his position in 1871. The Stockholm church baptized Hymander, age sixty-nine, and his daughter, following which he baptized his wife and several others back home. He died in 1877 with his church, if formed, apparently disappearing. A new church was established here in 1898.[10]

At the beginning of the 1870s, Baptist work had thus begun among both Swedish-speaking and Finnish-speaking people on the mainland of Finland. Unlike Baptists in Germany and Sweden, Baptists, dispersed in two language groups and lacking sufficient leadership, never had the same mass appeal and will not prove to be an entry point of any significance for Baptist work in Russia proper.

Courland

In contrast to the thrust to the Åland Islands and Finland, the Baptist penetration into Courland, just to the north of Memel, was far more successful. Courland was a Baltic province of Russia, today part of the country of Latvia, inhabited primarily by Latvians (or Letts) who were primarily peasants or members of the working class. A significant minority were the Germans, numbers of whom were artisans but who also were members of the upper ruling classes. Lutheranism was the established church for both Latvians and Germans.

As with the Åland Islands, the Crimean War also gave the opportunity for the entry of Baptists.[11] On September 1, 1855, the Memel church baptized Friedrich Jacobson (Frizis Jekabsons), a Latvian who was a helmsman from Courland who found work in Memel. At the end of the Crimean War in 1856, he returned to Libau (Liepaja), his native city, where he was a witness for the Baptist faith. Jacobson was not the only Courlander in the Memel church for up to that time nine others, all German, had become members. At the end of the war, economic opportunity beckoned inhabitants of Memel to cross into Courland and the neighboring city of Riga.

The city of Libau, seventy kilometers north of Memel by land, became the first mission point with the formation in 1856 of a mission circle that included besides Jacobson, Daniel Juraschka, a shipwright; August Meyer, a carpenter; Johann Brandtmann, a rope maker, who settled in Grobin about six miles to the east of Libau; and a woman by the name of Beutze. Juraschka, Meyer, and Brandtmann were German subjects. Juraschka and Meyer learned Lettish but Brandtmann used an interpreter.

---

10. For Baptist beginnings among Finnish-speaking Finns, see Aaltio, 12–14. For a contemporaneous account on Henriksson, see Sundell, 48, which provides an excerpt from the diary of Anders Wiberg, who visited Henriksson in 1871. Since there is no recorded date for the church in Luvia, it is unknown whether it preceded or followed the date of the church at Jakobstad.

11. A basic source of the spread of Baptists in Courland is the work on the church in Memel and its missions by Otto Ekelmann, *Gnadenwunder*, 49–100. For a critical Lutheran view of early Baptist activity, see "Die Baptisten in Kurland," in Busch (1867), 1:747–55. For another Lutheran critique of Baptist penetration into Courland, see "Die religiös-sektirerischen Bewegungen in den Ostsee-Provinzen," *SPES*, 1862, 42–45.

The Memel church in August 1858 baptized two converts from Libau and in June and August 1859 two more from Grobin. Earlier in 1859, upon a request from Meyer, Niemetz, the pastor of the Memel church, accompanied by Karl Deggie who spoke Lettish, crossed the border on March 22, 1859, to hold meetings in Grobin and Libau. At the time only fourteen Baptists resided in the area. For six successive days in Libau, Niemetz conducted his meetings with a particularly large crowd of hundreds on Sunday, March 27. The warning of the Lutheran pastor against Niemetz evidently brought out the curious. On Monday the next day, Niemetz was forced to go before the city council of three members and was ordered not to preach further. In regaining their passports, officials threatened Niemetz and his companion, accused them of upsetting the city, and condemned them as worse than "godless good-for-nothing Hottentots." Nevertheless that evening Niemetz bravely held one more meeting in a home but shortened his message with the word that soldiers were coming. He safely left the next morning.[12]

On August 14, 1860, at Hasau near Windau (Ventsplis), north of Libau, Baptists with Brandtmann present held a large meeting with messages and distribution of numerous tracts. As a result of the meeting, eight Latvians and an additional three from Libau and Grobin crossed the border in a farmer's cart, arriving in Memel on August 31. On the following Sunday on September 2, after giving their testimonies in Lettish but interpreted into German, they were accepted by the Memel church and baptized. Among the eight men and three women were Adam Gaertner (Gertners) (1829–1875) and his wife Anna. Gaertner will play a leading role in Baptist work in Courland.

The authorities now closed the border to those seeking baptism. In June 1861 sixteen from the region of Windau secretly arrived by fishing boat at the Memel seashore. Niemetz baptized fifteen of them in the middle of the night and conducted the Lord's Supper. They returned by sea. At the end of the month on June 30, another group—six men and one woman—came by boat and were baptized.

Lutheran Concerns

Lutheran writers of Baptist activity signaled out Brandtmann, who had settled in Grobin, as an aggressive emissary. They charged him with circuitous travels (generally at night), holding unauthorized meetings, distributing tracts, attracting a Latvian schoolmaster to his cause, and attacking infant baptism. The authorities accused Brandtmann for converting Latvians who lived in the interior and who in turn went to Memel to be baptized. About this time Baptists excluded Brandtmann from their fellowship, possibly for improper sexual conduct. The authorities on their part arrested him on September 15, 1860, imprisoning him for proselyting with no prospect of release. He was imprisoned at Windau for almost five months and then banished.

12. For Niemetz's visit to Courland, see *Missionsblatt*, May 1859, 86–87; QR, July 1859, 43–44; and Ekelmann, 51–52.

PART TWO—Prospects: German and Baltic Beginnings, 1855–1884

While imprisoned, Brandtmann's wife visited him, but she was imprisoned for a short time for alleged religious activity in Windau and then forced to leave the town.[13]

In August 1861, Gaertner came to Memel with a converted Latvian who was then baptized. Gaertner, who was a master tailor, gave up his vocation to devote himself full time to Christian ministry. Niemetz instructed Gaertner, having been baptized only the year before and just thirty-two years of age, in doctrine and church order. The Memel church charged Gaertner with the care of the Latvian members while Juraschka was given the care of the German members. In September the Memel church gave Gaertner the authority to baptize since it was felt that it was too dangerous for baptismal candidates to come by sea in the fall. On the night of September 21, Gaertner baptized seventy-two candidates, the first in Courland.[14]

The Courland Lutheran Consistory first received information of Baptist activity on March 13, 1857, from the Lutheran provost at Grobin and also from the Courland civil government. The police had already arrested on March 3 ten working-class women led by Meyer. They apparently were part of a group of thirty. Lutheran leaders became increasingly alarmed by its spread but were somewhat uncertain how to challenge it. The Consistory did not wish to make the Baptists martyrs and rather sought to meet the challenge with weapons of the gospel. But faced with Baptist aggressiveness that included open solicitation to their meetings on the street with no police interference, distribution of tracts, proselyting, and attacks considered defamatory, it is not surprising that Lutherans were ready to support police action. Lutherans charged Baptists for degrading infant baptism with "disgraceful names" and calling other religious groups "Sodom and Gomorrah" and their churches "heathen temples."[15]

Police measures, however, did not stop the movement. Lutheran leaders not only noted that Baptists ignored the regulations but also considered any punishment they might receive as a type of martyrdom. Baptists loudly complained of their punishments, calling such action suppression and persecution, with reports finding their way to Prussia. By 1864 Baptists were baptizing openly in the day, not as earlier secretly and at night, and performing weddings and conducting funerals.

Suppression

On the Baptist side, Otto Ekelmann, pastor of the Memel church in the early twentieth century, recounted in his history the numerous afflictions Baptists suffered. He listed beatings, imprisonments, fetters, transport, deportation, and slander, such as accusing Baptists of concubinage and communistic-political agitation. He maintained that Lutheran opponents charged Baptists with revolutionary intentions, claiming they

---

13. Busch (1867), 1:748. *SPES*, 1862, 43–44. *MM*, Apr. 1861, 105. *QR*, Apr. 1861, 23–24.
14. Ekelmann, 73.
15. See Busch (1867), 1:747–55, for the response of church and civil authorities to Baptist activity.

promised land to the peasants, ready to destroy relationships between landlord and tenant.[16]

The one who suffered most was Adam Gaertner, the native Lett. As a full-time missionary, he was the most successful leader in the first years of the Baptist movement in Courland.[17] In December 1860 while preaching to a large crowd, police officials placed Gaertner together with Juraschka and Maria Kronberg, who had accompanied the latter, in fetters, taking them to Windau, where they were imprisoned for eight days and forced to sleep chained. Soldiers then escorted the three, still chained and in the cold, to their respective homes. After thirty-two miles, Gaertner arrived at his home in Goldingen. The other two traveled over fifty miles further. They were finally unchained on the way, arriving in Libau fourteen days after their arrest.

In the fall of 1861 the authorities imprisoned Gaertner for preaching and baptizing and held him for a year except released for eight days to bury one of his children. Upon release the authorities insisted that he pledge never again to preach, conduct the Lord's Supper, or baptize, but upon refusing to accept this demand the authorities again imprisoned him but then finally released him. Although freed, he was under close surveillance. In the summer of 1863 after baptizing sixty-four candidates, Gaertner was again imprisoned with Unis Jannsohn, in whose home a meeting was held, with the threat of possible confinement from six to twelve months. But an imperial *ukas* dated August 8 but not taking effect until October would free them. The governor of Courland came to Gaertner's prison and ordered his immediate release and said: "You can go to your house and pray there, and no longer worship in the woods. It would be a disgrace to the Czar that pious people should have to go and worship tn the woods." Gaertner, however, was fined one silver ruble for having secretly visited Memel. Gaertner will once again be imprisoned, this time in 1865, but then released.

Others also faced repression. Meyer in Libau was held for four days before his hearing and then imprisoned for fourteen days for leading a small Baptist gathering. After a couple of years of quiet, in February 1865 he was again imprisoned, held for fourteen days this time without a hearing but then released. Juraschka, who had been seized with Gaertner in 1860, was again imprisoned with Andreas Jankowski on February 1, 1863. Niemetz wrote that the night before Juraschka had baptized fourteen individuals, who were also taken but released, but Juraschka and Jankowski remained in prison. When Jankowski's father came without a pass to visit his son, he was taken from a prayer service and imprisoned for four weeks. Jankowski was held for eight

---

16. See Eckelmann, 58, 61, 66–68, 70, for a description of persecution of Baptists and charges against them. Also see *QR*, Jan. 1868, 280.

17. For Gaertner's career and imprisonments, see *Missionsblatt*, Feb. 1861, 20–21, and Nov. 1863, 173; *QR*, Apr. 1861, 22–23; Oct. 1862, 62; Apr. 1863, 27; Oct. 1863, 62; Jan. 1864, 14–15; Oct. 1865, 121; and Feb. 1866, 53; Ekelmann, 58, 61, 62–63, 67, 73–78; and *EC*, Jan. 1, 1864, 51.

weeks, but Juraschka was imprisoned for sixteen and a half weeks and then he and his wife and five young children were banished to Germany.[18]

On some estates, rods or whips beat Baptist farmhands. Because of participation in a service, a middle-class woman by the name of Jacobson spent three weeks in prison. For attendance at a Baptist meeting and refusal to stop attending them, a workman by the name of Pfemfert was held for some weeks and then he and his family were banished.[19]

BAPTIST PETITIONS

In this period Niemetz took the lead in establishing a fund in the Memel church to provide financial aid to the oppressed and their families. But Niemetz did more by using his pen to arouse concern and protest from the Baptist and wider Christian community. His reports in *Missionsblatt*, which were then translated into English for Baptists in Great Britain and America, in *Neuen Evangelischen Kirchenzeitung* in Berlin, and in *Evangelical World*, periodical of the Evangelical World Alliance, were effective channels of propaganda, which helped to play up the negative aspects of the suppression. Niemetz hoped that the reports would bring forth petitions and deputations to the Russian government. He thought that possibly the Evangelical Alliance might help in this regard. In 1863 James H. Millard, secretary of the Baptist Union of Great Britain, presented to the Council of the Evangelical Alliance information on persecution of Baptists in Poland and Russia. The Council authorized its foreign secretary to approach the Russian ambassador in England with facts of the persecution and a petition for the Tsar.[20]

Soon after he returned to Prussia from his visit to Courland in 1859, Niemetz made a direct appeal to the civil authorities in Courland who told him instead to appeal to the spiritual authorities if he wanted freedom for his religious work in Courland. He then appealed to the Courland Consistory, stating he wanted to provide pastoral care for Baptists in the area and also preach the Word of the Cross, appealing to those who can differentiate such preaching from evil proselytism. The Consistory replied that it was outside of its competence to consider his case. Niemetz then appealed to the General Consistory, which declared it could not rule on the status of other confessions in the country. Niemetz then appealed to the Tsar. He finally received word in January 1861 from the Minister of the Interior, which was sent to the General Consistory, that since Niemetz claimed only fourteen Baptists from his church in Courland it was therefore not sufficient justification for a foreign minister to serve them. It suggested, however, the Memel church could authorize a Baptist in Courland to administer the

---

18. For persecution of Meyer, Jaraschka, and Jankowski (father and son), see Ekelmann, 56, 61, 67, 78–79; *Missionsblatt*, Apr. 1863, 60; and QR, Apr. 1863, 27–28, and July 1863, 45.

19. Ekelmann, 61, 67. QR, July, 1863, 45.

20. Ekelmann, 58, 60, 70. QR, Jan. 1861, 15; Apr. 1862, 26; and July 1863, 45. EC, Jan. 1, 1864, 51.

Lord's Supper for Baptists there. In addition, the General Consistory opposed any free entry of Baptists to enter the country and preach in Lutheran churches.[21]

In the winter of 1861–1862, two Baptists, J. Jankowski and Sinieck, traveled to St. Petersburg with a petition concerning Gaertner's imprisonment. The governor of Courland had told them to seek justice there with their petition. Fellow Baptists financed the trip. Ch. Plonus, a member of the Memel church residing in St. Petersburg, directed the two to a spot near the palace to await Tsar Alexander II. Here they became acquainted with a Lettish guard, who called to show them the way to meet the Tsar who was then taking a walk. The two presented the petition to Alexander who didn't take it but told them to go to the Chancellery. The two stood half frightened. The Tsar then turned them over to an attendant who delivered them to a guard who took them into a beautiful hall of the palace where they met a uniformed official. They gave the official the petition, who read it, and after some questions promised an answer. A guard led the two out of the palace, but with all this effort the two never received a response.[22]

Niemetz continued to petition for himself and for the persecuted. Around 1860 he appealed on behalf of Brandtmann to the German ambassador in St. Petersburg, who then was Otto Bismarck, who claimed he could do nothing to help. In response to one of Niemetz's petitions, the civil governor of Courland instructed the Russian consul in January 1862 to inform him that the prohibition of his entry into Russia remained in full force as well as forbidding the return of Brandtmann. The governor also declared that pending the question of the recognition of Baptists regulations against them have been strengthened and the authorities are ordered to keep them under the most stringent surveillance. At the end of September 1863 the Baptist Union of Germany sent a petition to the Russian ambassador in England to convey it to the Tsar. About this time the *ukas* of the Senate of August 8, 1863, that stated Baptist teaching was not prohibited in Russia and which freed Gaertner and Jannsohn, proved in the end disappointing as the *ukas* related only to the two who were freed.[23]

The Oncken Visit

On October 15, 1864, Oncken, the German Baptist leader, left Hamburg to travel to St. Petersburg to plead personally for the Baptist cause.[24] Oncken was motivated to go because of the persecution in Courland as well as the repression of Baptists in

21. Busch (1867), 1:749–51. Ekelmann, 54–55.

22. *Missionsblatt*, May 1862, 73. Ekelmann, 60. QR, Apr. 1862, 225–26, includes an observation by Niemetz on the visit to the Tsar and also a garbled version on the interview with the Tsar from a deacon of the Baptist church in Hamburg.

23. *Missionsblatt*, May 1862, 74–75. QR, July 1862, 45–46. Ekelmann, 54–57, 62–64.

24. On Oncken's visit to St. Petersburg, see QR, Jan. 1865, 73–79. See QR, July 1864, 49–52, for the letters of Schwan and Niemetz requesting someone to come to St. Petersburg to baptize. See Dalton, *Der Stundismus in Russland*, 27, for Dalton's comments on Oncken's visit with him.

PART TWO—Prospects: German and Baltic Beginnings, 1855–1884

Russian Poland. Another motive was the urgent request from F. Schwan, representing believers in St. Petersburg and supported by Niemetz, for someone to come to the city to baptize. Oncken met Niemetz in Memel, and the two traveled by steamer to Kovno and then by train to St. Petersburg, arriving on October 28, avoiding Courland, a territory Niemetz was forbidden to enter. They stayed at the apartment of Plonus. During his five weeks in St. Petersburg, Oncken made the rounds in visiting officials in government and leaders of the various Christian bodies, including Hermann Dalton, pastor of the German Reformed Church. He also held services in private homes.

After some difficulty, Oncken and Niemetz were able to get an interview with Count Sievers, the president of the Ministry of the Interior, which was followed by two further interviews with him. They, however, could never get to see the minister of the Interior Ministry himself. Count Sievers told Oncken that in Russia freedom of worship was permitted, but the major obstacle in recognizing Baptists was due to their proselyting, an activity strictly forbidden in Russia. Sievers also condemned what he alleged were secret Baptist meetings. Niemetz attempted to counter his charges against Baptist work in Courland, while Oncken tried to answer the charge of proselyting.

Oncken declared that the main purpose of the Baptists was to preach the gospel of faith in Christ among the millions of Europe who have repudiated all divine truth and are a danger to good government. Oncken repudiated the idea that the main purpose of Baptists was to baptize and stated that Baptists believe baptism in no way brings entry into heaven, a theology that differed from most other groups. Oncken also pointed out that many who have been converted through Baptist preaching have not become Baptists but some, of course, naturally have joined them. Oncken rejected the charge that Baptists were ignorant, claiming they were more knowledgeable in Scripture than any other denomination and that "it was proverbial that we have always a string of passages at our fingers' ends."

Oncken stressed his opposition to forcing any one to accept a belief contrary to conscience. He maintained that it would be most difficult to remove forcibly Baptists, whom he declared to be "a purely religious movement." He predicted that religious liberty would come to Russia and Baptists would be a blessing to the country. Oncken was careful to state that he had the highest respect for the Imperial government since the Bible admonished believers to obey, next to obedience to Christ, political authority.

Oncken's defense of the Baptist position was a masterful *tour de force,* portraying Baptists as loyal subjects who above all were revivalists who brought religious blessing even to the extent of converting potential revolutionaries. Although Oncken admitted that some joined the Baptist cause, he did not own up to the fact that Baptists were also establishing a counter church that aggressively attacked not only unethical behavior in the established churches but also with their insistence on believer's baptism and their anti-sacramentalism were questioning the very basis of these churches as Christian communions. Oncken also did not acknowledge that new religious movements might separate populations from traditional cultural and political ties.

In the last interview of Oncken and Niemetz with the Count, the latter advised them that it would be best to terminate their stay since questions were being raised concerning their presence and further delay would injure their cause. Oncken and Niemetz left three days later on Monday, December 5, but not before Oncken had immersed seven candidates between midnight and one o'clock, the first hour of Sunday, performing the first Baptist baptism in St. Petersburg.

A New Environment

Shortly thereafter in 1865 an intensive wave of persecution broke out against the Baptists in Courland. Suddenly, however, without official announcement the oppression began to cease at the end of the year not only against Baptists in Courland but also in Poland and Ukraine. The *Rigaschen Zeitung* reported in October 1866 from a report on the Courland Lutheran Synod that the government had forbidden any further police action against Baptists, and in the Baltic Sea provinces the same standard applied to them as between Lutherans and the Orthodox. In a polemical exchange of articles between Niemetz and Bishop D. Ulmann of the Lutheran Church, the latter revealed that the order had already been issued in November 1865, about a year before.[25]

From a handful in 1856, Baptists, in spite of repression, had grown ten years later by 1866 to around 900. Even though Lutheran hostility continued unabated, members and mission stations of the Memel church continued to multiply with Baptists spreading among Latvians in the neighboring province of Livonia. At its twenty-fifth anniversary in 1866, the Memel church ordained Gaertner. In 1875 the church reached 2,780 members with thirty-three mission stations, twenty-seven of them in Russia, a foreign land. Beginning in 1876 the Memel church began to grant independence to its stations, the first in Riga. In 1879 the Prussian Association authorized Latvian Baptists to form their own Baltic Association, which in 1881 had almost 4,000 members.[26]

A good portion of the success to the Courland mission must be given to the Memel church, which became known as the "Antioch" of the Baltic region, and its pastor, Ferdinand Niemetz.[27] The first Baptists in Courland came from the Memel church. It gave encouragement and financial support to the persecuted. It relayed the principles of Baptist faith and practice. The church undertook a supervising care of its mission stations, holding two-day consultations with leaders from Courland and after the repression sending mission workers into the area who might spend a month to strengthen the work. Such work was most important for the fledgling congregations in Courland, composed primarily of peasant stock who knew nothing of Baptist

---

25. Ekelmann, 68–69. *QR*, Jan. 1868, 279–83.
26. *Missionsblatt*, Apr. 1866, 63. *BMM*, Mar. 1867, 80. Ekelmann, 234.
27. Ekelmann, 83, 88. For references to the Memel church as an "Antioch," see *Der Sendbote*, Jan. 13, 1892, 2, and Newman, *A Century of Baptist Achievement*, 128.

PART TWO—Prospects: German and Baltic Beginnings, 1855–1884

church order and who needed to become self-supporting. In 1874 Martins Riss and Jekabs Rumbergs were the first Latvians to attend the Mission School in Hamburg.

Even with the support and example of the Baptists in Germany, much of the Baptist work in Courland was indigenous. The first German Baptists to cross the Russian border into Courland settled with family members for economic reasons, not coming as missionaries. For some of them as German subjects, their sojourn terminated with banishment. Their personal witness spread to the Latvians, who in turn, such as Gaertner, carried on much of the evangelistic work. Even though a few German-speaking Baptist churches were established, the far greater number were Latvian congregations, led by Latvian pastors.

By the mid-seventies, the Hamburg Baptist Confession had been translated into Latvian.[28] The first Latvian Baptist periodical, *Evangelists,* began in 1881 under the editorship of Rumbergs. In spite of the oppression, the work spread readily and spontaneously.

St. Petersburg

St. Petersburg, the imperial capital of Russia that Peter the Great had founded as a "window to the West," was a growing cosmopolitan center of half a million in 1860. Although the majority of its inhabitants were Russian, it included many other nationalities. It incorporated Dutch, Finns, Swedes, Latvians, and Estonians, and a large German minority of from forty-five to fifty thousand. At the end of 1864, E. H. Busch recorded a total Protestant population of Lutherans and Reformed of around 59,000 that included nationalities other than German.[29]

The first Baptist in the city was Ch. Plonus, a master tailor who settled in the city on October 4, 1855. He was a member of the Memel church, having been baptized in 1851. In a large city that was more tolerant of divergent views than other places of Russia, Plonus felt free to witness for his faith. As many Baptists he distributed tracts that he brought with him and those he later purchased at a Christian store in the city. Plonus attracted a circle around him that joined him in his tract ministry. They soon were meeting together for Christian fellowship, theological discussion, and prayer. The host of the meeting would provide a box for an offering for his mission interest. Plonus's box carried the transcription, "Gifts for the distribution of tracts."[30]

By 1857 a circle had gathered around Plonus on Sunday mornings at eight and Monday evenings that included W. Nürnberg, a sculptor from Riga, and his family as well as J. Schwan, an Estonian surveyor, a convert. Plonus was not only important for

28. *Missionsblatt,* Feb. 1876, 97.
29. Busch (1867), 1:46.
30. For the settlement and activity of Plonus, see Ekelmann, 86–87, and "Brief von Br. Schiewe," *Der Sendbote,* May 18, 1884, 170. Ekelmann gives the date of Plonus's arrival as 1856 but Schiewe's date of 1855 is no doubt correct. Neither source gives Plonus's first name in full although Diedrich, *Siedler, Sektierer und Stundisten,* 49, records it as Christophorus.

beginning the first German Baptist nucleus in St. Petersburg but also for both contact and accommodations for German Baptists and Mennonite Brethren who came to the city. As already noted, Plonus assisted in the early 1860s Jankowski and Sinieck in their petition and in 1864 lodging for Oncken and Niemetz.

The seven candidates whom Oncken baptized at the midnight hour early on Sunday, December 4, 1864, included Schwan, who had written the urgent plea for one to come to the city to baptize, and four members of the Nürnberg family. In addition, Oncken already found in the city besides Plonus three other German Baptists—Plonus's wife and a member each from Stettin and Courland. As a mission of the Memel church, the small group struggled for existence in its inability to support a pastor and because of internal difficulties.[31]

As a young convert, Plonus was at first not settled in Baptist doctrine, even maintaining that one could not be saved outside baptism. In 1869 the Memel church placed Plonus and his wife under discipline with the result that the work was divided for two years. Schwan will become a problem when he tried to exercise complete control as elder. While working as surveyor on the island of Oesel, part of the neighboring province of Estonia, Schwan got into difficulty in 1865 with the Lutheran Consistory, which forbade him to preach among native Estonians in prayer houses and private homes. The Estonian press attacked him and the police put him under surveillance.[32]

When Johann Wieler from Germany visited St. Petersburg in 1872, he found the small group scattered without meetings. He brought them together for mission work and regular services. In his visit from June 30 to July 9, 1874, Karl Ondra, a leading Baptist missionary in Ukraine, whom Schwan invited to his home, brought reconciliation to the divided members. Soon afterward from August 8 to 18, August Penski, another German Baptist missionary, stayed with Plonus and his wife and baptized four candidates, bringing the membership to twenty-three persons.[33]

Johann G. (Ivan V.) Kargel

In early 1875, Ondra again returned for another visit. This time he brought with him a close friend, a young man in his mid-twenties, Johann G. Kargel (1849–1937), who was to be engaged for a limited time in mission work in the city. Six years before in 1869 Martin Kalweit, who at the time headed a German congregation in Tiflis, had baptized him. In 1873 Ondra had introduced him to the mission work in Volhynia in Ukraine, which led him to accept the pastorate of the German Baptist church in Soroczin in August. During his pastorate there he attended in 1874 the Mission School in Hamburg. To the chagrin of the church in Soroczin, Kargel decided to stay in St.

---

31. *QR*, Jan. 1865, 79. Ekelmann, 87.

32. Ekelmann, 87. *Der Sendbote*, May 28, 1884, 170. *Missionsblatt*, Dec. 1865, 186–88. Ekelmann refers to Schwan as "L. Schwan."

33. *QR*, Nov. 1874, 10–12, and Mar. 1875, 13. *Missionsblatt*, Dec. 1874, 206–207.

PART TWO—Prospects: German and Baltic Beginnings, 1855–1884

Petersburg in spite of entreaties from his church members to return. After requesting a missionary/pastor for years, the St. Petersburg Mission now finally had a resident pastor who will prove to be a rising star in evangelical circles.[34]

Kargel was young and energetic with pastoral training and several years of pastoral service. He was unmarried, which thereby eased the burden of pastoral support. At this time, he was conversant in German and up to a point in Russian, unlike the many German Baptist ministers who were monolingual. He was born of a German father and reportedly an Armenian mother outside of Russia in Turkish territory. Although beginning his work in the city in early 1875, he was absent in the south from May through July but then picked up the work. The congregation began with thirty-six members. During his first year, he baptized eleven and restored one to membership, but with a number moving away his membership in early 1876 had decreased by two.[35]

Kargel began with no regular salary, receiving only small contributions, thus threatening his continuation at the post. The members had all they could do to pay the rent for a hall on the first floor in a private home, and in 1877 they began to rent larger premises at three times the cost. At the conference of German Baptists in Hamburg in July in 1876, Kargel made an appeal for assistance. Upon the church's application for support, the German-American Mission Committee began to provide aid. While on his trip to Germany, Plonus, Nickels, and Jacobson in turn conducted the services, while Jacobson regularly held an Estonian service after the German service. In July 1876 Kargel reported only twenty-seven members, but at the end of 1877 the number had risen to fifty. He complained it was difficult to get German tracts through the censor because of Lutheran control of the import of German literature. With the expulsion in 1877 by the Russian authorities of six German Baptists from Ukraine for allegedly proselyting Orthodox, Kargel took measures to be naturalized to avoid banishment.[36]

On September 12, 1879 (o.s.), the Ruling Senate of the Russian government recognized Baptists as a legal entity, which allowed Baptist churches to become corporate bodies and maintain a public registry of their members. The St. Petersburg congregation was the first to comply with the new law. On November 23, Kargel took an oath of allegiance, refusing, however, to kiss the cross or the gospel, as was the custom, but

---

34. *Missionsblatt*, May 1874, 10–12, and June 1875, 93–94. See Miller, *In the Midst of Wolves*, 62, for Kargel's departure from the Soroczin church.

35. For a comprehensive biography of Kargel, see Nichols, *The Development of Russian Evangelical Spirituality*. For a listing of biographical sources, see Wardin, *Evangelical Sectarianism*, 323–25. For a short biographical sketch from Kargel, see the introduction in Kargel, *Zwischen den Enden der Erde unter Brüdern in Ketten*, vii–xvi. The Orthodox author Val'kevich, *Zapiska o propagande*, 4:26, n. 1, claims Kargel was a Turkish subject and in app. 5:29–30, produces K. K. Kalweit's letter of June 17, 1889, that records Kargel's baptism in 1869. For Kargel's first year in St. Petersburg, see QR, Apr. 1876, 7–9.

36. QR, 1876, 8; Apr. 1877, 4–6; Jan. 1878, 8; July 1878, 7–8; and Apr. 1880, 6. German Baptist Union, *Bundeskonferenz*, 1876, 65, and 1879, 5. *Missionsblatt*, July 1878, 126. BMM, Nov. 1877, 376. It is not clear based on street addresses if the mission was able to continue renting new premises during the remainder of Kargel's pastorate.

nevertheless promised with his pulpit Bible on the table that he would faithfully obey the laws of the Empire as well as preaching and teaching only "the pure doctrine of the Baptists."[37]

In the middle of 1880 Kargel resigned his post as pastor. During his tenure he had baptized fifty-one. The membership was around seventy and services were held in three languages. Kargel suffered from the severe climate and felt a change was necessary. In the meantime, he had become acquainted in 1877 with V. A. Pashkov who headed an evangelical movement in St. Petersburg, begun through Lord Radstock from England who was invited to preach among the aristocrats of the city. While attending the German Baptist Conference in Hamburg in 1879, Kargel heard an appeal from August Liebig, pastor in Odessa, and H. Berneike, pastor in Königsberg in East Prussia, for a call of help from Bulgarians who wanted a Baptist to come to baptize them. With the financial assistance of Pashkov, Kargel settled in 1880 in Ruse, Bulgaria, recently freed from Turkish sovereignty, and in September baptized at Kazanlik five candidates, the first in Bulgaria. Evidently this trip, as it was in St. Petersburg, was to be limited, but he and his wife, whom he had just married, decided to stay and learn Bulgarian. In the month before on August 17, Kargel was in Tiflis, Georgia, with August Liebig helping to organize the Baptist church at that place and ordaining as its pastor Vasiliĭ Pavlov.[38]

Adam Reinhold Schiewe

Kargel's successor in St. Petersburg was Adam Reinhold Schiewe (1843–1930), born in Russian Poland, attended the Mission School in Hamburg in 1874, and followed Kargel at the Soroczin church in 1876. But his pastorate lasted less than a year when with others the authorities banished him in May 1877, alleging baptizing the Orthodox. He was banished to Poland but became pastor at Dirschau in West Prussia in Germany. In response to the call of the St. Petersburg congregation and the German-American Mission Committee, he moved to St. Petersburg in 1880.[39]

Schiewe, now thirty-seven, arrived on September 4 with his wife and five small children. On September 12 the Memel church released its members at St. Petersburg, which led on September 14 to the constituting the St. Petersburg body as an independent church. The church, however, was not self-supporting and depended on support from the mission committee. During the first year Schiewe received annual support of

---

37. *WHZ*, Apr 1, 1880, 54. *QR*, July 1880, 8–9.

38. *Der Sendbote*, May 28, 1884, 170. For Kargel's acquaintance with the Pashkov movement in St. Petersburg, see Kargel, viii–x; *Missionsblatt*, Oct. 1878, 183–88; and *BMM*, Nov. 1878, 408–9. For his visit to Tiflis, see Val'kevich, 113–14, and app. 1:45, and *WHZ*, May 1, 1882, 90, and May 15, 1884, 110. For his arrival and work in Bulgaria, see Wardin, "The Baptists in Bulgaria," *The Baptist Quarterly*, 34/4 (Oct. 1991): 148–50, and also *BMM*, July 1881, 263.

39. Miller, 66–69.

$400, the same as Kargel, but the next year received a raise of $100, a welcome increase in a city that Schiewe found very expensive.[40]

Schiewe was beset from the start with problems. Kargel had failed to resign his papers thus delaying Schiewe taking the required oath. Schwan, who tried to set himself up as elder whom all should obey but who had some time before been excluded, brought to the government charges to remove him. Schiewe also found it difficult to work with so many nationalities in the same church, all with their own distinct characteristics that included Germans, Estonians, Latvians, and Swedes. At the end of 1880 the congregation numbered only seventy-three with some living in Moscow. He also found the premises inadequate in size and no baptistry nor space for a Sunday school. In addition, its rent at 1,200 rubles, including heat and lighting, was a great burden, pressuring the congregation to find a cheaper place. A change in location, however, would involve the government that specified the location of all registered congregations.[41]

Although Baptists at the beginning of the 1880s had been in St. Petersburg for over twenty-five years, their presence in the city, even with formal organization and civil recognition, was very weak and dependent on foreign assistance. In comparison to the magnificent church structures of the Lutherans and Reformed in the city, their hall was inadequate and paltry. Their membership was small with some members living elsewhere. The pastor, having been exiled once before, could again suffer the same fate. In writing of the history of the congregation, Schiewe wrote: "Very slowly and meagerly it went further and often all appeared to perish." He also claimed that he took the post "under great difficulties." The great imperial metropolis was no friend, and only time would tell the congregation's survival.[42]

Baptist penetration into the Russian Empire first occurred in the Baltic area, unplanned and uncoordinated. Fortunately, the Memel church was strategically located and with its dedicated leadership played an import role. The church itself provided a haven for converts from the Empire and contributed financial support and mounted protest for the persecuted. The German Baptist center in Hamburg provided publicity and ministerial training. Except for occasional visits of German Baptist missionaries and pastors to the church in St. Petersburg, much of the work was indigenous, especially among the Lettish and Swedish believers. Although by the early 1880s the effort in St. Petersburg was problematic and the work in Finland weak, yet a mass movement of Baptist work had begun in Courland and an outpost had been made in the imperial capital itself.

40. *WHZ*, Nov. 1, 1880, 166–67. *QR*, Jan. 1881, 7–8. *Der Sendbote*, June 14, 1882, 186.
41. *BMM*, July 1881, 263. *Der Sendbote*, June 14, 1882, 186, and May 28, 1884, 170–71.
42. *Der Sendbote*, May 28, 1884, 170–71.

5

German Baptists in Russian Poland and Volhynia

Gottfried Alf

ABOUT THE SAME TIME Baptists were beginning to penetrate the Baltic area, another Baptist movement began south of East Prussia in Russian Poland. Although East Prussia will play a role in its origin, this movement was indigenous, led by a native of the area who began a revival movement, knowing nothing of Baptists. Gottfried F. Alf (1831–1898) was a Lutheran schoolteacher of German extraction, a native of Poland who spoke both German and Polish. In the absence of the minister in the parish, he was required to lead the service. In preparation for this responsibility and study of Scripture, he began to realize his own spiritually lost condition. Without the influence of others, he experienced in 1853 a personal conversion that led him to put his complete faith in the finished work of Christ.[1]

Upon his conversion, he began preaching to his students, beginning a revival that also spread to adults. Many parents became alarmed and began to keep their children from school. The pastor forbade Alf's discussions and prayer meetings. Upon Alf's refusal, the pastor brought to the Lutheran Consistory charges against Alf that led to

---

1. For bibliographic material on Alf and the beginnings of Baptists in Russian Poland, see Wardin, *Evangelical Sectarianism*, 199–205. For a biography of Alf, see Wardin, *Gottfried F. Alf*. A comprehensive history of Baptist in Poland is Kupsch, *Geschichte der Baptisten in Polen, 1852–1932*. A very valuable and early source is the work by Gottfried Liebert, *Geschichte der Baptisten in Russisch-Polen*, who was a deacon in the Kicin Baptist Church who personally knew Alf. Baptist periodicals published numerous reports from Alf that were also translated into English.

PART TWO—Prospects: German and Baltic Beginnings, 1855–1884

Alf's loss of his position as teacher as well as his home. Alf's appeal to the Consistory was met with a rude response. He then moved in 1854 with his wife and baby son to his parents where his father gave him land to make a living.

Alf continued his revival activity and undertook mission trips, but the Lutheran authorities tried to stop him. On one occasion he and a companion were seized, beaten, and held for three days. He began to think, where should he turn if his own church is persecuting him? Heinrich Assmann, a neighbor from Stolzeberg, East Prussia, who bought land near Alf, although himself not yet a Baptist, told him of Baptists in Germany. Although Alf had never heard of Baptists, he felt that his views and theirs were in agreement except on infant baptism. Alf and his group studied the issue, but with Alf's decision to become a Baptist his group divided. In addition, his father now turned against him, took away his land, and expelled him and his family. Alf's pilgrimage from a schoolteacher, to a revivalist, to becoming a Baptist was costly—twice the loss of income, repudiation by family, and division of his following. Alf now moved to Adamowo.

Assmann told Alf about Wilhelm Weist (1822–1903), first missionary of the German Baptist Prussian Association and pastor of the Baptist church in Stolzenberg, who might come to baptize him. After preliminary inquiries, Weist with Gnass, an assistant pastor, and Schimanski, a Polish interpreter, went to Russian Poland. At the border Weist's company prayed that a door be opened into Russia. They were admitted, carrying with them Bibles and tracts that were not confiscated. On November 28, 1858, Weist baptized nine candidates, including Alf, and on the following day an additional seventeen in a small brook. Before his departure, Weist baptized an additional eighteen.[2]

Alf, only twenty-seven years old, was not only the head of a revival movement but also the Baptist denomination in Poland. The Lutheran Consistory and district magistrate forbade Alf spreading Baptist doctrine. Alf wanted a pass to study at the Mission School in Hamburg in 1859, fearing he would never get it, but nevertheless received it since the authorities hoped he would never return. Alf was ordained on September 26 in Hamburg, the first Russian subject to receive Baptist ordination. He returned to Poland in October. Even though Baptist meetings were forbidden and petitions to the Tsar unanswered, Alf nevertheless addressed large crowds and began a Sunday school. He baptized forty persons in November and ten in December and made three missionary trips in the two months after his return. Alf found a receptive mission field, especially among the German Lutherans and Mennonites. The Lutheran Church at this time was beset by a shortage of pastors, large parishes, a membership of many nominal members, and handicapped with liberal theology and formal services. Revivalistic preaching also attracted numbers of Mennonites who were ready to break from their traditional worship.

2. For Weist's arrival, see *Missionsblatt*, Dec. 1858, 185–86, and the English version in *QR*, Jan. 1859, 5–8.

Persecution

Hostility toward Alf arose in proportion to his success. Almost fourteen months after his return, the authorities arrested him in December 1860. He was imprisoned, chained, and transported to two other prisons but was freed nine days later and placed under strict surveillance. Even though he faced for the next five years through 1865 imprisonment and transport, he continued his missionary work. Liebert, the early chronicler of Baptist work in Poland, claimed Alf was persecuted eighteen times, including thirty-two imprisonments of 278 days and transport of 1,728 kilometers.[3]

One of Alf's worst and yet rewarding imprisonments was for three months from September to December 1863 in the prison in Pultusk. He was forced to wear prisoner's garb, fed little food, and slept on bare boards. His fellow prisoners were about seventy, most of whom were thieves but included some women imprisoned for murder. On his entry into prison, the prisoners met him with ridicule. On the first night, the food he had brought for supper was stolen, and soon his neckerchief was taken. For a time despair overtook him as he was beset by hunger, evil companions, vermin, and satanic torment. But he began to return good for evil by sharing his bread with other prisoners and putting salt into their water. Theft of his possessions ceased, and some asked his forgiveness. He distributed Polish tracts brought by his wife as well as several copies of Scripture that he obtained and found opportunity to preach.[4]

Some of Alf's co-workers also suffered persecution, but Alf suffered more than others. He probably underwent more intense oppression than any other Baptist leader in the nineteenth century in Russia. At the end of 1865 the government ceased its general concerted oppression, although not publicly known until 1866, a policy also carried out in Courland and in Ukraine. Although Baptists were more or less tolerated, they still faced hostility from Lutherans, Old Mennonites, and Orthodox in Poland or Ukraine and still faced possible local attacks, imprisonments, and harassment. Alf wrote in 1874 that persecution had declined and the Lutheran clergy was more reasonable, realizing that persecution caused more harm than good.

Church Life

Alf was charismatic in his preaching, winning converts primarily from German Lutherans and Mennonites but almost none from the predominant Polish Roman Catholic population or Jews. Alf, however, was more than an itinerant missionary; he also was a pastor, a teacher, and a builder of a new denomination. With his educational background as a teacher, he was literate, and as a student of Scripture and training in Hamburg he acquired some knowledge of theology and church polity.

---

3. See Liebert, 163–249 for a description of the persecutions of Alf and others in Poland.
4. For Alf's account of his three-month imprisonment in Pultusk, see *QR*, Apr. 1864, 29–32.

PART TWO—Prospects: German and Baltic Beginnings, 1855–1884

Alf's first congregation at Adamowo was a mission of the church in Stolzenberg, East Prussia, gaining independent status on August 4, 1861. A second congregation followed at Kicin on August 25, which will supersede the congregation at Adamowo on the emigration of most of the latter's members. These two congregations were the first two independent Baptist churches on Russian soil except for the two small congregations in the Åland Islands. At the end of 1874, in spite of a migration of over 900, membership in Russian Poland was 1,570 in four churches that in turn had 75 mission stations with members at 136 different locations. As Baptists in Germany, but unlike Baptists in Sweden, Baptists in Poland took time and care in forming independent congregations. Seventeen Sunday schools enrolled 445 children with twenty-five teachers.[5]

Church life was patterned after Baptist churches in Germany. Churches accepted members only after a creditable confession of faith and exercised discipline for erring brethren. Members were expected to attend services regularly, read Scripture, engage in secret and family prayer, and witness. By 1874 members had distributed 6,410 Bibles and Testaments and almost 57,000 tracts. Baptisms in rivers, observance of the Lord's Supper, and love feasts with testimony and fellowship were important events.

It was not until 1868 before authorities permitted the Kicin church to erect a wooden chapel, but not too high as to resemble a church. By the early 1870s, three other chapels were erected. Money for chapels came from Germany and England.

Alf not only expected the members to act as missionaries but was fortunate to attract men, some of them schoolteachers, to enter regular mission service. The mission force was indigenous, not an import from Germany, which, in any case, would have been illegal. In 1874 eighteen missionaries were on the field. Mission work was difficult with travel generally by foot or wagon, and remuneration was poor. Following Oncken's example, Alf began to hold mission schools for his workers.

As noted, Baptists were very diligent in distributing Scriptures and tracts. Unfortunately, many Polish people were illiterate. In addition, the Lutheran Consistory placed an embargo on all Baptist literature, including Baptist periodicals from abroad.

It took time to develop stewardship among the new converts and financial assistance from abroad was needed. The American Baptist Missionary Union provided funds to the German-American Committee that in turn helped to support mission work in Russia. Moneys also came from the German Baptist Conference in the USA. Great Britain was also a contributor that included, because of Oncken's appeal, support from the Bristo Place Baptist Church of Edinburgh for Alf's salary.

---

5. For statistics, see Liebert, 250.

Migration to Volhynia

Very early in Alf's ministry a new field of endeavor opened up 800 kilometers to the east in Volhynia in northwest Ukraine. Beginning in 1859 and then with increased numbers, Baptists from Poland began to emigrate to this area for economic opportunity where land was available. Upon freedom of the serfs in 1861, landlords were happy to sell or rent their lands to new settlers. Other motives in migrating were the unsettled conditions from the second Polish Uprising in 1863 and prospects of greater religious freedom. Although Baptist migrants came primarily from Poland, others arrived from East and West Prussia. Other Germans, primarily Lutheran, had already settled in the area, but thousands more of them were also overtaken by the fever of migration.

The trek to the new territory was not easy. Horses pulled large wagons, including some covered, filled with all kinds of utensils upon which one or two families, numbering fifteen to twenty, sat on top. Singly or in caravans the trekkers made the trip in two to three weeks. After stopping for the night, the women prepared the meal; a boiling kettle rested on a roaring fire. At night men crawled under the wagons while women and children slept on top.[6]

Conditions in the new land were primitive. The area was heavily forested and required hard labor to remove the trees and clear the ground. The first houses were made of earth and scrub. There were no schools, and sons would be subject to Russian military service. Many lamented their move. In June 1867, *Missionsblatt*, the Baptist periodical in Germany, ran an article, "On a Warning before Emigration to Russia," that included a letter from a woman who claimed nothing existed there but misery and poverty and extremely low spiritual life.[7]

Whatever the conditions, the migration did not stop. Almost the entire membership of the church in Adamowo had migrated by 1863. Two of Alf's early coworkers, Mathias Kelm and M. Hartwich, also moved to the area. Liebert claimed by 1874 over 900 Baptists had migrated. In October and November 1862 Alf made his first trip to the region, staying in his host's home, a shelter with a roof of grass and hay in a dark forest. Alf held a meeting in the shelter that included Lutherans and Mennonites. On invitation, he also preached in a Mennonite church. On his second journey, beginning in February 1864, he traveled by horse and wagon through rain and snow and at times on roads that were only paths. On this trip, Alf not only preached and baptized but also led in forming two Baptist congregations. The first was on May 19 (n.s.) at Horczik with 203 members and three days later a church at Soroczin with 250 members, the first two durable Baptist churches in Ukraine. Alf was also invited to preach in a Mennonite colony. Alf was again in Volhynia for almost six weeks in 1874, attending the meeting of the Russian-Turkish Association at the church in Neudorf and

---

6. For a description of the trek to Volhynia, see *SPES* 8 (1865), 406.
7. *Missionsblatt*, Mar. 1867, 46–48, 86–87.

also conducting numerous meetings.[8] Baptists in Volhynia, however, faced their own internal difficulties. Theological dissension arose over sinless perfection and the restoration of all things and even over distribution of property among Polish-speaking Masurs from East Prussia. In 1866 the Prussian Association sent Bernhard Vogel and August Penski, two emissaries from the Prussian Association, who brought order with the exclusion of a great number of members. Nevertheless a third congregation at Neudorf was established in 1866.[9]

As early as 1801, Lutherans had established a parish at Zhitomer and then two other parishes respectively in 1864 and 1869 and then beginning in 1888 formed adjunct parishes. Their large parishes and too few clergy seriously handicapped Lutheran work. In 1876, with over 40,000 German colonists, the Lutherans maintained only three pastors. With such large numbers without adequate spiritual care, Baptists found Volhynia a most productive mission field. Baptists possessed a corps of consecrated itinerant missionaries, who could periodically visit the villages, and also a dedicated laity.[10]

Karl Ondra

One of the most effective and energetic missionaries in Volhynia was Karl Ondra (1839–1887), a man who, as Eduard Kupsch, a writer of Polish Baptist history, stated, possessed "a strong personality." His biography, written by friends shortly after his death, described him as "earnest and eloquent."[11] Toward the end of his ministry, he became particularly interested in the end times. He believed in the return of the Jews to Palestine, the conversion of Israel to Christ, and the near appearance of the Antichrist and his dominion. He also had a gift for poetry. He spoke both German and Polish and could understand Russian.

Ondra was born in Russian Poland, but when a child his parents moved to Volhynia. Ondra was confirmed in the Lutheran Church and, although seeking to convert Baptists from their errors, he himself became convinced to become a Baptist. Kelm immersed him in 1863. Ondra attended the Mission School in Hamburg in 1865. At the age of twenty-six, he began his ministry the same year in Neudorf. He experienced a great response to his preaching with numbers often mingling their joy with tears in public confession. Ondra reported in 1868: "Our public services are now so well attended that we are puzzled to find room for all who come, and on occasions of

---

8. *Missionsblatt*, Jan. 1863, 15–16; Sep. 1864, 141–43; Mar. 1875, 44–46; Apr. 1875, 70–72; and June 1875, 92. BMM, Apr. 1863, 108–9. QR, Mar. 1875, 11–12.

9. *Missionsblatt (Beilage)*, Apr, 1867, 2–3. Liebert, 112–14.

10. *Wandering Volhynians* 3 (1989), 11–12. SPES 19/44 (1876), 348–49, and 36/32 (1893), 252.

11. For sketches of Ondra's life, see Miller, *In the Midst of Wolves*, 11–20; Kupsch, 153–58; and Veltisov, "Nemetskiĭ baptizm v Rossii," MO (June 1902): 1020–21. A small booklet, *Kurz gefasste Lebens-Beschreibung*, includes data on his life and some of his poetry.

baptism not only is the chapel filled to overflowing . . . many stand outside listening, and many have to go away as they cannot get near enough to catch the sound." Crowds continued to come, and people not finding a seat would stand by the windows. After enlarging its chapel twice, in 1874 the congregation rebuilt its building with 1,500 people attending the opening ceremonies.[12]

In the mid-seventies Ondra was conducting large baptismal services. In one letter he reported baptizing his largest group—eighty-two composed of forty-three women and thirty-nine men. In a later letter he recorded baptizing thirty-four and that the Neudorf church had received during the year 221 by baptism. In spite of a large reponse to his preaching, care was nevertheless taken in receiving candidates for baptism. He reported on one occasion that a boy who was moved by the preaching wept because he was not considered "ripe for profession." He felt a great need for workers. At the end of 1872 he found himself almost alone with three churches in Volhynia and their stations. In February 1873 he conducted a small mission school to prepare evangelists. In 1875 he had acquired some coworkers, including Johann Kargel and L. Nasgowitz, but yet declared, "What is that among so many?!" He also heard the call, "Come over and help us." In 1873 he made three journeys—to Luzk near the Polish border, to the conference of the Mennonite Brethren in the Molochna Colony, and to Annenthal near Odessa. In 1874 Ondra with Kargel from the Soroczin church undertook a mission trip to St. Petersburg.[13]

Lutherans and Orthodox were particularly hostile toward the Baptist presence in Volhynia. Kelm wrote in November, 1863, "The members of the Lutheran and Greek Church would destroy us, 'the sooner the better,' if it were in their power. I am often alarmed at the rage and fury of the adversaries!"

When he was at Odessa in 1870, Ondra recorded that it was the first time he sat under "lock and key" for preaching and also charged for being an Anabaptist. He claimed this event was followed by "a long series of persecutions" in Volhynia. For a time in 1871 authorities forbade him to baptize, a prohibition that, however, was lifted. In an annual report, probably written around the beginning of 1872, Ondra complained of oppression from Treufeld, a Lutheran pastor, who caused "constant trials, expenses, and committals to prison." In December 1872 a magistrate summoned Ondra who informed him of many complaints of Baptist baptisms, an activity he claimed was forbidden. Ondra pointed out that Baptists had freedom in Russian Poland, Courland, and in the South. In response the magistrate requested him only to write down the names of those baptized, the jurisdiction to which they belonged, and their former religious affiliation. Ondra submitted the lists as well as a petition from his church.[14]

---

12. QR, Oct. 1868, 329–30, and Jan. 1876, 13. *Missionsblatt*, Jan. 1873, 12.

13. *BMM*, Jan. 1876, 22. *Missionsblatt*, May 1873, 80–81; Aug. 1873, 137–42; and June 1875, 93–94. QR, July 1875, 38–39, and Oct. 1876, 13.

14. QR, Jan. 1864, 13; Apr. 1872, 954; July 1873, 38–39; and July 1881, 10. *Der Sendbote*, Feb. 10,

PART TWO—Prospects: German and Baltic Beginnings, 1855–1884

In a mission report in 1876, Ondra wrote, "The black clouds which hung over our work, particularly in connection with the threatened proscription, have nearly passed away, and with less mischief than we feared, though not without leaving some trace; but we look for better days." He then noted the continuing evangelistic opportunities and baptisms. Little did Ondra realize, however, that in the following year the authorities will strike a serious blow against the German Baptist work in Volhynia, which will greatly impact his own ministry. He will also not realize that the status of German Baptists in the Empire will also significantly change before the end of the decade.[15]

1886, 50. *Missionsblatt*, July 1871, 116–21; Apr. 1872, 72; and May 1873, 80–81.

15. *QR*, Oct. 1876, 13.

6

Emergence of the Mennonite Brethren

BAPTISTS EMERGED, AS ALREADY noted, in the 1850s and early 1860s almost simultaneously in the Baltic, Russian Poland, and Volhynia in northwest Ukraine. About the same time in the Black Sea region of southern Ukraine and Dobrudja in Turkey (after 1878 in Romania), evangelical currents were also developing that resulted in the almost simultaneous appearance in this area of Mennonite Brethren, German Baptists, and Ukrainian Stundo-Baptists. These three bodies were closely related ideologically and regarded themselves as religious allies. The Mennonite Brethren will help lay the basis for the appearance of German Baptists who in turn will play a timely role in the development of Mennonite Brethren. Both German Baptists and Mennonite Brethren will be conduits for the appearance of a Ukrainian Stundo-Baptist movement.[1]

The Mennonite colonies of Chortitza (the Old Colony) and Molochna, although traditional in custom and religious practice, were not immune from outside influences. Johann Cornies, chairman of the Agricultural Improvement Society from 1817 to his death in 1848, was a forceful leader for improving agriculture and the educational system. The educational standards were woefully low, but standards for teachers and teaching increased and the curriculum expanded. The establishment in 1822 of a high

---

1. For a bibliography of works in English, German, and Russian on Mennonite Brethren, see Wardin, *Evangelical Sectarianism in the Russian Empire and the USSR*, 263–87. A primary and indispensable source of the beginnings and development of the Mennonite Brethren is Friesen, *Die Alt-Evangelische Mennonitische Brüderschaft in Russland*. An English translation of the work is *The Mennonite Brotherhood in Russia (1789–1910)*. A modern treatment and standard history of Mennonite Brethren is Toews, *A History of the Mennonite Brethren Church*.

PART TWO—Prospects: German and Baltic Beginnings, 1855–1884

school at Ohrloff in Molochna produced trained teachers.² Other secondary schools followed.

Outside religious influences made some impact from representatives of the Russian Bible Society or the British and Foreign Bible Society, the visits of Quakers, and pietistic influences that brought religious vitality and a broadened view of the world. In 1821 in the Molochna, the elder of the church in Ohrloff, Cornies's church, formed a branch of the Russian Bible Society, which, however, produced opposition and division. Other influences came through teachers who taught at the school at Ohrloff and in Chortitza, pietistic literature from Germany, and also Mennonites from Poland and Germany who settled in Molochna and whose congregations were open to pietistic thought and practice. Gnadenfeld, a Groningen Old Flemish congregation whose membership was infused with Lutheran pietists from Prussia and under Moravian influence, was a notable example.³

These influences, however, at this time brought no widespread religious revival. Mennonite society reflected much of society around it including tensions and conflicts between government and church authorities, landowners and the landless, and progressives and conservatives. Mennonites in South Russia had lost much of their character as a distinct Christian community. In 1812 a small division occurred with the establishment of the *Kleine Gemeinde* (the small church), whose adherents bemoaned the departure from the attributes of the forefathers of community, equality, humility, and sobriety. Heinrich Balzer (1800–1846), who in 1833 joined the *Kleine Gemeinde*, wrote scathingly of Mennonite society of his time. In his treatise, "Faith and Reason," he noted the push for wealth and pride and such vices as drunkenness, smoking, gambling, and singing of sensual songs. In the same year, his "A Poem in Farewell," composed of thirty-nine stanzas, included the same strictures. He noted the reading of frivolous literature, the festivals and weddings without any godly sentiment, and the lack of chastity.⁴

John Melville, a Scot who settled in 1837 in Odessa and a distributor of Bibles and tracts, wrote in 1842 in his travel in the Mennonite colonies that although the people were kind he noted a "cold-hearted Christianity" and a total lack of religious instruction in the schools and in most families. He recorded that young people are baptized "as a mere matter of course" and then rarely attend services in the church. He found, however, an exception in the Molochna Colony, evidently in the Gnadenfeld

---

2. For a valuable study of the first century of the development of life of the Mennonite colonies in the Russian Empire, see Urry, *None But Saints*. Also see his dissertation, "The Closed and the Open."

3. For outside evangelical influences, see Friesen, *The Mennonite Brotherhood in Russia*, 92–109, 141–42; Jantz, "Pietism's Gift to Russian Mennonites," *Direction* 36/1 (Spring 2007): 58–73; and Urry, "The Closed and the Open," 207–55. Also see Urry's article, "John Melville and the Mennonites," *MQR* 54/4 (Oct. 1980): 305–22, for information on networks of distribution of Bibles and tracts in the Russian Empire in the mid-nineteenth century that also impacted Mennonites.

4. For Balzar's treatise, "Faith and Reason," as translated and edited by Robert Friedmann, and "A Poem in Farewell," in the original German, see Plett, *The Golden Years*, 215–18, 237–47.

settlement where he found "spiritual worship," religious instruction in home and school, missionary meetings, and a temperance society. Another outside observer was Alexander K. Brune, a Lutheran, sent by the Minister of Internal Affairs upon the request of the Lutheran General Consistory to investigate economic and religious affairs in South Russia. Except in economic affairs, Brune criticized the Mennonite community for its bondage to custom. Although unduly judgmental but yet with substantial evidence, he criticized the Mennonite community for its "impaired level of intelligence, morality and religious education." He noted that the Mennonites, although attending church, "mechanically fulfill the requirement of their religion" and gave priority to material concerns. Brune also claimed that the divisions between Mennonite churches have produced "an indifference of faith."[5]

Jacob P. Bekker, one of the founders of the Mennonite Brethren, noted the distilleries and saloons in the colonies. He claimed drinking and drunkenness, also common at wedding celebrations and house-raising bees, were widespread. Young people attended taverns and fairs at neighboring Russian villages where they drank, sang, and danced. Bekker blamed the elders for turning a blind eye and failing to exercise any church discipline. David Epp (1781–1843) and his son Jacob D. Epp (1820–1890), devoted farmer-ministers from the Old Colony, were unhappy with moral conditions. David noted the declining morality and decried the "dead moralism," while Jacob hoped in 1862 that the then appearance of a new revival movement, although rejecting its extremism, might arouse the Mennonite Church from its "drowsy stupor."[6]

One, of course, must take care in evaluating the critical account of Russian Mennonite society at this time from critics with their own agendas. Of course, not all Mennonites in the colonies lived lives of luxury, debauchery, or moral indifference. Numbers lived quiet morally respectable lives led by dedicated elders. Along with their economic achievements, Mennonites in Russia were noted for their discipline, diligence, and dependability. But on the other hand, Mennonite society as a whole was increasingly accepting the loose lifestyle and worldly aims of society around them rather than existing as godly communities separate from the world. A religious revolt was almost inevitable.

Eduard Wüst

The main catalyst for an eruption came in the person of a Lutheran pastor of a Separatist Lutheran congregation, Eduard Wüst (1819–1859), who appeared on the Russian scene as a brightly burning meteorite.[7] After a thirteen-year ministry, which ended

---

5. BFBS, *Monthly Extracts*, Mar. 1843, 404–6. On Melville's career, see Urry, "John Melville and the Mennonites." Toews, *The Story of the Early Mennonite Brethren (1860–1869)*, 58, 107.

6. Bekker, *Origin of The Mennonite Brethren Church*, 18–21. Dyck, *A Mennonite in Russia*, 25, 166.

7. For a sympathetic biography of Wüst, see Kroeker, *Pfarrer Eduard Wüst*. An appraisal of his work is in Urry, "The Closed and the Open," 489–508. Also see Jantz, "A Pietist Pastor and the Russian Mennonites," *Direction* 36/2 (Fall 2007): 232–46.

PART TWO—Prospects: German and Baltic Beginnings, 1855–1884

shortly before his death, much of the blaze had dissipated but nevertheless left far-reaching consequences. He became a controversial figure in his native Württemberg in Germany and later in Russia, beloved by many but despised by others. Many in Germany were drawn to his call for repentance and faith, but others faulted him for his dramatic preaching and his participation in private meetings. His opponents criticized him for his mingling with common folk, failing to admonish them to stay in their own parishes, and his familiarity with children.[8]

With the door closed in Württemberg for ecclesiastical appointment, he accepted in 1845 the invitation of the Separatist Lutherans, independent of the Lutheran Consistory, to become pastor in Neu-Hoffnung near Berdyansk in southern Ukraine. His inaugural sermon set the tone for his ministry. He quoted from Isaiah 40:6, "The voice said, Preach. And he said, What shall I preach?" After reading further, he declared he would proclaim God's "eternally-abiding word." He stressed he would preach Jesus Christ, the crucified.[9] He drew great crowds, and many were converted. People of all classes came from all over southern Russia, from Odessa to the Caucasus, including Lutherans belonging to the General Consistory, Separatists, neighboring Mennonites, and some Catholics. He preached not only in Neu-Hoffnung but also in the other Separatist colonies as well as in regular Lutheran parishes and exchanged pulpits with the Mennonite church in Gnadenfeld. In 1849 he undertook a major trip to Kharkov, St. Petersburg, and Reval (Tallinn).[10]

Wüst also held mission festivals for support of missions across confessional lines. One corespondent wrote in 1849 to *Evangelical Christendom* that around 1,000 Lutherans and Mennonites attended an annual mission festival that collected 300 guilders. On the following day after a mission festival, Wüst would convene a conference of people from various denominations, stressing oneness in Christ. In addition, a women's mission society met during the winter months in which women sewed and knitted for missions and also included intercessory prayer, singing, and reading of mission news led by a brother. Members of the Mennonite church of Gnadenfeld held monthly meetings with Wüst on Saturday for mutual edification. Weekly edification meetings also met in a number of villages.[11]

Abraham Kroeker, Wüst's biographer, claimed that his ministry also had social benefits in the rise of educational standards with the calling of trained teachers and

---

8. For an excellent account of Wüst's career in Germany, see Doerksen, "A Second Menno?," *MQR* 74/2 (Apr. 2000): 311–25.

9. For an English translation of Wüst's inaugural sermon, see Friesen, *The Mennonite Brotherhood in Russia*, 213–23.

10. For the extent of Wüst's ministry, see Alexander Brune's report in Toews, *The Story of the Early Mennonite Brethren*, 59, and Kroeker, *Pfarrer Eduard Wüst*, 42, 75.

11. For Wüst's relationship to the Mennonites in Gnadenfeld, see Friesen, *The Mennonite Brotherhood in Russia*, 206–207; *EC* 3 (1849), 220; and Bekker, 24–27.

improvement in economic life. He also exercised strict church discipline. The moral tone of the surrounding colonies was raised.[12]

But numbers in the Lutheran clergy were unhappy with Wüst's activity. In 1851 charges were brought to the General Lutheran Synod in St. Petersburg that he was "a disturber of the peace," even claiming that several individuals had taken their own lives because of his preaching. After a visit of the General Superintendent, two school teachers were dismissed and one imprisoned. The Superintendent, although having no jurisdiction over Wüst, forbade him to preach outside his own congregations, but his attempt to get the Russian government to expel him was overruled. Further complaints to the General Consistory and the Guardian's Committee resulted in September 1857 of a ruling from the Ministries of the Interior and State Domains forbidding Wüst to minister outside his own congregations. But Wüst had his defenders, and the investigation that considered his banishment came to nought.[13]

Wüst was not only beset by strong opposition from without but also beset by inner turmoil within his own congregations. Wüst had been too one-sided in his preaching of free grace and neglected, as he later recognized, sanctification of the believer after conversion. According to Kroeker, an opposition party, led by Kappes from the Lutheran Mariupol colonies, in its stress on justification by faith also began advocating antinomianian views, freeing the believer from moral restraint. The opposition also advocated more freedom in church practice, desiring elimination of traditional Lutheran practices in baptism, the Lord's Supper, and confirmation. Kappes and his followers charged Wüst with "rigid pharisaism."[14] The opposition gained Joseph Hottmann, who, according to Jacob Bekker, was a schoolteacher and an official of a Wüst church and had been converted under Wüst's ministry. In preaching in Wüst's absence, he departed from the prescribed sermon and spoke extemporaneously with a stress on free grace. According to a correspondent to the Lutheran *St. Peterburgishes evangelisches Sonntagsblatt*, Hottmann was a colonist from the Crimea who introduced as well a new style of worship. Earlier Wüst himself had shifted away from traditional Lutheran hymnody, and, in fact, Wüst, in leading a caravan of wagons to a mission festival with members singing and praying, would occasionally stop for rest, wave a red banner, and lead in a popular Christian song. But Hottmann went beyond Wüst. He led people to beat the time with their fingers as they sang, which became more and more enthusiastic, leading finally to springing and hopping. Because of this type of worship, the opposition became known as *Hüpfer* or Jumpers.[15]

Wüst now faced a great crisis. He now began to stress sanctification and tried to counter both Kappes and Hottmann, even removing the latter from his church position. In the fall of 1858, a decisive break occurred between Wüst and the opposition at

12. Kroeker, *Pfarrer Eduard Wüst*, 70–73.
13. *EC* 6 (1852), 221–22. Kroeker, *Pfarrer Eduard Wüst*, 94–96.
14. Kroeker, 88–90. *SPES* 8 (1865), 221–22.
15. Bekker, 27–30. *SPES* 5 (1862), 142.

a conference tied to a mission festival. The opponents condemned Wüst for his stress on sanctification and for allowing both converted and unconverted to partake of the Lord's Supper. In his inaugural sermon in 1845 Wüst declared the need for the separation of believer and non-believer but inconsistently did not require close communion. Wüst's opponents left singing an insulting song, calling the Wüst followers Pharisees, alleging they cursed the law with hearts full of sin. Wüst was devastated by the defection. He became sick, and beginning in the spring of 1859 could not leave his bed. He died in July 1859 from dropsy at the age of forty-one, but no doubt the heartache from the opposition hastened his death.[16]

Mennonite Brethren Secession

The 1850s and early 1860s, fueled by the ministry of Wüst, were times of great spiritual upheaval in southern Ukraine. The Wüst phenomenon not only created Wüst brethren or supporters among Württemberg Separatists, Lutherans, and Mennonites but also the rise of a movement of free grace with ecstatic exercises that brought division and alienation from Wüst himself. A further complication was the influence of a Mennonite Templer movement, "The Friends of Jerusalem," furthered by the influential paper, *Süddeutsche Warte,* published in Württemberg by Christof Hoffman, that also found adherents among Wüst's followers. This movement was pietistic but also activistic and eschatological. It promoted educational reform and the formation of a new world, including the establishment of a Christian community in Jerusalem.[17]

At the time of Wüst's death in 1859, it was problematic what channels Wüst's followers or former adherents would take. In any case, the fermentation of the time demanded change. But would the "old wineskins" hold the "new wine" of new religious experiences and new visions? The path of the Kleine Gemeinde of attempting to return to a pristine past of corporate communities of simplicity and humility, rejecting the world without requiring an immediate experience of regeneration, had no appeal. Some Wüst adherents, such as Elder August Lenzmann of the Gnadenfeld church, saw no need to separate from the larger Mennonite community. While a number of Gnadenfeld members will remain, others, however, will leave. Although initially not seeking withdrawal, some will help to initiate a Mennonite Brethren secession in 1860, while others became Templers in 1863.

The Mennonite Brethren secession was a laymen's movement in face of opposition from the elders of the Mennonite Church. As a critic of Wüst in the "free grace movement" and an advocate of exuberance in worship, Hottmann became a key figure in moving some Mennonites to separatism. Hottmann, a strong advocate of

---

16. Bekker, 29–30. Kroeker, *Pfarrer Eduard Wüst,* 89–90, 96. Friesen, *The Mennonite Brotherhood in Russia,* 385. *SPES* 5 (1862), 142.

17. See Friesen, *The Mennonite Brotherhood in Russia,* 223–25, for divisions in the Wüst movement. For the Mennonite Templer movement, see Friesen, 106–8; Sawatzky, *Mennonite Templers*; and Doerksen, "Mennonite Templers in Russia," *JMS* 3 (1985): 128–37.

separation of believers from non-believers, convened a council in the spring of 1859 with Mennonites in attendance in which he condemned the decadence of the Christian church with its inclusion of believers and apostates at the Lord's Table. Mennonite dissidents from Wüst were already meeting with other believers in separate conventicles. In addition, Hottmann administered communion with consecrated wafers as in the Lutheran Church but passed the broken bread among the participants.[18] Some Mennonites of the Wüst Brethren, spiritually energized, conscious of the unconverted in the churches, and participants in devotional meetings of fellow believers, began to consider private communion for themselves. They then asked Lenzmann, the elder of the Gnadenfeld church, to lead separate communion services for them, a request that Lenzmann refused, believing it was disruptive of regular church order. In November Abraham Cornelsen, member of the Rudnerweide (Frisian) church, presided at a communion service in a home in Elizabethtal, which included not only members of the Flemish church but also six from the Gnadenfeld church. The Flemish church put its members under a church ban, but the Gnadenfeld church only admonished them. But in two church meetings in December at the Gnadenfeld church, all adherents of the new movement were attacked, particularly Johann Claassen (1820–1876) and Jacob Reimer, (1817–1891), both of whom, however, had been absent from the communion service. As a result Claassen and Reimer and their supporters left the meeting.

On January 6, 1860, at a meeting in Elizabethtal, eighteen brethren signed a document of secession, which was followed on January 18 by signatures of nine others.[19] The document pointed out the decadence and godlessness in the Mennonite community without any ministerial reproof. It declared that its adherents would separate from their respective churches, although continuing to pray for the salvation of their brethren. It appealed to the sanction of Scripture, claiming to be in agreement with Menno Simons, upholding a baptism based on a living faith, communion of believers only, and footwashing for its blessing. The church was to ban unrepentant sinners from its fellowship.

The signers of the document clearly saw themselves as Mennonites, feeling they were the true Mennonites who adhered to Menno's teaching of a vital faith, establishment of a believer's church, and the practice of the ban. In spite of these Mennonite elements, were they attempting to recreate the Anabaptism of the sixteenth century? Not at all. Their principles were not based on a community founded on Kingdom ethics separate from the political and religious elements of the world. Their type of separatism was based on the new pietism that included revivalism, personal conversion, expressive if not exuberant worship, individual accountability, mission outreach,

18. For a detailed recital of events from primary sources of the Mennonite Brethren secession, see Friesen, *The Mennonite Brethren Brotherhood in Russia*, 227–62, 280–84, 341–401. Bekker, one of the founders, in his *Origin of the Mennonite Brethren Church*, presents first-hand observations and primary sources. Also see Toews, *A History of the Mennonite Brethren Church*, 32–50.

19. For an English translation of the document, see Friesen, *The Mennonite Brotherhood in Russia*, 230–32.

and an activism that sought to change the world through the distribution of Scripture, moral action, and an openness to educational initiatives. They accepted economic and social advancement. Their separatism was a separatism of a believer's church, not a traditional separatism from other denominations, and recognition if not fellowship with the converted in other communions.[20]

Although social and economic conditions opened doors for a new religious movement, the movement was not simply a social revolution in religious guise. It is true it incorporated the characteristics of a new age of individualism, rising educational expectations, and capitalistic enterprise, but it imbibed the new religious currents of individual religious experience, accountability, and activity. Although the movement will attract a cross-section of society, including the poor, its leaders were not from the landless. Although not traditional landholders who held political and ecclesiastical control, they nevertheless were part of a rising entrepreneurial and rising educational class. Their leaders included merchants, teachers, millers, or a combination of these occupations.[21]

Immediately the Mennonite Brethren faced opposition. Five elders of the *Kirchenconvent* (Council of Elders), including Lenzmann, in spite of the protest of Bernhard Fast, elder of the Ohrloff Church, signed a statement that the new group could not be accepted and the *Gebietsamt or* Administrative Office should attempt to dissuade it to stop its endeavor. The Administrative Office, gaining no satisfactory response from the Mennonite Brethren leaders, sent out a directive to all village mayors forbidding all unauthorized meetings.

In an effort to gain recognition, Johann Claassen, who in the 1850s had previously made two trips to St. Petersburg on educational matters, secretly went to the capital. He was unable to accomplish much but realized the group needed to organize formally as a separate church. Soon after his return in May, the Mennonite Brethren elected Heinrich Huebert (1810–1895) minister and Jacob P. Bekker (1828–1908) his associate.

Claassen's trip to St. Petersburg, however, brought also an unexpected turn of events in the ecclesiastical development of the Mennonite Brethren. One of Claassen's contacts in St. Petersburg was Ch. Plonus, a master tailor and member of the Baptist church in Memel, who distributed tracts. Claassen returned with a tract on believer's

20. For a contrast been the Anabaptism of the sixteenth century and later pietism, see "Retrospect: Contacts and Contrasts Between Anabaptism and Pietism," in Friedmann, *Mennonite Piety Through the Centuries*, 72–77. Also see Doerksen, "Pietism, Revivalism, and the Early Mennonite Brethren," in Longenecker and Arnett, *The Dilemma of Anabaptist Piety*, 69–84, which emphasizes the impact of revivalism in the creation of the Mennonite Brethren Church. Also see Goertzen, "The Influence of Radical Pietism on Russian Mennonites," *The Covenant Quarterly* 38/4 (Nov. 1980): 19–26.

21. See Toews, "Cultural Background of the Mennonite Brethren Church," 215–20. Also see Urry, "A Religious or a Social Elite?," paper at the symposium "Dynamics of Faith and Culture in Mennonite Brethren History," Winnipeg, Nov. 14–15, 1986, 24–29, on the social background of the leaders and supporters of the Mennonite Brethren movement, including charts with biographical information on leading members.

baptism by immersion, which was a startling revelation to the new group. Since Mennonites were baptizing by pouring, Bekker, although never having heard of Baptists, was convinced of the biblical argument and on September 23, 1860, he immersed Heinrich Bartel who in turn baptized Bekker. This act, together with the practice of close (or exclusive) communion, will put another divisive wedge between Mennonite Brethren and other Mennonites. It will also push them toward the Baptists.[22]

In the Old Colony of Chortitza, at Neu Kronsweide, a revival movement had broken out in 1853 led by Johann Loewen, converted by reading a sermon of Ludwig Hofacker, a pietist in Württemberg. But the revival fell into disrepute for its antinomianism with the result that both guilty and innocent came under church discipline. But from this a more permanent movement of prayer and mission meetings emerged in the late 1850s in Einlage under Abraham Unger (1820–1880), Heinrich Neufeld, and Cornelius Unger that included reading *Missionsblatt*, the mission periodical of the German Baptist Union. Abraham Unger owned a large carriage factory, and Heinrich Neufeld was a silk manufacturer. Possibly as early as 1859, Abraham Unger began to correspond with Oncken, the Baptist leader in Germany, which brought up questions of baptism and secession. In one of his letters in 1860 to Oncken, Unger requested that Baptists send two or three men to work with them. In 1861 the brethren in Einlage contacted the Molochna Brethren and discovered that they were immersing. Gerhard Wieler (1833–1911), who had already been immersed in November 1861 by Mennonite Brethren in the Molochna, persuaded Unger not to wait for baptism from the German Baptists. On March 4, 1862, Wieler baptized Unger, Neufeld, and a third brother in Molochna and then shortly following on March 11 a group of eighteen in the Dnieper River at Einlage itself, thereby constituting the Einlage Mennonite Brethren Church. Another baptism of seventeen persons followed a week later.[23]

In their effort to gain recognition, Mennonite Brethren faced serious opposition from both church and state. In Molochna the Administrative Office summoned in October 1860 thirty-two members, who had earlier in March responded in their defense to the Ohrloff Church Council, to appear in court. Five elders and five ministers attempted to persuade them to return to their former fellowship. With failure the administrative official warned them that if they not return within a month they were subject to be banned by the church and thus banished from the colony itself. Shortly afterwards the Mennonite churches placed forty-two Mennonite Brethren

22. On the introduction of immersion among Mennonite Brethren, see Wardin, "Baptist Influences on Mennonite Brethren with an Emphasis on the Practice of Immersion," *Direction* 8/4 (Oct., 1979), 33–38. Also see Bekker, 69–73, and Friesen, *The Mennonite Brotherhood in Russia*, 284–91.

23. For the revival movement in Chortitza, see Friesen, *The Mennonite Brotherhood in Russia*, 280–84; Hildebrand, "Aus der Kronsweider Erweckungszeit," *Der Botschafter* 8/6 (1913), 8–19, tr. by Toews in "The Early Mennonite Brethren: Some Outside Views," *MQR* 58/2 (Apr. 1984), 83–124; and Toews, *The Story of the Early Mennonite Brethren*, 117–28. For a biography of Unger, see the translation into English of the booklet by Heinrich Epp, *Notizen aus dem Leben und Wirken des verstorbenen Aeltesten Abraham Unger*, in *Direction* 19/2 (Fall, 1990), 127–39, and 20/1 (Spring, 1991), 125–40. For Unger's letter to Oncken, see *QR*, Jan. 1862, 14–15. For the early baptisms, see Friesen, 285, 289–90.

PART TWO—Prospects: German and Baltic Beginnings, 1855–1884

under church ban, which not only excluded them from the church and its worship and other activities but if strictly implemented included the prohibition of attending community events, denial of civil rights, and termination of all social intercourse with family and friends. It was also a threat to one's economic security. Two schoolteachers lost their positions, which forced them to move. One of them was Wieler, who by the end of 1861 moved to Chortitza, his original colony, and moved in with Unger. One member received a prison term with hard labor. On the other hand, the five elders and their congregations that opposed the Brethren did not have enough votes in the Mennonite Church Assembly to force their exile. The seceders, however, received word that their case was being transferred to the Security Committee in Odessa to consider depriving them of their rights as colonists. Claassen now felt the need to travel again to St. Petersburg to appeal there to the highest authorities. He left in November but did not return until a little over a year and a half later in June 1862. Otto Forchhammer, a Bible colporteur of Danish descent, accompanied Claassen as an adviser and secretary in German.[24]

The Mennonite Brethren in Chortitza faced especially hard opposition from the administrative officials. In February, 1862, the Administrative Office issued an order for the dissidents to cease their meetings, and the church in Chortitza put them under the ban. Jacob Janzen was imprisoned for a time and seriously beaten. In July 1862 Abraham Unger, Heinrich Neufeld, Gerhard Wieler, and Peter Berg were arrested and held for about two weeks but then released on bail. Shortly before Wieler had returned from St. Petersburg, sent there by the Brethren in Chortitza, where he worked with Claassen.[25]

In St. Petersburg Claassen and Forchhammer worked diligently in contacting government officials. In 1862 both Claassen and Wieler presented petitions to the Tsar, who in any case would turn them over to an appointed official. At first Russian officials viewed the Mennonite Brethren negatively as a "divisive sect" that endangered the Russian Church itself and were now focused on implementing measures for the emancipation of the serfs. Claassen and Forchhammer met with other believers and were particularly close to Plonus, the resident Baptist. Claassen also attempted to help Jankowski and Sinieck, two Baptists from Courland, who were in St. Petersburg at the same time with their own petition, and who, as noted earlier, were with the help of Plonus able to approach the Tsar personally.[26]

In June 1862 both Claassen and Wieler returned without getting a final verdict on their appeal for state protection. In November Johann Harder, elder of the Ohrloff

24. Bekker, 75–80. Toews, *A History of the Mennonite Brethren Church*, 45–46. Friesen, *The Mennonite Brotherhood in Russia*, 244–45, 264–65. For the effects of a ban, see the report of Brune in Toews, *The Story of the Early Mennonite Brethren*, 66.

25. Friesen, *The Mennonite Brotherhood in Russia*, 312–24. Toews, *The Story of the Early Mennonite Brethren*, 117–18, 126. Bekker, 143.

26. Friesen, *The Mennonite Brotherhood in Russia*, 318–20, 344–52, 359–71. For relations with Plonus and the Baptists from Courland, see Friesen, 345, 359, 362, 370, and 371.

Church, the mother church in the Molochna, wrote to the colony administrator that his congregation opposed exile of the Brethren and was willing to recognize them as an independent congregation since the Mennonite Brethren and his church were in doctrinal agreement. This action of the Ohrloff Church greatly helped to gain tolerance for the Brethren. But it was not until May 1866 that Claassen received word that the Russian government had granted the Brethren full rights.[27]

Claassen and Wieler also sought approval for settlement of their co-religionists elsewhere in Russia, which would be a safety net if they were forced to leave the colonies. Claassen petitioned the government for land in 1862. After their return, Claassen with letters of recommendation and Wieler, both serving as agents, traveled in August in two wagons to the Kuban in the northern Caucasus to inspect lands for possible settlement. In March 1864 the Land Office granted permission for the settlement, and the first village was established that year. Only a minority of the Brethren, however, moved to this area.[28]

Exuberance

With roots in the Wüst movement with its more exuberant worship, the young Mennonite Brethren exhibited the same joyful and extemporaneous expressions in their gatherings. Instead of High German, *Platt-deutsch* or Low German, the language of the people, and popular songs became standard. Such a pattern was not unusual in revival movements. Methodism and Pentecostalism, among others, are prime examples. One of the prime movers in exuberant worship was Wilhelm Bartel, musically talented and an adherent of Kappes but not theologically astute. Even Claassen was favorable toward the movement, although never an advocate of its excesses and became a mediator between contending factions that arose over it. The movement of exuberance among Mennonite Brethren went through several stages beginning with a degree of acceptance but moving to extremism and fanaticism that brought reproach from within and outside Mennonite Brethren ranks and then finally a repudiation.[29] Unfortunately, opponents were able to tar the new movement with the name of *Hüpfer* or Jumpers.[30]

In the summer of 1861 members of the Ohrloff Church Council visited Mennonite Brethren services on three occasions. Although they noted exuberant singing, some clapping, and use of musical instruments, they found the services orderly and

---

27. Toews, *A History of the Mennonite Brethren Church*, 48–49.

28. Ibid., 75. Friesen, *The Mennonite Brotherhood in Russia*, 401–16.

29. An excellent study of the exuberance movement among Mennonite Brethren is by Harry Loewen, "Echoes of Drumbeats," *JMS* 3 (1985), 118–27. See Friesen, *The Mennonite Brethren Brotherhood in Russia*, 262–78, for a description of the movement from primary sources.

30. See an early appraisal of Mennonite Brethren, "Ueber die Secte der Hübfer in den Colonien Süd-Russlands," in Busch (1867), 1:256–65.

incorporated sound biblical teaching.[31] But not all meetings were so subdued. Bekker wrote about two months earlier that in another home in Gnadenfeld the members leaped and danced. At about the same time Katherina Claassen, in a disapproving tone, wrote to her husband in St. Petersburg that at Pentecost in 1861 in a vacant mosque in a former Nogai village some of the participants leaped and danced, played and sang, and with most shouting for joy scarcely anything could be understood. In his account in 1867 on the "*Hüpfer*," the Lutheran writer E. H. Busch alleged that "at the close of the gathering, they gave way to a noisy gaiety, sang spiritual songs with worldly melodies," which were accompanied by violin and harmonica and wild dancing. The intensified exuberance was not confined to the Brethren in Molochna but was brought by Gerhard Wieler to Chortitza, the Old Colony.[32]

But worse was yet to come. An antinominian movement that a number called a "false freedom" appeared in 1862 among some of the leaders, including Jacob Bekker and his younger brother, Benjamin (1833–1920), who taught that the truly converted could no longer sin. They and others also favored the kiss of peace or "sister kiss," which Jacob Bekker claimed came from the Molokans. The mixed kissing led to questionable behavior among some of the worshipers. The antinominian movement soon came under condemnation, but the movement of exuberance, however, continued, although after the spring of 1862 it became more moderate.[33]

Another serious threat to the integrity of the new movement was the appearance in both Molochna and Chortitza of a spiritual despotism. Gerhard Wieler and Benjamin Bekker, both claiming apostleship, and Bernhard Penner were the primary leaders. In the Einlage church in Chortitza, Wieler was able to win over Heinrich Neufeld. Their fanatical iconoclasm resulted in the destruction of pictures on walls and Christian books, including the burning such pietistic treasures as Hofacker's *Sermons*, Arndt's *Wahres Christentum*, and Starck's prayerbook as well as old church hymnals. Wieler held the Bible aloft and declared that the Bible was the only book necessary for salvation. They forced young women to wear a head covering, excluded non-participants in exuberant worship, and shunned anyone not of their party. The Einlage Church excluded, among others, Abraham Unger, and even Gerhard's father, Johann, and his two brothers, Johann and Franz. The church in Molochna excluded its elder, Heinrich Huebert, and Jakob Reimer.[34]

Finally the moderates under the leadership of Claassen, who in May 1865 returned to the Molochna from the Kuban where he was then living, restored order. The congregation in Molochna adopted what were called the "June Reforms," forbade arbitrary excommunications by an individual or group, limited excessive exuberance by denouncing the loud music, the tambourine, and dancing, and gave thanks that the

---

31. Bekker, 89–94.

32. Friesen, *The Mennonite Brotherhood in Russia*, 266–67. Bekker, 84–85. Busch (1867), 1:257. Toews, *The Story of the Early Mennonite Brethren*, 120–21.

33. Friesen, *The Mennonite Brotherhood in Russia*, 271–74. Bekker, 97–98.

34. Friesen, *The Mennonite Brotherhood in Russia*, 274–75.

"false freedom" in their midst was dead and its adherents had repented. Claassen also brought the reforms to Einlage where they were also accepted.³⁵

Separated brethren were also reconciled. A few, however, remained aside, including Bernhard Penner and Gerhard Wieler. At the time of the reconciliation, Gerhard was in prison for baptizing Russians and thus made reconciliation easier. After his release, he attempted to associate with the few remaining enthusiasts in Molochna, such as Hermann Peters. Peters earlier had made a drum, which he used in adding to the noise of the exuberant gatherings. With failure of collaboration, Gerhard returned in 1866 to the Old Mennonite Church and then will settle in the USA. Peters himself will lead a group of about twenty in 1865–66 to withdraw, and his so-called "Hermann Peters Church" will move to the Crimea and then to Siberia, to the USA, and finally Canada.³⁶

For four years from 1861 to 1865, the Mennonite Brethren went through a crucible that threatened to engulf them. Internal threats seemed to come from every side—emotional excesses, antinomianism, dictatorial leadership, iconoclasm, and division. Self-appointed leaders shunted aside moderate leadership and swayed members more by emotional appeal than rational argument. A report on Protestant sects in South Russia, signed by Vice-Director Sievers of the Ministry of Internal Affairs, stated that the *Hüpfer* were beginning to disintegrate, maintained no proper church organization, and had no civil registers of births, baptisms, and marriages, thus handicapping them in matters of inheritance and property.³⁷

Mennonite Brethren were a small group. The Brethren in Molochna in January 1861 numbered around 190 and those in Chortitza in May 1862 included 76. By 1865/6 the Brethren had baptized in Molochna and Chortitza around 500 and then from that date to 1871/2 a significantly reduced number of a little over 200. With death, exclusions, migration, and a reduced baptismal rate, Mennonite Brethren numbered, according to Friesen, 600 in Molochna, Chortitza, and Kuban, although the number was probably closer to 500.³⁸

Fortunately healing came from within, and moderate and sensible leadership began to assert itself and saved the movement. In addition, contacts with Baptists, already begun in Einlage, will soon be a steadying influence on the young movement.

---

35. Ibid., 275–77, 436–41.

36. Ibid., 277–78, 444–45. Bekker, 84–85. Kornelius Hildebrant in Toews, "The Early Mennonite Brethren: Some Outside Views, *MQR* 58/2 (Apr. 1984), 111. Toews, *A History of the Mennonite Brethren Church*, 70.

37. Toews, *The Story of the Early Mennonite Brethren*, 163.

38. Ibid., 25–26, 35. Friesen, *The Mennonite Brotherhood in Russia*, 468–69, 475–76, 489–90. Friesen took the top numbers of the estimated memberships of Molochna, 150 to 200, and Kuban, 100 to 150, and all baptisms (except one) in Chortitza from 1862 to 1871.

7

Mennonite Brethren and German Baptist Relations

GERMAN BAPTISTS AND MENNONITE Brethren were close ideologically and interacted on each other, but also differences emerged between the two groups. In his correspondence with Mennonite Brethren in the Molochna in 1860–1861, Gottfried Alf, the German Baptist leader in Poland, condemned Peter Ewert, a Mennonite Brethren in Poland, for his manner of immersing—the candidate first kneeled in the water and then was submerged face forward. Alf insisted the correct method was once backward, claiming the way Baptists practiced it everywhere. The Baptist practice became the norm. From the start Mennonite Brethren in Chortitza practiced close communion as Baptists, but Mennonite Brethren in Molochna only later adopted this practice. Alf opposed the Mennonite Brethren adherence to non-resistance and footwashing, differences that were never overcome.[1]

MENNONITE BRETHREN OUTREACH

As a new religious movement, imbued with enthusiasm and the desire to proclaim the truth to others, Mennonite Brethren as with Baptists reached out beyond their own immediate community. Shortly before the formation of the Mennonite Brethren Church, Benjamin Bekker and Heinrich Bartel, members of the Wüst movement, left the Molochna for the District of Saratov in the Volga region to distribute Bibles and Testaments and engage in evangelism among the Lutheran population. They arrived

---

1. Friesen, 285–86, 288–91. Wardin, *Gottfried Alf*, 74–75.

in October 1859 and soon located Otto Forchhammer, a Lutheran colporteur, with whom they worked. They gained access to stundist gatherings. Bekker and Bartel not only distributed Scripture but, according to the Lutheran authorities, introduced the kiss of peace and wild frenzied worship. In addition to calling themselves "new brethren," they insisted that believers be baptized by the Holy Spirit, separate from the corrupt church, and refuse to participate with other "dead Christians" in the sacrament of the Lord's Supper. After three months, they were forced to leave.[2]

In March 1860 the two Mennonites and the Lutheran colporteur sent letters to the Saratov District, continuing their agitation, and called the Lutheran Church "Babel." Their agitation resulted in a separatist movement. In 1874 Mennonite Brethren accepted from this area a church from a Lutheran colony and one from a Mennonite colony, but by 1880 the two congregations ceased to exist. Many emigrated to America and the rest joined the Baptists.[3]

Neu-Danzig and Alt-Danzig

A far more important Mennonite Brethren thrust occurred in 1864 into the Lutheran colonies of Neu-Danzig near Nikolaev and Alt-Danzig near Elisabetgrad (Kirovograd), both in Kherson Province in Ukraine, west of the Mennonite colonies. In 1787 German migrants from Danzig in Prussia established Alt-Danzig, at first called Danzig. Because of the need for more land, a second colony, Neu-Danzig, was established in 1839 about one hundred miles to the south on the Ingul River. The Mennonite Brethren effort will bring some unexpected results. It will establish a German Baptist outpost in Dobrudja, then in Turkey, form two German Baptist congregations in Kherson Province, and will give an impetus to the rise of a Stundo-Baptist movement.

Colonists from Neu-Danzig developed ties with Mennonite Brethren in Einlage in Chortitza when they purchased wagons at the carriage factory of Abraham Unger. Some from Neu-Danzig began to meet in stundist gatherings. In the winter of 1863 two Mennonite Brethren, Gerhard Wieler and Benjamin Bekker, visited Neu-Danzig and held meetings, convincing a number to accept believer's baptism by immersion. On Pentecost Sunday, May 3 (o.s.), Wieler and Bekker met with a group in a prayer meeting in a private home. On May 5 at ten in the morning, Wieler baptized seven women and four men. The candidates included not only Lutherans but also those of Roman Catholic and Reformed background. They elected Friedrich Engel as elder, and the group grew with additional baptisms. Alexander Brune, a Lutheran state instigator, reported in September that the new group in Neu-Danzig included twenty

---

2. For a Mennonite description of the mission to the Volga, see Bekker, 33–39. For the Lutheran reaction, see Busch (1867), 1:364–68. Also see S. D. Bondar, *Sekta Mennonitov v Rosssii v svyazi s istorieĭ nemetskoĭ kolonizatsii na yuge Rossii.*

3. Friesen, 513–14, 522.

PART TWO—Prospects: German and Baltic Beginnings, 1855–1884

families of sixty-six people besides two families of ten people in two Swedish colonies and four families in the Jewish colony of Dobraya.[4]

The appearance of an Anabaptist sect with ties to the Wűst revival and Hűpfer movements, noted for their proselytizing activity, caused an uproar from both Lutheran and government authorities. The government forbade further meetings of the group and refused passports for them to bring their case before the authorities in St. Petersburg. In August the authorities imprisoned in the storehouse of the village until evening everyone, including women and children, who were present in one of the meetings. Members now met in the fields to pray. Five men were transported to Kherson where they were imprisoned and then marched to Odessa. With refusal to abjure their faith, they chose exile in Turkish territory and on recommendation by Christian friends went to the German colony of Catalui near Tultscha in the Dobrudja. Two brothers, Friedrich and Martin Engel, both elders, were also exiled to Catalui.[5] Three who had been exiled returned at the beginning of 1865 to Neu-Danzig, furnished with Turkish passports and Russian visas, to sell their property and claim their families, but under a pretext the authorities took away their passports. The authorities imprisoned in Kherson two of them, Karl Edinger and Franz Linowski, and ordered them exiled to Siberia. According to the law, individuals exiled abroad and who return were to be sent to Siberia. The two got sick on their way to Siberia and were then hospitalized in Nikolaev. In March the two Engel brothers in Tultscha sent a petition, forwarded as well to the Evangelical Alliance, that publicized it in its periodical, *Evangelical Christendom*, requesting release of the prisoners and requesting the right of the group to reside in Russia or at least the right to sell their property and leave with their families. In any case, on formal renunciation of their sectarian errors, the three who had returned from exile were allowed to remain in the colony. In February eight additional brethren were imprisoned for exile to Turkey but received a reprieve. Ten families, twenty-two men and twenty-two women, requested in the fall release from Russian citizenship and exile to Dobrudja. One making the request was Karl Edinger, who had earlier been exiled, then returned, threatened with exile to Siberia, then signed a retraction, and will finally settle in Dobrudja![6]

---

4. Ibid., 327. Bekker, 104, 182. Toews, *The Story of the Early Mennonite Brethren*, 25–26. Bondar, *Sekta Mennonitov*, 159–61. Although Bekker and Brune imply that both Wieler and Bekker baptized, it was probably Wieler himself who did the baptizing. A later account in *Der Sendbote*, April 1, 1874, 51, mentions only Wieler as baptizer. More important, the obituary of Jakob Klundt, one of those baptized, states in a footnote in the Bulgarian periodical, *Evangelist* 2/2 (Mar.–Apr., 1921), 1, that Wieler baptized him.

5. See *EC*, May 1, 1865, 258–60, for a detailed account of the persecution of the believers in Neu-Danzig. Also in *Missionsblatt*, June 1865, 92–94. Toews, *The Story of the Early Mennonite Brethren*, 137–48.

6. *EC*, May 1, 1865, 258–60. Toews, *The Story of the Early Mennonite Brethren*, 138, 154–55. Veltistov, *MO*, Mar. 1902, 467–68. Dorodnitsyn, "Nemetskie missionery neobaptizma (Neo-Baptismus)," *ChOLDP*, 1893, no. 3, 330–35.

In spite of the persecution, including imprisonment, transport, exile, and renunciations, individuals of the movement still remained. Although formally renouncing their sectarianism and outwardly showing proper conduct, they rarely attended the parish Lutheran church. Some practiced their sectarianism secretly. The sectarian movement did not die out in Neu-Danizg but survived with its later becoming a preaching station of the Alt-Danzig Baptist Church and then becoming an independent congregation in 1875. As will later be shown, the exiles in Dobrudja thrived, gained converts, and will become an independent Baptist church in Catalui in 1869.[7]

The Lutheran colony of Alt-Danzig, about one hundred miles north of Neu-Danzig, was located many miles away from other German settlements amongst a Russian-Ukrainian population. As elsewhere, the stundist movement of private gatherings of prayer and Bible study also reached the settlement. According to Johann Pritzkau (1841–1924), a native of Alt-Danzig and chronicler of the German Baptist work in southern Ukraine, the first stundist thrust came from Karl Bonekemper, a Reformed pastor, in a visit in 1840 and then followed in the mid-forties by other stundists, who helped to bring revival, such as Friedrich Engel (later exiled from Neu-Danzig in 1864) and a missionary by the name of Kuss, a friend of Wűst.[8]

After a close brush with death from a typhus epidemic, Pritzkau in 1859, at the time seventeen, underwent a conversion experience. He became a leader with three other schoolmates in a circle for devotional reading, prayer, and singing, which attracted other young people, leading to another great revival. Unexpectedly at this time the community approved him at his young age to be teacher in the village school of eighty pupils, a position he filled for six years. As teacher he also was the assistant to the parish minister, which required him in the absence of the pastor to lead the service and Sunday school and serve at infant baptisms and funerals. Without knowing that Charles Spurgeon of England was a Baptist, Pritzkau read in the morning service Spurgeon's sermons, which now had appeared in German.[9]

In the middle of September 1864, J. Kowalsky, Mennonite Brethren, arrived in Alt-Danzig. Two days after his arrival, probably on Sunday, September 18, in the afternoon, he baptized at least seventeen if not possibly twenty-seven, both men and women. In his accounts of the baptism, Pritzkau does not specifically state he was baptized in this group but probably was included. The authorities imprisoned Kowalsky at Kherson and then exiled him to Turkey. After his arrival in Turkey, he traveled to Jerusalem, then under Turkish control, to preach to Russian pilgrims. He soon, however, appeared in Dobrudja among the exiles where he continued his preaching and baptizing activity.[10]

---

7. Toews, *The Story of the Early Mennonite Brethren*, 154–55. Dorodnitsyn, ChOLDP, 1893, no. 3, 334–35. Pritzkau, 124–30. *WHZ*, Aug. 15, 1883, 165.

8. Pritzkau, 3–5.

9. Ibid., 5–9.

10. Ibid., 12. *Missionsblatt*, Oct. 1865, 157. *QR*, Apr. 1866, 165–67. *BMM*, Feb. 1868, 54.

PART TWO—Prospects: German and Baltic Beginnings, 1855–1884

Although the meetings of the newly baptized group were forbidden, it was fortunately spared the persecution meted to the believers in Neu-Danzig. For one thing, the leaders of the colony, such as the village mayor and the churchwarden, as well as the village as a whole were sympathetic to the pietist cause.[11]

The group, however, was left an orphan, weak in knowledge and lacking proper organization. It was not organized as a Baptist church, knowing nothing of Baptists but only Mennonite Brethren.

Authorities forbade outside assistance. In May 1866 its members sought help by going to Aron Lepp, then administrator in a Jewish Colony, who then went with them to Einlage, the home of Abraham Unger. Although they found a church with officers, yet they were disturbed with its condition, having gone through the extremes of the exuberance movement and the despotism of Gerhard Wieler and Heinrich Neufeld that split the church. Unger gave them the address of Oncken to write for help. After his return home, Pritzkau wrote a letter asking for Oncken to come or to send someone in his place. Oncken replied with a letter of encouragement but could not promise to send any help.[12]

After about a year in prayer and hope, in January 1868 a leader proposed sending Prizkau to Hamburg. Funds were raised. Pritzkau traveled on his first train on the newly built track into Odessa where with the help of pietist brethren he obtained the necessary travel documents. He arrived in Hamburg in February, but finding no mission school in session spent fourteen months in valuable practical training, preaching at mission stations, working with youth and music societies, assisting in the Sunday school, and attendance at sessions for teacher preparation.[13]

Before his departure in April 1869, Oncken ordained Pritzkau for mission service. On his return he stopped in Dobrudja where he met August Liebig, the leader, who became a close friend. He arrived in Alt-Danzig a few days before Pentecost. He found the congregation had recently been through an exciting time of revival but was now ready for a more regulated church life. He entered immediately into the work and began examining candidates for the large baptismal service that occurred on June 11 (o.s.) with Abraham Unger from Chortitza performing the ordinance. Pritzkau also

---

Mitteilungen und Nachrichten, June 1869, 278. *WHZ*, May 15, 1883, 107. In all accounts of Kowalsky, his first name is never recorded except his first initial is given as "J" in the manuscript of Georg Teutsch, "Kurzgefasste Geschichte der deutschen Baptisten in der Dobrudscha, 1864–1940, und besonders ueber die Gruendung der Gemeinde Cataloi," in the compilation of Klukas, *Geschichtliche Quellen der Deutschen Baptistengemeinde Cataloi*, 38–43. The accounts in *Missionsblatt* and *Mitteilungen und Nachrichten* record a baptism of twenty-seven but Pritzkau in his account in *WHZ* in 1883 records only seventeen and then in his history of 1914 records twenty. Pritzkau also records September 15, a Sunday, as the day of baptism, but in 1864 Sunday occurred on the eighteenth.

11. Pritzkau, 18–20.
12. Ibid., 31–33.
13. Ibid., 34.

learned that Oncken himself would soon come to Alt-Danzig on a visit, a trip that he had encouraged Oncken to make.[14]

August Liebig in Dobrudja and Ukraine

In Dobrudja, then part of Turkey, Friedrich and Martin Engel served as elders for the exiled community from Neu-Danzig. As earlier noted, J. Kowalsky, who in 1864 had been exiled to Turkey for baptizing in Alt-Danzig, also arrived in Dobrudja after his trip to Jerusalem. Although the two Engel brothers had baptized in Russia, they now became concerned about proper church order. They were disturbed when Kowalsky baptized on Easter 1865 four candidates and forbade him to baptize further until the issue of church order was settled. The Engel brothers prepared to write to Charles Spurgeon in London, the only Baptist they knew, but on the advice of Frederick W. Flocken, Methodist missionary in the area, they instead wrote to Oncken for help. Oncken sent August Liebig (1836–1914) to investigate, who was stationed as a missionary in Bucharest, Romania.[15]

Liebig, a German subject, was born in February 1836 in Neumark, Prussia, near the border of Pomerania. He was baptized in 1854 and will settle in Hamburg where he caught Oncken's eye. After limited instruction and ordination, Oncken sent Liebig in 1863, only twenty-seven, to lead the small German Baptist mission in Bucharest, Romania. Although united in 1862 under its own prince, Romania was still under Turkish sovereignty. Liebig, a locksmith or possibly a mechanic, was one of Oncken's *Handwerker* or artisans who provided their own support. In 1865 in Hamburg, Liebig attended Oncken's mission school, attended as well by Liebig's two brothers, Friederich and Hermann. In September he married and then in October arrived in Dobrudja where he not only consulted with Kowalsky but also held services, instructed in Baptist church order, and in November conducted two baptismal services. He also itinerated north into southern Bessarabia, then also controlled by Turkey where he found converts whom Kowalsky had baptized but persecuted and without spiritual leadership.[16]

In addition to Bucharest in 1863 and then Dobrudja in 1865, Liebig now on behalf of Oncken engaged in a third mission assignment—a ministry in 1866 to Mennonite Brethren in Chortitza. On Unger's appeal for assistance, Oncken sent Liebig to undertake the challenge. On his way to Ukraine, he again ministered in Dobrudja and then went to the Russian consulate at Tultscha (Tulcea) for a Russian passport. The official in charge questioned Liebig at great length as to his purpose for the trip,

---

14. Ibid., 34–35. *WHZ*, June 1, 1883, 117. In his 1883 account, Pritzkau was off one year in his dates of his stay and return from Hamburg.

15. *Missionsblatt*, Jan. 1866, 11–13. *QR*, Apr. 1866, 165–67.

16. For Liebig's career, see Wardin, "August G. A Liebig," *JMS* 28 (2010), 167–86. Donat, *Das wachsende Werk*, 383–84.

suspecting he was a missionary. On the basis of his statement that he was a "workman," the consulate finally provided him with a passport. A Russian ship took him to Odessa and another ship to the Dnieper River, arriving in Einlage in Chortitza on May 5.[17]

Liebig found the Einlage congregation in division and disorder. He preached at the business meeting, provided instruction in proper conduct, insisting that minutes be recorded, one must rise to speak, take one's turn without interruption, and refrain from talking on the same point more than three times. He played no favorites, seeking harmony from all factions. A correspondent from Einlage wrote to Oncken on Liebig's ministry, "The dear Brother took much trouble to unite and order our disturbed church and thanks to the Lord his efforts have been crowned with success and a rich blessing has been the result. We see therefore how necessary it is that we should have amongst us a Brother who is both talented, modest and devoted, who should form our church on the model of the New Testament."[18]

Liebig's stay was only two weeks. The vice-consul had sent a report to Kotzebu, the governor-general, that Liebig was a "dangerous man," a "chief spreader" of his sectarian sect, and he was bound for the German colonies. On the basis of the report, the administrative office in Chortitza was alerted to arrest Liebig if he should appear. Consequently, the authorities arrested Liebig, who was taken to Yekaterinoslav for a hearing before the governor. On his way the inspector told him he was under suspicion for advocating sectarianism and a new teaching. After being held for four days and five nights, he was sent to Odessa, arriving on May 12. On June 12 he reported he was free. Liebig blamed the Old Mennonites for his arrest, not knowing the report of the vice consul. Immediately after the trip he wrote a strong criticism of Mennonites who persecuted fellow Mennonites, accusing them of esteeming the privileges from the Russian government more than God's word and wishing God might replace such privileges with the privilege of leading sinners to Christ.

Liebig was not the only German Baptist to assist the Mennonite Brethren in Einlage. In the following spring, Karl Benzien, a deacon from West Prussia, who migrated to the area of Einlage for business reasons, also presided at congregational meetings. Under his leadership in 1868, the Einlage church established mission stations, a feature of German Baptist work, and chose officers. He also presided at the meeting that chose Unger as elder of the Einlage church. A son of Unger married Luise, a daughter of Benzien.[19]

Both Liebig and Benzien brought the Mennonite Brethren the standards of the German Baptist movement for a stable church order. They were unlike a Gerhard

---

17. For Liebig's visit to Einlage, see *Missionsblatt*, Aug. 1866, 125–28; QR, July 1866, 179–80; and Friesen, 339–40. See Dorodnitsyn, *Materialy dlya istorii religiozno-ratsionalisticheskago dvizheniya na yuge Rossii vo vtoroï polovine xix-go stoletiya*, doc. 35, for the statement of the vice-consul in Tultscha.

18. QR, Jan. 1867, 215.

19. Friesen, 459–61. Löwen, *In Vergessenheit geratene Beziehungen*, 21–22.

Wieler or a J. Kowalsky, who after baptizing left believers without proper organization or instruction. Liebig himself saw the results of Kowalsky's activity in Dobrudja and Bessarabia. It was fortunate that Unger in Chortitza, Pritzkau in Alt-Danzig, and the Engel brothers in Dobrudja could appeal to Hamburg for help.

The Oncken Visit

At the end of 1869, Oncken, almost seventy, undertook an arduous journey to southern Ukraine and the Dobrudja. Although part of the journey was by rail and steamer, much of it was by wagon and carriage without springs. He was beset by clouds of dust and at times traveled at night to avoid the burning heat of the sun. Although he complained of the "barbaric travel" and the "lack of nourishing food," he arrived in good shape. Oncken was struck by the poverty of the recently emancipated serfs, poorly clothed with women with bandannas but wearing no shoes, and homes surrounded by filth and afflicted with drunkenness. He noted what he considered was the avarice of the Jews who everywhere appeared to control commerce. Nevertheless he held the hope that the gospel and schools will bring great changes to the people. Unlike his first trip to Russia in 1864, visiting Russian officials on behalf of suffering Baptists and other evangelicals, he came to consult and fellowship with his missionary sons, such as Liebig and Pritzkau, visit with such Mennonite Brethren as Unger and Johann Wieler (the brother of Gerhard), and provide counsel and encouragement. He arrived as a missionary to preach and baptize as well as to instruct in church order, organize churches, and ordain leaders. With his prestige and discernment, he helped to bring stability to both the German Baptist and Mennonite Brethren movements. His correspondence answering appeals for help went back at least ten years. According to Aleksii Ya. Dorodnitsyn, the Orthodox author, the arrival of Oncken was puzzling to the police on how they should deal with the noted foreigner. Officials sent reports on Oncken's activities in preaching and baptizing and were very concerned to what extent he might subvert the Orthodox population.[20]

Oncken arrived in Alt-Danzig on Wednesday, September 16 (o.s.), where he preached and baptized. A regular Baptist church was constituted here, and Pritzkau was chosen as one of the elders. The Baptists had been so successful in the village that the Lutheran church was almost empty. The Lutheran pastor had recently left so that the Baptist leadership took his place in the registration of births, marriages, and deaths. He noted that twenty-eight Ukrainians had been baptized and were meeting separately. Three of them visited him one morning. An officer, however, ordered Oncken to report to the mayor for an interrogation. On the next day the officer ordered him to the police office where he was questioned at great length as to his purpose in

---

20. For Oncken's letters of his trip in English translation, see QR, Jan. 1870, 797–806, and *Missionsblatt*, Nov., 161–64, and Dec.1869, 177–85. For the reaction of the Russian administration to Oncken's visit, see Dorodnitsyn, docs. 61–62 and 67–70.

coming to Russia. On the following day, he underwent another hearing and regained his passport but through it all lost two days of travel.

Oncken also visited other sites, including Neu-Danzig, and arrived in Einlage in October, staying in Unger's home. Here Oncken stayed in the area around ten days, preaching, bringing edification, and instruction. He ordained Unger as elder, Aaron Lepp and Benzien as ministers, and two deacons. Because of approaching winter, he cancelled his plans to visit the Molochna. From Einlage, Johann Wieler accompanied Oncken to Odessa, where the latter preached among Germans with a Lutheran and Reformed background and spent an evening with John Melville, the Bible colporteur. Upon leaving Russia, he looked upon the nation as "a most inviting field," and wrote that if he were forty years younger he would devote himself to its cultivation.

In November he arrived in Dobrudja. In his short stay, Oncken established the work in Catalui as an independent congregation with Liebig as pastor, ordained leaders and deacons, conducted services, attended a love feast, and consecrated the opening of a chapel at Admadja. The Catalui church, numbering 111, with two preaching stations, occupied a new building with an assembly room, schoolroom, and quarters for the pastor.[21]

The church at Catalui, a number of whose first members were exiles from Ukraine, in turn became a center of expansion for Baptist work not only in Dobrudja but other parts of the Balkans. It helped to place colporteurs in the field who worked with the British and Foreign Bible Society in European Turkey. Two outstanding colporteurs were Martin Heringer and Jakob Klundt, both exiles from Neu-Danzig, who had notable careers in Bulgaria. Russian authorities looked upon Baptists in Dobrudja as a "viper's nest" and a "lightning conductor" for Baptist work in Russia. Officials accused Liebig and Klundt of sending tracts and hymnals into Russia. Dobrudja was also a sanctuary for Baptist and Mennonite refugees.[22]

ORGANIZATON AND CONSULTATION

On the recommendation of Aron Lepp, the Einlage church again invited Liebig to come and minister. In June 1871 Liebig arrived with his wife and one-year-old daughter Marie. The hosts provided Liebig and his family with a small house at Andreasfeld, located northeast of Einlage across the Dnieper River, where the Einlage church had formed a daughter congregation. Liebig remained one year.[23]

The Einlage church still suffered from division over such issues as military service and the use of tobacco. With his even temper and non-partisanship, Liebig brought order. He again set standards for business meetings and also for the Sunday school and introduced a prayer hour on Sunday mornings. Since Liebig had been reared in

21. *Missionsblatt*, 1870, no. 1, 3–5, and no. 4, 68–69. QR, Apr. 1870, 814–16, and July 1870, 835–36.
22. *Missionsblatt*, 1872, no. 10, 162. Veltistov, 1022–23. Val'kevich, 54.
23. Friesen, 466–67.

a Platt-deutsch or Low German area, he had the advantage of speaking with Mennonites who used a similar dialect. Liebig later wrote that he was able to work at Einlage in "undisturbed peace and delightful harmony."[24]

At the same time, Liebig did not neglect German Baptist affairs. He presided at the first Baptist association in Russia, the Russian-Turkish Association, which met at Alt-Danzig in 1872 on Sunday, May 3, and continued until Tuesday. As presiding officer, Liebig explained the purpose and need of an association, which, although not impinging on the independence of the churches, could propose resolutions on mission extension and combat discord and misunderstandings.[25]

Liebig also made a significant contribution toward the organizational life of Mennonite Brethren when a week later, from May 14 to 16, he presided at the first general conference of the Mennonite Brethren at Andreasfeld. Three congregations—Einlage, Molochna, and Kuban—with a membership of 600 were represented. Under his direction, the conference formed a missions committee of seven members for itinerant missionaries and a system of collection for their support. Each missionary was to keep a diary and send it in quarterly. The conference approved five missionaries.[26]

In 1872 Liebig returned to Dobrudja and the church in Catalui, but in the following year his brother Ludwig became pastor at the church. Liebig moved to Bucharest but soon was called to serve in Odessa. Liebig continued for some years presiding at Mennonite Brethren conferences.

---

24. Epp, 132–34. *Missionsblatt*, Dec. 1874, 221.

25. *Missionsblatt*, Sep. 1872, 148–50. *BMM*, Jan. 1873, 25–26. Pritzkau, 76–82. Pritzkau somewhat confused the first associational meeting with the meeting in Neudorf in Volhynia two years later.

26. Friesen, 466–67, and 475–76. *Missionsblatt*, Aug. 1873, 140. QR, Oct. 1873, 60.

8

Mennonite Brethren and German Baptists

Identity and Stability

IN 1872 AT ITS first convention, Mennonite Brethren numbered around 600 members in three congregations—Einlage in Chortitza, Molochna, and Kuban. One of the missions of the Einlage church was at Andreasfeld, northeast of Einlage across the Dnieper River. Here the Einlage church constructed the first Mennonite Brethren meeting house, which also served as a school and where for a number of years the annual Mennonite Brethren conventions met when the Einlage church was host. The Molochna church established a mission at Spat in the Crimea. In 1874 the church transformed a saloon into a meeting house but in 1883 built at Rüchenau a large new structure.[1] In spite of emigration, in 1885, at the time of their twenty-fifth anniversary, Mennonite Brethren claimed 1,800 members and a constituency, including family members, of 4,000. Although under five percent of the Russian Mennonite population, Mennonite Brethren were showing steady growth. The three congregations had increased to six and with missions the total number of communion groups was fifteen.[2]

MENNONITE BRETHREN RESTRAINTS AND IDENTITY

Potential growth, however, was primarily limited to natural growth among its own members and converts from other Mennonites. As an ethnic-religious group settled

---

1. Friesen, 476, 483–84, 487, 493–94, 499–500. Toews, *History of the Mennonite Brethren Church*, 71.
2. Friesen, 522–23. Ehrt, *Das Mennonitum in Russland*, 61.

in closed colonies with special privileges, Mennonite Brethren, as other Mennonites, were prohibited from recruitment from either the native population or from other religious confessions. Converts with non-Mennonite background would, if not by choice at least by necessity, become Baptist rather than Mennonite Brethren.[3]

Another negative factor in Mennonite Brethren growth in Russia was the emigration movement to North America. In an attempt to integrate its German minority, the Russian regime issued in 1870 a *ukase*, which would terminate the special privileges of all German colonists, including the abolition of the *Fürsorge-Komitee*, the Guardian Committee, that looked after their particular needs. The Russian language would become the official language in local administration and was to be introduced as a subject in the German schools, which had been independent but now would come under direct control of the government.

Most threatening for Mennonites was the termination of the military exemption promised to them as settlers, even though the government was willing to grant alternative service in hospital and sanitary service and the forestry. Numbers of Mennonites, including some Mennonite Brethren, fearing their loss of autonomy and Russification, fuelled by the prospects of free land in the New World, opted for migration. Between 1874 and 1800 about 18,000 settled in the United States, primarily in Kansas, and in Canada in Manitoba. By 1880 the number of Mennonite Brethren in America had grown to around 1,200.[4]

Mennonite Brethren not only faced the threat of Russification but also the problem of maintaining an identify apart from Baptists. German Baptists looked upon the Mennonite Brethren with their revivalism, gathered churches, and adoption of immersion as co-religionists. Many German Baptists no doubt felt as Karl Ondra when he wrote in his report of the German Baptist Russian-Turkish Association in 1874 that Mennonite Brethren were "essentially nothing other than Baptists."[5] Abraham Unger in the Einlage church closely identified himself with Baptists, and he with others accepted in 1869 ordination from Oncken himself. Baptists and Mennonite Brethren attended each other's meetings. In 1876 Jakob Jantz, a Mennonite Brethren itinerant missionary traveled to a Baptist associational meeting in Neu-Danzig in company with Christian Fischer, a Baptist minister. Mennonite Brethren provided support for Johann Kargel, then serving as a Baptist pastor in St. Petersburg. Kargel's report for 1876–1877 found its way into a copybook with reports of other Mennonite Brethren missionaries, which was circulated among the churches. Even the Russian government was wondering if Mennonite Brethren should not be counted as Baptists.[6]

---

3. See Friesen, 513–14.

4. For the emigration, see Smith, *Smith's Story of the Mennonites*, 283–84, and Leibrandt, "The Emigration of the German Mennonites from Russia to the United States and Canada in 1873–1880," *MQR* 6/4 (1932), 205–26, and 7/1 (1933), 5–41.

5. *Missionsblatt*, Mar. 1875, 45.

6. Friesen, 520–22.

PART TWO—Prospects: German and Baltic Beginnings, 1855–1884

Not all Mennonite Brethren, however, were comfortable with close identification with Baptists. First, they were descendents of an Anabaptist heritage and were part of a distinct religious fraternity recognized by the government. They also had exemption from military service, while Baptists accepted it. Some Mennonites were also critical of Baptists who tolerated the use of tobacco. In fact, Oncken himself smoked, a practice that some Mennonite Brethren copied. Contention over this issue rose to such a point that the Einlage church, although opposed by Unger as too severe, excluded ten to twelve members for the habit.[7]

Edward Leppke, a former Baptist, entered another wedge when he insisted that anyone not accepting nonresistance could not be saved. His contention began to influence a segment of members that moved them to separate themselves from Baptists. The issue became so contentious that when Liebig attended the Einlage church as a visitor in the mid-seventies, he was not even allowed to observe the Lord's Supper with the congregation. Although invited, Liebig then declined to preach the communion sermon.[8]

In 1873 a government official visited the Mennonites in South Russia to ascertain the relationship of Mennonite Brethren to the impeding compulsory military law that will be issued in 1874. After discussion, the Einlage church, under Unger's influence, sent the German Baptist Confession of 1847. The document, printed in Basel in 1876, however, included *Bemerkungen* or annotations that noted that Mennonite Brethren differed from Baptists on the latter's rejection of nonresistance and footwashing and their acceptance of the oath. Even with these differences, the appendix stated that with Baptists they confessed one and the same faith, immersed only the born again, and disciplined by exclusion until repentance members who practiced ungodly behavior. They also explicitly differentiated themselves from other Mennonites who accepted young people in their teen years into membership without evidence of regeneration, baptized by pouring instead of immersion, and only disciplined individuals for the most egregious sins such as adultery and possibly drunkenness and then for only a limited time.[9]

When Baptists in 1879 received recognition, the Russian government wished to determine their number. In the Chortitza area, the Russian administration counted the Mennonite Brethren as Baptists, which brought an inquiry from Mennonite Brethren leaders. As a result, they produced a document that differentiated Mennonite Brethren from Baptists that Abraham Unger, Aron Lepp, Johann Siemens, Peter M. Friesen, and Johann Wieler helped to produce with the latter two also providing a Russian translation as demanded by the government. In May 1880 the government

---

7. Ibid., 463–64.

8. Ibid., 476–77. Pritzkau, 116.

9. Friesen, 478–79. Toews, *History of the Mennonite Brethren Church*, 74–5. *Glaubens-Bekenntniss und Verfassung der gläubiggetauften und vereinigten Mennonite-Brüdergemeinde in Südlichen Russland* (1876).

issued an order that informed the Einlage congregation that they would be considered Mennonites as other Mennonites.[10]

German Baptist Expansion and Organization

Alt-Danzig and Neu-Danzig were not the only German Baptist centers in southern Ukraine. To the west in the Black Sea region, Odessa and the nearby Schwabian colonies became another center. A few German Baptists began to settle in the area. Odessa was located near numerous German colonies that had been influenced by pietism as well as revival movements. It is thus not surprising that German Baptists and Mennonite Brethren leaders found the area attractive. On the other hand, the beginnings of the Baptist church in Odessa proved to be difficult.[11]

Johann Wieler (1839–1889), a younger brother of Gerhard Wieler, arrived in Odessa at the end of 1869. In the spring of 1870 he invited Heinrich Maier (Meyer) from Alt-Danzig to assist in the mission he had begun. In May of the same year Pritzkau undertook a mission tour of five weeks to Neu-Danzig and then to the Schwabian colonies where he found a ready response and conducted a baptismal service in Annenthal. Pritzkau also attempted to mediate between the warring factions in the mission Wieler had begun, then numbering scarcely ten members. Some wanted to ordain Maier as elder, charging Wieler was a Mennonite, while the other party supported Wieler as the one who had begun the work. No solution was found, and Wieler separated with his own party.

On Pritzkau's suggestion, Karl Ondra now came South to strengthen the work in Annenthal and Odessa. On June 17 he baptized in Annenthal two brethren from Odessa, which was also the date for founding the Odessa Baptist Church. Authorities arrested Ondra in Annenthal, who was then imprisoned for two weeks in Odessa. After his release, he continued his ministry before returning to Volhynia. Wieler provided bail for him. In addition, Maier cut his ministry short at the church, which ended before the end of 1870.[12]

On Ondra's encouragement, the next pastor was Wilhelm Schulz, a German subject from Königserg, East Prussia, who came in May 1871. He had been in Ukraine since about 1867, serving the church in Hortschick. According to K. I. Veltistov, the Orthodox writer, Schulz was forced to leave the Hortschick church because of his "severity and sharpness in manner and preaching." While in Odessa, he crossed the

---

10. Friesen, 479–80.

11. For sources of pietist and revivalistic influences in southwestern Ukraine, see Wardin, *Evangelical Sectarianism*, nos. 179–82, 185–87. For the turbulent beginnings of the German Baptist work in Odessa and vicinity, see Pritzkau, 55–60, 62–63, and *Istoriya Evangel'skikh Khristian-Baptistov v SSSR*, 434–35.

12. For Ondra's ministry in Odessa, see *Der Sendbote*, Feb. 10, 1886, 50, and Pritzkau, 62–63. See Dorodnitsyn, *Materialy*, doc. 91, for the bail that Wieler provided Ondra. In 1873 Maier will become the founder of Baptist work in Hungary.

Southern Bug River where in ministering at Steingut, a station of Alt-Danzig church, a mob stopped his meeting and then was held for investigation for several weeks. He also gained converts in the Roman Catholic colony of Landau in the Beresan District, where again he was arrested. In addition, his ministry in the Odessa church was marred in a conflict with a young brother from Germany named Ziehl. He left the church near the end of 1872. Many years later Pritzkau wrote that Schulz had been the wrong man for the Odessa church.[13]

Schulz now settled in the Mennonite colony of Chortitza in Einlage. He served as a traveling missionary among Mennonites and Lutherans, traveling as far east as the Don region. With Lutheran instigation, an order in 1873 forbade him to hold further meetings. He was arrested in Yekaterinoslav Province and then released on bail until his trial. In June he received an order from the acting governor that in the meantime he was to remain in Einlage under village arrest. In September he was escorted to the chief town of the district and imprisoned for almost a month. Through the influence of a Lutheran clergyman, the Lutheran Consistory in St. Petersburg persuaded the government to banish him. He was sent to Odessa where on November 6 Schulz and his wife and daughter were put on a train to Germany with a warning never again to return.[14]

After all the conflicts and short pastorates in the Odessa church and the turbulent career of Schulz, it was fortunate that August Liebig, the Baptist leader in Dobrudja, would now become pastor in Odessa. He had been a peacemaker among the Mennonite Brethren, preceptor in church and association polity for both Mennonite Brethren and German Baptists, and exhibited a humble spirit. On the encouragement of Pritzkau, Liebig accepted the call of the Odessa church and arrived in April 1874. At first he lived in Annenthal, thirty-two kilometers from Odessa, where many of his members lived, leaving Odessa a station, but then will later move there.[15]

Liebig found a very productive field in the surrounding Schwabian colonies. Soon he was responsible for thirty-two sites, which entailed extended travel and hurried visits by horse and wagon. Liebig faced opposition from Lutheran leaders and pietistic brethren who resented Baptist intrusion as well as competition from Seventh-day Adventists. But membership grew rapidly from 62 members to 875 in 1884, which led to forming three new churches the following year.[16]

---

13. Pritzkau, 63. *Istoriya Evangel'skikh Khristian-Baptistov v SSSR*, 435. *Missionsblatt*, Sep. 1868, 139–41; Jan. 1869, 11–12; Apr. 1870, 77; Apr. 1872, 71–72; Nov. 1872, 178–81. *BMM*, Feb. 1869, 59–60; Feb. 1873, 57. Dorodnitsyn, *Nemetskie missionary neobaptizma*, 727–29. Veltistov, *MO*, June 1902, 1021–22.

14. *Missionsblatt*, June 1873, 100–101; Aug. 1873, 139; July 1874, 121–23. *QR*, July 1873, 44–45; Jan. 1874, 5–7. Pritzkau, 115.

15. For Liebig's ministry in Odessa, see Pritzkau, 64–74. *BMM*, Jan. 1878, 18. *Missionsblatt*, Dec. 1874, 221.

16. *BMM*, Sep. 1874, 325–28; Jan. 1878, 18–19; May 1887, 140. *Missionsblatt*, 1875, no. 4, 66; 1877, no. 5, 79–81. *WHZ*, Apr. 15, 1884, 85.

Although most Baptist converts came from those with a Lutheran heritage, some Roman Catholics became Baptist converts, as noted already in Schulz's ministry in Landau colony, where pietism was present. In his association with pietistic circles, Christian Fischer became a convert, but faced strong opposition and physical attack, including several beatings from his own father. He nevertheless persevered, winning coverts, including members of his own family. Authorities attempted to forbid his meetings and fined those who attended. In 1869 he and his wife with other Catholics were baptized in 1869 at Alt-Danzig at the time of Oncken's visit. He and his small band leased land near Alt-Danzig. He engaged in mission work in Landau and other parts of southern Russia, supported with a small monthly stipend from the Alt-Danzig church.[17]

Fischer continued to face violence from the populace and strong opposition from Roman Catholic priests, which brought him into conflct with the police. In January 1872 Fischer with Karl König, a Saxon German subject, were arrested for "subversion of the Catholic peasants into Anabaptism." They were let go on bail but were almost immediately again engaged in their evangelistic work. The administrator and dean of Landau from 1873 to 1877, Father Johannes Burgardt, was powerless in stopping the evangelical movement. His gruffness and scolding did little good, failing to win the confidence of his flock. Fischer became a pastor in Johannesthal, near Landau, a mission of the Odessa church. He later became a co-pastor in the Michailowka church in Yekaterinoslav Province.[18]

German Baptists also gained a few Jewish converts. On Easter Sunday in 1871, Ondra baptized a brother and two sisters. In 1873 at Annenthal, Ondra baptized a Jewish woman, who for a short time had been in the Lutheran Church. The baptism in September 1871 of Israel Zimmerman, a youth of sixteen, became part of a *cause celebre* that attracted much attention in the colonies. Because of the testimony of a Russian fellow servant, Zimmerman began to seek salvation, recognizing Christ as the Messiah, but because of opposition fled to Alt-Danzig. After six weeks here, he fled to Odessa and then was illegally spirited to Dobrudja in Turkey. He was required to return to Russia, going again to Alt-Danzig, but the Baptists here, fearing for his safety, sent him to Ondra who baptized him. His Jewish opponents found him here and under arrest was brought to his home. Years later the Russian historian Veltistov used the case as an example of Baptists kidnapping and seducing children, giving the victim a false Turkish identity, and a willingness to provide false testimony.[19]

---

17. Pritzkau, 97–102. Giesinger, "The Landau Baptists," *JAHSGR* 17/4 (Winter, 1994), 18. *Der Sendbote*, Apr. 15, 1874, 58. *BMM*, Aug. 1874, 300.

18. Pritzkau, 21–23, 97, 101–2. Giesinger, 19–20. Dorodnitsyn, *Nemetskie missionary neobaptizma*, 729–30. Keller, *Die deutschen Kolonien in Südrussland*.

19. *Missionsblatt*, Nov. 1870, 202–3; Feb. 1871, 28–29; July 1871, 117; Aug. 1873, 141. *QR*, Apr. 1871, 890–91. Veltistov, *MO*, June 1902, 1024–25. See correspondence between Wieler and Klundt on Zimmerman in *Kievskaya starina* 10 (Oct. 1884), 315–16, 319.

PART TWO—Prospects: German and Baltic Beginnings, 1855–1884

The establishment of associational life was a demonstration of the growing strength of the German Baptist movement and its growing independence from Germany. The first one, the Russian-Turkish Association, was established in May in 1872 in Alt-Danzig. Besides the Alt-Danzig church, it included three churches in Volhynia, the Odessa church, and Catalui in Dobrudja. Pritzkau was the host pastor and Liebig the moderator. Speakers included Ondra, Ziehl, Schulz, as well as Jakob Klundt from Catalui, who had been exiled from Neu-Danzig in the mid-sixties. The association ended with a love feast.[20]

The next meeting of the association opened in September 1874 at Neudorf in Volhynia with Ondra as host pastor. It proved to be a gala affair in attendance and the galaxy of German Baptist leaders who participated. Although without a roof, the newly enlarged chapel building was dedicated. On the Sunday before the opening of the associational meeting, around 1,500 were present, crowding every space with many pressing from the outside at the open windows. Among the participants of the association was the patriarch from Russian Poland, Gottfried Alf, as well as Pritzkau, August and Ludwig Liebig, and Johann Kargel, who conducted a baptismal service. Such guests as H. Berneike, the influential pastor of the Baptist church in Königsberg and in the Prussian Association, and the Mennonite Brethren leader, Abraham Unger, who was given voting rights, also spoke. Also present was the Stundo-Baptist leader, Ivan Ryaboshapka, with other Russians. The presence of Mennonite Brethren and Russian Baptist leaders was also evidence of a close identify of these bodies with German Baptists.[21]

Because of fear that the authorities might prohibit the association, Ondra spoke to the *Ispranik* or magistrate, who suggested sending a petition, which, including the agenda of the association, was subsequently approved by the highest authorities in St. Petersburg. The magistrate with the mayor attended the associational sessions with an interpreter. The magistrate even engaged with the representatives in a time of questions and answers and after the meeting wrote a favorable report on the proceedings. On the wall behind the pulpit in the chapel was not only in Russian and German the Baptist motto from Ephesians, "One Lord, one faith, one baptism," but also from I Peter, "Fear God: honor the king" in German but in Russian, "Honor the Tsar." Shortly after the conference Ondra, Kargel, and Berneike visited the governor with whom Berneike addressed in German since he was German, thanking him and other officials for their permission for holding the association. The governor requested that they express their concerns to him.[22]

The next association was held in October 1875 in Annenthal with Liebig as host. A large crowd gathered that filled every cottage with carriages in every yard. Liebig and his wife hosted at least fifteen in their home. The association met in a large wooden

20. *Missionsblatt*, Sep. 1872, 148–50. *BMM*, Jan. 1873, 25–26.
21. *Missionsblatt*, Mar. 1875, 44–46; Apr. 1875, 70–72. *QR*, Mar. 1875, 11–12. *BMM*, Feb. 1875, 47.
22. *QR*, Mar. 1875, 11–12. *Missionsblatt*, Apr. 1875, 71. *BMM*, June 1875, 181.

tabernacle, quickly constructed for the occasion. The main topic at the association was missions—how to promote it in Odessa and in Bulgaria where some people in the latter place were requesting believer's baptism. The association condemned the use of tobacco, which was in line with Mennonite Brethren views. As at the association in Neudorf, a baptismal service was also held. When Liebig, standing in the Black Sea, was about to immerse a woman, a wave suddenly immersed both of them.[23] Mennonite Brethren from the Molochna were present as guests as was August Penski, pastor from the Hohenkirch church in West Prussia, Germany. Before arriving in Annenthal, Penski had undertaken an extensive tour of four to five weeks, visiting Odessa; Mennonites in Chortitza colony, speaking at Rückenau, the Mennonite Brethren center, and the church in Halbstadt of Old Mennonites; Mennonites in Molochna; and Baptists in Alt-Danzig. In Alt-Danzig, where Baptists were in the majority, the Lutheran church was locked up, and the Lutheran schoolteacher sent by the Consistory was unable to serve since the parents of the village sent their children to the Baptist school.[24]

In the meantime the German Baptist churches in Russian Poland were still members of the Prussian Association. In early 1875 the brethren in Poland considered sending a petition to the Prussian Association for dismissal. Some argued that crossing the German-Russian border was difficult for delegates from Russian Poland and that they were treated somewhat as stepchildren. Another factor was the use of tobacco. Because of Alf and Penski's influence, Baptists in Poland forbade smoking, which, however, was tolerated by missionaries from Prussia. The petition, however, was not sent until two years later, which the Prussian Association will accept. The churches in Poland formed in Kicin in September 1877 the Russian Polish Association.[25]

German Baptists in Russia felt a need for Bible training. The Russian-Turkish Association passed a resolution for a need of annual one-month Bible courses for its pastoral leadership, including lay members who assisted the ordained ministers with their many mission stations. The first Bible course was at Annenthal with subsequent courses elsewhere in Ukraine. Early teachers included, Liebig, Ondra, and J. Kessler. Mennonite Brethren also participated.[26]

Although Baptists outside Russia looked upon Russia as a mission field, German Baptists in Russia themselves looked to foreign fields. In 1875 five German Baptist churches contributed to China and Africa, and in 1876 the churches in Volhynia and elsewhere as well as the Mennonite Brethren community at Einlage gave to either or both foreign fields. German Baptists also had an interest in the Karen Baptist mission in India.[27]

---

23. *BMM*, Apr. 1876, 117–18.
24. Ibid., Mar. 1876, 78–80; Apr. 1876, 117–18.
25. Kupsch, 427–28, and ft. 17.
26. Pritzkau, 84–91.
27. German Baptist Union, *Bundeskonferenz*, 1873, 14–15; 1876, 22–23. *WHZ*, Jan. 15, 1882, 21.

PART TWO—Prospects: German and Baltic Beginnings, 1855–1884

At the end of 1881, German Baptists in Russia reported 6,900 members that included the church in Catalui in Romania with 137 members. Most churches were in a Russian-Turkish Association (1872) or a Russian-Polish Association (1877) and now also in a Baltic Association of Latvian Baptist churches that first met in 1880 in Preekuln. In 1875 the church in Memel, Germany, reported 2,780 members including thirty-three mission stations but with twenty-seven of them in the Baltic region of Russia. Beginning in 1876 the church began releasing its members in the Baltic to form independent congregations.[28]

German Baptist Relations with the State

The relations of German Baptists with the state went through several stages. In the first half of the 1860s, as already noted, government policy with the incitement of Lutheran officials was extremely harsh in attempting to stop the new movement with imprisonment, fines, and exile. Government officials began to realize that its policies were increasing sectarian fanaticism instead of stopping it. The adverse publicity that Russia was receiving in the press concerning its policy toward evangelicals possibly also played a factor. Since it was the government's policy to accept other religious traditions of foreign origin if they did not proselyte among the Orthodox, it was thus logical to tolerate sectarians as long as they were law abiding and fulfilled their civic duties. In 1865 the governor-general of the Baltic issued an order to cease persecution of Baptists, an order, however, not known by them until the following year.[29]

In light of the disruption in Neu-Danzig in 1864–1865, which brought imprisonment and exile to new followers accused of becoming Anabaptists, the Minstry of Internal Affairs undertook an investigation. It concluded that punitive measures should be stopped with possible resettlement in Russia itself but not exile abroad that might establish a sectarian base that could prove inimical to Russian interests. In 1867 the Ministry of Internal Affairs declared a policy of toleration with governor-general Kotzebu, even though he had favored prosecution of sectarians, supporting the policy.[30]

Officials, however, were directed to be particularly wary of foreigners who might proselyte. Some officials, urged on by Lutheran or Roman Catholic authorities, might bring charges and arrest for proselytism, such as in the cases of Ondra, Fischer, and Schulz, but generally such actions proved limited and ineffective with the exception, however, of the exile of Schulz in 1873. Although Russian Poland also witnessed some further arrests and imprisonment, also here the oppression was much less. Alf wrote in 1874 that persecution had declined and the Lutheran clergy had become more reasonable. At the end of the same year August Rauschenbusch of Rochester, New York, although disturbed at the persecution of Russian stundists, noted the excellent

---

28. *QR*, July 1882, 16. Ekelmann, 98.
29. Toews, *The Story of the Early Mennonite Brethren*, 170–71. Veltistov, *MO*, Mar. 1902, 464.
30. Toews, *The Story of the Early Mennonite Brethren*. 170–74. Veltistov, *MO*, June 1902, 1026–27.

relationship between the Russian authorities and German Baptists in the associational meeting that year in Neudorf. Crossing the border between Russia and Germany or the reverse for both German and Russian pastors apparently was no insurmountable obstacle. In reviewing German Baptist missionary activity in this period, Veltistov, the Orthodox historian, lamented the government's leniency and lack of following through on a clear-cut policy as well as en effective counter activity on the part of the Protestant clergy.[31]

The Banishment of 1877

With the great improvement in relations with the regime, it came as a great shock and surprise to the Baptist community in Volhynia when unannounced and without trial the authorities banished almost overnight three of their pastors and three lay members.[32] The pastors included Ondra of the Neudorf church, A. R. Schiewe, the new pastor of the Soroczin church, and Ludwig Nasgowitz, pastor of the congregation at Toporischtsch, composed of Masuren migrants from East Prussia. The laymen were Gottlieb Schirrmann, Wilhelm Langhans, and Adolph Neumann, lay preachers of the Neudorf church. It was ironic that at the outbreak of the Russian-Turkish War in 1877 the Baptists of Volhynia not only had pledged loyalty to Emperor Alexander II but also agreed to send without cost several men and women to serve the sick and wounded in the war zone for two or three months.

At their summons, the police officials told the apprehended that they were prisoners and were to be banished immediately, leaving behind their wives, children, and farms. The presumption was that they had spread Baptist views among the Orthodox population. Upon request, the departure was delayed a day or two. Under military escort, the six traveled by train, paying their own expenses. As their birth was in Russian Poland, the authorities sent Ondra and Schiewe to that part of the Empire, while the others, German subjects who resided under a Russian pass, were taken to the Austrian border, finally making their way to Berlin.

All proclaimed their innocence, claiming they never worked with Russian stundists nor baptized any Orthodox.[33] In his lengthy essay on stundists in South Russia, the Orthodox author, signed V. V., claimed that Ondra was not all that innocent, at least guilt by association. He claimed Ondra wrote to Oncken that he witnessed the baptism of a Russian woman in Neudorf, performed by Lyasotskiï, a Ukrainian recently freed from prison, and in Hamburg he had received 212 marks for the use of Russian brethren.

---

31. Veltistov, *MO*, June 1902, 1027–28. *Missionsblatt*, June 1874, 96. *BMM*, Feb. 1875, 47.
32. For a contemporary account of the exile of the six from Volhynia, see *BMM*, Nov. 1877, 376–78.
33. For Ondra's personal defense, see *Missionsblatt*, May 1878, 81–85. For charges against Ondra by an Orthodox critic, see *TsV*, 1882, no. 43, 11.

PART TWO—Prospects: German and Baltic Beginnings, 1855–1884

Ondra, although understanding Russian did not preach in Russian; Schiewe came from German parentage in Poland and knew Russian; Nasgowitz spoke a Polish dialect in his ministry among the Masurens. The three lay pastors scarcely knew a word of Russian.[34]

It was later determined that a former member of the Neudorf church and former Lutheran schoolteacher had turned against his former co-religionists, claiming the banished had baptized Orthodox and encouraged them to leave their faith. Whatever the truth of the allegations, Lutheran and Orthodox leaders were more than happy to stop the advance of Baptists in Volhynia by seeking to cripple their leadership. The Orthodox were becoming increasingly aroused by the growth of a Russian stundist movement that some alleged had direct ties with Baptists. Soon after deportation, two local officials with a high ranking official from St. Petersburg arrived at Neudorf at the end of July. The official from the capital spoke with disdain against Baptists and asked why they were converting native Russians. The visit was no judicial inquiry but just an inspection. Some years later in 1902, Veltistov, in justifying the events of 1877, alleged that the Baptists, who preached conversion, were also inducing the converted to leave "Babylon" and "Egyptian bondage" (a long-standing Lutheran charge) and thus break their former confessional ties.[35]

The two Russian subjects, Ondra and Schiewe, sent a petition to the Tsar, while the four German subjects petitioned the Emperor of Germany. In Berlin, Joseph Lehmann appealed to Bismarck. In addition, Ondra and Schiewe drew up a statement, which a committee of the Prussian Association sent to the Minister of the Interior, declaring that they worked only among fellow Germans and took care not to proselyte Russians. The Neudorf church sent two representatives to the Russian embassy in Turkey with a petition to present to the Tsar and also a petition to the government in St. Petersburg. The wives of the banished sent their own petition to the Russian empress, describing their anguish, and asked for her intercession.[36]

All efforts to gain the return of the banished were of no avail. Their families joined them at their new locations. Oncken appealed for financial help for the families. In January 1880 *Der Sendbote*, the German Baptist paper in America, printed a letter of thanks from Ondra for the support for the banished received through the efforts of August Rauschenbusch. The authorities removed Ondra's police supervision, and he became pastor of the Baptist church in Lodz, beginning here a very successful pastorate. After three and a half years in exile, Ondra traveled to Ukraine, stopping in Odessa and in January 1881 visiting Neudorf for an emotional homecoming. Schiewe became pastor of the Baptist church in Dirschau Germany, and then no less in 1880

---

34. For Ondra's knowledge of Russian, see his biography, *Kurz gefasste Lebens-Beschreibung*, 16, and for Schiewe's competency in the language see Kiefer's letter in *Texas Baptist*, March 6, 1884, 1. For the lack of knowing Russian by the lay pastors, see *Missionsblatt*, May 1878, 83.

35. BMM, Nov. 1877, 377. QR, Oct. 1877, 2–5. MO, June 1902, 1033.

36. BMM, Nov. 1877, 377–78. QR, Oct. 1877, 5, and Apr. 1878, 9.

pastor of the German Baptist church in St. Petersburg, a remarkable turn of events for one who earlier had been banished.[37]

In the absence of their pastors, lay leadership provided some preaching and led prayer services for the Neudorf church. In the fall the church gained the services of Severin W. Lehmann (1847–1918), who at the time was unmarried and came from serving in Odessa. In 1871 in Coblenz, Germany, he had become a convert and was baptized by Eduard Schiewe, but his Roman Catholic family repudiated him. He served the church for seventeen years. The congregation in Soroczin received Julius K. Vogel from Lodz. In 1878 the Toporischtsch congregation, then a mission of the Neudorf church, was constituted as an independent church and was served by J. G. Gargulla who came from Poland. The German Baptists simply shifted their pastors between Germany, Poland, and Ukraine.[38]

Lehmann, Vogel, and Gargulla all had successful pastorates in their respective congregations. In the following year after the banishment, the Neudorf church experienced a great revival and Lehmann baptized 200. In 1877 the membership of the three affected congregations reported 1,446 members; in 1879, 1,627. The banishment at the time was a blow to the work and very stressful, but in the end proved to be only a blimp in the road.[39]

Recognition of 1879

At the associational meeting in Neudorf in 1874, the delegates raised the question of legal recognition of German Baptists in the Russian Empire. The magistrate who was present responded that the churches should petition by sending delegates to St. Petersburg. In his history, Pritzkau claimed he expedited the gaining of recognition in 1879. He wrote that upon his arrest in 1871 for baptizing, he was brought before a police-officer but then referred the officer to the order Governor-General Kotzebu had issued forbidding the police to molest Baptists for their religious practices. As a consequence, Pritzkau was summoned in January 1872 to the governor in Kherson who informed Pritzkau that Kotzebu's order gave no right of propaganda. Pritzkau then explained to him the basic principles of the Baptist faith, which led the governor to suggest that Pritzkau send a petition and a copy of the Baptist confession to the central authority in St. Petersburg. He also stated he would also give his support to Baptist concerns. With the work of a lawyer in drawing up the petition and the acceptance of the offer from Johann Wieler of translating the confession into Russian, the documents were sent.[40]

---

37. *QR*, Apr. 1878, 9; July 1880, 10; Apr. 1881, 10. *Der Sendbote*, Jan. 28, 1880, 40.
38. For biographical information on Lehmann, Vogel, and Gargulla, see Miller, *In the Midst of Wolves*, 20–25, 69–71, 89.
39. *WHZ*, May 15, 1884, 110. German Baptist Union, *Jahrbuch*, 1878, 18, 20, and 1879, 20–21.
40. Pritzkau, 28–30.

Finally in September 1879 the government issued the recognition of German Baptists as a corporate body with legal rights along with other denominations. They rejoiced in receiving the recognition. It gave them the freedom of faith and practice and the right to establish a civil registry of births, marriages, and deaths. Earlier the Lutherans were responsible for recording Baptist data but would not as they considered them sectarians. On the other hand, the government expected Baptists to abide by their regulations for approval for registration of churches, calling of pastors, and erection of church buildings. The recognition granted rights only to those of non-Orthodox background and no right to proselytize members of the Orthodox Church.[41]

A writer in the Lutheran periodical, *St. Petersburger evangelisches Sonntagsblatt*, observed editorially that the Baptists will with the recognition renew efforts to increase their number at Lutheran expense. On the other hand, the writer, trying to make the best of the situation, claimed that he did not begrudge Baptists the recognition and, in fact, Lutherans for years had recommended this action. Henceforth Lutheran clergy could now concentrate their energies in struggling against Baptist error with spiritual weapons rather then police measures. Although opposing Lutherans becoming Baptists, nevertheless the writer acknowledged that Baptists confess the Lord Jesus and "among them are also many upright and sincere believing souls." In a time of such intense denominational rivalry with charge and counter charge, such words from either side were few and far between.[42]

---

41. *WHZ*, May 15, 1879, 87; Nov. 1, 1879, 182–83. *BMM*, Feb. 1880, 53. *QR*, Jan. 1880, 11. *SPES* 20 (1879), 319–20.

42. *SPES* 20 (1879), 336.

PART THREE

Prospects

Ukrainian and Russian Beginnings,
1860–1884

9

The Stundist Movement

Preparation and Obstacles

WHILE THE EVANGELICAL SECTARIAN movement found a base in Russia among German Baptists and Mennonite Brethren, practically in parallel was the emergence of a Russo-Stundist movement among the native population in Ukraine. As with the German population, pietism and revivalism helped to prepare the way. One center was in western Ukraine north of Odessa nurtured first by German pietism. A second center was in central Ukraine, fed by Mennonite Brethren and German Baptists.

SOCIAL AND ECONOMIC FACTORS

Although the Russo-Stundist movement emerged with the help of pietism within Russia, a number of other factors—social, economic, and religious— made it possible for it to emerge. The succession to the throne of Alexander II, who reigned from 1855 to 1881, ushered in a period of Great Reforms that shifted the Russian regime away from the rigid authoritarian rule of Nicholas I. Even with their limitations, these reforms brought to the peasant hopeful expectations.

The manifesto in March 1861 that abolished serfdom freed fifty-two million peasants who had been bound to the land. Although the lot of the peasant was still difficult with limited land and resources, yet the emancipation brought a sense of individualism with more economic opportunity, freedom of movement, and circulation of new ideas. The establishment in 1864 of zemstvo assemblies and boards provided more democracy and initiative on the local level. Among their responsibilities was education, and the number of elementary schools notably increased. Although Russia lagged far behind Western Europe in literacy with about fifty-five percent still illiterate in 1917, nevertheless popular literature greatly increased. The reform of the legal system, also in 1864, gave Russia an independent judiciary, and except for military and ecclesiastical courts all Russians were now equal before the law.[1]

As Sergeï M. Kravchinskiï, writing under the pseudonym "Stepniak," wrote in 1884, the peasants began to think of themselves as citizens. The despotism of a patriarchal head of the entire family began to subside with children increasingly forming their own independent households. In his report to the Church Missionary Society in 1865, "Missionary and Religious Progress in Russia," J. Long declared that the emancipation of the serfs "is literally the waking up of a nation. Schools are multiplying among the peasantry . . . and, in consequence the circulation of the Bible is rapidly increasing."[2] The improvement in communication and transportation furthered the dissemination of new ideas. Although under Nicholas I the regime built over 5,000 miles of hard-surface roads, the system of roads was inadequate and generally poorly maintained. Beginning in 1837, Russia began building railroads but by 1855 still had only 650 miles. By 1881, however, railway mileage had increased to 14,000 miles.[3]

In 1874 Johann Pritzkau wrote to Oncken that railroad travel had become much improved and comfortable since Oncken's trip in 1869, which Oncken himself described as "oriental." Pritzkau declared that one could now reach by railroad all the points that Oncken had visited and that he could also visit by rail almost all his preaching stations. In a six-day tour, Pritzkau stated that he had traveled around 400 kilometers, visited four stations, and preached ten times.[4]

Bibles and Tracts

The termination by the regime of the Russian Bible Society in 1826 ended the distribution of the Russian Bible in the Russian Empire. The Holy Synod published limited editions of the Slavonic Bible but no Scripture in the language of the people. The Evangelical Bible Society and the British and Foreign Bible Society (BFBS) continued distribution of Scripture, but they were largely confined to the Protestant population and to versions other than Russian.

A new day dawned with the accession of Alexander II in 1855, who favored a translation of the Bible into Russian and its availability for the populace. At a conference in Moscow in 1856, the Holy Synod recognized the need for a translation from the original manuscripts and gave the work of translation to the four spiritual academies. Imperial approval was granted in 1858. In 1861 the Four Gospels appeared and

---

1. For the impact of the Great Reforms, see Riasnovsky, *A History of Russia*, 408–19, 484–87.
2. Stepniak, *The Russian Peasantry*, 74–75. *BMM*, Mar. 1865, 86.
3. Florinsky, *Russia*, 2:789, 934.
4. *QR*, Apr. 1874, 4.

in 1862 the New Testament. In 1876 the full Bible was completed. In 1877 Alexander wrote to the Holy Synod expressing his thanks for its work and stated, "I pray to the Almighty, that he reveals the holy strength of his Word for the growth of the Russian Orthodox people in faith and in godliness, on which the true happiness of the Empire and the people rests." The Holy Synod published its version and distributed it by its own commission agents and colporteurs, forbidding the circulation of other Russian versions.[5]

In 1862 or the following year a private circle formed to further the distribution of Scripture, which included both Orthodox and Protestant participation. Protestants included Dalton, the German Reformed pastor, the pastor of the Moravian Brethren in St. Petersburg, and two Lutherans. In 1869 the government granted the organization its approval as the "Society for the Distribution of the Holy Scripture in Russia," but now an entirely Orthodox organization. It could not publish on its own, but with depots in St. Petersburg and Moscow and its own colporteurs it became an important agency in Bible distribution. By 1893 it had distributed over one and a half million copies of the Scripture.[6]

Although the British and Foreign Bible Society was not allowed to circulate its own Russian Bible, which, by the way, differed from the Bible of the Holy Synod by excluding the Apocrypha, it, however, now enjoyed an expanded field for its work. It could purchase the Holy Synod version and distribute it along with versions in other languages that it imported without paying duty. It expanded its staff of colporteurs and depots. The state railways and many commercial firms granted free passes to its colporteurs and waived charges for the transport of Scripture. On the twenty-fifth anniversary of Alexander's accession in 1880, the BFBS sent an address through the British ambassador expressing gratitude for "the protection and facilities" it enjoyed.[7]

In the distribution of the Bible and Christian literature, some individuals who began as independents will enter the service of the BFBS. One was the indefatigable John Melville, the Presbyterian Scotsman who settled in Odessa in 1837. He continued his work into the 1880s, but age and health finally ended his notable career. Otto Forchhammer, the pietistic Lutheran who had accompanied Johann Claassen, the Mennonite Brethren, to St. Petersburg in 1860, will settle in the city. He obtained copies of the Russian New Testament, selling them on commission. He also received a large supply of tracts from a lady in England and distributed them at the great fair at Nizhnii Novgorod. Forchhammer not only entered the service of the BFBS but became closely allied with the Pashkovites.[8]

---

5. Korff, *Am Zarenhof*, 54. Astaf'ev, *Opyt istorii biblii v Rossii*, 3.

6. Astafev, 3–5. Benford, "Evangelical Bible Society in the Russian Empire," *MERSH* 11, 10. "The Entrance of the Bible into Russia," *MRW*, May 1899, 363–64. Kean, *The Bible in Russia*, 13–14. Astaf'ev claims 1862 but Benford claims 1863 for the beginning of the society.

7. Kean, 11–16. BFBS, *Report*, 1880, 99.

8. RTS, *Report*, 1882, 100. Friesen, 264. *EC*, Sep. 1, 1870, 275–76.

PART THREE—Prospects: Ukrainian and Russian Beginnings, 1860–1884

Another notable colporteur and evangelist who later served with the BFBS and was closely aligned with evangelicalism in the Russian Empire was Jakob D. Delyakov (1833–1898). He was an evangelical Nestorian from Persia who was converted in a Protestant mission school. After ministering in Tiflis, he began in 1862 work as an independent colporteur in Ukraine, supporting himself by selling household items. On his first tour he held successsful revivals in Karlovka near Elizavetgrad and at Rohrbach that contributed to the nascent Russian stundist movement. After suffering arrest twice, he began to concentrate his work among the Molokans in Taurida *guberniya* (Province).[9]

Although a great field for the distribution of Scripture had now opened, obstacles remained. Russia was an extremely large country with a population in 1860 of sixty million that was overwhelmingly rural in thousands of villages and in many thinly populated areas. Even with the growth of railroads and use of steamers, problems of distributions were daunting. Difficult travel conditions, poor accommodations, and cold winters were serious handicaps. A popular place of distribution was at the annual fair at Nishnii Novgorod that drew large crowds.[10]

An important handmaiden to Scriptural distribution was the ministry of tracts, small brochures that often in story form presented biblical truths. It was the Internet of the nineteenth century for the spread of the gospel. The Religious Tract Society (RTS) of London was the premier agency for the publication and distribution of tracts and successfully entered the Russian field. Although distribution of the Russian Bible had largely stopped under Nicholas I, the distribution of tracts by and large continued with the approval of the authorities. As will be seen later, the formation by the Pashkovites with the assistance of the RTS of a Russian society, The Society for the Encouragement of Spiritual and Ethical Reading, in St. Petersburg in 1875 will be a great boon to production of tracts and their distribution

Evangelical Relations

The social and economic conditions and the distribution of the Bible and tracts in the language of the people will be important factors in the emergence of the Russo-Stundist movement, but other components will be the influence of evangelicalism already in Russia as well as the spiritual state of Russian Orthodoxy. Pietism as expressed in the stundist movement was well represented within the German Lutheran and Reformed bodies in Russia and, as will be noted later, will play a significant role. The two evangelical sectarian bodies, Mennonite Brethren and German Baptists, will

---

9. For Delyakov's career, see his autobiography in *The European Harvest Field*, Mar.–June, Sep.–Dec., 1935.

10. Pike, "The Bible in Russia," *The Sunday Magazine* 18 (n. s.), 1889, 634–36. BFBS, *Report*, 1871, 134; 1877, 109; 1880, 100–102; 1883, 99. *BMM*, Mar. 1865, 85–86.

also play their own roles, particularly in moving the Russo-Stundist movement from a movement within Orthodoxy to evangelical separatism.

Even though the Russian government granted recognition to the Mennonite Brethren and then later to German Baptists, the regime was always concerned about their influence on the native Russian/Ukrainian Orthodox population. In the eyes of the authorities their evangelistic enthusiasm and revivalism could easily spill over among the Orthodox. According to Russian law, it was strictly forbidden either to alienate an Orthodox member from his faith or lead this person to join another confession. The penalty for breaking the law could be harsh, either exile or imprisonment. In 1864 a Mennonite Brethren who had earlier suffered some imprisonment for his alleged evangelistic activity wrote in 1864 to the German Baptist headquarters in Hamburg, "A young Russian wishes to be baptized on profession of his faith; but here a mountain towers aloft in our way. It is well known that every Russian who changes his faith is to be exiled to Siberia, as well as the person leading him to such a change."[11]

Although the Ukrainian population lived apart from the Germans in their own villages with cultural barriers between the two nationalities extremely high, some interaction was possible, particularly in the economic sphere. Besides trade, Germans, including Mennonites, employed numbers of Ukrainians in their homes, farms, or businesses, who in turn might acquire some German. Some of them began to be influenced by the evangelical examples or views of their German employers or neighbors or may even begin to attend a stundist gathering in a German home. In addition, an evangelical, although at great risk, might begin to witness to an adherent of the Orthodox faith.[12]

The foremost leader in specifically targeting Orthodox with the gospel was Gerhard Wieler (1833–1911), a young Mennonite, born in 1833 in the Mennonite colony of Chortitza.[13] He was a son of Johann Wieler, Sr., and six years older than his brother Johann. He was well educated in German and unusual for the time in Russian. He became a schoolteacher.

In the account of the Mennonite Brethren, the reader has already come across Gerhard's career of radicalism beset by *Sturm und Drang*. He was an early convert to the Mennonite Brethren movement, baptized in November 1861 in Berdyansk, but

11. *BMM*, 1864, 275.

12. For the German influence on Russian laborers and their employment, see Rozhdestvenskiĭ, *Yuzhnorusskiĭ shtundizm*, 48, and Dalton, *Der Stundismus in Russland*, 10.

13. For disjoined references to Gerhard Wieler's background and activity, see Friesen, 274–75, 285, 278–90, 318–26, 373–76, 401, 433–34. For his initial activity in Chortitza, see Toews, *The Story of the Early Mennonite Brethren*, 119–28, and Dorodnitsyn, *Materialy*, doc. 4. On the Wieler family as well as Gerhard's youth, early teaching experience, and later fanaticism, see Toews, "The Early Mennonite Brethren: Some Outside Views," *MQR* 58/2 (Apr. 1984), 101–11, translated from the reminiscences of Hildebrandt, "Aus der Kronsweider Erweckungszeit," which appeared in *Der Botschafter* 8 (1913). For Gerhard's own defense in 1862, see Toews, *The Story of the Early Mennonite Brethren*, 86–87, and Dorodnitsyn, *Materialy*, doc. 16. At his defense, Gerhard said he was twenty-eight years old.

PART THREE—Prospects: Ukrainian and Russian Beginnings, 1860–1884

was forced to leave his teaching position of six years in Libenau in the Molochna and then moved to Chortitza. In 1862 he appealed to Tsar Alexander in St. Petersburg for religious rights, which was soon followed by his arrest and imprisonment with others for his views and the suspicion of proselytizing Orthodox. Later in the year he went to the Kuban to check out the area for Mennonite Brethren settlement. In May 1864 his baptism of eleven German converts in Neu-Danzig caused a great uproar. He participated in the exuberant excesses that beset numbers of Mennonite Brethren at this time and displayed his fanaticism in 1864–1865 in his dictatorial control in the Chortitza church, even excluding both his father and brothers from the church. As if all of this were not enough, his activity with the Orthodox will bring him into serious conflict with the government.

While still teaching in Libenau, Gerhard engaged in ministry among Orthodox in the village of Ostrikov across the Tokmak River. A group of fifty gathered to read the New Testament. One of those who attended was Efrosiniya (or Priska) Morozova, a servant in the household of Heinrich Huebert in Liebenau, an early minister of the Mennonite Brethren Church in the Molochna. Besides the Bible reading in Ostrikov, she had also earlier learned enough German to hear the Bible read in the Huebert household, a home that at times included Russian peasants for worship. In 1862 the authorities interrogated and beat her and then transferred her to another Mennonite home, but she kept steadfast in her faith and even brought about conversions in her new home. Upon her request for baptism, Abram Dyck (as was later revealed), just on the point of leaving for the Kuban, secretly baptized her in July. Huebert and two others were also present. In an attempt to discover the baptizer, the authorities interrogated Huebert who refused to reveal his identity. In 1865, almost three years after the baptism, Huebert was imprisoned for twenty-two weeks, then released but kept under surveillance, allowed to resettle, finally moving to the Kuban in 1873. Efrosiniya was delivered to a Russian deacon and rejoined the Orthodox Church.[14] On suspicion of proselytizing Orthodox, the Yekaterinoslav District Court in 1862 tried and imprisoned for about fourteen days four Chortitza residents—Abraham Unger, Heinrich Neufeld, Peter Berg, and Gerhard Wieler. It, however, could not sustain the charge of their converting Orthodox and turned the case over to the Guardian Committee to make a final decision. The Guardian Committee noted a number of encounters between the Mennonite Brethren and the Orthodox with Gerhard appearing particularly active. The report stated that he attempted to convert thirteen workers in Unger's factory, Tatiana Filipova (his mother's servant girl), and Andrey Khomutenko, and instructed Demyan Veletsky, a peasant who had received a Russian New Testament from another German. It also appeared that Johann Claassen had sold

14. For a letter by Unger on Gerhard's activity among the Russians across from Liebenau and interrogation of the Russian believers, see QR, Apr. 1862, 27. On the Huebert case, see Toews, *The Story of the Early Mennonite Brethren*, 155–59, and also "Two Letters of Heinrich Huebert," *Direction* 25/1 (Spring, 1996), 55–59. Also see Bekker, 99–102, 169–73, who claims Efrosiniya's baptism was in 1865, but Huebert's letters clearly indicate 1862.

books to some villagers near Liebenau, who had earlier been influenced by Gerhard but here unnamed in the report. According to Alexander Brune, the Lutheran State Investigator, the fact that Gerhard suffered no repercussions from this evidence made him even bolder.[15]

In a memorandum to the Russian authorities, probably in 1864, Gerhard admitted baptizing two members of the Orthodox Church. In October 1863 he baptized near the Dnieper River a peasant boy, Matthew Serbulsky (Matveï Serbushenko), who had been converted through August Willms, his employer, and reading the New Testament. In April 1864 he baptized in Einlage Andrey Patashenko (Andreï Pedasenko), a twenty-two-year-old from Kharkov who was converted by his employer, Conrad Weis (Weiss), a shoemaker. Ten days later as noted earlier, Gerhard with Benjamin Bekker went to Neu-Danzig to baptize German believers in this village. The authorities held Serbulsky and Willms for two weeks but released them. According to Heinrich Epp in his account of Unger's life, Serbulsky, facing persecution, fled to Turkey. Weiss will be imprisoned for three months, but Patashenko will remain longer. After release, Patashenko, although under police supervision, still preached his new faith.[16]

After these baptisms Gerhard went again for about two months to the Kuban for business, but upon his return home in July he discovered the government was searching for him as a dangerous person. He went into hiding for a time. At the Chortitza church in the winter of 1864-1865 he brought havoc through his despotic control. Finally, in May 1865 the authorities imprisoned him for an extended period in Yekaterinoslav. After his release, Gerhard went to the Molochna and attempted to work with Hermann Peters and his enthusiasts, but confict developed between them. In 1866 in Chortitza, he joined the old Mennonite Church, a body that he had earlier mercilessly assailed. In 1877 he will settle in America, live in Kansas, and finally move to Ridley, California. It was reported that he had joined the United Brethren in Christ in North America, a German body. A year before his death, he was admitted to the Bethel Deaconess Hospital, a Mennonite institution in Newton, Kansas, and will pass away here in June 1911. For five short years in Russia he was an exploding meteorite in Mennonite Brethren affairs with repercussions for Russian stundists, but a career that burned itself out.[17] After Gerhard disappeared in 1864 after the baptism

15. Toews, *The Story of the Early Mennonite Brethren*, 22-24. Friesen, 322-24. The account of the criminal investigation in Toews is placed in June while Friesen, based on the diary of one of the defendants, is placed in July.

16. Toews, *The Story of the Early Mennonite Brethren*, 24-25, 51, 132-33. Dorodnitsyn, *Materialy*, docs. 23-25. Bekker, 147-48. *Missionsblatt*, Oct. 1864, 154. *Direction* 20/1 (Spring, 1991), 132. Lehmann in *Geschichte der deutschen Baptisten*, 2:315, is in error in ascribing the baptism of the two members of the Orthodox Church in 1863-1864 to Johann Wieler instead of to Gerhard and also recording that Gerhard had baptized as many as five.

17. Bekker, 143. Friesen, 278, 433-34, 445, 454. Toews, *MQR* 58/2 (Apr. 1984), 111. Dorodnitsyn, *Materialy*, docs. 27, 32, and 33. Also see the Family Group Sheet on Gerhard Wieler, California Mennonite Historical Society, Fresno, California, and information on the final years and death of Gerhard received from John Thiessen, Mennonite Library and Archives, North Newton, Kansas, March 18, 2008.

of Patashenko, the authorities turned their wrath on three who had only witnessed the baptism. They placed Abraham Unger and Heinrich Neufeld under police supervision and imprisoned Peter Berg. In early 1865 Unger wrote to Hamburg that Berg had already been in prison for five months but in the meantime had converted in the prison a Russian who wanted baptism after his freedom. In June 1865 an order was issued to investigate Peter Freze (Froese) in Chortitza for subverting Jakob Saran from Orthodoxy and for blasphemy against the Orthodox Church.[18]

The Russian authorities were properly concerned about the influence of Mennonite Brethren on the Orthodox, yet it was often difficult to prove specific cases of conversion. The number of baptisms of Orthodox was minuscule—apparently only three bona fide cases. In these cases the authorities either could not at first discover the baptizer or immediately find him but instead apprehended those who were merely observers. Because of their desire for recognition as a legal body and the great fear of imprisonment or banishment, Mennonite Brethren were inhibited in converting and baptizing Orthodox. It is unrealistic to think that there may have been a number of unreported secret baptisms. For one thing, there were no subsequent reports of such baptisms, and besides baptism for both Baptists and Mennonite Brethren was a public rite in open water.

Although Efrosiniya Morosova and Andrey Patashenko were heralds of their new faith, the former returned to the Orthodox Church, and the regime placed the second under surveillance. The third convert, Serbulsky, was harried out of the land. The rise of a Russo-Stundist movement will not arise from these early cases but from other sources.

---

18. Toews, *The Story of the Early Mennonite Brethren*, 51. Bekker, 171. *Missionsblatt*, Oct. 1864, 154, and Mar. 1865, 40. QR, Apr. 1865, 101. Dorodnitsyn, doc. 31.

10

Ukrainian Stundism

THE 1860S NOT ONLY witnessed the appearance in Ukraine of Mennonite Brethren and German Baptists but also concurrently the rise of Ukrainian stundism, a native evangelical movement. With the emancipation of the serfs, the increasing availability of the Bible and popular theological knowledge, together with increasing mobility and literacy, the times were right for its appearance. Ukrainian stundism exhibited indigenous characteristics in its search for spiritual reality, including the development of its own leadership and use of the Ukrainian language. Their appropriating or even rejecting certain theological concepts and ecclesiastical practices from their German neighbors helped to produce a unique amalgam of both native and foreign elements. Ukraine is a vast territory stretching from Volhynia in the northwest to the Don region in the southeast. It is therefore not surprising that Ukrainian stundism appeared almost simultaneously in more than one region.

ROHRBACH AND OSNOVA

An early and important center for the origins of the Ukrainian stundist movement was rooted in the Reformed/ Lutheran parish of Worms-Rohrbach, located over some sixty miles northeast of Odessa in the Beresaner region. Germans settled Rohrbach and Worms in 1809–1810. In June 1824 Johannes Bonekemper (1795–1857), born in Rhenish Prussia and an alumnus of the Basel Mission Seminary in Basel, Switzerland, arrived shortly before his twenty-ninth birthday as the new pastor. He was an

PART THREE—Prospects: Ukrainian and Russian Beginnings, 1860–1884

evangelical, influenced by the pietist movement, and held Reformed convictions. His inaugural sermon was on the gospel, speaking of the lost sheep and the lost coin.[1]

Bonekemper found a low spiritual level, but through his preaching and support of German stundist gatherings revival broke out and spiritual life revived. He traveled not only through his own parish with its scattered population but also to other places, including Odessa, Nikolaev, and Kherson, and into Bessarabia and to Alt-Danzig and Neu-Danzig in the neighboring *guberniya* of Yekaterinoslav. He had to defend himself against the charge of introducing hard-line Calvinism and struggled against the imposition of Lutheran worship practices. After twenty-four years, he left in 1848 to Dobrudja in Turkey and after serving there for five years returned to Germany where he died in 1857.

Bonekemper's son, Karl (1827–1893), born in Russia but who also lived in Turkey, America, Germany, and Switzerland, was truly international. He knew not only German and English but also Russian, including Ukrainian. After graduating from Mercersburg Theological Seminary in America in 1849, he pastored in Philadelphia, then served in Germany from 1851 to 1854, and then taught at St. Chrischona in Switzerland from 1857 to 1865. He served his father's parish in Russia from 1865 to 1876. In 1859 the Rohrbach-Worms Parish became entirely Reformed, while Lutherans soon formed their own parallel parishes.[2]

As his father, Karl supported the German stundist ministry. He entered into friendly relations with his Ukrainian neighbors and day laborers, engaging them in conversation on spiritual matters, even teaching them to read and providing them with Scripture. Karl, however, was no schismatic, and as pastor of an established church he always advised Russian stundists to remain in the Orthodox Church.

Between the departure of Johannes Bonekemper and the arrival of his son Karl, Hermann Dalton, pastor of the German Reformed Church in St. Petersburg and superintendent of the Reformed churches in Russia, visited Ukraine in 1862. After preaching on a hot July Sunday in Rohrbach and Worms, he gladly accepted the invitation to attend a German stundist gathering, a first in his experience. The schoolhouse was packed full. After singing from a hymnal, a white-haired farmer led in a free prayer, read Scripture, and then expounded on the passage. In the gathering were two Ukrainian day laborers from Osnova who had come to Rohrbach for work.

---

1. On the life and ministry of Johannes Bonekemper, see Bonekemper, "Johannes Bonekemper und seine Familie," in *Immanuel! Eine Hütte Gottes bei den Menschen*, 15–40, tr. into Eng. by Wenzlaff, Germans from Russia Heritage Society, *Heritage Review*, Sep. 1979, 14–20; Bonekemper, "Stundism in Russia," *MRW*, Mar. 1894, 201–4; and Roemmich, "Der Ursprung des ukrainischen Stundism," *Heimat der Deutschen aus Russland*, 1967/1968, 65–74.

2. For Karl Bonekemper's career, see Bonekemper, "Stundism in Russia;" Dalton, *Evangelische Strömungen in der Russischen Kirche in der Gegenwart*, 10–11, in *Catholic Presbyterian* 6 (1881), 13–14; and Rozhdestvenskiï, 59–60. The short biography, "Karl Bonekemper," *Diakonissen Freund*, Jan. 1906, 3–6, must be used with care because of wrong dating and other errors.

At the time Dalton did not know their names but later claimed they were Mikhail T. Ratushnyï and Teodor Onishchenko.³

After Karl preached his first sermon in his father's parish on July 4, 1865, he met and conversed with Ratushnyï. After a lecture in German to the youth, Karl met again with Ratushnyï and four of his friends and conversed in Russian with them about Christ.⁴

Two years later in 1867 the Russian periodical *Golos* in St. Petersburg reported that in the Odessa and Anan'ev districts a sect of stundists existed, exclusively Ukrainian, numbering up to 100 families or 300 souls. It also noted that their meetings, as other stundists, included the reading of the New Testament, preaching, and singing. It stated their adherence to the Orthodox Church was only external, showing no reverence for ikons, holy days, fasts, or other church rites. Positively, drunkenness was unknown among them, and they exercised mutual care for each other. Their German character was evident by their intercourse with the German colonies, the singing of German psalms, and the translation from German Scripture by a German in their midst, which was followed by his explanation.⁵

In the same year the *Odesskiï vestnik* commented on the article and again in a few issues later. This periodical contended that this stundist body did not come from the Germans, who, in any case were not interested in Ukrainian religious life, but from the desire of the Ukrainian peasant for a more simplified worship, which was a trend of the last hundred years. About the same time Aleksandr Znachko-Yavorskiï sent a memorandum to the governor-general of New Russia, P. E. Kotzebu, which was published in *Odesskiï vestnik*, labeled, "The Sect of the Stundists," and also published elsewhere. He took an entirely different approach, contending this group was a conspiratorial communistic sect, more devoted to economic and political rather than religious aims and an interest in land distribution. With alarm, Karl Bonekemper wrote a lengthy rebuttal, published in many papers, defending stundism as a church within a church and "salt and light in all colonies," not a sect or schismatic movement. In the eyes of dissenters, Karl was a hero, but the Orthodox establishment regarded him a schismatic. Although exonerated from all charges after his appearance before Kotzebu, the pressures and persecution against him became so great that he returned to the United States in 1876.⁶

Mikhail Ratushnyï (1830–c. 1915) was the leader of the group. He was born in the village of Osnova in the Odessa *uyezd* (district) of Kherson *guberniya*. In his

---

3. Dalton, *Der Stundismus in Russland*, 8–10; Dalton, *Evangelische Strömungen*, 8–9; and in *Catholic Presbyterian* 6 (1881), 12–13.

4. Bonekemper, "Stundism in Russia," 203.

5. *Golos*, 1867, no. 331, 2.

6. *Odesskiï vestnik*, 1867, no. 273, 917; no. 277, 933; 1868, no. 35, 112; no. 56, 184. Dorodnitsyn, *Materialy*, docs. 47, 190. Bonekemper, "Stundism in Russia," 203–4. See. Klibanov, *History of Religious Sectarianism in Russia* (1860s–1917), 259–60, for a Marxist appraisal of Znachko-Yavorskiï.

PART THREE—Prospects: Ukrainian and Russian Beginnings, 1860–1884

youth he was poor, engaged in agriculture but learned to repair shoes. As an adult, he learned to read. According to Johann Wieler, who knew him well, Ratushnyï became alarmed in 1859 about his lost spiritual state. Through prayer, finding lonely spots while at work, buying a Bible, which he studied, and meeting with Reformed brethren in neighboring Rohrbach, eight and a half miles distant, he became grounded in the evangelical faith. In Ratushnyï's letter to Hermann Fast in 1893, he wrote he had been reading a Bible, which he bought in 1857, and with instruction from a German stundist in Rohrbach who, according to Val'kevich, was "Kepel" (Kepple), he experienced conversion in 1860. According to a report many years later in 1912 on Ratushnyï, he was of medium height with a high forehead, intelligent-appearing gray eyes, and sported a small white beard.[7]

Soon after the emancipation of the serfs in 1861, Ratushnyï, who at the time was headman or *starosta* of his village, began his leadership of the stundist group. He was a man of religious passion, a successful evangelist, and under the guise of a merchant traveled to various localities in spreading his views. The Orthodox acknowledged that he was a man of ability. The governor of Kherson agreed with Archbishop Dmitrii in 1870 that Ratushnyï should be brought back to the Orthodox Church and in addition be encouraged to enter the Orthodox priesthood.[8]

Ratushnyï was married to Matrena and had two sons, Nikita, born around 1860, and Avram, born eight years later. His main support came from his farm. By the mid-eighties he had become a successful farmer, possessing an allotment of fifteen acres as well as purchasing with an association fifty-four more acres, which was mortgaged to a land bank. He had a stone house and nine draught animals.[9]

Among Ratushnyï's colleagues was an older friend, Teodor Onishchenko, born possibly around 1817, who settled in Osnova. Arsenii Rozhdestvenskii, Orthodox historian of Ukrainian stundism, who knew him personally, considered him, however, a marginal figure in the stundist movement. He appears to have been a herdsman of sheep and a vagrant, wandering among the German farmers in the vicinity of Nikolaev. He possibly became a stundist in 1858. Rozhdestvenskii claimed in the late 1880s that he had been separated from the Orthodox Church for some thirty years. Before his conversion, Onishchenko felt he was even worse than a beast. On at least two occasions, while praying out to God in a field, he personally and dramatically felt God's presence. Rozhdestvenskii called him a mystic, eccentric in lifestyle, living apart from his wife and son, and providing his own food and clothes. He and Ratushnyï

---

7. For an account of Ratushnyï's life, see E. Sokolov, "M. T. Ratushnyï," *BV*, 1980, no. 6, 41–45. For Ratushnyï's letter to Fast in 1893, see Val'kevich, App. 5:133–36, and 134, ft. 6. Also see Rozhdestvenskii, 53, ft. 1; Johann Wieler, "Letter from Odessa," QR, July 1874, 5; and *Utrennyaya zvezda*, 1912, no. 2, 1, 2, 4, tr. into Eng. in *Christian Standard*, April 16, 1913, 8, which recorded Ratushnyï's conversion on New Year's 1861.

8. Stanyukovich, *Polnoe sobranie sochinenii*, 7:153–54. Dorodnitsyn, *Materialy*, docs. 65, 76. Klimenko, "Anfänge des Baptismus in Südrussland," 37–38.

9. Dorodnityn, *Materialy*, doc. 235.

read Scripture together and conferred on religious themes, but he did not attend the stundist gatherings. Onischchenko said "God gave him light and Mikhail [Ratushnyï] understanding." In his study, based on official documents, Michael Klimenko came to the conclusion that, although Onishchenko may have had some influence on Ratushnyï, he had no influence on the development of stundism as a whole.[10]

In spite of the lack of documentation, Lev Zhapko-Potapovich in his work in 1952, *Krystove svitlo v Ukraïni*, raised Onishchenko to progenitor of Ukrainian stundism. He claimed Onishchenko was baptized in 1852 and in the following year baptized others, thus undercutting the claim that the first Russian baptism was in 1867 and the first Ukrainian in 1869. Zhapko-Potapovich used two articles by F. A. Shcherbina on Ukrainian stundism, besides two additional articles to which he credits Shcherbina, for his documentation, but Shcherbina lists Ratushnyï, Ryaboshapka, and Balaban as the leaders. In fact, none of the articles list Onishchenko at all. Besides, there were no Baptists in the Ukraine in 1852 to baptize Onishchenko. The work perpetuated for Ukrainian Baptists a false centennial, not the first time in Baptist history ideology has trumped historical reality.[11]

It appears that the Ukrainian group in Osnova was at first of no concern to the civil authorities and only began to arouse the suspicions of the Orthodox Church only some years after it began. In January 1865 Kiriakov, a rural dean in Kherson Diocese, reported to Archbishop Dimitriï in Odessa that some inhabitants in Osnova were suspected of belonging "To the sect of Reformers, namely stundists." In February Stoïkov, the local priest, reported that meetings had been held in the home of Ratushnyï for four years, which included seventeen men and three women; they neither visited foreign churches nor foreign pastors came to them. In April Stoïkov stated that he found nothing suspicious; services consisted of reading Scripture and singing. In October he reported that ikons were visible and were rendered with proper worship. In February 1866 Stoïkov communicated that the stundists regularly attended Sunday services and other holy days and fasted during Lent. They had suspended their house gatherings but had not come to him for discussions as promised.[12]

In March the *mirovoï posrednik* (arbitrator) of Odessa reported to the governor of Kherson that a sectarian group of twenty existed in Osnova, gathering at night and singing hymns from Russian and German books. He noted that some of its adherents had worked for the German colonists and acquired German customs and even

---

10. Rozhdestvenskiï, 52–53, 170–71. *TrKDA*, 1887, no. 3, 399. For references to Onishchenko in Dorodnitsyn, *Materialy*, see docs. 72, 75, 124. For an evaluation of Onishchenko based on Rozhdestvenskiï and Dorodnitsyn, see Klimenko, 39–41.

11. Zhabko-Potapovich, *Khrystove svitlo v Ukraïni*. 105–9. For Zhabko-Potapovich's documentation, see Shcherbina, "Malorusskaya shtunda," *Nedelya*, 1877, no. 1, 22–32, and no. 2, 54–61, as well as "Novo- shtundisty," *Nedelya*, 1885, no. 26, 941–45, and "O shtundistakh," *Nedelya*, 1885, no. 45, 1586–87.

12. Rozhdestvenskiï, 56–58. Klimenko, 8–11.

PART THREE—Prospects: Ukrainian and Russian Beginnings, 1860–1884

learned German. He named Mikhail Ratushnyï as leader. Converts were found in the neighboring villages of Ignatovka and Ryasnopole.[13]

On the basis of the report of the *posrednik*, the governor of Kherson demanded of the *ispravnik* (police chief) of Odessa *uyezd* detailed information on the group, which was not delivered until February of the following year in 1867. It was a rather damning report. It stated that the stundists read church-slavonic books, which they themselves interpreted or by a Reformed schismatic from the colony of Rohrbach. Also the group's adherents did not attend the Orthodox Church, showed no reverence to the ikons, or fulfilled any church rites.[14]

In the following month the rural dean, Kiriakov, visited the three villages where the stundists resided. The inhabitants admitted that they met Germans many times but only for counsel on economic questions. The inhabitants in Osnova claimed that Germans came as guests to their house gatherings and they visited German churches out of curiosity. In Ignatovka the dean asked them to sing their new hymns and recognizing their German source told them the hymns were dangerous to their souls. They possessed a Psalter, New Testament, a church calendar, Book of Hours, and a hymnal, *An Offering to Orthodox Christians*, published in St. Petersburg in 1864, but no German or Russian books from abroad.[15]

On its part the Orthodox Church was becoming increasingly alarmed, regarding the stundists as a dangerous sect rejecting the sacramental system of the church. The civil authorities, however, were little concerned with the religious views of the sectarians and claimed without the initiative of the church they could take no action on their own. But events were moving to where even the civil authorities felt compelled to take administrative action.[16]

On January 6, 1867, a number of peasants in Ignatovka brought to the parish priest slanderous charges against the stundists. The priest went to the *starosta* (village headmaster), who in turn brought in the regional authorities, who arrested Alexandr Kapustyan, pastor of the Ignatovka congregation, Ratushnyï, Gerasim Balaban (also called Vitenko), and Ilya Ossadchiï. Kapustyan was subject to particularly harsh treatment with blows to his face and a beating with birch rods. The authorities kept the four under arrest until June 5 when the judicial investigator ordered their imprisonment in Odessa; they were finally released on September 18. Johann Wieler later wrote an account that verified Kapustyan's treatment but also that two English travelers in Crimea obtained their release by approaching Tsar Alexander II who was there on a visit. Wieler's account, written over six years after the event, however, has not been verified. In any case, the incarceration was real, which led the four to appeal in July

---

13. Dorodnitsyn, *Materialy*, doc. 34. Klimenko 13–14.
14. Dorodnitsyn, *Materialy*, doc. 34. Rozhdestvenskiï, 59. Klimenko, 14–15.
15. Rozhdestvenskiï, 61. Klimenko, 17.
16. Dorodnitsyn, *Materialy*, doc. 66. Klimenko, 21, 34–35.

1868 to Kotzebu, the governor-general of New Russia, for protection from affliction by church and state officials.[17]

In March 1868 Archbishop Dimitrii reported to Kotzebu that the priest in Osnova stated the stundists attend church and fulfill their ecclesiastical obligations. Meetings, however, continued in the home of Ratushnyï with German colonists in attendance. Dmitrii appealed to Kotzebu to forbid German colonists from assembling with the stundists and to exile Ratushnyï from the village. In October the *ispravnik* from Odessa reported that in their meetings Ratushnyï, Balaban, and Kapustyan imitate the German colonists in word and gestures and also in their style of shirts and boots. Ratushnyï admitted to the *ispravnik* that he did not observe a number of the fasts, including fasts on Wednesdays and Fridays, generally not observed in any case by the peasant population. Some months before Ratushnyï also did not observe Lent. He excused himself by stating that persecution disrupted care for his family and work and the reproaches of the villagers, who called him stundist, heretic, and Anti-Christ, deflected him from his first duties as a Christian.[18]

The stundists were moving toward a break with the church, which finally occurred in 1870. In May 1870 the *ispravnik* reported that although some stundists from Osnova might attend the church at times they will leave as soon as the priest began to preach. The priest no longer visited the homes of the stundists where he was met with disrespect or the inhabitants would leave if the priest came to visit. In May the stundists delivered their ikons to the church. They claimed that they did this to counter the charge that they were guilty of disrespect for them.[19]

Karlovka and Lyubomirka

A second important center of Ukrainian stundism developed about ninety miles from Osnova east of the Bug River in the north of Kherson *guberniya* in the district of Elizavetgrad. As already noted, J. Kowalsky in 1864 immersed in the German colony of Alt-Danzig a group of believers. In not finding a suitable relationship with Mennonite Brethren, they looked for support from German Baptists. The two major leaders were Ephraim Pritzkau and his son, Johann, who went to Hamburg for training. As early as 1862 the Pritzkau home was a center of a mixed gathering of Germans and Russians that participated in the reading and explaining of Scripture and song. Johann, if asked, would read the Scripture in Russian and then explain it. Ephraim claimed that those who attended came on their own and were not invited. Johann said he never asked anyone to leave the Orthodox Church.[20]

17. Dorodnitsyn, *Materialy*, doc. 52. Klimenko, 29–31. For Wieler's account see, QR, 1874, Jan., 2; Apr., 6.

18. Dorodnitsyn, *Materialy*, docs. 50, 54. Rozhdestvenskii, 65–66. Klimenko, 28–29, 31–32.

19. Dorodnitsyn, *Materialy*, doc. 80. Rozhdestvenskii, 68. Klimenko, 35–36.

20. Dorodnitsyn, doc. 64, and Dorodnitsyn (Episkop Aleksii), *Religiozno- ratsionalistichesko dvizhenie na yuge Rossii*, 237–43. Klimenko, 41–42.

PART THREE—Prospects: Ukrainian and Russian Beginnings, 1860–1884

In 1868 Demidenkov, the rural dean, reported that because of the Pritzkau meetings ten Ukrainian peasants from the village of Karlovka had been seduced from Orthodoxy. One of the leaders was Efim (or Yukhym) Tsimbal (c. 1833–1880), about thirty-five years of age. He claimed he kept Lent but in the previous year in his study of the Bible had rejected ikons as idols. Stundism also spread to the neighboring village of Lyubomirka. Here Ivan Ryaboshapka (c. 1831–1900) and Maxim Kravchenko were leading meetings in 1866. The two of were influenced by stundism while serving in the German colonies.

Ryaboshapka will become the foremost Ukrainian stundist leader. The *ispravnik* of Elizavetgrad *uyezd* in 1886 reported that Ryaboshapka occupied the preeminent position among the stundists, considered a "protopresbyter," who was tireless in placing his stamp on the development of the movement. Ryaboshapka traveled outside his own environs to adjoining provinces. In an 1873 report, he is described as above average in height with brown hair, a round face, and a beard. Rozhdestvenskiĭ described him, when fifty-seven, as plain in appearance, stooped, middle height, with a pleasing voice with a drawl, and noted for "great ability." As an adult he learned to read and write.[21]

In 1857 Ryaboshapka settled in Lyubomirka near Karlovka and the German colony of Alt-Danzig. At first he was a sheepherder but became a blacksmith and locksmith. In 1859 he became a miller, managing a mill owned by a German, Martin Huebner of Alt-Danzig. Here he learned to read and write and evidently came in contact with German stundism. In 1862 he became a farmer, acquiring his own cottage and married a woman from a neighboring village. He and his wife had three children, but all died at a young age. With three other comrades, he worked in 1864 for Germans in building a water mill in Bessarabia but after more than a year returned to Lyubomirka. Although he will engage in a very active pastoral ministry, he continued to maintain his own farm. On his own allotment and around eight additional acres, which he leased, he had in 1886 a cottage, two sheds, two forges, a horse-driven threshing machine, as well as horses and cattle.[22]

In his testimony in 1868 to Governor-General Kotzebu, Ryaboshapka stated he had purchased two New Testaments, which he read in his spare time and shared with his comrades. In his account of stundism, Johann Wieler recorded Ryaboshapka purchasing a Testament in 1866. Ryaboshapka said he was spiritually transformed from a life of hard drinking and debauchery. With Bible in hand and going from house

---

21. For accounts of Ryaboshapka's life in *BV*, see 1947/5, 34–36, and the article by Koval'kov and Sokolov, 1981/6, 57–58. For contemporary accounts from Orthodox sources, see Dorodnitsyn, *Materialy*, docs. 180, 236, and Rozhdestvenskiĭ, 72–75, including footnotes. Various reports give different ages for Ryaboshapka, but Rozhdestvenskiĭ's statement (p. 72, ft. 5) that he was fifty-seven at the time of writing gives a date of c. 1831. Koval'kov and Sokolov accept 1831, based on those who state Ryaboshapka was one year younger than Ratushnyĭ.

22. Dorodnitsyn, *Materialy*, doc. 236. Rozhdestvenskiĭ, 72, ft. 5.

to house, Ryaboshapka began preaching to fellow villagers that they were lost and needed repentance. He attracted up to twenty individuals of both sexes.[23]

In 1867 the authorities arrested Ryaboshapka and his co-laborer, Maksim Kravchenko, and ten others. All were held a week with little food. Ten were released but Ryaboshapka and Kravchenko were held for ten more weeks. In the following year, the two were again arrested and sent to work in other colonies. Ryaboshapka was held this time for seven weeks under hard labor.[24]

Ryaboshapka and Kravchenko sent a petition to the governor-general of Kherson *guberniya* with complaint against the village priest and authorities. The Provincial Office on Peasant Affairs found that the justice of the peace had unlawfully exceeded his authority. But in his report to the Governing Senate, the governor believed that the offending officer had not acted from any improper motive but simply from religious zeal and a judicial review of the prosecution might give the wrong impression to the stundists that the highest authority provided them protection. He nevertheless admitted that administrative measures against the stundists might force them only to lie low and not disappear.[25]

The arrests, however, did not stop the movement. A report in March 1871 from the *ispravnik* of Elizavetgrad *uyezd* recorded a total of 224 stundists, 108 men and 116 women. Lyubomirka had 131 and Karlovka 58 with the remaining in four other localities.[26] In the previous year the same *ispravnik* had reported the deepening division between the Orthodox Church and the stundists with the latter placing their ikons in storerooms. One of them even cut up an ikon, and another covered a window with his ikons in place of a shudder. The break had come.[27]

Kiev Province

As early as 1868 authorities discovered that stundism had also entered into Kiev *guberniya*, north of Kherson, in Tarashchanskiï *uyezd* from contact with stundists in Kherson. Pavel Tsybul'skiï, often visiting in Kherson *guberniya*, held meetings in his home for instruction in Scripture and singing. Although Tsybul'skiï and his colleague, Yosif Tyshkevich, kept ikons in their homes, they nevertheless considered ikons and relics idolatry. In January 1870 the authorities imprisoned them and admonished them for heresy. Tsybul'skiï and Tyshkevich were received back into the church.[28] According to Rozhdestvenskiï, the arrival of Gerasim A. Balaban (Vitenko) in Tarashchanskiï

---

23. Rozhdestvenskiï, 72, ft. 6, and 73–74. Johann Wieler, "Erweckungen und Verfolgungen in Süd-Russland," *Der Sendbote*, Apr. 8, 1874, 55.
24. Rozhdestvenskiï, 72, ft. 6, 74. *Razsvet'*, 1904, no. 1, 14.
25. Dorodnitsyn, *Materialy*, doc. 93. Klimenko. 46.
26. Dorodnitsyn, *Materialy*, doc. 108. Rozhdestvenskiï, 75.
27. Dorodnitsyn, *Materialy*, doc. 87.
28. Rozhdestvenskiï, 75–79. Dorodnitsyn, *Materialy*, doc. 74. Klimenko, 48–49.

uyezd in 1870 ignited a flame that spread stundism far and wide. Balaban was about the same age as Ratushnyï, born in Chaplinka in Tarashchanskiï *uyezd*. He moved probably in 1865 to Ignatovka, four to five miles from Osnova in Kherson *guberniya*, as a worker on a widow's farm. He married the widow, who had children, and became a proprietor. He and his wife apparently had a daughter. By the 1880s he had become a prosperous farmer with ninety acres, but mortgaged, a stone house, two adobe cottages, ninety-seven head of cattle, and a number of horses. At this time Rozhdestvenskiï described him as tall, fat, with a fleshy face, and appeared clumsy but nevertheless possessed native intelligence, a gift of speech, and knowledge of Scripture.[29]

Upon his acceptance of stundism, Balaban became a co-worker with Ratushnyï and Kapustyan. Because of his zeal, the police chief was determined to deport him from Ignatovka. Before the formal order was issued, Balaban left his family in Osnova and went to his birthplace of Chaplinka to obtain a passport. The Kherson governor warned the church authorities to keep Balaban under surveillance. Balaban took the opportunity to preach in his home territory, speaking in a tavern with attacks on the priesthood and church practices. On the charge of breaking an ikon, the authorities imprisoned him in May 1871. He claimed he was a true Orthodox believer and was released in August.[30] Balaban resumed his preaching, attracting youth, villagers, and soldiers up to sixty in attendance. Stundism also spread elsewhere in the *guberniya*. In January 1872 authorities imprisoned Balaban for a second time, not releasing him until May 1873. In the meantime other leaders arose to continue the work. While still in prison, the stundists in Chaplinka audaciously took their ikons to the church and cast them in the church tower as unnecessary. The break with the Orthodox Church had now occurred here as already in Osnova and Lyubomirka.[31]

---

29. Rozhdestvenskiï, 54, ft. 1, and 79. Dorodnitsyn, *Materialy*, docs. 80 (pp. 95–96), 235. Klimenko, 38.

30. Rozhdestvenskiï, 79–81. Dorodnitsyn, *Materialy*, doc. 80 (pp. 95–96). Klimenko, 49–50.

31. Rozhdestvenskiï, 66.

11

Stundo-Baptism, Mladostundism, and State Relations

THE INTRODUCTION OF BELIEVER'S baptism by immersion in Ukraine among Mennonite Brethren, German stundists, and Ukrainian stundists came not through Baptist missionaries from Germany. The initial baptism among Mennonite Brethren in the Molochna was among Mennonite Brethren themselves who were influenced by a Baptist tract from St. Petersburg and who knew little or nothing about Baptists. Mennonite Brethren performed the first baptisms among German stundists in Neu-Danzig and Alt-Danzig who knew nothing of Baptists. In its beginning the Ukrainian stundist movement knew nothing of Baptists and only began to accept believer's baptism through Mennonite Brethren or German Baptists in Ukraine or fellow Ukrainians. Mennonite Brethren and German stundists reached out first to Baptists in Germany rather than Baptists from abroad reaching out to them.

N. I. Petrov is an example, however, of charging German Baptist missionaries from Germany subverting Ukrainian workers, whom he claims were already alienated from society and the church. Such writers fail to note sufficiently the numerous indigenous factors that gave rise to Ukrainian stundism. They also fail to recognize that German stundism in Ukraine, which initially influenced Ukrainian stundism, did not practice believer's baptism by immersion. In fact, numbers of Ukrainian stundists resisted German Baptist polity and practice. German Baptist influence on Ukrainian stundism will not have an appreciable effect until almost a decade after Ukrainian stundism began. In addition, German Baptist missionaries, by and large, could not

PART THREE—Prospects: Ukrainian and Russian Beginnings, 1860–1884

stay for any length of time in Russia, and as Rozhdestvenskiĭ pointed out such missionaries if found were shown the door, expelled without ceremony.[1]

When believer's baptism by immersion first appeared in the Russian Empire, it was strongly resisted. The Lutheran and Reformed Churches fought against it, and only a comparatively small minority of the stundists in these churches ever accepted it. The Orthodox Church regarded the rite as schismatic and imposed penalties on any Orthodox who adopted it, which made its adoption by the Orthodox particularly difficult.

Even among Ukrainian stundists it was no foregone conclusion that as a movement they would accept believer's baptism by immersion. In rejecting the rites of the Orthodox Church, some of them were not interested in rites from any other body. Baptists also had to contend against Molokans and some Ukrainian stundists who spiritualized baptism. Also for some Ukrainian stundists, the tradition of infant baptism was still valid. It was only after some years that evangelical Ukrainians, by and large, accepted believer's baptism by immersion as the biblical norm.

The adoption in the Russian Empire of believer's baptism by immersion was a gradual process—step by step from one national group to another and in different parts of the country. The first such baptisms on Russian soil occurred first among Swedes in the Åland Islands (1856), Germans in Poland (1858), Mennonite Brethren in Ukraine (1860), Latvians in Courland (1861), German stundists in Ukraine (1864), Russian Baptists in Caucasus (1867), and finally Ukrainian stundists in Ukraine (1869–1871). A few other baptisms were interspersed, such as that of a few Ukrainians by Mennonite Brethren in the early 1860s and a few German Baptists in St. Petersburg in 1864, but were comparatively insignificant in their impact.

THE 1869 BAPTISM

Even though Ukrainian stundists were moving increasingly to an evangelical sectarian position in faith and practice with their rejection of the sacraments and rites of the Orthodox Church, before 1869 they had not taken the decisive step of becoming Stundo-Baptists by observing believer's baptism by immersion. In the eyes of the Orthodox, it was a flagrant act of rebellion against church and state. For the baptizer it could result in a long prison sentence or deportation to Siberia or exile from the country. For the one baptized it could result in ostracism, if not imprisonment.

The opportunity for the baptism of an Orthodox believer occurred at Alt-Danzig on the second day of Pentecost, June 11 (o.s.) 1869. Here Ephraim Pritzkau and his son Johann held meetings that included both Germans and Ukrainians. In March a correspondent from Alt-Danzig reported that a great revival movement was in

---

1. For Russian writers who considered Ukrainian stundism primarily a product of German propaganda, see Wardin, *Evangelical Sectarianism in the Russian Empire and the USSR*, 81. For N. I. Petrov's article, see "Novyya svedeniya o shtundisme," *TrKDA*, 1887, no. 3, 383. Rozhdestvenskiĭ, 101.

progress that included both Germans and Ukrainians. Johann Pritzkau, who had been in Hamburg for fourteen months and ordained in April by Oncken for mission service, arrived a few days before Pentecost and became immediately engaged in the revival.[2]

Although Pritzkau, who had been ordained and could have performed the baptism, Abraham Unger, the Mennonite Brethren pastor from Chortitza and closely aligned with Baptists, was invited to baptize. It took some days, including Pritzkau's participation, for the careful examination of the candidates. At the baptism both Germans and Ukrainians gathered to observe the event. Unger read from the gospel, joined in song with the assembled group, prayed, and then brought separately into the water each candidate, clothed in white linen. After prayer, he immersed each one. All the candidates were German except one Ukrainian man, Efim Tsimbal, and a Ukrainian girl, reared in a German home and the daughter of Postaushchin, a discharged soldier.[3]

In his first account immediately after the baptism, Pritzkau reported on the "glorious baptism" of eighty-nine candidates conducted by Unger but no mention of Tsimbal or the girl. Some months later in the following year, Pritzkau reported that upon the baptism of fifty Germans, a Russian brother, although previously unexamined, no longer resisting the urging of his heart, entered into the water where he was baptized by Unger. Many years later in his history of German Baptists in Russia, Pritzkau pointed out that Mennonite Brethren, with whom they were at the time closely aligned, were invited to the baptism, including Unger, their elder. He also stated that the national Russian, no longer resisting his desire for baptism, intermixed himself among the baptismal candidates and was baptized without Unger knowing his identity.

In 1873, Karl Ondra, a leading German pastor from Volhynia but not present at the baptism, wrote that the national Russian, without anyone saying anything to him, quickly undressed, entered the water without Unger realizing who he was. Five years later, Ondra will add that Unger, soon realizing what had happened, became alarmed, did not remain for the Lord's Supper that followed, and immediately left for home.[4]

Was Tsimbal's baptism so inadvertent as German Baptists claimed? Michael Klimenko raised the question many years ago in his dissertation on Ukrainian stundism. According to his report, the police chief noted that only thirty had been baptized and that the village magistrate was under suspicion and found himself in trouble for failing to stop Tsimbal. Why did Unger baptize instead of Pritzkau, who, by the way, was baptizing a short time later? Was Pritzkau protecting himself from engaging in an

---

2. QR, Sep. 1869, 359–60. Pritzkau, *Geschichte*, 34–35.

3. For the report of the chief of police, see Dorodnitsyn, doc. 58. For Pritzkau's reports, see *Missionsblatt*, Sep. 1869, 143–44, and Apr. 1870, 66–68; QR, Oct. 1869, 394–95, and July 1870, 836–38; and Pritzkau, *Geschichte*, 13–14. For information on the Ukrainian girl, see the report from *Odessa Zeitung* in *Mitteilungen und Nachrichten* 25 (Sep. 1869), 419–20, and *Direction* 20/1 (1991), 132.

4. *Der Sendbote*, Oct. 29, 1873, 171. *Missionsblatt*, May 1878, 84.

act that could mean exile or imprisonment? Was it then expedient to have an outsider, who could claim he did not know personally all the candidates? By the way, Unger himself was probably engaged in the interrogation of candidates. Did Tsimbal decide on baptism on the spur of the moment? Would he not have had to be wearing a linen garment under the outer garments he removed to be an acceptable candidate? Why did Unger leave so precipitously and not remain for the Lord's Supper?

Whatever the circumstances, Tsimbal's baptism was done. The diocesan authority ordered the local priest to exhort the sectarians in the village of Karlovka where Tsimbal resided, but this action was fruitless. An appeal was made to the Kherson governor to bring to trial Tsimbal and the one who had seduced him. The governor did not follow through, arguing that he could not prosecute without a formal request from the spiritual authority.[5]

Pritzkau reported that a few weeks later Tsimbal immersed three candidates and then later an additional twenty-one. He also went to another village, probably Lyubomirka, where he baptized three more, including Petr Griva and Yakov Taran as well as Ivan Ryaboshapka, who told Rozhdestvenskiĭ he had been baptized in 1869. The Lord's Supper was also observed. Baptist immersions were now taking root among Ukrainians in northern Kherson *guberniya* and will spread elsewhere in Ukraine.[6]

Johann Wieler and Ukrainian Stundists

Johann Wieler (1839–1889), a Mennonite Brethren, will play a very constructive and far-reaching role among Ukrainian stundists. He was the younger brother of Gerhard Wieler who had played such havoc among Mennonite Brethren and was imprisoned for baptizing stundists. Johann was born in the Mennonite colony of Chortitza and was converted in the 1850s. He attended the secondary school in Chortitza and possessed a command of both German and Russian. In 1859 the Guardians' Committee for Foreign Colonists in Odessa employed him as a secretary. In 1860, when only twenty-one, with his Bible he began to share the gospel with natives in the city with the result that six were converted and a group of about twenty emerged. This first evangelistic effort, which was discovered by the police, did not lead to any permanent work. After three years Wieler moved to Chortitza and joined the Mennonite Brethren.[7]

    5. Rozhdestvenskiĭ, 101–2.

    6. *Missionsblatt*, Apr. 1870, 66–67. QR, July 1870, 836–38. Rozhdestvenskiĭ, 102. The report in Dorodnitsyn, doc. 87, that Tsimbal baptized Ryaboshapka in April 1870 is no doubt in error; see Klimenko, 64.

    7. For a biography of Johann Wieler, see Johannes Dyck, "Moulding the Brotherhood." For an account by Wieler of his evangelistic activity, see the Eng. tr. of Wieler's manuscript, "Einige kurze Mitteilungen über die Entstehung des Stundismus und Baptismus unter der russischen Bevölkerung im Süden Russlands," in the Pashkov Papers by Klippenstein, entitled, "Johann Wieler (1839–1889) Among Russian Evangelicals," *JMS* 5 (1987), 44–60. A third biographical source is Kroeker, "Prediger Johann Wieler," *Christlicher Familienkalender*, 1908, 1–2.

From 1865 to 1868 he taught at a German school in Berdyansk and then went to Switzerland where he spent eight months at a Christian pedagogical institute. He also traveled in Germany that included meeting Oncken in Hamburg and went to St. Petersburg where he was unsuccessful in appealing for freedom for oppressed sectarians in Ukraine. Before leaving St. Petersburg, he met Jacobson, a native Estonian, and baptized him in a lake near the city. In 1869 he again met Oncken upon the latter's visit in Russia and accompanied him from Chortitza to Odessa where he decided to stay.[8]

As already noted in an earlier chapter, Wieler began a German mission in Odessa and in the spring of 1870 invited H. Maier from Alt-Danzig to assist him in the work. But unfortunately dissension erupted between those who wanted to ordain Maier as elder, charging Wieler was a Mennonite, while others supported Wieler. In spite of Pritzkau's mediation, no solution could be found and Wieler left with his own party. His congregation included relatives of Martin Kalweit's wife, individuals from Kovno *guberniya* who stayed in Odessa while Martin Kalweit and his wife continued to the Caucasus where he introduced the Baptist faith.[9]

Far more important than his work among Germans was Wieler's relationship with Ukrainian stundists who were breaking their ties with the Orthodox Church. In 1870 the stundists, who included such leaders as Ratushnyï, Kapustyan, Ryaboshapka, and Kushnerenko, appealed to Wieler for counsel. He not only told them, contrary to Karl Bonekemper's advice, to break completely from Orthodoxy and form their own congregations, but he also helped them in church organization. He drew up a confession of faith of ten articles, called *Pravila veroispovedaniya novoobrashchennago russkago bratstva* (Regulations of the Confession of the Newly Converted Russian Brotherhood). Although it was not a reproduction of the German Baptist confession, it was in accord with its principles. The confession was then circulated among the stundists for discussion with most approving a fellowship on the doctrinal statement.[10]

To obtain legal recognition, Wieler drew up a petition, attaching the confession, which was signed by 103 heads of families, to submit to Alexander II in St. Petersburg. Wieler claimed Mennonite Brethren provided the emissaries financial support, including travel costs, and requested Jacobson to help them. According to Wilhelm Schulz, the German Baptist missionary, three emissaries went to St. Petersburg, two of whom were evidently Ratushnyï and Balaban, with one of the three collecting funds for the trip. The emissaries arrived in early 1871 and, although unable to approach the

---

8. Klippenstein, "Johann Wieler," 49. Kroeker, "Prediger Johann Wieler," 1. *Missionsblatt*, Dec., 1869, 181–83.

9. Pritzkau, *Geschichte*, 55–60, 62–63. Dyck, 64. Kroeker, "Prediger Johann Wieler," 1.

10. Klippenstein, "Johann Wieler," 49–50. For copies of the "Regulations," see Dorodnitsyn, doc. 301 (pp. 477–82), and Dorodnitsyn (Episkop Aleksiï), *Religiozno-ratsionalisticheskoe dvizhenie*, 262–70, with the second reference providing a comparison with the German Baptist confession.

Tsar, were able to give the petition to a court official, who said he would acquaint the Tsar with it.[11]

The Ukrainian stundists moved ahead with a public baptism on June 8, 1871, conduced by Ryaboshapka, who had already been baptized by Tsimbal. The fifty who were baptized included Ratushnyï and Kapustyan, thus bringing believer's baptism by immersion to stundists in the Odessa region. The authorities were under the impression that the regime had granted the stundists recognition and at this point did not hinder the baptism nor formation of their congregations, although this would soon change. At least five Stundo-Baptist congregations now existed—Karlovka and Lyubomirka near Elizabetgrad and three now in the Odessa area.[12]

Wieler also assisted the stundists in other ways. He provided certificates for baptism, weddings, and burial. In 1870 he communicated with Jacob Klundt and August Liebig, then in Turkish territory, to obtain the hymnal, *Spiritual Songs*, that contained ninety hymns in Russian and was published in Constantinople. The work was compiled by Frederick W. Flocken, a Methodist missionary born in Odessa, but served in 1859–1870, 1873–1878 in Turkish territory in the Balkans, including time in Dobrudja, and by Alexandr Storozhev, a Baptist. The work included many hymns translated from the German. Wieler suggested the hymnbooks be sent by steamer to avoid the censor.[13]

Stundo-Baptists and Mladostundists

The impact of the Baptist movement on stundism was particularly strong in 1869 with the arrival of Johann Pritzkau from Hamburg, the baptism of Tsimbal, the visit of Oncken, and the settlement of Wieler in Odessa. The above mentioned four men were at a strategic time and place to establish Stundo-Baptism. Stundo-Baptism was more than introducing believer's baptism by immersion since it brought this segment of the stundist movement in line with the faith and polity of Baptists. Before 1869 Ukrainian stundism was a spiritual movement of individuals with ties, even though tenuous, to the Orthodox Church. But as Baptists elsewhere and with German Baptists setting the example, Stundo-Baptism adopted confessional standards; introduced church discipline; established congregations with officers—elders and deacons;

---

11. Klippenstein, "Johann Wieler," 50. According to Wieler's account in *Der Sendbote*, Apr. 8, 1874, 55, the petition was submitted in early 1871 not in 1870, as stated in Wieler's later manuscript. *Missionsblatt*, July 1871, 125. Dorodnitsyn, *Materialy*, doc. 106. According to the government report, two emissaries were Ratushnyï and Balaban but does not name a third. Schulz refers to three emissaries but does not name them except that one had already been immersed. Wieler names Ratushnyï, Kapustyan, and Ryaboshapka but not Balaban. See Klippenstein, "Johann Wieler," 53, on Balaban's rejection as an emissary.

12. Klippenstein, "Johann Wieler," 50. Dorodnitsyn, *Materialy*, doc. 124. Rozhdestvenskiï, 102.

13. *BMM*, Aug. 1874, 301. Stanyukovich, *Polnoe sobranie sochineniï*, 7:156. Rozhdestvenskiï, 245, ft. 3. *QR*, July, 1874, 6, 8. See Val'kevich, App. 1:2, for the spelling of Storozhen's name.

observed two ordinances—believer's baptism and the Lord's Supper; and practiced close communion.

The movement had its own succession of baptizers from Tsimbal to Ryaboshapka to Ratushnyï. The elder or presbyter or "elder brother" of the congregation, in some cases ordained with the laying on of hands, played a leading role as head of the congregation, directed its operation, and led in prayer and the interpretation of Scripture. The elder baptized and presided at the Lord's Supper and conducted the rites of marriage and burial. In time the followers of Ryaboshapka and Ratushnyï considered them protopresbyters or arch-presbyters. The elder was expected to be literate, mature, upright, and methodical and consistent in his conduct. The deacons were his assistants.[14]

The move towards a stronger organization with recognized leaders and standardization in belief and practice brought cohesion. As a movement, stundism had been beset by the threat of increasing disunity and endless debate over polity and Christian practice, some consequential but others trivial. On the other hand, however, divisions between elders and congregations at times resulted in the formation of a second congregation.[15]

In 1873 Ryaboshapka's congregation called itself "Brethren of the Evangelical Faith." With the attempt to gain the same privileges as the German Baptists in 1879, Stundo-Baptists used terminology that identified themselves as Baptists. In its petition to the government in 1881, Ryaboshapka's congregation took the name, "Society of Baptized Christians Baptists." In its petition, Ratushnyï's body called itself "The Society of Christians Baptists" or "Christian Baptists of Russian Nationality."[16] With its centralization, authoritarian leadership, church discipline, new rites, and appeal for support of missions, Stundo-Baptism produced a counter movement called Mladostundism, young or early stundism. The Mladostundists wished to preserve the original character of stundism, a movement of people meeting for prayer, study of Scripture, and song with direct access to God and led by gifted leaders. The officiating officers and rites of the Stundo-Baptists reminded them of the sacerdotalism and sacramentalism of the Orthodox Church.[17]

In one of six letters seized from him, Daniel Kondratskiï in 1870 expressed the thought that "baptism in water was not necessary and completely without use" and stressed instead the baptism of the Holy Spirit. He also claimed that elders in Stundo-Baptist congregations called for material sacrifices for support of rites and mission

---

14. Shcherbina, "Malorusskaya shtunda," *Nedelya*, 1877, no. 1, 28, and no. 2, 57. Dorodnitsyn, *Materialy*, docs. 215, 217. Rozhdestvenskiï, 177.

15. Shcherbina, "Malorusskaya shtunda," 1877, no. 2, 57. Brown, *The Stundists*, 54.

16. Dorodnitsyn, *Materialy*, doc. 171. Dorodnitsyn (1909), 261.

17. For differences between Mladostundism (or stundism) and Stundo-Baptism, see Rozhdestvenskiï, 104–7, 143, 174–78, 201, 204, 266–67; Shcherbina, 1877, no. 1, 28, and no. 2, 57; V. V., "Shtundisty na yuge Rossii," *TsV*, 1882, no. 48, 6–8; and Klippenstein, "Johann Wieler," 53.

work. A letter in 1878 from another writer bitterly attacked a certain Baptist elder for insisting that each male member pay annually two rubles and female member one ruble for his mission travels. The letter also charged him for taking money from the treasury for his own necessities and for his high style of living in horses, new clothes, watches, and use of tobacco.[18]

A historic confrontation occurred in 1872 in a prison in Kiev *guberniya* between Gerasim Balaban (Vitenko) and Ivan and Gavriil Lyasotskiĭ over baptism and the Lord's Supper. Balaban was a leader in opposing believer's baptism and the call for contributions to missions. Lyasotskiĭ was a clerk, one of Balaban's converts, and in turn had converted his brother Gavriil, a teacher. Both brothers lost their positions, moved to a farm near Odessa owned by a stundist. Here they became acquainted with the Stundo-Baptist movement and Gavriil copied out the ten regulations composed by Wieler. In the spring of 1872 the brothers returned to their native district in Kiev *guberniya* but, because of their stundist activity, they with seven others were arrested in July, moved to a civil prison, and then finally to the tower in Tarashcha. Here they met Balaban, a fellow prisoner.[19]

The Lyasotskiĭ brothers were comforted to see Balaban, but after two or three months a hot debate erupted over the ordinances. Although having early accepted the validity of baptism and the Lord's Supper, Balaban now rejected both, while the Lyasotskiĭ brothers defended both. In the conflict Balaban gained the support of eight others in the tower while the brothers, who were even subjected to ridicule, gained only one other for their side.[20] Balaban was quoted as declaring, "Rites—this is theater." For him as other Mladoststundists, baptism was only an external sign with no power. One needed to receive the living water that Christ offered the Samaritan woman at the well. In apostolic times baptism played only a secondary role. Christ sent the disciples to preach the gospel and Paul baptized very few. Christ's baptism was for himself alone. According to Scripture, believers are to be baptized by Christ in the Spirit and fire.[21]

Because of Balaban's preaching in Kiev *guberniya* after his release, Mladostundism became very strong in the area. The Lyasotskiĭ brothers, although facing criticism, finally, however, got a following of their own. In 1876 they went to Osnova where Ratushnyĭ baptized them. A Stundo-Baptist church of baptized believers now existed in Kiev *guberniya* at Kosyakovka with Ivan Lyasotskiĭ as elder.[22]

---

18. Rozhdestvenskiĭ, 105, 174–76.

19. Lehmann, "The Russian 'Stundists,'" *BMM*, Apr. 1877, 85–86. Lyasotskiĭ, "Kak ya otpal ot pravoslaviya," *Baptist*, 1908, no. 1, 20.

20. Lehmann, "Stundists," 86–87.

21. Rozdestvenskiĭ, 105, 201, ft. 2. Kutepov, *Kratkaya istoriya i verouchenie russkikh ratsionalisticheskikh i misticheskikh ereseĭ*, 59.

22. Lyasovskiĭ, 21. Lehmann, 'Stundists,' 88. Rozhdestvenskiĭ, 106, ft. 3, 177.

One of Ivan Lyasotskiï's strongest opponents was Yakov Koval, a peasant from Chaplinka, who headed his own Mladostundist body in this village. Koval, thin, of medium height, fair-haired, and expressive eyes, was an ardent propagandist, who also had been imprisoned. He attracted the attention of the Pashkovites in St. Petersburg who will send him money and assistance for the brotherhood at large. Ivan Andreev headed another Mladostundist congregation in Dymievka, a suburb of Kiev, who also received support from the Pashkovites. Upon Andreev's exile, this center, however, will lose its significance.[23]

In 1873 Balaban was sent to Osnova for trial. Here Balaban again came in contact with his old colleague Ratushnyï. Conflict erupted between the two over the ordinances with the result that the Osnova congregation divided almost in half between Ratushnyï and Balaban. Balaban lived eight and a half kilometers from Ignatovka on his farm with Anton Strigun as his assistant.[24]

Although Mladostundists resisted the institutional trends of the Stundo-Baptists, they, however, were not entirely immune from the same trends, such as accepting elders and deacons. Even with their belief in the equality of believers, it was natural for leaders to rise who were literate with gifts of speaking and leadership. Koval, the fiery preacher in Chaplinka, served from the beginning as an elder of his flock. Another leader, of course, was Balaban, who was even regarded as a protopresbyter. After his return to Osnova, women of his congregation presssured him to observe the breaking of bread as practiced among the Stundo-Baptists. Also they began to perform weddings. Some Mladostundists, although rejecting believer's baptism by immersion, however, accepted infant baptism by sprinkling while others with only a spiritual blessing.[25]

In time the division between Mladstundists and Stundo-Baptists lessened until it finally disappeared with Stundo-Baptism establishing the norm. Stundo-Baptism had the advantage of much stronger cohesion and a doctrinal standard, while Mladostundism was unsystematic in its theology, depending upon the individual views of its leaders. According to A. D. Ushinskiï, an Orthodox observer, it tended to diverge from classical Protestantism toward the spiritualist views of traditional Russian dissent.[26]

With examples in Scripture and the drama of its execution, believer's baptism by immersion increasingly took the field. Nevertheless John Brown, a Congregationalist from England, and Hermann Dalton of the German Reformed Church, both advocates of infant baptism and possibly also thinking of German stundists, wrote that infant baptism was widespread among Russian stundists. Brown in 1893 claimed two-third observed it, while the latter in 1896 stated that the "true stundists" kept the rite. But in his report in 1890–1891, Konstantin Pobedonostsev, the Ober-Procurator of

23. Rozhdestvenskiï, 16, 136–38, 144, 196, ft. 1. Kutepov, 59.
24. Rozhdestvenskiï, 105–6, 144, 176–77.
25. Ibid., 109, ft. 1, 177–78, 204, 257, 263. Shcherbina, "Malorusskaya shtunda," 1877, no. 1, 26–27.
26. Rozhdestvenskiï, 208. A. D. Ushinskiï, *Verouchenie malorusskikh shtundistov*, viii–ix.

the Holy Synod of the Orthodox Church, reported that the "overwhelming majority" of Russian stundism had shifted over to "pure Baptism," openly naming it as its creed, furthered by the possibility of gaining legal recognition by the legislation for German Baptists in 1879. In 1896 Georges Godet, a Reformed theologian of Neuchâtel, Switzerland, probably gave one of the best appraisals of Russian stundists when he wrote, "To-day almost all the Stundists hold the beliefs of the Baptists, and in the south of Russia Baptist and Stundist are practically synonymous terms."[27]

Repression in the Seventies

In the 1870s not only were Stundo-Baptists and Mladostundists contending between themselves over church polity and ordinances but also both faced increasing pressure and suppression from the authorities of church and state. The introduction of Baptist principles among the Ukrainian stundists heightened the confrontation.

Because of his close relations with Russian stundists, Johann Wieler became a marked man. He not only had counseled them in their break with Orthodoxy but also became a public advocate for their cause. In 1874 he wrote that he had frequently traveled on behalf of religious freedom and had written numerous petitions, both in Russian and German, which were sent to the Tsar and to the public. He not only had sent the 1871 petition to the Tsar but a second one in October of the same year and a third in October 1873. He sent reports to *Missionsblatt* in Germany and *Der Sendbote* in America and also to the Evangelical Alliance.[28]

On the request of Ratushnyï and Kapustyan, Wieler was asked to meet with Ukrainian believers in the house of Heinrich Stoller in Rohrbach on February 6, 1872, to speak on the gospel in Russian. Wieler not only spoke but also presided at the Lord's Supper. The authorities then arrested Wieler for subverting the Orthodox, and while his case was pending they placed him on parole, restricting his leaving his home without permission. In a search of his home, the police discovered two rough drafts of petitions for the Ministry of Interior, a copy of the "Regulations," photographs, and his diary in German that provided data on his activities and names and places of his acquaintances.[29]

During his two years of parole, he continued his small German congregation in his home. In May he attended in Andreasfeld in Chortitza the first Mennonite Brethren conference and in the same month married Helena Thielmann. She served as hostess for many visitors who came to the home, including Johann Kargel, who stayed

---

27. Brown, 56. Dalton, "Stundismus in Russland," 21. Procurator of the Holy Synod, *Report*, 1890–1891, 247 Godet, "The Russian Stundists," *MRW*, Oct. 1896, 742, 746.

28. *BMM*, Aug. 1874, 301. *Der Sendbote*, Apr. 8, 1874, 55. Klippenstein, "Johann Wieler," 51. Dyck, "Johann Wieler," 45–46.

29. Dyck, "Johann Wieler," 46. Dorodnitsyn, *Materialy*, docs. 122, 124. *QR*, Apr. 1874, 4–5. Stanyukovich, "Ratushnyï trial," in Stanyukovich, *Polnoe sobranie sochenenii*, 3:154–55.

from December 1872 to April 1873, and Peter M. Friesen, a Mennonite Brethren who spent the summer of 1872. Their first child, a daughter, was born in April 1873, which will be followed by nine more, but many will die in infancy or early childhood. He upset the authorities for illegally residing in St. Petersburg from December 1872 to January 1873 where he had gone to petition the Minister of Interior for a speedy trial. After his return, he was fined 400 rubles. In January 1874 authorities caught him and three other Germans in the colony of Alt-Helenthal and ordered him never again to return to the area. Although he faced the prospect of exile to the Transcaucasus, by his appeal to the Minister of Internal Affairs and the decision of the Odessa Court he was freed. In July 1874 he moved with his wife and daughter to Friedensfeld, the Mennonite village of his wife, where he soon opened a private school.[30]

The authorities also became very alarmed with the stundists in the Odessa area after their large baptism in June 1871. According to Wilhelm Schulz, the authorities discovered a stundist gathering in which each one present was required to pay a fine of fifteen rubles. In addition, stundists not yet immersed had already paid over one thousand rubles and one of the emissaries to St. Petersburg in 1871 suffered imprisonment for six months. In his account in 1884, Wieler claimed that Ratushnyï, Ryaboshapka, Kapustyan, and Balaban were imprisoned in Odessa, although later released, while others were heavily fined and suffered physical abuse.[31]

A year later in 1872 Schulz wrote that in many places stundists in the Odessa region were no longer subject to persecution but others had suffered severely. He reported that one baptized believer had received over 150 lashes, lacerating his body, but the government removed the *starosta* for this brutality. In Ignatovka the *ispravnik* forbade the congregation headed by Kapustyan to continue unlawful assemblies. The congregation defiantly refused, declaring that they had already paid over 800 rubles in fines and would pay even ten times more if necessary. Ratushnyï even declared that the stundist brotherhood in the area would request permission to construct its own prayer house.[32]

In January 1873, a former police officer, assisted by an accomplice, raided Ratushnyï's home, shouting at his wife and frightening his children. They ordered the opening of a chest in which they discovered fifty rubles, which they took, and found books, documents, and photographs. The books included a Bible, Testament, and a hymnal. Documents included lists of births and deaths, certificates of birth, baptism, burial, and marriage that Wieler had composed, rough petitions, a certification of oppressed stundists in Kiev *guberniya*, evidence of a special treasury, and

30. Dorodnitsyn, *Materialy*, docs. 144, 151. *Der Sendbote*, Apr. 15, 1874, 58. QR, Apr. 1874, 4–5. Martens, "Grandmother's Letter," Eng. tr. of "Grossmutters Brief," typed mns., Mennonite Heritage Centre of Winnipeg, 3–4. Friesen, 475. Klippenstein, "Johann Wieler," 52. Dyck, 46–47, 71–72. Johannes Wieler, Family Group Sheet, California Mennonite Historical Society.

31. *Missionsblatt*, July 1871, 25. Klippenstein, "Johann Wieler," 50.

32. *Missionsblatt*, Nov. 1872, 180. BMM, Feb. 1873, 57. Dorodnitsyn, *Materialy*, doc. 156. Dorodnitsyn, "Nemetskie missionery neobaptizma," ChOLDP, 1893, no. 6, 737–38.

PART THREE—Prospects: Ukrainian and Russian Beginnings, 1860–1884

correspondence. Correspondence was conducted through Heinrich Klundt, a German stundist in Rohrbach. Photographs were of Ratushnyï, Ryaboshapka, and Wieler taken in St. Petersburg.[33]

On February 22 Ratushnyï and Kapustyan sent to the Kherson governor a petition of eighteen points, recounting grievances beginning in 1867, and on March 18 a second petition of ten points. They complained of the hostile conduct of priests and oppression from the police. They reported attempts to forbid their meetings, bringing them to court, and fines. They complained of officials stopping them from burying their own children in the cemetery, failure to receive passports, and prohibiting them from acquiring land. Repression nevertheless continued. Wieler reported in letters in December 1873 and February 1874 that Ratushnyï, Kapustyan, Radion Arichipov and his wife were imprisoned on September 23 where they will also find Ryboshapka who had already been imprisoned in July. They will be released on bail on November 22.[34]

The German Baptist paper, *Missionsblatt*, printed a letter from Odessa, written in April 1872, which claimed that Russian Baptists now had full liberty and were beginning under the leadership of Ryaboshapka at Lyubomirka in building a house of worship, the first Russian Baptist chapel in the empire. Ryaboshapka appealed to fellow German Baptists for financial assistance. The structure, however, was not all that it appeared to be. On June 10, 1873, the police chief (*ispravnik*) of the district with other officials and villagers inspected the building. The structure included two rooms, separated by vestibules. On the left lived Alekseï Soloveï and on the right was a room with wooden benches for worshipers. Fellow brethren had assisted Soloveï with their work and money in the building's construction. The services of the group included the exposition of Scripture and also the Lord's Supper with the breaking of bread and drinking of red wine from a white metallic cup. On the following day, the authorities removed books and letters, gave the communion cup into the custody of the village headman (*starosta*), locked the building, and affixed with sealing wax a formal seal. If the group attempted to meet again, the authorities threatened to send Ryaboshapka to Siberia and fine every participant fifteen rubles.[35]

Authorities will not send Ryaboshapka to Siberia but will send him to the regional court in Odessa. Wieler reported in February 1874 that Ryaboshapka was imprisoned from July 9 to November 22 and then released. August Rauschenbusch reported that Ryaboshapka and four others were imprisoned with common criminals and at the beginning of the imprisonment deprived of food. In the meantime thirty members

---

33. Dorodnitsyn, *Materialy*, docs., 149, 155. Stanyukovich, "Ratushnyï trial," 155, 156, 158. QR, Apr. 1874, 6. Klimenko, 70.

34. QR, Jan. 1874, 3–4; Apr. 1874, 6.

35. *Missionsblatt*, July 1872, 113–14. BMM, Oct. 1872, 427; July 1873, 285. Dorodnitsyn, *Materialy*, doc. 171. ABMU, "Persecution of the Baptists in Southern Russia," mns.

of the Lyobomirka congregation were required to pay 450 rubles and later sixty-three members were forced to pay 2,395 rubles.[36]

Another area in Kherson *guberniya* where revival had produced a stundist movement was east of Odessa in the vicinity of Nikolaev. Upon their failure to attend the Orthodox Church and refusal to reverence ikons, stundists here suffered a backlash. In his letters, Wieler brought the unfolding incidents to the Christian public outside Russia. In the village of Konstantinovka, a mob attacked a stundist prayer meeting on January 1, 1872, with worshipers dragged to prison. Five men and a woman were severely beaten with rods. The justice of the peace of the village also placed heavy fines on the believers. In the village of Bashtanka some stundists suffered as much as 150 blows with rods. In the village of Peski, seven stundists, including the wife of one of them, were flogged. In this case, the village elder who had ordered the flogging was removed from office and sent for judicial prosecution for exceeding his authority and inflicting the punishment.[37]

As difficult as it was for the stundists in Kherson *guberniya* in the first half of the 1870s, the confrontation between stundists and the authorities in Kiev *guberniya* was worse. As noted earlier, in January 1872 authorities imprisoned Balaban, the leading apostle of stundism in the province, holding him almost a year and a half. The regime with threat of fines forbade house gatherings, and stundists were under strict surveillance. The spiritual authorities attempted to win back stundists through exhortations, which resulted in some success, but also requested the governor for a police official to carry out the law. Popov, described as coarse, a petty tyrant, intellectually backward, and a drunkard, with his assistants struck fear by breaking into homes and whippings. Nevertheless night meetings continued, new leaders arose, such as Yakov Koval and Kliment Tereshchuk, and Balaban wrote letters of encouragement from prison. As noted earlier, in July the two Lyasotskiĭ brothers with seven others, including Koval and Tereshchuk, were taken to the prison in Tarashcha where they met Balaban.[38] With the coming in late 1872 of a new priest, D'yakovskiĭ, into the Chaplinka parish and the order banning stundist gatherings with the threat of arrest for non-compliance, the stundists, according to an official report, revolted on November 17, 1872, and continued to meet. On the following day the authorities arrested stundists for allegedly abusing ikons in one of the homes. On the nineteenth, stundists created a new scuffle in which they cast their ikons from their homes, shouted that they no longer revered them, brought them to the church, and threw them into the bell tower. The

---

36. "Persecution of the Baptists in Southern Russia." QR, Apr. 1874, 7. *Der Sendbote*, Oct. 29, 1873, 171.

37. QR, Jan. 1874, 3; Apr. 1874, 6–7. *Der Sendbote*, April 8, 1874, 55. Dorodnitsyn, *Materialy*, docs. 113, 116, 118. Klimenko, 89–91.

38. Rozhdestvenskiĭ, 83–85, 87, 94, 97, ft. 2. Klimenko, 50–52. EC, Apr. 1, 1874, 118.

PART THREE—Prospects: Ukrainian and Russian Beginnings, 1860–1884

authorities arrested the ringleaders but at the time of sentencing stundists attacked the regional authorities, threatened their lives, and freed their co-religionists.[39]

In December after an almost full day of admonition from the priesthood, only two stundists signed a statement returning to the Orthodox Church, while the rest remained steadfast. Rozhdestvenskiĭ recorded that at the end of December, Balaban, Koval, and Ivan Lyasotskiĭ were on trial along with nine others. Balaban was sentenced for a year, a minor of nineteen was given two months, and a third was on bail, while the rest were freed.[40] It appears, however, that Koval and Lyasotskiĭ were not freed at this time. In a report in the April 1873 issue of *Missionsblatt*, Wieler listed thirteen names, including both Lyasotskiĭ brothers, also noting that nineteen others had been imprisoned whose names he did not know. In the middle of 1873 an unsigned document in English, "Persecution of the Baptists in Southern Russia," sent to the American Baptist Missionary Union in America, listed the same thirteen names. Except for Balaban and Agafia Musokovia, a woman, both imprisoned at the beginning of 1872, at least nine of the remaining eleven were individuals incarcerated in July 1872. In April 1873, the governor general of Kiev wrote that the Kiev courts had acquitted twelve of the Kiev prisoners, removing, however, Balaban to Kherson for his spread of heresy. Another source about the same time, however, recorded that eight or nine were still in prison but their release had been ordered. From other sources it appears that all the Kiev prisoners, even including Balaban, were released in May 1873. Balaban became active again in his ministry but was soon again imprisoned and was returned in October of the same year to Osnova for a judicial investigation for spreading stundism.[41]

Although Koval was free, he did not remain out of the sight of the authorities. In 1876 authorities sent him to Mikailovskiĭ, a monastery in Kiev, where it was reported he was "intractable" and "troublesome" and stoical under the exhortation of the monks. In fact, he proved to be a threat to newly admitted monks who were influenced by his views.[42]

In addition to the above confrontations in Kiev *guberniya*, Wieler in his missives to the West and August Rauschenbusch in a letter in 1874, filled with information from three correspondents in Russia, described additional incidents of oppression in this area. Wieler wrote in a letter in December 1873, information described also in the document sent to the ABMU, that eleven men and three women, after their Bibles had been taken from them and upon their refusing to accept crucifixes and saints' pictures, were flogged and imprisoned. In February 1874 he stated that four men and four women were flogged with twenty-five blows each and robbed of their clothes and household goods. On his part, Rauschenbusch described a group of stundists

39. Rozhdestvenskiĭ, 88–89.

40. Ibid., 89–92.

41. *Missionsblatt*, Apr. 1873, 67–68. QR, Apr., 1874, 7, and July 1874, 3–4. BMM, Apr. 1877, 86–87. Rozhdestvenskiĭ, 96.

42. Rozhdestvenskiĭ, 121–22.

gathering in the forest, which included wives whose husbands were imprisoned with one husband having recently died. He also reported the flogging in a village of six men and six women, forty-eight to fifty blows for the men and twenty-five to thirty for the women, as well as the suffering Balaban had endured in his imprisonments.[43]

Counterpoint—Home and Abroad

The repression of stundism or Stundo-Baptism during the reign of Alexander II did not follow a simple trajectory. Although the cases of repression may give such an impression, a number of currents were at play for both oppressor and oppressed. The regime wanted to stop the spread of stundism, but at the same time it tried to project to the world that it tolerated, much more than other nations, a diversity of religions among its various ethnic groups. In addition, it liberated its serfs, established an independent judiciary, and introduced other reforms. In an editorial of the *Quarterly Reporter of the German Baptist Mission* in April 1881, Martin H. Wilkin admitted, in spite of the limitations of the autocracy, Alexander II "must be associated with great strides in liberty and general progress."

What was the relation of stundism to the larger society? In an autocratic regime with a state church with each supporting the other, any threat to either or both was a threat to the social fabric. The regime feared a coalition within the nation of evangelical forces. With its aggressive proselytism and its frontal attack on the faith and practice of the Orthodox Church, was stundism unnecessarily provocative, inviting retaliation? Or were the stundists simply a self-effacing movement of lambs to be devoured by ravaging wolves?

In his defense in his trial in 1878, Balaban asked: Was his crime simply for reading the gospel? He declared he believed in Christ and one God as others, did not drink, nor engage in anything that was impious. He claimed his gospel was that all might find salvation for their souls.[44] But were stundists simply Bible readers who wished to share their biblical insights with others? It was true as far as it went, but as Stundo-Baptists and Mladostundists, unlike German stundists, they rejected the sacraments and rites of their traditional faith, which included repudiating ikons that venerated the saints and attacking the priesthood. The epithets they cast on their opponents and separation from the normal social life of the community helped to produce resentment if not enmity. Although they subscribed loyalty to the government, their insistence that they were not bound to obey directives contrary to Scripture, which they themselves interpreted, also placed them under suspicion. The stundist movement included indigenous elements, but it also carried the charge it was a foreign import, alien to the life and culture of the nation. To what degree did stundism adopt western influences and was shaped by it? Did it go too far in aping western worship and western lifestyles?

43. *QR*, Jan. 1874, 4, and Apr. 1874, 7. *EC* Apr. 1, 1874, 113–14. *BMM*, Feb. 1875, 47–49.
44. Stanyukovich, "Ratushnyï trial," 159–60.

PART THREE—Prospects: Ukrainian and Russian Beginnings, 1860–1884

What were the effects on it from its associations with the western evangelical world? Were reports of oppression to the evangelical press over stated to gain support? Orthodox critics, such as Vasiliĭ Skvortsov, believed so. What effect did the petitions from the stundists themselves and from the West have on the Russian government? In comparison to other periods of Russian history, the oppression was somewhat limited and even somewhat muddled because of ineptness of the regime and conflicting views over measures. As noted, a number of cases of suppression if also not brutality were perpetrated by over zealous officials, or by the instigation of a priest, or the passions of a mob. Officials prohibited gatherings, arrested and imprisoned worshipers, engaged in beatings, exacted excessive fines, and threatened exile. The appearance of the Baptist movement among the stundists also intensified measures against them. But such efforts had their limitations. An over zealous official might be removed for going beyond regulations. In 1876 the governor of Kherson *guberniya* complained of priests, including Mikhael Kozakevich, the priest in Lyubomirka, who were incapable of conciliating the stundists and unnecessarily arousing the populace against them. Some felt, as this same governor, that oppression may prove more harmful than helpful. In his trial in 1878, Ratushnyĭ argued that his imprisonment even helped to spread the gospel as it directed people's attention to it.[45]

Although exile was recommended or threatened in this period, it was never put into effect. In 1870 the Kherson governor refused to confirm the decision of an administrative assembly to remove certain stundist leaders from their homes in Osnova and Ignatovka. Upon the recommendation in 1873 of Vladimir Terletskiĭ, a missionary priest, for the exile of heretical "ring-leaders," the Minister of the Interior responded that such a measure would only produce harm. He argued that exile would bring such leaders greater prominence in the eyes of their followers, the leaders would find new followers in their place of exile, and new leaders at home would arise. In the 1860s the chief administrative deputy of the Trans-Caucasus, which in the past had been a dumping ground for dissidents, forbade resettlement of sectarian leaders into his region.[46]

Ecclesiastical authorities began to realize that spiritual means were necessary to meet the stundist challenge. Some effort was made to raise the level of the clergy, providing copies of the gospels, opening Sunday schools, printing Orthodox materials, sending missionaries, and engaging in discussions with their opponents. As additional assistance, the Orthodox formed church brotherhoods to work among the people. Around 1879 they established the Kiev Holy-Vladimir Brotherhood that provided relief and fostered schools. In 1880 in Kherson *guberniya*, the Orthodox formed the

---

45. Rozhdestvenskiĭ, 100, 110, 126–27. Dorodnitsyn, *Materialy*, docs. 76, 198. Klimenko, 97. Stanyukovich, "Ratushnyĭ trial," 159.

46. Dorodnitsyn, *Materialy*, docs. 72, 77. Klimenko, 33, 54. Rozhdestvenskiĭ, 94–96, 112, 116.

Brotherhood of the Holy Apostle Andrew the Great, subsidized by the Holy Synod, a society to spread Orthodox teaching and fight moral vices.[47]

Although the Orthodox Church tried to take some positive steps in meeting the stundist challenge, it was unable to stop its spread. It was difficult to find properly trained priests. In his study, Pavel Kozitskiĭ noted a decline in the authority of the priests since they had become more aloof from the people, losing their religious goals for more material concerns. Priests were engaged in the ritual of the divine office conducted in Church Slavonic and notably lacked preaching skills. They were often ill equipped to meet the biblical arguments of their opponents and many of them didn't even have Scripture in their homes. Instead of speaking the language of the people, priests would use technical language that was not always understood and failed to preach in Ukrainian. Priests were also handicapped in ministering to scattered parishioners who lived at great distances. In addition, the church was slow in developing materials on the stundists that priests could utilize. Admonitions generally produced few results, and the sending of stundists to monasteries for reformation failed.[48]

In its confrontation with the stundists, the Orthodox Church met a stubborn foe. Its members were willing to suffer for their beliefs, even to the extent of developing a cult of suffering that authenticated the truth of their message. They were also intrepid missionaries. They were always ready to discuss and dispute their faith. In a letter in 1883 sent to the governor of Kherson, the stundists were described as openly and fearlessly conducting their propaganda in contrast to the Orthodox who were so wavering and irresolute. The letter went on to say that when opportunity arose "they not only try to subvert the Orthodox in meeting them on the streets, at the markets and at work but even digging themselves into their homes, reviling the Orthodox with their own startling expressions."[49]

Stundist services attracted numbers of ordinary Ukrainians in contrast to the liturgy in the Orthodox Church in Church Slavonic that few could understand. In 1889 Pavel Kozitskiĭ wrote that stundism attracted people by the simplicity of its preaching as well as its harmonious singing of the Psalms and songs of praise and thanksgiving. In addition, their interpretation of Scripture was natural, not artificial. By prayer and faith one came to Christ, whose sacrifice cleansed from all sin.[50]

On the legal front, the stundists were at a disadvantage as an illegal sect. But on the other hand, the legal means that church and state used against them were limited. For one thing, as Rozhdestvenskiĭ noted, the state had no special law dealing

47. Rozhdestvenskiĭ, 112, 117, 140–63. Petrov, "Svedeniya o dvizhenii yuzhno- russkago sektantstva v" poslednie gody, "*TrKDA*, 1886, no 11, 537–40.

48. Rozhdestvenskiĭ, 112, 115, 117, 121–22, 150, 283. *TsV*, 1880, no, 47, 11; 1882, no. 48, 8; 1891, no. 6, 86–87. Dorodnitsyn, *Materialy*, doc. 79. Wallace, *Russsia*, 305. Kozitskiĭ, "O prichinakh," *TsV*, 1890, no, 7, 122–23, and no. 8, 137–39.

49. Nesdoly, "Evangelical Sectarianism in Russia," 170. Stanyukovich, "Ratushnyĭ trial," 160. *TsV*, 1882, no. 48, 8. Dorodnitsyn, *Materialy*, doc. 216.

50. *TsV*, 1889, no. 50, 858.

PART THREE—Prospects: Ukrainian and Russian Beginnings, 1860–1884

with stundists. Kozitskiĭ stated that authorities lacked constancy in their prosecution, which included the carelessness if not sympathy for sectarians from judicial authorities and the inertia of lower officials. Some stundists were released on bail and some even acquitted.[51]

A most remarkable judical proceeding against the stundists in this period was the trial in 1878 of Ratushnyĭ, Kupustyan, Balaban, Archipov and his wife in the Odessa Circuit Court. As early as 1870 the ecclesiastical authorities brought up the charge of the illegal spread of stundism, but the case was not finally considered until seven years and three months later. As already noted, Balaban made the defense that he was orthodox in his views of God and Christ and that he was only trying to follow the gospel. Ratushnyĭ stressed that he did not subvert anyone from the Orthodox Church but only read and explained the gospel to those who were interested in it. Kapustyan and Balaban refused to admit any guilt of subverting Orthodox and the latter even denied ever interpreting Scripture or preaching. Ratushnyĭ artfully defended himself against spreading stundism by stating first of all that its principles spread because of knowledge generated about it because of his earlier imprisonment. He maintained he had no time to travel to the main villages where stundism had spread since he had to expend his energy on his farm, receiving no money from any other source.[52] After the testimony of numerous witnesses, the trial finally ended. The jury, after only five minutes, reached the unanimous decision of not guilty, and the defendants were released. It was a great victory for the stundists but a bitter defeat for the Orthodox party. The stundists had put up an effective defense although spinning the truth. In its comments on the trial, the Orthodox periodical, *Pravoslavnoe obozrenie*, pointed out that Ratushnyĭ as an arch presbyter observed religious statutes, performed pastoral duties, including baptism, and sent missives to others. The periodical called the defendants outright liars, notoriously discrediting their alleged high morality.[53]

As already noted, the stundists used petitions to the Tsar. But beyond this traditional approach for redress in Imperial Russia, correspondents in Russia used the press in the West to describe disabilities and repression, a means of publicity that might generate financial contributions and the gaining of international support. As information was disseminated on repression, groups in the West felt motivated to make their own appeals to bring relief.

An international assembly of thirty-seven members of the Evangelical Alliance, including Baptists and a wide range of other denominations, met in 1871 in Stuttgart, Germany, to approach the Tsar, who would be on a visit to Friedrichhafen on Lake Constance, on behalf of religious liberty. Philip Schaff, distinguished church historian from America, led the group and met with the Tsar's chancellor, Prince Alexander

---

51. Rozhdestvenskiĭ, 100, 118–20, 128–29. *TsV*, 1891, no. 5, 72–73.

52. For an account of the trial, see "sudebnaya khronika," *Golos*, 1878, no. 108, 3. For a republication of the trial, see Stanyukovich, *Polnoe sobranie sochineniĭ*, 3:153–61, in *BV*, 1947, no. 5, 51–54.

53. *Pravoslavnoe obozrenie*, 1878, II, nos. 5–6, 382–84.

Gorchakov. The delegation presented two memorials, one from the Americans and a second from the Europeans, but since Gorchakov found that the European memorial contained objectionable language he felt it would be best if both memorials be withdrawn. The attempt was apparently a failure even though Gorchakov promised to report to the Tsar the concerns of the deputation and insisted the Tsar was fully in favor of religious toleration but not "propagandism."[54]

Through the efforts of August Rauschenbusch, the Rochester branch in New York of the Evangelical Alliance presented in October 1873 three papers on religious suppression in Russia to the Evangelical Alliance at the meeting of its Sixth General Conference in New York City. The leadership of the Alliance decided it would not serve the cause of the sufferers or toleration to publicize the issue at this time but to consult with the British Alliance as to future action. In January 1874, George W. Samson, noted Baptist pastor and former president of Columbian College, wrote a learned and extremely detailed essay, "Religious Freedom in Russia, Consisting of An Argument in Behalf of Russian Baptists." He marshaled arguments from the past, even from Greek and Roman times, to justify religious liberty in Russia. In January 1874 he submitted his memorial to the Russian ambassador in the United States, Henri, Baron d'Offenberg. Although the ambassador transmitted the paper's issues to St. Petersburg, *Evangelical Christendom* reported, however, that "the memorial was politely returned."[55]

In April 1873 Dr. Edward J. Steane, London pastor, presented to the Baptist Union of Great Britain a resolution on persecution and in the summer went to Switzerland to discuss the issue with the Russian ambassador there. The interview went well, but nevertheless the ambassador made the point that in matters of religious liberty the government "liked to do it themselves, and apart from foreign interference." In April 1874 the Baptist Union sent a memorial to the Russian ambassador in Great Britain to present to Tsar Alexander II on his visit to the country. The attempts by individuals to approach the Tsar directly while on his visit apparently failed. Also in April Edward Young, chief of the Bureau of Statistics in Washington, DC and a Baptist, approached Baron de Rosen, an advisor of Alexander II, on behalf of the stundist prisoners in Kiev. Rosen took up the issue with Count Sievers and shared with Young correspondence from the governor general of Kiev that the Kiev prisoners, except for Balaban, had been released.[56]

In a lengthy recital of persecutions in Russia, the editor of the *Quarterly Reporter* in London wrote in July 1874 that if the stundists "refrain from needless attacks on the Orthodox Church, and show more zeal for the spread of the Gospel than for the propagation of their views on one of its ordinances, the authorities will put a liberal

---

54. *Report of the Alliance Deputation of the American Branch of the Evangelical Alliance*, 10–29.

55. Evangelical Alliance, *Sixth General Conference*, 1873, 729. *Missionsblatt*, Apr. 1874, 69–70. For a copy of Samson's memorial, see *Religious Freedom in Russia*. EC, Aug. 1, 1874, 236.

56. QR, July 1874, 1–4. EC, Aug. 1, 1874, 234–37.

construction on their own terms." In an article on religious persecution in Russia in the *Baptist Missionary Magazine* in 1875, Samson noted the government's agreement with the Mennonites, granting them continued exemption from military service in exchange for forestry and hospital service, and the report of the release of Baptist prisoners. For continuing cases of repression, he counseled that quiet diplomacy was the best policy in approaching such autocratic regimes as the Russian and Ottoman Empires.[57]

According to Joseph Lehmann in Berlin, the Minister of the Interior in Russia suddenly released all prisoners on December 22, 1874. He also noted that violence against stundists had ceased, even though the government made no public announcement, which, according to Lehmann, was customary. Lehmann was not sure if the attempts for redress from abroad made a difference but felt that at least prayer had been answered. He felt that the adverse publicity that the government received from abroad, possibly helped by the more discreet behavior of the stundists, had now brought a time of comparative toleration.[58]

German Baptists in both America and Germany provided funds for suffering brethren in Russia. In September 1873, August Rauschenbusch wrote that the German Baptist churches in America had up to this time sent on six different occasions a total of $1,000 for the persecuted in Russia. He also wrote to Baptist papers in Boston and New York to awaken their readers for contributions. In 1876 Rauschenbusch wrote that the gifts sent to Russia were divided in thirds—first, to the imprisoned and their families; secondly, to freed prisoners; and finally to freed preachers among the native population. The Baptist Union in Germany maintained a treasury for the persecuted, and their triennial conventions in 1873 and 1876 heard reports on the persecution. The fund in February 1873 had a balance of around 348 marks and by 1876 another 2,719 marks had been contributed. From this fund Pritzkau received a gift in 1873, Wieler in 1875, and August Liebig in 1876.[59] Stundists received moral and financial support from fellow evangelicals in Russia itself. German and Russian stundists attended each other's meetings. Ryaboshapka and other Ukrainians attended the German Baptist associational meeting at Neudorf in 1874. It was claimed that stundists in Kiev *guberniya* received money from the German colonies. It was reported in early 1873 that Ratushnyï received books from the store of the German stundist Max in Odessa. Vasiliï Pashkov in St. Petersburg cultivated ties with the stundists and provided funds for such stundist ministers as Koval and Andreev. Stundists had no better friend than Johann Wieler, the Mennonite Brethren, who counseled them, defended them, and provided bail. Wieler, however, was an exception. Culture proved to be a barrier for Mennonite Brethren and German Baptists, and the desire to protect

57. QR, July 1874, 3. BMM, June 1875, 172–73.

58. BMM, Apr. 1876, 118; Apr. 1877, 88.

59. *Der Sendbote*, Sep. 17, 1873, 146; Mar. 15, 1876, 85. German Baptist Union, *Bundeskonferenz*, 1873, 9, 62; 1876, 13, 67–68.

their status as tolerated bodies made them were very careful to avoid any charge of proselytism among the native population. The baptism in 1875 by a well-known but unnamed Mennonite Brethren pastor of the Ukrainian farm laborer, Peter I. Lysenko, along with German candidates at Friedensfeld, was most exceptional.[60]

Stundists also helped fellow stundists. After Balaban's arrest, in 1872 Ryaboshapka visited Chaplinka and distributed funds to the sufferers, inspired them, and promised to assist them in the future. In December 1874 August Rauschenbusch reported from a corespondent that a stundist undetected from another area found stundists in the Kiev area, met them in a forest, brought them funds, and told them that others were praying for them.[61]

---

60. QR, Apr. 1874, 5. BMM, Feb. 1875, 47. Dorodnitsyn, *Materialy*, docs. 79, 154. Dorodnitsyn, "Nemetskie missionery neobaptizma," ChOLDP, 1893, no. 6, 734, 738. Rozhdestvenskiĭ, 93, 106, ft. 1, 137, 143. "Persecution of the Baptists in Southern Russia," 1. For Lysenko's baptism, see BV, 1955, no. 5, 62–63.

61. Dorodnitsyn, *Materialy*, doc. 180. BMM, Feb. 1875, 48.

12

The Stundist/Stundo-Baptist Community

THE FIRST GATHERINGS OF Ukrainian stundists were like the gatherings of the German Stundists. They met for Scripture, prayer, and song. At first they were still members of the Orthodox Church without the purpose of forming a new organization. With increasing alienation from the Orthodox Church, stundism became more self-consciously a dissenting religious body but still with a simple organizational structure. Stundist groups, however, even including a number of Mladostundists, who resisted organizational trends, began to define membership and accept officers. Among Stundo-Baptists, church ordinances became an integral part of church practice.

FAITH AND ORDER

In 1875 Archbishop Leontiï of Kherson Diocese entered into a dialog with Ivan Ryaboshapka who was accompanied by Petr Griva and Maxim Kravchenko. The stundist leaders declared that the Bible led by the Holy Spirit taught everyone. They declared they did not need to go to an Orthodox church or temple where they claimed they did not understand anything. They stated the temple is in the heart and the Lord, who is everywhere and present even where two or three gather in His name. In teaching the Word of God and discussing divine things, they denied subverting anyone nor forbidding anyone from hearing them. In an article on stundism in *Trudy Kievskoï Dukhovnoï Akademii* in 1886, stundists were quoted as saying that the Word of God not tradition was the basis of their faith. They asserted that the obligations of the Orthodox Church are not only troublesome for the believer but at times almost unrealizable and may even be harmful. They said that such rites as fasts, confessions, and requiems do not compose the essence of faith and should be abandoned.[1]

Stundists therefore rejected the authority of the Orthodox Church, its priesthood, church tradition, the sacraments, and its rites and ceremonies. Some went so far as to regard the church a daughter of Babylon and called the priests abusive terms. In their belief that the Holy Spirit indwelled each believer and in the priesthood of the believer, they rejected the need for intercessors as the Virgin Mary, saints, and angels and the need for relics, reverence for the cross, and worship before ikons. They identified ikons with idols and called those who revered them idolaters. They rejected The Holy Eucharist and confession and for most infant baptism as well.[2]

In their rejection of sacerdotalism and sacramentalism, the stundists moved even beyond their German stundist mentors in their views of the church and the role of ministers. Mladostundists rejected not only the sacraments but also initially ordinances as well, and the Stundo-Baptists regarded their ordinances of baptism and Lord's Supper as memorials and not channels of grace. Mladostundists and Stundo-Baptists rejected the concept of clergy as a class, while some of the former even rejected the role of elder.

Unlike the Orthodox, Lutheran, and Reformed Churches, but like the Mennonites, Russian Baptist polity was congregational. Members of a congregation elected the officers, including elders and deacons, determined its theology, and adopted its own type of services. Each congregation was independent but followed generally a similar pattern of practice as other congregations of like origin and ideology.

The elder (or elder brother) was the presiding officer. He was expected to be literate and spiritually mature and consistent in his spiritual life. He led in the reading and interpretation of Scripture, although others in the congregation might also assume this responsibility. Some but not all were ordained. Among Stundo-Baptists he conducted the ordinances and officiated at weddings and funerals. Because of their ability in leadership and preaching, some elders, such as Ratushnyï, Ryaboshapka, and Balaban, were recognized as "protopresbyters." Deacons were the assistants of the elders and led the services in his absence. Elders were not on salary but might receive gifts of food or money. They were, by and large, self-supporting, dependent on their own farms. Fellow believers might help in their farming operation, especially if the elder was gone for any length of time in a circuit of preaching.[3]

Women outnumbered men among the stundists and were, as one observer noted, a "more suffering and ennobling" presence among them. They could engage in prayer and song but were forbidden to be elders and would not debate men in church gatherings. F. A. Shcherbina recorded, however, but probably only in some places, women

---

1. *TsV*, 1875, no. 41, 12–14. *TrKDA*, 1887, no. 2, 402.
2. Rozhdestvenskiï, 179–86.
3. Shcherbina, "Malorusskaya shtunda," *Nedelya*, 1877, no. 1, 28. Rozhdestvenskiï, 264. Dorodnitsyn, *Materialy*, docs. 172, 215, 217. Brown. 52–54.

may even preach and comment on and explain the Holy Scripture. In the absence of men, some women formed heir own stundist gatherings and thus assumed the responsibilities as men.[4]

From the start stundists established treasuries, sustained primarily by freewill offerings. Money was expended for ill members or for loss from fire or some other adversity. Treasuries also provided support for traveling brethren in their preaching or legal help for imprisoned brethren.[5]

Johann Wieler's compilation in 1870 of his "*Pravila veroispovedaniya novoobrashchennago russkago bratstva*" (Regulations of the Confession of the Newly Converted Russian Brotherhood) provided the emerging Stundo-Baptist movement with its first constitution. Although Wieler claimed he followed the Confession of Faith of the Baptists in Germany, the Rule was not a simple replication of the German document. It is shorter, ten articles over the fifteen articles of the latter. The Rule began with an article on God, followed by an article on the Word of God, while the Confession began with an article on the Word of God. Both the Rule and Confession stressed sin and confession, but the Rule had no separate articles on redemption and the means of grace. Both documents devoted considerable space to baptism and the Holy Supper. The Rule had separate articles on the church, its officers, and church discipline, while the Confession put all three topics in one article. The Rule listed presbyters (elders), teachers, and deacons, while the Confession listed presbyters, preachers, and deacons. Both had articles on marriage, civil order, the Second Coming, the Resurrection, and Final Judgment, but the Rule had no articles on sanctification and the Divine Law that called for observance of the Sabbath.[6]

Worship

As with German stundism, Ukrainian stundism and Stundo-Baptism sought a relationship with the Divine through knowledge of God's Word, fervent prayer, and hymns of praise and devotion. In contrast with Orthodox worship that was sacramental and conducted by a priest with a prescribed ritual in a language not understood, stundist worship, conducterd by lay leadership in the language of the common people, sought lay participation, understanding of God's Word, and a response. Even today evangelical services among Slavic peoples in Eastern Europe are generally held in structures called prayer houses, not churches or temples, where preaching of God's Word, cycles of fervent prayers led by lay members, and hymns compose the service.

4. *TsV*, 1883, no. 1, 10–11. Shcherbina, "Malorusskaya shtunda," *Nedelya*, 1877, no. 2, 60.

5. Shcherbina, "Malorusskaya shtunda," *Nedelya*, 1877, no. 2, 56. Rozhdestvenskiĭ, 264. *TsV*, 1882, no. 48, 8.

6. For the Rule and Dorodnitsyn's comparison with the German Baptist Confession and comments, see Dorodnitsyn (1909), 262–69. For the German Baptist confession of faith in Eng. tr. see W. J. McGlothlin, *Baptist Confessions of Faith*, 333–54. A few years later, Wieler mistakenly referred to the Rule as consisting of twelve instead of ten articles (*QR*, July, 1874, 5–6).

In arriving at the place of worship, generally in a home, worshipers greeted each other as "brother" or "sister," extending their hands with men kissing men and women kissing women. Worshipers sat on benches, men on the right and women on the left, possibly along a wall. In a corner, a small table covered with a white tablecloth held a Bible and possibly some hymnals. The elder or presider of the service sat at the table, reading the Russian Bible and interpreting in Ukrainian the Scripture passage verse by verse. One priest pointed out that one reason for the spread of stundism was its use of Ukrainian, "the language of the people," in preaching. Rhetoric was avoided, but Shcherbina noted that some expositors, such as Ryaboshapka or Balaban, were skilled in language, expressing even shades of meaning from the Church Slavonic and using poetic turns of speech. Since the lay preachers were untrained, stundist theology was unsystematic except for treatises, which may have come from elsewhere. Interpretation was generally literal consistent with a normal reading of the text but might veer off into the allegorical. After the reading and explanation of a passage, the meeting was opened to the men for discussion or questions.[7]

Prayer, so basic, was improvised and may appear at the beginning, inspersed throughout, or at the close of a service. Worshipers knelt in prayer with both men and women leading out in prayer. Prayers were generally long and repetitious, concerned with confession of sin and self-examination. Prayers were frequently expressed with extreme emotion and laden with tears but this lessened in time.[8]

Although often difficult to acquire, stundists were eager to gain hymnals. An early hymnal from an unknown compiler was *Prinoshenie pravoslavnym khristianam* (An Offering to Orthodox Christians). It included ninety-four hymns, based primarily on German Protestant compositions, but with its title it passed the ecclesiastical censor. A second edition was published in St. Petersburg in 1864, and it appeared among the stundists at least by 1867. As noted earlier, Johann Wieler in 1870 made an effort to import *Dukovnyya pesni* (Spiritual Songs), a hymnal of ninety songs, many translated from the German, printed in Constantinople. The Pashkovites in St. Petersburg produced two small hymnals, *Lyubimye stikhi* (Beloved Verses) in 1880 and *Radostnyya pesni Siona* (Joyful Songs of Zion) in 1882. N. I. Voronin, Baptist leader in the Caucasus, produced in 1882 *Golos very* (The Voice of Faith). This hymnal also appeared in the Ukraine.[9]

The music of stundists and Stundo-Baptists was strikingly different from the Orthodox who had no congregational singing or the Molokans who sang chapters from the Bible for hours in a monotonous tone. Stundists and Baptists sang congregationally.

---

7. Shcherbina, "Malorusskaya shtunda," *Nedelya*, no. 2, 57. Rozhdestvenskii, 208, 251–52. *TsV*, 1883, no. 1, 9; 1889, no. 50, 858; 1890, no. 20, 248. Brown, 71, 73. *Strannik*, 1890, no. 7, 404–5. Dalton, *Der Stundismus in Russland*, 18–19.

8. Rozhdestvenskii, 247–49, 251–52. *Strannik*, 1890, no. 7, 404–5; 1895, no. 1, 218–19. Brown, 72–73. *TsV*, 1883, no. 1, 9.

9. Rozhdestvenskii, 244–46. QR, 1864, 6–7. *Strannik*, 1890, no. 7, 405. Brown, 71.

Hymns were uplifting and related to the experiences of the believer. Andrew Dubovy wrote that when his father attended in Chaplinka his first service he found the house filled with people on benches, on the floor, or standing against the walls. The singing was completely new to him. He later said, "They all sang with a single heart, inspired and joyful." The singing made a deep impression on him, and he felt he was "in some grand cathedral, like heaven itself."[10]

Although many of the hymns came from German Protestant sources, some, however, came from Ira Sankey's hymns, while others were original stundist or Pashkovite compositions. Many melodies came from the West, but some, however, were Orthodox or Ukrainian folk melodies. With the lack of hymnals and for the inability of numbers who could not read, it was common for the song leader to line out a hymn, reading each verse in turn with the congregation singing after each verse.[11]

In the services, letters were read from stundists from other localities and from the imprisoned. After the end of a service, particularly men of the congregation would continue visiting, discussing economic, societal, or religious issues. Topics included concern for the needs of some brother or relations to the state or the Orthodox priesthood. During the winter, stundists met on Sundays and Wednesdays but in summer only on Sunday. They met twice on Sunday at nine or ten in the morning and at four in the afternoon. Besides Sundays, stundists might make special note of Christmas, Easter, Ascension Day, and Pentecost. Worship was not confined to the church. Stundists were known to set aside a time for devotion in the home, singing before a meal verses from Psalm 18 and after a meal with song and prayer.[12]

Stundists tended to meet in a large room of a house or a barn or during intense persecution a clearing in the forest. As congregations grew, a growing self-confidence led to the consideration of erecting their own houses of worship. German Baptists had some success in building. In Neudorf in Volhynia, German Baptists built a chapel as early as 1864, a structure that was doubled in size in 1872. Only after much discouragement, Gottfried Alf in Russian Poland was finally allowed to build a wooden chapel in 1868, a building that could not appear as a church. For Ukrainian Stundo-Baptists it was impossible to gain permission. As noted earlier, the chapel that Stundo-Baptists under Ryaboshapaka completed in the spring of 1873 was soon confiscated. Ratushnyï considered asking permission to build in 1873, but no such effort at this time was possible.[13]

---

10. Dubovy, *Pilgrims of the Plain*, 5.

11. Rozhdestvenskiï, 246–47, 250–51. Dalton, *Der Stundismus in Russland*, 22. *Strannik*, 1890, no.7, 405. Brown, 72. *TsV*, 1883, no.1, 9.

12. *TsV*, 1883, no. 1, 10–11. *Strannik*, 1890, no. 7, 406–7. Rozhdestvenskiï, 246, 249–50. E. von der Brügen, "Die evangelisch-religiöse Bewegung in Russland," *Deutsche Rundschau*, Jan. 1883, 120.

13. Rozhdestvenskiï, 243. Brown, 243. Dalton, *Der Stundismus in Russland*, 22. Dorodnitsyn, *Materialy*, doc. 171. Dorodnitsyn, "*Nemetskie missionary neobaptizma*," *ChOLDP*, 1893, no. 6, 738.

The Ordinances

The Stundo-Baptist view of the ordinances, as other Baptists, was on the one hand, between the sacramentalism of the Orthodox and magisterial Protestant Churches, which held to sacraments as channel of grace, and, on the other hand, the Molokans and Mladostundists who in spiritualizing them rejected the observance of all sacraments and ordinances. With the Mennonites they regarded their ordinances of baptism and the Lord's Supper not only as memorials but also a testimony and commitment of the believer who participated in them.

Baptism for believers was a solemn but yet joyful affair. The event took place generally at night in a river or creek. The candidate clothed in white linen and for men in a white shirt and trousers entered the water up to his or her waist. The elder prayed and then immersed the candidate in the name of the Father, Son, and Holy Spirit. Although the subject and design of the baptism differed from Orthodox practice, yet the mode was similar as both churches, as today, practice immersion. On the other hand, Orthodox practiced trine immersion while Baptists dipped only once. A report in 1877 described Ryaboshapka, however, as immersing a candidate three times for each person of the Trinity. Gottfried Alf, the Baptist leader in Russian Poland, took Mennonite Brethren to task for immersing candidates three times facing forward, declaring the universal practice for Baptists is one time backwards. In a discussion with the son of an Orthodox priest after a baptism in Neudorf, Karl Ondra argued for a single immersion, declaring there was one new birth, one resurrection, and on the basis of Ephesians 4:5 only one baptism.[14]

The Lord's Supper or "the breaking of bread" was also a significant ordinance of Stundo-Baptists, observed generally once a month. The Lord' Supper was also observed immediately after baptism, thereby allowing the newly baptized to partake for the first time. The church obligated members to attend. The Lord's Supper was not closed but close—only immersed believers may partake, which also included Mennonite Brethren. Stundists who had not been immersed were not permitted to partake but could attend as observers.[15]

In the observance of the Supper, the elder might first read from Exodus 12, the institution of the Passover, and then from I Corinthians 11 and Matthew 26. A deacon brought on a tray or plate broken bits of bread to the table and upon the words of the elder, "take eat" and words following, the elder then returned the plate to the deacon. The deacon then took the plate to each worshiper separately, or it was passed from one worshiper to the next. While the bread was passed, the congregation sang a hymn. After the bread, the elder read from the gospel concerning the cup. When he said,

14. Shcherbina, "Malorusskaya shtunda," *Nedelya*, 1877, no. 1, 26. Dorodnitsyn, *Materialy*, docs. 155, 164. Stanyukovich, "Ratushnyï Trial," 154, 157. *Elisabetgradskiï vestnik*, 1877, no. 22, 2. Rozhdestvenskiï, 218–20. Friesen, 288. *Missionsblatt*, Nov. 1872, 183.

15. Rozhdestvenskiï, 254–55, ft. 4. Dorodnitsyn, *Materialy*, doc. 164. The proper word for the communion is "close" not "closed."

"drink from it all of you" and words following, the deacon took the metallic or glass chalice of wine, which had been standing on the table covered with a napkin, to the worshipers who passing it from person to person took a sip from it. The congregation again sang. The service ended possibly with a prayer of thanksgiving and a general hymn. According to one source, Ryaboshapka evidently followed his own pattern. Without a deacon he himself broke the bread in a plate and poured wine into a cup with participants then approaching the table to partake each element.[16]

Although unrecognized by the government, elders of both the Mladostundists and Stundo-Baptists performed weddings. Marriage was not a sacrament but a contract. Elders also performed burials. On the third day after death, the elder and brethren would wrap the corpse in white linen, put it into a coffin and carry it to the cemetery, placing it in the grave. No cross was put on the grave.[17]

Morality

Congregations expected members to have had a personal conversion experience through repentance and faith and lead a godly life. At his trial in 1878, Ratushnyï stated that one entered the Kingdom of God by being born again by repentance of his sinful past and to feel "in his heart and soul his previous sins that he ought to live only for righteousness and holiness."[18]

Stundists imposed a strict personal code on their followers, a standard that distinguished them from society. They strongly condemned drunkenness, which was widespread in Russian society and also common among the Orthodox clergy. Vodka was strictly forbidden, except for use as a medicine. Unlike German Baptists, many stundists, although not all, abstained from beer and wine. For many, coffee and tea were preferred drinks. They prohibited the use of tobacco, which, however, many German Baptists tolerated. Their opposition to alcohol and tobacco, which included refusal to participate in religious holidays where drunkenness was widespread, further alienated them from society. Stundists were also noted for opposing such common evils as theft and indecent language. One of the non-stundist witnesses at Ratushnyï's trial stated he found no drunkenness or thieves among them. In his description of stundists, Kozitskiï stated neither drunkenness nor foul language were in their midst. Stundists seriously upheld the marriage bond. They also condemned the taking of usury.[19]

---

16. *Strannik*, 1890, no. 7, 407. Rozhdestvenskiï, 254–56. *TsV*, 1882, no. 48, 6. *Elisabetgradskiï vestnik*, 1877, no. 22, 2.

17. Rozhdestvenskiï, 107, 254–55. Dorodnitsyn, *Materialy*, doc. 155.

18. Stanyukovich, "Ratushnyï Trial," 157.

19. Rozhdestvenskiï, 34. Shcherbina, "Malorusskaya shtunda," *Nedelya*, 1877, no. 2, 59. Dubovy, 49. Brown 61–62. Stanyukovich, "Ratushnyï Trial," 156. *TsV*, 1889, no. 50, 858. *Delo*, 1883, no. 2, 91. *MRW*, Oct. 1896, 743.

Members who violated the moral strictures of the church community were subject to church discipline. If the procedure of admonition as outlined in Matthew 18 failed, then the case might be brought to the church, which may temporarily suspend the erring member from church fellowship. Only after several other attempts brought no repentance, the church excluded the member. Excluded members who were formerly Orthodox would find themselves in a rather untenable situation, ostracized at the same time by two religious bodies. Members with quarrels among themselves were also subject to church discipline. The church opposed going to the civil courts, following 1 Corinthians that forbade taking cases before unbelievers.[20]

The Orthodox writer, P. Kozitskiï, however, claimed stundism was an easy path to salvation. One only needed to pray and believe in Christ the redeemer from sin. It did not demand any "heroic deeds" or "self-denial," such as fasts, standing in church for prayer, or giving alms. He felt that their outer side "for show," such as objecting to certain types of behavior and support for each other, attracted outsiders.[21]

Although evangelicals as well as some Orthodox recognized the high morality of stundists, some of the latter, however, were ready to charge them with immoral behavior. Because of their denunciation by church and state as heretics, the reputation and morality of stundists were automatically blackened. Probably Mikhael Kozakevich, a priest in Lybomirka who was very antagonistic toward them, brought the most detailed case against them. He divided his memorandum into five sections: slanderers, deceivers, drunkards, thieves, and robbers. He also tried to discredit Ryaboshapka by claiming he collected money on the pretext that he was going to St. Petersburg and other places but then who knew where he went. In the meantime his followers worked on his farm and even acquired new equipment for him.[22]

One might brush aside these allegations by pointing out that Lyobomirka was a center of intense conflict between Orthodox and stundists, and for centuries opponents have used the tactic of discrediting enemies by alleging their immorality. The governor of Kherson notably used Kozakevich as an example of a priest improperly arousing the antagonism of villagers against the stundists. The priest's own lack of balance is in evidence when he charged stundists for associations with Quakers, Anabaptists, Mormons, and German emissaries. Even with all of these considerations, the priest probably had some grounds for his allegations, especially in cases of slander (four of the cases here involved one man), theft, and drinking where the culprits were either found guilty, fined, kept under arrest. or jailed. Stundists themselves recognized that they did not have a perfect membership. Otherwise, why then the need for church discipline.

---

20. Rozhdestvesnkiï, 265–66, *TsV*, 1883, no. 1, 11.

21. P. Kozitskiï, "O prichinakh, sposobstvuyushchikh rasprostraneniyu shtundizma v malorusskikh guberniyakh," *TsV*, 1889, no. 50, 858.

22. Dorodnitsyn, *Materialy*, doc. 186. Klimenko, 94–95.

Rozhdestvenskiĭ, the Orthodox priest who was unusually careful and balanced in his study of stundism, but as a chronicler and not evaluating the sources of the charges, listed Kozakevich's allegations as well as noting other charges of immoral behavior. Nevertheless he attempted to be more nuanced in his appraisal. He said that reports were contradictory, suggesting that perhaps not enough data had been collected. He suggested supporters of the stundists may exaggerate their good qualities and their poor behavior may result from the waning of the enthusiasm of new converts. On behalf of the stundists, Rozhdestvenskiĭ listed their peaceable nature, opposition to injustice, strong work ethic, rejection of idle pleasure, opposition to strong drink, avoidance of stealing, disapproval of lying, and benevolence toward the needy. On the other hand, he listed against them and without noting their frequency spite, slander, fraud, falsehood, cupidity, and pharisaical boastfulness as well as theft, drinking, and adultery. He also charged Ryaboshapka for exploiting the generosity of his followers and Koval for sharp business practices and drinking.[23] Rozhdestvenskiĭ concluded that stundists stood out from the common people in moral qualities, but, on the other hand, he claimed they exhibited a low level of moral development and a morality that was too narrow. He noted that stundists majored on not drinking, not smoking, and not buying and selling on the Sabbath, while at the same time they failed in charity, in their acquiring the property of others, and in lacking such high moral Christian truths as love of the enemy and self-denial.[24]

Social and Economic Life

In evaluating the social and economic life of stundists, one must as with observations on stundist morality take as much care in considering the reporter as the report itself. Too often people reported what they wished to see, promoting their own agenda, rather than what is seen. As with morality, stundists received conflicting reports.

Stundism arose in a changing social and economic world and in part was a product of it. The new religious values of the stundists helped to raise their social and economic standing as is seen today among various groups in the developing world. An interplay of a number of factors was at work.

Although some were artisans, the average Ukrainian stundist in the 1860s and 1870s started as a poor peasant, a member of the lowest class of society. In the eyes of Westerners, such as Dalton, the German-bred pastor of the Reformed Church in St. Petersburg, the condition of the average Ukrainian peasant was dire. In his description, a Russian village was more often than not disorderly with wretched houses, unkempt courtyards, and frequently lacking a church not to speak of a school. Around the village was poorly tilled farmland. The inhabitants were slovenly with little energy, lacked incentive for change, and fatalistic. Dalton pointedly contrasted the Ukrainian

23. Rozhdestvenskiĭ, 269–79.
24. Ibid., 269, 284–85.

village with the neighboring German village, prosperous with its clean houses, tree-lined street, church and school, and surrounded by well cultivated fields. Other observers besides Dalton also noted the contrast.[25]

Whether the contrasts were overdrawn, the German settler in Russia was nevertheless on a higher social and ecoomic level than the Russian peasant. The German came from a society that experienced the Reformation and Renaissance, provided incentives for self-advancement and greater educational opportunities, and had eliminated serfdom in contrast to a society that for centuries suffered under despotism, the shackles of serfdom, and widespread illiteracy. The psychologies of the German and Russian were also radically different. The German was noted for efficiency, orderliness, punctuality, and cleanliness. The Russian peasant with lack of incentive tended to be lax and disorderly and given to drink. Although apparently lazy, yet he might follow his inactivity with sudden bursts of energy.[26]

The Ukrainian who became a stundist, however, adopted religious values that affected his lifestyle. His emancipation from serfdom already brought a significant change in self-worth and the possibility of change, and such biblical values as honesty, responsibility, purpose, fruitful labor, orderliness, rejection of idleness, and sobriety were additional incentives for a different standard of life.

The stundist attachment to the Bible was a strong incentive to become literate. In 1861 only eight percent of the population could read and in 1881 less than nine percent of children of school age attended school. With their eagerness to read the Bible, stundists made a great effort to learn to read with parents insisting their children read as well. Stundists were eager to read anything available, and their children also attended village schools if available.[27]

Another factor in the stundist lifestyle was the influence of the German settlers nearby, such as the colony of Rohrbach in the Odessa region. In their association as farmhands and domestics of Germans, they not only were influenced by German stundist values but also observed their prosperous status and began to emulate them. With a combination of influences, stundist households began to portray an air of prosperity. Stundists planted trees and flowers and became noted for orderliness, cleanliness, and punctuality. They went even so far as to emulate German patterns in personal appearance, clothes, home furnishings, and clocks. As the Germans, they adopted warm and comfortable clothing, wearing jackets, shirts, cloth trousers, and high boots. They even cut their hair shorter, and beards were either trimmed or shaved.[28]

25. Dalton, *Der Stundismus in Russland*, 9–10.

26. See Ronald Hingley, *The Russian Mind*, 33–34, 148–50, 196, 208, for Russian as over against German characteristics.

27. Brown, 62–63, 67. *MRW*, Oct. 1896, 742. Rozhdestvenskiï, 173, 268. Stanyukovich, "Ratushnyï Trial," 157.

28. Rozhdestvenskiï, 67, 269. Brown, 63, 66–67. *TsV*, 1883, no. 1, 11. *MRW*, Oct. 1896, 743. E. von der Brügen, 120. Dorodnitsyn, *Materialy*, doc. 54. Shcherbina, "Malorusskaya shtunda," *Nedelya*, 1877, no. 2, 59.

PART THREE—Prospects: Ukrainian and Russian Beginnings, 1860–1884

As other peasants, it is not surprising that stundists felt the need for a more equitable distribution of land. In a report to the Kherson governor in 1873, the *ispravnik* of the Odessa *uezd* stated that stundist leaders avoided giving straight answers on the ownership of property. Although some stundists considered forming artels for common work, these never came to pass, but they nevertheless practiced mutual help. As already noted, Ukrainian stundists opposed usury, and some of them, as some German stundists, opposed keeping fellow stundists as farm laborers.[29]

In a memorandum in 1867 to P. E. Kotzebu, governor-general of New Russia, Znachko-Yavorskiĭ, a landowner, charged Ukrainian and German stundists of promoting communism. Besides describing their rejection of Orthodox rites and high moral character, he alleged their support of communism as a bait to attract adherents, appealing to Russians dissatisfied with their allotment of land at the time of emancipation and to Germans who desired more than their original allotment of *desyatiny*. He claimed they argued that since Christ suffered for all mankind and loves all people equally, then the blessings of the world should be divided among all people.[30]

Charges of socialism or communism continued to surface against stundism. In a letter in 1873 to the governor of Kherson *guberniya*, a Marshal of the Nobility wrote that stundism "carries in itself clear germs of socialism." In 1883 the Minister of Internal Affairs wrote to the governor of Kherson that stundism, which "daily develops and increases" maintains "a dogma full of spiritual socialist rationalism, imperceptibly stealing into the ignorant popular masses and undermining in their feeling respect to the legal authority." They teach that all natural resources are from God and, as all men are equal, all land should be divided equally.[31]

On the other hand, other reports denied that stundists were advocates of socialism. In May 1883, the *ispravnik* of Odessa *uezd* wrote that although stundists looked upon themselves as equals and spiritual brethren, socialism had not penetrated their ranks and they fulfill all their civic responsibilities with some of them even elected to civil posts. The *ispravnik* of Elizabetgrad *uezd* reported to the governor of Kherson that the spirit of socialism had not invaded them with each possessing land of their own, while at the same time the more affluent were not forgetting to help the poor brethren.[32]

One evidence that stundism was not a social revolutionary movement in religious disguise was its attitude in 1873–1874 toward the *Narodniks* or Populists, young people with revolutionary fervor. They instituted a movement "to the people" to teach and assist the masses in the villages with many of them also seeking to arouse them

---

29. Dorodnitsyn, *Materialy*, doc. 157. Rozhdestvenskiĭ, 262–63. Shcherbina, "Malorusskaya shtunda," *Nedelya*, 1877, no. 2, 58. MRW, Oct. 1896, 743.

30. Dorodnitsyn, *Materialy*, doc. 47. For a discussion of Znachko-Yavorskiĭ's views, see Klibanov, 259–60.

31. Dorodnitsyn, *Materialy*, docs. 166, 209.

32. Ibid., docs. 213, 215. Also see Klibanov, 257–58.

to revolutionary action. In 1874 Catharine Breshkovsky, who was later dubbed, "The little grandmother of the revolution," and a companion entered Lybomirka to contact stundists for the cause. They met with stundist gatherings in a stundist home where they stressed the abject poverty and brutality that the peasants endured and who also were robbed not only of their religious rights but also their political and social rights. In their use of Scripture, the two insisted that it taught to help the oppressed and faith without works is dead. They also used texts to attempt to refute the words of Christ, "Render unto Caesar the things that are Caesar's."

The stundists, although greatly interested, would make no commitment until they heard from their leader Ryaboshapka, who arrived at the second meeting. Ryaboshapka rejected their revolutionary arguments, declaring that he and others of his flock had been severely persecuted, including imprisonment, but he was not going to jeopardize himself or his flock further through revolutionary activity. The *Narodniks* soon left the village.[33]

In his reminiscences, Solomon E. Lion, a revolutionary *Narodnik*, attempted to spread revolutionary propaganda among stundists in the vicinity of Odessa. He claimed that some stundists became "politically conscious, useful revolutionaries."[34] Whatever number of stundists may have been recruited, it would have been small. The *Narodnik* movement collapsed, and stundists as well as the peasants of the time were not attracted to it.

In spite of the ideal of equality in their ranks, as in all organizations some become more equal than others. Among both German and Ukrainian stundists some were acquiring wealth and engaged in usury. Shcherbina pointed out in 1877 that Ryaboshapka, Ratushnyï, and Balaban had become *kulaks*, rich farmers, while the mass of stundists pursued "microscopic goals." Shcherbina also wrote that displeasure and murmuring began to rise against these leaders.[35]

In his study of the social and economic status of nineteen stundist and Stundo-Baptist leaders in Kherson *guberniya*, A. I. Klibanov, a Marxist scholar on Russian sectarianism, used the reports of *ispravniki* in three districts that Aleskiï Dorodnitsyn had assembled. Among the leaders were Ratushnyï, Ryaboshapka, Kapustyan, and Balaban. Klibanov noted that sixteen were *kulaks* or wealthy farmers and only three were poor peasants. The wealthy leaders collectively possessed extensive land holdings, stone houses, horses and other livestock, threshers, and mills. In contrast to the peasant masses, the top leaders were becoming capitalist entrepreneurs, breaking from the communal past and exhibiting class differentiation in their ranks.[36]

33. For the relations of the *Narodniks* to the stundists, see Blackwell, *The Little Grandmother of the Revolution*, chapter five. Another version of the same account is in Hutchinson, *Hidden Springs of the Russian Revolution*, chapter four.
34. Lion, "Ot propagandy k teroru," *Katorga i ssylka*, 1924, no. 5, 19–20.
35. Shcherbina, "Malorusskaya shtunda," *Nedelya*, 1877, no. 2, 57–58. Rozhdestvenskiï, 273.
36. Dorodnitsyn *Materialy*, 234–36. Klibanov, 243–44.

PART THREE—Prospects: Ukrainian and Russian Beginnings, 1860–1884

Denominational and State Relations

Stundist communities sent each other letters, written even as epistles in Scriptural style. Such communications were then shared with the entire congregation. Stundo-Baptists even went further by holding regional meetings. Such meetings, lasting two or three days, occurred two or three times a year, generally at Christmas, Easter, or Pentecost, and held at a farmstead or in the steppe. Such meetings were an enlarged gathering of a local assembly with preaching, prayer, and singing but also included communications and news, which were shared, and practical considerations such as relations with fellow stundists and the Orthodox or establishing a general treasury.[37]

Even though after the mid-1870s, stundists were able to function in comparative peace, even winning in 1878 a notable legal victory in the Odessa Court, and German Baptists gaining legal recognition in 1879, the regime continued to consider Ukrainian stundists a heretical sect with no legal rights. In 1880 a secular court fined Ryaboshapka and twenty other stundists fifteen rubles each but with an appeal to the court in Elizabetgrad the fine was reduced to only fifteen kopeks each. Instead of being satisfied with such a ridiculously insignificant fine, Ryaboshapka appealed to the Senate. The Senate revoked the decision of the Elizabetgrad court and sent the case to the Aleksandr Assembly (*Zemstvo*) that affirmed the original fine of the secular court. Ryaboshapka not only was required to pay the far higher original fine but failed to get from the Senate recognition of the legality of stundist gatherings.[38]

In the following year in 1881, both Ryaboshapka and Ratushnyï submitted petitions to the Minister of Internal Affairs for legal recognition as Baptists, based on the recognition German Baptists received in 1879. Ryaboshapka with Grigoriï Kusherenko submitted a petition signed by 278 persons. The petition asked permission to open prayer houses, the right to choose elders, maintain books of registry, and the right to be called, "Congregation of Christian-Baptists." The examiner of Ryboshapka considered him lacking in literacy and deficient in Baptist dogma. At the same time, Ratushnyï with two others and the signatures of 324 submitted two petitions, one from Ryasnopol and the other from Osnova, calling themselves the "Society of Christian-Baptists" or "Christian Baptists of Russian Nationality." They also requested opening prayer houses and the right to elect their own elders. As the petitioners were natives, obviously schismatic from the Orthodox Church, the petitions were denied.[39]

But such rebuffs did not stop further developments. As he had been in the past in Ukrainian stundist affairs, a chief player was the Mennonite Brethren teacher/evangelist Johannn Wieler. After he had directed many Ukrainian stundists in the Odessa region 1870–1871 into Stundo-Baptism and after his own two-year period

---

37. *Strannik*, 1890, no. 7, 406. *TsV*, 1883, no. 1, 10. Brown, 51. Shcherbina, "Malorusskaya shtunda," *Nedelya*, 1877, no. 2, 56.

38. *Delo*, 1883, no. 2, 190–91.

39. *Delo*, 1883, no. 2, 192. Dorodnitsyn, *Materialy*, docs. 204, 205. Klimenko, 85–86.

of administrative arrest, he left Odessa in 1874. He began a school in Friedensfeld but then in the following year established a school in Nikopol. From 1879 to 1883 he taught at the Mennonite Central School in Halbstadt. Because of teaching responsibilities he was restricted in his evangelistic activities, but during holidays he ministered among the Ukrainians.[40]

Wieler began to correspond with Colonel Vasilii Pashkov, an aristocrat who headed an evangelical movement called Pashkovism in St. Petersburg. Through his preaching, benevolent, and tract ministry, Pashkov was interested in spreading the gospel throughout Russia and sought links with the stundist movement in the south of the country. Pashkov began to provide some support for stundist leaders, and leaders would travel to St. Petersburg for consultation and financial help. By 1879 Pashkov himself had visited Ukraine and would visit again. Pashkov invited Wieler to St. Petersburg to view the work there, and he and Peter M. Friesen, teacher and principal at the school in Halbstadt, arrived in December 1881. The three consulted on mission strategy. Pashkov persuaded Wieler and Friesen to accept open communion for all evangelical believers, a position of the Pashkovites but contrary to the views of German Baptists and Mennonite Brethren.[41]

In May 1882 at Rückenau in the Mennonite colony of Molochna, Wieler invited stundist leaders to meet at the annual Mennonte Brethen Conference. It was a remarkable assembly of both Germans and Ukrainians. With their own associational organization, German Baptists as a group were not represented. It was a good place and time to meet. As Molochna was a Mennonite German colony, it was comparatively immune from imperial interference. It was also a time of comparative peace for the Stundo-Baptist movement. When Ryaboshapka reported, he noted that although the government had persecuted the stundists for a long time, yet during the last two years people were no longer afraid to attend their services. Since the minutes of the conference were kept secret and were found by the government only later by chance in searching the home of Alexandr Storozhev from Kuban, one of the participants, the government was kept from the results of the meeting for some time.[42]

The minutes listed the names of sixty-two Mennonite Brethren messengers from five congregations, including the Molochna church whose center was at Rückenau; the Einlage church in Chortitza Colony; the Friedensfeld church in Yekaterinoslav

40. Klippenstein, "Johann Wieler," 52, 55. Dyck, 47–48.

41. For material on the Pashkovite movement, see chapters fifteen and sixteen of this work. Klippenstein, "Johann Wieler," 54–55. Dyck, 76. Friesen, 499.

42. Minutes of the Conference of Mennonite Brethren and Stundo-Baptists in 1882 may be found in several sources. The accounts of Kal'nev in *Russkoe obozrenie*, 1897, no. 4, 818–64, and in his work, *Nemtsy i shtundobaptizm*, and in Skvortsov in *MO*, Sep., 1900, 209–25, show variation in content in addition to their own critical remarks. Val'kevich, *Zapiska*, app. 1, 1–8, and Dorodnitsyn, *Materialy*, doc.322, also include the minutes. An Eng. tr. of the minutes with both Kal'nev's and Skvortsov's comments is in Dueck, *Moving Beyond Secession: Defining Russian Mennonite Brethren Mission and Identity 1872–1922*, 37–54.

PART THREE—Prospects: Ukrainian and Russian Beginnings, 1860–1884

guberniya; the Don church; and the Kuban church in addition to affiliated stations. Wieler and Friesen were messengers from the Molochna church.

The eighteen Ukrainians/Russians from thirteen locations included a good cross section of Stundo-Baptist/Baptist life. Among these were Ratushnyĭ from Osnova; Aleksandr Kapustyan from Ignatievka; Ryaboshapka and Petr Griva from Lybomirka; Trifon Khlystun from Karlovka; Grigoriĭ Kushnerenko from Poltavka; Andreĭ M. Mazaev from Tiflis; Egor M. Bogdanov and Ivan N. Skorokhodov from Vladikavkaz; Arkhip Romanenko from Bessarabia; and Andreĭ A. Stoyalov from Novo-Vasilyevka. In addition two guests were present—Christian Fischer, a German Baptist evangelist, and Yakov Delyakov, the Nestorian evangelical serving in Ukraine.

Seven Mennonite Brethren and seven Stundo-Baptist/Baptists gave mission reports. Of the latter Egor Bogdanov from Vladikavkaz reported on his ministry and Nikita Voronin of his among Molokans in Taurida *guberniya*. Ratushnyĭ told of his work in trying to unite brethren who disagee on numerous petty subjects and visiting brethren in Bessarabia and Kiev *gubernii*. He stated that mission contributions were only sixty rubles in two years. Pavel Peretyatkin and Yakov Saranov from Yekaterinoslav *guberniya* complained of brethren who refused to give anything to missions. Andreĭ Mazaev, deacon from the Tiflis church, reported on the work of Vasiliĭ Pavlov, the leading elder of Russian Baptists in the Caucasus but not present at the conference. Although not in the reports, Ryaboshapka noted in his remarks of his visiting Kiev *guberniya* where there were around a hundred baptized believers but some of them were engaged in improper behavior and needed instruction.

The conference agreed on a sliding scale for salaries of missionaries—450 rubles for eight months; 175 rubles for four months; and 75 rubles for two months of work. Fifty rubles would be added for lodging. In addition to the election of a number of Mennonite Brethren missionaries, the conference appointed Ratushnyĭ, Ryaboshapka, and Kushnerenko for four-month terms and Pavlov for eight months—four months in Taurida guberniya and four months in the Caucasus. The conference, however, instructed Pavlov that he not make an issue of observing Sunday, the Sabbath day, from midnight to midnight, the custom among German Baptists and the West, but let believers observe the Sabbath from evening to evening as they had done as Molokans and as recorded in the Bible.

A far more contentious issue was when Wieler reported that Pashkov desired that fellow believers who were baptized only as infants be invited to the Lord's Supper, that is, open communion. Strong opposition came from the Baptists from the Caucasus who supported the traditional Baptist position of close communion, arguing that if communion were open it would then acknowledge that baptism of infants was valid. The issue could not be settled and was tabled for a future time.

In the election of officers and members to the Mission Committee, Johann Wieler was elected chairman and Nickel Hiebert treasurer, and nine Stundo-Baptists/Baptists were added to the Committee. At the end of the Conference, the Lord's Supper was observed. On Sunday morning the German and Russian brethren held separate services. In the afternoon Christian Schmidt, a Mennonite Brethren from the Kuban Church, gave the final sermon on giving. Three hundrd rubles were raised.

More funds, of course, were needed. The Mennonite Brethren were in a strong position to raise their own funds from their churches, but the Stundo-Baptists and Russian Baptists, coming from a lower economic level if not poverty, with no tradition of stewardship and from strong opposition in their own ranks to giving to missions, would need outside support. Fortunately, Baptists in the West were willing to provide some support and above all Pashkov in St. Petersburg had the resources to make significant contributions.

In the summer of 1882 Pashkov again visited Ukraine, visiting Christians of the Evangelical Faith (New Molokans) as well as Wieler in his home. Pashkov proposed to Wieler that he become a full-time evangelist among the native population.[43]

It appeared that the Pashkov program and Mennonite Brethren cooperation with stundists were on the way, but it suffered a setback in the following year in May 1883 at the Mennonite Brethren Conference at Friedensfeld. The conference rejected Wieler's plea for cooperation in mission work with the stundists. Any mission activity with the native population would be entirely Wieler's own responsibility. For opponents, the risks with confrontation with the regime were too great. Nevertheless some individuals on their own provided financial support for Wieler's efforts. Mennonite Brethren also rejected Wieler's advocacy of open communion, although both Wieler and Friesen continued to maintain their convictions on the issue.[44]

Whatever the setbacks, Wieler continued with Pashkov's program. He terminated his teaching position in June and began his work as a full-time missionary with Pashkov providing a salary of 1,000 rubles and 600 rubles for travel. He moved to a house in Tiege, Molochna. Shortly before Easter in 1884 he was in St. Petersburg at the unity conference for evangelical sectarians. Here Wieler discussed plans for a mission conference in Ukraine for Russian evangelicals to follow almost immediately after the St. Petersburg conference. As will be later noted, the conference in Ukraine will result in the formation of the Russian Baptist Union.[45]

How Indigenous Was Ukrainian Stundism?

A major historical question among Russian Baptists is to what extent were stundism and Stundo-Baptism indigenous? It is much more than just a theoretical question for its answer carries far-reaching implications for the essence, self-identity, and relation to Russian life and culture of these bodies. It becomes a very sensitive issue when enemies of the movement disparage them as simply a foreign import and an import

---

43. Dyck, 43.
44. Friesen, 498–99, 514. Friesen, *Konfession oder Sekte?*
45. Dyck, 77. Klippenstein, "Johann Wieler," 54.

PART THREE—Prospects: Ukrainian and Russian Beginnings, 1860–1884

no less from Germans who increasingly from the last decades of the nineteenth century and in the twentieth century Russians have viewed as an enemy of the Russian people.[46]

Both Orthodox researchers and native Russian/Ukrainian Baptists have wrestled with the question of stundist and Baptist origins in the Russian Empire. The Orthodox have presented a wide range of views. They have seen stundism as primarily a Russian phenomenon, influenced by native sects, or a movement developing from German propaganda but secondary causes as more important in preparing the ground for its arrival, or seeing it simply as a product of German influences, such as from German stundism, or a direct foreign import from the German Baptist movement itself.[47] In an effort to avoid German if not Russsian origins, some Ukrainian Baptists with no documentary evidence have developed a theory of native Ukrainian origins, while with limited evidence some Russian Baptists in the Caucasus have found their origins in the so-called Water Molokans.

As one peruses the documentary evidence from government reports, studies of researchers, newspaper and journalistic accounts, and personal testimony, the evidence is overwhelming that German stundism and the Mennonite Brethren in Russia itself were important factors in the development of Ukrainian stundism. In addition, the German Baptists in Germany through their leadership, literature, and training center in Hamburg were a significant factor in the rise of the Stundo-Baptist movement. But even if one accepts this evidence, it still is far from providing a full answer as to the character of either stundism or Stundo-Baptism. Many other factors were also at work.

A foreign movement that will have any long-term support cannot be simply imposed without individuals in the native culture ready to receive it. The soil needs to be ready. If Baptists from the West would have attempted to penetrate Russia a century earlier, they probably would have met with utter failure. With changing social conditions, people in Russia in the nineteenth century were beginning to look for social and moral change. Numbers of individuals regarded the existing ecclesiastical establishment as deficient with many in the priesthood lacking credibility and failing to provide a personally satisfying religion that common people could understand and appropriate for themselves. With increasing literacy, the Bible in Russian, another potent force for evangelicalism, was now becoming increasingly available.

The German Baptist, Ukrainian stundist, and Stundo-Baptist movements produced their own native-born leadership. Johann Wieler, the Mennonite Brethren, wrote in 1874, "Notwithstanding all persecutions, the awakening is spreading through

---

46. See Wardin, "How Indigenous was the Baptist Movement in the Russian Empire?," *JEBS* 9/2 (Jan. 2009), 29–37, for a discussion of the indigenous nature of stundism/StundoBaptism.

47. For a discussion of the various theories of origin of stundism/Stundo-Baptism, see Wardin, *Evangelical Sectarianism in the Russian Empire and USSR*, 81–82.

the feeble instrumentality of simple brethren."[48] By and large, the foreign missionary did not establish the evangelical sectarian movement in Russia, but the movement emerged through channels within Russia itself. The foreign missionary found it most difficult to stay any length of time within the Empire and was expelled if he tried. August Liebig was the only German missionary who remained for any great length of time but even he was expelled twice in his career in the country. Native-born Ukrainians and German-Russians, not missionaries, formed the churches.

Ukrainian stundism also followed its own path, choosing its own examples and associations. Although influenced by German pietism, Ukrainian stundism rejected its polity. German pietists were generally members of the Lutheran and Reformed Churches, established denominations with their own creeds, sacramental, practicing infant baptism, and with centralized structures. Even meeting in their own gatherings, German pietists, by and large, did not separate from their denominations. Ukrainian stundists, on their side, did not become either Lutheran or Reformed. Unlike most German pietists they became separatists, leaving the Orthodox Church, formed independent congregations, opposed sacramentalism, and, by and large, rejected infant baptism. Also Ukrainian stundism was very nationalistic. Even with a Russian Bible, it used the Ukrainian language and Ukrainian folk melodies. It followed its own Ukrainian leadership and confined itself to its own ethnic base, not even reaching out to the Great Russian population.[49]

The rise of Mladostundism was another sign that Ukrainian stundism was forging its own identity. Beginning in 1869 the Baptist movement began to make a strong impact, but the Mladostundists rejected not only believer's baptism by immersion, a basic Baptist and Mennonite Brethren tenet, but most of them spiritualized all sacraments. They generally rejected the dominating role of the elder as well as the financial demands of a cooperative mission work.

As previously noted, the appearance of the Baptist movement in the empire did not come all at once but appeared step by step from one national group to the other, beginning with Swedes in 1856 and not reaching Russians until 1867 and Ukrainians until 1869. For their influence on Russians and Ukrainians, Baptists were comparative latecomers. The rite of believer's baptism by immersion in Russia came primarily by peoples within the Empire seeking it for themselves rather than its being brought to them from the outside. The evangelical sectarian movement in Russia looked far more to others for guidance than foreigners bringing a new creed to them. Whether providentially or fortuitously, Baptists just happened to be at the right place at the right time.

---

48. *QR*, July 1874, 6.

49. For the nationalistic character of the Ukrainian stundist movement, see Dorodnitsyn, *Materialy*, doc. 205; Dalton, *Der Stundismus in Russland*, 17–18, 22; and *TsV*, 1890, no. 17, 289–91, and no. 20, 248.

PART THREE—Prospects: Ukrainian and Russian Beginnings, 1860–1884

For evangelicals who accepted the Baptist faith, it was not a foregone conclusion that they would automatically accept foreign Baptist leadership or all Baptist practices. For many years many Baltic Baptists threw off their German Baptist relations. Numbers of Russian Baptists in the Caucasus with Molokan roots resisted the wholesale adoption of German Baptist standards and made an effort to retain their more familiar Molokan ways. Today Russian Evangelical Christians-Baptists worship in an entirely different mode than their fellow Baptists in Western Europe and America, continuing to portray if not betray their original stundist roots.

The adoption of a foreign creed in non-western nations produces a religious movement that is a hybrid of foreign and native elements.[50] Likewise evangelical sectarianism in the Russian Empire was also a hybrid. To what extent it was indigenous depends in part on the weight one gives to various competing factors and possibly also on the point of view of the beholder.

---

50. See Cox, "What I Have Learned About Missions from Writing *The British Missionary Enterprise Since 1700*," *International Bulletin of Missionary Research* 32/2 (Apr. 2008), 86–87, on the hybrid nature of mission movements.

13

Baptists from the Caucasus

CONCURRENTLY IN UKRAINE, A Baptist movement arose in the Caucasus in the vicinity of Tiflis (Tbilisi), today in the nation of Georgia. The movement occurred from no effort of Oncken in Hamburg or by German Baptist missionaries but by the fortuitous arrival in the Caucasus of a Baptist layman, Martin K. Kalweit (1833–1918). Kalweit was a German Baptist of Lithuanian extraction who was born a Russian subject in the Province of Kovno, near the Russian-German border. He was baptized in 1858 at Ickschen near Ragnit in East Prussia, Germany, also not far from the border. Ickschen was then a mission station of the great mission-minded Baptist church at Memel. Kalweit was born in poverty, lost his mother in infancy, and received no formal education but learned to operate a lathe. While living at a mill, he met the daughter of the miller, Carolina Val, whom he married. Because of the Val family, Kalweit was converted and joined the Baptist church.[1]

In July 1869 Kalweit sent Oncken a letter, written for him by his brother Karl, relating his move to the Caucasus seven years before in 1862. Kalweit, his wife, two sisters, and family members of his wife, twelve in number, left for the Caucasus, 1,800 miles away, lured by words of opportunity from Kalweit's uncle and a brother who served in the army. Eight of them, after 600 miles of travel, decided to stay in Odessa, but Kalweit, his wife and sisters, assisted by fifty rubles from fellow Baptists, arrived in the Caucasus in September. The small band was worn out with little financial resources and met Kalweit's brother and some prosperous relatives who lived some

---

1. For details of Kalweit's early life, see "50-ti letnii jubeleï Martyna Karlovicha Kal'veïta," *Baptist*, Aug. 1908, 20–22. Also see the manuscript of Keshe, "Semeïnoe vospominanie o Martine Karloviche Kal'veï t," and his own memoirs in *BV*, 1947, no. 5, 36–37.

miles from Tiflis. The relatives charged them for accommodations, and one year later Kalweit moved with his family to Tiflis. Here they felt almost abandoned, cut off from fellow believers, and even fearing the Russian people. Four years after arrival, Kalweit again received *Missionsblatt*, the German Baptist paper, bringing him again in touch with the Baptist world.[2]

Kalweit attempted mission work in the military barracks among lower classes of Latvians and Finns but with no success. He nevertheless held worship services in both German and Russian, singing in both languages, and used the German hymnal, *Glaubensstimme*. In his letter of July 1869, he reported that his little group now numbered eleven with the recent baptism of T. F. Kielblock, a German Prussian youth, age nineteen, and a man of forty who fifteen years before had been transported to the Caucasus in chains because of his faith. Kalweit also urged Oncken to come to Tiflis on his journey to Russia, laying out the mission opportunities among German colonists. Apparently some fanaticism had also broken out among the Baptists in Tiflis.[3]

Later in the year on October 6, 1869 (o.s) at eleven at night in the Kura River, Kalweit baptized his brother Karl and Johann (Ivan) Kargel (1849–1937). Kargel was a young man of twenty, born in the Turkish Empire, and was at least half German and probably half Armenian. As earlier noted, he became a German Baptist pastor in Volhynia and St. Petersburg. The introduction to his work, *Zwischen den Enden der Erde unter Brüdern in Ketten*, stated he was converted in Tiflis in 1869. Viktor L. Val'kevich, the Orthodox researcher of Protestants in the Caucasus, reproduced a letter by Karl Kalweit, Martin's brother, written almost twenty years later, which gave an account of his and Kargel's baptism. It has generally been assumed that Nikita Voronin, a Russian Molokan convert, had baptized Kargel, but this is in error. Voronin in a letter in 1889 recording his early baptisms and Pavlov in his record of baptisms by Voronin from 1867 to 1871 make no mention of Kargel at all.[4]

THE MOLOKAN CONNECTION

Martin Kalweit's letter of July 1869 did not tell of his baptizing on August 20, 1867 (o.s.) in the Kura River of Nikita I. Voronin (1840–1905), a merchant and elder in the Molokan community. This was the first baptism of a native Russian and marks the beginning of the Baptist movement among native Russians, almost two years before the first Ukrainian baptisms. The baptism occurred through the agency of Kalweit, a German Baptist, and Yakob D. Delyakov (1833–1898), a native of Persia,

---

2. For Kalweit's letter to Oncken, see *Missionsblatt*, Sep. 1869, 129–32. For an Eng. tr., see *BMM*, Jan. 1870, 19–21.

3. *Misssionblatt*, Sep., 1869, 129–32, and Dec. 1869, 162.

4. Kargel, *Zwischen den Enden der Erde unter Brüdern in Ketten*, viii. Val'kevich, 107, and App. 5:29. Pavlov, "Pravda o baptistakh," *Baptist*, Oct. 19, 1911, 337–38.

an evangelical Nestorian and baptized as an infant, who worked as an independent missionary among Russians.[5]

Molokans were a native Russian sect but divided into many sectarian divisions. Many of them lived in the Caucasus, forced to settle there by the government. They accepted the Scripture with the Apocrypha but rejected the sacraments and rites of the Orthodox Church. The great majority of them spiritualized the sacraments, thus observing no baptism or Lord's Supper. A small minority in what today is Azerbaijan, called "Water Molokans," however, accepted baptism and the Lord's Supper. Worship included reading the Bible, expounded by lay elders, a cappella singing with words from Scripture, and memorized prayer only from Scripture. In a letter in 1874, Johann Wieler described a Molokan service as follows: "To a monotonous tune they sing for hours a chapter, then pray a chapter kneeling, then again sing a chapter; thus they usually sing nine chapters standing, and pray nine chapters kneeling, all in chorus, and by memory." He noted that the service ended with bowing and the kiss of peace unrestricted between men and women.[6]

Molokans lacked a full Christology and rejected justification by faith since both faith and meritorious work were necessary for salvation. They adopted Jewish dietary laws, such as rejecting the eating of pork. They met in homes or halls, forbidden by the government to erect chapels. In a letter written about twenty years later, Voronin recounted that in 1863 he had met two Water Molokans, Nikita I. Severov and Yakob I. Tanasov, who encouraged him to seek the truth of salvation. In the mid-sixties he became acquainted with Delyakov, who helped him in his quest. When he felt fully convinced concerning his salvation, he wanted baptism without delay and instead of turning to the Water Molokans asked Delyakov to perform it. Delyakov refused, fearing his mission work among Molokans would be put in serious jeopardy. He suggested Kalweit do it. With his Molokan antecedents, Voronin at first resisted, declaring he could not allow a German who ate pork to baptize him. Delyakov said that Kalweit and his family were the only evangelical believers he knew and changed Voronin's mind. They went to Kalweit's home where they waited for Kalweit to return from his tinsmith shop. Delyakov served as interpreter since neither Kalweit nor Voronin knew each other's language. Kalweit was more than happy to baptize Voronin, who would be the first fruit from the native population. As customary with Baptists, Kalweit with his wife and Delyakov examined Voronin and then all four knelt in prayer. They then

---

5. For Delyakov's career, see his autobiography, "The Autobiography of Jacob Dilakoff," in installments in *The European Harvest Field* 16 (1935), Mar.–June, Sep.–Dec.

6. For a short survey of Molokan beliefs and divisions, see Bolshakoff, *Russian Nonconformity*, 105–12. Also see Diedrich, 231–34, and Delyakov, *The European Harvest Field*, June 1935, 10–11. For similarities and differences between Molokans and Baptists, see Khakhanov, "Molokane i baptisty Zakavkaz'ya," *Etnograficheskie obozrenie*, 1909/1, 45–46. For Wieler's account, see QR, July 1874, 6–7. For information on Water Molokans, see *Baptist*, Sep. 1908, 24.

PART THREE—Prospects: Ukrainian and Russian Beginnings, 1860–1884

went to the Kura River where Voronin was baptized. In the following year Kalweit baptized Voronin's wife.[7]

The Orthodox priest Nikolaï Kallistov later described Voronin as a man with dark hair, tall, and small bright black eyes. Kallistov wrote that Voronin had an excellent command of the Bible, was well read in the theological literature, a gifted speaker, and a successful businessman. At first Voronin and his wife met with Kalweit's group, but Voronin began to reach out to other Molokans. In 1869 he baptized two Molokan couples, forming on April 18, 1869, his own Russian Baptist congregation of six members. Soon afterwards Voronin baptized Semen G. Rodionov, a noted Molokan leader, and Gerasim U. Gorbachev.[8]

In 1871 the congregation gained two notable young men from Molokan families. One was Vasilii G. Pavlov, baptized with three others in April, which brought the membership, according to Pavlov to ten, but probably twelve. Later in October, Vasilii V. Ivanov, the other young man, was baptized. Pavlov and Ivanov will become the two leading Baptist missionaries from the Caucasus region.[9]

Vasilii G. Pavlov (1854–1924) was born in Vorontsovka, about one hundred miles southwest of Tiflis, the only child in the family. He was precocious, reading the Slavonic Bible at the age of five. In his youth he eagerly purchased books. He not only knew Russian but mastered German and was acquainted with other languages of the Caucasus and later in life learned English through self-study. At the age of sixteen, he became a shop assistant to Voronin in Tiflis. In spite of strong opposition from his parents, he was converted and baptized. Upon his conversion he began to witness and a short time later began to speak at Baptist gatherings. With the help of Kalweit, Pavlov went in May 1875 to Hamburg for training. Although no mission school operated in Hamburg at the time, Oncken provided him with the services of Peter Willrath, who instructed him in theology and German, opened preaching engagements for him, and gave him opportunity to participate in the life of the German Baptist Union. From the start, Oncken was impressed with Pavlov and wrote in 1875, "He is apparently strong and healthy in body, intelligent and anxious to increase his knowledge in every thing, and to make himself useful to the millions in his fatherland." After a year, Oncken in 1876 ordained Pavlov to serve as a missionary. On his return to Tiflis, Pavlov visited Stundo-Baptists in Ukraine. On his arrival home, the church had grown to forty members, which now included his parents.[10]

---

7. For Delyakov's own account of the baptism of Voronin, see Delyakov, *The European Harvest Field*, Sep. 1935, 11. For Voronin's letter on his baptism, see Val'kevich, App. 5:27.

8. Val'kevich, App. 5:27. Pavlov, "Pravda o baptistakh," *Baptist*, Oct. 19, 1911, 337–38. Kallistov, "Russkaya obshchina baptistov v Tiflise," *TsV*, 1879, no. 49, 2–5.

9. Pavlov, "Pravda o baptistakh," *Baptist*, Oct. 19, 1911, 337–38. Pavlov was in error in recording Ivanov's baptism in 1873; see *BV*, 1982, no. 1, 48.

10. For Pavlov's early life and career, see Pavloff, "The Christianizing of the World—Russia," Baptist World Alliance, Congress, *Proceedings*, 1911, 23–31; Rushbrooke, "Vasili Pavlov: A Russian Baptist Pioneer," *The Baptist Quarterly* 6/8 (Oct. 1933), 361–67; and Pavlov, "Vospominaniya ssyl'nago,"

Besides preaching, Pavlov now opened a Sunday school, introduced Bible studies, presided at the church's business meetings, and kept its minutes. In the fall of 1876, he and Semen Rodionov traveled by horse and oxen in the Caucasus in what today are Armenia and Azerbaijan, reaching the Caspian Sea. Authorities arrested them for spreading Lutheranism, and on their return to Tiflis Pavlov denied the charge. At the end of 1877 Pavlov married.

Pavlov was a rising star in Baptist ranks. In an article in 1886, V. Zavitnevich, an Orthodox writer, stated that without exaggeration one could describe Pavlov as "a star of the first magnitude" in the sectarian world. He claimed Pavlov, while still a shop assistant, showed rare ability in public disputes with the Molokans. The article included a lengthy description of Pavlov at age thirty from a certain V. P., who had personally heard Pavlov. V. P. described Pavlov as one of medium height, thin, with a dark complexion, a long, lean face, and sporting clean-shaved sides and a black beard. He tried somewhat to downgrade Pavlov, stating, although he received a good education, he did not impress one as coming from the professional class and failed to display strength of character or will. On the other hand, V. P. admitted that with his loud and sonorous voice Pavlov spoke with unusual energy and conviction, keeping his audience at close attention for two hours. He contrasted Pavlov with Voronin, declaring that the latter tried to move his hearers to weeping.[11]

Vasiliĭ V. Ivanov (1846–1919), the other Molokan youth baptized in 1871, was only second to Pavlov in mission outreach. Because of persecution in Tambov *guberniya,* his father, Efim Trefilovich Klyshnikov, moved to the Caucasus, adopting the name of Vasiliĭ Semenovich Ivanov. His son Vasiliĭ carried the name Ivanov, while the grandson, Pavel, hyphenated the name to Ivanov-Klyshnikov. Ivanov spent his childhood in the village of Novoivanovka, Elisavetpol *guberniya,* south of Georgia, today in Azerbaijan. When seventeen, he lost his father and as the oldest child was forced with his mother to assume family responsibilities.[12]

In 1872 and 1873, Ivanov and Pavlov traveled among Molokans in evangelistic tours that included Novoivanovka where Ivanov established the next congregation after Tiflis. In the latter year Ivanov traveled as far as Lenkoran, today in Azerbaijan, on the Caspian Sea. In 1879 the Tiflis church sent Ivanov to Baku *guberniya,* where in the following year he established the Baku congregation that he pastored for thirty-seven years, almost to the time of his death.[13]

---

in Vladimir D. Bonch-Bruevich, *Materialy k istorii i izucheniyu rosskago sektantsva i raskola* (SPB, 1908), 1:1–24; and Val'kevich, 108. For an extended bibliography on Pavlov, see Wardin, *Evangelical Sectarianism,* 153–57. For Oncken's remarks, see *QR,* Oct. 1875, 3.

11. Zavitnevich, "Svedaniya o dvizhenii yuzhno-russkago sektantstva v" poslednie gody," *TrKDA,* 1886, no. 11, 506–8. Also in Rozhdestvenskiĭ, 140, ft. 3.

12. For a biography of Ivanov, see Sokolov, "V. V. Ivanov," *BV,* 1982, no. 1, 47–52. For the change of the family name, see the footnote in *Baptist,* 1925/3, 8.

13. *BV,* 1982, no. 1, 49. *Istoriya,* 78, 498.

PART THREE—Prospects: Ukrainian and Russian Beginnings, 1860–1884

At the beginning of their careers, Pavlov and Ivanov were close co-workers, but the two will represent different trends within the Baptist community. After his return from Hamburg, Pavlov introduced the standards of faith and practice of the German Baptists, while Ivanov, as well as Voronin, were more traditional and closer to Molokan roots. Pavlov contended that the day of worship (the Sabbath) was from midnight to midnight, as in the West, while other Caucasian Baptists followed the Molokan and Jewish custom of reckoning it from sunset to sunset. In his unpublished memoirs now in the State Museum of the History of Religion in St. Petersburg, Ivanov admitted that, although with cultural differences German and Russian Baptists expressed the same faith, the former, however, wished to discard such Molokan practices as singing the Psalms and bowing during prayer and singing. Ivanov continued to urge a more Russian path of spirituality and avoid simply looking to the West for doctrinal standards.[14]

In an article in 1908 in the Russian periodical, *Baptist*, Ivanov went so far as to present a counter thesis to the views of Bishop Alexiï that German Baptists brought the Baptist movement to Russia, stating that the Baptist movement had its roots already in the 1840s and 1850s among the Molokans.

Ivanov claimed that from a study of Scripture a group of "Water Molokans" in Azerbaijan accepted baptism and the Lord's Supper. Vasiliï M. Sitnikov from Lenkoran carried the new views to the Volga where he organized something of a mission circle. Without documentation, Ivanov stated that Voronin became "enamored" with the teaching of the Water Molokans and thus was prepared to accept baptism from Kalweit. Ivanov, however, far overstated the influence of the Water Molokans on Voronin. In Voronin's own account of his baptism, he states that in 1864 he was in contact with Water Molokans who directed his attention to the need for baptism, but at the time he instead turned his attention to find salvation with the help of Delyakov. Voronin will not turn to the Water Molokans for baptism and will develop his own Baptist group apart from them.[15]

Ivanov also claimed that in the organization of the Tiflis church Pavlov borrowed only some features from the Germans, which also somewhat distorts the picture. For Ivanov the true roots of Russian Baptists sprang from the unique religious life of the Russian people themselves in their search for the one true path to God through the Holy Spirit and the assistance of the New Testament in the native tongue.

Congregatonal Relations

In 1877 the Tiflis congregation moved into the newly constructed home of Voronin, which was in a more visible section of the city. The church was drawing a diverse

---

14. *MO*, Sep. 1900, 21. See Coleman, *Russian Baptists and Spiritual Revolution, 1905–1929*, 96–97, on Ivanov's views.

15. Ivanov, "Kniga episkopa Aleksiya," *Baptist*, Sep. 1908, 23–27. Val'kevich, App. 5, 27. Also see Diedrich, 236–37.

group of both the educated and the uneducated. At the outbreak of the Russo-Turkish War in 1877, the congregation provided two female nurses and two male medical attendants, who received the insignia of the Red Cross.[16]

While the Tiflis Russian church was doing well under Voronin and Pavlov, the German-Russian congregation under Kalweit was beginning to disintegrate. The Kalweit group divided over its relations with the Voronin body. According to a letter of Pavlov to Ivanov in 1873, Kalweit, his wife, two of his first cousins, and Kielblock (absent now in Yerevan) were favorable toward fellowship with Voronin's body. On the other side, Kalweit's brother, Karl, his sister, Henrieta, another male, and three other women refused fellowship with this body, even looking on them as not reborn. Kalweit, losing support because of emigration, soon joined the Voronin congregation where he became a respected member. Kalweit was especially helpful in music, using melodies from the hymnal, *Dukhovnye pesni*, and taught the worshipers to sing.[17]

According to Val'kevich, the Orthodox historian, an intense rivalry erupted between Voronin and Pavlov. Voronin wished to maintain more of the Molokan tradition, while Pavlov sought to introduce the dogmatic and organizational standards of the German Baptists. The conflict came to a head at the time of the recognition by the state of Baptists as a legal body.[18]

In light of the 1879 recognition, state authorities in Tiflis believed the Tiflis congregation, composed of non-Orthodox members with Molokan antecedents and some Germans, was eligible for recognition and asked for a Baptist representative. On October 7, 1879, the Baptist conference in Tiflis with delegates from the Tiflis church and only one other congregation approved the election of a presbyter and formation of one Baptist congregation for the entire Caucasus. On October 21 the Tiflis church then elected Pavlov as its presbyter, arguing, even if other congregations did not approve one presbyter for all, it might be deprived the right of preaching if a presbyter were not ready to be confirmed by the government. On December 13 the church elected Pavlov, Voronin, and two others to represent the church before the government.[19]

Only three days later on December 16 matters reached another level. At a business meeting of the Tiflis church, Pavlov brought a disciplinary charge against Voronin. Voronin was a partner in a trading company that loaned money at interest and was accused for being a hypocrite in the light of his earlier stand of taking interest as sinful. The charge was made even though earlier in October the church, although declaring the taking of interest from the poor was sinful, had approved as lawful the taking of moderate interest in business. Voronin was taken by surprise. He heatedly raised his voice and said "What?" He declared that he had provided his own home as a

16. QR., Oct 1878, 8–9. *Missionsblatt*, Sep. 1878, 164. *Baptist*, Oct. 19, 1911, 338, and Oct. 26, 1911, 345.
17. Val'kevich, 108, and App. 5:1. *Istoriya*, 75–76.
18. Val'kevich, 108.
19. Ibid., 112–13, and App. 1:38–40.

meeting place and had helped Pavlov when only an apprentice to get a start in life. Voronin stated he invested in the company not to gain interest but for a business return and was willing to return his interest to the poor brethren. If the church judged his actions sinful, he would return his money. Kalweit felt that since Voronin promised to return his money he should be forgiven. But the Pavlov party prevailed, and Voronin was excluded from the congregation. Voronin contended that Pavlov brought the charge maliciously to remove any competition for presbyter for the Caucasus. In a vote for such a position, Voronin would probably have won, receiving support from Baptists outside Tiflis. P. Z. Easton, the Presbyterian missionary and friend of Pavlov, wrote that division occurred because of the effort of "a man of means," i.e., Voronin, "to control the congregation," a statement that clearly indicates a power struggle.[20]

A schism now occurred with Pavlov heading the Tiflis congregation and Voronin his own followers. The Pavlov body excluded supporters of Voronin, and the Voronin body excluded leaders of the Pavlov party. Outside of Tiflis, Baptists condemned the exclusion of Voronin, thus bringing the division elsewhere. Ivanov fraternized with Voronin and as a consequence lost his mission support from the Tiflis church.[21]

The schism occurred on the eve of the recognition by the government of Baptists in Tiflis. The Tiflis congregation invited August Liebig from Odessa and Ivan Kargel, now leaving his charge in St. Petersburg for Bulgaria, to assist the church in organizing on August 17, 1880 (o.s.) as a regular Baptist church. Liebig, who presided, began to give theological instruction but was cut short when the congregation declared it was already familiar with Baptist principles. As early as 1873, the Tiflis church had ordered from Odessa the German Baptist confession of faith, which Pavlov proposed to translate, and a history of Baptists. Liebig then explained the purpose of the German Baptist Union, which the congregation agreed to join. The church accepted Pavlov as presbyter, Rodionov as teacher, and Andreï Mazaev and Kalweit as deacons. Liebig and Kargel ordained them in the evening. The government recognized the Pavlov church as the First Baptist Church of Tiflis and the Voronin body as the Second Baptist Church of the city with Voronin as presbyter.[22]

With the realization that the schism was hurting Baptist work and the desire for reconciliation, in July 1882 the Voronin body joined the First church. It was stipulated, however, that Pavlov would be recognized as presbyter, and Voronin returned as an ordinary member. With permission of the censor, Voronin published in the same year in Tiflis a hymnal, *Golos very* (The Voice of Faith), which was designed as a collection of spiritual songs and Psalms for the Baptist church and home services. V. N. Treskovskiĭ, an editor and teacher at the Tiflis First Gymnasium, edited the

---

20. Ibid., 113, and App. 1:37–38, 40–41. *TsV*, Aug. 9, 1880, 5. *BMM*, Feb, 1883, 36.
21. Val'kevich, 113, and App. 1:43–45.
22. Ibid., 109, 113–14, and App 1:45–47. *TsV*, Aug. 9, 1880, 5. *Baptist*, Oct. 26, 1911, 345.

volume for which he was paid 240 rubles. The volume found its way into Ukraine, but in 1886 a government circular forbade its circulation.[23]

Because of its strength and strong leadership, the Tiflis church became a leading center of Baptist work to which other Baptists inside and outside the Caucasus looked for counsel. Even Ratushnyĭ in the Osnova church in Kherson *guberniya* in Ukraine communicated with it. The church began a missionary treasury and provided missionary support. It was the first Russian church to hold a church conference, even though only one other church sent representation.[24]

Church Life

During the division, the two congregations met in separate areas—the Pavlov group in the soldier's market while the Voronin group in a residence in the Churguretakh area. Baptists also held meetings in other areas, such as in Kakakh, a wealthy sector of the city, or in Molokan villages at the edge of the city.[25]

Baptists congregated on Sundays and Wednesdays as well as other days, meeting at nine in the morning and seven in the evening. Services included the reading of Scripture by the elder or one chosen from the congregation, a sermon, singing and extemporaneous prayer with worshipers standing with bowed head and folded arms. Sermons related to the Scripture. The service ended with a final benediction.

Worshipers sat on benches, men on the right and women on the left. During the service, women were to cover their heads. In observing the kiss of peace, the church forbade kissing between men and women. As other Baptists, the church rejected footwashing and anointing.[26]

The church expected worshipers to observe complete silence, no speaking or turning around. At the entrance was a statement on proper conduct, including the need to remain until the end of the service as not to disturb others. Once while Pavlov was preaching, stressing the words of Christ to preach the gospel to the whole world, he incidentally declared that baptism was a symbol, not a means of rebirth, and no godparent could substitute for a child at baptism. A simple Russian peasant suddenly interrupted by shouting aloud: "The Lord punishes you for such a lie." Very quickly members of the congregation picked up the offender and ejected him from the meeting. A service, however, might lead worshipers crying out for grace. On one such occasion while preaching among Molokans in Taurida, Pavlov asked those so moved to stand for prayer and then asked all to kneel. It was reported everyone was so moved

23. Val'kevich, 117–18, and App. 1:40, ft. 1, and 52–54.
24. Ibid., 110, 112, 115, and App. 1:33–34, 37–38.
25. *TsV*, Aug. 9, 1880, 4.
26. Ibid., 5. Val'kevich, 112, and App. 1:38.

that "no eye remained dry." As already noted, Voronin was also noted for moving his hearers emotionally."[27]

Baptists observed the Lord's Supper twelve times a year, the first Sunday of each month. Kallistov, the Orthodox priest, recorded that Baptists regarded the Supper as a symbol, rejecting the transubstantiation of the elements, but yet feeling they received Christ spiritually. Tiflis Baptists held a love feast at least once a year, if not more. The Pavlov congregation invited Kallistov to attend a love feast on February 19, 1880 (o.s.), the nineteenth anniversary of the emancipation of the serfs and to commemorate the twenty-fifth anniversary of the reign of Alexander II. It was a festive occasion with colored lamps decorating the entrance. Two rows of large dinner tables laden with an abundance of desserts and other tasty morsels replaced the benches. Conversation was convivial. The service included singing spiritual songs, three speeches, one each from Pavlov, Treskovskiĭ, and Abraham Amirkhanianz, an evangelical Armenian. Treskovkiĭ spoke on the Great Reforms and lauded Alexander for the publication of the Bible in Russian and granting in 1879 legal recognition to Baptists. The love feast ended with a prayer of thanksgiving and a benediction.[28]

The church received new members on their confession of faith, followed quickly by baptism. As in Germany, the Tiflis church exercised strict discipline. The Presbyterian missionary, P. Z. Easton, noted that some individuals accused Russian Baptists of exercising discipline for trivial matters, but at the same time, while admitting something of the truth of the charge, yet lauded them for their effort to follow Scriptural principles compared to the laxness of others. The church admonished members to avoid tempting food and drink as well as smoking. It prohibited marriage with non-believers and the disfellowshiped as well as burial of the same. Riding to church with animals was breaking the Sabbath, but the church made exception for those who lived at a great distance or in poor health.[29] Anyone could be subjected to discipline. Even Treskovskiĭ was repeatedly excluded for wrongful behavior. The church charged him of needlessly piling up debt. In 1879 it restored him on his promise of payment of his liabilities and requested that he list his debtors and obligations. In 1885, Otto, the son of Kalweit, was brought before the church for smoking and playing billiards. Although he acknowledged his wrong doing, the church nevertheless excluded him for his betrothal to a non-believer, in this case a Lutheran. His sister, Ottiliya (Ottilie), intended to marry an officer, but with her declaration that the wedding would not occur the congregation expressed its gratitude for her "repentance and courage." Ottilie will later marry the Armenian evangelical Sembat Bagdasarjanz.[30]

---

27. *TsV*, Aug. 9, 1880, 5. *WHZ*, May 1, 1882, 90.

28. *TsV*, Aug. 9, 1880, 6–7.

29. *BMM*, Feb., 1883, 35. Val'kevich, 111–12, and App. 1:37–38. For reception of members, see App. 1:45, 49.

30. Val'kevich, 116, and App. 1:40, ft. 1, and 61–62.

The congregation was also concerned about economic behavior. As noted, it excluded Voronin, allegedly accepting usury and his hypocrisy over the matter, and Tserkovskiĭ over debt. In 1890 the church established an economic council that provided support for members who faced loss or ruin in business enterprises because of imprudence or lack of capital.[31]

Men dominated the business meetings and filled the offices. Women participated in church meetings, speaking out on occasion and giving their own confessions of faith.

Misssion Expansion

The broad spread of the Baptist movement from Tiflis was remarkable in its rapidity from the early 1870s to the early 1880s. By the latter date the movement had spread over much of the Trans-Caucasus, crossed the Caucasus into the Terek and Kuban *guberniyii*, and was reaching up the Volga into Samara and westward into the Don region and as far as Taurida *gubeniya* in southern Ukraine. As German Baptists and Ukrainian stundists, the Russian Baptists in the Caucasus also produced a coterie of young zealous missionaries, such as Pavlov, Ivanov, and E. M. Bogdanov, who itinerated and formed congregations.

As elsewhere in the empire, the spread of Scripture helped prepare the way. Not only Melville in Odessa and Delyakov in Ukraine, Baptist colporteurs were important purveyors as well. Easton, the Presbyterian missionary, wrote in 1883 that top officials of the British and Foreign Bible Society (BFBS) told him the zeal of Baptists in Scriptural distribution far outpaced the Lutherans. Easton also felt that the Baptist school in Hamburg and the publications of Charles Haddon Spurgeon also strengthened the Baptist cause. At first travel for missionaries was by horse, but in 1883 the opening of a Transcaucasian railroad between the Black and Caspian Seas made travel easier. Pavlov took advantage of the railroad one day after it opened.[32]

With their own Molokan heritage, the Baptists in the Caucasus used the bridge of the scattered Molokan population to gain converts. Baptists faced little or no interference from the government in evangelizing a non-Orthodox body. As in St. Petersburg, the Orthodox attempted to thwart Baptists through public disputation, such as in Vladikavkaz, but with no evident success. The recognition in 1879 of Baptists as a legal entity was a benefit. Aside from the very early leaders, other notable leaders from Molokan ranks appeared, such as Deï and Gavriil Mazaev, Fedor P. Balikhin, Ivan S. Prokhanov, and Il'ya A. Golyaev.

The Baptist penetration among the Molokans included both opportunities and obstacles. Although Baptists and Molokans possessed a number of affinities, rejecting the sacraments, rites, and traditions of the Orthodox Church, the acceptance of

31. Ibid., App. 1:65–66. Klibanov, 262–63.
32. *BMM*, Feb., 1883, 34–35. WHZ, Sep. 15, 1883, 185.

baptism was a great stumbling block for many Molokans. Pavlov noted that in Molokan thought the accepting of believer's baptism was rejecting its own pure spiritual teaching that rejected the external and was thus a step back toward Orthodoxy with its rituals. In their hostility, Molokans sometimes took violent measures, such as beatings, to prevent a family member from immersion. In his review of sectarians, V. Zavitnevich claimed that to stem the Baptist tide Molokans resorted "not only to moral but also crudely material means."[33]

For Molokans who became Baptists, the Baptist movement, besides incorporating such rites as baptism and the Lord's Supper, also brought a dynamic lacking in traditional Molokanism. Baptist worship was far more spontaneous and lively with its evangelistic and expository preaching, extemporaneous prayers, and rhythmical singing. Unlike Molokanism, Baptists had a full Christology and preached the doctrine of justification by faith alone.[34] Baptists represented the new spirit of personal decision and accountability, rejecting the traditional communalism of the past. Baptists also had organizational skills that included full-time and part-time pastors, trained missionaries, and a missionary organization and program.

Baptists crossed northward across the Caucasus to Vladikavkaz (Ordzhonikidze) in the late 1870s with the settlement there of E. M. Bogdanov from Tiflis who formed a circle of believers. I. N. Skorokhodov also worked with Bogdanov. In 1879 Pavlov visited the town and baptized some believers. The police incarcerated him for three days, forcing him on the first night to mingle with common criminals from the street. Vladikavkaz will become an important Baptist center, attracting the Molokan Prokhanov family from which Ivan S. Prokhanov will emerge later as the leader of the Evangelical Christian movement. Bogdanov also worked in Kuban and in the Taurida *guberniya*.[35]

The Taurida *guberniya* in Ukraine near the Mennonite colony of Molochna became an important field of Baptist advance. Molokans had settled here in three villages in the 1820s, growing to 10,000 by the 1890s. Molokans had divided into five sects, three of them basically Molokan (including Pryguny or Jumpers); two of them, called Don sects, had adopted sacraments, including infant baptism.[36] Delyakov, the evangelical Nestorian from Persia, will become an influential evangelist among the Molokans in this area. In 1863 the Nestorians had ordained him a deacon and then in 1867 with consent of the Protestant missionaries ordained him a minister. In 1862 he had worked among Nestorians in Tiflis but later began work as an independent

---

33. *Baptist*, Oct. 19, 1911, 338. Zavitnevich, *TrKDA*, 1886, no. 11, 507.

34. For a Baptist convert's view on Molokan Christology, see Uspenskiĭ, *Polnoe sobranie sochenenii*, 8:209, quoted in Klibanov, 27.

35. Val'kevich, 110. *BV*, 1945, no. 3, 29. *Istoriya*, 77–78.

36. For information on the Molokans in the Molochna area, see "Donskie tolki v molokanstve i v stundizme," *MO*, 1897, Nov. (1), 991–1007. Also see Delyakov's description in *The European Harvest Field*, June 1935, 9–11.

missionary and colporteur in Ukraine and Bessarabia, supporting himself as a peddler of household goods. After suffering arrest twice, he began in 1867 concentrating his work among the Molokans in Taurida, where he already had some success the year before.[37]

Because of the impact of Pashkovite and stundist influence and Delyakov's activity, a second Don sect arose, known as New Molokans or Christians of the Evangelical Faith. Their center was the village of Astrakhanka in the district of Berdyansk. Their leader was Zinoviï D. Zakharov, a wealthy landowner and later member of the Russian Duma. Except for infant baptism and footwashing, their beliefs and worship were very similar to Baptists.[38]

Baptists also entered the area. In 1877 they won Alexeï A. Stoyalov, son of a Molokan elder, and in 1878 Ivan I. Popov who in turn was baptized by Johann Wieler. In 1880 Stoyalov organized a conference at Novovasil'evka in which Pavlov and Wieler spoke as well as holding conversations with Molokans. In August 1881 Wieler baptized ten believers. In October a love feast was held in Novovasil'evka attended by Pavlov as well as by Wieler and Peter M. Friesen, both of whom at the time were teachers at the Mennonite school in Halbstadt in the neighboring Molochna Colony. Bogdanov and Voronin also ministered in the area. Baptists organized churches in Novovasil'evka, Astrakhanka, and Novospasskoe.[39]

In 1881 Pavlov returned, noting that from his first visit the church in Novovasil'evka had grown from fourteen members to 100 and at a cost of 1,600 rubles had converted a mansion into a prayer house of 500 seats. He worked for two months, often preaching before large crowds, gaining converts who "wept bitterly" over their sins. After visiting Einlage in the Mennonite Colony, preaching in both Russian and German, and visiting several other villages, he returned to Astrakhanka for the consecration of the new chapel of the New Molokans. Because of remarks by Abraham Amirkhanianz, the evangelical Armenian, on the necessity of infant baptism and from discussion of others on the subject, Pavlov with Stoyalov and V. R. Kolodin debated Amirkhanianz and Zakharov before a crowd of 500 up to midnight for three hours or more.[40]

The Baptist influence was becoming so strong that Ivan G. Mazaev, whose sons Deï and Gavriil will become Baptists, called the Molokans to a meeting to discuss measures to restrain Molokans from becoming Baptists. The assembly decided to accept such Baptist principles as examination, exclusion, and heart prayer but not their view of baptism.[41] Delyakov, who had continued to accept infant baptism, began

37. For Delyakov's ministry in Ukraine and Bessarabia, see his autobiography in *The European Harvest Field*, May 1935, 12–16, and June 1935, 8–9. Also see the letter of Delykov to Pashkov, Nov. 2, 1884, as recorded in Dyck, 58.

38. For information on the New Molokans, see Klibanov, 210; *Istoriya*, 71; and Skvortsov, *Missionerskoe posokh* (SPB, 1912), part 1, 289–92.

39. *Istoriya*, 71–72. WHZ, May 1, 1882, 90. *Baptist*, Oct. 26, 1911, 345–46.

40. BMM, Sep., 1883, 344–46. Val'kevich, App. 5:8.

41. Val'kevich, App. 5:8.

PART THREE—Prospects: Ukrainian and Russian Beginnings, 1860–1884

to debate the issue in his own mind. Finally in 1886 he accepted believer's baptism and joined a Baptist church. This decision helped him to become more acceptable to Baptists.[42]

A critical need for Baptist work was monetary support for itinerant missionaries. At first Pavlov received no mission support. In 1877 he wrote that as the only child he lived at home and worked nine months of the year in business with his father. In 1880 he reported that his father's business was not doing well. Two years later he wrote that with the reversal of his father's fortunes and illness and the inability of the Tiflis church (only barely able to maintain its prayer hall) to provide support, he was forced to work to support his wife and two children. He also wrote that his business brought in no income, he was beset with debt, and he must spend time at home to keep his household from going to pieces. He complained to the Baptist brethren in Germany about his need in 1880 and again in 1882, pointing out that in all Russia not one Russian preacher can spend full time in ministry.[43]

In 1879 the Tiflis church divided its treasury into general and missionary funds. In 1879 Baptist congregations in Baku *guberniya* promised to pay one half of Ivanov's salary with the other half paid by F. V. Bergeman, a Lutheran friend in Prussia, a contributor to Baptist work on the continent.[44]

At the Mennonite Brethren-stundist conference in Rückenau in Taurida *guberniya* in 1882, Pavlov was appointed missionary for one year with a small salary. Pavlov also moved with his family from Tiflis to Vladikavkaz to be more centrally located for his mission work. In the fall of 1883 Pavlov went to Samara *guberniya* where he baptized sixteen believers. In the following year he traveled to the Don Cossacks where V. V. Ivanov had already begun a revival movement. Pavlov also baptized converts here, laying the foundation of Baptist work among the Cossacks.[45]

Pavlov's mission activity included a trip to Saratov on the Volga; in recrossing the Volga he went eastward to the steppes of the Kazakhs, returning to Tiflis in 1885. At the Baptist congress of 1884 at Novo-Vasil'evka, he was appointed one of the evangelists, receiving support from Vasilii Pashkov in St. Petersburg. Rozhdestvenskii reported in the mid-1880s that Pavlov received 600 rubles from abroad and 200 from the Tiflis church.[46]

In their mission work, Baptists were strong protagonists for their cause. P. Z. Easton reported that two top agents of the BFBS, although appreciating the energetic work of Baptist colporteurs, had commented "that there was a certain narrowness in

---

42. *The European Harvest Field*, Oct. 1935, 13, 18. Also see Delyakov's correspondence with Pashkov on the issue of baptism in Dyck, 58.

43. *BMM*, Mar. 1878, 83. *QR*, Oct. 1880, 2–4, and July 1882, 11–12. *WHZ*, May 1, 1881, 90.

44. Val'kevich, 110, and App. 1:33.

45. *BV*, 1945, no. 3, 30. *BMM*, Feb. 1885, 47.

46. *BMM*, Sep. 1883, 344, and Apr. 1884, 103. *Baptist*, Oct. 26, 1911, 346. Rozhdestvenskii, 140, ft. 3.

the brethren in their relations with Christians of other denominations."[47] Baptists, however, were not an exclusive cult but recognized that genuine Christians may exist in other denominations. Baptists felt very close to Mennonite Brethren. They could express warm fraternal feelings toward evangelicals who were in accord with them in revivalism and conversion but with whom they disagreed on baptism, such as with pietists, stundists, Presbyterians (as Easton and Melville), New Molokans, evangelical Nestorians (as Delyakov), evangelical Armenians (as Amirkhanianz), and Pashkovites. In 1885 Pavlov held some meetings in Tiflis that included Easton, Amirkhanianz, and Easton's assistant, Moses, a Nestorian evangelical.[48]

When Kalweit wrote his letter to Oncken in 1869 that he said he was enclosing seven rubles for evangelization in Spain and three for China, missions far away, he himself did not realize he was helping to lay in the Russian Empire a mission field that would reverberate throughout the empire. But it did not seem that way at first. The beginnings of Baptist work in the Caucasus were indeed small. In 1869 Kalweit's group had only thirteen while Voronin's only eight. The Baptist movement from the Caucasus had grown by 1883 to a bit over 400 members with, according to Pavlov, about 150 in Transcaucasus, 107 in Terek *guberniya*, and 150 in Taurida *guberniya*. The report of Pobedonostsev in 1884 reported 529 Baptists in Trans-Caucasus.[49] Its growth was primarily from Molokans, and it failed to make inroads in the German and the Russian Orthodox communities. Even though it started a decade later, it did not exhibit the same Baptist success as other areas at this time—3,500 Baptists in the Baltic; 6,000 German Baptists in Poland and Ukraine; or 5,000 Ukrainian stundists (2,000 in Kiev *guberniya* and 3,000 in Kherson *guberniya*). Nevertheless with its strong leaders who were willing to go far afield in the preaching of the gospel, the Baptist movement from the Caucasus will in time be one of the strongest contributing streams to evangelicalism in the whole Empire and will help to bring cohesion to the Baptist movement as a whole.[50]

47. *BMM*, Feb. 1883, 35.
48. Ibid., Aug. 1885, 342.
49. *Missionsblatt*, Sep. 1869, 130. Val'kevich, App. 5, 29. *Baptist*, Oct. 19, 1911, 337–38. *BMM*, 1883, 346. Procurator of the Holy Synod, *Report*, 1884, 221.
50. German Baptist Union, *Statistik*, 1884, 18, 20. Rozhdestvenskiĭ, 145–49.

PART FOUR

Prospects

The Aristocratic Impulse, 1874–1884

14

The Radstock Phenomenon

IN THE SPRING OF 1874, evangelical Christianity suddenly and surprisingly entered into the ranks of the Russian aristocracy in St. Petersburg. The penetration of evangelicalism in the 1850s and 1860s was primarily among the lower classes in the borderlands. Many of the first adherents were non-Russians—Germans, Swedes, and Latvians—along with some Ukrainian peasants and Russians from the Molokan sect. In contrast, the adherents of the Radstock movement were from the ranks of high society in the capital with ties to the center of imperial power. The Orthodox reviewer of the movement, G. I. Terletskiĭ, noted the stark contrast, recognizing that one could not point to uneducated and unskilled commoners as a source, which generally portrayed sectarian movements. Unlike the first leaders of evangelicalism in the empire, the initiator, Lord Radstock (1833–1913) was an English nobleman, not ordained, claimed no allegiance to any denomination, spoke no Russian or German but instead English and French.[1]

Lord Radstock (in Russia, called Lord Redstock), otherwise known as Granville Augustus William Waldegrave, Third baron Radstock, came from a distinguished line, including a grandfather, a vice admiral in the British navy. Radstock attended Harrow and Balliol College in Oxford, receiving an MA degree with honors in history

---

1. A standard Russian Orthodox work on the Radstock-Pashkov movement is Terletskiĭ, *Sekta pashkovtsev*. The most scholarly study of the movement in a Western Language is Heier, *Religious Schism in the Russian Aristocracy, 1860–1900*. A comparatively recent and well-researched thesis is Corrado, "The Philosophy of Ministry of Colonel Vasily Pashkov," which has been published in Russian as *Filosofiya sluzheniya polkovnika Pashkova*. For a bibliographic listing of the Radstock-Pashkov movement, including both Russian and Western sources, see Wardin, *Evangelical Sectarianism*, 287–315.

PART FOUR—Prospects: The Aristocratic Impulse, 1874–1884

and second honors in physical science. Between 1860 and 1866 he was colonel commandant of the West Middlesex Volunteers. Upon the death of his father in 1857, he inherited his title at the age of twenty-four. Under the influence of the evangelical revival in England, he relinquished his position as commandant and with his substantial fortune began in 1866 a full-time life of lay ministry.[2]

Although a member of the Church of England, he considered himself simply a member of the universal church of Christ. He was "low church" in his evangelical views. Baptism and the Lord's Supper were of no sacramental significance; the former was only a "public declaration" and the latter only a commemoration."[3] Although closely associated with the Open Brethren branch of Plymouth Brethren, he never formally joined this group and will later separate from it.[4] His preaching centered on justification by faith; good works did not produce salvation but were its fruit. Evangelism was his first priority, but he also encouraged the knowledge and distribution of Scripture, prayer, personal witness, and social work among the poor and needy. Radstock lived a simple life of self-denial. At times he was impetuous as well as single minded, lacking in give and take in conversation, and careless in dress, yet a man of moral principle and fully devoted to his calling.[5]

In 1867 he attended the Fifth General Conference of the Evangelical Alliance in Amsterdam in The Netherlands and held successful meetings in the country. In 1868 he conducted his first meetings in Paris, a ministry he continued there until the end of his life. He also ministered in French Swizerland and eventually will cover much of Europe, visit the USA, and between 1880 and 1910 undertook seven trips to India.[6]

Before Radstock's arrival, some members of the St. Petersburg aristocracy were already attracted to evangelicalism. In a lengthy article in 1864 on religious progress in Russia, the writer claimed that Russians of the upper class were enamored with English institutions and many of those who traveled abroad attended English churches. He wrote of meeting a Russian princess who had translated the life of Hannah More into Russian, and while in Moscow met a Princess Lieven and her daughter, who showed a great interest in missions in India. In England, Russian aristocrats attended the "Drawing Room Mission" of Sir Arthur Blackwood (1832–1893), who became financial secretary of the Post Office in 1874 and then secretary in 1880. In

---

2. For a biography of Radstock, including his beliefs and personal characteristics, see Trotter, *Lord Radstock, an Interpretation and a Record*. A somewhat objective but still critical work of Radstock and his ministry in Russia is by the Orthodox literary figure Leskov, *Velikosveskii raskol*; translated into English and edited by Muckle as, *Schism in High Society*. For a short but helpful account of his background and ministry, see Jones, "Dostoyevsky, Tolstoy, Leskov and Redstokizm," *Journal of Russian Studies* 13 (1972), 3–4.

3. Leskov, *Schism in High Society*, 159.

4. Coad, *History of the Brethren Movement*, 193.

5. For Radstock's personal characteristics, see Trotter, 22, 58–60, 71, 73–74, 101, 105–107, 120–21, 134–35, 151–52.

6. Trotter, 141. Jones, 3–4.

1862 he began publishing his Bible addresses. Aristocratic women who attended the Blackwood meetings included Madame Elizaveta Ivanova Chertkova, Princess Nathalie Lieven, and her sister Princess Vera Gagarina von der Pahlen. The latter two experienced personal conversion in the meetings.[7]

In Paris and in the area of Lake Geneva in French Switzerland visiting Russian aristocrats also had the opportunity of hearing the gospel from foreign evangelicals. One was Reginald Radcliffe (1825–1895), a solicitor from Liverpool England, who beginning in 1859 became an active evangelist. In 1861 with another evangelist, he held meetings with an interpreter in Paris and then in the following year in the region of Lake Geneva. As a result of six weeks of Radcliffe's meetings in Paris in 1867, a French banker organized in thirteen districts of Paris groups for reading and prayer. Lord Radstock led one of them. Radstock also ministered in French Switzerland. Terletskiĭ claimed Radstock arrived in 1872 in Vevey on Lake Geneva where he not only preached but with the help of his mother and sister accosted foreigners, including Russian women, to attend the services. Another source records that in the following year Radstock with other Englishmen and two pastors of the Union of Evangelical Free Churches in France, which had separated from the Reformed Church, held services in French Switzerland that were attended by Russian aristocratic women.[8]

For ten years Radstock had hoped to enter Russia and began to despair it would ever happen. The door, however, finally opened with an invitation from one or more of the aristocratic women. Nikolaĭ Leskov believed that the invitation came from Yulia Zasetskaya, who came to know Radstock in London and was one of his most ardent supporters in St. Petersburg. A number of sources point instead to Elizaveta Chertkova for whom Radstock provided spiritual help in her grief over the loss of two sons. In any case, Radstock arrived in St. Petersburg during Holy Week in 1874 with supporters awaiting his arrival.[9]

Some of Radstock's friends thought that the authorities would not allow him to speak or, even if permitted, comparatively few would benefit from his coming. He began services in the American Chapel, speaking in both French and English. Soon after his arrival, he received an urgent call from England that his mother was dying and should return, but he felt compelled to continue his mission. Radstock not only received a warm reception from his friends, but crowds began to attend the six to seven public services he held weekly in the chapel. Radstock received numerous

---

7. *BMM*, Mar. 1865, 84–89. Lieven, *Eine Saat, die reiche Frucht brachte*, 12–13. *Dein Reich Komme*, July–Aug. 1923, 156. For the career of Blackwood, see "Sir (Stevenson) Arthur Blackwood," *Oxford Dictionary of National Biography*, 6:37–38.

8. For information on Radcliffe's evangelistic career, see Radcliffe, *Recollections of Reginald Radcliffe*, and Orr, *The Second Evangelical Awakening in Britain*, 157–61, 235–36. For Radcliffe's meetings in Paris and French Switzerland, see Radcliffe, 158–76, 179–86, and Trotter, 178. For Radstock in Paris and French Swizerland, see Trotter, 178; Terletskiĭ, 11; *EC*, July 1, 1880, 207–8; and QR, July1880, 11.

9. Trotter, 180. Leskov, 63, 99. Lieven, 8–9. Korff, *Am Zarenhof*, 13–14. Krusenstjerna, *Im Kreuz hoffe und siege ich*, 79. *Dein Reich Komme*, July–Aug. 1923, 156.

PART FOUR—Prospects: The Aristocratic Impulse, 1874–1884

invitations to the homes of aristocrats where he held personal conversations from eight and even to fourteen hours a day. Later he conducted services in the salons of these homes, which were labeled "drawing-room stundism." His first visit to Russia lasted about three months. He returned with his family in 1875–1876 and thereafter several additional times.[10]

For St. Petersburg's high society, Radstock's services became the top fashion of the day. They were not in the splendor of an Orthodox church structure or part of the beauty and familiarity of the Orthodox ritual. They began in a chapel with services composed of a Bible message, extemporaneous prayer, and the singing of English psalms. Radstock's messages were generally in French, which critics claimed lacked proficiency, delivered in a conversational style, lacking homilectical or oratorical skill, buttressed with numerous biblical references, not necessarily in context, and illustrations from everyday life. Nevertheless both the messenger and the message were great attractions. Radstock, who himself was a nobleman, an attraction in itself, came as a lay preacher with great earnestness and sincerity, expressing a love for Christ and Christ's Word. The simple message of justification by faith, so foreign to Orthodox ears, had great appeal to people looking for spiritual reality in unsettled times. Numbers of them were already alienated from the Orthodox Church or were only nominal adherents.[11]

In his letter at the end of his first visit in 1874, Radstock declared that the Orthodox Church put no obstacle in the study of Scripture and, although noting persecution in the south of the country, it was absent in the capital. On the other hand, he wrote that since liberty was controlled only by a few, "Therefore there is the greatest need for prudence and wisdom from the Lord, lest by injudicious zeal opposition should be provoked, which should bring trial on others." He was very careful not to debate theological questions or attack the Orthodox Church. In 1878 he wrote to a friend that workers need "to preach Christ only" and not attack what the Orthodox consider divine.[12]

After a sermon, Radstock usually arose from his seat and asked if anyone desired to stay and continue the discourse. Radstock, after silent prayer, asked those who remained to pray aloud and then personally moved among the prayers, asking each one whether he or she wanted to accept Christ. Upon a positive response, he then

---

10. Trotter, 188–189. *Missionary Echo*, May 1874, 63, and Sep. 1874, 126. *EC*, July 1, 1874, 202–3. Latimer, *Under Three Tsars*, 73. Leroy-Beaulieu, *The Empire of the Tsars and the Russians*, 3:471. For dates of Radstock's visits to St. Petersburg, see Heier, 44; Lieven, 25; Stead, *Truth about Russia*, 377; and *Missionary Echo*, April 1882, 49.

11. Leskov, 45–46, 48, 50, 99–100, 105. Dalton, *Catholic Presbyterian* 6 (1881), 105. Tolstoï, "Samozvannii missioner v pravoslavnoï Moskve," *Dushepoleznoe chtenie*, 1877, 2:79. Trotter, 64–65, 70. Korff, 14. *Missionary Echo*, May 1874, 63. *EC*, July 1, 1874, 202–3. Leroy-Beaulieu, 3:471–72. Latimer, 71–73.

12. Leskov, 52. *Missionary Echo*, Sep. 1874, 126–27, and Apr. 1878, 59.

dealt personally with the individual with texts and prayer.[13] A number of aristocratic women became converts. Among them were Katherine Galitsin, who was a cousin of Princess Lieven, Baroness Nathalie von Kruse, and her sister Baroness Maria N. Yasnovsky. Three very notable male converts during Radstock's first visit were Vasilii Pashkov (1831–1902), one of Russia's richest men, who was retired from the Guards, having risen to colonel, its highest rank; Count Modest M. Korff (1842–1931), lord chamberlain at the imperial court; and Count Aleksii P. Bobrinskii (d. 1894), minister of communications from 1871 to 1874. Radstock did not confine his preaching to the American chapel or salons of aristocrats. It was reported in July, 1875, soon after his second arrival in St. Petersburg, that he had preached three times in the French church in French and in his own lodging held prayer meetings each morning as well as services twice a week in the evening in the French language. His later visits, however, did not receive the same enthusiastic response as the first one. His three-day trip in 1876 to Moscow, the citadel of Orthodoxy and immune from the westernized aristocracy of the capital, netted only Nathalie von Kruse and three of her siblings as converts. In a subsequent visit of about two months to Moscow in 1878 gained no converts at all.[14]

Radstock also extended his ministry to the streets of St. Petersburg. Instead of riding, he generally walked. After filling his pockets of his overcoat with copies of the Russian New Testament and even unable to communicate in Russian, he would attempt to put a copy into the hands of passerbys. Radstock also encouraged his followers to spread the gospel. Female adherents had numerous opportunities for witness not only among their own aristocratic acquaintances but also among the many domestic servants in their households. Dalton recorded that one princess began to hold weekly meetings for her female domestics. At the Lieven mansion devotions were held that included the servants. Women also began to evangelize the poor of the city, which also expanded into a social ministry.[15]

The changed orientation in the Radstock aristocrats superseded the worldly activities of high society with its balls, drinking, and other social pursuits. Devotional services, study of Scripture, and social service took precedence. In her memoir of the movement, Sophie Lieven recorded that swearing, drunkenness, gambling, immorality, and family strife were put aside. Her aunt, Vera Gagarina, no longer wore her fine jewelry, giving some to family members and selling other items for Christian work, and wore plain dresses, although still of fine material. Radstock followers, however, did not become ascetics, giving up their wealth and a comfortable life style, but directed their wealth to what they considered were more suitable purposes.[16]

---

13. Leskov, 47.

14. *Missionary Echo*, August 1875, 101–2, and June 1876, 77. Korff, 37. Heier, 53. *The Friend of Missions*, Mar. 1928, 46–47. Also see Tolstoï, 78–87.

15. Leskov, 38–39, 98. Terletskii, 21. Dalton, *Catholic Presbyterian* 6 (1881), 112. Corrado, 85.

16. Lieven, 16, 29.

PART FOUR—Prospects: The Aristocratic Impulse, 1874–1884

THE CRITICS

Opposition to Radstock appeared about as instantaneously as his reception. A leading critic was Vladimir P. Meshcherskiĭ, a writer who had founded a reactionary paper, *Grazhdanin* (The Citizen). *Grazhdanin* attacked "The New Apostle" or "Lord Apostle" and his followers. Meshcherskiĭ's novel, *Lord-Apostol v bol'shom petersburgskom svete* (Lord Apostle in Petersburg High Society) was a satire. It began in serial form in *Grazhdanin* in 1875 before its publication in 1876. Meshcherskiĭ attacked Radstock as a charlatan, a romantic who was after the ladies, and that his followers in their acceptance of free grace continued to live in frivolity and lacked high moral standards. He also attacked Petersburg's high society for its fascination with the West.[17]

In defense of his novel, Meshcherskiĭ also published in 1876 "Pisma k Lordu Redstocku," an open letter to Radstock in French and Russian, a version of which was also published in *Grazhdanin*. He charged that Radstock's meetings were not just simply religious conferences but introduced a new cult with its own songs, confessions, and dogmas of salvation that fundamentally contradicted the morals and teachings of the Orthodox Church.[18]

Another severe critic was Count M. Tolstoy, who reacted negatively to Radstock's visit to Moscow in his letter, "Samozvaniĭ missioner v pravoslavnoĭ moskve (The False Missionary in Orthodox Moscow). Although he admitted Radststock's sincere advocacy of the merits of redemption, he nevertheless criticized him for his easy path to salvation—simply just to have faith. He hoped that the Lord would bring him into "His true flock—into the Holy Orthodox Church."[19]

Two great Russian literary figures of the age, Fedor M. Dostoevskiĭ (Dostoyevsky) and Leo N. Tolstoĭ (Tolstoy), also took cognizance of the Radstock movement. As an ardent follower of the Orthodox Church and a critic of western society, Dostoyevsky opposed the Radstock movement. He attended one of Radstock's meetings and wrote of his preaching: "I found nothing startling; he spoke neither particularly cleverly nor in a particularly dull manner." From informants he concluded that Radstock treated Christ and His blessing "quite trifingly." He noted, however, that people flocked to him and he miraculously changed people to seek to minister to the poor and needy of society. He admitted that Radstock "does produce extraordinary transformations and inspires in the hearts of his followers magnanimous sentiments." Dostoyevsky blamed the attraction of Radstock to the alienation of Russian people from their own society and ignorance of their own religion.[20]

---

17. Heier, 47–48, 63–67. Jones, 4. See *Missionary Echo*, May, 1874, 63, for an account of an early attack on Radstock in *Grazhdanin*.

18. Meshcherskiĭ, *Lettre au Lord Redstock/Pisma k Lordu Redstoku*. For copy in Russian in *Grazhdanin*, see 1876, no. 13, 345–49.

19. Tolstoĭ, 78–87. Heier, 53–54.

20. See Dostoyevsky, "Lord Radstock," *Diary of a Writer*, 1:267–69. For an evaluation of Dostoyevsky's views on Radstockism and his relationship with Yuliya Zasetskaya, see Heier, 58–62, and Jones, 5–9.

Although Leo Tolstoy evidently never met Radstock, his ministry, however, alerted his interest. The mother of his associate V. G. Chertkov, Elizaveta Chertkova, was an ardent Radstock follower. In his visit to Tolstoy in 1876, Count Aleksiï P. Bobrinskiï, a committed Radstock convert, impressed Tolstoy with his testimony of faith. In his own religious quest, however, Tolstoy rejected the dogma and rites of the Orthodox Church, including Christ's divinity, and fashioned his own ethical and rational religion based on the Sermon on the Mount and the Epistle of James. He claimed Radstockism was so attractive because it did not insist on a fundamental transformation of life, such as rejecting property, the use of force, and "the Princes of this world." His repudiation of justification by faith is evident in his novel, *Anna Karenina*, and his hostility toward evangelical Christianity in his caricature of the evangelist in his novel, *Voskresenie* (Resurrection).[21]

The Russian novelist Nikolaï S. Leskov in his work, *Velikosvetskiï raskol: Lord Redstok i ego posledovateli* (Dissent in High Society: Lord Radstock and His Followers), attempted to present an objective portrayal of Radstock and his movement as over against the slanderous attacks of Meshcherskiï's novel. Leskov was very interested in the Radstock movement and attended its meetings, which he described in some detail, and even incorporated two of Radstock's sermons. He was also a friend of Yuliya Zatsetskaya who supplied him with information on the Radstock movement, although she later felt betrayed by his use of her material. For a time he became an advisor and editor of the non-denominational Radstock publication, the *Russkiï rabochiï* (Russian Workman).[22] Leskov rejected the slanderous attacks on Radstock and showed a certain sympathy toward him, believing him to be a man of sincerity with a good heart. At the same time, however, he portrayed him as limited in intellect, scholarship, and oratorical skills as well as immune from the social questions of the day. Leskov also faulted Radstock for rejecting church tradition and prayers for the dead. Leskov rejected the idea of instant salvation and felt that justification by faith had no relevance for the common Russian who needed, as in James, to show his faith by his good deeds. Although he recognized the faithfulness of Radstock women in their witness and philanthropic work, at the same time he felt their results were negligible because of the sad state of the recipients and their inability to grasp the theological message.

In contrast to the foremost literary writers, one author, Elizabeth Ward de Charrière, who wrote *Serge Batourine*, a novel in French, portrayed the Radstock movement in a positive light. It was first published in Lausanne, Switzerland in 1879, republished in Paris in 1882 and in a German edition in 1894. The work presented

---

21. For an evaluation of Tolstoy's views on Radstockism, see Heier, 82–102, and Jones, 10–14.

22. See Leskov, *Schism in High Society*, for the English translation of Leskov's work by Muckle, which also includes an "Afterward," an evaluation of Leskov and this work. For additional evaluations, see Heier, 67–76, and Jones, 15–18.

free grace sympathetically and characters who can be identified with leading figures of the movement.[23]

One early defense came from an Orthodox priest, Ivan Stepanovich Bellyustin, who in 1876 wrote in *Tserkovno obshchestvennyï vestnik* that demands for Radstock's expulsion were not justified. Although he claimed that Radstock's convictions belonged to the realm of fantasy, he was neither a charlatan or pharisee nor dangerous for either society or the church.[24]

In spite of the attacks and criticism, the government did not see fit to expel him. After his initial visit, he was able to return on more than one occasion, even able to enter St. Petersburg when the political climate turned decidedly more hostile. The movement did not stop with his departure but took even deeper root in Russian soil with Russian leadership.

---

23. Heier, 76–82. Dalton, *Evangelische Strömungen*, 30.
24. Heier, 47–48. Leskov, 67–68. Terletskiï, 24–25.

15

Pashkovite Ascendancy

ONE OF THE REMARKABLE developments of the Radstock movement was not only the gaining of a body of devoted followers but the rise of native Russians into its leadership. Although evidently attaining some knowledge of Russian, Radstock was always the foreigner, never ministering in the native language. The Russian leadership possessed the advantage of familiarity with Russian Orthodox culture and a command of the language. As members of high society, it had invaluable connections with government, even extending to the Tsar himself. Collectively their wealth was immense with the ability to finance their own programs in contrast to other evangelicals in the country who were much less affluent and dependent on financial support from abroad.

The person who assumed the top leadership was Colonel Vasiliĭ A. Pashkov (1831–1902), who rose to such prominence that adherents of the Radstock Movement became known as "*Pashkovtsy*." Pashkov possessed great wealth, including two mansions in the capital, three large estates in the provinces of Nizhniĭ Novgorod, Moscow, and Tambov, and copper mines in Ufa *guberniya*. With his wealth and indulging in worldly pleasure, Pashkov had been indifferent to any spiritual life. His wife, Alexandra, the sister of Elizaveta Chertkova, had earlier become an evangelical believer in England, but he intentionally avoided meeting Lord Radstock. After remaining on his Moscow estate for two months, believing that by then Radstock would have left, he discovered on his return home that his wife had invited Radstock for a service and could not avoid meeting him. He listened courteously but unmoved to Radstock's message. But in joining others on his knees for prayer, a new and unusual experience for him, he experienced a radical change. As he was listening to the prayer, he later

PART FOUR—Prospects: The Aristocratic Impulse, 1874–1884

said, "It was as if a ray from heaven shot through my breast. I arose from my knees, ran into my bedroom, and gave myself to God."[1]

In an exchange of letters in 1880 with the rector of the Theological Academy of St. Petersburg, Ioann Yanyshev, Pashkov wrote in his letter of April 9/21 that he was no theologian but substantiated his statements with a multitude of biblical passages. He declared that, although alienated from God and "a friend of the world," he received the forgiveness of sin through Christ's redemption. He insisted one is not justified by works but only by faith in Christ. In response Yanyshev pressed Pashkov to justify his activity in a land with an ecclesiastical establishment but was independent of it. He also asked Pashkov to clarify his views on the efficacy of the sacraments and the Orthodox Church. Although not denying the sacraments, Pashkov insisted that they were only for believers, not a means of grace for the unbeliever and a judgement on him if he partook without faith. He sidestepped his views on the Orthodox ecclesiastical establishment, expressing the view that the church is the body of all true believers. Pashkov admitted to Yanyshev a limitation of knowledge and that his answers would not be completely satisfactory to him in form or precision. He also did not wish to engage in further theological discussion since this was not his goal in his preaching.[2]

PREACHING AND WORSHIP

Pashkov brought the Radstock movement to a new level. He expanded it from its aristocratic moorings to become a mass movement among the common people, although aristocrats still held their private Bible studies. Pashkov, Count Korff, and Count Bobrinskiĭ, unlike Radstock, preached in Russian and opened their stately homes for the preaching of the gospel. Pashkov's mansion on the Gagarin Quay at the Neva River with its manorial entrance and great hall of white columns, well lighted with chandeliers and wall lamps, drew great crowds. In 1880 Konstantin Pobedonostsev, procurator of the Holy Synod, reported one gathering numbered as many as 1,500. Princess Nathalie Lieven opened her mansion near the Winter Palace on Ulitsa Morskaya. It was noted for its hall of Corinthian malachite pillars and other halls with Italian paintings on the ceilings, parquet floors, silk-lined walls, and ornate furniture. Her sister, Vera Gagarina, opened her home next door.[3]

---

1. For a listing of biographical sources on the life of Pashkov, see Wardin, *Evangelical Sectarianism*, 300–301. Also see Cheryl Corrado, "The Philosophy of Ministry of Colonel Vasiliy Pashkov," and the Russian translation, *Filosofiya sluzheniya polkovnika Pashkova*. For Pashkov's conversion, see Latimer, *Dr. Baedeker and His Apostolic Work in Russia*, 81–82; Lieven 13–14; and Korff, 17–18.

2. For a reproduction of the exchange between Pashkov and Yanyshev in English, see *The Christian Week*, July 21, 1880, 673–76, and in German in Korff, 67–77. For sources in Russian see Wardin, *Evangelical Sectarianism*, 298–99. For a discussion of the correspondence, see Heier, 111, and Corrado, 61–62.

3. Corrado, 74. Krusenstjerna, 80. Korff, 31. Lieven, 44, 60.

Social barriers crumbled as civil officials, domestic servants, cab drivers, factory workers, peasants, and even priests and beggars worshiped with aristocrats and other members of high society. On one occasion when Korff visited the Lieven mansion, he noted an unusual smell of odor from the stables. Princess Lieven explained that just before she had held a prayer meeting for cab drivers, justifying the service by saying, "My house belongs to my Savior, I am only his steward." On another occasion and different social level in the home of Count Bobrinskiĭ, F. W. Baedeker was startled at the end of his message when he heard scratching and smell of sulfur. Aristocratic women were lighting their cigarettes. The count finally ended the custom except for one countess who insisted she was too old to stop.[4]

Services were held throughout the winter months but terminated at the end of May when aristocrats went to their estates in the summer. At his mansion, Pashkov would commence the service by giving out a number of a hymn from a hymnbook after they became available. The hymn was apt to be a Russian translation of a familiar English hymn with a tune from the West but adapted to Russian taste. The Moody-Sankey hymnal was an important source. Pashkovites came to use such hymnals as *Lyubimye stikhi* (Favorite Verses), published in 1880, and *Radostnye pesni Siona* (Joyful Songs of Zion), published in 1882. Pashkov's wife played a harmonium or reed organ, accompanied by the three Pashkov daughters. On other occasions, other girls would join the daughters, forming a choir. Miss A. I. Peuker might also play the organ.[5]

Pashkov prayed extemporaneously and then brought a message, earnestly expressed and after Radstock's style ladened with biblical texts. According to one reporter, Bobrinskiĭ was more animated in his preaching, while Korff appealed more to the intellect. The sermon was orderly and without emotional eruption. After the sermon another hymn was sung.[6] Pashkovites often held services on their estates in summer. Pashkov and Bobrinskiĭ were noted for such efforts, although other aristocrats might do the same. Bobrinskiĭ also held services in his home in Switzerland. Workers on the various estates attended, and villagers from surrounding areas would also congregate.[7]

Social Service

Although Pashkovites rejected works for salvation, they as other evangelical believers felt an obligation to minister to the social needs of society, an impulse closely intertwined with their commitment to share the gospel message. Such a ministry demonstrated the conviction that good works follow genuine faith.

---

4. Korff, 31. Latimer, *Baedeker*, 81.

5. Lieven, 36–37. Corrado, 79–81. Muckle, "Charlotte Elliott and the Beginnings of Russian Evangelical Hymnody," *Bulletin* of the Hymn Society of Great Britain and Ireland 10/2 (May 1982), 33–38. QR, July 1880, 11–12. Lieven, 15–16.

6. QR., July 1880, 11–12. Lieven, 16.

7. Latimer, *Under Three Tsars*, 75. Lieven, 90. Corrrado, 85–89, 92–93.

PART FOUR—Prospects: The Aristocratic Impulse, 1874–1884

Pashkov himself was a prime example in programs of mercy and social amelioration, using not only his fortune but also becoming personally engaged. At his meetings Pashkov provided sumptuous meals for those who attended and gave money to those in need. He did not confine his ministry to his home but visited prisons and hospitals and went to the public houses of cab drivers where he witnessed and distributed Testaments and tracts. In his home in the working class district of Viborg, he opened a dining hall that provided food at low prices, which attracted workers as well as many students, numbers of whom were under nihilistic and atheistic influences. Bible texts adorned the walls, and Bibles and tracts were distributed. Serving girls inquired of patrons of their relationship to Christ. Pashkov also opened two other restaurants.[8]

At the restaurant in Viborg, Pashkov preached and held personal conversations. An inspector of students provided a visiting card with his recommendation to those students who wished to learn more about the Christian faith. Pashkov met with inquiring students and discussed spiritual issues with them. For needy students who embraced the evangelical faith, he provided material help.[9]

In the Viborg district by his home, he established a workshop for poor children. In the same district he provided a home for poor women at low cost. He also founded a crèche for infants of working women and a daily kindergarten. On his Nizhnii Novgorod estate, he established a hospital, which performed surgeries, as well as a pharmacy. Mia Salberg, the director of the hospital, organized a weaving school for village women and led a Sunday school for children. On his Moscow estate he opened a school and a hospital, a school on his Tambov estate, and schools near his copper mines.[10]

Along with Pashkov, Count Korff also visited the cabmen. He also served on a prison committee and had free access to preach to the prisoners. On her own initiative, Yulia Zasetskaya gave a large sum of money for a hostel for the homeless in St. Petersburg and undertook its management. A number of Pashkovite women not only visited prisons and hospitals but also visited the worse tenements to speak of Christ to the poor. Some women opened on their estates private schools to teach peasants.[11]

Princess Vera Gagarina, Madame Elizaveta Chertkova, and Madame Alexandra Pashkov undertook responsibility for four workrooms for women in various parts of the city, which another woman had founded earlier but had to give up. A committee was formed with Dr. Karl von Mayer of the St. Petersburg Evangelical (Protestant) Hospital as secretary and treasurer. Poor women received material from the workroom and worked at home, returning then their finished handicraft items. Pashkovite

---

8. Lieven, 16, 38–40. Korff, 32. Heier, 115–16.

9. Terletskiĭ, 64. Heier, 116–17.

10. Corrado, 120–22. Heier, 115, 130. *The Friend of Missions*, May 1931, 58. *Den evangeliska rörelsen i Ryssland*, 78–79.

11. Lieven, 38, 43. Korff, 30–31. Leskov, 93, 104. Stead, 355–56. Dillon, "A Russian Religious Reformer," *The Sunday Magazine*, Apr. 1902, 332.

women visited these women in their homes to bring the word of God. Someone might also read spiritual material while individuals worked in the workroom. Pashkovite women also established two sewing classes where women engaged in fine linen work. Women were paid, and their work was sold. At first the handicraft items were sold in the Lieven mansion, but some individuals in the mixed crowd began to chip off bits of malachite from the columns, and the goods were then moved to their own shop. More expensive items, such as clothes and linen work, were sold in their own small shop but then later brought to the Lieven mansion.[12]

Unlike others in their philanthropy, Pashkovites did not raise money for the poor through such entertainments as dancing and singing. Leskov strongly condemned those who "cannot do good otherwise than through the allurement of pleasure." Pashkovites were personally involved in their ministry of charity, witness, visitation, and instruction. Pashkovites, who formerly were caught up in the social whirl of society, began to lead a more sober life, avoiding worldly enticements.[13]

Leskov praised the Pashkovite aristocratic women for their good intentions, but he noted their philanthropy was with few exceptions often unskillful and appeared more as a "pastime than real Christian action." He claimed they were unable to bridge the religious and cultural chasm between society and the poor peasant. Was Leskov unduly harsh? The Pashkovite movement was primarily spiritual, seeking individual transformation on a one to one basis. It did not seek or expect any immediate revolutionary social change of society but sought to change society with new principles. Leskov also failed to acknowledge the significant efforts in time and money that personally benefited many poor and needy. But yet with all this, Leskov was correct that Pashkovite efforts did not seek structural change to meet the great disparities between the rich and the poor that will bring Russia to revolution and civil war.[14]

Leo Tolstoy believed that Radstock was successful since he himself was in high society and did not insist, as already noted, that his followers change their lifestyle to the extent of a "renunciation of force, of property and of the Princes of this world." In a comparison between Pashkov and Tolstoy, Heier made the trenchant observation that with all of Tolstoy's renunciation of the world, Pashkov was more consistent than Tolstoy and in application Pashkovism was far more practical than Tolstoyism.[15] It is true the Pashkovites now followed a far more sober and purpose-driven lifestyle. Also, unlike other aristocrats, they associated with classes far beneath their social status. On the other hand, they continued, by and large, to maintain, even with their generosity, the lifestyle commensurate with their economic and social status. Unless exiled, they continued to live in their mansions, retire to their country estates in summer, maintain a bevy of servants, and travel abroad. Even upon exile Pashkov and Korff kept

12. Lieven, 40–42, 44–45, 71.
13. Leskov, 99–100.
14. For Leskov's criticisms of Pashkovite philanthropy, see Leskov, 93, 98.
15. Heier, 92–93, 114.

their estates and lived comfortably abroad. In her memoir, Sophie Lieven admitted that while on their country estates they worked less diligently for the Lord, a sign she said of the danger of riches for a Christian. She also spoke of her aunt Vera Gagarina with an associate visiting repulsive quarters but yet the two were taken to the area by a sledge driven by thoroughbred horses to be later picked up by the coachman at an appointed time and taken back home.[16]

The widespread philanthropy of the Pashkovites also brought, as Stead pointed out, the "knave and the hypocrite" who exploited their generosity. Pashkov was well known for his beneficence, providing meals in his mansion, reasonable meals in his eating houses, and gifts to poor and needy. For skeptics and enemies of the Pashkovites, their philanthropy produced questions as to its real purpose. Rumors easily arose, such as the one that Pashkov was paying peasants to listen to his messages. In his indictment against Pashkov, Pobedonostsev stated that with his wealth he was attempting to "lure" the common people and mistakenly claimed he had opened a "free eating house." And the purity of some philanthropy could be questioned when, for instance, aid to a needy student would be terminated if he or she no longer showed interest in the gospel.[17]

Publication

With the appearance of an official version of the Russian Bible, completed between 1861 and 1876, the great interest in religious material, and the rise in literacy, the times were right for spreading Scriptural knowledge through religious publication. J. Craig, agent of the Religious Tract Society (RTS) of London and stationed in Hamburg, suggested along with Radstock the formation of a society to publish and distribute tracts and distribute Scripture. Craig had sent tracts to centers in St. Petersburg and Riga and between 1870 and 1874 frequently visited these cities. The Religious Tract Society also had a center in Warsaw. But a tract society in Russia itself, supported by Russians, would be a great boon to its work.

In April 1875, at the parsonage of Hermann Dalton, the German Reformed pastor, a mixed group of men and women formed the Society for the Encouragement of Spiritual and Ethical Reading. Besides Pashkov, who was elected director, and Korff, vice-president and then director in 1861, the meeting included such leading Pashkovite women as Elizaveta Chertkova, Vera Gargarina, and Maria Peuker. In addition to Dalton and Radstock, other members included G. H. Hall of the Religious Tract Society, William Nicolson of the British and Foreign Bible Society, Prince Paul Lieven, and Nikolaï Astaf'ev, president of the Society for the Distribution of the Holy Scripture in Russia (the Russian Bible Society).[18]

16. *The Friend of Missions*, May 1931, 58. Lieven, 43–44, 90.
17. Stead, *Truth about Russia*, 360–61, 377–78. Corrrado, 123–25. Terletskiï, 64–65.
18. Jones, "A Note on Mr. J. G. Blissmer and the Society for the Encouragement of Spiritual and

At the first meeting, the new society's supporters enthusiastically raised a large sum for its operation. On Craig's recommendation the RTS granted in addition £1,000 for the new society's disposal, and in the following years the RTS matched funds raised by the society on the field. The RTS stipulated that all publications must adhere to evangelical doctrine and prohibited any suggestion of salvation through the sacraments. The new society soon purchased the stock and copyright of tracts published by J. G. Blissmer. By June the society had printed 150,000 tracts, about a year and a half before its legal authorization in November 1876. The British and Foreign Bible Society offered the new society permission to draw from its store of Bibles at a large discount. It also reported that the new society was planning to engage colporteurs, some who would serve on the estates of the supporters of the society.[19]

At about this time, old mainline Protestants, Lutherans and Reformed, formed a St. Petersburg Evangelical City Mission with Dalton as a leading director. The mission engaged missionaries to work among the Protestant population and distributed Scripture and other devotional material.[20]

The new society, however, immediately faced a problem. The Pashkovite supporters, members of high society and western in outlook, unfortunately failed to consider the culture of the Russian peasant, so far removed from St. Petersburg. The tracts were simply translations into Russian from English or German originals without even, as Dalton pointed out, a change in names, such as James or John to a current Russian equivalent, or teapot to samovar. Dalton also criticized the tracts that Radstock wrote, noting that he was unable to enter into the inner psyche of the Russian populace and filled them, as in his sermons, with Biblical references that only confused the average reader. Dalton soon left the society, not wishing to take responsibility for the poor translations. He observed later, however, that the society made improvements and admitted that not all tracts were so affected.[21]

Regardless of their foreign coloration, stundists ardently welcomed the tracts, and they began to have wide circulation. The Russo-Turkish War of 1877–1878 provided a grand opportunity for the Pashkovite society and the Religious Tract Society to spread tracts and books and for the BFBS to distribute Scripture. Lutherans also entered into distribution, and the Red Cross was also of great assistance. The tract and Bible societies found an inviting field among soldiers in the Balkans, veterans on furlough, and sick and wounded soldiers in the hospitals. Korff gained permission from the Ministry of War to circulate Scripture to veterans in the hospitals as well

---

Ethical Reading," *Slavic and East European Review*, 53, no. 130 (January 1975), 92–96. Dalton, *Der Stundismus in Russland*, 23, and *Evangelische Strömungen*, 24–25. Corrado, 130–31. RTS, *Report*, 1882, 97.

19. Jones, *J. G. Blissmer*, 92–96. Dalton, *Der Stundismus in Russland*, 23. BFBS, *Report*, 1877, 109.

20. BFBS, *Report*, 1877, 108, and 1881, 85. Lenker, 445.

21. Dalton, *Strömungen*, 25–26; *Lebenserinnerungen*, 2:217–54; and *Der Stundismus in Russland*, 25.

as to Turkish prisoners of war. Korff was also able to persuade the censor to allow the Religious Tract Society to reprint such tracts as "The Roll Call," "Good News," and "Conversation on the New Birth." Other tracts as "Are You a Christian?," "The Lord's Prayer," "Christ and the Two Thieves," and "Heaven and Hell," as well as some of Charles Spurgeon's sermons were circulated. A popular book was *The Life of Christ*. The Religious Tract Society also brought in tracts in Turkish and Arabic for Moslem prisoners of war.[22]

Pashkov eagerly promoted the Pashkovite society not only through energetic leadership and financial spport but also provided a hall in his mansion for the society. The society's hired colporteurs distributed both Scripture and tracts. Women went to hospitals, prisons, military barracks, and homes for the poor. Tracts were distributed on railroads and at the annual fair at Nizhnii Novgorod. The society employed some women as Bible women. One of the most successful distributions was at the Exhibition of Trades and Arts in Moscow in 1882, where Count Bobrinskii gained a favorable location for two stands and underwrote expenses. With two women at each stand and the assistance of three colporteurs and in spite of attacks from the secular and church press, 1,250,000 tracts were distributed of which 50,000 were sold. Applications for tracts came from Orthodox priests and school teachers. From an appeal of Lord Radstock, in 1883 the Religious Tract Society granted £200 for distribution of tracts among the elementary schools of the country.[23]

A Pashkovite publication, *Russkii rabochii* (the Russian Workman), a non-denominational illustrated monthly, appeared from 1875 to 1886. Maria G. Peuker and later Alexandra Ivanovna, her daughter, were editors. For a time Leskov became an advisor and even editor for part of one year. Much of its stories and religious illustrations came from the Religious Tract Society.[24]

Although the society was legal, its publications were still subject to civil and ecclesiastical censorship. M. G. Peuker and her daughter frequently struggled with the censors. Korff often found the spiritual censor particularly difficult and would often go to his office to meet his argument that the publications represented the views of the Protestant reformers. Korff argued that it was not the censor's duty to be a defender of Orthodoxy but only to determine whether the publication incorporated a danger to society. In any case, the censor approved many of the tracts.[25]

At the beginning of his tenure as procurator of the Holy Synod, Konstantin Pobedonostsev did not oppose the publications of the society. In reviewing a number of its publications that had been confiscated, he wrote in 1881 to Korff that he approved their continued circulation. He liked the material taken from the Orthodox saint,

---

22. RTS, *Report*, 1878, 94–102, and 1879, 92–93. BFBS, *Report*, 1879, 93.

23. BFBS, *Report*, 1878, 88; 1880, 105; and 1881, 85. RTS, *Report*, 1882, 97–98, 1883, 88–91, and 1884, 96–99. Leskov, 93. Corrado, 143.

24. Heier, 71–74.

25. Korff, 51.

Tikhon Zadonskiĭ, but believed that the hymnal, *Lyubimye stikhi* (Favorite Verses), was written in a disgraceful style and should be withdrawn. He also wrote that many tracts with their poor translations, English names, and way of life were alien to the soul and life of the common people.[26]

In later years the populist author, Alexander S. Prugavin, sympathetic toward sectarians, nonetheless penned a critical review of the Pashkovite brochures. He alleged the tracts were "hazy, cloudy mysticism," simply looking to heaven but avoiding the harsh reality of the world of evil and injustice. This view is not surprising from one who favored transforming Russian social life.[27]

In spite of censors and critics and the great difficulties of distribution over such a large and under developed territory, the Society for the Encouragement of Spiritual and Ethical Reading thrived. G. I. Terletskiĭ, the Orthodox chronicler of the Pashkovite movement, attributed its great success to several factors. He pointed out that the society came at a time of increasing literacy when the demand for literature, particularly religious, was increasing. He also noted that the society produced huge quantities of tracts, many of which were provided free or sold at a very low price. Colporteurs helped in their dissemination in all areas of the Empire. Also the society provided tracts earlier than other organizations and outclassed them, such as the Society for the Spread of the Holy Scripture in Russia, the Vladimir Brotherhood of Saint Alexandr Nevskiĭ, and the Brotherhood of St. Andrew.[28]

The British and Foreign Bible Society continued its own distribution of Scripture as well as assisting the Pashkovite Society in the same effort. Yakov Delyakov, the energetic Nestorian evangelical who served as an independent colporteur in Ukraine, joined the BFBS in 1876 together with his stepson, Ivan Ivanovich Zhidkov.[29]

A notable distributor of Bibles and tracts was Henry Lansdell (1841–1919), an evangelical Anglican who from 1874 to 1888 traveled seven times to the Russian Empire. He went to prisons, hospitals, and other public institutions. In 1882 he wrote, *Through Siberia*, describing his four-month trip there in 1879. In 1885 he wrote, *Russian Central Asia*, about his six-month trip in 1882 in this area, and in 1893 a third book, *Chinese Central Asia*, a trip he undertook in 1888–1890. The Religious Tract Society provided him grants for thousands of tracts.[30]

On his 1879 journey, Lansdell engaged a Russian interpreter who had received training at the East London Institute for Home and Foreign Missions, founded by Henry Grattan Guiness (1835–1910). Guiness and one of his sons visited the Pashkovites

---

26. Corrado, 133.

27. Prugavin, *Religioznye otshchepenstsy*, 2:151. See Klibanov, 246, ft. 4, for the quote from Prugavin.

28. Terletskiĭ, 32–36.

29. BFBS, *Report*, 1877, 123–24. *Istoriya*, 525–26.

30. For an article that provides a scholarly evaluation of Lansdell's ministry in Russia, see Muckle, "Henry Lansdell, Leskov and Tolstoy," *Neue Zeitschrift für Missionswissenschaft*, 1978, no. 4, 291–308. For Lansdell's books and other sources of his career, see Wardin, *Evangelical Sectarianism*, 42–43.

PART FOUR—Prospects: The Aristocratic Impulse, 1874–1884

in Russia, and Pashkov provided recommendations for some Russian students who will study at the school.[31]

As has been noted the Pashkovite movement was closely connected with evangelicalism from abroad, particularly with Great Britain. Some of its early supporters when abroad were influenced by British evangelicals and the movement itself began in Russia itself through the ministry of a British lord. The British and Foreign Bible Society and Religious Tract Society from London found Pashkovites strong supporters for their own ministries in the country and even some Russians found training in England. The time, however, will soon come when this door of evangelical opportunity will be sorely tested.

---

31. Muckle, 306–307.

16

Pashkovite Denouement

ALTHOUGH THE PRESS AND intellectuals continued to evaluate Radstockism critically, the movement, now headed by Pashkov, was thriving. Crowds attended Pashkovite services, and Pashkovite distribution of Scripture and tracts continued at an accelerated pace. The Russo-Turkish War of 1877–1878 provided Pashkovites even greater opportunity for propagation and benevolent activity. The Pashkovites also had protection in high places. General F. F. Trepov, military governor of St. Petersburg, was a relative of Pashkov, and Aleksandr Y. Timashev, Minister of Internal Affairs, was a husband of Pashkov's sister, Yekatrina.[1]

In spite of toleration, the forces against the movement, particularly defenders of Orthodoxy, were becoming increasingly alarmed at the success of the Pashkovite movement. The government had final control over religion and exercised state censorship of printed material. It did not interfere as along as it felt the movement was confined to aristocrats who, in any case, were loyal subjects. When it perceived that the movement was reaching the common people who might be alienated from the Orthodox faith or become linked with evangelical dissidents, the movement then appeared to pose a threat to society itself.[2] In defense of state policy, Olga Novikov declared in an article that "Russia is primarily a Church, not a State" and cannot allow "the cement which binds together our mighty empire to be dissolved by a propaganda of iconoclasts, whether political or religious."[3]

---

1. Korff, 47–48. Heier, 113. Corrado, 25.
2. Leroy-Beaulieu, 472–73.
3. Novikoff, "A Cask of Honey with a Spoonful of Tar," *Contemporary Review*, Feb. 1889, 209.

PART FOUR—Prospects: The Aristocratic Impulse, 1874–1884

In 1878 the Orthodox Church ordered Pashkov and his followers to stop their activity with an admonition to return to the Orthodox Church. According to the law, Pashkov was operating illegally without ecclesiastical authorization and engaged in unauthorized meetings. Even though the Metropolitan Police received orders to stop the meetings, they still continued with the number of attendees even increasing. The Orthodox now attempted to counter attack. In some of the larger churches in St. Petersburg and Moscow, higher clergy lectured on Sunday evenings in defense of Orthodoxy with an exposure of the Pashkovite heresy. The lectures were published and circulated gratis. In April 1880 twenty-five priests formed an anti-Pashkov Society to engage in conferences and exhortations with the use of apologetics for the educated class and catechetical instruction for the masses. The effort, if started at all, was negligible.[4]

In the early 1880s two events adversely affected the Pashkovite movement—the appointment of Konstantin Pobedonostsev (1827–1907) as procurator of the Orthodox Church and the assassination of Tsar Alexander II in the following year. Pobedonostsev tutored the future Tsars, Alexander III and Nicholas II, and served until 1905, exerting an unforgettable influence on church-state relations for twenty-five years. He was well educated—a writer, editor, translator of English books, and professor of law. He was unsympathetic toward the Great Reforms of Alexander II, opposed additional reforms, and was an arch supporter of the Autocracy and the authority of the Orthodox Church.[5]

Pobedonostsev painted a romantic picture of the church. He blamed the corruption, superstition, and the ignorance and lethargy of the clergy on external political and economic conditions, which he claimed would soon disappear. The divine service, which excluded a sermon, was the best sermon of all since in it one heard the words of God, not man. The church was a national church for the population with church and state mutually supporting each other. He opposed granting rights to such schismatics as Old Believers or sectarians as threats to church and state.

In 1880 Pobedonostsev got a chance to strike a blow against the Pashkov meetings. From a report of Count Michael Loris-Melkov, head of the Supreme Executive Commission to fight terrorism, which recommended suppression of Pashkov's meetings, the Tsar ordered on May 10 a meeting of a special commission of ministers, which included Pobedonostsev. The ministers approved suppression and an order to watch carefully any manifestations of Pashkovite propaganda. At this time, Pobedonostsev sent the Tsar a memorandum outlining his concerns concerning Pashkovite

4. Stead, 376. *Novosti*, 1880, no. 129, 2. Terletskii, 66–68. Dalton, *Catholic Presbyterian*, 112–13.

5. For Pobedonostsev's views, see his work, *Reflections of a Russian Statesman*, published in English in 1898 and later published by the University of Michigan in 1965, with an excellent foreword on his career by Murray Polner. Also see Adams, "Pobedonostsev's Religious Politics," *Church History* 22/4 (Dec. 1953), 314–26, and Warth, "Konstantin Petrovich Pobedonostsev," *MERSH* 38, 139–42, which includes a helpful bibliography. For additional bibliographical material, see Wardin, *Evangelical Sectarianism*, 355–56.

activity. On May 25 the Tsar issued an order forbidding all Pashkov gatherings, which was followed by another order that for a time exiled Pashkov.[6]

Pashkov left for England but then returned in the summer to his estate in Moscow *guberniya* and then allowed to return to St. Petersburg. At a service in Pashkov's mansion on March 1, 1881, word came that Tsar Alexander II was wounded. For some time, nihilists had attempted to assassinate him and finally succeeded. Pashkov prayed fervently for the Tsar and the Fatherland, and many other prayers were offered in the assembled gathering. Pashkovites showed their loyalty and sought no revolutionary change. Under the successor, Alexander III, who was greatly influenced by Pobedonostsev, the reform agenda ended, and a period of reaction ensued with no relief for evangelical sectarians.[7]

Although large gatherings were now forbidden, Pashkovites continued to be active. In the meantime Pashkovites had spread to all parts of St. Petersburg. They now worked more secretly and spread to the outskirts of the city. Women were the main missionaries, maintaining their sewing circles in various parts of the city and continued to visit the poor. In his memorandum to the Minister of Internal Affairs in April 1882, Pobedonostsev complained that Pashkov had extended his activity and recruited new workers, including Count Bobrinskiĭ who was preaching openly in the city. Before Lent even Lord Radstock had reappeared with the support of his women supporters. Pobedonostsev urged his immediate removal. He noted that Pashkovites were spreading elsewhere in the empire and particularly pointed to their contacts with sectarians centered in Prishib in Ukraine.[8]

Pashkovites also continued to be under attack from the press and under government surveillance. Bogdanovich, church warden (*starosta*) of St. Isaac Cathedral, wrote "Open Letters to Pashkov," in which he briefly described Pashkovite teaching, attacked its improper means of enticing people into the sect, and pointed out the dangers of the sect.[9]

In March 1882 Frederick Baedeker, residing in St. Petersburg at the Lieven mansion, reported holding meetings in German and English. He also wrote that at the same time meetings in French, apparently by Lord Radstock, and other meetings in Russian were conduced in the city. All meetings, however, were only by invitation by cards and in private. When George Müller was in the city in 1883, the authorities at first allowed him only to use English but then permitted him to use German in the German churches and speak to Swedes with an interpreter. Müller also reported that

---

6. For the May 10th meeting of ministers, the regime's orders, and Pobedonostsev's memorandum, see Stead, 373–77. See Heier, 125–30, for a reproduction of Pobedonostsev's memorandum and the Tsar's order to terminate Pashkovite meetings and propaganda. See *Pis'ma Pobedonostseva k Aleksandru III*, ed. by Pokrovskiĭ, 1:284, on Pobedonostsev's report to the Tsar of the May 10 meeting.

7. *EC* Aug. 2, 1880, 248. Heier, 130–32. Korff, 48–49.

8. Terletskiĭ, 65, ft. 2, and 77. Korff, 49–50. Stead, 377–78.

9. Terletskiĭ, 78.

Pashkov was followed everywhere, not allowed to have more than twenty for meetings in his home, and suffered the breaking up of a meeting by a policeman when he was speaking to seven poor Russians in their language. When Müller spoke in the Pashkov mansion with a Russian interpreter in Russian, authorities stopped Müller from speaking further in the residence.[10]

On May 3, 1883, the regime granted toleration to Old Believers and sectarians, but who were still subjected to the discretion and regulations of the Ministry of Interior. The law, however, provided no relief for stundists, Stundo-Baptists, or Pashkovites since their mission activity was considered illegal as subverting the Orthodox population. From an appeal in 1886 by a group of stundists, it was ruled that the law did not apply to them since they were not dissenters from birth but had been seduced from Orthodoxy.[11]

Problems in Publication

In its report in 1880, the Religious Tract Society noted that in the previous year censorship had restricted the activity of the Society for the Encouragement of Moral and Religious Reading. The society nevertheless continued its work with tracts stamped by the censors and its own licensed colporteurs. It continued to receive a subsidy from the Religious Tract Society of London that matched the revenue it itself raised. In 1880 Count Ignatev, then governor of Nizhnii Novgorod, ordered the distribution of its tracts stopped. After reviewing them, Pobedonostsev, feeling they were harmless, gave permission for their continued distribution. Later he will reverse himself, claiming he did not realize at the time their "secret aim."[12] In his memorandum in April 1882 to the Minister of Internal Affairs, Pobedonostsev expressed his alarm at the activity of the Pashkovite society. Besides tracts, which the civil censor approved but unknown to the ecclesiastical censor, he noted hymnbooks translated from the German and English and New Testaments with underlined texts. He was upset at an edition of John Bunyan's *Pilgrim's Progress* with edited notations, which bypassed the ecclesiastical censor's review though its contents were "religious, dogmatic, and purely Protestant."[13]

Lars E. Högberg, missionary in Russia from the Swedish Mission Covenant Church, later wrote that censorship was erratic and could be circumvented. If one censor disapproved, one might then change the title and introduction and get approval from another censor. Terletskii pointed out that although tracts or brochures were to receive reviews from both civil and spiritual censors, numbers of brochures

---

10. *Missionary Echo*, April 1882, 49. Müller, *The Life of Trust*, 537–38.

11. Blane, "The Relations between the Russian Protestant Sects and the State, 1900–1921," 23–30. Stead, 383–84. Dorodnitsyn, doc. 244.

12. RTS, *Report*, 1880, 95. *Religious Tract Society Record*, Sep. 1884, 79. Corrado, 146.

13. Stead, 378.

received approval only from the civil censor. He noted that tracts printed in Warsaw and Odessa received only the approval of the civil censor, which thereby suggested they avoided a more careful scrutiny if they had been reviewed in St. Petersburg.[14]

In 1883 *Tserkovnyï vestnik* published an article listing titles of Pashkovite books and brochures. It noted on their covers, aside from the title, the Greek symbols of alpha and omega, signifying the beginning and end of our salvation. The article stated that the brochures were, by and large, printed in Warsaw, the majority translated from English and German. The brochures were also annotated with biblical texts. It claimed the texts were chosen without sophistication, highlighting only the beliefs of the author, were printed with gaps, eliminating anything contrary to the author's belief, and were placed out of context. In his analysis of the brochures, Terletskiï wrote that their teaching was one-sided, not presenting Christian truth "in all its fullness and purity." They stressed justification by faith alone, failed to mention the need for Christian piety, and omitted such texts as "faith without works is dead." In addition, they made no mention of churches, church tradition, the church hierarchy, the sacraments, ikons, and the worship of saints.[15]

In 1885 the Holy Synod classified the tracts in three categories. The first were tracts whose authors were Orthodox or were not contrary to Orthodoxy. A second category were brochures with something of a sectarian coloring. A third category were those that were boldly sectarian. In 1886 the Holy Synod specifically listed forty-one titles that were dangerous and to be withdrawn. They included such tracts as, "Who Is a Christian?," "Come to Jesus Christ," "Are You Saved, or Lost? And Be Ready," and "Two Paths and Their Limits."[16]

In a review in 1888 by an Educational Committee, it was admitted that if read individually and without systematic order the brochures did not appear particularly sectarian, but when read in their entirety and arranged in sections their sectarian nature was clearly evident. It was not so much what they stated but how much they deliberately left out.[17]

In their New Testaments Pashkovites underlined or marked in red verses that highlighted their views, a practice that upset Pobedonostsev and other Orthodox critics. Frederick Baedeker underlined verses in red ink and placed crosses on margins in Scriptures he distributed in prisons across Russia. A prison officer forced him to stop the practice as he was under license, but he continued to distribute marked Bibles elsewhere. At times Pashkovites did not underline passages but drew horizontal and vertical lines to direct the attention of the reader.[18]

14. Högberg, *Skuggor och dagrer från missionsarbetet i Ryssland*, 79. Terletskiï, 35.

15. *TsV*, 1883, no. 24, 13. Terletskiï, 56–57.

16. Heier, 119–20. See Terletskiï, 37–56, for a detailed description of fifty-four tracts and Terletskiï, 79–80, for forty-one titles that the Holy Synod listed in 1886 as dangerous.

17. Skvortsov, *Sovremennoe russkoe sektantstvo*, 126.

18. Stead, 378. *TsV*, 1883, no. 24, 13. *The Gospel Call*, Jan. 1939, 7. Latimer, *Dr. Baedeker*, 51–53. Corrado, 139–41.

PART FOUR—Prospects: The Aristocratic Impulse, 1874–1884

Relations with Sectarians

It was inevitable that Pashkovites would enter into relations with evangelical sectarians, who generally accepted the same basic theological principles. Before becoming a Pashkovite, Count Bobrinskiĭ had had an early contact with local stundists. According to Korff, the government sent Bobrinskiĭ in 1864 with a detachment of troops to subdue a riot because of the unjust treatment of a stundist. Through negotiation, the matter was settled peaceably. In the summer of 1874 Count Korff traveled to Kiev to learn at first hand the life and faith of the stundists there. The authorities, however, required him to visit under an assumed name. After visiting twelve stundist men imprisoned in a cloister, he appealed to the civil and ecclesiastical authorities for their release. Although at the time he was unsuccessful in his appeal, the authorities will later free them.[19]

Pashkovites provided financial support to stundists. Terletskiĭ wrote that Count Korff on his visit to the Kiev area in the mid-seventies assisted the stundists there. Terletskiĭ also reported that Yakov Koval, a leader of stundists in Kiev *guberniya* who rejected sacraments, corresponded with Pashkov and received support from him, such as 200 rubles in 1879. According to the same source, Koval not only took money for himself but also funds disgnated for fellow stundists, began to drank heavily, and then lost his position as elder. Ivan Andreev in the Kiev suburb of Dymievka led a group of stundists with Pashkovite ties. In 1883 an Orthodox priest reported that Pashkov was their patron, supplying them with large amounts of money for propaganda. Andreev was successful in gathering workers, railroad men, and soldiers, besides a couple of Kiev women, producing a proletarian body, unusual for stundists at that time. The regime exiled Andreev to Orlov *guberniya*.[20]

Pashkovites not only had ties with stundists in Kiev *guberniya* but also in other areas. Orthodox observers noted that stundist leaders in Kherson *guberniya*, such as Mikhail Ratushnyĭ and Anton Strigun, traveled each year to St. Petersburg with others for instruction and financial assistance. In the 1880s August Liebig, the German Baptist minister in the Odessa region, was a conduit for funds for Russian Stundo-Baptist believers, funds that he might himself dole out but more often distributed through such leaders as Mikhail Ratushnyĭ and Ivan Ryaboshapka. In his report in 1884, Pobedonostsev reported that in Mogilev Diocese stundists were receiving material aid from Pashkov and his supporters.[21]

By 1879 Pashkov had visited stundists in Ukraine and in 1881 or possibly 1882 Molokans in Novosvil'evka, Taurida *guberniya*. Earlier a leader of the Don sect of

---

19. Korff, 18–19, 38–47.

20. Terletskiĭ, 123–24. *WHZ*, Oct. 1, 1884, 201. Rozhdestvenskiĭ, 136–38. Diedrich, *Ursprünge und Anfänge des russischen Freikirchentums*, 419–20.

21. Terletskiĭ, 127. Letters of Liebig to Pashkov, 1883, Apr. 5, Apr. 7/19; 1885, Sep.21/Oct. 3; 1886, Jan. 7/19, July 11/23, Pashkov Papers. Procurator of the Holy Synod, *Report*, 1884, 207.

Molokans in Taurida had become acquainted with Pashkovism on business in St. Petersburg and began to preach Pashkovite doctrine on his return. In his report in 1883, Pobedonostsev stated that Pashkovites in 1882 and 1883 began to preach among Molokans in Astrakhanka and surrounding areas in Taurida *guberniya*. In addition, Dimitrii Udarov, a leader in the Baptist church in Vladikavkaz in the Caucasus, corresponded in 1880 with Pashkov.[22]

The literature of the Pashkovites, distributed by colporteurs and by means of the railroad, spread not only Pashkovite teachings but were also a tie with sectarians, including Molokans, stundists, and Stundo-Baptists. Vasilii Pavlov, the Baptist evangelist, provided a mass of tracts to Molokans in Samara *guberniya*. Religious hymns of the Pashkovites also had an impact on both stundists and Baptists.[23]

THE ST. PETERSBURG CONGRESS

One of Pashkov and Korff's audacious efforts was the calling in St. Petersburg a unity congress of evangelical sectarian believers. With their ties with sectarians and the belief that all true believers were members of the one universal church of Christ, it was natural for them to seek a common platform. It was particularly daring in light of the growing hostility of the regime toward Pashkov's activity among the masses and for its location in the capital city itself. The scope of its invitation was broad, including not only Pashkovites but all independent evangelicals—Molokans, New Molokans, stundists, Stundo-Baptists, Russian Baptists, German Baptists, evangelical Armenians—as well as evangelical leaders from abroad. The regime was already nervous about such a linkage. As early as 1880 Pobedonostsev had written in his memorandum that Pashkov, among other things, was dangerous "because he calls into existence a new sect" and "threatens to coalesce with the *Stunda,* which sprung among the peasants of the south-west of Russia."[24]

According to Stead, General Oryevskii, head of the political police, summoned Pashkov and Korff to sign a statement to refrain from preaching, distributing tracts, or receive sectarian delegates from the South. The authorities also ordered Princess Lieven not to receive sectarians into her home.[25] Since the congress began and continued some days without police intevention, such an order may not have been issued at this time, or the regime was unusually inept in its surveillance. Stead suggested that the authorities did not make inquiry concerning the congress until Orthodox priests, at first thinking the delegates had gone to St. Petersburg to petition for religious liberty, became suspicious and alerted them.

22. Corrado, 148–49. *MO*, Mar. 1902, 606. Terletskii, 130. Procurator of the Holy Synod, *Report*, 1883, 261. Dyck, 77.

23. *TsV*, 1886, no. 45, 714. Terletskii, 125, 128, 131. Rozhdenstvenskii, 178.

24. Stead, 375.

25. Ibid., 365.

PART FOUR—Prospects: The Aristocratic Impulse, 1874–1884

In any case, according to Korff the invitation to the congress, which would begin on April 1st, was dated March 24, which assumes that many had such information much earlier because of their need to prepare and travel great distances whether within the country or from abroad. The invitation declared that those who are members of one body and baptized with one spirit should fulfil the prayer of Christ that "They all may be one" and "that they may be made perfect in one." It would not be a mass meeting but composed of delegates from congregations. The invitation provided the address of Pashkov's home where delegates could receive information on accommodations and if needed even free quarters and support.

Since the congress produced no official minutes, the accounts of three of the participants, Korff, Vasilii Pavlov from Tiflis, and the Swedish missionary A. P. Larsson, are the most valuable, although other accounts are helpful. Pashkov recorded the first five days of the congress in his diary, which was seized by the police and later reproduced by such Orthodox authors as Rozhdestvenskii and Terletskii. Larsson's account, incorporating in part Pavlov's account, provides some valuable details. Korff's record, written in 1922, unfortunately is foreshortened and appears unreliable in its chronology.[26]

Korff reported that over seventy persons arrived. Stead stated that twenty-five were Russians while forty-five were Germans, English, and Swedes. Around one hundred were at the initial assembly, which would include Pashkovites of the area. The conference was international and included a galaxy of evangelical leaders from inside and outside Russia, demonstrating that Russian evangelical sectarianism was clearly linked with a worldwide movement. Pashkovite participants included, besides Pashkov and Korff, Nathalie Lieven and Vera Gagarina. Russian stundists and Stundo-Baptists included Ratushnyii, Ryaboshapka, Balikhin, Kolodin, Delyakov, Bogdanov, and Kiselev. Others from within the Russian Empire were Vasilii Pavlov from the Russian Baptists, Z. D. Zakharov from the New Molokans, and A. F. Amirkhanianz from the evangelical Armenians. German Baptists included Karl Ondra from Lodz, August Liebig from Odessa, and Johann Kargel from Bulgaria. Mr. and Mrs. F. W. Baedeker, and Mr. and Mrs. Reginald Radcliffe with a daughter arrived from England. From Sweden were N. F. Höijer and A. P. Larsson, Mission Covenant missionaries. P. Z. Easton, an American Presbyterian missionary in Persia, also attended.

The congress was planned for eight days, Sunday to Sunday, from April 1 to April 8. According to Larsson, sessions were held in the homes of Lieven, Korff, and Pashkov. The host usually treated the guests to dinner. Korff wrote that the first gathering was in the eating house in the vicinity of Pashkov's home. Pavlov, however, recorded that the first meeting was in Princess Lieven's mansion. Almost immediately a serious

---

26. For accounts or details of the congress, see Korff, 56–62; Larsson, *Tjugufem år i Ryssland*, 113–20; Rozhdestvenskii, 139–43; Terletskii, 132–38; Stead, 363–66; Dalton, *Der Stundismus in Russland*, 43–45; Ondra's report on the conference in *Der Sendbote*, June 11, 1884, 182; Latimer, *Dr. Baedeker*, 36–38; and Kmeta, *With Christ in America*, 36.

fault line appeared. According to Pavlov and Dalton's accounts, the Baptists and most of the Stundo-Baptists refused to participate in the observance of the Lord's Supper, adhering to their position of close communion, i.e., communing only with immersed believers. Princess Lieven provided dinner for the guests, which was followed by another session with numerous messages on the themes of unity and prayer.

On April 2, also in Lieven's mansion, the morning session was devoted to singing, spontaneous prayers, and messages from Bible texts. After dinner, a statement of six points was introduced, which earlier a committee of five, composed of Korff, Pashkov, Kargel, Delyakov, and Baedeker, had formulated, feeling it would be accepted without controversy. After prolonged discussion on voting, the assembly voted unanimously to accept the first point that the body of Christ consists of those redeemed through the blood of Christ and born by the Holy Spirit through God's Word. All then ate dinner at Pashkov's mansion.

On April 3 a service was held at Korff's home, followed by dinner at Pashkov's home. In the afternoon the guests met at Lieven's home and discussed the second article on baptism. The statement recognized baptism as an ordinance of God, but its fulfillment was to be left to "the conscience of each individual and his knowledge of the Word of God." But strife ensued. Even though one of the guests from England called on all to fall on their knees and pray, declaring unity is in Christ, yet unity was not achieved. Ondra reported that an article recognizing God's Word as the only standard be placed before all other articles was not adopted. On April 4 the assembly met again at Lieven's home. Since the controversy over baptism had not ended, Pashkov asked for prayer and went into consultation with the committee of five; Pashkov returned with Baedeker stating that the committee had agreed to eliminate the statement of baptism from the agenda.

After a repast, Count Korff invited the guests to his home where they discussed practical matters, such as how to be more effective in extending the Kingdom of God. Both Liebig and Pavlov spoke. In the evening Korff invited the guests to an elegant dinner. Larsson described the occasion, stating that all dined on the finest china, a set that the Tsar had given Korff's father and previously used only when the Tsar was present. A nobleman, who was a trained opera singer, sang several songs with his magnificent voice. The assembly was diverse, including nobility, women in high society, manual workers, and peasants. Ryaboshapka, the simple Ukrainian with long hair and beard, attracted much attention, arriving in his sheep fur. His dress was Ukrainian with wide pants and one pant leg tucked into a heavy boot and the other on the outside, a red shirt hanging outside the pants, and a rope around the waist. Instead of sleeping in the richly furnished bed that Countess Gargarina had provided for him at her home, scaring the chamber maid by his absence, he was found sleeping in the servants' quarters.

On Thursday, April 5, the assembly met three times in Lieven's home. Reginald Radcliffe from England spoke at one of the sessions, warning against paying preachers a salary and opposed women speaking in public assemblies. In a private conversation,

Pavlov expressed his disapproval of his views. Lieven hosted the evening meal, praying aloud and also speaking, which included the theme, "Do not love the world."

Through the last session on April 5 the congress had proceeded without police interference, but Pavlov's diary ends with this day since he with others were arrested that evening. What transpired afterwards must be gleaned from a number of reminiscences of those in attendance. The accounts differ in sequence of events, in part because there were two separate arrests in which events were evidently indiscriminately mixed. There is also a question of dates and the total number arrested.[27]

Pavlov's account, written in his autobiography in 1899, appears to be the most reliable. Pavlov wrote that on his return with others to their hotel, they discovered the police had entered their rooms and searched their trunks. The police arrested thirteen of them, finally brought them to the Kazan police station where they were examined and here spent the night. Dalton claimed the authorities sharply questioned them but handled them with much more consideration than authorities at home. The authorities released them, and according to Stead they returned to the congress where there was much rejoicing on their appearance.

Pavlov, Dalton, and Stead recount a second arrest, probably on Saturday evening, which included again Pavlov. The police had found incriminating type, linking them to nihilists, which Pavlov will later contend was an invented charge. Nevertheless the police held those arrested until Easter Sunday, April 8. Dalton and Larsson claim that Pobedonostsev was at the hearing on Easter, but as Pavlov does not mention it and because of the Easter holiday it is somewhat questionable. The authorities released them but took them to the train station, took away their money, and bought train tickets for their return home. In the meantime the assembled guests in the Pashkov home waited for some time for the missing delegates but then decided to meet without them. By a ruse, one of the arrested, Amirkhanianz, avoided deportation and toward evening was able to return to report to the other delegates what had occurred. Almost immediately after the close of the congress, Baedeker wrote a report that was very upbeat, stating that the police after interrogation had "requested" the thirteen who were arrested to return home, declaring it was "a wonderful answer to prayer." Baedeker, not knowing all the details, may very well have unduly conflated the two arrests.

Dissolution and Exile

Whatever the sequence of events, the congress, in spite of the two arrests, continued almost to its conclusion with a minimum of disruption. The police did not arrest any of the Pashkovites nor expel any of the foreign guests. At the moment the government's main concern was to remove the sectarian delegates who had come from the south. If

---

27. For accounts of the arrests, see Pavlov, "Vospominaniya ssyl'nago," in *MKIsI*, 1:4–5, and *BV*, 1945, 3, 30; Dalton, *Der Stundismus in Russland*, 45; Stead, 365–66; Latimer, *Dr. Baedeker*, 37–38; Larsson, 117–18; and Baedeker's report in *Missionary Echo*, June 1884, 89.

nothing else, the congress proved the fear of Pobedonostsev and other authorities of a growing alliance between Pashkovites and sectarians.

The consequences of the congress in St. Petersburg will be far greater than the expulsion of delegates. The authorities now felt that it could not wait to destroy the Pashkovite enterprise, which was fueling a sectarian insurgency. Pobdedonostsev now had his opportunity for suppression.

On May 24, 1884, the regime suppressed the Society for the Encouragement of Spiritual and Ethical Reading. It confiscated its books and tracts and their further distribution. The authorities searched the country to destroy remaining copies. Later in the year Pashkov wrote to Pobedonostsev for compensation of the tracts taken from the home of his brother-in-law, Count Chernishev-Kruglikov, claiming a loss of 21,000 rubles—12,000 to the society and 9,000 to himself. Pobedonostsev rejected the claim, stating the publications were dangerous and the confiscation legal. The Religious Tract Society of London could continue distributing tracts in foreign tongues but its distribution of Russian tracts now ended.[28]

For the present the *Russkiï rabochiï* continued, but its end soon came. The ecclesiastical censor became extremely exacting, criticizing the paper for what it allegedly omitted, such as the role of the church, or material that appeared to support sectarian belief. The Holy Synod finally brought about its demise in 1886 by ordering the censor not to approve any material the editor sent him.[29]

With the closing of the Pashkovite society, the police carefully watched Pashkov and Korff. In June the regime ordered both Pashkov and Korff to appear separately before the Minister of Police to sign a statement not to engage in unauthorized religious meetings to preach, to engage in free prayer, nor maintain relationships with stundists or other religious communities. If they failed to sign, the government threatened immediate exile from Russia. For the sake of conscience, both refused to sign and were given fourteen days to leave. With a wife expecting a child, Korff asked for an extension, which was refused. Pashkov went to England. Korff and wife left on June 27 to settle near Paris where his wife's parents lived. Here Korff's wife gave birth to a son. The regime, however, did not confiscate Pashkov and Korff's estates, which saved their wealth.[30]

The minister of police also went to the home of Princess Lieven for her to sign the same demand that had been presented to Pashskov and Korff. She also refused. Alexander III, however, ordered that she and the other Pashkovite widows, such as Elizaveta Chertkova and Vera Gagarina, were not to be molested and were able to continue meetings in their homes. Count Bobrinskiï who often went abroad and evidently abroad at the time of the St. Petersburg Conference and who largely confined

---

28. RTS, *Report*, 1885, 83, and 1887, 89. Högberg, 79–81. Corrado, 146. *Pobedonostsev i ego korrespondenty*, ed. by Pokrovskiï, 2:456–57.

29. Stead, 342–44. RTS, *Report*, 1887, 89.

30. Korff, 62–66. Stead, 366–72.

himself to his estate in Tula *guberniya* while in Russia, was also not exiled. Edward Hilton, a British subject and a Protestant and a manager of Pashkov's property, including property at his copper mines in Ufa *guberniya*, however, suffered expulsion in 1884. Hilton had gotten into a controversy with the Orthodox priest over church holidays and was accused of distributing Pashkovite literature. In Tambov *guberniya*, where Pashkov had an estate, the governor also accused Edward of the same activity. Edward's brother, Henry Hilton, succeeded him but one or two years later he was also given an order of expulsion. Although the order was rescinded as unjust, even Pobedonostsev admitting the same, Henry had already left the country.[31]

EVALUATION

In his evaluation of the Radstock movement in 1876/1877, Leskov concluded it was not a schism, i.e., a division from the church, in his work with the ironic title, *Schism in High Society*. He believed it was only potentially schismatic if the religious establishment did not meet the spiritual needs of its parishioners. Leskov claimed the Radstock followers centered their interest on Scripture and salvation, expressed no enmity toward the church, nor sought to establish a sect of their own. Whatever their evangelical beliefs and associations, neither Radstock nor Pashkov formally repudiated the church in which they were baptized as infants. Both of them sought to bring people into the universal church of Christ and worked above and outside ecclesiastical organizations. Terletskiĭ pointed out that the Pashkovitess taught it was unnecessary to join any denomination; one need only to commit oneself to Christ. Only one Radstock follower, J. D. Zasetskaya, openly broke with the Orthodox Church and upon her death abroad in 1883 had forbade Orthodox burial rites. On his visit to St. Petersburg in 1883, George Müller, a member of the Plymouth Brethren, had immersed Pashkov, Princess Lieven, and the Lieven governess, Miss Klassovskaya, a testimony of faith but not looking to the establishment of a new church with its own ordinances.[32]

In some ways the Pashkovite movement was too successful for its own good. If it had remained a revival movement within the Orthodox Church with a select clientele, it may not have brought on itself the wrath of the regime. It had influence in high circles, financial resources, and a successful publishing enterprise. But it was becoming a mass movement that extended its ties and support to sectarian movements condemned by both church and state as heretical and inimical to the unity of the state. Its benevolent activity began to be regarded as subversive as a means of buying the allegiance of the lower classes and thus alienating them from the church.

---

31. Korff, 65–66. *The Friend of Missions*, Mar. 1928, 47. For information on the Hilton brothers, see Stead, 344–53, and *EC*, Feb. 1, 1884, 63–64.

32. Leskov, 106–8. Heier, 59, and 74, ft. 46. For the baptisms by Müller, see Waldemar Gutsche, *Westliche Quellen des russischen Stundismus*, 60; *Der Sendbote*, May 1884, 171; and *Missions*, Oct. 1911, 666.

Pashkov's largesse appeared especially threatening. His free meals in his mansion and the reasonable meals in his eating halls were material inducements.[33]

Although Radstock and Pashkov and their followers avoided condemning the Orthodox Church, but their teaching, although not explicitly rejecting the sacraments and rites of the Orthodox Church implicitly repudiated them. With its emphasis on justification by faith, one needed no priesthood, sacraments, prayer to saints, and observance of fasts and holy days. Reports surfaced of workers or peasants discarding ikons and crucifixes. It was reported that Pashkov distributed wall plaques with verses that replaced ikons in the homes. His dining halls displayed texts on the walls.[34]

Authorities also began to feel that much of the Pashkovite literature included more than simply teaching ethical behavior in its appeal to faith alone and failure to include the sacraments and rites of the church. Its sources and illustrations often came from abroad. Even its Bibles were not just simply the text but with their markings led one toward the theology of the movement.

Pashkovism appeared to be simply a foreign implant with no concession to Orthodox theology or worship. Western evangelicalism was the norm. Critics felt there was too much emphasis upon simple faith without a proper balance between faith and works and a disregard of the rich heritage of Orthodox piety. Preaching by laymen was central with no formal liturgy; music was often translations of foreign hymns; and singing, now generally congregational and accompanied by a musical instrument, was contrary to Orthodox practice. Their leaders, laypersons without theological training, expounding Bible texts and stressing Christian experience, were in no position to enter into any meaningful dialog with Orthodox thinkers. One Orthodox critic claimed that Pashkov went even beyond usual Protestant norms in rejecting a historical and church basis, thereby standing above any church.[35]

Was Pashkov too reckless or foolhardy or too fanatical? Did he overreach? With his political and social connections and wealth, did he feel immune? Before his final exile, he had warnings, including an order in 1878 to stop his activity, which was not carried out, an exile in 1880, which proved to be temporary, and personal admonitions from Pobedonostsev himself.[36] The St. Petersburg Conference under the very nose of the government showed great insensitivity in the face of political reality.

The exile, the suppression of the Society for the Encouragement of Spiritual and Ethical Reading, and the following repression of the Pashkovites with other evangelicals will prove to be a serious blow. Could it have been avoided? Perhaps not. In any case, the Pashkovites, whatever their strengths and weaknesses, made a unique contribution to evangelicalism in Russia. Upon their exile, Paskhov and Korff wrote a letter to The Tsar, stating, "The Lord's work in Russia will not be hindered or stopped

---

33. Stead. 377–78. Heier, 115–16.
34. Stead, 358–59, 376–77. Terletskiĭ, 103–4. Leroy-Beaulieu, 473. *MO*, March 1902, 605.
35. Leskov, 63–67. Heier, 48–49. Corrado, 190–91. *Strannik*, 1883, I, no. 3, 515.
36. Stead, 375–77. Dalton, *Catholic Presbyterian*, 114. Heier, 139.

by our exile." The letter predicted that the Kingdom of God will grow in Russia "with still more power," carried on by many others, and that "Our undeserved exile will serve to consolidate this work." Time will tell the truth of these assertions.[37]

---

37. Stead, 390–91.

PART FIVE

Peril, 1884–1905

17

The Attack

IN 1884 AUGUST RAUSCHENBUSCH wrote an article, "Good News from Russia," in which he was most upbeat on Baptist prospects in the Russian Empire. He declared, "As no other Protestant denomination has at present an influence with the Russian people, there is a golden opportunity for the Baptists; and, if they seize it, our denomination will have a great future in Russia."[1] Rauschenbusch wrote the article before the dissolution of the Pashkovite publication society and the banishment of Pashkov and Korff in 1884 and had every reason to be optimistic. As noted earlier, Johann Wieler in 1882 invited Russian Baptist leaders to meet with Mennonite Brethren in conference where both gave mission reports. They approved four Baptists missionaries with salaries determined by length of service on the field, a pattern that Russian Baptists themselves will soon follow in their own conferences. At the conference Ivan Ryaboshapka noted that, although stundists for a long time had been subject to government suppression, people were not now afraid to attend services. In November 1885 Ryaboshapka wrote to Pashkov that his congregation continued to increase with attendance at times of about 300 with many forced to stand outside. A year earlier, Michael Ratushnyï wrote to Pashkov that in the south of Russia the brethren were living at peace and were not hindered in their services.[2]

The authorities disrupted in April 1884 the St. Petersburg Congress, sponsored by the Pashkovites, but the many Stundo-Baptists and other evangelicals who attended, although temporarily detained, were allowed to return to their homes without

---

1. *BMM*, Sep. 1884, 237.

2. MO, Sep. 1900, 219. Letters of Ryaboshapka, November 21, 1885, and Ratushnyï, Nov. 1884, Pashkov Papers.

penalty. As previously planned, Russian Baptist delegates met in Novo-Vasil'evka on April 30 and May 1, 1884, where they formed their own Russian union. The acquittal of the stundists in the landmark case of 1878 emboldened them and helped to spread the rumor that stundist beliefs conformed to Christian teaching. The legalization of the German Baptists in 1879 and the new legislation of 1883–1884 for dissidents provided a possible basis for legalization of Russian stundists and Baptists.[3]

In a letter printed in *Nedelya* in 1885, the writer asserted that one could fight stundism only with moral weapons. To oppress it would further its organization and resolve, popularize its teaching, and transform it into an underground movement outside any control. He noted inconsistencies in attitude and policy toward them. Some officials pointed to stundists as examples while other officials severely beat and insulted them. Some schools accepted stundist children while others expelled them or refused them altogether. Some courts levied small fines while others laid on them excessive penalties.[4]

In spite of hopeful signs, Stundo-Baptists themselves noted that not all was well. Although Ratushnyï wrote to Pashkov in 1884 that his congregation was at peace, yet a year earlier he wrote that authorities had fined a number of them fifteen or twenty rubles. Vasilii Pavlov wrote in 1882 of the inability of the church in Vladikavkaz to gain legal status. John Brown noted that in 1882–1883 local police chiefs (*ispravniki*) were fining stundists and even auctioning their goods for attendance at stundist meetings. In 1883 *Der Wahrheitszeuge* reported the beating by birch rods of a stundist who refused to kiss the cross. In 1883 Ryaboshapka and Ratushnyï appealed to the authorities in Kiev, Moscow, and St. Petersburg for freedom of worship.[5]

As noted earlier, both Ryaboshapka and Ratushnyï also unsuccessively petitioned the government for recognition as "Christian Baptists." In Stavropol region and Taurida *guberniya* some Russian Baptists were able to gain recognition as Baptists, but this was an exception.[6] The authorities insisted the 1879 law did not apply to Russians who had defected from Orthodoxy. For them there was no such thing as Russian Baptists.[7]

Under Alexander II the regime formed in 1858 a commission to study reforming legislation on dissidents but nothing was issued before Alexander's assassination. The new law of May 3, 1883, with the rewording in a new edition on May 1, 1884, at least on its surface appeared to provide relief for Old Believers and sectarians. Such persons could now worship in their own places, gain passports, engage in commercial enterprises, and serve in minor offices, but they still faced numerous restrictions.

3. I. Strebliskiï, *Kratkiï Ocherk shtundizma i svod tekstov, napravlennykh k ego oblicheniyu*, 27.

4. *Nedelya*, 1885, no. 45, 1586–87.

5. Letter of Ratushnyï to Pashkov, August 9, 1883, Pashkov Papers. WHZ, May 1, 1882, 90; Mar. 1, 1883, 52. John Brown, 28. Val'kevich, 85.

6. *Beseda*, Feb. 1895, 30.

7. Melgunov, "*Tserkov i gosudarstvo v Rossii*," I, "Shtundisty ili baptisty," 57–66. Hourwich, "Religious Sects in Russia," *The International Quarterly* 8, Sep.–Dec. 1903/Dec.–Mar. 1903–1904, 171.

For instance, the Ministry of Internal Affairs granted permission for new structures, which must, however, differ from Orthodox houses of worship, and reserved the right to issue regulations for each sect. The law continued to forbid all proselytizing of Orthodox. The Old Believers, who were aligned with Orthodoxy in theology but differed in ritual, were called "*Raskolniks*" or "dissenters" and benefited from the new law. Stundo-Baptists in Saratov, Samara, and Baku Provinces utilized the May 1883 law for the right of worship, but this was an exception. The regime called Russian free church evangelicals "sectarians," making it a term of opprobrium, considering them apostates without any rights under this legislation.[8]

Growing Antagonism

Unfortunately the times were now against the Russian stundists and Russian Baptists. The assassination of Alexander II in 1881 led to the reign of his son, Alexander III, from 1881 to 1894. It ushered a regime of reaction, fearful of further liberalization with a determination of repression of revolutionary threats and dissent. Alexander II was regarded as "The Tsar Liberator," but E. B. Lanin in his biting indictment of Russia's religious policies called Alexander III "The Tsar Persecutor."[9] The same policies continued until shortly before the Revolution of 1905 under Nicholas II. As noted earlier, the procurator of the Holy Synod from 1880–1905, Konstantin Pobedonostsev, upheld the autocracy and the religious monopoly of the Orthodox Church and regarded toleration of dissenters a threat to both church and state.

The climate of suppression for Russian stundists and Baptists became very apparent in the mid-1880s. One factor was that the Stundo-Baptist movement was growing at such an accelerated pace that measures of church and state were failing to check it. In his report in 1888–1889, Pobedonostsev declared that stundism from its origin in Ukraine had grown to "dangerous dimensions." He noted that the movement was not only in numerous districts in Ukraine but had crossed into various provinces of Great Russia and even penetrated into the "middle belt of Russia." Pobedonostsev listed active Baptist missionaries from the Caucasus with Vasilii Pavlov the most significant. In his work on stundism, first appearing in 1893, I. Strel'bitskii noted that they were successful in carrying their message to "inns, railroad coaches, field workers, weddings, peasants, funerals, evening parties . . . and in a word always and everywhere."[10]

In his report of 1889–1890, Pobedonostsev noted that the first stundists, although adopting some features of Protestantism, attended the Orthodox Church,

---

8. Leroy-Beaulieu, *The Empire of the Tsars and the Russians*, 3:497–98. Blane, "The Relations between the Russian Protestant Sects and the State, 1900–1921," 28–30. Curtis, *Church and State in Russia*, 135–36. Bobrishchev-Pushkin, *Sud i raskol'niki-sektantry*, 178–79. "A Voice from Russia," *MRW*, Oct. 1894, 756.

9. E. B. Lanin, "The Tsar Persecutor," *Contemporary Review* 61 (Jan. 1892), 1–25.

10. Procurator of the Holy Synod, *Report*, 1888–1889, 109. Strel'bitskii, 43.

partook of the sacraments, and were more subdued in their propaganda. But now with growing confidence stundism "openly with fanaticism propagates its heresy, tries to subvert the Orthodox into the sect, and uses for this every possible means." As much controversy as the leaders of Orthodoxy had had with the schismatic Old Believers, they recognized them as far less dangerous than stundism. The conflict with Old Believers was over ritual; with stundism it was over a whole range of issues, leading to the rejecting entirely of the authority and sacramentalism of the Orthodox Church. Victor L. Val'kevich condemned stundists for excessive conceit and sanctimoniousness, comparing themselves with the holy apostles and sending out "church epistles," covering them authoritatively with texts of Scripture.[11]

The antagonism between Orthodox and evangelical sectarians grew so great that both sides disparaged the other without recognition of any Christian virtue in the other, using epithets that were scurrilous. Although serious issues divided them, both held many Christian dogmas in common. Orthodox and stundists were Trinitarian, recognized Christ as Savior, Scripture as divinely inspired, the validity of the Ten Commandments, and for Orthodox and Baptists immersion as the biblical mode of baptism. But both sides regarded the other as false purveyors of the faith. In the attacks there may have been elements of truth in the charges and counter charges, but the attacks were hurled to destroy. All Christian charity was lost.

In the battle some village priests attempted to ignore the stundist threat and made no charges against it. On the other hand, other priests sent in reports, denouncing stundists as blasphemers who revile all that was sacred. Such priests urged civil action against them.[12] Stundists took advantage of the widespread anticlericalism in the Russian population. Strel'bitskiï claimed that to get a hearing stundist propagandists first began with an attack on the priests and then later will condemn Orthodox teaching. Val'kevich charged that stundism engaged in vilification, calling "the Orthodox Church—a whore, ikons—idols, and priests—stallions." Pobedonostsev wrote that stundists at Sunday discussions were impertinent toward priests, calling them blasphemers, and also mocked "the Orthodox faith, ikons, and sacraments." Paul Kozitskiï declared stundism was an "anti-church sect," expressing animosity toward the priests and condemning them as poor pastors and "predatory wolves." He accused stundism as simplifying the road to salvation without the rules and rituals of the church. N. Zaozerskiï declared that stundism in essence was "church nihilism," fueled by its opposition to the church hierarchy and church rites.[13]

---

11. Procurator of the Holy Synod, *Report*, 1888–1889, 111. *TsV*, 1891, no. 25, 385–86. Val'kevich, 199.

12. Kozitskiï, "O prichinakh, prepyatstvuyushchikh uspeshnoï bor'be so shtundizmom," *TsV*, 1891, no. 21, 325. *Leisure Hour*, Mar. 1890, 306.

13. For a description of the widespread anticlericalism among the masses, see Evans, *The Churches in the U.S.S.R.*, 18–29. Strel'bitskiï, 28–29. Val'kevich, 199. Procurator of the Holy Synod, *Report*, 1888–1889, 111. Kozitskiï, *TsV*, 1891, no. 21, 324. Zaozerskiï, "Chem silen' shtundizm?," *Bogoslavskiï vestnik*, 1893, no. 10, 184–85. For a justification by an evangelical of attacks on Orthodoxy for idolatry

The level of invective reached another level when the Orthodox began charging stundism not only as a subversive religious movement but attempted to denigrate it further by associating it with clearly deviant movements. In this way, the critics broadened the name "stundist" to mean a body that was deviant even from Protestant norms as bad as these were in the critics' minds. In his article in the evangelical periodical, *Beseda,* Ivan S. Prokhanov (under the pen name of Upovayushchiï), "What Is Stundism!," pointed out that earlier researchers recognized stundism as a Protestant evangelical movement. But others, he noted, are associating stundism with the Malevantsy, clearly heretical and repudiated by stundists themselves and through this sect associating them with the Khlysty, a mystical and pantheistic sect. Critics also tried to associate stundism with Tolstoyism, a rationalistic ideology.[14]

In his 1888–1889 report, Pobedonostsev claimed that "so-called prophets" were within stundism, and some stundists have passed over into the Khlysty "with its wild rites." He also asserted that some stundists rejected the divinity of Christ and even the sacrament of marriage. An article in *Tserkovnyï vestnik* in 1893 maintained that missionaries have found strong rationalistic thinking among stundists, even atheism; in some places they state that neither Christ nor the Holy Spirit are divine.[15]

Critics also attacked stundism as a serious danger to society from its disputatious and scandalous behavior within its own ranks as well as holding to social and political views that threatened the state. Victor L. Val'kevich, one of the major Orthodox researchers on evangelical sectarians in his monumental work, *Zapiska o propaganda protestantskikh sekt v Rossii i, v osobenosti, na Kavkaze* (A Memorandum on the Propaganda of Protestant Sects in Russia and in Particular in the Caucasus), published in 1900, is a carefully crafted narrative that used primary source material collected in six appendices of the work. The final section of the narrative, "The Injurious Social-Political Significance of Sectarianism," is entirely negative with no redemptive features for the movement as in Rozhdostvenskiï's work, written in the 1880s. Val'kevich's work was written in the 1890s at the height of the conflict. As previously noted, Val'kevich condemned the apostolic pretensions of stundists and Stundo-Baptists and recorded their epithets on the Orthodox Church and its priests. In using church minutes and correspondence, he pointedly recorded the quarrels of their leaders and portrayed them as a people who engaged in scandal and who portrayed a degraded morality.[16]

An old and unfounded charge that Val'kevich and others used was that the stundist movement advocated socialist if not communist ideals. Some contended that under the guise of religion stundists advocated political and nihilistic principles. Such charges were most damaging as the regime was then in a struggle with revolutionaries who wished to overthrow it. This attack was one more weapon in its arsenal against

---

and misconduct of priests, see, "A Voice from Russia," *MRW,* Oct. 1894, 757–59.

14. "Chto takoe shtundizm!," *Beseda,* July 1895, 101–5.
15. Procurator of the Holy Synod, *Report,* 1888–1889, 111–12. *TsV,* 1893, no. 11, 174.
16. Val'kevich, 199–209.

its foe. Both Val'kevich and Pobedonostsev wrote that stundists in 1880 predicted that after thirty years the Orthodox Church would be abolished and a brotherhood established in which all property would be held in common. In his 1890–1891 report, Pobedonostsev claimed stundism advocated a general equality and rejected civil authority, military service, and oaths. Val'kevich maintained that the revolutionary intelligentsia and Tolstoyism influenced stundism, which were both hostile to the regime. He faulted *Beseda* for its advocacy of religious liberty, which made stundism even more dangerous.[17]

Another instrument that critics used against stundism (by the way, a German name) was the charge that it was a foreign import that made it a threat to national security and the country's religious integrity. Critics pointed out Germanic ties stundism may have had with Germans from abroad or within the nation itself and any indication of its approval of German culture. The Germanophobia of the time fed on itself. Foreign relations between Russia and Germany began to deteriorate in the 1880s that led in 1892 to a convention that pledged mutual military support between Russia and France. In addition, the growing resentment of German influence and culture, reflected in the prosperity and lifestyle of German inhabitants within the nation, also nurtured the German threat.[18]

Some writers charged stundism/Stundo-Baptism was a product of German propaganda and Germanization. Such Russian authors as P. G. Lebedintsev (1885), I. Strel'bitskii (1890), A. A. Velitsyn (1893), and Aleskii Dorodnitsyn (1893, 1903, 1908, 1909) propounded this thesis. In his article on stundism, N. I. Petrov claimed Hamburg deliberately sent out in the 1870s missionaries to German colonies in Russia where they influenced Ukrainian workers. He pointed out the influence of a German mill owner, Chesse, in Volhynia as well as Friedrich Müller, an agent of the British and Foreign Bible Society at Rostov-on-Don, and the German colony of Friedensfeld.[19]

Val'kevich made a long list of the foreign associations of the stundists, including Germans as well as English and Swedes. He listed Stundo-Baptist attendance at foreign schools or with German colonists in Russia, learning German, translating from German, admiration of foreign propagandists from abroad, looking to Hamburg as its spiritual center, imitation of the German way of life, including dwellings and furniture, and even hanging the pictures of German figures, such as Bismarck. He also noted donors from the German colonists and Pashkovites, ties with Bible societies in Germany and England, articles on stundists in the foreign press, and the migration of stundists abroad. In 1894 Vasilii Skvortsov, a leading missionary of the Orthodox

---

17. Procurator of the Holy Synod, *Report*, 1888–1889, 112, and 1890–1891, 249–50. Val'kevich, 215, 217–20.

18. For an extensive listing of bibliographic entries on Germanophobia and the stundists, see Wardin, *Evangelical Sectarianism*, 370–71.

19. Petrov, "Novyya svedeniya o shtundizme," *TrKDA*, no. 3, 1887, 383, 389, 395. See BFBS, *Report*, 1886, 128, for a laudatory report by the BFBS on Müller.

Church and recognized as an expert on stundism, declared that it was a foreign creed and was "resolutely alien" to the national soul and the religious outlook of the Russian people, "forcibly imposed first by German propagandists and later by Russian associates."[20]

Pobedonostsev in his report in 1890–1891 quoted stundists as saying "the Germans are rich and more clever than we, their faith more pure, better customs." Strel'bitskiĭ described the striking similarity in appearance between the stundist and the German colonist with his clean shaven face, similar style of clothing, the same trousers in high boots, which at times made it difficult to distinguish a Ukrainian stundist from a German.[21]

A. A. Velitsyn in his work in 1890 with the provocative title, *Nemetskoe zavoevanie na yuge Rossii* (The German Conquest in South Russia) pointed out not only the phenomenal purchase of land by Germans but also the threat of stundism, which not only attacked the Orthodox Church but also made the peasant a German. On his conversion the peasant adopted German ways and a German allegiance. A. P. Liprandi in his work in 1890 on the German question also linked stundism and Germanization. A. M. Dondukov-Korskov, head of the administration in the Caucasus, not only was concerned that Baptist converts lost their Russian character but in addition posed a security threat to the Empire on its southern border.[22]

The evangelical paper, *Beseda*, tried to counter the charge of foreign allegiance of stundists by writing in 1895: "In our teaching there is not any slyness or impure motives: for the Lord Emperor we pray and serve him more faithfully than the Orthodox, and although in the papers they write that we have greater love for the German lord, but this is a lie and slander, imputed to us by the spiritual authorities."[23]

Orthodox Counter Measures

In this period the Orthodox Church continued to counter stundism through missionary means. Pobedonostsev helped to establish the Inner Mission with a cadre of missionaries to work in areas where its threat was greatest. The missionary force, although it grew, was not large for the size of the country and in comparison with the mission force of the stundists with their pastors and laity. In 1897 the missionary force included only 197 persons. In his report for 1886, Prokhanov stated that the Holy Synod appropriated for the effort 1,500 rubles for the year.

A rising star of the Inner Mission was Vasiliĭ M. Skvortsov (1859–1932). In 1884 he completed his academic training at the Kiev Spiritual Academy with a degree of

---

20. Val'kevich, 221–23. Skvortsov, "Organizatsiya shtundistkoĭ propagandy," *Moskovskiya vedomosti*. Aug. 10, 1894, 1–2.

21. Procurator of the Holy Synod, *Report.* 1890–1891, 250. Strel'bitskiĭ, 50–51.

22. Breyfogle, *Heretics and Colonizers*, 150–51.

23. *Beseda*, June 1894, 95.

master of theology and will marry the following year. While still a student, he engaged in missionary work and became a lecturer. After serving a short time in a seminary in Podolia, he held the chair of homiletics and pastoral theology as well as pedagogy in two women's institutions. The rector of the Kiev Seminary then called him to Kiev to write for two periodicals, *Leadership for Village Pastors* and *Church and School.* On his initiative Skvortsov established at the Kiev Seminary the chair of missionary sciences and was is first lecturer. He then introduced in the Kiev diocese a missionary congress and afterwards congresses in other dioceses. He served as secretary of the Second All-Russian Missionary Conference in 1891 as well as subsequent conferences. In his missionary activity, Skvortsov openly and secretly attended stundist meetings, studied the movement's worship, teaching, morals, and literature, and became a recognized authority of the movement. He served as an expert witness at judicial trials of dissidents.[24]

Ivan S. Prokhanov was very critical of Skvortsov and other missionaries of the Inner Mission, asserting they were spies who sought to provide information for the police to imprison or exile stundist leaders. He claimed that in disputations with the missionaries, evangelical preachers who participated were exiled soon afterwards. In his periodical, *Beseda,* Prokhanov bitterly attacked them in 1895 for not going to places of debauchery or to seek to win Orthodox who were still enmeshed with paganism or to Moslems. Prokhanov noted that the name Skvortsov meant "starling" and so stundists called all Russian missionaries "starlings." In his evaluation of missionaries, Pavel Kozitskiĭ, an Orthodox defender, pointed out that they often failed to adapt and lacked proper training. Some missionaries, he wrote, addressed sectarians with biting and even mocking remarks. Other missionaries were unable to come down to the level of the common people, speaking in bookish and pompous language, incorporating abstract concepts. Some parish priests were known to dread the coming of the missionary from a sense of false pride and initially failed to regard him as a coworker.[25] Stundo-Russian Baptists had a jump on the Orthodox for nation-wide mission conferences, a fact that Skvortsov himself noted in 1894. As early as 1884 the Holy Synod charged the metropolitan of Kiev to convene a conference of bishops of the southwestern dioceses to consider measures to counter heresy and especially stundism. In 1888 the Holy Synod proposed to the bishops regulations on the structure of the mission and method of operation of missionaries and pastors. The Orthodox finally called their first All-Russian Missionary Conference in Moscow in 1887. A second Missionary Conference convened in Moscow in 1891, a third in Kazan in 1897, and a fourth in Kiev in 1909, which were supplemented by regional conferences. Such congresses

---

24. For a sympathetic account of Skvortsov and the Inner Mission, see Maevskiĭ, *Vnutrennyaya missiya i ee osnovopolozhnik.*

25. *Beseda*, Feb. 1895, 28–29. Prokhanov, *In the Cauldron of Russia*, 82, 133–34. *TsV*, 1891, no. 211, 215–26. Maevskiĭ, 80–81.

were not only a means of rallying the mission forces but also discussed policies for church and state and practical measures for the mission task.[26]

Under the guidance of Pobdonostsev, the Second Missionary Conference in Moscow in 1891 adopted recommendations for increasing repressive measures. It discussed Pashkovites and Mlado-Stundists, considering them identical, as well as Stundo-Baptists and Baptists, both also considered identical. The congress noted that these groups were in agreement on the atonement of Christ but accused some stundists with incorporating mysticism and Tolstoyan ideas. It also charged stundism for not pursuing perfection of faith but rather paving the way for economic prosperity. It concluded that Baptists and Pashkovites along with Molokans were in the ranks of the most dangerous sects.[27]

For practical measures against sectarians, the congress recommended that ecclesiastical judges not juries try offenders and to prohibit them from renting, buying, or holding real property. It recommended removal of their children to be educated in Orthodoxy and to forbid them to leave their own villages.[28]

The third All-Russian Missionary Congress in 1897 in Kazan repeated past descriptions of stundism with nothing new. The conference was disturbed that stundists were using Russian translations of German works approved by the censor and attending German congregations where services included the Russian language. Although Mennonites were not generally considered a body that evangelized among Russians, nevertheless Aleksiï Dorodnitsyn, then missionary in Yekaterinoslav Province, presented a report which condemned the Mennonite Brethren. He charged it for its affinity to Stundo-Baptism and for spiritually and materially supporting it. He recommended the regime close their prayer houses and forbid their publications.[29]

In its fight against sectarianism, the conference recommended forbidding sectarian schools, sending adherents of especially dangerous sects to Siberia, declaring dangerous the publication of Lutheran religious books in the Russian language, and the use of Russian in Lutheran services in the vicinity of stundists. A whole day was devoted to the issue over sending children of sectarians to asylums, but the proposal was finally rejected because of the difficulty in erecting such facilities.[30]

Adjuncts to the Inner Mission were the Brotherhoods, subsidized by the Holy Synod, to retain Orthodox in the church and regain apostates. The most important was the St. Andrew Brotherhood in Odessa. The Brotherhoods provided missionaries who with knowledge of Scripture and the teaching of the Orthodox Church and stundism sought to engage in conversations with stundists and Orthodox on the Christian faith and life. In his criticism of the anti-sectarian program of the Orthodox,

26. Procurator of the Holy Synod, *Report*, 1888–1889, 112–15.
27. Skvortsov, *Vtoroï missionerskoï s'ezd Moskve*, 25–33.
28. Latimer, *Dr. Baedeker*, 190.
29. Skvortsov, *Deyaniya 3-go* Vserossiïskago *missionersago s"ezda Kazani*, 154–57, 320–23.
30. *St. Petersburger evangelisches Sonntagsblatt* 40 (1897), 271–72.

E. B. Lanin claimed that the Brotherhoods offered financial assistance to converts and the education of their children.[31]

In 1884/1885 the St. Andrew Brotherhod distributed 40,000 copies of six publications, including such titles as "What is the Temple of God?" and "On the Worship of the Holy Ikon of Christ the Savior." Two other leaflets were "How to read the Holy Scripture on the Holy Tradition" and "Conversation on Defectors from the Holy Orthodox Church." Two of the most popular brochures were "No Salvation Outside the Orthodox Church" and "The Damned Stundist," a hymn of ten verses. The last two verses were: "Dark and gloomy, demon-like, He shuns the flock, the Orthodox He sulks in nooks and corners dark, God's foe, the damned Stundist. The simple sheep who venture near The lair of this evil-working beast, Shudder at his blasphemy, And are entrapped by the damned Stundist."

Anti-stundist poems included, "Chto takoe shtunda?" (What is the Stunda?); "K zabludshim brat'yam—shtundistam" (To Lost brethren—the Stundists); and "Pravda o shtunde" (The Truth Concerning the Stunda).[32]

Another organization in the defense of the Orthodox Church was the Society for the Spread of Religious-Enlightenment in Kiev. Its active members were required to have had theological training and engaged in teaching and discussions. Its candidate members may be any Orthodox, male or female. It also published brochures and leaflets. One very active churchman was the bishop of Yekaterinoslav Diocese who in 1886 undertook the circulation of brochures, undertook liturgical teaching and conversations for the populace, formed missionary committees of priests, removed ineffectual priests, and replenished church libraries. Schools in the local parish also were a support to the Orthodox Church.[33]

The chief organ of the Inner Mission was *Missionerskoe obozrenie* (The Missionary Review), first published in Kiev (1896–1898) and then in St. Petersburg (1899–1916), edited by Skvortsov. The periodical was a journal of substance that included apologetical and polemical articles, mission methods, book reviews, historical data on sectarians, and a chronicle of the Inner Mission.[34]

The institutions and resources of the Orthodox Church were formidable in protecting its own flock, especially with its support from the state and in the choking off the spread of evangelical literature. Its efforts no doubt helped to keep some in the

31. Zavitnevich, "Svedeniya o dvizhenii yuzhno-russkago-sektantstva v" poslednie gody," *TrKDA*, 1886, no. 11, 537–38. Lanin, "The Tsar Persecutor," 15.

32. Zavitnevich, 538–39. Petrov, "Novyya svedeniya o shtundizme," *TrKDA*, 1887, no, 4, 619. Lanin, "The Tsar Persecutor," 15. Lanin includes in English translation all verses of "The Damned Stundist," while Brown, *The Stundists*, 48, contains the last two verses, and *Review of Reviews* 3 (Apr. 1891), 273, contains three verses both of them in another version. For the other anti-stundist poems, see *MO*, Jan. (2), 1897, 70–72; Sep.–Oct. (2), 1897, 539–42; and Nov.(2), 1897, 648–50.

33. *Beseda*, May 1890, 80. *MO*, Mar. 2, 1903, 844. *TsV*, 1886, no. 42, 652. Procurator of the Holy Synod, *Report*, 1893, 121–22.

34. Maevskii, 93–159.

Orthodox Church and even helped to reinvigorate the church itself, a factor, of course, its supporters would be loathe to credit its opponents for forcing such measures. But, on the other hand, these measures did not stop the continuing growth of stundism nor were able to reclaim many of them for the church. In his report in 1887, Pobedonostsev wrote that the missionaries and the parish priests regained from sectarianism over twenty families and some individuals for around 100 souls, an infinitesimal number for the whole country. Because of such failure, the church increasingly turned to the state for police measures to eliminate the stundist heresy. In 1893 N. Zaozerskiï observed, however, the polemical exhortations and criminal suppression are only palliatives that do not eliminate the evil in the heart. He suggested the need to increase more churches and schools, and priests should not just major on theology and edification but be "fathers and mothers" of the flock and care for the orphan, the sick, and the oppressed.[35]

Legal Action

The penal law, article 187, subjected a defector from the church with loss of civil and personal rights and transport to Siberia or for milder cases work in a reformatory. In article 189, those who by writing or preaching subvert one from the Orthodox faith were subject to the loss of certain rights and imprisonment from eight to sixteen months; for a second offense, imprisonment from thirty-two to forty-eight months; and for a third offense, the loss of all rights and transport to Siberia. In Article 196 for spreading heresy, the penalty was loss of all rights and transport to the Caucasus, from the Caucasus to Siberia, and from Siberia to remote regions beyond.[36] The Holy Synod confirmed the resolutions of the meeting of the conference of bishops in Kiev in 1884. In 1889 the Holy Synod instructed the bishops to take vigilant care to see that the priesthood fulfill all approved measures and inform their superiors on the appearance of any heresy. At the same time, Pobedonostsev approached the Minister of Internal Affairs to order the civil authority to render assistance to the priesthood in weakening stundism and propose to the general-governors of the provinces that means be used to give full assistance to the priesthood in its struggle with heresy. On September 29, 1889, the Minister of Internal Affairs issued a circular to the governors.[37]

In the spring of 1891 the bishop of Kiev drew up a memorandum of proposals for the civil authorities to implement the following:[38] 1. Forbid stundists to work in factories. 2. Post notices in offices and railroad work stations forbidding employment of stundists on railroads. 3. Place children of stundists under the guardianship of

---

35. Procurator of the Holy Synod, *Report*, 1887, 75–76. Zaozerskiï, 187, 190.
36. *Review of Reviews* 3 (Apr. 1891), 272. Latimer, *Dr. Baedeker*, 190–91.
37. Procurator of the Holy Synod, *Report*, 1888–1889, 116–18. *Free Russia*, April 1, 1893, 58. Val'kevich, 120.
38. *Chronik*, April 9, 1891, 17.

Orthodox relatives or those of the Orthodox faith. 4. Forbid stundists from erecting prayer houses and holding services. The general-governors of Kiev, Podolia, and Volhynia raised the question of enforcing the law against the Stunda since the law of May, 1883 (apart from the Skoptsy), did not help distinguish which dissidents were the most harmful. Also they noted that stundist meetings strengthened the heresy and were also a means of spreading it among the Orthodox. The Council of Ministers proposed to the Minster of the Interior with concurrence of Pobedonostsev that stundists be declared "the most dangerous" sect and their meetings be forbidden. In 1894 the imperial authority approved such a law on July 4 and on September 3 the Minister of Internal Affairs issued a circular on the law. In justification the Minister of Interior Affairs maintained that the Stunda rejected all church rites and thus rejected all authority, the oath, and military service and preached socialist principles, thereby undermining the Orthodox faith and Russian national character. Although the new law did not mention Baptists, the Ministry of Interior Affairs declared that the law of May 1883 had given no rights to stundists or Russian Baptists.[39] Pobedonostsev was now finally able to get into law a final blow to outlaw stundism/Stundo-Baptism. In his report in 1894–1895, Pobedonostsev reported, "it was impossible not to welcome with joy" the new law, which he claimed remedied the defect of the 1883 law that had not designated the most dangerous sects. *Tserkovnyï vestnik* defended the new legislation in the face of criticism of the foreign press that declared that relations with the stundists now had shifted from a powerless church to a civil authority that was now engaged in an unjustified persecution of an industrious part of the population that only wanted to satisfy its own religious needs. *Tserskovnyï vestnik* replied that the priesthood would still be active in the fight against heresy, and the role of government was justified in that stundism was undermining the authority of the state.[40]

One of the Orthodox missionaries, Mikhail Kal'nev, reported that he found stundists reacting indifferently to the circular or even mocking it, declaring that circulars are only inventions of the priests and missionaries. Some claimed that the sudden death of Alexander III on October 20 nullified the circular, and, in any case, the circular did not apply to them since they were Baptists and not stundists. In any case, the new tsar, Nicholas II, signed the new legislation.[41]

The new law pushed stundists even more toward declaring themselves Baptists since it seemed to be the only alternative for legal recognition, a status that German Baptists who were of foreign origin had already attained. But as already noted, the regime refused to recognize Russian stundists or Stundo-Baptists were Baptists.

---

39. For the law of July 4 and its application, see Skvortsov, *Denaniya 3-go Vserossiïskago missionerskago s"ezda v Kazani*, 339–42. "Das neue Gesetz gegen die Stundisten," WHZ, Feb. 16, 1895, 52–53. *Beseda*, Feb. 1895, 31–32.

40. Procurator of the Holy Synod, *Report*, 1894–1895, 229. *TsV*, 1894, no. 46, 748.

41. *TsV*, 1894, no. 10, 304. *EC*, April 1, 1895, 127.

18

The Suppression, 1884–1905

THE GROWING ANTAGONISM TOWARD stundists and Stundo-Baptists led to outright suppression. The suppression lasted twenty-one years, only ending in 1905 with the grant of toleration as a result of the Revolution of 1905. The Russian regime had always been hostile toward such sectarian groups as the Khlysty, Skoptsy, and Dukhobors (many of whom will migrate to Canada in 1899), but this period will come to brand Russian evangelical sectarians as the most dangerous religious body to church and state. Earlier the regime had oppressed them only sporadically and on a local level but had not attempted to suppress them throughout the empire.

The suppression caused Russian evangelicals much suffering and curtailed their activities, yet because of the size of the country, differences in degree of enforcement, and the ability of the sectarians themselves to avoid the full impact of the regime's efforts, the suppression in the end did not meet its final goal. Nevertheless its impact was severe. In an article in *Evangelical Christendom* in 1894, the author claimed that over 3,000 were now exiled or imprisoned, while "tens of thousands" have lost their civil rights with loss of passport, the right to engage in business, or migrated.[1] The evangelical press in the West provided extensive coverage. Besides *Evangelical Christendom*, *Der Sendbote* (the German Baptist paper in the USA), *Baptist Missionary Magazine*, *Echoes of Service* (which carried Frederick Baedeker's reports), and the underground evangelical periodical, *Beseda*, the general press in the West carried reports of the oppression as well as such evangelical authors as John Brown and Georges Godet. Liberal periodicals and books also provided material.[2]

---

1. Gritton, "The Stundists and their Sorrows," *EC*, March 1, 1894, 79.
2. See Wardin *Evangelical Sectarianism*, 371–85, for a listing of bibliographical sources on the suppression.

PART FIVE—Peril, 1884-1905

THE OPENING YEARS

In spite of some restriction, such as the assessment of fines, stundists and Stundo-Baptists found little or no restraint during the first half of the 1880s, but conditions changed decidedly for the worse in the mid-1880s, beginning in 1884 with the suppression of the Pashkovite movement. At the opening session of the congress of the Russian Baptist Union in Vladikavkaz in 1885, Johann Wieler, the president, presided, but at the session the following morning Wieler left for safety, forcing Vasilii Pavlov, the vice-president, to replace him. In May of the previous year, Wieler was arrested for baptizing thirteen converts from Orthodoxy and although released was no doubt under police surveillance. Five months after the 1885 congress, Wieler fled to Berlin.[3]

Mikhail Ratushnyï and Ivan Ryaboshapka had attended the 1884 congress and the latter also the congress in 1885, but because of police surveillance and forbidden to attend neither came to the third congress in 1886. In May 1886 *Der Sendbote* printed a lengthy letter from "Adolphos" in Tiflis (almost certainly Pavlov), with a call for financial support and a description of the beginning of "strong persecution" for stundists and Baptists. He pointed out that the regime singled them out over other sects, which were left in peace for their passivity. He pointed out that believers in Kherson Province had been heavily fined, paying over 3,000 rubles. In November of the previous year the regime had removed the legal status of the Baptist church in Tiflis, closed its place of meeting, forbade further services, forcing the members to meet elsewhere but not as publicly. He also stated that in 1885 Leon Primachenko from Mogilev Province was suddenly exiled to Orsk in Orenburg Province in Siberia without trial, leaving his wife with three small children and his elderly father with no means of support. Trofim Babienko from Kiev (unduly indiscreet in his attacks on Orthodoxy) was exiled to Stavropol and separated from wife and child. The author declared that the law of May 3, 1883, providing rights to dissidents, "remains only a dead letter."[4]

As indicated in the above letter, one of the regime's targets was Tiflis. In 1885 Paul, the exarch of Georgia, submitted to the governor an inquiry on Baptists and the means of struggle against them, insisting that they were a danger to both the church and the Russian people. On March 1887 without warning, the authorities ordered Pavlov, pastor of the Tiflis church, and Abraham Amirchanjanz, an Armenian evangelical, to report to the police station where they learned they were to be exiled for four years in Orenburg Province for spreading Stundo-Baptism. Soon afterwards the authorities also made the same charge against Nikita Voronin, a founding member of the Tiflis church, who had been absent from Tiflis. Without saying farewell to their families, Pavlov and Amirchanjanz were thrown in with common criminals but after two days were allowed to put on their own clothes and given better accommodations.

---

3. Val'kevich, App. 1:17–19. Dyck, *Wieler*, 92–93.

4. *Der Sendbote*, May 19, 1886, 162. Brown, 32. Packer, *Among the Heretics in Europe*, 46. *Baptist*, Nov. 2, 1911, 353.

Ten days later, the three of them went into exile with their families, accompanied by a single policeman, to travel, largely by steamer and rail, over 2,000 kilometers to Orenburg. A crowd of over 1,000 friends accompanied them in their own vehicles to outside the city.[5]

An author of a letter from Orenburg in November 1887, probably again from Pavlov, declared that persecution continued. He noted that five men in Mogilev, in the same village from which Primachenko had been exiled, were, after a year in prison, deprived of all civil rights and permanently exiled to Transcaucasus as well as a man from another village in the same area. Other men were given various terms of imprisonment, eight months or less, as well as women for the short period of three days.[6]

On the other hand, Sumbat Bagdasarjanz, also an Armenian evangelical, wrote a letter in January 1888 to Frederick Baedeker that portrayed a much calmer situation. Bagdasarjanz had accompanied Baedeker in the Caucasus the previous year, and Baedeker now wanted a report on conditions in the region. Bagdasarjanz was upbeat, noting continuing services in Tiflis among various nationalities, even though services were held in different locations. He made no reference to the exile of Pavlov and Voronin and fellow Armenian Amirchanjanz, although he noted that in Tiflis an uproar had arisen over the possible exile of his father-in-law, Martin Kalweit.[7]

Increasing Pressure

With increasing hostility, the entire stundist/Baptist community was affected, not only those who were apprehended. Baedeker, who had the freedom of crossing Russia in his prison ministry, wrote in January 1892 in *Echoes of Service*:

> A very heavy and more and more thickening cloud is hanging over Russia. From a programme recently published by the ruling powers there is more persecution in prospect, and no toleration for those who will not or cannot say *shibboleth* according to the manner of the Orthodox Church. The atmosphere is heavy with espionage, and the truth of God is at a discount, whilst the cause of superstition is upheld by all the forces of government, and, alas! often with a brutality which does not find its equal in the middle ages.

In the same issue, the section entitled, "The Stundists," recorded—

> The cry has gone forth from headquarters that the Stundists are inimical to the State and to the Church, and therefore ought to be suppressed by force

---

5. Breyfogle, 150. For accounts of Pavlov's experiences in exile, see his manuscript written in 1899, "Vospominaniya ssyl'nago," in Bonch-Bruevich, MKIsI, 1:1–24. Also see "Pravda o baptistakh" by Pavlov in *Baptist*, Nov. 2, 1911, 353–55.

6. *Der Sendbote*, January 25, 1888, 2.

7. Kahle, "Ein Bericht über Allianz- und Baptistengemeinden des Kaukasus aus dem Jahr 1888," *Kirche im Osten* 25 (1982), 121–22.

both by the means which the Church has at her disposal and also by the powers of the Government. . . . Even governors who till quite lately favoured and encouraged them have suddenly turned against them and persecute and exile them, and every under-official seeks to please his superior and the head of the government, by lending a helping hand to stamp out such anti-Russian and anti-Christian people. . . . The dear people are not [only] exiled or banished, but what is much worse, they are not allowed to earn an honest living. The name Stundist disqualifies them for any situation. . . . In the most arbitrary manner they have been driven from their employments, put into prisons, fined heavily, even beaten, and there is no appeal against all this injustice.[8]

From other sources, the spirit of hostility was becoming rampant. In the report in 1886 of the Procurator Pobedonostsev, it stated that the peasants in a village in Podolia demanded the eviction of those who were bringing in stundism, and in a village in Chernigov the inhabitants expelled stundist intruders. John Brown wrote that peasants in villages in Kherson and Kiev Provinces, encouraged mainly by the priests, rose up against stundists where they were physically abused, beaten, and imprisoned. Mobs attacked homes and windows and crockery were broken. Andreï L. Evstratenko, born in Mogilev Province, admitted that previous to his conversion in 1890 and becoming a stundist leader, he felt stundists merited only "scorn and contempt." He led rioters who threw stones and broke windows. Writing years after the event, one writer recorded that in 1895 in Kiev the authorities on behest of the consistory pressured the believers by forcing them to undertake exhausting labor in construction and digging out weeds and then took them to a trade fair where they were shamed before the people.[9]

In his work, *Red Wedding*, Damon L. Orlow, wrote that when a boy two families in his village converted to stundism. The priest began to denounce and preach against them. The two families were brought to the square where they were admonished to recant and cursed and threatened. One of the husbands was cruelly treated by twisting his body with a long rope and small pole, a *tsurka,* until he fell unconscious. Several weeks later the authorities exiled the two stundist families to Siberia.[10]

One notorious case of brutality in 1896, written by the victim, Josif A. Semerenko, was published in several publications. When it become known that Semerenko and his wife had converted to stundism, a mob assembled before their home, broke the windows and doors, and seized and beat him. His brother, Ivan, a village elder, seized all his possessions. By refusing to reverence the ikons, he was beaten by rods. Later the brother and priest tortured him by burning his body with two cigarettes,

8. *Echoes of Service*, Feb. (I) 1892, 36.
9. Procurator of the Holy Synod, *Report*, 1886, 97–98. Brown, 46–48, who claims Evstratenko was born in Saratov Province. Prestridge, *Modern Baptist Heroes and Martyrs*, 32, 36. Bonch-Bruevich, "Sredi sektantov," *Zhizn*, 1902. no. 5, 186–87. *Istoriya*, 525.
10. Orlow, *Red Wedding*, 115–21.

pricked him with a needle, beat him, and put his left hand into a vise, scorching it with an iron and then did the same with the right hand. Finally the authorities arrested him, but he broke a window in the prison and with his wife and young child fled, finally arriving in Odessa and then to Tulcha in Romania.[11]

Children also faced difficulties at school. Ratushnyï reported that the regime ruled it was forbidden to teach stundist/Baptist children in the local school if they failed to observe Orthodox rites. Consequently such children were removed from the school, or the parents did not send them at all.

Beseda reported that in Kherson Province the stundists/Baptists built their own village school and paid their own teacher. At times children who had not been baptized were forcibly taken and baptized according to the Orthodox rite.[12]

Fines and Imprisonment

For years stundists/Stundo-Baptists had been fined for meeting illegally, a practice that continued in this period. As noted, Ratushnyï complained about the heavy fines believers were forced to pay. In his article on Baptist persecution, Vladimir D. Bonch-Bruevich, a sympathetic Marxist researcher, included a report written by Ratushnyï in 1901 who claimed from 1897 to 1899, according to data Bonch-Bruevich summarized, 122 Baptists were arrested in Osnova, forced to pay 5,995 rubles or imprisoned in a penal home for 4,839 days. John Brown wrote that in 1882–1883 the *ispravniki* (police chiefs) levied fines that amounted to confiscation. He claimed it was not uncommon to see stundists in villages auctioning their clothes, bedding, and furniture to pay the fines. In one village the authorities fined within twelve months twelve families with the huge sum of 2,600 rubles. If one refused to pay, the authorities resorted to imprisonment and sale of personal possessions.[13]

After he began preaching, Andreï Evstratenko suffered numerous hard knocks with imprisonment and fines before his exile to Siberia. In the 1890s the authorities imprisoned him with the heads of five families without trial and with beatings. After their leaving prison, the authorities forced them to pay fines for meeting illegally. Evstratenko was again imprisoned for his inability to pay. Pinkov, who headed a village church in Samara Province, was arrested and then imprisoned for two years awaiting trial. The authorities freed him for a year due to a friend who stood bond for him. The court finally tried him, sentencing him to the Caucasus for twelve years. As already

---

11. Bonch-Bruevich, *Presledovanie baptistov evangelicheskoï sekty*, 58–64. Bonch-Bruevich, "Sredi sektantov," *Zhizn'*, 1902, no. 5, 187–93. *Der christliche Orient* 5 (1903), 136–41. Latimer, *Dr. Baedeker*, 195–97 (a summary).

12. Bonch-Bruevich, "Presledovanie baptistov" v" Rossii," *Vestnik evropy*, June 1910, 163. *Beseda*, May 1894, 79; June 1894, 96; July 1894, 11.

13. Bonch-Bruevich, "Presledovanie bapistov," *Vestnik evropy*, June 1910, 163–65, and in Bonch-Bruevich, *Presledovanie baptistov* (1902), 55–58, where the data is summarized. Brown, 28–29.

noted, five believers were imprisoned in Mogilev Province for about a year before their exile to the Transcaucasus, while others were imprisoned for shorter periods.[14]

Transport

Convicted stundists/Stundo-Baptists who were exiled faced transport to their new domiciles. The transport for some could be by regular transportation, but for others it was by convoy. As noted, Pavlov traveled with his family, using normal means of transportation, with the escort of one officer. Four years later in 1891, after his refusal to sign the statement he would no more preach, the authorities suddenly arrested and exiled him without his family, transported him largely by rail in a coach for prisoners, coupled with his left hand to another prisoner, staying in prisons where he was unchained, and after forty days arriving again in Orenburg.[15]

Authorities allowed Andreï Leushkin in 1891, traveling from Tiflis to Geokchaï in Baku Province, to pay his own passage, including the fare of the two policemen who escorted him. In contrast, Trifon Khlystun, one of the first stundist believers in Karlovka in Kherson Province in Ukraine, endured in 1892 three months of travel. He visited ten prisons, traveling in part by rail, but in the Caucasus was forced to go on foot for about 100 kilometers before his arrival in Shusha. While in prisons in Tiflis and Elisavetpol, brethren furnished him with basic necessities. In the last leg of his journey from Shusha to Gerusy, other brethren gained permission to take him and others in his party by donkey at their expense.[16]

G. N. Morozov in his letter in 1891 to a friend in Odessa did not find anything positive to record of his trip from July 7 to September 7 when he arrived in Gerusy. He stated his "sufferings were very great and arduous," which included passing through seven prisons and eight *étape* houses (transport stations). In some prisons he had to sit six or more days and in Tiflis the entire month of August. He wrote that crossing the high mountains in the Caucasus scared him so much as to make his hairs rise on his head.[17]

In March 1891 the periodical, *Leisure Hour*, printed the case of Egor N. Ivanov, who after ten months in prison was finally sentenced in a trial in Kharkov Province for exile for life in the Caucasus. Ivanov tramped in chains and stayed in transport stations, consisting of small-unventilated rooms in which large groups of prisoners were crowded into a single room for the night. Authorities in 1891 exiled Sazont E. Kapustinskiĭ of Kiev Province to the Transcaucasus. After leaving the train at Vladikavkaz, he tramped across the mountains to Tiflis with soldiers forcing the prisoners to

---

14. Prestridge, 32–35. Byford, *Peasants and Prophets*, 139–140. *Der Sendbote*, Jan. 25, 1888, 2.

15. Pavlov, "Vospominaniya ssyl'nago," 10–12. Prestridge, 99.

16. Val'kevich, 93. Bonch-Bruevich, *Presledovanie baptistov* (1902), 45–46. Prestridge, 43, misspells the name of Leushkin as "Levuchkin."

17. Bonch-Bruevich, *Presledovanie baptistov* (1902), 43–44.

carry their baggage and prodded with bayonets if any resisted. He endured additional stretches of walking before he reached Gerusy.[18]

When Vasilii V. Ivanov was transported in 1895 from Elisavetpol in the Transcaucasus to Kalisz Province in Western Poland, he passed through fourteen prisons. At the thirteenth stop, after several hours in prison, he was shifted to a prisoner's home where he was now freed from the armed convoy and received his own clothes that had been taken from him near the beginning of his journey. He then discarded his torn prisoner's dress and cap.[19]

Prokop Gaponchuk (Haponchuk), born in Volhynia in 1853, was imprisoned for two years in Kherson and then exiled to Transcaucasus for fifteen years. On his trip, he stayed in thirty prisons on the way. A report, evidently from Baedeker, recorded seeing in a prison in Tiflis a party of twenty-seven stundists that included seven families with children. Among them was a grandmother who said she had gone through seven prisons and then will go to another in Elisavetpol before she would know the place of exile for her and her family.[20]

John Brown and Georges Godet, writing in the 1890s when the suppression was reaching its intensity, highlighted the terrible conditions of transport, describing stundists marching as common criminals in chains and shaven heads. Their aim was to arouse as much sympathy for the oppressed and abhorrence toward the regime. If these cases existed, they were nevertheless far from the norm.[21]

Exile

One of the major components in the regime's program of suppression was the exile of leaders to places distant from their homes. This practice of exiling political and religious dissidents was a common practice in Tsarist Russia, a means of isolating them from society to minimize their influence and stop their opportunities for propaganda. Although the effort was directed primarily against leaders, it also affected family members who were then separated or also went into exile and was even extended to lay members of entire congregations.[22]

---

18. *Leisure Hour*, Mar. 1891, 303. Brown, 35, 39. Bonch-Bruevich, *Materialy k istorii i izucheniyu russkago sektantsva i raskola*, 1:41–51.

19. "Put V. V. Ivanova [Klyshnikova] v ssylku," *Seyatel' istiny*, July, 10–12; Aug., 10–11; Sep.–Oct., 8; and Nov. 1925, 9–11.

20. *The Friend of Russia*, July 1922, 107–8. Also in *Seyatel' istiny*, Jan. 1922, 8–9. *EC*, Dec. 1, 1894, 390.

21. See Brown, 35, 41–43, and Georges Godet, *Persécutions actuelles en Russie*, 23–24, for descriptions of stundists exiled as common criminals.

22. For the development of isolating religious dissidents during the reigns of Alexander I and Nicholas I, see Breyfogle, 35. *Svobodnaya mysl'*, 1901, no. 14, 221–23. For affects on churches, see Byford, 90, 122.

PART FIVE—Peril, 1884-1905

The Tsarist program was far less oppressive than the later Stalinist oppression in the 1930s and 1940s where dissidents, if not immediately executed, were sent to labor camps of the Gulag under harsh conditions where they were worked to death and frequently did not survive. Although the Tsarist program was more humane it was not particularly benign. Exiles came from various parts of Russia but with Tiflis and Vladivakaz in the Caucasus, Kiev and vicinity, and the Lower Volga supplying substantial numbers. The years 1887, 1890–1892, and 1895–1896 were high points for transporting exiles but individuals were in exile every year from 1884 to 1905. Some were exiled for life, but others for terms of four or five years. The regime would often add an additional term of exile for individuals who continued to be recalcitrant or refused to promise never again to engage in propagating their faith.

After a trial, a court might order exile but frequently such an order was frequently issued without any trial but by "administrative order" of an official who deemed the dissident a threat to the community and must be removed. The purpose was to send the exile as far as possible from his native surroundings and to an alien environment and among people with different cultures and languages. Stundists and Stundo- Baptists from Ukraine might be sent to the Caucasus, while those in the Caucasus might be sent to Siberia in the east or Poland in the west. Exiles had to sell their property and begin anew to make their own livelihood. Some managed successfully but many were placed in areas of little or no employment or with limited resources. The program was particularly hard on families with wives and children accompanying the husband or later coming to his place of exile. In some cases, the regime forbade the removal of children, and wives had to make the agonizing decision to stay with her children or go with her husband. In some cases the authorities just simply took the children by force and gave them to the guardianship of Orthodox relatives. Almost all leaders survived, but some wives and children died.

The exile of the first three from Tiflis in the Caucasus in 1887—Vasilii Pavlov, Nikita Voronin, and Abraham Amirchanianz—demonstrates different results. As already noted, Pavlov went into exile with his wife and family to Siberia with one police escort and did rather well for himself with financial support from abroad and fellow Russian believers. He was free to preach and sent missives to fellow believers. His second exile from 1891 to 1895 did not turn out nearly as well. This time the regime sent him without his family as a chained prisoner. His wife and children arrived in March 1892, but with the Asiatic cholera in July his wife and four of his children died within a week, while in the week before a daughter at age twelve drowned in the Ural River, leaving him with only one child, Paul, age nine. In January 1893 Pavlov remarried, continued his ministry, and returned to Tiflis in 1895. With a call from the Baptist church in Tulcha, Romania, he left Russia, remaining for the most part outside the country until 1901.[23]

---

23. Val'kevich, 80–81. Pavlov, "Vospominaniya ssyl'nago," 10–16. Prestridge, 99–100.

The Suppression, 1884–1905

As Pavlov, Voronin was also in exile in Orenburg where he also received support from within and outside of Russia. On his return from his first exile in 1891, he signed a statement that he would relinquish all preaching activity. Although he spent much of his time in construction, the authorities charged him with continuing to propagate the Baptist faith. N. F. Höijer, a Swedish Mission Covenant missionary, believed the authorities were considering sending Voronin to Arkhangelsk and tried to assist Voronin's escape. But Voronin's wife "called him back with tears and prayers." The authorities imprisoned him, and on October 1, 1894, he went in a convoy of prisoners with his wife to Vologda, not to Arkhangelsk, but still far north from Tiflis.[24]

Amirchanianz, an evangelical Armenian who had studied at Basel in Switzerland, had also served an Armenian church in Constantinople, translating for the British and Foreign Bible Society the Scripture into Ararat-Armenian and Transcaucasian Turkish. He settled in Tiflis in 1875 and preached in Transcaucasus and South Russia. The authorities deported him with his wife and seven children to Orenburg where the family suffered in the cold climate. His two oldest sons did not survive. Because Grand Duke Constantine recognized his use as an orientalist, the regime allowed Amirchanianz to settle in Helsingfors (Helsinki), Finland, where he stayed for seven years from 1891 to 1898, then going to Varna, Bulgaria, where he worked for a couple of years with the Deutsche Orient Mission.[25]

The fates of Ivan Ryaboshapka and Michael Ratushnyï, the two-leading Stundo-Baptist leaders in the Ukraine, were in stark contrast. Both of them were under police surveillance in 1886 and unable to attend in that year the congress of the Russian Baptist Union. On the other hand, neither were exiled in 1887 as were the leaders in the Caucasus. In 1891 the authorities decided to exile Ryaboshapka and Trifon Khlystun, an early co-worker with Ryaboshapka, but Ryaboshapka's exile was delayed one year because at the time he was in court facing the charge of conducting weddings illegally. With difficulty Ryaboshapka gained permission to move at his own expense. He rented his farm and mill, sold his movable property, and on January 29, 1893, he and his wife with a van and pair of horses with a police attendant began their journey. Ryaboshapka collected a rather large sum from each peasant household in Lyubomirka for the trip. The authorities, however, soon turned him back for signing himself as the Baptist presbyter of Lyubomirka. He and his wife then started again with stops on the way, including a stay in a prison in Kharkov, but finally arrived in Yerevan in the Caucasus, where he was in exile from 1894 to 1899.

Ryaboshapka's exile in Yerevan proved miserable where he felt isolated, suffered material need, and was under constant surveillance of the police. At the end of his exile in 1899, he was not allowed to return home as an "incorrigible stundist"

---

24. Val'kevich, 89–90. Larsson, *Tjugufem år i Ryssland*, 380. *Beseda*, Jan. 1895, 15.

25. BFBS, *Monthly Reporter*, Feb. 1889, 21–22. Wright, "The Training of a Translator; or, Amirkhanianz and His Work," *Der christliche Orient*, Feb., 21–22, and Mar. 1889, 42–43. "Abraham Amirchanjanz," *Der christliche Orient*, June–July 1900, 100–102.

but permitted to emigrate with the promise never to return. He and his wife took a steamer from Batum to Constantinople, arriving sick and broken, where the authorities arrested them as Russian spies. With the help of a Bulgarian, they were released and given a ticket to Sofia, Bulgaria. At a Baptist conference in Rustchuk (Russe) in April 1899, he met Pavlov, where they jointly led an evening meeting. Pashkov supplied Ryaboshapka some small financial assistance. Fellow Baptists, however, refused to allow Ryaboshapka to participate with them in the Lord's Supper for breaking the practice of close communion by his communing with Bulgarian Congregationalists. Ryaboshapka died in Sofia in February 1900. In September Ryaboshapka's wife returned to Lyubomirka where believers in the area sustained her.[26]

In contrast to Ryaboshapka, no evidence exists that Ratushnyï suffered exile but continued to minister in Osnova. As already noted, he wrote about Baptists in the area in the 1890s who suffered payment of fines and imprisonment but made no mention of any problems he faced personally, although in his earlier career he had suffered arrest and imprisonment.[27]

As Ryaboshapka, John Wieler, the Mennonite Brethren who helped to bring the stundists in the Odessa region into the Baptist orbit and served as first president of the Russian Baptist Union, also greatly suffered because of the increasing suppression. As already noted, after the first evening session of the Russian Baptist congress at Vladikavkaz in 1885, he suddenly left and then fled to Berlin. After spending time in Bucharest and Tulcha in Romania and then in Odessa, he returned to his home in February 1886 in the Molochna. The police were again on his trail, and after hiding with relatives he appeared again in Berlin in August where his wife and three children joined him. As refugees the Wielers could not stay more than one year and went to Tulcha and then back to Berlin and then in late summer in 1887 again to Tulcha where a fouth child was born in March 1888. Wieler became one of the preachers in a chapel in Tulcha, a station of the Baptist church located a short distance away in Catalui. Each Sunday Wieler preached twice in German and twice in Russian.[28]

With a growing congregation, Wieler decided to build a chapel, seating 450 to 500, which was then dedicated in October 1888. In the construction, Wieler injured himself by jumping off a ladder and possibly also due to his strenuous activity suffered further medical complications. By the end of the year he was confined to his room. He was taken to Bucharest for medical help where he died on July 30, 1889 (o.s.), a few

---

26. Koval'kov and Sokolov, "I. G. Ryaboshapka," *BV*, 1981, no. 6, 64–65. Christophilos, *Ein Blatt aus der Geschichte des Stundismus in Russland*, 19–20. Byford, 75–76.

27. Val'kevich, 85. Bonch-Bruevich, *Presledovanie baptistov* (1902), 55–56.

28. For Wieler's changing locations, see Dyck, *Wieler*, 92–93, and his wife's autobiography, Martens, "Grandmother's Letter," mns., 10–12. For his ministry in Tulcha, see the report of Marcheff from Bulgaria, *WHZ*, 1889, no. 1, 6.

days before his fiftieth birthday. An autopsy revealed a large tumor, an enlarged liver, a rolled up spleen, and malnutrition.[29]

As noted by the above cases, the places of exile could be anywhere. Although Siberia was one notable place of exile, it was not the regime's major site of exile for evangelical dissidents. Frederick Baedeker, who knew Siberia well in his travels, felt that western Siberia was not a bad place for exiles. He wrote in 1893 that he had found brethren there who were prospering. He even suggested indirectly to Russian authorities to send exiles to Siberia rather than Transcaucasus since Siberia was a rich land where settlers could prosper.[30]

But all exiles to Siberia did not find it desirable, and western Siberia differed from eastern Siberia. John Brown recorded the fate of Ivan Golovchenko, a stundist preacher from Yekaterinoslav, who was imprisoned for three years. On advice of the priest, the authorities by administrative order exiled him for life to Siberia where according to Brown the experiences of his family "on the long and desolate road to Siberia were terrible." R. S. Latimer recorded the exile of A. Stoyanov, a pioneer Baptist preacher in the Crimea in the 1880s, who was exiled in 1902 to Turokhansk on the Yenisey River. In a letter soon after his arrival, Stoyanov noted, after traveling about 1,150 miles, that he had arrived in territory where the soil never properly thawed with a population primarily of tribal peoples, such as the Yakuts. He was unable to ply his trade and felt desolate and alone.[31]

On the extreme west from eastern Siberia, the authorities exiled two stundist leaders in Russian Poland. Vasiliĭ V. Ivanov, whose long transport has been noted, settled from 1895 to 1899 in the small town of Sluptsy in Kalisz Province near the Prussian border, and E. M. Bogdanov, a pioneer Baptist preacher in Vladikavkaz, was exiled near Lodz in 1890. After Ivanov's arrival, Bogdanov walked over thirty-five miles for a joyful meeting with his friend whom he had not seen for many years. The authorities freed Bogdanov by 1898 if not earlier.[32]

The regime exiled some stundists in the area of Stavropol in the northern Caucasus. One of the earliest exiles around 1886 was Trofim Babienko from near Kiev. K. Popov, diocesan missionary, visited him and other stundists, including Novosil'tseve and Goshchapov. The missionary reported that the stundists were "pernicious and out-and-out fanatics" and continued with their heretical teaching. When called to converse with the Orthodox priests, they claimed illness or lack of time or flatly said they were Orthodox while the priests were those who preached heresy. Popov wrote that Babienko was "extremely coarse, impertinent in word and abusive in language of

---

29. See Martens. 13–15, for Wieler's accident, medical problems, and death, 13–15. For a report on Wieler's last days, including his kidney problems but nothing of the accident, see Isler's report in *WHZ*, 1889, no. 19, 187–88.

30. *Echoes of Service*, Oct. (I) 1893, 218–19.

31. Brown, 35–36. Latimer, *Three Tsars*, 163–65.

32. *Seyatel' istiny*, Nov. 1925, 11. For Bogdanov's release, see *Der Sendbote*, April 12, 1899, 230.

the Orthodox Church and priesthood." Babienko portrayed himself a martyr and was particularly proud of his exile.[33]

The most notorious region for exiles was the Transcaucasus (today, Georgia, Armenia, and Azerbaijan) because of its remoteness, rugged terrain, and non-Slavic populations, located in the extreme south and bordering Persia (Iran) and Turkey. Such places as Elizavetpol (today Kirovabad), Kuba, Geokchaï, Dzebrail, Nakhichevan', and Terter in Azerbijan; Yerevan, Shusha, and Gerusy (today Goris) in Armenia or under Armenian control; and Artvin and Akhalkalaki in Georgia were all places of exile for stundists and Stundo-Baptists.[34] Elisavetpol was an important center for exiles. Living condition here were difficult for many and some survived only by donations. On the other hand, some found work on the railroad or as carriers; one even sold milk from his cow.[35]

The most notorious place remembered as a byword by stundists and Baptists was Gerusy for its isolation, literally at the end of the road, and its harsh living conditions. From the *Quarterly Reporter of the German Baptist Mission,* the *Baptist Missionary Magazine* printed in 1898 a detailed article, "Baptist Exiles at Gerusi." In more recent years in 1996 Yu. S. Grachev produced a book, *Gerusy,* which described an expedition in 1972 to rediscover Gerusy and included biographical material on a number of the exiles.[36]

The regime sent the first Baptist exiles to Gerusy in 1890. They included Sazont E. Kapustinskiĭ from Kiev as well as Ananchuk and Vityuk from Volhynia. Kapustinskiĭ was forced to dig out his own mud hut. His wife and children arrived the next year, but after the difficult trip over the mountain in an open cart the wife contracted typhoid fever and died soon after her arrival. At the end of 1897, Gerusy held thirty Baptists. Other Baptists who were in Gerusy included Martin Kalweit, Trifon Khlystun, Stepan A. Prokhanov, Grigoriĭ Morozov, as well as Teodor Kostromin, a Cossack, and Ivan Lyasotskiĭ from Kiev for short periods.[37]

The article on Gerusy in the *Baptist Missionary Magazine* described the road, about one hundred kilometers from Shusha to Gerusy, as a hazardous mountain passage with ravines and passes. Armenians and Tartars primarily inhabited the area, who were descried as "wild, cruel, ignorant, and dirty," living in poor mud huts. It was most difficult to make a living from the barren and stony soil, although some found work at extremely low wages as servants of government officials. A few obtained some limited support from the government or from donations from abroad. Stundists who cultivated watermelons or cabbages were subjected to thieves who stole the produce

---

33. *TsV,* 1891, no. 48, 760–61.
34. See Warns, *Russland und das Evangelium,* 125, for additional places of exile in Transcacasus.
35. *Beseda,* Feb. 1895, 2. Bonch-Bruevich, *Presledovanie baptistov* (1902), 44. *BMM,* 1898, 493.
36. *BMM,* Aug., 1898, 492–94. Grachev, *Gerusy—Giryusy (Goris).*
37. Bonch-Bruevich, *Presledovanie baptistov* (1902), 26. Prestridge, 115–35. *BMM.* Aug. 1898, 494.

and then destroyed the rest. As the exiles were held in strict confinement, it was forbidden to find work in neighboring areas.[38]

After a visit to Gerusy, Baedeker most unrealistically claimed that the brethren "bear their sufferings nobly ... without a murmur against the authorities." Because of harsh conditions, some returned to the Orthodox Church and thus released from exile. At the end of 1897, the administration released only six and extended the terms of the others from three to five years. Six in exile now attempted to escape, three reaching Tulcha in Romania, but the others were caught and tried. The Orthodox sent a priest, Nicolaï Mikhailov, to Gerusy to covert the stundists, but none attended his services in a house he had converted into a place of worship. The priest left with indignation and persuaded the police to prohibit all religious meetings.[39]

For those who broke the rules, even a worse fate awaited them by being sent to Terter, a very isolated postal station on the Persian border, which was worse than Gerusy. According to Val'kevich, Kapustinskiï "exerted a dangerous influence" on the settlers in Gerusy. After a police office discovered that the brethren were meeting in the home of Kapustinskiï, he and his children were transferred to Terter where he again had to dig out his home. He married another exile but after unable to work he finally died in January 1898, survived by his widow and six children.[40]

The regime sent Martin Kalweit to Gerusy in 1891. According to Bonch-Bruevch, the visit in 1892 of Isidor Kolokolov, a synodal missionary who came to admonition the exiles, led to the removal of Kalweit to Yerevan. In his autobiography, Kalweit claimed he was exiled to Yerevan for sharing funds he received from other believers.[41]

In 1902 Bonch-Bruevich wrote an article in 1902 in which he claimed that the passive resistance and insubordination of authority of stundists was very significant in undermining the autocratic authority.[42] For Bonch-Bruevich, an adherent of Marxism, any resistance was socially revolutionary. Whatever the social consequences of their resistance, stundists never renounced the authority of the Tsarist regime, and resistance, if any, was passive except for those who attempted to flee the country.

Pashkovite Restriction

The exile of Vasiliï Pashkov and Modest Korff and the termination of the Society for the Encouragement of Spiritual and Moral Reading in 1884 was the beginning of the suppression that soon engulfed all evangelical sectarians. No more meetings were

---

38. *BMM*, Aug. 1898, 492–93. *EC*, Jan. 1, 1896, 19–20. Bonch-Bruevich, *Presledovanie baptistov* (1902), 25–28.

39. *EC*, Jan. 1, 1896, 19. *BMM*, Aug. 1898, 493–94. Latimer, *Three Tsars*, 161.

40. Prestridge, 133–35. Bonch-Bruevich, *Presledovanie baptistov* (1902), 26. Latimer, *Three Tsars*, 158–61. Val'kevich, 86–87.

41. Bonch-Bruevich, *Presledovanie baptistov* (1902), 29. *BV*, 1947, no. 5, 37. Grachev, 42.

42. *Zhizn'*, 1902, no. 5, 196.

held in the great Pashkov mansion. The regime removed Bible texts from the walls of Pashkov's canteen, and later the canteen itself was closed. It forbade the circulation of Pashkovte literature and Pashkovite meetings outside of St. Petersburg.

Tsar Alexander II, however, protected the aristocratic women, the widows, of the Pashkovite movement and permitted them to continue meetings in their homes. From outside appearances, it appeared the movement was in a state of atrophy. The *Sankt-Peterburgskiye vedomosti* reported in 1888 that the Pashkovites were now only a small circle, composed primarily of women. In his evaluation of the Pashkovite movement, Edmund Heier in his insightful study of the movement in 1970, stated it "failed as a nation-wide force," and although it helped to revitalize Orthodoxy it simply evolved into another evangelical sect. He noted its divisions, internal disintegration, and the continuing opposition of church and state that sapped its strength. His observations have much validity especially if one assumes the premise that the movement had regarded itself as more than just an evangelistic effort. It may have simply evolved into an evangelical sect, but in tracing its later history it did not die but in the end made a significant contribution at the time and later to the evangelical movement in Russia.[43]

Although in exile, Pashkov and Korff continued to maintain their assets within Russia, which enabled them to continue not only evangelical efforts abroad but also to provide encouragement and financial aid to the evangelical cause in Russia itself. Although the Pashkovite movement lost much of its male leadership, it was fortunate in its coterie of aristocatic women, living in St. Petersburg and on their estates, such as Nathalie Lieven, Elizaveta Chertkova, and Vera Gagarina, who gave strong support for the cause and continued an evangelical witness in spite of the general suppression of evangelicalism in the country. Pashkovite meetings outside of St. Petersburg, however, were forced to meet secretly. If caught, Pashkovites were arrested and tried for illegal assembly. In his work, *Sovremennoe russkoe sektantstvo*, published in 1905, Dmitrii I. Skvortsov devoted an entire chapter on Pashkovite judicial cases in Tver Province in the 1880s and 1890s.[44]

On three different occasions from 1897 to 1899, Jessie Penn-Lewis of London, England, a Keswick holiness speaker and writer, visited St. Petersburg. In her first trip in January and February 1897, she openly engaged in meetings and interviews, primarily at the homes of Princess Nathalie Lieven and Baron Paul Nikolay, and at the British-American (Congregational) Church. Her second visit, at the beginning of the year in 1898, was shorter and conduced with great circumspection. The chaplain of the British-American Church suggested that she find places other than the church since the church authorities had indicated to him because of the number of sectarians who attended her meetings their discomfort with her presence. She realized it was better not to engage in public work and to conduct drawing-room meetings for Germans only and other meetings for English only and meetings for Russians by

---

43. *Sankt-Peterburgskiye vedomosti*, Sep. 9/21, 1888, 2. Heier, 145–49.

44. Skvortsov, *Sovremennoe russkoe sektantstvo*, 71–123. Also see *Nedelya*, June 25, 1893, 816–17.

invitation only. Russian meetings were held secretly with covered windows; those in attendance left by different exits. In early 1899 she made a third trip for rest and held no meetings. During this time she became deathly ill but for ten days and nights the prayers of four Russian women sustained her. She did survive.[45]

Changing Conditions

Some hoped that with the accession in 1894 of the new tsar, Nicholas II, change might come in religious policy. Instead of relief, Nicholas II affirmed the legislation of 1894 that declared stundism "an especially harmful sect" with no indication of chartering a new course. In 1896 the *Baptist Missionary Magazine* published an article, "The Non-Conformist Movement in Russia" by "a prominent Christian Exile in Transcaucasia." The writer declared, "There is no sign on the part of the Government of relaxation in the barbarous persecution of the Russian non-conformists, especially those known under the name of stundists. A considerable number of common criminals were pardoned at the accession to the throne of the present Czar, but none of the non-conformist exiles shared in the imperial clemency."[46]

Pobedonostsev continued until 1905 as Ober-Procurator of the Holy Synod. He consistently continued his policy of suppressing heretical dissent. Although he recognized the legality of Baptists of non-Russian descent, he continued to demonize stundists as a sect subversive to both church and state, insisting that Russian Stundo-Baptists were simply stundists who attempted to masquerade as Baptists. He wrote to the Minister of Internal Affairs in 1900 that "there are and must be no Russian Baptists." Through the prodding of Pobedonostsev, the Minister of Justice issued a circular to the criminal courts to punish stundists according to the laws, including the conducting of prayer meetings. Because of Pobedonostsev, the Minister of Internal Affairs sent a secret circular to the governors disallowing the claims of stundists that they were Baptists.[47]

In spite of official policy, times were beginning to change as seen in the lives of three outstanding evangelical leaders. Vasilii Pavlov, who had experienced two periods of exile and lived abroad in Romania, undertook a remarkable journey in 1898–1899 that included a tour of his old homeland. After a short trip to Bulgaria, Pavlov and his wife were able to obtain a visa that enabled them to travel by train and ship in Russia, and Pavlov preached without arrest. They traveled in Taurida Province among Molokan evangelicals and Mennonite Brethren. In the territory of the Cossacks they visited Deï and Gavriil Mazaev (but closely watched by the government), the Volga, and finally, after crossing the Caucasus by post, finally arrived in November

---

45. Penn-Lewis, "Reminiscences of My Visit to Russia," *The Friend of Russia*, June 1921, 10–21. Garrard, *Mrs. Penn-Lewis, A Memoir*, 83–145, 174–75.

46. *BMM*, May 1896, 142.

47. Curtiss, 164–65. *Evangelical Alliance Quarterly*, Oct. 1, 1902, 294–95.

in Tiflis, his home territory, where he stayed almost two months. Two years later in 1901 Pavlov will return permanently to Russia.[48]

Johann (Ivan) Kargel, formerly German Baptist pastor in St. Petersburg but who associated with the Pashkovites and engaged in a teaching ministry throughout Russia, lived for many years in the Duchy of Finland. In 1898 he returned to live in St. Petersburg, working with the Pashkovite circle.

Fedor P. Balikhin (1854–1919) had a remarkable ministry. He was born in a Molokan family but was baptized in the Baptist faith in 1882 and soon began preaching. In 1885 the Russian Baptist Union appointed him one-fourth time for missionary work in Taurida Province, which was followed in subsequent years by regular appointments. In the 1890s he visited prisons and exiles in various provinces and even alleged that through attorneys he helped to liberate the condemned. In 1908 he claimed to have brought into the Union over 1,300 converts. During the time of suppression, except for one term of imprisonment, he was generally able to avoid the authorities. In 1897 he visited Romania and Bulgaria and in 1903 undertook a fifty-day trip to England and Germany, visiting in the latter country the triennial convention of the German Baptist Union and the Blankenburg Conference.[49]

Change also began to occur in the political sphere. An article in 1900 "By a Russian" in the *Evangelical Alliance Quarterly* stated that the Tsar issued an order to cease "administrative banishment" that had sent numbers without trial into exile and also freed those who had suffered under this type of exile, such as those in Gerusy. The same correspondent also noted that the Senate had set aside the verdict of a lower court that found a group of worshipers as stundists with the observation that it must be proved that such a group rejected Orthodoxy, opposed military service, and accepted socialist principles. The case, however, did not result in any general change.[50]

At the same time, however, not all cases went in favor of the evangelicals. In 1903 a group, claiming to be of the "Evangelical Faith" in Kharkov Province, submitted a petition, signed by 225 individuals, asking for relief from persecution, alleging they recognized civil authority, prayed for the Tsar, and accepted military service and the taking of oaths. The governor of Kharkov, however, rejected the petition, declaring them to be stundists for their adherence to justification by faith and rejection of the sacraments and obedience to civil authority only if not contrary to God's law. In spite of their petition, he still claimed they rejected military service and oaths.[51]

---

48. *Der Sendbote*, April 5, 218, 1899, and April 12, 1899, 230.

49. For Balikhin's autobiography, first printed in Rostov-on-Don in 1908, see *BV*, 1955, no. 1, 64–66. For his trips abroad and his work for the imprisoned and exiled, see his autobiography. Also see, "Moya poezdka zagranitsu," *Baptist*, June 1907, 13–20, for his 1903 trip.

50. *Evangelical Alliance Quarterly*, Oct. 1, 1900, 87–88, and Oct. 1, 1902, 294–95. Latimer, *Three Tsars*, 163.

51. Curtiss, 173–74.

Although upholding the supremacy of Orthodoxy, the Tsar issued on February 26, 1903, a manifesto that declared the government favored the toleration of non-Orthodox faiths with the right of worship according to their own rituals. The manifesto did not, however, make any mention of Old Believers or sectarians but apparently was moving in their direction. In December 1904 the regime issued a decree that ordered a review of laws for reform and the establishment of toleration for dissenters. Ivan Prokhanov, who had been the editor of *Beseda*, wrote a report to the Ministry of Internal Affairs on the legal status of evangelical sectarians. Ivan Kushnerov, judicial counsel for Stundo-Baptists, and Vasilii V. Ivanov, Stundo-Baptist leader, went to St. Petersburg detailing sectarian persecution.[52]

With the birth in 1904 of Alexis, a male heir to the throne, the Tsar liberated a number of prisoners. Among them was Leon D. Primachenko, a notable Baptist evangelist, who had been exiled for two years in 1886 to Orsk, Orenburg Province, Siberia, and then in 1893 exiled for life to Elisavetpol in the Transcaucasus. Fedot P. Kostromin, a Cossack, who was arrested in 1890 and then spent a short time in Gerusy and then went to Shusha and then to Artrim in Kutais Province, finally received permission in 1904 to settle in Burgas, Bulgaria. With a full pardon in 1908, he returned to Russia.[53]

---

52. Blane, 40–41. Prokhanov, *In the Cauldron*, 130–31.
53. Kostromin, "Moya zhizn' vo Khrist," *Baptist*, 1909, no. 11, 17–18.

19

Evangelical Substratum

IN ITS SUPPRESSION OF the Russian stundists/Baptists, surprisingly a number of resources were available that helped the evangelical movement to survive. As a consequence, an evangelical substratum existed with numerous interrelations both inside and outside Russia. Unlike the later Soviet regime that was anti-God and attempted to destroy religion, the Russian Empire regarded itself as "Holy Russia," a protector of the Christian faith and values. The Empire fought what it considered heresy but yet it was limited by certain Christian standards and thus constrained in its attempt to eliminate it. Although administrative exile undermined judicial legality, nevertheless exile was far different from the Stalinist Gulag where thousands lost their lives.

The regime continued to further the distribution of Scripture, and some evangelical literature and books slipped through. It legalized such evangelical non-Russian denominational groups as the Mennonite Brethren and German Baptist Union. Numbers of Pashkovites and evangelical Armenians were able to continue in ministry. The government, although not permitting missionaries from abroad, permitted some non-Russian evangelicals to engage in a prison ministry among Russian prisoners and a teaching ministry among non-Russians if they avoided overtly proselytizing the Orthodox. Although the Tsarist regime was autocratic, yet because of these limitations, lack of administrative controls, and its own inefficiencies, an evangelical substratum was able to exist. In its program of suppression, the Russian government was more like a leaking sieve than an exterminator.

Evangelical Substratum

Scripture and Christian Literature

The regime of Alexander III continued the policy of his father that encouraged the distribution of Scripture and its translation into the Russian language. The Scripture had been the lifeblood of the evangelical movement, an important factor in its growth in Russia. The regime stipulated, however, that the Holy Synod of the Russian Orthodox Church alone had the right to print the Bible in Russian and Slavonic, requiring also the inclusion of the Apocrypha. The government established printing establishments in St. Petersburg and Moscow.

The British and Foreign Bible Society (BFBS) could not import its own version of the Russian Bible, but, on the other hand, could purchase copies of Russian Scripture from the Holy Synod for distribution through its depots and colporteurs. In addition, it had the right to circulate also its own non-Russian versions of Scripture. In 1892 it was reported that the BFBS with approval of the Holy Synod could import Scripture free of duty. In 1899 the BFBS circulated 578,000 copies of Scripture and employed almost eighty colporteurs, many of whom received free passes on railways and steamboats. All state railroads transported Bibles of any quantity free of charge, and even private railroads and steamers up to a certain limit did the same.[1]

As a foreign institution with Protestant principles and support, the BFBS, however, was subject to suspicion as an agent of evangelicalism. Some felt that its depots were centers of evangelical propaganda and its colporteurs were evangelical agents. Val'kevich, the Orthodox critic of the evangelical movement, noted that Walter Davidson, the sub-agent of the BFBS in Siberia and Turkmenistan, assisted Baedeker in his prison activity in Siberia. He was critical of the activity of the Armenian, Abraham Amirchanianz, in Tiflis; Frederick Müller in Rostov-on-Don; Peter Perk in Saratov; E. F. Kirsch in Kazan; Vasiliĭ N. Ivanov in Kharkhov; I. I. Sherer in Odessa; and Kilius in Kiev, who was removed by the governor-general of Kiev in 1893 for his sectarian activity.[2]

One very active and troublesome colporteur was Ivan I. Zhidkov, (1858–1928), a co-worker with V. N. Ivanov in Kharkov. His grandfather was Sazont Kapustinskiĭ, who had been exiled to Gerusy and then died in Terter. His mother was Pelageya Sazontovna, who also lived in exile. She first married Ivan Zhidkov and secondly Yakob Delyakov, the evangelical Nestorian missionary, who thus became Ivan's stepfather. Ivan first began his work as colporteur with the BFBS in 1876 distributing Scripture during the Russo-Turkish War in 1877. He then served in the Lower Volga and Odessa and then returned to the Lower Volga. It was reported in 1883 that he had been in trouble with the police for a whole year, and his work stopped for some months. In 1884 he moved to Kharkov where he distributed Scripture but also

---

1. *MRW*, Nov. 1898, 874; Dec. 1898, 959; July 1900, 567; June 1901, 470. BFBS, *Monthly Reporter*, May 1900, 105.

2. Val'kevich, 174–79.

attended evangelical services in homes. From pressure from the police, the new head of the Bible Society in 1896 removed him from service, which forced him to move to the Volga with his seven small children. In 1901 he settled in St. Petersburg. Years later his son Jacob (Yakov) will become president of the Union of Evangelical Christians-Baptists, and a grandson, Mikhail, an official in the same union.[3]

In 1887 M. A. Morrison, the director of the agency of the BFBS for South Russia, issued a "Bible Policy in Russia, An Explanation and Defense" to allay charges and remove suspicions against the society. He wrote, "We are not proselytisers for Protestantism.... Our object is solely and alone to circulate the Scriptures, not to expound them." He declared that the agents of the BFBS "seek the recognition and assistance of the local authorities" and "invite the re-examination of our Scriptures, already authorised by the Censor or printed by the Holy Synod." To show his alignment with the regime, he attacked evangelical sectarians, even by name, declaring, "There are perfervid agents of German and Russian Baptist societies, travelling preachers from local Stundist communities, and others, all earnestly endeavoring to carry on a propaganda among the Russian Orthodox and the German Lutherans. With these missionaries the Bible Society has absolutely no connection open or hidden.... Indeed, we have a rule that expressly forbids our *employés* from mixing themselves up in any movement which is hostile to the Russian Church, and the infringement of this fundamental rule is visited with dismissal forthwith."[4]

In 1893 the Minister of Interior ordered the depot of the BFBS in Kiev closed for six months. But worse was to come when the governor-general of Kiev not only opposed reopening the depot but also prohibited colportage in the four provinces where he had jurisdiction, claiming that the colporteurs were engaged in stundist propaganda.[5]

In 1897 *The Mission World* reported that the Holy Synod was debating whether the circulation of Scripture should be encouraged; Pobedonostsev and the metropolitans of Kiev and St. Petersburg believed that the free circulation of Scripture endangered the church. The article pointed out, however, that the Holy Synod, which was always in need of financial support, reaped a great income from the circulation of the Bible and its curtailment would produce financial consequences. In any case, the Tsarist regime never attempted to limit the distribution of the Bible.[6]

A Russian organization, the Society for the Distribution of the Holy Scripture in Russia (*Obshchestvo rasprostraneniya Svyashchenogo Pisaniya v Rossii*) (ORSPvR) also distributed Scripture. In 1869 Orthodox and Protestants formed the society but

---

3. Grachev, *Gerusy*, 32–33. BFBS, *Report*, 1883, 113, and 1884, 132. *Khristianin*. 1924, no. 4, 48–51. *BV*, 1948, no. 6, 58–59.

4. BFBS, *Report*, 1888, 131.

5. *The Missions of the World*, I (1894), 350. *Nedelya*, 1894, no. 50, 1616. Canton, *A History of the British and Foreign Bible Society* 5, 41–42.

6. *The Mission World* 4 (1897), 312.

it became an entirely Orthodox organization. Its president was N. A. Astaf'ev, who in 1892 wrote a work on the history of the Bible in Russia. In 1895 the society claimed 1,389 members. Val'kevich claimed the society was sympathetically inclined toward sectarians in its correspondence and included in its membership such Pashkovites as Pashkov, Bobrinskiĭ, and E. I. Chertkova as well as Baptists, Molokans, Tolstoyans, and Protestant pastors.[7]

The ORSPvR had a special relationship with the American Bible Society that, according to Val'kevich, had been forbidden in the 1870s to work further in Russia. Evidently since 1881 the American Bible Society provided the ORSPvR from five to eight thousand rubles a year, which enabled it to circulate Scripture at a reduced price. Other donors to the society were Mennonite communities in southern Russia, the Dutch Reformed Church in St. Petersburg, Protestant pastors, Pashkovite leaders, and the stundist missionary Yakob Delyakov.[8]

In addition to the circulation of Scripture, an important lifeline in nurturing and spreading of evangelicalism was the publication and distribution of literature. The closing of the Pashkovite Society for the Encouragement of Spiritual and Moral Teaching and the seizing of its brochures and tracts was a serious blow. The work of the Religious Tract society (RTS) of London, which was closely aligned with this society, came almost entirely to a halt except for its agency in Warsaw, which was able to issue tracts in Polish and German. The RTS continued to grant funds for tracts in German in Volhynia, tracts in the languages of Finland and the Baltic provinces, and small grants for tracts in Yiddish or Hebrew to Joseph Rabinovitz, a Christian Jew in Kishinev. Tracts in Russian, however, were prohibited.[9]

Distribution of Pashkovite and other evangelical literature had to be done privately or surreptitiously. In 1891 an Orthodox missionary in *Tserkovnyĭ vestnik* complained that various sectarian brochures continued to circulate, such as "Are You Reconciled to God?" and "Do You Love God?". In an article in *Missionerskoe obozrenie* in 1896, the author noted that, although the Pashkovite society no longer existed, a significant collection of its publications undoubtedly remained to poison the populace. *Missionerskoe obozrenie* reported in 1900 on a recently published series of stundist brochures but with no indication by whom or from where. In April 1904 *Missionerskoe obozrenie* recounted how stundist leaders increased their spread of brochures, leaflets, doctrinal expositions, and collections of songs, including those with notes. The author was concerned about the translation of German works into Russian for the needs of the German population that were increasingly using Russian, but material that could be used for sectarian propaganda.[10]

---

7. Val'kevich, 180–81.
8. Ibid. *MRW*, 1897, 793.
9. RTS, *Report*, 1888, 92; 1889, 93; 1892, 89; 1898, 100; and 1908, 79.
10. *TsV*, 1891, no. 25, 385. *MO*, Feb. (I), 1896, 42, and Oct. 1900, 229.

Criticism was directed toward the journal *Bratskaya pomoshch'* for publishing evangelical material. An article in *Missionerskoe obozrenie* claimed it included Pashkovite brochures and articles from the former Pashkovite publication, *Russkii rabochii*. Val'kevich pointed out that the publication published sermons of Charles H. Spurgeon and contributions from V. G. Pavlov and E. V. Kirchner, news on the work of Protestant mission societies in Russia, and articles translated from foreign languages and in addition supported the doctrine of justification by faith alone.[11]

The censor approved some publications that were acceptable to sectarians. One was a work by Y. M. Burmistrov from Ryazan Province, a Pashkovite, who with other contributors published in 1891 in Moscow, *Sbornik statei dukhovnago soderzhaniya* (Collection of Articles of Spiritual Content).[12]

Lutherans gained permission to publish a hymnal in Russian, which was followed by a second edition. This volume, *Sbornik dukhovnykh stikhotvorenii* (Collection of Spiritual Poems), published in Sevastopol in 1892, was a collection of 416 songs, most accompanied by a Bible verse, from the Psalms, German hymnody, and Moody numbers. The hymnal found its way among the stundists and *Beseda,* the underground evangelical publication, listed it. In 1895 the authorities forbade its circulation.[13]

In the early 1890s *Beseda* published a long list of books and leaflets with prices. In spite of the restrictions of availability of books and brochures among evangelicals, it is surprising how much appeared on the market. One factor was that a number of firms in the book trade carried evangelical works in Russian and imports from abroad. One such firm was Grothe in St. Petersburg. Others were in Riga, Revel, Warsaw, Odessa, Saratov, and the Mennonite colony Chortitza. In the Transcaucasus in Baku and Shusha, firms related to evangelical Armenians also provided evangelical publications. Book peddlers within the country also sold evangelical works.[14]

Mission Figures

A number of non-Russian evangelicals were able to engage in an evangelical ministry, some more freely than others, in a variety of ways in spite of the prohibiton against foreign missionaries. Some of these individuals were born outside Russia, while several of them were Russian subjects by either birth or naturalization and others never became subjects of the country. Whatever status, their contributions in teaching, Bible distribution, prison ministry, and witness were significant.

---

11. *MO*, Sep. (I) 1896, 144. Val'kevich, 167–68, and App. 3:69, ft. 4. Also see *TsV*, Sep. 7, 1895, 1145–48.

12. Val'kevich, App. 5:74, ft. 2.

13. Dalton, *Der Stundismus in Russland*, 22. Val'kevich, App. 3:12, ft. 1.

14. Val'kevich, App. 3:10–12, 183–84, and App. 5:75, ft. 1. Val'kevich claims the list in *Beseda* was circulated in 1892 when it was probably 1893. *TrKDA*, 1887, no., 3, 383.

Evangelical Substratum

The foremost representative of this class is *Frederick Baedeker* (1823–1906), an international phenomenon in the evangelical world. He was born in Germany but a resident in England beginning in 1859, a convert of Lord Radstock, and a member of the Open Plymouth Brethren. He was able to relate to all evangelicals, including Baltic peoples, German Mennonites, Armenians, Stundo-Baptists, Pashkovites, exiled sectarians, and the like. At the same time he retained good relations with the Russian regime. He undertook a remarkable ministry in Russia of twenty-five years from 1876 to just after the turn of the century.[15]

After an evangelistic tour in Germany in 1875, Baedeker entered Russia for the first time in 1876. Radstock introduced him to his aristocratic friends in St. Petersburg. In 1877 he returned to Russia with his wife and adopted daughter for three years to serve primarily among the German community. Later in an evangelistic tour to Sweden and the Duchy of Finland, Mathilda Wrede, a resident of the latter territory, introduced him to a prison ministry. Soon afterwards in Riga he gained permission to speak to prisoners in the city and gave them New Testaments, opening his eyes to such a ministry within Russia proper. Through the influence of a countess, whose husband was the Director of the Prisons' Department, the government granted him a license in 1887 to visit any prison in the Empire and distribute Scripture in them. The BFBS supplied Baedeker with Bibles and Testaments. The regime continued to renew his license as late as 1901, when soon afterwards because of age he terminated his work. Aside from trips outside Russia, he covered much of the Empire, including two journeys across Siberia as far as Sakhalin Island and trips as well into the Transcaucasus and other regions.[16]

Baedeker's preaching was instructional and inspirational. He also provided material assistance to exiled believers. His extensive reports in the evangelical press and speeches, such as at the Evangelical Alliance (for instance at the Jubilee Congress in 1896) and the Blankenburg Conference in Germany, brought not only information but also support to the evangelical cause in Russia.

In his critical review of evangelicalism in Russia, Val'kevich described in great detail Baedeker's many visits, particularly in the Caucasus. He looked upon Baedeker negatively as one who was a propagandist for Protestant dogma but also for his moral and material support for local propagandists in their fanaticism and proselytizing activity. Another critic was Leo Tolstoy, who portrayed Baedeker with hostility in his characters "Kizewetter" and the "Englishman" in his novel *Resurrection*.[17]

---

15. See Latimer, *Dr. Baedeker*, for his early life and ministry in the Russian Empire. See Wardin, *Evangelical Sectarianism*, 38–41, for an extensive bibliography of Baedeker's ministry.

16. Latimer, *With Christ in Russia*, 207–98. BFBS, *Monthly Reporter*, Mar. 1901, 64. For Baedeker's first trip across Siberia, see Latimer, *Dr. Baedeker*, 109–63. *Bratskiï listok*, 1906, no. 10, 10–12. Tatford, *Red Glow Over Eastern Europe*, 217–25. *Echoes of Service*, Aug. (I) 1901, 299. For an address by Baedeker on his earlier experiences in visiting the prisons, see *Echoes of Service*, June, 166–69; July, 213–16; and Aug. 1889, 231–33.

17. Val'kevich, 192–99. See Latimer, *Dr. Baedeker*, for the chapter, "Dr. Baedeker and Count Leo

PART FIVE—Peril, 1884–1905

In spite of negative criticism, Baedeker, who clearly did not hide his evangelical mission and support for evangelicals, was still very successful in a hostile environment toward evangelicalism. He nevertheless took care in his personal and official relations with the regime. In a letter in 1887, printed in *Echoes of Service,* January 1888, Baedeker admitted, however, he had had scrapes with the police and had been just arrested for attending a meeting of Russian sectarians in the Caucasus, but on appeal the governor released him. He was a foreigner who spoke no Russian but only though interpreters, which somewhat isolated him from the Orthodox population. But more important, the government had provided him a license for Bible distribution and visitation of prisoners, often the most often neglected and debased segment of society, while at the same time not proselyting the Orthodox.

Another man in a similar ministry as Baedeker and at times his associate was *Johann (Ivan) Kargel* (1849–1937). He has been noted earlier as a German Baptist pastor in Volhynia and St. Petersburg. Kargel was born in Turkey of a German father and probably an Armenian mother and became a Baptist in the Caucasus in 1869. In St. Petersburg he associated with the Pashkovites and in time will reject the strict ecclesiology of the Baptists and accept open communion. He became a noted teacher and writer, advocating the doctrine of holiness and premillennial eschatology. He became a naturalized citizen of Russia and acquired the ability to speak Russian. Kargel traveled widely throughout Russia speaking to both Russian and German groups. He accompanied Baedeker to the Transcaucasus in 1886 as well as across Siberia in 1890, then short trips from 1891 to 1895 with again a trip to the Transcaucasus in the latter year. In 1901 he again traveled to Siberia with Baron Paul Nicolay.[18]

A third outstanding mission figure in this period is *Yakob D. Delyakov* (1833–1898), as has already been noted a Nestorian from Persia. He was converted in a mission school and became an evangelist and colporteur. He began work as an independent colporteur in 1862 and ended his ministry only at his death thirty-six years later. As noted earlier, he introduced Nikita Voronin to Martin Kalweit for baptism. He served among the Molokans in Taurida Province, during which time he claimed the authorities brought him to trial eight times. With the help of friends, he escaped the authorities ten times. In 1874 he married Pelageya Sazontovna Zhidkova. Because his marriage entailed increased responsibilities, he became a colporteur for the BFBS, serving with this society three years. In 1886 he himself finally accepted believer's baptism and became a Baptist.[19]

Tolstoy," 198–207, for a review of Tolstoy's portrayal of Baedeker.

18. For limited biographical data on Kargel and a description of his trip in 1890 across Siberia with Baedeker, see Kargel, *Zwischen den Enden der Erde unter Brüdern in Ketten.* Also see Val'kevich, 193. See Nichols, *The Development of Russian Evangelical Spirituality: a Study of Ivan Kargel (1849–1937),* for a well-documented work on the life and theology of Kargel.

19. For Delyakov's early life and career, see his autobiography, "The Autobiography of Jacob Dilakoff, Independent Missionary in Russia," in issues of *The European Harvest Field* from March to December, 1935.

In 1889 the congress of the Russian Baptist Union (Christian Brotherhood) at Nikol'skoe, Stavropol Region, appointed M. D. Chechetkin to visit the Molokans in the Amur area in the Far East for 600 rubles as well as Delyakov, who volunteered to accompany him for 300 rubles because of limited funds. After two months of travel of over 9,000 kilometers, the two reached Blagoveshchensk. Chechetkin did not remain but Delyakov remained until 1891 and established Baptist work in the region. Authorities imprisoned Delyakov twice, once in a village some fifty kilometers away for two days and a night and then in another village for only a couple of hours.[20]

In an effort to gain ministerial training for his son Joseph, now fifteen, Delyakov enrolled him in the new Moody Bible Institute in Chicago with Dr. A. J. Gordon and his church, the Clarendon Street Baptist Church of Boston, assuming the financial expense. Delyakov's heart was still with his ministry in the Amur. He returned but while preaching there took cold and after confined to a bed for approximately a month died on February 28, 1898. He was buried in the village of Gil'chin, eighty kilometers from Blagoveshchensk, where a monument was erected on his grave.[21]

Val'kevich wrote in the 1890s that Delyakov was "one of the most dangerous" colporteurs of the BFBS. Elsewhere he also stated that Delyakov was "the oldest and most popular propagandist" among all Protestant sectarians, one who was known to propagandize "with remarkable energy and dexterity."[22]

Two Lutheran pietists of the nobility in the Duchy of Finland who made significant contributions to the evangelical cause in this period were Baroness *Mathilda Wrede* (1864–1928) and Baron *Paul Nicolay* (1860–1919). Mathilda's father was Baron Karl G. Wrede and a brother was Henrik Wrede, who from 1883 to 1885 established for the BFBS Bible depots in Siberia. Beginning in 1884 and until the end of her life, Mathilda was noted for her prison ministry in Finland. As already noted, she introduced Baedeker to this ministry.[23]

While living in St. Petersburg as a student, Nicolay attended meetings in the homes of V. A. Pashkov and Nathalie Lieven, becoming a fully committed Christian by the end of 1888. He participated in German meetings led by the bookseller Grothe and conducted similar meetings in his own home. With his yacht "Lady" he engaged in mission cruises in distributing tracts and conducted Bible talks, taking on board evangelists to conduct meetings on the small islands of the area. From 1896 to 1905 he was also engaged in a prison ministry.[24]

20. Val'kevich, 91, and App. 1:29. Delyakov, "Autobiography," Dec. 1935, 14–15. *BMM*, Apr. 1898, 130.

21. Delyakov, "Autobiography," Dec. 1935, 15–16. *BV*, 1947, no. 6, 47; 1993, no. 2, 72. Wiens, "Essay on the Baptist Movement in the Far East of Siberia," mns., Archives of the International Mission Board of the Southern Baptist Convention.

22. Val'kevich, 91, 177.

23. For a standard biography of Wrede in English, see Stevenson, *Mathilda Wrede of Finland, Friend of Prisoners*. For other biographical material on Wrede, see Wardin, *Evangelical Sectarianism*, 43–44.

24. A standard biography of Nicolay is Langenskjold, *Baron Paul Nicolay*.

PART FIVE—Peril, 1884-1905

Nicolay was an intellectual, trained in law, and besides Russian was fluent in English, French, German, Swedish, and Finnish. At a meeting in 1899 of John R. Mott, General Secretary of the World's Christian Federation, in the home of Nathalie Lieven, Nicolay felt called to student work, which led to his leadership in the movement. It was, however, not an auspicious time to begin any new evangelical initiative. Mott later reported that at this time he himself gave only one public address, attended also by spies, while other meetings were held secretly between midnight and four in the morning. Nevertheless in the home of Grothe Nicolay began with five students. In 1902 Russian Orthodox students began joining, and in 1903 it was decided to conduct eleven meetings in Russian. In 1905 Nicolay gave up his prison ministry to devote more time to his ministry with students.[25]

Beginning in the 1880s, the Swedish Mission Covenant, a new pietistic mission movement within the Lutheran Church of Sweden, with evangelistic zeal began to send missionaries to Russia. It recognized no one form of baptism and did not require its missionaries to subscribe to the Augsburg Confession. At its second conference in 1880, the Mission Covenant sent Frans Hammarstedt and A. E. Karlsson to work among the nomads around Archangelsk, Lars E. Högberg to St. Petersburg, and N. F. Höijer (Hoyer) to Kronstadt, a naval base near St. Petersburg. While learning the language, Hammarstedt and Karlsson undertook mission work among both Scandinavian sailors and Russians, but the authorities imprisoned them in Moscow and deported them back to Sweden.[26]

Both *Lars E. Högberg* and *N. F. Höijer* had lengthy careers in Russia, both traveling even to Central Asia. Högberg went to St. Petersburg to work among the Swedes in the city. By 1883 he had settled in Lenkoran, Baku Province, studied Russian, and became a Baptist. Because of a threat from the authorities, he moved elsewhere in the Caucasus, which included traveling with Vasilii V. Ivanov. He then served in Persia from 1889 to 1893 and Chinese Turkmenistan from 1894 to 1916.[27]

N. F. Höijer (1857-1926) had an extended mission career of forty-six years from the time he went to Kronstadt in 1880 at the age of twenty-three until his death in 1926 in a hospital in Alaska. His assignment was to work among the sailors on Scandinavian ships. He also held meetings in Kronstadt, but the authorities forced him to flee to St. Petersburg. He participated in the Pashkov movement in the city and held services in private homes. With concern from the Swedish ambassador, the Swedish

25. For Nicolay's work among Russian students, see Langenskjold, 91-157. Also see "The Story of the Conversion of Prof. V. Ph. Marcinkovsky," written in memory of Nicolay and published in *The European Harvest Field*, Aug. 1928, 11-13. *MRW*, Feb. 1914, 88. For the work of the World's Student Christian Federation in Russia, see Wardin, *Evangelical Sectarianism*. 58-59.

26. See Olsson, *By One Spirit: A History of the Evangelical Covenant Church of America*, 410, for the formation of the Mission Covenant in Sweden and its early work in Russia. Also see Val'kevich, 184-88.

27. For Högberg's career, see Val'kevich, 185-86, and App. 1:30, ft. 1, and two autobiographical works: *Skuggor och dagrer från missionsarbetet i Ryssland* and *En missionärs minnen*.

Evangelical Substratum

government requested Höijer to return to Sweden, but he didn't remain long. He returned to Russia with seven additional missionaries, which in a short time grew to seventeen missionaries who worked in Archangel, Ural Mountains, and St. Petersburg, while Höijer and Adoph Lydell went to Baku Province. The authorities, by and large, forced the missionaries to flee, while some were imprisoned.[28]

Höijer soon returned to St. Petersburg, but was watched by the police. He attended the St. Petersburg Conference of 1884, sponsored by Pashkov and Korff. He rented an apartment on the third floor of a building for services, one floor above a club; those who attended fooled the police since the latter thought all entering the building were headed for the club.

Höijer will flee to Odessa and then to Tiflis, where he became acquainted with Amirchanianz, translator for the BFBS. Division occurred in the Tiflis church over baptism with Höijer and Amirchanianz supporting infant baptism. Nevertheless, Höijer initiated the Evangelical Oriental Society, which sought united action of all Christian believers in the region. He became its second chairman in 1890. As a craftsman of pianos, he traveled under the guise of a repairer and tuner of organs and pianos and other instruments.[29]

Against his mission board and with no permission from the Russian or Chinese governments, in 1892 Höijer sailed across the Caspian Sea, crossed Central Asia, and went to Kasgar (Kasgi), Sinkiang, China, where he established a mission. In 1901 he came to Kiev where he interested evangelicals in forming a committee to cooperate in a common mission cause. He then went to Sweden where he initiated the formation in 1903 of the Committee for Evangelical Mission in Russia.[30]

Pashkovite Activity

Although the Pashkovites suffered significant loss with the exile in 1884 of two of their foremost leaders, V. A. Pashkov and M. M. Korff, and the closing of their Society for the Encouragement of Spiritual and Moral Reading, yet even while suffering repression, they continued to be an important element in the evangelical substratum. Their leaders were able to retain their estates, and within Russia itself Pashkovites could still exercise some influence and retain limited religious privileges.

Because of the exile of the two Hilton brothers, Edward and Henry, Englishmen who were managers of Pashkov's properties, the regime allowed Pashkov to return for

---

28. An excellent source for Höijer's career are his two articles in Brooks, *Good News for Russia*, "Forty Years in Russia," 159–168, and "Among the Mohammedans and Kurds at Ararat," 173–179. Also see Val'kevich, 186–87, and App. 5:11, ft. 6, and Larsson, *Tjugufem år i Ryssland*.

29. For Höijer's move to Tiflis and the formation of the Evangelical Oriental Society, see Höijer, "Forty Years in Russia," 165–66; *Den evangeliska rörelsen i Ryssland*, 28–30; and Val'kevich, 186. See Val'kevich, App. 5:11, ft. 6, on Höijer's work as a repairer of musical instruments.

30. For Höijer's trip to Central Asia in 1892, see "Forty Years in Russia," 166–67. For his work in forming mission committees in Kiev and Sweden, see *Den Evangeliska rörelsen i Ryssland*, 30–36.

PART FIVE—Peril, 1884–1905

three months to help settle his affairs. Pobedonostsev, who was not consulted on his return, became alarmed and sent a letter to Alexander III opposing Pashkov's petition to remain in the country, claiming he was causing "new evil" and was continuing his propaganda on his estates. The Tsar summoned Pashkov for an interview, informing him he would not have been permitted a visit if it were thought he would continue his former activity. He was never again to return to the country.[31]

In spite of his failure to remain, Pashkov continued to provide financial assistance to evangelicals within Russia, including such Stundo-Baptists as Ryaboshapka and Ratushnyï as well as Wieler and Kargel. He apparently corresponded with all evangelical leaders of any party. He ceased, however, not later than 1890, financial aid for the mission work of the Russian Baptist Union.[32]

Outside Russia Pashkov became a traveling missionary in a number of European countries. In France and Austria he distributed Scripture from a Bible wagon and will finally settle in Salzburg. He provided funds for the "East London Institute for Home and Foreign Missions," led by H. Gratten and Fanny Guiness. In France he was a supporter of the "Pont de Brique," a mission led by Spencer and Cecilia Compton in Paris as well as the McCall Mission.[33]

After an extended illness, Pashkov died in Paris on February 12, 1902 (n.s.) and was buried in the Protestant Cemetery in Rome. Family members attended along with three daughters of Nathalie Lieven, including Sophie Lieven, and a few others.[34]

M. M. Korff spent much of his time in exile in Germany and Switzerland. He accepted believer's baptism by immersion in 1887. He continued to be active in evangelical circles and served on the staff of the Russian Missionary Society. He died on November 9, 1933, at the age of ninety-one. His funeral was in Basel, Switzerland, also attended by Sophie Lieven, and was buried in Lausanne.[35]

As already noted, Alexander III granted the aristocratic Pashkovite women, the widows, to hold meetings in their homes. Elizaveta Chertkova even built a meeting house on her property on Vasiliï Island in the St. Petersburg area. These women also held services on their estates. Vera Gagarina continued to hold services on her estate in Tula Province although meetings in her school were terminated and distribution of brochures ceased. Men were often absent. Women generally worked in small groups

---

31. Pobedonostsev, *Pis'ma Pobedonostseva k Aleksandru III*, 2:163. *Pobedonostsev i ego korrespondenty: Pis'ma i zapiski*, 2:795–96. Nichols, "Pashkovism: Nineteenth Century Russian Piety," 124. Latimer, *Dr. Baedeker*, 35–36.

32. Corrado, 163. Dyck, *Wieler*, 91.

33. Corrado, 165. Nichols, "Pashkovism," 122–23. *The Friend of Missions*, Mar. 1928, 46–47. Lieven, 54. Packer, 63–64.

34. Dillon, "A Russian Religious Reformer," *The Sunday Magazine*, Apr. 1902, 336. *Evangelical Alliance Quarterly*, July 1, 1903, 350. Lieven, 55–56.

35. Lieven, 56. *The Friend of Missions*, Jan. 1934, 2. Val'kevich, App. 3:24, ft. 2.

Evangelical Substratum

and might say a word in the general assembly. A couple of women were noted for leading Bible studies where men might be present.[36]

Alexandra Ivanovna Peuker, when unable to edit further the *Russkiï rabochiï*, worked among women and girls and then among students and later with a hospital, mainly for poor and needy, that one of her friends founded at her suggestion. Countess Helena Ivanovna Shuvalova, a Radstock convert, who had been married to the Chief of Police for Russia, provided material help to sectarians and funds for evangelism. She would invite an official to dinner where she would appeal to him to modify if not liberate some believer who had been exiled.[37]

A man who was closely allied with Shuvalova was Hermann I. Fast (1880–1935), who served as tutor in her family and lived in Tsarskoe Selo (The Tsar's Village), outside of St. Petersburg. His father was Isaac Fast of Gnadenfeld in the Mennonite colony of Molochna. Fast received training at the missionary school of St. Chrischona in Switzerland. He assisted in managing a children's orphanage, established in 1886 by two Swedes, which included children whose stundist families had suffered exile. He held meetings with Pashkovites in his home, where he also educated sectarian youth. He helped enroll Russian students at St. Chrischona with three of them attending in 1893. He became a missionary of the Russian Baptist Union but turned negatively against Baptists for their "superficiality" and adherence to "outer forms," and even advocated the removal of A. R. Shiewe from his post as pastor of the German Baptist Church in St. Petersburg.[38]

Fast was an advocate for persecuted sectarians who appealed to him for help. In turn, he requested material aid for them from Shuvalova, Paul Nicolay, and others. He traveled widely, including a trip with Quakers to exiles in Transcaucasus. In reports on his travels in *Glaubensbote,* the organ of St. Chrischona, Fast played up evangelical suppression. He also collaborated with I. S. Prokhanov in the publication of *Beseda.* For a short time in 1894 Fast with Prokhanov and others lived in an agricultural commune in Crimea, "Vertograd." When authorities searched his home in 1894, they discovered letters, manuscripts, printed leaflets, a copying press, and a lithographic stone. He conducted a broad correspondence that included Pashkov and Korff, Wieler, Baedeker, Julius Herrmann (German Baptist pastor in Riga), representatives of the BFBS, publishers in Sweden, Germany, and Kansas, USA, and with others. The authorities forced Fast into exile, moving first to Romania and then to Canada.

Some men who lived outside St. Petersburg, as Ivan Kargel and Frederick Baedeker, frequently visited the home of Nathalie Lieven. Baedeker also visited the widow of Count Bobrinskiï on her estate in Tula Province upon the death of her husband, a Radstock convert, in 1895. In the same year he visited the estate of Pashkov,

---

36. Lieven, 62–63. Terletskiï, 80. Procurator of the Holy Synod, *Report*, 1887, 79–80.

37. Lieven, 62–65. Val'kevich, 71.

38. For the career of Fast, see Val'kevich, 158–59, 169–73, and App. 3:96, ft. 1, and Prokhanov, "G. I. Fast, Posmertnoe slovo," *Evangel'skaya vera* 4/7–9 (July–Sep. 1935), 27.

Vetoshkino in Nizhniĭ Novgorod Province, which maintained a hospital frequented by nearby residents.³⁹

The regime prohibited Pashkovite meetings outside of St. Petersburg and arrested worshipers if caught. Maria Yasnovsky wrote some years later that she and others would go into the woods for communion services, hiding behind bushes for protection. One of the men would be appointed to be at a tram stop and without a word would point to a path for those arriving for the service. When Lars E. Högberg visited Pashkov's estate, Vetoshkino, he found that the authorities forbade gatherings for prayer and singing. He nevertheless conducted services in the absence of the supervisor, a man fearful of offending the authorities and who would have probably not allowed the services if he had been present.⁴⁰

In spite of the prohibitions and harassment, Pashkovism continued to spread. In his report in 1887, Pobedonostsev reported the spread of Pashkovism in Novgorod, Tver, Tula, Yaroslav, and Olonets dioceses and the continuing distribution of Pashkovite books and brochures. In his report for 1888–1889, Pobedonostsev recorded that laborers who had come to St. Petersburg for work carried the Pashkovite heresy back to their home areas. He also noted that members of the cultured gentry in the provinces also spread the teaching. In 1897 the periodical *Tserkovnyĭ vestnik* reported that the clergy in St. Petersburg were struggling with the Pashkovites, who continued to spread among the upper and lower classes, especially among the factory workers. They also appeared to be more prepared in their propaganda than in the first decade of their existence. Their missionaries were penetrating apartments and inns, and even the coachman or footman might become a sectarian preacher.⁴¹

At the Kazan Missionary Congress of the Orthodox Church in 1897, time was allotted for an exchange of opinions from anti-sectarian missionaries, and four teachers of the Tver Seminary presented papers. The congress noted that a close relationship existed between Pashkovites and stundists. Pashkovites in St. Petersburg sent stundists in Tver Province brochures and leaflets and sometime monetary assistance. They also maintained ties with stundists in Kiev. The editor of the Orthodox periodical in St. Petersburg, F. N. Ornatskiĭ, reported that the Pashkovites were conducting prayer meetings in up to forty homes in the city. He declared that they grow unrestricted because the 1894 law that outlawed stundism did not apply to them.⁴²

The session noted also that in Pashkovism as in stundism factionalism existed between those who rejected rites, particularly the necessity of baptism, such as the Mladostundists, and those who insisted on believer's baptism and a church structure

---

39. *Echoes of Service*, Sep. (II), 1895, 228.

40. *The Friend of Missions*, June 1926, 62. Högberg, *Skuggor och dagrer*, 283–85.

41. Procurator of the Holy Synod, *Report*, 1887, 78–82, and 1888–1889, 118–19. *TsV*, 1897, no. 4, 121.

42. See "Pashkovshchina i stundism," in Skvortzov, *Deyaniya 3-go Vserossiĭskago missionerskago s'ezda v Kazani*, 119–28.

as did Stundo-Baptists and German Baptists. It was also pointed out that Pashkov had been in close communication with Koval the Mladostundist, but he himself was evasive on baptism. As already noted, believer's baptism began to spread among the Pashkovites, but whatever their views on baptism they continued to differentiate themselves from Stundo-Baptists over close communion.[43]

Evangelical Armenians

An important segment of the evangelical substratum was the Protestant Armenian community in the Transcaucasus. It began in the early nineteenth century through the work Felician Zaremba and Heinrich Dietrich, missionaries of the Basel Missionary Society. The regime terminated the mission in 1835 but in 1866 permitted the formation of an Armenian Lutheran Church in Shusha. Protestant Armenians were nominally Lutheran, but with Lutheran pastors attempting to exercise ecclesiastical control some of them, strongly evangelistic, attempted to form their own free assemblies. The evangelical Armenians produced several outstanding leaders.[44]

Evangelical Armenians were valuable in the work of the BFBS in Bible distribution and in translation. Abraham Amirchanianz, a preacher among the Armenians, translated the Bible into Ararat-Armenian and Transcaucasian Turkish. They were also valuable interpreters, as in the ministry of Baedeker.[45]

Sumbat G. Bagdasarjanz, who attended a Methodist seminary in Frankfurt am Mainz in Germany, joined the Baptists and married Ottilie, the daughter of Martin Kalweit. He accompanied Baedeker in his trip in the Caucasus in 1887. Baedeker stated in 1888 that he was to him "a gift of God for the work," such as in prison ministry and interpreting in Armenian churches.[46]

One of the most active evangelical Armenian was Patvakan Tarajanz, a merchant and an evangelist among his own people. He spoke Russian, Tartar, Armenian, German, and Swedish. He was a traveling companion of Baedeker, which included accompanying Baedeker across Siberia in 1893. Val'kevich reported that Tarajanz was in Tulcha, Romania in 1894, migrated to Constanta in 1897 but was resolved to return to Russia. In 1901 Tarajanz, who received a special permit to visit Caucasian prisons, spent two months with Baedeker. For many years he served as head of an Armenian evangelical assembly in Baku.[47]

---

43. Ibid., 126–28.

44. BFBS, *Monthly Reporter*, Sep. 1886, 154–59. Letters of Baedeker in *Echoes of Service*, Feb. 1889, 43–44, and Feb. (I), 1892, 35–46.

45. BFBS, *Monthly Reporter*, March 1889, 42–43.

46. *Kirche im Osten* 25 (1982), 121–28. *Echoes of Service*, Jan. 1889, 5–7.

47. *Echoes of Service*, Feb. (I) 1892, 35; Aug. (I), 1901, 299; Oct. (II) 1905, 389–90; and Jan. (I) 1917, 9–10. Val'kevich, 53.

Another leading Armenian evangelical was K. A. Ter-Asaturov of Shusha, who provided material help to exiles in Elizavetpol Province. He served as an intermediary between sectarians on the one side and Baedeker and Tarajanz on the other side.[48]

The evangelical suppression also affected evangelical Armenians. Tarajanz lived outside Russia in Romania for some years. Others initially faced exile within Russia. Amirchanianz was exiled to Orenburg in 1889 and settled for seven years in Finland. Bagdasarjanz was exiled in 1891 to Akhalkalaki, today in Georgia, and then to Romania. Baedeker wrote in 1893 that one who was closely watched by the regime reported that the government was then beginning a persecution among the Armenians.[49]

Jewish Missions

Although Peter the Great permited Jews to settle in Russia, the regime expelled them in 1795. As Russia expanded further to the south and west, it gained an increasing number of Jews. With few exceptions Jews were not allowed to settle in Russia proper, but the regime permitted them to reside in a so-called "Jewish Pale" that included Russian Poland and fifteen provinces in western and southern Russia. Evangelism among Jews was difficult, at least partly because of the prohibition of foreign missionaries, general apathy, and the jealousy of the Russian Orthodox Church of other Christian faiths. But even more was the resistance of the Jewish population itself, attaching their identity to their religion as well as bitterness toward Christians for discrimination and persecution.[50]

Anti-Semitism was widespread in Russia with pogroms from time to time erupting against Jews. But according to Charles T. Byford, villages where stundists were a substantial part of the population avoided anti-Jewish attacks. Byford claimed that Ivan Ryaboshapka, the Stundo-Baptist leader in Ukraine, delivered several sermons on the topic. Although Ryaboshapka declared that the Jews were perhaps suffering for their sins, he said that believers were to refrain from "participating, even in thought, in such deeds. The Jews are the eldest sons of God. He punishes them more severely than the others. Woe to the man who will take upon himself to be the instrument of God's wrath."[51]

The Lutheran Church in Russia, as a recognized body, was able to engage in some mission work among the Jews, forming, for instance, a Baltic Central Jewish Mission Society in 1870. On the other hand, the regime restricted Lutheran and Reformed pastors from aggressive evangelism among the Jews and only with permission of the government were they allowed to instruct and baptize Jews and distribute Scripture

48. Val'kevich, App. 5:11, ft. 1.
49. *Echoes of Service*, July (I) 1893, 160.
50. Gidney, *The History of the London Society for Promoting Christianity amongst the Jews*, 92–93. Wilkinson, *In the Land of the North*, 24, 30–32, 89.
51. Byford, *The Soul of Russia*, 347.

among them. In the nineteenth century, several societies for Jewish evangelism were able to enter the country. The London Society for Promoting Christianity amongst Jews, formed in 1809 as an interdenominal evangelical society, but becoming entirely Anglican in 1815, established a mission in Russian Poland that continued with one break until the beginning of the Second World War. Other missions included the Mildmay Mission in London and the Zion Society for Israel, founded by Norwegian Lutherans in America. The Mildmay Mission was unique in that it employed only individuals in Russia itself who received governmental permission to distribute Scripture and government-approved tracts. It also opened depots.[52]

According to the *Missionary Review of the World* in 1890, the Minster of the Interior ordered authorities to prohibit foreign missionaries to evangelize Jews, which was a prerogative of the Russian Church. In 1894 the same periodical reported that evangelistic work among Jews was now more limited than a few years ago. It also stated that the government recognized only one foreign missionary, O. J. Ellis in Warsaw.[53]

Nevertheless some Jews were won to the Christian faith. Two notable Jewish converts were Dr. Adolph Althausen (1820–1904), for twenty-five years an army physician, and his son-in-law, Theodor Carl Meyerson (1850–1913). Althausen settled in St. Petersburg in 1882 and became a missionary of the Zion Society for Israel. He became the first permanent missionary of the Mildmay Mission in 1887 and was in charge of the depot in Vilnius from 1888 to 1896. Meyersohn opened a depot in Minsk, gaining authorization for its establishment and continued in this post until his death in 1913. After thirty-three years as missionary, he baptized 438 Jewish converts.[54]

Beginning in 1859 Rudolph Faltin (1829–1918), a Lutheran minister, began a ministry in Kishinev in Bessarabia. Through ministering to inquirers and distributing Scripture, he helped to lay the foundation of Jewish Christian work in South Russia. One of his notable converts was Rabbi Rudolph Gurland, baptized in 1864, who after training in Berlin and ordination served for a time as Faltin's assistant but then moved to the Baltic area. Faltin won 300 Jewish converts.[55]

The one Jewish work that caught the attention of the evangelical world in the late nineteenth century was the ministry of Joseph Rabinowitz (Rabinowich) (1837–1899), a Jewish lawyer in Kishinev, Bessarabia. While in 1882 in Palestine to consider a Jewish settlement in Palestine, he felt, while on the Mt. of Olives, that the solution to the Jewish problem was to recognize Jesus as the Messiah. He was familiar with the life of Jesus through a Hebrew Bible that had been given to him. On his return to Kishinev, he began to proclaim his new views with the result that a group developed

---

52. Lenker, 453–54. Wilkinson, 89–93. See Wardin, *Evangelical Sectarianism*, 22–23, 36–37, for bibliographic entries on Jewish missions in Russia.

53. *MRW* 13 (1890), 799, and 17 (1894), 759.

54. Roi, de le, *Geschichte der evangelischen Juden-Mission seit Entstehung des neueren Judentums*, 1:335–37. Wilkinson, 73–77. Solberg, *A Brief History of the Zion Society For Israel*, 27–31, 39–45.

55. Roi, de le, 340–44. Gidney, 42–43. Thompson, *A Century of Jewish Missions*, 148–49.

calling itself, "Israelites of the New Covenant." In October 1882 A. Venitianer, a pastor of the Reformed Church, baptized the first converts, including Rabinovitz's three daughters, but Rabinovich himself was not baptized until March 1885 and then at the Moravian church in Berlin by a professor from Andover Seminary in America. In December 1884 the authorities allowed Rabinowitz to open his own Jewish Christian synagogue.[56]

Rabinowitz's work did not identify with any one Christian denomination and developed its own thirteen declarations and ten articles of faith. Although he taught that the Law had been fulfilled in Christ, yet he believed that a Christian Jew as a Jew was to keep the Law as part of his national identity, a position that many Christians criticized. At first he held services on the seventh day of the week and approved circumcision but a rite without spiritual significance.[57]

Rabinowitz faced strong resistance and even persecution from fellow Jews. He was forced to leave his residence and lost all his clients. He nevertheless had a wide impact on the Jewish community in his preaching and in his writings, tracts, and sermons, which were published in Russian, Hebrew, and Yiddish.[58]

The death of Rabinowitz in 1899 and the removal of Faltin to Riga in 1904 left a serious void in leadership in Jewish work in Kishinev. It was impossible to find a successor to Rabinowitz's work, which was unique, and his congregation dispersed. The hall in which he ministered was used from time to time for gospel services but sold in 1921 as a private residence.[59]

---

56. An excellent biography of Rabinowitz is Kjaer-Hansen, *Joseph Rabinowitz and the Messianic Movement*. For the beginnings and development of Rabinovich's work, see *EC*, Aug. 1, 1883, 280–83; *BMM*, May 1885, 139; Wilkinson, 77–78; and de le Roi, 344–53, which includes a list of early documents on the movement. See Wardin, *Evangelical Sectarianism*, 36–37, for bibliographic entries in evangelical periodicals.

57. *BMM*, Oct. 1885, 396–97, and Sep. 1886, 368–69. *MRW* 8/2 (Mar.–Apr. 1885), 101–102. Thompson, 149.

58. *Missionary Herald*, May 1885, 203. Schonfield, *The History of Jewish Christianity*, 225–26. *EC*, Apr. 1, 1890, 113–15.

59. See Kjer-Hansen, 206–20, for the aftermath of Rabinowitz's ministry.

20

Survival

CHURCH HISTORY IS REPLETE with religious bodies that have failed to survive such as the Montanists in the Ancient World, Albigensians in the Middle Ages, and the Malevantsy, an offshoot of Russian stundism that appeared in the late nineteenth century. A number of factors, however, enabled Russian Stundo-Baptism to survive its suppression, some external and others internal. Stundo-Baptism was part of a worldwide evangelical movement with support from Baptists and other evangelicals in Great Britain, Germany, and the USA. An evangelical substratum within Russian itself also helped to sustain it. But its own internal resources and conception of itself proved to be most crucial of all.

Although the regime attempted to brand stundism/Stundo-Baptism as a social-political threat to the state and a supporter of socialism, it was not a political movement. Its main political goal was for religious toleration or liberty of conscience. It had no social agenda except for the class interests of its individual members. It always expressed loyalty to the Tsar with the reservation that it was not bound to any measures contrary to God's law or their conscience.

In taking an oath to Nicholas II, the new Tsar in 1894, some stundists refused by objecting to all oaths, the Mennonite position. Other stundists took the oath with some change in its wording or its administration. Such persons refused to kiss the holy cross, considering it idolatrous, and some also refused to repeat the words, "swear by Almighty God." Some stundists thought the taking the oath would give the government a legal basis for punishing them as stundists. Whatever their reaction to swearing an oath to Nicholas, it was not because of disloyalty to the regime.[1]

---

1. *TsV*, 1894, nos. 51–52, 822–23.

PART FIVE—Peril, 1884–1905

Stundists and Stundo-Baptists bore their suffering not because they felt they were innocent of any crime but suffering for God and the gospel, believing they were in the ranks of Christians who suffered for the faith since apostolic times. Although under great pressure and even with complaints, legal challenges, and even subterfuge, they never revolted against their lot. One of the stundists who was exiled to the Transcaucasus, wrote to a friend during the height of the suppression:

> Pray for us that we may have strength given us to bear our cross uncomplainingly. Although we have lost our liberty, and are confined here among high, gloomy mountains, we have not yet lost that liberty which God has given us in his dear son: and we are reminded to look up to the hills whence cometh our aid. Often we ascend the hills, and there bend our knees in praise of our God, perfect freemen.[2]

In spite of church splits, one of the great strengths of the Stundo-Baptist movement was its cohesion. The movement was a confessional body with doctrinal standards. The members were under church discipline, which also included pastors.[3]

Although the movement was under male leadership, it nevertheless provided a spiritual equality for women who provided a significant portion of the membership in their attendance and contributions to the work and to charity. The stundist publication, *Beseda,* noted that in the congregation in Tambov women bought materials and knitted socks and made shirts and from the proceeds, although retaining a portion to continue the enterprise, contributed to the poor and other charitable causes.[4]

Orthodox observers noted the inner strength of the movement. Pavel Kozitskiĭ wrote of its communal nature, its strong cohesion. Members assisted each other in misfortune. They informed each other of the arrival of Orthodox missionaries, even providing information on their personalities. Val'kevich claimed stundists created a "state in a state" with their separatist tendencies, establishing organs for control of moral and economic life, opening their own schools, forming their own treasuries, and their support of underground publications. In an article in 1889 on the difficulty of struggle with stundism, one particular author was very critical of A. Ushinskiĭ in his efforts in collecting information on stundism. He called him a dilettante and disparaged his claim that a powerful refutation of their heresy and an explanation of Orthodox faith and rites would win them over. The author countered by asserting that stundism was "a very complex phenomenon" and could not be overcome with one or two conversations. He added, "stundism is not a soap bubble, destroying it with a light shaking of the air."[5]

2. *Missionary Herald.* April 1894, 142.
3. For discipline of church leaders for drinking or other improper behavior, see Val'kevich, 74, 98.
4. *Beseda*, Aug. 1895, 121–22.
5. Kozitskiĭ, "O prichinakh, prepyatstvuyushchikh uspeshnoĭ bor'be so shtundizmom," *TsV*, 1891, no. 21, 324. Val'kevich, 220. "Shtundistskie tolki i trudnost' bor'be s nimi," *TsV*, 1889, no. 46, 790–91.

The Russian Baptist Union

One of the important institutions that provided cohesion to the Stundo-Baptist movement was the Russian Baptist Union. Its congresses and mission committee provided an organizational center for the widespread independent congregations. The financial support of the Union helped to place missionaries on the field. It was fortunate it was founded not later than 1884, the year of the beginning of the suppression. It had before it the examples of German Baptist associations and the Mennonite Brethren Conference, which began as early as 1872, and the conference at Rückenau in 1882 when Russian Baptists joined Mennonite Brethren at the latter's annual conference.[6]

The congress in 1884 at Novo-Vasil'evka in Taurida Province met in comparatively safe territory, near the Mennonite colony of Molochna and in an area where Baptists had been successful in gaining converts from the Molokans.[7] A preliminary meeting chose the following officers: Johann Wieler, a Mennonite Brethren leader among stundists, for president; Johann (Ivan) Kargel from St. Petersburg, the German Baptist who recently completed establishing Baptist work in Bulgaria, for vice-president; Minaï Khanin and Mikhail Koloskov for secretaries; and Vasilii Kolodin and Maksim Balikhin for treasurers. The congress enrolled thirty-three delegates and six guests. Taurida Province was well represented with seventeen delegates with six, including Wieler, from the Mennonite colony of Molochna. Ratushnyï and Ryaboshapka came from Kherson Province. No delegates were present from the Caucasus, including V. G. Pavlov, but correspondence was sent from there.

Because of fear of interference from the police, outsiders, including Kargel, went for safety to a German colony before the official opening. On Sunday April 29 a great rally, estimated at 2,500, of Stundo-Baptists, Molokans, and even some Orthodox gathered at Novo-Vasil'evka, which included a message on missions by Zinovii D. Zakharov, leader of the New Molokans, that produced a collection of seventy-six rubles. On Monday the outside guests felt safe enough to assemble for the opening session. Wieler opened the congress with the singing of a hymn from "Lyubimykh stikhov," reading Ephesians 4:1–16, with an exposition of the tenth verse that stressed unity, a prayer, and the presentation of an agenda of twenty-three items. The congress followed the pattern of the Mennonite Brethren with a missionary for eight months receiving 500 rubles; for four months, 175 rubles; two months for 75 rubles, and payment of traveling expenses for all. The conference approved eight missionaries, including such veterans as Ratushnyï, Ryaboshapka, Vasilii V. Ivanov, and Pavlov as a general missionary. Pavlov received 400 rubles but also from the German-American

---

6. For sources for the congresses of the Russian Baptist Union before 1905, see Wardin, *Evangelical Sectarianism*, 144–47. Val'kevich, App 1:8–31, provides data on congresses of the Russian Baptist Union from 1884 to 1890 (except for the one in 1887–1888).

7. For a valuable account of the 1884 congress written in a letter by Kargel, May 3, 1884, translated into English, see Klippenstein, "Russian Evangelicalism Revisited: Ivan Kargel and the Founding of the Russian Baptist Union," *Baptist History and Heritage* 27 (Apr. 1992), no. 2, 42–48.

PART FIVE—Peril, 1884–1905

Committee a supplementary 200 rubles and about 100 rubles for traveling expenses. The conference elected a mission committee, which was responsible for collecting funds, and also heard reports from various missionaries. The Zakharov brothers, who were New Molokans that practiced infant baptism, left after the mission reports. The conference discussed a variety of local church issues. Wieler described the significance of washing feet among Mennonite Brethren, but Kargel pointed out it was not an apostolic custom. The conference resolved to permit it, leaving it up to each church to decide on the practice. After Kargel read of examples of the laying on of hands in the Acts of the Apostles, the conference resolved that presbyters not receiving this rite should be in harmony with the Word of God. On the question of open communion with those who were not in agreement on baptism, it was resolved to keep the question open and to make it a matter of prayer for those who did not have clarity on the issue. On the question to what extent resolutions of the congress were binding on the churches, Wieler outlined three categories. Resolutions on missions were binding because of the nature of the congress; resolutions on theology were not obligatory although it was desirable to accept unanimity; and other issues were up to the discretion of the local church. Church members without the local church's knowledge were admonished not to go to the civil court to prosecute for debt. Members were to give to the poor without charging interest and not charge more than six percent in commercial transactions.

The second congress at Vladikavkaz in April 1885 included nine churches with Wieler again president. But on the second day with the sudden departure of Wieler, who will soon go into exile, Pavlov, the vice-president, now presided. By a rising vote, the congress expressed its heartfelt thanks to Wieler for his work. In the absence of Wieler and also Kargel, both accepting the Pashkov position of open communion, the strict Baptist position prevailed that open communion was contrary to the statement of faith, and footwashing was not to be introduced. Except in cases of necessity, members should avoid traveling on Sunday.[8] The third congress with sixteen delegates met in the Kuban in December 1886. Except for five delegates from Taurida Province, one from the Volga, and one undetermined, the remaining nine came from the Caucasus or adjoining areas. Because of police surveillance, Ratushnyĭ and Ryaboshapka from Kherson Province were not present. Four of the delegates came from the Kuban congregation, including the two wealthy Mazaev brothers, Deĭ and Gavriil. The congress selected Deĭ as president and Andreĭ M. Mazaev of another Mazaev family and member of the Tiflis church as vice-president. Pavlov, who was absent, had written that he declined the position of president of the mission committee, while Wieler wrote a letter proposing Deĭ for president. The Congress, however, retained Wieler as president and elected Deĭ over Pavlov as assistant. In the absence of Wieler, Deĭ now held the two chief positions in the Union.[9] With the growing suppression, the conference

8. Val'kevich, App. 1:16–22.
9. Ibid., App. 1:22–28.

unanimously agreed that arrested missionaries would not forfeit their support while imprisoned. The congress resolved to place defenders or counsel for accused missionaries without distinction of confession. The president proposed to open a subscription for donations for defense of the missionaries under judgment. At the conclusion, the congress expressed its heartfelt thanks to the Kuban church and especially Gavriil Mazaev for rendering hospitality. Although absent, the congress also expressed to Wieler sincere thanks "for all his indefatigable labors and for the Church." In spite of the increasing suppression, the Russian Baptist Union continued to maintain a treasury, appoint missionaries, hear reports, and provide money for those suffering persecution. Congresses were not held in Ukraine but in northern Caucasus or the Don and Volga regions, areas that were closer to properties of the Mazaev family and also probably less chance of interference or detection by the authorities.

The congress from December 29, 1887 to January 1, 1888, location unrecorded, was called the "Christian Brotherhood." Sixteen delegates from ten congregations attended. The congress elected Deï Mazaev "leader of common brethren affairs." It created it as a permanent office with five brethren as assistants. The congress extended its authority in the ordination of elders by declaring it was "always desirable" ordination be in agreement with the annual congress and neighboring brethren and with the participation of the leader of common affairs.[10]

The 1889 "Christian Brotherhood" congress in January 1889 in Nikol'skoe, Stavropol region, as noted earlier, approved M. D. Chechetkin and Yakob D. Delyakov for a mission to the Molokans in the Amur region. The congress in 1890 met again in Nikol'skoe. It allocated almost 2,900 rubles for thirteen evangelists for various terms of service. Five others volunteered their services for short periods with payment of traveling expenses, while Gavriil Mazaev volunteered for an indefinite time without salary or payment for travel.[11]

The congress first scheduled to meet in January 1891 in Vladikavkaz was moved to Gor'skaya Balka. The congress endorsed the new publication, *Beseda*, and wished it success. It approved F. P. Balikhin and Vasiliĭ V. Ivanov (although unable to attend) as evangelists for a year, while seven others were appointed for two months each.[12] Although the Union of Evangelical Christians-Baptists was unable to list between 1891 and 1898 any congresses in its history published in 1989, there is evidence that congresses continued to operate through the entire period of the suppression. Pavlov wrote in 1906 from Tiflis, "In account of persecutions the Union could not, as it would to develop its activity in proclamation of the Gospel, but it never ceased to meet to send and to support the evangelists." In his recording of the congresses, Val'kevich maintained there was a congress at the end of 1892 and the beginning of 1893 but did not know the location. In searching for Baptist material in Russia, the author of

10. Dyck, *Wieler*, 92–93. *Istoriya*, 129.
11. Val'kevich, App. 1:28–31.
12. *Istoriya*, 130–31.

this work discovered in the March 1896 issue of *Der Sendbote*, the periodical of the German Baptist Conference in America, an account of a congress in "M" near Rostov-on-Don in December 1895. Wilhelm Weber, a former Mennonite Brethren who joined the Baptists in the Volga region, submitted the article. The account followed a regular agenda of election of officers, appointment of missionaries, mission reports, and assistance for the exiled brethren.[13] For congresses that may have met from 1892 through 1904, no extant minutes have survived. Except for the congress in December 1895, already described, practically nothing or little is known of these congresses before 1902. The congress in 1898 at Tsaritsyn invited Pashkovites to attend. In 1902, at Rostov-on-Don, leaders of the Evangelical Christian (Pashkovite) congregation of St. Petersburg, V. I. Dolgopolov and G. M. Matveev, attended. Evangelical Christians also attended the congress in 1903 at Tsaritsyn and the one in 1904 at Rostov-on-Don.[14]

THE MAZAEVS

The congress in 1886 that elected Deï I. Mazaev (1855–1922) president of the congress and assistant president of the mission committee began a new era in the life of Russian Baptists. First, it signaled that with the exile of Wieler the movement was now in the hands of Russians and not led by Mennonite Brethren or German Baptists. The locus of the Stundo-Baptist movement had now moved from Ukraine eastward to the Don, Volga, and north Caucasus regions. It also meant the control of the movement by the Mazaevs led by Deï and accompanied by his brother Gavriil (1858–1937). The Mazaev era will last a generation. Deï will serve as president, except for one interval until 1920, shortly before his death. Gavriil will serve as treasurer of the Union in 1887 and 1888 and as president of the Siberian Baptist Union. Russian Baptists were fortunate to have such talented and wealthy leaders at this time. Deï was noted for his organizational abilities, wisdom, and writing. Gavriil was noted for his services as a missionary and administrative leadership. Both contributed significant sums to the Baptist cause.[15] The Mazaev brothers were born into a prosperous Molokan family in Taurida Province. The father, Ivan G. Mazaev (d. 1897), was a very successful breeder of sheep; at the time of his death, *Beseda* wrote that the father had a fortune of a million. The father

---

13. Letter of Pavlov, August 7, 1906, ABMU/ABFMS, *Correspondence*, Russian Mission, 1900–1919. Val'kevich, 164. Weber, "Reisebericht aus Russland," *Der Sendbote*, March 11, 1896, 3, and March 18, 1896, 2–3. On Weber's preaching activity and persecution, including his own difficulties with the authorities, see March 15, 1899, 167.

14. *Istoriya*, 131.

15. For the life of Deï I. Mazaev see Levindanto, "Pamyati Deya Ivanovicha Mazaeva," *BV*, 1953, 2–3, 95–98, and Nagirnyak, "Deï Ivanovich Mazaev," *Materialy nauchno-bogoslovskoï* konferentsi Rossiĭskogo *Soyuza evangel'skikh khristian-baptistov*, 152–71. For the life of Gavriil I. Mazaev, see his autobiography, *Obrashchenie na istinnyĭ put' i vospominaniya baptista G. I. M.*, and references to him in Val'kevich, 92, and App. 1:27, ft. 2. For references to Ivan G. Mazaev, the father of the Mazaev brothers, see Val'kevich, App. 3:128–29, which quotes *Beseda*, March, 1897, and *WHZ*, April 22, 1899, 118. For other material on the Mazaev family see Wardin, *Evangelical Sectarianism*, 152–53.

bought a large area of land from Count Pletov, a hetman of the Cossacks, and divided it among his sons. As the father, Deï and Gavril were also wealthy not only through family inheritance but also by continuing to enlarge their wealth through leasing additional land. Val'kevich recorded that the two brothers leased land in the Don and the Kuban besides land in the vicinity of Omsk in Siberia and in Stavropol, Tambov, and Samara. N. Kutepov, an Orthodox writer, recorded that the father and his four sons possessed sixty thousand *desyatiny* or 162,000 acres. Deï became noted for his expertise in sheep breading by developing a special breed called "Mazaev sheep."[16] Both Deï and Gavriil came under Baptist influence through the ministry of Baptists among the Molokans in Taurida Province. Both accepted baptism, which was contrary to Molokan belief. Their uncle, Timofeï G. Mazaev, a Molokan elder, and their father opposed baptism, but the latter, however, did not forbid it outright. In November 1884, Vasilii Kolodin, a Baptist elder from Novo-Vasil'evka, baptized the two brothers with their wives and three others. The Molokans in Novo-Vasil'evka severely chided the father for allowing his sons to be baptized. The father felt greatly pained in the charge and his inability to reconcile himself to the conduct of his sons. In December the father reproached the two sons, exiling Deï from the home for being the chief instigator, but left Gavriil, hoping by threats and his exercise of parental authority to change his mind. The father even considered disinheriting Deï but will finally receive him back in 1888. The sons soon were preaching and quickly rose to prominence in Baptist ranks. The two men were part of a remarkable number of Baptist leaders who came from the Molokans such as Nikita Voronin, V. G. Pavlov, V. V. Ivanov, F. P. Balikhin, and I. S. Prokhanov.[17] In his account of Deï Mazaev, N. Kutepov, the Orthodox writer, noted his gifts as a preacher and his willingness to travel everywhere in the Don, Kuban, and Terek regions spreading the Baptist faith among the common people. A source of Baptist converts came from the two hundred workers who served on the Mazaev estates all year along with the two thousand summer seasonal workers. In the newly formed congregations, Deï instructed the new converts. In his visit, probably in the mid-nineties, to the Mazaev brothers, N. F. Höijer, the Swedish Mission Covenant missionary, went to a neighboring village where one of the brothers had built a prayer house where he regularly preached; on this occasion Höijer preached in German and the Mazaev brother in Russian. In 1899 Pavlov visited the estate of Gavriil. On the Sunday he was there Pavlov preached twice in Russian and once in German.[18] The Mazaevs were able to rise to such prominence so rapidly as new converts because of their natural abilities, evangelistic work, and wealth but also the need for strong

---

16. Val'kevich, App. 1:27, ft. 2, and App. 3:128–29. Levindanto, 98. N. Kutepov, "Sovremennaya baptistskaya, shtundistskaya i molokanskaya propaganda na yuge Rossii," *Pribavleniya k Tserkovnym vedomostyam*, Feb. 13, 1888, 174.

17. G. I. Mazaev, *Obrashchenie*, 23–27.

18. Kutepov, 175. Larsson, *Tjugufem år i Ryssland*, 379. WHZ Apr. 22, 1899, 118. Also see Val'kevich, 92, on the success of the Mazaev brothers in their evangelistic work among their farmhands.

leadership with the growing supression of the Russian Baptist movement. Wieler was now in exile and leaders from Ukraine could not lead because of strict surveillance. Such possible leaders as Pavlov and Voronin in the Tiflis church will soon be exiled and the suppression will increase to the extent of causing much of the movement to go underground. It is rather ironic that the Mazaevs could function as leaders of a suppressed movement while they continued to live in affluence and seemingly immune from exile, while at the same time many of their co-religionts were imprisoned, lost property, and sent far away into exile and often in degrading circumstances. It again shows the conflicting and inconsistent conduct of the Tsarist regime in their religious policies, providing, even inadvertently, a number of loopholes for a movement it wished to limit or destroy. The fact that in their religious journey the Mazaev brothers shifted from Molokanism, a heretical group, to another heretical group and not from Orthodoxy possibly helped, although this trajectory did not shield other Baptist leaders who followed the same path. Perhaps they were more discreet than others or just more fortunate. Above all probably their social and economic prominence and great wealth helped to shield them. In 1888 the Orthodox writer N. Kutepov noted that Deï Mazaev's authority among Baptist propagandists came from his wealth and broad education.[19] Whatever the failure of the Tsarist regime to follow a consistent policy in respect to the Stundo-Baptist movement, it, however, was not blind to the role of the Mazaevs in the movement. Val'kevich wrote that Deï was under surveillance. When N. F. Höijer visited one of the Mazaev brothers' homes, probably the residence of Deï, the brother he was visiting informed him that the authorities had harrassed him. During the visit, the local priest demanded that the Mazaevs come to him for an interrogation and threatened serious consequences for failure to comply.[20]

Today with more critical evaluation of the Russsian Baptist movement, the role of the Mazaevs is coming under more scrutiny. This is seen particularly in the biographical study in 2007 of the life of Deï Mazaev by A. P. Nagirnyak. He admits that the writing of the biography was difficult because of Deï's wealthy status, which was particularly condemned by Soviet writers, and also Deï's strong opposition to the Evangelical Christian movement that arose in the early twentieth century, a movement that became united in 1944 with the Baptists to form the Union of Evangelical Christians-Baptists. Deï tenaciously held to a rigid view of Baptist polity.[21] With their opposition to both religion and capitalism, it is understandable that Soviet writers would point to Deï as a severely flawed religious leader. They used the letters of Vasilii V. Ivanov, an early and very successful Baptist evangelist who also came from Molokan roots, who severely condemned Deï's leadership. One first needs to understand, as already noted, Ivanov's own personal views or biases. He was very critical of the growing centralization of the Baptist movement and also the Germanic influences

19. Kutepov, 173.
20. Val'kevich, 139. Larsson, 379.
21. Nagirnyak, 152.

that were crowding out early Molokan religious traditions. Any forceful leadership that strongly upheld Baptist norms as borrowed from the German Baptists would automatically bring Ivanov's disfavor.[22] Ivanov's criticism of Deï was harsh. In a letter to Pavlov, Ivanov was critical of Deï's imperious conduct within the Russian Baptist Union and claimed his workers "groveled" before him. In 1900 he complained that the Baptist administration was like a Holy Synod only in one person; with all squabbles thrust on him, he felt he was over all.

Ivanov also probably had a class bias against the Mazaevs. When Höijer visited the Mazaevs in Rostov-on-Don, he was ushered into a lovely room of one of the Mazaev homes with its fine beds, already made up, and other furniture, although strangely enough his host preferred sleeping on the hard floor. On Sunday he rode with his host in a "comfortable coach pulled by strong, black horses."[23] The average stundist and Stundo-Baptist preacher, including Ivanov, could not imagine living on such a level. Ivanov charged Mazaev for putting his own personal interests before the concerns of the Baptist Brotherhood, and as a millionaire he almost never met with self-denial the demands of individual believers. In his biography, Nagirnyak claimed from the testimony of several brethren that Deï became increasingly involved in his economic pursuits to the detriment of the Union.[24]

As Nagirnyak pointed out, Deï Mazaev must be put in historical context, a man who felt the necessity of defending the Russian Baptist Union from all competition and enemies. One must also take into account the motivations and biases of his critics. No doubt many believers felt that the Mazaevs with their wealth did not give enough and possibly could have been more generous but which, of course, would never be enough. Nevertheless the Mazaevs shared their wealth and helped to sustain the Baptist Union at a most difficult time. Deï provided funds for spiritual literature and support for the journal *Beseda*. In 1906 at the congress of the Russian Baptist Union at Rostov-on-Don when the travel treasury was in deficit, Deï stepped forward and stated he was ready to cover it. He continued to provide support in subsequent years.[25]

Worship and Evangelism

Exile and dispersal of congregations were disruptive but yet worship and evangelism continued. In his report in 1892–1893, Pobedonostsev reported that if stundism is

---

22. See Lyalina, *Baptizm: Illyuzii i real'nost*, 75, for excerpts of Ivanov's letters by a Soviet author. See Tverskaya, "Iz arkhiva sektantskikh vozhakov," *Antireligioznik*, July 1939, 36–38, for items from Ivanov's correspondence and minutes of the Baku Baptist Church.

23. Larsson, 379.

24. Nagirnyak, 164.

25. *Christlicher Familienkalender*, 1907, no. 1, 1. Nagirnyak, 163–64, for other examples of Deï's generosity.

not as public as before and appears more restrained it is not that it has laid down its weapons but has engaged in more secret propaganda.[26]

Deï Mazaev stated at the Baptist World Alliance in 1905:

> The Kingdom of the Lord in Russia had at this time to grow in an underground way... in Russia the Bread of Life could only be transported under the earth. The children of God could only meet together to pray and praise God in the night, when the windows were quite closed.... The meetings were only of five or six persons, and often when the police came in the preacher had to hide under the bed or escape through the window. But they had not forgotten their duty to preach the Gospel, and there was nothing that could hold them back.[27]

Sumbat Bagdasarjanz, the Armenian evangelical who returned on a visit to Russia after twelve years in exile recalled in a speech: "We had to come together in cellars or some little hidden place, and never could sing loud for fear of being heard by the police." Another witness was Ivan Saveliev (b. 1858), born in a Molokan family but joined the Baptists in 1883 and immediately began preaching. He was imprisoned seven times for short terms. When all of his meetings were forbidden, he reported that services always continued at times deep in the forests or in secluded areas on banks of rivers.[28]

One of the most successful evangelists during this period, who generally avoided the police, was Fedor P. Balikhin. In 1885 the Russian Baptist Union appointed him a missionary one-fourth time in Taurida Province and received subsequently additional appointments.[29] Balikhin described his activity before 1905 as follows:

> For four years I carried on the work of making converts despite orders from the police to stop it. I was constantly under suspicion, but by exercising great care in my work and holding secret meetings away from the towns I was able to keep out of the hands of the authorities until 1886. Then I was sentenced to a term in prison, and at the end of my sentence released with a warning that I would be sent back if I was found preaching again. I still carried on the work, but had to be more careful than before, because I was constantly under suspicion. We would meet in some lonely spot in the depths of the forest late at night, stealing there one by one, and post sentinels to avoid being surprised by the police. Of the more than sixteen hundred persons I have baptized, by far the greater majority were converted at such meetings.[30]

26. Procurator of the Holy Synod, *Report*, 1892-1893, 265-66.
27. BWA, Congress, *Proceedings*, 1905, 184-85.
28. *Echoes of Service*, May, 1909, 188-89. Prestridge, 47.
29. For Balikhin's short autobiography, see "Kratkaya avtobiografiya presvetera-propovednika evangel'skikh khristian-baptistov Fedora Prokhorovicha Balikhina," *BV*, 1955, no. 1, 64-66, first printed at Rostov-on-Don in 1908. For reports of Balikhin in *Beseda*, see Mar. 1895, 37-42, and July 1895, 110. For his 1894 report see *MO*, Mar. 1900, 418-28. For his other activity in the 1880s and 1890s, see Val'kevich, 84.
30. Prestridge, 39-40.

With these examples of secret meetings, one, however, must not assume that the entire stundist or evangelical movement at this time was underground. In his description of meetings in Osnova, Ratushnyï made no reference to underground meetings; instead those who attended were fined. The Mazaevs themselves did not lead secret meetings and even provided a chapel that was open for services. Even though the Baptist church in Tiflis suffered severely with the removal of its leaders, yet, according to Val'kevich, it continued to carry on with attendance in 1894 of up to seventy persons. Val'kevich named six men, including Frederick Kielblock from the original Kalweit congregation, who served as a core group that collected support for those in exile and who were still engaged in ministry. Pashkovites in St. Petersburg continued to meet in their homes. As Baedeker wrote in 1898, "There are ups and downs in this big Russian Empire, and one has to seize opportunities as they present themselves. The open door in one part is no security for one elsewhere, nor does the permission at one time give a right for another time."[31] Individuals who speak of suppression often do not give an overall picture and highlight only their own experiences or the most extreme cases. In his speech at the Congress of the Baptist World Alliance, Deï Mazaev heightened the intensity of his remarks by quoting Hebrews 11:32–34 (verses, however, not included in the official record of the Congress), which graphically detailed the persecution of Christians in Apostolic times. His remarks also included the greatly exaggerated statement that "many of them, blessing the persecutors died in exile in Russia and abroad."[32]

Exile of some leaders stopped their ministry, such as the case of Andreï Leushkin who in his exile could not communicate with the Tartars because of the language barrier. On the other hand, to the discomfort of the authorities, the ministry of other exiles continued if not augmented. In 1896 the *Missionary Review of the World* noted: "The very dispersal of these brethren must tend to their rapid increase. Filled with zeal for his cause the banished man and his family at once start to make known to their neighbors the great truths which have done so much for them." Although this statement is overstated yet there were a number of cases that substantiate it. Andreï M. Mazaev evangelized among Molokans while in exile. P. D. Odnol'ko influenced other exiles in Gerusy and after his transfer to Yerevan spread evangelical views among Cossack troops. Andreï Evstratenko ministered in Siberia, where after his release in 1905 he remained to evangelize. Upon his second exile to Orenburg in Siberia, Vasilii Pavlov immediately baptized fourteen and in the remaining four years formed three churches.[33]

---

31. Val'kevich, 122–23. *Echoes of Service*, Apr. 1898, 108.

32. Compare the text of Mazaev's speech in the BWA, Congress, 1905, 185, with the speech in Nagirnyak, 160.

33. Prestridge, 35, 43–44, 100. *MRW*, Oct. 1896, 728. Val'kevich, 73, 94.

PART FIVE—Peril, 1884–1905

Mutual Assistance

The Stundo-Baptist community also survived through the mutual assistance provided by the community in Russia and from abroad. As previously noted, the Russian Baptist Union established a fund for the sufferers in exile. Balikhin recorded that he furnished material help to poor believers. Vasilii N. Ivanov, dressed as a peasant, secretly traveled in Ukraine to stundist believers in remote areas, ministering to them spiritually as well as providing material assistance. He collected information on the persecution and sent it to sympathetic officials in Kharkov and also sent or brought it to Prokhanov, editor of *Beseda*, then in St. Petersburg.[34]

Frederick Baedeker, who traveled widely throughout Russia in a prison ministry and a visitor to evangelical groups, added to his activity a ministry to exiles and provided material assistance to them from funds received from abroad. In September 1887 Baedeker visited Pavlov and Voronin in Orenburg, only exiled several months before. He then returned to the Volga and crossed the Caspian Sea to Baku. Under his license, he visited in Transcaucasus prisons in Shusha and Tiflis but also evangelical believers outside his mandate. In 1888 and 1889 he again was in the Transcaucasus and after a trip across Siberia in 1890 with Kargel again entered this territory in 1891 to assist the exiles.[35]

Baedeker's journey in 1891 across the mountains to Gerusy was difficult. Patvakan Tarajanz, the multilingual Armenian evangelist, accompanied him. They found the exiles often living in limestone caves and in abject poverty. After locating evangelicals, Baedeker distributed the material aid he had brought, which was joyfully received.[36]

Soon after his visit, Baedeker wrote from Odessa, "The atmosphere is heavy with espionage." He dared not preach to any native Russians "for fear of bringing persecution upon the resident Christians. But the prison doors are still open to me." After receiving distressing communications from some of the exiled, he wrote in April that he was able to send further assistance from Moscow to both Elisavetpol and "other far away places." Later in the year he wrote that because of assistance from England and other places from abroad he was able to send aid "to meet the most pressing needs."[37]

With the help of the depository of the BFBS in Tiflis, Baedeker used Taranjanz and other agents, such as K. Ter-Asaturov, in distributing funds. According to Val'kevich, in 1892–1893 Baedeker was sending at least 1,000 rubles monthly but in 1894 lesser sums. In a letter to Taranjanz, Baedeker wrote, "I do not wish that the money for the brethren fall into other hands or turned to other goals: they ought to be

---

34. Prokhanov, *In the Cauldron*, 165.

35. *Echoes of Service*, Oct. 1887, 149–51; Jan. 1888, 5–7; Jan. 1889, 5–7; Jan. 1890, 5–7; and Feb. (I) 1892, 35–36. Val'kevich, 193, and App. 5, 49. *MRW*, Mar. 1892, 181.

36. *Echoes of Service*, Apr. (I) 1892, 82. *EC*, June 1, 1892, 173.

37. *Echoes of Service*, Feb. (I) 1892, 36; May (I) 1892, 107; and Nov. (I) 1892, 250.

evenly divided among them who are needy." He also wrote that money "should be to help only those who are exiled for the sake of the Gospel." In August 1893 Baedeker reported that he had made a visit to the Caucasus and made it short "not to cause any fresh difficulties to the brethren." He also wrote "several brethren were tempted to look for more money, and as it was not forthcoming, they behaved in a very unseemly manner. . . . But out of the great number are only a *few*." In the same letter he stated that he tried indirectly to influence the authorities to direct exiles to Siberia as a more desirable location than the Transcaucasus. Baedeker also provided funds and supplies for travel expenses for wives with children who were joining their husbands.[38]

In 1894 Baedeker with Kargel was again in Transcaucasus providing relief. He again returned with Kargel in 1895, meeting with Armenian believers but now making another trip to Gerusy. As recorded by Kargel, this is probably the finest documented journey of outsiders to this notorious place. When first arriving in Shusha, the district chief asked Baedeker why he came there, this end of the earth? Baedeker replied that he had now come four times to Transcaucasus, but Shusha had been off his path. When the chief found out that he planned to continue on to Gerusy, he asked why at his age he would undertake such a trip. Baedeker replied that he had crossed Siberia in springless carriages (*tarantasses*). When Baedeker was asked whether he was armed, he said he relied only on God's protection; the chief, however, insisted he would provide protection.[39]

Upon their arrival in Gerusy, Baedeker and Kargel found no hotel but only a caravansary with only one room crowded with men for accommodations. After meeting the district chief and explaining they came to visit inmates in the local prison, the chief insisted they be his guest, which concerned them as limiting their freedom to approach the evangelical exiles, the main purpose of the visit. Since the chief could not be with them on Friday and Saturday, Baedeker and Kargel then had the opportunity of making contact with one of the believers. This brother complained of lack of work and also that with a mixture of Baptists, stundists, Molokans, and Sabbatarians dissension existed along with dissatisfaction over the distribution of aid.

At four in the afternoon on Saturday, Baedeker and Kargel met with a group of the exiles. Baedeker spoke of their suffering for Christ's sake and that the Children of God in the West had much compassion for their lot and prayed for them. Baedeker was much disappointed when he discovered that only Baptists had been invited to the meeting. Those present excused their conduct by stating that if all were invited the news of the meeting would have been trumpeted everywhere. In distributing the aid, Baedeker insisted that women and children must first be considered, then those who receive nothing from home, then those who do receive aid from home, and finally

---

38. Val'kevich, 197–98, and App. 5, 85. *Echoes of Service*, Oct. (I) 1893, 218–20.

39. For the account by Kargel of the 1895 trip to Gerusy, see Kargel, *Zwischen die Enden der Erde*, 191–218. Also see *Echoes of Service*, Nov. (I) 1895, 260–61. For the 1894 trip to the Transcaucasus, see *Echoes of Service*, Dec. (I) 1894, 279.

PART FIVE—Peril, 1884–1905

those who require no support at all. He also stipulated that non-Baptists be allowed to share.

Before the meeting ended, the police found Baedeker and Kargel meeting alone with the exiles. In attempting to justify their conduct to the district chief in meeting exiles in a group, they said they did not have time to meet each of them one by one. In describing the situation at Gerusy, the district chief said that the exiles have much more freedom than they should have, but they are dissatisfied. He said their correspondence, which he must read, is full of complaints and accusations, which are often false. He then shows the complaints to his subordinates and reprimands them if he finds they are in the wrong. Before leaving, Baedeker and Kargel did visit the prison that held not more than fifty prisoners.

But times began to change. In December 1900 Baedeker wrote that Russian Christians were now caring for most of the exiles and only a few cases now came to his attention. In 1901 he received a permit for 1901 and 1902 with a special permit for Tarajanz to visit prisons in the Caucasus. Baedeker's ministry, however, was soon coming to a close.[40]

Baedeker and his companions were not the only evangelicals to visit the exiles in Gerusy. Hermann Fast from St.Petersburg, who served as interpreter, and two Quakers, an Englishman and an Australian, undertook an inspection trip in the winter of 1892–1893. The Quakers had gone to petition Alexander III for religious freedom for sectarians but were not allowed to see him. The authorities, however, granted them permission to visit the exiles. They met Baptists in Tersk *oblast;* Baptists, Molokans and Jews in Tiflis; and exiles in Elisavetpol Province. The chief officer in Gerusy did not allow the Quakers to speak to the exiles alone but speak only to one or two at a time in a special office. The visitors not only provided material aid, leaving 300 rubles, but also encouraged the exiles by saying the whole world was praying and pleading for them. They also met Tolstoyan exiles.[41]

Funds for the persecuted stundists also came from other sources. The editor of *Der Wahrheitszeuge*, the Baptist paper in Germany, told his readers of his willingness to forward their gifts. Money also came from Sweden, including funds from missionaries of the Swedish Mission Covenant. A concert in Stockholm, Sweden, by the Fisk Jubilee Singers, an African-American choir of seven voices from Nashville, Tennessee, USA, raised 400 rubles followed by a free-will offering of over twenty-seven rubles. A contribution came from Baedeker that he received from a lady he met in China; and German Baptists in Russia itself also contributed.[42]

---

40. *Echoes of Service*, Jan. (II) 1901, 24, and Aug. (I) 1901, 299.

41. Val'kevich, 171–72. Grachev, *Gerusy,* 69–70.

42. *Echoes of Service*, Feb. (I) 1895, 27, and May (I) 1895, 107. *WHZ, Missionsbeilage*, Feb. 1892, 7–8. *Beseda*, Sep. 1894, 144, and Jan. 1895, 16. Val'kevich, 197–98.

The Evangelical Alliance

In London in 1846, evangelicals formed on Protestant principles the Evangelical Alliance. In other nations, evangelicals formed their own alliances, such as in the USA, with ties to the Alliance in London, which served as a world headquarters. With an international network of evangelical leaders, its international and national conferences, and its publication, *Evangelical Christendom*, the Alliance became a potent force worldwide for evangelical principles and an advocate for religious liberty. Membership was not by denomination but by individuals, including evangelicals from both Protestant state churches as well as free churches. Among its members were J. G. Oncken, Lord Radstock, Frederick W. Baedeker, and I. S. Prokhanov. The latter three addressed the jubilee conference in London in 1896. Radstock spoke on the unity of the church, while Baedeker in two addresses and Prokhanov in one address spoke on religious liberty and the stundists in the Russian Empire.[43]

With reports from Baedeker, a member of the Council of the Evangelical Alliance, the Alliance began to take a special interest in the 1890s on the plight of the stundists in Russia. In May 1893 Baedeker wrote that he had "many opportunities of speaking words of comfort to the persecuted ones, and spending the money entrusted to me to supply the urgent needs of our brethren and of the families of the banished ones."[44]

In January 1894 *Evangelical Christendom* reported that the Council of the Evangelical Alliance in Great Britain urged Christians in the country to pray earnestly for the persecuted believers in Russia. It also reported that the British Alliance had raised privately among its members in the past year £900 for the exiles, money that has been distributed almost entirely by agents in Russia and others who traveled to the country for this purpose. In April 1896 the periodical also reported that in the last two or three years the Alliance had raised a significant amount of money that was distributed. Funds came not only from Britain but also large amounts from French and German Switzerland. The publication in 1896 by Georges Godet, professor of theology at Neuchâtel, Switzerland, on the persecution in Russia (soon translated into German), and letters on the subject to the papers helped to increase support for the cause.[45]

Besides serving as a conduit of material aid to evangelical sufferers in Russia, the Evangelical Alliance played a valuable role in its petitions and direct appeals for religious liberty in this country. In 1871 it appealed on behalf of Lutherans in the Baltic area and in 1874 on behalf of Baptists. Through its branch in Switzerland the

---

43. For historical information on the Evangelical Alliance, see D. S. Schaff, "Evangelical Alliance," *The New Schaff-Herzog Religious Encyclopedia*, 4:221-23, and Ewing, *The Goodly Fellowship*. For the addresses of Radstock, Baedeker, and Prokhanov, see Evangelical Alliance, *Conference*, 1896, 105-8, 307-13, and 410-15.

44. *EC*, Apr. 1, 1893, 126; July 1, 1893, 220-22; and Aug. 1, 1893, 253-55.

45. Ibid., Jan. 1, 1894, 31-32, and Apr. 1, 1896, 117.

Alliance in 1888 sent a petition to Alexander III on behalf of religious liberty for all Christian churches. The Tsar gave the petition to Pobedonostsev for a reply. Pobedonostsev rejected the petition on the grounds that Russia's national strength came from the Orthodox faith, and it was the duty of the Russian state to protect its security. Russia cannot thus allow its people to be lured into alien faiths. In January 1889 the Swiss branch of the Alliance wrote a response to Pobedonostsev. Ivan S. Prokhanov, editor of *Beseda*, who spoke some years later at the jubilee conference of the Evangelical Alliance in 1896, claimed that although the petition was rejected it nevertheless encouraged the evangelical believers and led some papers in Russia to print articles on religious liberty.[46]

In 1893 123 leading clergy and laypersons in the Church of England and free churches sent confidentially a letter in Russian to the bishops of the Russian Orthodox church where oppression was particularly severe but no replies were received. Also in 1893 both the Baptist Union and Congregational Union in Great Britain invited A. J. Arnold, secretary of the Evangelical Alliance, to address respectively their annual assemblies on persecution of Christians in Russia and Turkey. Both unions passed resolutions expressing sympathy and appealed for prayer for those suffering for their faith and appreciation to the Alliance for its efforts.[47]

Although the Alliance provided aid to the sufferers and expressed their prayerful and sympathetic support, yet frustration began to appear with the feeling that God was apparently permitting all efforts to alleviate the persecution to fail. John Gritton, however, in a lengthy article in *Evangelical Christendom* in 1894 urged Christians to unite everywhere in an appeal to the Russian authorities and heartfelt prayer to the Lord. Later in the year E.V. Bligh wrote in *Evangelical Christendom* that in the failure of the 1888 petition it was fruitless to contend with Pobedonostsev and persecution had even increased but believed that the time had now come to speak out more boldly, a sentiment he noted that was coming from America. On the other hand, he noted that some felt such an approach, even supported by many of the persecuted themselves, would cause more harm than good for the oppressed.[48]

Lord Radstock, the evangelist of twenty years earlier in St. Petersburg, wrote from Biarritz, France, in early 1895 that he feared that proposed plans for "united action and demonstration" would cause more harm than good. He felt that any effort from England would be "stigmatised as an effort to bring in English ideas, and would not only increase the already existing prejudice, but cool the ardour of Russians who desired religious liberty."[49]

46. For Pobedonostsev's response see Leroy-Beaulieu, 514–15, and *Unitarian Review*, Aug. 1891, 115. For the response of the Evangelical Alliance to Pobedonostsev, see *Die christliche Welt*, Feb. 24, 1889, 165–66. Evangelical Alliance, *Conference*, 1896, 311–12.

47. *EC*, Nov. 1, 1893, 357–58, and July 1, 1895, 219–20.

48. Ibid., Mar. 1, 1894, 77–80, and Aug. 1, 1894, 245–46.

49. Ibid., Apr. 1, 1895, 127–28.

Shortly after on March 1 the quarterly meeting of the Council of the Alliance discussed the plight of the stundists. Baedeker presented a report on his recent journey in Russia, stating he was able to engage freely in his prison ministry but met stundists on their way to exile and described the severe suffering of the oppressed. He was greatly disturbed that the new Tsar, Nicholas II, signed the 1894 decree on the stundists issued just before his father's death. Baedeker pled for "earnest and continuous prayer" for the persecuted and felt that if the Alliance did anything that "it ought to be done quickly."[50]

For the moment the Council attempted to make efforts of a confidential nature. In its annual report for 1896, the Alliance noted change moved slowly in Russia, the power of its officials, and the difficulty to bring facts to the Tsar himself. Within the last several months the Council had nevertheless attempted to bring an appeal to the Tsar with certain prominent and influential persons supporting the effort. At this time the American Baptist Home Mission Society also sent its own petition to the Tsar.[51]

In October 1898 William Sears Oncken, the son of Johann Oncken, while on business in Copenhagen, Denmark, took his chances by sending a petition to the Tsar while he was attending the funeral of the queen of Denmark, his maternal grandmother. Oncken felt such a direct attempt would bypass the usual officialdom. Oncken described the cruel suffering of the stundists, who he wrote were law-abiding subjects, asked for clemency and an imperial investigation of their case. He commended the Tsar's call for world peace and a possible decrease in armaments, which, by the way, led to The Hague Peace Conference in 1899. He claimed his own father had influenced Dean Stanley in England to influence Alexander II, the Tsar's grandfather, when on a trip to England in 1873, to stop persecution of the Baptists at that time. Although Oncken never received a reply, he claimed a bit later that whether it was his petition or other petitions the Tsar had ordered authorities not to disturb the Baptists in their services.[52]

Hermann Dalton, the highly respected pastor for thirty years at the German Reformed Church in St. Petersburg, published in 1889, shortly before his retirement, a lengthy *Offenes Sendschreiben* or *Open Letter* to Pobedonostsev, whom he knew personally, with a plea for freedom of conscience in Russia. Dalton was a member of the Evangelical Alliance, wrote sympathetically on stundists and Pashkovites, and cooperated with foreign preachers who visited St. Petersburg, although warned against Baptists for their aggressive sectarianism. The work was a sensation when it appeared and was translated into Russian, French, and English. Benjamin Benford, his biographer, noted Dalton was an outstanding author but a poor polemicist, concentrating primarily on the conflict between Lutherans and Orthodox in the Baltic and making

---

50. Ibid., Apr. 1, 1895, 127.

51. Ibid., Apr. 1, 1897, 122. American Baptist Home Mission Society, *Minutes*, 1896, 14. *WHZ*, July 25, 1896, 220.

52. *QR*, Jan. 1899, 5–8. Latimer, *Under Three Tsars*, 190–91.

no impact on the reactionary regime of Alexander III. Pobedonostsev made no personal response.[53]

The Emergence of Ivan S. Prokhanov—Underground Publications

Another means of survival was the continuing appearance of illegal publications. Val'kevich listed a number of these publications in hectograph form, which included three produced by Vasilii V. Ivanov, *Obryad sochetaniya braka* (The Rite of Marriage), *Pravila soversheniya Sv. Kreshcheniya* (Regulations for the Performance of Holy Baptism), and *Pravila zasedaniya obshchiny* (Regulations for a Meeting of the Church). He also listed *Verouchenie baptistov* (Confession of Faith of Baptists) and *Zhitel' Sarmatskoï zemli i khristianin. Razgovor*, which was a brochure of a religious conversation that ridiculed Orthodox teaching. Val'kevich noted the distribution of tracts and brochures by Hermann Fast, the circulation by the editor of *Bratskaya Pomoshch'* of sectarian publications, the use of prohibited hymnals, and the appearance of Bible texts, highlighting evangelical teaching, that adorned walls and served as bookmarks.[54]

Ivan S. Prokhanov (1869–1935), who played a leading role in underground publications, was an emerging leader with a far broader view of the world than the first generation of evangelical leaders. He was a man of great size, an intellectual, energetic, adaptive, and visionary. Although trained as an engineer, he became a preacher, writer, editor, publisher, composer of hymns, denominational leader, and Christian educator.[55]

Prokhanov was born in 1869 in Vladikavkaz in the Caucasus into a Molokan family in Tersk *oblast*, the oldest son of Stepan, a merchant, and Nina Prokhorov. The father became a member of the new Baptist congregation in Vladikavkaz, where he was a leading member, and served on the mission committee of the Russian Baptist Union. In 1894 the authorities exiled him to Gerusy for five years.[56]

Prokhanov was converted in November 1886 and baptized in January of the following year. From 1,200 candidates for 200 places in the St. Petersburg Technological Institute in 1888, Prokhanov entered the school among the top five students,

---

53. See Benford, 260–80, for his analysis of Dalton's *Open Letter* and his relations with the Evangelical Alliance and other religious leaders and movements. For an English translation of the first part, see *Lutheran Church Review*, Jan. 1890, 43–71. *EC* printed summaries of the *Open Letter* in the September and October issues, 1889, and its entirety in its May, June, August, and September 1890 issues.

54. Val'kevich, 168–69. See *Beseda*, June, 81–85; July, 103–4; and Oct. 1894, 151–57, for the publications from Ivanov.

55. A major source of the life of Prokhanov is his autobiography, *In the Cauldron, 1869–1933*. A scholarly article on his life is Steeves, "Ivan Stepanovich Prokhanov," *MERSH*, 30, 8–14. The most scholarly and comprehensive biography of Prokhanov is the work of Kahle, *Evangelische Christen in Russland und der Sovetunion*. Also see Val'kevich, 160–66. See Wardin, *Evangelical Sectarianism*, 325–27, for a list of biographical sources.

56. Val'kevich, 74, and App. 1, 16, ft. 2.

graduating in 1893. As part of his requirements at the Institute, he served two months in 1890 on a railroad. In the summer of 1892 he was an apprentice on a steamship, the "Russia," that took him to Constantinople, Alexandria, and Beirut, a journey he claimed greatly enlarged his mental horizons.[57]

While he was a student in St. Petersburg he joined the Pashkovites but rarely attended their meetings in the home of Nathalie Lieven. He generally met secretly and often preached to small groups in the city. At the same time he became acquainted with the ethical teachings of Leo N. Tolstoy, a system based on the Sermon on the Mount, incorporating love of neighbor and non-resistance to evil but rejecting the supernatural elements of the gospel. Shortly after his graduation from the institute in 1893, he and a companion visited Tolstoy at Yasnaya Polyana, his estate. Although Prokhanov greatly admired Tolstoy as a literary genius and was stimulated by his views on moral issues, he never accepted Tolstoyism as a religious philosophy.[58]

While still a student and only twenty-one years of age, Prokhanov with his brother Aleksandr began in 1890 *Beseda* (Conversation), an underground monthly periodical. It was a journal for all evangelicals—Pashkovites, stundists, and Baptists—and covered a wide range of interests. The name of the journal was chosen to appear as innocuous as possible. Writers of articles used pseudonyms or initials to cover their identity, but not always successfully. For its first six months in 1890, the journal appeared in manuscript in Vladikavkaz, but then in January 1891 moved to St. Petersburg, appearing in lithographic and hectograph form. Prokhanov moved into the home of Hermann Fast from where he issued the journal. It was temporarily suspended in 1893 but then from January 1894 through February 1896 it was printed in Stockholm, Sweden. It then was moved to London with issues appearing as late as 1897. In his correspondence with Pashkov, it appears the journal still existed in 1898 but no doubt ended upon his return to Russia that year. The date of its last issue is unknown. Subscribers received copies as registered letters.[59]

A publishing council supervised *Beseda*, which included, besides Prokhanov, Hermann Fast and Grigor P. Ivanenko. Elena V. Kirchner, a former teacher at the Transcaucasus Girls' Institute, moved to Stockholm and directed its publication while it was printed in this city. Jonas Stadling, Swedish Baptist pastor and author, assisted her. Kirchner then moved to Tulcha, Romania, where she helped to form a school. The journal now moved to London where Prokhanov again took charge.[60]

---

57. Prokhanov, *In the Cauldron*, 48, 69–70. Steeves, "Prokhanov," 9.

58. Lieven, 86, 91. Prokhanov, *In the Cauldron*, 62–64, 76–81. See *Beseda*, Apr. 1894, 55–62, for a report on Prokhanov's visit to Tolstoy.

59. For a history and description of *Beseda*, see Val'kevich, 161–67, App. 3, 1 ft. l. For reprinted excerpts of the journal see Val'kevich, App. 3, 1–69, 119–29. Also see Prokhanov, *In the Cauldron*, 67–69, 91, 98, and *Beseda*, Nov. 1894, 167–70, and Dec., 180–89. See Wardin, *Evangelical Sectarianism*, 309, for a listing of extant copies or reprints of the journal. Puzynin, *The Tradition of the Gospel Christians*, 130–31.

60. Val'kevich, 50, 120–21, ft. 3; App. 1, 30, ft. 2; and App. 3, 1, ft. 1. Prokhanov, *In the Cauldron*, 91.

The periodical was not a narrow sectarian journal but sported a broad agenda. Its editorial council stated that its first purpose was the encouragement of unity among believers; secondly, the encouragement of the spiritual life through an interchange of ideas; and thirdly, to solve world problems and undertake the organization of God's people. In January 1895 *Beseda* proposed a program under ten divisions: edification, narratives, social life, defense against irregular teaching, life of Christian communities and other people, material for the Sunday school, letters, news and notes, popular articles from science, and recommended books. It also began to include Tolstoyan and Molokan material.[61]

Besides the two Prokhanov brothers, Fast, and Kirchner, its contributors included V. G. Pavlov, V. V. Ivanov, F. P. Balikhin, L. E. Högberg, Petr Perk, and Prince D. A. Khilkov, a leading Tolstoyan advocate. Subscribers included I. I. Zhidkov, Deï Mazaev, V. A. Pashkov, M. M. Korff, N. I. Voronin, I. V. Kargel, the wife of Y. D. Delyakov, and V. T. Nicolson of the BFBS, and other subscribers from the German Baptists, Russian Baptists, Mennonites, Armenian Evangelicals, New Molokans, old Molokans, and Tolstoyans.[62]

After a short time as an assistant manager of a sugar factory, Prokhanov's idealism led him to help found with Hermann Fast an agricultural commune based on the principles of the apostolic church in Jerusalem with the financial assistance of Zinaida Nekrasova, widow of the poet N. A. Nekrasov, and a Pashkovite. The commune, called "Vertograd" (The Vineyard) settled on an estate near Simferopol in the Crimea, purchased from the Jerusalem Friends. Prokhanov participated wholeheartedly in the work of the commune, but with the exile of his father in 1894 Prokhanov left the commune for Vladikavkaz to assist his mother and the commune soon ceased. Under compulsion from the government, Fast will migrate in 1894 to Romania and then Canada, and Nekrasova returned to Saratov, where, by the way, she later will be excluded from her Baptist church.[63]

The year 1894 was very critical for Prokhanov and all Russian stundists and Baptists. *Beseda* began publishing abroad, the anti-stundist decree was passed, Prokhanov's father was exiled, and Prokhanov himself feared arrest by the secret police. In January 1895 he fled to Finland and at the end of April sailed to Sweden. He now spent a remarkable three and a half years in travel and further education in England, Germany, and France, acquiring also linguistic skills in the three countries before returning to Russia by the end of 1898. In London he visited Baedeker and Adams, secretary of the Evangelical Alliance, spoke at the jubilee conference of the Alliance in 1896, and will again assume responsibility for *Beseda*. He attended the Baptist College in Bristol for a year (1895–1896) and then in 1897 studied at the New Congregational College

---

61. *Beseda*, Jan. 1895, 6–7. Val'kevich, 163.

62. Val'kevich, 163, and App. 3, 67–69.

63. Prokhanov, *In the Cauldron*, 187–91. Later in Saratov the Baptists will exclude Nekrasova. See Nikolaï Nekrasov, "Sud'ba Ziny Nekrasovoï," *Nauka i religiya*, 1971, no. 12, 70–72.

in London and Hamstead New College. He spent a half-year each at Berlin University (1897–1898) and the University of Paris (1898) for theological studies. His exposure to liberaal theology in the universities of Berlin and Paris was limited for time spent but more important for his rejection of it as rationalistic speculations. In Paris his brother Alexandr had been studying at the Faculty of Medicine and attending lectures on theology at the University of Paris.[64]

On a call for help for Doukobors who were stranded in Cyprus on their way to Canada and with the encouragement of Sergius Tolstoy, the son of Leo Tolstoy, he went in 1898 to the island. On the way he visited the pyramids in Egypt. In Cyprus he became deathly sick with typhus. He was now determined to return to Russia and fortunately the Russian officials allowed him to settle in his home in Vladikavkaz. In January 1899 he visited his father in exile in Gerusy. He became assistant manager on the Riga-Orel Railroad, and then in 1899 assistant professor at the Riga Polytechnic Institute. After his dismissal in 1901 because of his stundist views, he became a mechanical engineer of the Westinghouse Electric Company in St. Petersburg.[65]

In the meantime he continued his religious activity. He persuaded the Printing Bureau of the Ministry of the Interior, a firm that took outside orders, to print in 1902 20,000 copies of his hymnal, *Gusli* (The Psaltery), and thus bypass the censor. The book was distributed before it could be stopped. The hymnal included 571 selections, including some of his own compositions and his translations of other hymns. Shortly afterward, Westinghouse sent him to the USA with their engineers for training in America, which probably saved him from prosecution.[66]

Sympathetic Publications and the Intelligentsia

Prokhanov pointed out at the 1896 conference of the Evangelical Alliance that some Russian periodicals were now beginning to discuss the issue of religious liberty. In his report in 1892–1893 Pobedonostsev noted that the foreign press included correspondence and news from Russia on the Stunda, portraying it as oppressed. In 1898 Pobedonostsev pointed out that numerous articles were appearing in support of the *Raskol* (Old Believers) and sectarians, while criticizing the Orthodox mission against them. He also noted that Baptists from Germany were circulating brochures and leaflets, supporting propagandists, educating Russian Stundo-Baptists at the Hamburg Seminary, and highlighting the persecution of their co-religionists.[67]

Even though liberal organizations generally had their own agendas opposing the Orthodox regime and used sectarians for their own ends, nevertheless their publications helped the stundist cause. Pobedonostsev was concerned about the publishing

---

64. Prokhanov, *In the Cauldron*, 92–101. Puzynin, 129–32, 168.
65. Prokhanov, 107–18.
66. Ibid., 121–23.
67. Procurator of the Holy Synod, *Report*, 1892–1893, 265, and 1898, 91–92.

efforts of Tolstoyans, such as Vladimir Chertkov, the son of the Radstock supporter, Elizabeta I. Chertkova, who established in England in 1898 a printing establishment. He edited from 1901 to 1905, *Svobodnoe slovo*, in Hampshire, England, a periodical sympathetic toward sectarians that also appealed for archival materials from them. Pavel Birykov edited from 1898–1899 in Essex, England, an earlier *Svobodnoe slovo*, and issued as a supplement *Listki Svobodnago slova* from 1898 to 1902. Birykov also edited from 1899 to 1901 at Onex near Geneva, Switzerland, *Svobodnaya mysl'*.[68]

Vladimir D. Bonch-Bruevich (1873–1955), a Marxist and supporter of Lenin, who cultivated sectarians for the Marxist cause, for a time contributed to Tolstoyan publications. Because of his revolutionary and anti-pacifist views, Tolstoyans broke with him. For a short time in 1904 he published in Geneva, *Razsvet* (The Dawn). He became an authority on sectarians, collected their materials, and became a leading writer on the sufferings of stundists and Baptists. His notable work on sectarians, *Materially k istorii i izucheniyu russago sektantsva i raskola*, included a most valuable collection of primary materials from sectarians themselves. It appeared in seven volumes from 1908 to 1916 except that volume six, *Presladovanie baptistsov evangelicheskoï sekty* (The Persecution of Baptists of the Evangelical Sect), was published earlier in 1902.[69]

Sergeï M. Kravchinskiï (1851–1895), who took S. Stepniak as a pseudonym, was a Russian revolutionary and founder in London in 1890 of the Society of Friends of Russian Freedom. It published in its periodical, *Free Russia*, in London and New York articles on stundist suppression. Kravchinskiï wrote in 1888, *The Russian Peasantry: Their Agrarian Condition, Social Life and Religion*, which included a sympathetic appraisal of stundism. He also published in Geneva in 1900 a novel, *Pavel Rudenko*, which described stundist persecution.[70]

Ukrainian writers who supported Ukrainian culture and freedom also supported the stundist cause, seeing in Ukrainian stundism a democratic movement of the Ukrainian people. Mykhaïlo P. Drahomanov (1841–1895), a socialist, political thinker, and folklorist, published a number of articles and booklets. Another sympathetic Ukrainian author was Trokhym Zin'kivs'kyï (1861–1891), whose work on stundism was published posthumously in 1893 and in 1896 outside of Russia. Ivan Ya. Franko with Mikhaïlo Pavlik edited, from 1890 to 1895, *Narod* (The People), the

---

68. Ibid., 1898, 92. See Wardin, *Evangelical Sectariansim*, 384–85 for Tolstoyan periodicals.

69. For an extended bibliography on Bonch-Bruevich's works, see Wardin, *Evangelical Sectarianism*, 380–82. For a helpful account on Bonch-Bruevich's relationship with sectarians, although very dependent on secondary sources, see Freeman, *Bonch-Bruevich and the Development of Bolshevik Policy toward the Sectarians*.

70. See *Beseda*, Dec. 1894, 191–92, for an account of the Society of Friends of Russian Freedom. For an account of the life of Kravchinskiï, see Good, "Sergei Mikhailovich Kravchinskii," *MERSH* 18, 54–56.

organ of the Russian-Ukrainian Party in Galicia in Austria-Hungary, which included articles on Stundo-Baptism.[71]

A Russian writer who was sympathetic toward religious dissenters was Alexandr S. Prugavin, a populist. The government confiscated his book, *Raskol vnizu i raskol vverskhu* (Dissent Below and Dissent from Above), which was published in St. Petersburg in 1882, but was unable to destroy all copies. V. I. Yasevich-Borodaevskaya was a woman, sympathetic toward populism, who wrote a monumental work, *Bor'ba za veru* (Struggle for the Faith), published in St. Petersburg in 1912. She dedicated her work to defenders of the persecuted for their faith. The book included two of her previous works published in 1897 and 1902.[72]

Western authors were also very important in informing the Western world of Russia's oppressive religious policy. Anatole Leroy-Beaulieu in volume three of his, *The Empire of the Tsars and the Russians*, contained a careful and critical analysis of Russia's policy toward religious dissidents. The work was translated from the French and was published in New York and London in the mid-1890s. William T. Stead, an English journalist, wrote a sympathetic account of the Pashkovites in his work, *Truth about Russia*, published in London in 1888. Evangelical writers in the West who highlighted the suppression were John Brown, *The Stundists: The Story of a Great Religious Revolt* (1893); H. v K., *A Short History of the Stundists* (1895); Georges Godet, *Persécutions actuelles en Russie* (1896); and Hesba Stretton, *Highway of Sorrow at the End of the Nineteenth Century* (1894), which was a novel.

In addition to books, the general press in the West also in the 1890s and after the turn of the century included from time to time articles on religious dissent and persecution in the Russian Empire. The Baptist press in Germany and the USA; *Echoes of Service*, Plymouth Brethren mission journal in England; *Evangelical Christendom*, journal of the Evangelical Alliance; and general missionary periodicals provided valuable material.[73]

The intelligentsia with liberal views of church and state also proved to be a source of support. Other than Pobedonostsev, others also noted the support of the intelligentsia for them. In his article on the rapid spread of stundism in South Russia, P. Kozitskiĭ wrote that the intelligentsia has looked upon the appearance of stundism as "the awakening of the people from everlasting hibernation in its attempt to be liberated from under the dead form of Byzantinism and on the display of the people's self-consciousness though also in religious form." He noted how the intelligentsia encouraged stundism and counseled priests not to persecute such honest working people. He averred that the indifference of the intelligentsia to Orthodoxy has also

---

71. See Wardin, Evangelical *Sectarianism*, 379–80, 382–83, for Ukrainian authors.

72. See Wardin, *Evangelical Sectarianism*, 353, on a description of the contents of Yasevich-Borodaevskaya's work, *Bor'ba za veru*.

73. See Wardin, *Evangelical Sectarianism*, 373–77, for a listing of evangelical publications in the West.

cleared the way for stundism among the common people. He claimed the press lauded verdicts of "not guilty" in stundist cases. A priest, I. Fudel', wrote a lengthy article, "*Intelligentnoe sodeïstvie shtunde*" (The Assistance of the Intelligentsia to the Stunda) in 1895 in the *Moskovskiya vedomosti*. Although the article included misinformation on the Stunda, it nevertheless recognized the strong sympathy of the intelligentsia for the movement.[74]

Migration

If the pressure of survival became too difficult to bear, migration was one avenue of escape for some. Not all migrations left the country but might be within the nation itself. Andreï Evstratenko, baptized in 1886, soon became pastor of the church upon the imprisonment of the pastor, L. D. Primachenko. On the advice of the Mazaev brothers, claiming less persecution in their area, Evstratenko with a congregation of twenty-five moved in 1887 to the Caucasus, founding a settlement named Garkusha. Some believers sold their possessions and moved to provinces adjacent to Siberia.[75]

Because of the suppression, some attempted to flee abroad. Six of the exiles in Gerusy decided to flee to Romania and three of them succeeded, but the frontier guard at the Prut River caught three of them. After three months of imprisonemnt, two were freed but under surveillance with one of them forbidden to live in four provinces and the other to live one year in exile but will finally move to Romania. The third one, Konygin, was sent again to the Transcaucasus, passed through a series of prisons, resided in a village for three months, and then exiled again to Gerusy for three years and then finally freed.[76]

As previously noted, Ivan S. Prokhanov fled in 1894 from St. Petersburg through Finland to Sweden and then to London and on to study on the continent before returning to Russia. The Council of the Evangelical Alliance with other friends assisted in his expenses. Another evangelical believer in 1884, after a series of warnings, escaped Russia, settled in America where he was naturalized, but about ten years later returned to southern Russia, attempting to preach from place to place and visit persecuted Christians. In May 1894 the authorities arrested him, sent him to St. Petersburg and as a former Russian seaman placed him in a naval prison. With the monetary assistance of the Alliance, he escaped to London and then returned to America![77]

In his report in 1892–1893, Pobededonstsev wrote that cases of stundism migrating abroad were increasing, claiming that fellow believers abroad provided assistance. He was disturbed that emigrants, writing to their former homeland and extolling their

---

74. *TsV*, 1891, no. 6, 87–88. *Moskovskiya vedomosti*, Apr. 1, 1895, 3–4. Also see *Beseda*, Apr. 1895, 64, and *Missionary Herald*, Oct. 1895, 414.

75. *Aquila*, Oct.–Dec., 2003, 21. Brown, 46.

76. Bonch-Bruevich, *Presledovanie Baptistov*, 31–32.

77. *EC*, Sep. 1, 1894, 279.

new lives, caused further unrest among the sectarians. In 1895 the Minister of the Interior, concerned about the growing number of sectarians in the Caucasus, which was causing problems of space and surveillance, recommended giving passports to sectarians who wished to emigrate with the promise never to return. In his study of the issue, Bonch-Bruevich claimed that although the government received many applications for passports none were granted. But this was not entirely true as seen in the exile of Ryaboshapka.[78]

One of the important havens abroad was the Baptist community at Tulcha in Romania on the border of the Bessarabian Province of Russia. Because of the exile there by the authorities in the 1860s of German believers in Ukraine who adopted believer's baptism by immersion, this settlement, as earlier noted, became inadvertently a serious thorn in the side of the authorities in limiting Stundo-Baptist influence penetrating back into Russia. Such leading evangelicals as Johann Wieler, V.G. Pavlov, and E. V. Kirchner all found refuge here with the latter two forming here a school.

The Russian community in Tulcha encouraged exiles to come, providing monetary assistance and even itineraries. Val'keich noted that Ivan Kolesnikov from Taurida Province went to Tulcha in 1890 where he lured Russians to settle. He also noted that a Russian, E. Herasimenko, born in Bessasrabia and a student in Hamburg who then served as a missionary of the Russian-Romanian Association, also served the Tulcha church before the arrival of Pavlov.[79]

Migration to another land could be difficult. John Schiek, harbor missionary for the American Baptist Home Mission Society in New York, met a destitute group of twenty Russian stundists, three families and a single man, including thirteen children, who came to America fleeing persecution. They all wanted to return to Russia, but Schiek could only send them to Louisville, Kentucky, the location of the German Baptist orphanage, where they might receive help.[80]

Baedeker wrote in 1893 that one family, after arriving in Romania, became so homesick that it wanted to return to Russia even if it meant facing imprisonment or punishment. A couple of years later Baedeker wrote that some of the exiles who escaped to Romania, although at liberty, faced great difficulties in adjustment. Teodor P. Kostromin, who had been exiled to Transcaucasus, escaped with his wife and three children to Tulcha where he was unhappy and went to Burgas, Bulgaria. As a result of a second petition, the regime allowed him to return to Russia, regaining his full rights. In 1900 the *Quarterly Reporter of the German Baptist Mission* reported that many of the exiles had arrived destitute in Romania with the police trying to force them to

---

78. Procurator of the Holy Synod, *Report*, 1892–1893, 264. *EC*, July 1, 1895, 221. Bonch-Bruevich, *Presledovanie Baptistov*, 30.

79. Val'kevich, 96, 98.

80. *Der Sendbote*, June 17, 1891, 3.

move into the interior of the country. At the time famine in the country added to the misery.[81]

Another place of refuge in Romania was Constanta, south of Tulcha. Such Armenian evangelicals as Patwakan Tarayanz and Sumbat Bagdasarjanz and Seventh-day Adventists as Theofil Babienko and Georg Wagner, both of whom were former Baptists, resided here.[82]

Although a number of exiles remained in Europe, some reached America. Schiek met in New York a refugee who had left Russia the last moment before being transported in Russia. Schiek sent him to Madison, South Dakota. Both German Baptists and Russian Baptists settled in the state.[83]

North Dakota also became a sanctuary for exiles from Russia. In a letter in 1916, Andrew Dubovy (Dubovoï) wrote that in 1899 around 1,500 sectarians left Kiev Province and settled here. In 1901 Ukrainian Baptists organized their first church and erected their first house of worship in what was later called Kiev. In 1902 a small group of Russian-Ukrainian Baptists settled in Winnipeg, Canada. In 1903 newly arrived emigrants from Russia, including Ivan Kolesnikov, who had earlier migrated to Romania and Bulgaria, founded a mission in New York City.[84]

The Legal System

With their suppression, one might easily assume that Stundo-Baptists had no rights under the legal system of the government. In spite of administrative exile, fines, imprisonment, flogging, and arbitrary extension of sentences and the law outlawing their existence, it would appear that Russian stundists and Baptists would have no legal recourse. A possible defense for evangelical sectarians, however, was the legal system itself. One of the Great Reforms of Alexander II was the reform of the judiciary in 1864 that established the principle of equality before the law, an impartial tribunal, judicial independence, and trial by jury. Even though the principles were not consistently observed, they were nevertheless a barrier to the arbitrary power of the state.[85]

Because of sympathy for their cause, courts not infrequently found stundists not guilty, a verdict, as earlier noted, supported by the liberal feelings of the intelligentsia. At the Third Missionary Congress in Kazan in 1897, the unreliability of legal measures

---

81. *Echoes of Service*, Oct. (I), 1893, 219, and Jan. (II), 1896, 18. Prestridge, 214. Byford, *Peasants and Prophets*, 117–18. *The Mission World* 7 (1900), 31–32.

82. Val'kevich, 54–55, ft. 13.

83. *Der Sendbote*, March 16, 1892, 3. Shanafelt, *The Baptist History of South Dakota*, 186–98.

84. Harsch, "The Multicultural Heritage of North Dakota Baptists," 85–88, 115–18. Dubovoï, "Vzglyad na russkikh sektantov," *Svobodnoe Slovo*, July 1916, 597–99. Dubovy, *Pilgrims of the Prairie*. 17–27. Hayne, "The Twenty-fifth Anniversary of Russian Baptists in North America," *Missions*, Nov. 1926, 587–89. Kmeta, *With Christ in America*, 42–43, 45–49. Also see Wardin, *Evangelical Sectarianism*, 196.

85. See Florinsky, 902–6.

was felt since laws were often interpreted liberally in favor of the sectarians. In a lecture at the congress, Professor Ivanovskiĭ expressed the need to give great attention to the judicial process. Too many judicial cases against sectarians were stopped because no crime was found or resulted in verdicts of not guilty or even reversed by the Governing Senate, the final court of appeal.[86]

In 1903 V. M. Skvortsov noted that sectarians collected written records, went to court with experts, sent their grievances to the Governing Senate, and spent years in lawsuits. He was upset that the Governing Senate almost always reversed the verdict of guilty in sectarian cases by requiring a review by another judicial sector, which he considered a waste of time and "profanation" of the jury system.[87]

Cases, however, brought mixed results. The agent of the Evangelical Alliance wrote a report, published in January 1902, on 144 persons brought before the courts. At two of the trials where there was no defense, fifteen persons were fined or went to prison. At the remaining nine trials, a poor evangelical believer who had managed to gain some practical legal knowledge represented the defense. In four of the cases the defendants were freed but in five cases 106 were fined or imprisoned but through outside intervention their cases were appealed.[88]

One of the major issues that Stundo-Baptists faced was their attempt to prove to the courts that they were Baptists, as recognized by the law of 1879, and not stundists, which the law of 1894 condemned as an illegal sect that supported socialism, denied all church rites, and opposed military service. Stundo-Baptists contended they were faithful to the Tsar, served in the military, and paid taxes. Stundists who became Stundo-Baptists already attempted to make this case in the early 1880s. *Beseda* reported in 1894 that in the last year 240 stundist families in Kiev, Kherson, and Chernigov Provinces in northern Ukraine petitioned to be recognized as Baptists, but the authorities rejected the petition as unlawful. In an article in 1895, *Beseda* pointed out that the application of the law in respect to recognition of evangelical sectarians was not consistent. It claimed authorities in Saratov, Samara, the Volga, and Baku Province recognized sectarians as legal sects under the law of 1883, while in a village in Stavropol Region and villages in Taurida Province sectarians were tolerated under the 1879 law for Baptists. On the other hand, in Tersk and Vladikavkaz Regions in the Caucasus and all of Ukraine the authorities regarded all sectarians as stundists.[89]

In a review of sectarians, *Missionerskoe obozrenie* in 1899 complained that Stundo-Baptists were utilizing the legal system for their benefit, such as declaring in

---

86. Maevskiĭ, *Vnutrennyaya missiya i ee osnovopolozhnik*, 187. Skvortsov, *Third All-Russian Missionary Congress*, 1897, 245.

87. *MO*, Jan. 1903, 124–25.

88. Ibid., Mar. 1902, 607.

89. On the issue of Stundo-Baptist identity, see Mel'gunov, *Tserkov i gosudarstvo v Rossii*, 1:57–66, who quotes Bobrishchev-Pushkin in his essay, "Shtundisty illi baptisty?" The essay appeared earlier in *Russkaya mysl'*, 1903, no. 11, 159–66. Procurator of the Holy Synod, *Report*, 1887, 76–77. *Beseda*, June 1894, 96, and Feb. 1895, 30.

their passports that they were "of the Baptist faith." It also recorded that a certain Romanteev had copies of all the judicial verdicts of the Governing Senate favorable to stundists, excerpts of which were attached to walls of homes where they gathered. On an appeal of a verdict in a case of two Baptists in Rostov-on-Don, the Governing Senate ruled that the 1894 law applied exclusively to stundists and not to other confessions, including Baptists, and Baptists were not identical with stundism. Stundo-Baptists who claimed they were Baptists and not stundists hailed the decision but alarmed the Orthodox authorities.[90]

The missionary congress of the Kherson Diocese in 1898 made a concerted effort to differentiate between stundism and the Baptist movement. It declared the Baptists were a non-Russian sect but stundism was Russian. Baptists had books on their creeds but stundism had none. Stundism showed "socialist, atheistic, and nihilistic aspirations" and possessed no official documents from the government that demonstrate its identity with German Baptists. In 1900 the regime issued two circulars that made it clear that the 1879 law for Baptists did not apply to stundists and there was no such thing as Russian Baptists. According to Bonch-Bruevich, cases against sectarians greatly increased.[91]

A land captain charged eighty-five peasants in Yekaterinoslav district for attending a stundist prayer meeting, requiring them to pay eighteen rubles each or three days arrest. At the district assembly the defendants denied they were stundists but Baptists. The assembly accepted the witness of the diocesan missionary and local priest and affirmed the land captain's decision. But the provincial authority found the witness of the experts worthless and acquitted the defendants. The Ministry of Internal Affairs now intervened and based on circulars issued in May 1900 stating the law did not recognize Baptists as a Russian sect reversed the decision.[92]

In the mid-1880s the Russian Baptist Union resolved that it would provide counsel for the defense of accused believers. The foremost judicial advocate of Stundo-Baptist rights was Ivan P. Kushnerov, a Baptist. He was born in 1861, the son of an Orthodox priest. He became a road surveyor but upon meeting a traveling Baptist minister became a believer and was baptized the following year in 1893 and joined the Kiev church. In 1894 he began his career of defending Stundo-Baptists by writing petitions, visiting prisoners, and representing them in court. The Russian Baptist Union appointed him as its official advocate, paying his traveling expenses but no salary. At times the authorities confiscated his furniture but he managed to continue

---

90. *MO*, May 1899, 617–18. See Skvortsov's review of the decision of the Governing Senate in *MO*, Nov. 1899, 1371–85.

91. *TsV*, 1899, no. 4, 128–30. Bonch-Bruevich, "Sredi sektantov," *Zhizn'*, 1902, no. 2, 284–88. Bonch-Bruevich, "Presledovanie baptistov v Rossii," *Vestnik evropy*, June 1910, 167–68. Also see "Stundisten-Prozesse," *Das Reich Christi* 7 (1904), 189–90.

92. *Evangelical Alliance Quarterly*, Jan. 1, 1902, 251.

his efforts with a career that continued after the decree of toleration of 1905. In 1905 he published a work on the evangelical movement and its needs.[93]

Friends and Opponents

With a strong organization and confessional base and aggressive leadership, the Stundo-Baptist movement was very competitive with other sectarians. Unlike groups mired in traditionalism, Stundo-Baptism was a new force, modern in approach in organization and tactics, in tune with the growing individualism of the modern age, and trumpeting a clear message of salvation. Although its advocacy of believer's baptism by immersion met strong resistance from Lutherans and Orthodox, the rite, supported by New Testament examples, appealed to those looking for biblical precedent. By the turn of the century believer's baptism by immersion had become the norm for most stundists and the greater number of Pashkovites, both groups that had included those who opposed the rite as unnecessary along with opposition to a centralized ecclesiology.

Pashkovites

At first the Pashkovites were a body of evangelical believers who were nominally members of the Orthodox Church, accepting infant baptism, with a program that did not seek schism or formation of a new denomination. Radstock and Pashkov believed in a universal church and the Lord's Supper was open to all true believers in Christ. For them baptism was to be no barrier for evangelical fellowship. Although George Müller immersed Pashkov, Nathalie Lieven, and the governess of her children in St. Petersburg in 1883 and Korff was baptized in Switzerland in 1887, the German Baptist minister in St. Petersburg, A. R. Schiewe, would have no association with the Pashkovites for their open communion views.[94]

In her history, Princess Sophie Lieven noted a growing cleavage in Pashkovite ranks between the more cultured and aristocratic ladies and the more uneducated men from lower ranks who insisted on rejection of all alcohol and tobacco and ostentatious dress. Differences also arose between those who saw no need for further baptism after their infant baptism and those insisting on believer's baptism. In his report in 1898, Pobedonostsev wrote that the majority of the Pashkovites were now accepting "rebaptism of adults and non-baptism of children," bringing them into close

---

93. Prestridge, 18–20. *Istoriya*, 533. See Wardin, *Evangelical Sectarianism*, 76, no. 559, on Kushnerov's 1905 publication.

94. For early believer's baptism among Pashkovites, see *Der Sendbote*, May 14, 1884, 171; *Missions*, Oct. 1911, 666; Gutsche, *Westliche Quellen des Russischen Stundismus*, 60; and Procurator of the Holy Synod, *Report*, 1888–1889, 121.

relations with the stundists in South Russia.[95] As seen in the letters in 1890 of P. S. Bezzubov, a member of the Pashkovite congregation in St. Petersburg, a formal division in Pashkovite ranks occurred in the late 1880s over church polity. In 1890 Bezzubov wrote to brethren in Elizavetpol Province to support those opposed to ecclesiastical organization. He asked, where is it written that apart from the body of Christ one should belong to another church? He called it slavery and admonished them to "remain firm in the freedom which Christ has given you." In a December 1890 letter he described division in the St. Petersburg congregation between the majority, who followed Kargel, which introduced church regulations, which Deï Mazaev and the Russian Baptists followed, including election of presbyters and deacons, and those who opposed. Bezzubov declared they have "dismissed Christ, the chief pastor."[96] On the other hand, Kargel accepted open communion for both baptized as infants and those baptized as believers.

Closer union between Pashkovites and Baptists occurred in 1898 when Pashkovites sent representatives to the Russian Baptist congress in Tsaritsyn. In 1902 at the Rostov-on-Don congress Pashkovites were again present. In the following year in 1903 at Tsaritsyn, the congress accepted the Pashkovites from St. Petersburg and Kiev into membership and changed the name of the Union to "The Union of Evangelical Christians Baptists." In 1904 at the congress in Rostov-Don, Pashkovites from St. Petersburg, Kiev, Konotop, and Sevastopol, calling themselves "Evangelical Christians," were accepted into the Baptist Union. At this time the congregation in St. Petersburg contributed 500 rubles to the Baptist mission. In 1906 Pavlov wrote that Pashkovites were still "fluctuating" and not conforming to a written confession but yet agree with Baptists on the fundamentals of the faith, including rejection of infant baptism, and are beginning to organize into churches.[97]

Brethren [Plymouth Brethren]

The Brethren, popularly known as Plymouth Brethren, arose in England in the early nineteenth century advocating a non-hierarchical and non-liturgical Christianity that stressed Bible teaching and missions. They opposed an ordained clergy and favored a plurality of lay leaders. Their weekly Lord's Supper was a "breaking of bread" with prayer and thanksgiving and shared by all believers. As with Baptists, they practiced believer's baptism.

Although an Anglican, Lord Radstock associated with the Brethren and brought into his ministry a Brethren pattern of teaching and worship. Frederick W. Baedeker

---

95. Lieven, 88–91. Procurator of the Holy Synod, *Report*, 1898, 92. Also see "*Pashkovshchina i shtundizm*," *MO*, Sep.–Oct. (1), 1897, 797–806.

96. See Val'kevich, App. 5, 34, 38, for Bezzubov's letters and excerpts from them in English in Klibanov, *Religious Sectarianism*, 271–73.

97. *Istoriya*, 131. *Baptist*, 1925, nos. 6–7, 39. Letter of Pavlov, August 7, 1906.

was the chief representative of the Brethren in Russia with his itinerant preaching and Bible distribution, ministering without distinction to all evangelical believers. Later in the century, Edmund H. Broadbent (1861–1945), a Brethren from England who traveled extensively in Europe and Asia, including Russia, engaged in a fifty-year ministry, but unlike Baedeker sought to establish groups on Brethren principles. In the 1890s the police often stopped his work and increasingly restricted his activity.[98]

Although Baptists had much in common with the Brethren, they looked unfavorably upon them, especially like Broadbent who established Brethren assemblies, along with their polity and open communion. In his turn, Broadbent in his work, *The Pilgrim Church*, showed his anti-Baptist bias. Even though some Brethren assemblies with the "breaking of bread" appeared in Russia, the Brethren movement proved to be negligible. They lacked mission leaders and a cohesive organization that could even begin to match the German Baptist and the Russian Stundo-Baptist movements. They were also too late on the scene in establishing an alternative denominational structure.[99]

Molokanism

One of the reasons for the growing strength of Stundo-Baptism, even in a time of suppression, was the vulnerability of Molokanism. Molokanism not only provided Stundo-Baptists with members but also some of its strongest leaders—N. I. Voronin, V. A. Pashkov, V. V. Ivanov, T. P. Balikhin, Deï and Gavriil Mazaev, Stepan Prokhanov, and his son I. S. Prokhanov. Since the Molokans themselves were a sect, Baptist missionaries were less subject to attack from the authorities for mission work among them. So strong was the Stundo-Baptist appeal that Pobedonostsev reported that missionaries expressed the conviction that Molokanism would inevitably cross over to stundism. In 1900 Pobedonostsev wrote that over 3,000 Molakans had become stundists in Taurida Province during the last fifteen to twenty years. Val'kevich noted before the century that in no Molokan settlement in the Caucasus "the Baptist sect has not twisted itself a solid nest."[100]

Although the rejection of all ecclesiastical rites by the Molokans was a barrier for many of them to become Baptists, but for others it had a special appeal. The dynamic character of Baptist worship was very attractive in contrast to traditional Molokan worship with its monotonous and ungrammatical reading and interpretation of Scripture and nasal singing. Pobedonostsev noted that Stundo-Baptist success, aside from similarity to Molokon beliefs, came from their prayer meetings with exalted preaching and prayer, engagement of beautiful choirs and mixed voices, and the fanaticism of

---

98. Stunt, et. al., *Turning the World Upside Down*, 63–65. Lang, *Edmund Hamer Broadbent*, 71. *Echoes of Service*, Jan. (I), 1900, 3–5.

99. Broadbent, *The Pilgrim Church*, 341–42.

100. Procurator of the Holy Synod, *Report*, 1898, 98, and 1900, 237. Val'kevich, 125.

their leaders. The centrality of Christ in salvation in Baptist preaching contrasted with the weak Christology of Molokanism. V. V. Ivanov noted in 1911 that old Molokan men and women indignantly whispered: "Now all has become Baptist: all is Christ, Christ!"[101] The Molokans in Taurida Province became fertile ground for the new evangelical currents. In the 1860s Yakob Delyakov, the Nestorian evangelical but not yet a Baptist, evangelized among them. His efforts helped to give rise to what was called the Second Don Sect or Trend or Christians of the Evangelical Faith, a movement led by Zinoviĭ D. Zakharov. They differed from Stundo-Baptists by practicing infant baptism, immersing the child one time, unlike the Orthodox who immersed the infant three times. They debated Baptists, resisting absorption by them. A Diocesan Missionary Committee in Taurida reported in 1896 that Christians of the Evangelical Faith numbered 953 while Baptists had 827.[102]

Malevantsy

In the late 1880s a mystical religious sect appeared that brought condemnation from both Orthodox and evangelicals. The movement was comparatively short-lived but attracted a diverse range of writers from Orthodox, evangelicals, Tolstoyans, Marxists, and psychiatrists. The Malevantsy, named after its founder, Kondratiĭ A. Malevannyĭ (1844–1913), a wheelwright in Kiev Province and father of seven children, converted to stundism in 1884. An old stundist raised the question: why the presence of universal death and illness if Christ had come to establish his Kingdom? Malevannyĭ, after conversing with mystics and reading the Book of Revelation and the prophetic scriptures, claimed he received a vision proclaiming him "the Firstborn, the Son of God," and announced he had come to establish the Kingdom of God. His appearance in white clothes preaching repentance and good works and proclaiming the Kingdom was at hand attracted crowds of people, both stundists and Orthodox. In 1889 the police received complaints that Malevannyĭ was calling himself Jesus Christ. When the investigator A. Yushchenko questioned him about it, he denied the charge but said that others believed it and they could not be wrong.[103]

---

101. Skvortsov, *Missionerskiĭ posokh*, part 1, 287. Procurator of the Holy Synod, *Report*, 1900, 237. Ivanov, "Polozhenie baptistov," *Baptist*, Feb. 23, 1911, 69.

102. "Donaskie tolki v Molokanstve i v shtundizme," *MO* (Nov. (1), 1897, 997–1007, and *Third All-Russian Missionary Congress*, 1897, 138–55. Val'kevich, App. 3, 36, ft. 1.

103. The Malevantsy movement began to appear in the Orthodox press in 1890. Skvortsov wrote extensively on the movement in his series "Novoshtundizm" in the *Moskovskiya vedomosti* in 1892, which Dillon, an evangelical, summarized but critically reviewed in "The Quasi-Spiritualist Revival in Russia," *Review of Reviews*, Apr. 1893, 317–21. Latimer, a Baptist, wrote a chapter, "Lo, Here Is Christ! Or, There!," in *With Christ in Russia*, 154–66. The report of Yushchenko is "Kondratiĭ Malevannyĭ," in *Istoricheskiĭ vestnik*. 1913. T. 132, no. 4, 237–42. For a psychological analysis at the time, see Sikorskiĭ "Psikhopaticheskaya epidemiya 1892 goda v Kievskoĭ Gubernii," St. Vladimir Imperial University, *Universitetskiy izvestiya* 33 (1893), 1–46. For a modern psychiatric review see, Windholz, "Psychiatric Commitments of Religious Dissenters in Tsarist and Soviet Russia," *Psychiatry* 48 (1985), 329–40,

The meetings of the Malevantsy were ecstatic with shouting, screaming, jumping, dancing, and speaking in tongues. They spiritualized the ordinances and did not observe them. The Malevantsy preached a community of goods and equality, even in families. They interpreted the Bible allegorically, and there was no historical Christ. The Malevantsy denied a physical resurrection with the spirits of the dead entering into another body; those living at the end of the world would live forever. They looked forward to the soon establishment of the Kingdom with total equality and no more human toil.[104]

The movement, arising in Kiev Province, soon reached 300. After repeated arrests in 1891, the authorities sent Maevannyï to a psychiatric ward in St. Cyril Monastery Hospital in Kiev. Upon his smuggling letters to his followers, the authorities sent him in 1893 to Kazan Psychiatric Hospital, which removed him 900 miles from his adherents. Kazan became a place of pilgrimage. Because of the efforts of Leo Tolstoy and one of his followers, they gained Malevannyï's release in August 1905.

While he was incarcerated, Malevannyï continued to communicate with his followers with his tracts. The movement continued to grow and split stundist congregations in Kiev Province and also gained adherents from both Orthodox and Roman Catholics. The movement did not confine itself to Kiev Province but appeared in Kursk Province and in Odessa. In 1900 Pobedonostsev reported almost 4,400 sectarians in Kiev Diocese; about three-fourths were stundists but one-fourth or around 1,000 were Malevantsy.[105]

In his evaluation of the Malevantsy, A. I. Klibanov, the Marxist writer, claimed in Marxist fashion the movement showed the beginning of an awakening for equality and justice. R. S. Latimer, however, claimed the Malevantsy arose from those who had suffered severely from the regime and in the absence of spiritual leaders fell prey to esoteric ideas. The regime judged Maelvannyï as suffering from paranoia, but George Windholz in his study noted that others, including Yasevich-Borodaevskaya and Tolstoy, did not consider him mentally ill.[106]

Although the movement initially showed dynamic growth, according to the Department of Police in 1916, three year's after Malevannyï's death, it numbered 2,000, not a great number. It will fade away as a potent religious body.[107]

---

which includes a significant list of references. See Wardin, *Evangelical Sectarianism*, 334–37, for an extensive bibliography.

104. For beliefs and practices, see Skvortsov, Dillon, and Latimer.
105. Procurator of the Holy Synod, *Report*, 1899. 126–29, and 1900, 233–34.
106. Klibanov, *Religious Sectarianism*, 168–271. Latimer, 156. Windholz, 331–32.
107. Klibanov, 269, ft. 11.

PART FIVE—Peril, 1884–1905

Seventh-day Adventists

Seventh-Day Adventism was a new religious movement from the West that entered Russia in the 1880s. Initially it was not a strong a threat to Stundo-Baptism as the Malevantsy, but it will outlast the latter. It exhibited a number of characteristics similar to the Stundo-Baptist movement in its adherence to Scriptural authority, believer's baptism by immersion, strict discipline, and aggressive evangelism. They differed significantly, however, in their observance of the seventh day (the Jewish Sabbath) as the day of worship and rest, which was more than a choice but a sign they were the true church. It also stressed the imminence of Christ's Second Coming. As a foreign sectarian body the Russian regime strongly opposed its entrance, and it proved to be a threat to both German Baptists and Russian Stundo-Baptists.

German-Russians who had settled in America and had become Adventists began to send Adventist literature to Germans in the empire. In November 1883, Phillip Reiswig, a German-Russian from America, returned to Russia and traveled with Adventist literature. He returned to America two years later and then went back to Russia in 1887, continuing to work for several more years. In 1886 the Adventist General Conference sent at age thirty Louis Richard Conradi (1856–1939), a German who had lived in the USA, to serve in Europe. He traveled to Russia in July, teamed up with Gerhard Perk, a Mennonite who had been a colporteur of the BFBS but now an Adventist convert, who served as his interpreter and guide. In the Crimea they held meetings with German Baptists, but also found here and there Sabbath keepers. They traveled to Berdebulat, near the Black Sea, forming here the first Adventist church on Russian soil with nineteen members, most of them former German Baptists and Mennonite Brethren but also included two women who were immersed on profession of faith. Authorities imprisoned Conradi and Perk for forty days but with the efforts of the American ambassador in St. Petersburg they gained their release.[108]

Heinrich Loebsack, an Adventist convert from the German colonies in the Volga, began in 1890 as a colporteur who undertook an extensive ministry in the Volga, Crimea, Volhynia, Caucasus, and Latvia. Up until 1895 Adventist work was primarily in rural areas, but it now began to enter such towns as Riga, Vilnius, and Reval (Tallinn). Gerhard Perk in 1897 led Bible studies in St. Petersburg where in 1898 a church was formed. In this period it was difficult to import Adventist literature and colporteurs were subject to imprisonment.

Adventism also began to penetrate into the Russian population, initially through Theofil Babienko, an inhabitant of Tarashcha in Kiev Province. He became a Stundo-Baptist leader and at the congress in Vladikavkaz in 1885 was named missionary for four months in Kiev Province. In the same year, however, by administrative order the

---

108. The article, "Union of Soviet Socialist Republics," in the *Seventh-day Adventist Encyclopedia*, 1344–62, includes an excellent survey of Adventist beginnings in the Russian Empire. Also in the encyclopedia see articles on Conradi, 302–303, Loebsack, 709–10, and Perk, 975–76. For a detailed account by an Orthodox researcher see "*Adventistskaya propaganda*," in Val'kevich, 139–56.

authorities moved him to Stavropol in the Caucasus where he gained Baptist converts and formed a church. In his study of the Bible he began to keep the Sabbath even before he knew about Adventists. At the end of the 1880s Babienko and his church became Adventists. The first Adventist tract in Russian was published in 1888. At the first general meeting of the Adventists in Russia, held in 1890 in Eigenheim in the Caucasus, Babienko was ordained the first Russian elder. By administrative order in 1891, Babienko and seven other members of his congregation were exiled to Gerusy. While here Babienko continued his active mission work, gaining numbers for the Adventist cause. In 1896 he settled in Constanta in Romania, which became a haven for Adventists from Russia.[109]

As for Baptists, Hamburg became an important center for the European work of Adventists. In 1889 Conradi and associates moved to Hamburg, which became the headquarters of the European mission. Conradi was the president of the German mission, presiding over its annual conferences in Hamburg and in Russia as well as over the tract society. He was also editor of the chief periodical of the German mission. In 1889 Adventist printing in Europe was moved from Basel to Hamburg. From 1889 to 1899 Adventists supported a mission school in Hamburg but was superseded by a mission school in Friedensau in Germany. Another agency was the Sabbath School Society.[110]

Growth was steady but not spectacular. In 1890 Adventists numbered 356 and in 1900 a bit over 1,000 with twenty-eight churches in addition to possibly 300 who had migrated to America, Romania, or other areas. After many years of service in the Adventist cause, including travels world-wide, Conradi will leave Adventism in 1932 at the age of seventy-six and became a pastor of the Seventh-Day Baptists in the USA.[111]

Appraisal

In spite of suppression for twenty-one years from 1884 to 1905, the evangelical movement of stundists, Stundo-Baptists, and Pashkovites maintained its vitality and even grew. In the mid-1880s Stundo-Baptists in Ukraine numbered about 5,000 and Baptists in the Caucasus a bit over 500. In 1906 Pavlov claimed that the Russian Baptist Union had possibly 20,000 members, besides the Pashkovites whom he estimated to be between three and five thousand.[112]

A review of the reports of Pobedonostsev, procurator of the Holy Synod, reveal his continuing lament over the penetration and growth of the stundist movement. In his report of 1884, he wrote that the stundists were most spread in Kherson Diocese and were penetrating all its districts. In 1887 he noted their activity among soldiers in

109. Val'kevich, 95, 148, and 148, ft. 1. *Seventh-day Adventist Encyclopedia*, 1347, 1349, 1350–51.
110. Val'kevich, 143, 146–47.
111. *Seventh-day Adventist Encyclopedia*, 303, 1349, 1353.
112. Letter of Pavlov, August 7, 1906.

PART FIVE—Peril, 1884–1905

the northern Caucasus and their propagation in the Transcaucasus among Orthodox, Molokans, and Armenians. In his report for 1890–1891 he listed stundism as numbering over 16,000 and claimed that if it weakened in one area it strengthened in another and was quickly advancing from the south to western regions and to St. Petersburg. For its part, Pashkovism had spread from St. Petersburg to central and southern provinces and even into Siberia. As early as 1881–1882 Pashkovite colporteurs began to preach in Moscow with Baedeker, Kargel, and Pashkov coming as visiting preachers. A more formal circle emerged in 1897 that led to the leadership of Teodor Savel'ev, who was immersed in 1903.[113]

Pobedonostsev noted that stundists were not just Ukrainian peasants or simple workers but also semi-cultured who worked on the railway and in banks, offices, and commercial establishments. Kharkov, where evangelical believers in the 1880s began to hold meetings in the apartment of Vasiliĭ N. Ivanov, a BFBS colporteur, had become in 1899, according to Pobedonstsev, the chief center of stundism where its members were employed in factories, mechanical workshops, and on the railroads. In his 1900 report, he noted that in Kiev stundists were shop assistants, typesetters, and clerks. Stundists had also been settling in the Don area, buying and leasing land and spreading here their religious views. Moreover in reports in 1898 and 1899, Pobedonstsev recorded that stundists were in Omsk Diocese in central Siberia and also at Vladivostok on the Pacific shore.[114]

In 1900 Pobedonostsev wrote that the Russian Orthodox Church had never faced "such a dangerous enemy" in the new rationalistic sectarianism, particularly in Tolstoyism and stundism. In his 1903–1904 report he recorded that stundists were now in thirty-six of the sixty-three dioceses of the country, more than any other sectarian group.[115]

The failure of the Orthodox Church to stop the stundist movement was not for want of trying. Pobedonostsev reported in 1886 that the Holy Synod allocated to the anti-stundist mission 1,500 rubles a year with missionaries visiting infected parishes where they conducted discussions among both Orthodox and stundists. Brotherhoods, such St. Andrew, supported the effort. The church also had the support of much of the press and distributed leaflets and brochures. As already detailed, the church also had the power of the Russian state to suppress the movement.[116]

Pobedonostsev portrayed the stundists as people with pride and conceit, calling themselves "saints" or "people of God," and pointing out their "fanatical hatred" of

---

113. Procurator of the Holy Synod, *Report*, 1884, 297–98; 1887, 76; and 1890–1891, 245–46. For the beginnings of the Pashkovites/Evangelical Christians in Moscow, see *BV*, 1957, no. 3, 74, and 1996, no. 4, 65–68, and *Das Reich Christi*, I (1898), no. 8, 251–52.

114. Procurator of the Holy Synod, *Report*, 1898, 96–98; 1899, 124–25; and 1900, 234. *Baptist Ukrainy*, 1926, no. 11, 30–31.

115. Procurator of the Holy Synod, *Report*, 1900, 229–30, and 1903–1904, 141–42.

116. Ibid., 1886, 100–101.

the Orthodox Church and their mockery and insults of the Orthodox. On the other hand, the evangelical press lauded the stundists for their perseverance under persecution and their joy in the privilege of suffering for the gospel. Both portrayals even with elements of truth were one-sided and exaggerated. In the struggle both sides had strengths and weaknesses that the other side could exploit. Numerous internal and external factors were at work, countering each other, whereby neither side could finally win out until the Revolution in 1905 significantly changed the political situation.[117]

---

117. Ibid., 1890–1891, 248–49, and 1901, 177–78. *Missionary Herald*, Oct. 1893, 418.

21

Tolerated Confession

Mennonite Brethren, 1885–1905

THE MENNONITE BRETHREN as well as the German Baptists in the Russian Empire were tolerated confessions. Since both were not outshoots of Orthodoxy but Protestantism and of foreign origin, the barriers to their toleration were not as high as for others. Although limited to outreach among non-Russians, the Mennonite Brethren and German Baptists increased in number and institutional development at a time Russian evangelicals suffered suppression.

At its twenty-fifth anniversary in 1885, the Mennonite Brethren Conference numbered 1,800 but claimed a constituency, including family members, of 4,000. As an ethno-religious body living in closed communities with special privileges, its increase was confined primarily to biological growth and the gaining of converts from other Mennonites. At the end of 1904 its membership was around 5,400.[1]

Much of the Mennonite Brethren strength continued in the first colonies of Chortitza and Molochna. The church in Rückenau in the Molochna with its affiliates now superseded the church in Einlage in leadership. The Rückenau church began a branch at Spat in the Crimea, which became an independent congregation in 1899. With the establishment of daughter colonies by settlers from Molochna or Chortitza, Mennonite Brethren expanded to other areas. They established work at Memrik in the Don; Ignatjewo in Yekatarinoslav Province, which became independent in 1895; and

---

1. For statistics in 1885 see Friesen, 522, and for 1904 see Dueck, *Moving Beyond Succession: Defining Russian Mennonite Brethren Mission and Identity 1871–1922*, 28, based on the statistical work of Heinrich Braun.

at Terek in the Caucasus, an affiliate of the Rückenau church in 1901. With Mennonite settlements in the Volga, Mennonite Brethren affiliates appeared in Neu Samara in 1891 and in Orenburg and Ufa in 1894. In addition, Mennonite Brethren formed, probably in 1886, a congregation at Alt Samara. In Western Siberia in 1900, an affiliate of the Rückenau church appeared in Omsk. At the opposite extreme of the country, Mennonite Brethren formed about 1884 a congregation at Deutsch-Wymyschle in Russian Poland in a region where German Baptists had absorbed the earlier Mennonite Brethren work.[2]

IDENTITY AND RELATIONSHIPS

Since its beginning in 1860, Mennonite Brethren struggled for decades over its identity. As an amalgam of Anabaptist, pietistic, and Baptist elements it sought to keep a Mennonite identity in spite of a powerful pietistic base and ecclesiastical trends that pushed them toward a Baptist orientation. When Russian officials in the Chortitza area counted Mennonite Brethren as Baptists after the regime extended legal status to German Baptists in 1879, Mennonite Brethren leaders, including Abraham Unger, Johann Wieler, and P. M. Friesen, all with special ties to Baptists, sent a petition and the Mennonite Brethren Confession of Faith to the authorities. In response, the authorities recognized the members of the Einlage church in Chortitza as Mennonites by birth.[3]

The issue of Mennonite Brethren identity, however, continued to rise. In 1896 the *Mennonitische Blätter*, a periodical in Danzig, published an article from an unidentified writer, "Was sind die Mitglieder der mennonitischen Brüdergemeinde?" (What Are the Members of the Mennonite Brethren Church?). The article strongly affirmed the Mennonite credentials of the Mennonite Brethren, which was seconded by *Zionsbote*, the Mennonite Brethren publication in America in its May 20, 1896 issue.[4]

Up to this time the Mennonite Brethren had recognized only the confession adopted by the Einlage church in Chortitza under the influence of Unger and printed in Basel in 1876. It was basically the 1847 German Baptist confession with the statement that it was one in faith with German Baptists but with annotations that it differed from Baptists on military service, the oath, and footwashing. Because of the discomfort of a number of Mennonite Brethren with the confession, the Mennonite Brethren in 1902 produced one that was entirely their own. The new confession included the same articles as the German Baptist confession with the same evangelical emphasis on God, sin, and redemption, the local church and its officers, believer's baptism by immersion, the Lord's Supper, marriage, the Sabbath, and the end of the age. As the

---

2. For Mennonite Brethren expansion see J. A. Toews, 86–93, and Friesen, 528–30, 551–68.

3. Friesen, 479–81.

4. See Harms, *Geschichte der Mennoniten Brüdergemeinde*, 48–57, for a reprint of the article and the response.

German Baptist confession, it supported its statements with copious Scriptures. On the other hand, it included a number of quotations from Menno Simons as well as separate statutes on the washing of feet, the oath, and non-resistance. Unlike the Baptist confessions, it included an extended section on the universal church that included all believers.[5]

In the meantime, however, the question of Mennonite Brethren identity continued to arise. In 1900 Joseph Lehmann, professor in the Baptist Seminary in Hamburg, produced his *Geschichte der deutschen Baptisten* in two volumes. As professor from 1883 until his death in 1907, he personally knew Mennonite Brethren students from Russia who studied at the school in the 1880s and 1890s. In his history, he wrote regarding Mennonite Brethren, "After some indecision it was also determined that only baptized should partake in the Lord's Supper and so here in South Russia a true Baptist church had come into existence." He also wrote that Mennonite Brethren called itself the Mennonite Brethren Church "no doubt not to forfeit any privileges, which the Mennonites in Russia possess." He also noted that although they observed several "Mennonite peculiarities" as refusing the oath and military service and observing footwashing, they were, "in full agreement with true Baptist churches."[6]

In the following year, the *Odessaer Zeitung* published an article by an anonymous author, "Baptisten oder nicht" (Baptists or Not), who cast a critical eye on Mennonite Brethren, quoting Lehmann, the Baptist professor. The author concluded with the telling observation that Lehmann was describing two Baptist bodies, which included a Mennonite Brethren one that was Baptist in essentials and a Mennonite one in non-essentials. It did raise the question, to what extent were the so-called Mennonite peculiarities such as the oath and military service vital to its identity? They came from a sixteenth-century radical Anabaptist *Weltanschauung* that rejected the world system both religiously and politically but were now retained largely to preserve privileges not granted to other populations. Did not Mennonites enter Russia as a privileged minority not challenging the status quo? Ironically in their closed communities, they were forced to use measures of the state to maintain law and order.[7]

Peter Friesen (1849–1914), the Mennonite Brethren historian who wrote the magisterial work, *Die Alt-Evangelische Mennonitische Brüderschaft in Russland (1789–1910)*, publishing it in Russia in 1911 after twenty-five years of research and writing, showed the often convoluted relations between Mennonite Brethren and Baptists. As mentioned, he was one of the Mennonite Brethren in 1880 who helped to differentiate for the authorities differences between Mennonite Brethren and Baptists and was an author for the Mennonite Brethren Confession of 1902. In his 1911 history, although

---

5. For the 1902 Mennonite Brethren confession, see Loewen, *One Lord, One Church, One Hope and One God*, 162–73, and a short commentary on the confession, 29–30.

6. Friesen, *In Defense of Privilege: Russian Mennonites and the State Before and During World War I*, 111–13, 411, ft. 123. Lehmann, *Geschichte der Deutschen Baptisten*, 2:312.

7. *Odessaer Zeitung*, Apr. 7/20, 1901, 118–19.

acknowledging Baptist contributions, he heightened Mennonite origins and pietistic influence but played down the Baptist role, particularly in the Molochna, but possibly lacked primary sources.[8]

But this is not the whole story since Friesen's ties with Baptists were very close, showing a near identity between Baptists and Mennonite Brethren. Various Orthodox writers noted these ties. Val'kevich recorded that Friesen participated in the Rückenau conference of Mennonite Brethren and Russian Stundo-Baptists in 1882 where he discussed mission service and proposed the sending out of V. G. Pavlov for one year. At the beginning of 1890 Friesen attended a short mission course at the Hamburg Baptist Seminary. In his notes on the Rückenau Conference, V. M. Skvortsov noted that Friesen was pastor of the Odessa Baptist congregation, where, by the way, he served from 1888 to 1895, as well as his special training at the Hamburg school. In his account of the Rückenau Conference, M A. Kal'nev noted that Friesen had great influence over the stundists in Kherson Province but was at present less bold than previously, especially because of his surveillance by the mayor of Odessa.[9]

Friesen maintained a very close relationship with August Liebig, pastor for many years of the German Baptist church in Odessa, with Friesen becoming his successor. In a letter to *Zionsbote*, Friesen wrote that he appreciated the fact that the Mennonite Brethren in America were as in Russia sitting at the feet of the dear worthy brother August Liebig in his Bible courses. He also cherished the mutual relations between Mennonite Brethren and Baptists in "evangelisation, ministerial aid, foreign missions, schools, publications, gift parcels and the like. Without the latter (that is Baptists) the Mennonite Brethren Church is impoverished and dries up into a Mennonite 'sect,' without the former (that is Mennonites) they would lose their good Mennonite character." At least for Friesen, Mennonite Brethren were not simply either Baptist or Mennonite but an amalgam of the best features of both.[10]

At the same time the Mennonite Brethren were growing closer to the Old Mennonites from whom they had separated. This was partly due to religious change within the Old Mennonite Church itself. Also the old intense antagonism of the early days began to abate when both groups recognized their common roots and advantages for cooperation. Mennonite Brethren began to fill positions in the schools of other Mennonites. Friesen himself was a teacher and a principal from 1873 to 1886 in the Zentralschule in Halbstadt, a secondary school. With the establishment of the Forestry Service for Mennonites that provided an alternative program to military service, Mennonite young men of both groups developed common bonds. In 1895 the

---

8. See Wardin, "Mennonite Brethren and German Baptists in Russia: Affinities and Dissimilarities," 101–2, on Friesen's treatment of Baptists and Mennonites. Also see Friesen, 289.

9. Val'kevich, 51, 92–93, and App. 1, 4–5. For an English translation of the Rückenau Conference that draws from the accounts of both Kal'nev and Skvortsov, see Dueck, *Moving Beyond Secession*, 37–57. For Kal'nev's account, see *Russkoe obozrenie*, 1897, no. 4, 818–64, and for Skvorsov's account, see *MO*, Sep. 1900, 209–25.

10. *Zionsbote*, May 14, 1902, 2–3.

Mennonite Brethren Conference rescinded its rule forbidding marriage outside the Mennonite Brethren Church.[11]

Some Mennonite Brethren, like Friesen and Johann Wieler, under Pashkov's influence had advocated as early as 1882 at Rückenau open communion. Mennonite Brethren and German Baptists generally observed communion between themselves, but some now wanted to commune with Mennonites who did not practice immersion. In 1899 Johann Reimer, evangelist of the conference, invited at a service at Steinbach all believers to the Lord's Table, creating a great controversy in the Rückenau church of which Reimer was a member. The conference, however, did not exclude Reimer or others of this view. In 1903 the conference by a vote of 59 to 13 with 10 abstaining sustained close communion, but at the same time counseled mutual forbearance over the issue.[12]

Mennonite Brethren became connected to the wider evangelical world through the ministry of Frederick W. Baedeker and Johann Kargel. Both men were closely aligned with the Pashkovite movement, adherents of open communion, and operated on a broad evangelical base. Kargel became a noted theologian, advocating the Deeper Life and dispensational eschatology. Hermann A. Neufeld (1860-1931), who became a Mennonite Brethren traveling missionary, recorded in his journal that he met Kargel at annual Mennonite Brethren conferences in 1887 and 1898 and attended a four-week course of Bible study led by Kargel at Friedensfeld in 1889 and at Andreasfeld in 1894. Neufeld met Baedeker at a mission conference in 1896 who in turn invited him to attend the annual Alliance conference in Blankenburg, Thuringia, Germany, in 1897. Blankenburg conferences strongly supported the Deeper Life and eschatology. At the conference, where Baedeker presided, Neufeld met Heinrich J. Braun and Heinrich Unruh, Mennonite Brethren studying at the Hamburg Seminary.[13]

Jakob W. Reimer (1860-1948), a Mennonite Brethren evangelist and advocate of open communion, at times also attended the Blankenburg conferences where he also spoke. He became a foremost advocate of dispensational theology among Mennonite Brethren. Reimer was a convert of Baedeker and served with him as an interpreter on his tours.[14]

As among Russian Stundo-Baptists and German Baptists, the Adventists were also troubling Mennonite Brethren and Old Mennonites. Hermann Neufeld reported in 1898 that two Adventist missionaries from America were successful in obtaining a number of converts in the German settlements. In 1910 he noted difficulties in his church over Adventist encroachment.[15]

11. J. A. Toews, 93-95, 100-101.
12. Ibid., 100-101. Toews, *Perilous Journey*, 68.
13. Neufeld, *Herman and Katharina*, 28-29, 33, and 35-37.
14. Lohrenz, *The Mennonite Brethren Church*, 318-19. J. A. Toews, 377-78. Neufeld, 29-30, 32.
15. Neufeld, 36-38.

STATE RELATIONS

As a tolerated body, Mennonite Brethren could hold their annual conferences and elect their itinerant missionaries without governmental interterference. Nevertheless the Russian regime continued to be concerned over the influence of German colonists on the Russian/Ukrainian population, numbers of whom worked for Germans. In 1886 *Tserkovnyï vestnik,* the periodical of the Orthodox Church, reported with alarm that a large number of sectarians were appearing in the neighboring German colonies in Yekaterinoslav Diocese. The province included many Mennonites with the article pointing out among others the influence of Friedensfeld, a Mennonite center. Also Val'kevich pointed out that the Mennonite colony of Woldemfürst in the Kuban attracted such Baptist propagandists as V. V. Ivanov and Deï Mazaev for Christian fellowship.[16]

In 1885 a newly appointed official reported to the governor of Taurida that the Rückenau church was a Baptist congregation that had no authority to meet. David Schellenberg and P.M. Friesen appealed to the Ministry of Affairs that as a Mennonite congregation it legally existed and requested that the officer be informed it was not a Baptist congregation. The Rückenau church, however, had a building that had not been confirmed. In 1887 Friesen was able to get the necessary confirmation as well as for the church in Spat. An antagonistic Mennonite in 1895 went to the authorities with the charge that the annual meeting of the Mennonite Brethren in the Rückenau church was an unauthorized Baptist meeting. The authorities suspended the session but after investigation found no basis for the allegation.[17]

At the Orthodox Missionary Congress in Kazan in 1897, Aleksiï Ya. Dorodnitsyn (Later Bishop Alesksiï), diocesan missionary in Yekaterinoslav Province, reported on the spread among the German population of the Stundo-Baptist religious movement under the name of the "Baptized by Faith Mennonite Brotherhood." In the strongest terms, he described their sectarian repudiation of other Mennonites and were "literally alike" with the Stundo-Baptists in worship, organization of congregations, means of propaganda, and spiritual proselytism. He charged them with having an "enormous influence" on the spread of the stundists in South Russia, whom the Committee of Ministers in 1894 characterized as a specially dangerous sect in church and social-political relations.[18]

Dorodnitsyn proposed eradication of the Mennonite Brethren by (1) closing their prayer houses, (2) forbidding construction of new prayer houses and prayer meetings in private homes, (3) forbidding keeping minors of Orthodox and other Christian faiths as workers and domestic servants, establish for Orthodox adults

---

16. *TsV,* 1886, no. 42, 651–53. Val'kevich, 133.

17. Friesen, 525–27.

18. Skvortsov, *Third All-Russian Missionary Congress,* 1897, "*Krestyashcheesya po vere soedinennoe Mennonitsko bratstvo,*" 154–57.

pastoral-missionary supervision, and erecting near workers churches and schools, (4) deprive exemption from military service, and (5) forbid their publications and spread of foreign publications of Stundo-Baptists. He also added to discontinue its spiritual and material assistance to the Stunda. The commission at the congress felt these proposals were well grounded and just. The regime, however, did not follow up on the recommendations, and the Mennonite Brethren continued as before. In the discussion one delegate brought up the issue of Russian stundists attending German services. The commission thereupon expressed the view that the regime should forbid Russian translations of Lutheran worship books, approved by the Lutheran consistory but used by stundists, as well as forbid Lutheran pastors and German Baptist and Mennonite leaders to use Russian in their services. *Zionsbote* reported in full the session, which was then reproduced in *Der Sendbote*, the German Baptist paper, from *Zionsbote*. Neither publication made any comment.[19]

Foreign Missions

Although Mennonite Brethren were limited in outreach to native inhabitants of the Empire, they nevertheless began to provide support for missions abroad and prayed for the heathen in other lands. As a small group with no mission organization or experience in foreign missions, the opportunity for them, however, came through the Baptists. The German Baptist Seminary in Hamburg provided training and the American Baptist Missionary Union (ABMU) in America contributed the organizational structure.

From mission literature from Germany, Mennonite Brethren became conscious of the Baptist mission fields and contributed funds for them. The desire arose, however, to send their own missionaries abroad. In 1885 Abraham J. Friesen (1859–1919) and his wife Maria in Chortitza volunteered for foreign service. They went to Hamburg where he studied for four years at the seminary, while his wife received training for three years in other institutions. With his attempt to improve his English, Friesen read the publications of the ABMU, becoming familiar with its work. With the encouragement of the leaders of the seminary, he approached the ABMU for service. In his last year of study, he wrote in 1888 to Mennonite Brethren congregations in Chortitza, Molochna, and Friedensfeld for support, noting that Mennonite Brethren could establish their own field under the ABMU. The response was encouraging.[20]

Friesen decided to serve among the Telugus in South India, which was a most productive field of the ABMU. In 1889 the ABMU appointed him and his wife to serve in Nalgonda, a new and promising field. After receiving funds for support and travel expenses from several Mennonite Brethren congregations they visited, the Friesens arrived in India in November, finally settling permanently in Nalgonda in October

---

19. *Der Sendbote*, June 29, 1898, 409.
20. Harms, 44–45. Peters, *Foundations of Mennonite Brethren Missions*, 24, 36–37.

1890. Earlier, American Baptists had engaged in very limited mission work in this field and Mennonite Brethren in America had provided, beginning in 1883, funds for native workers, but the Friesens were the first permanent missionaries and the only ones for some years.[21]

When the Friesens settled in Nalgonda station, a large number of new Christians were already awaiting them. In January 1891 a congregation with 129 members was formed. By the mid-nineties the church numbered 700 with twenty stations, a prayer house, two school buildings, a hospital, a mission residence, a Sunday school, youth society, and women's mission society. Native preachers and evangelists and Bible women contributed to the mission effort. In 1896 the Nalgonda church became three independent congregations.

Other Mennonite Brethren joined forces, including Mr. And Mrs. Abraham Huebert (1898) and Mr. And Mrs. Heinrich Unruh (1899). Also in 1899 Mr. and Mrs. N. N. Hiebert and Elise Neufeld arrived from the Mennonite Brethren in America but soon had their own field to the west in 1900. In 1900 Friesen began publishing *Das Erntefeld* (The Harvest Field) on the work of the mission.

Mennonite Brethren from Russia and America provided much of the support, but the ABMU was willing to assist the Unruhs when Mennonite Brethren at the time were unable to supply their full support. In 1904 the Mennonite Brethren and the ABMU agreed that the former would assume one-half of the cost of missionary salaries and the financial responsibility for evangelistic work, while the latter would provide the other half of the salaries and the costs for medical and children's work. Friesen was very appreciative of the support of the ABMU, while at the same time granting him full independence and never interfering with his work. The board of the ABMU in Boston welcomed the Friesens when they visited when on furlough.[22]

Publications

The Mennonite Brethren published no periodical of its own in the nineteenth century but received from Germany the Baptist periodicals of *Missionsblatt* and *Der Wahrheitszeuge*. From America came the German Baptist paper, *Der Sendbote*, and the Mennonite Brethren paper, *Zionsbote*. Abraham J. Kroeker (1863–1944), born in Molochna and a Mennonite Brethren minister, farmer, and writer, and his cousin Jakob Kroeker (1872–1948) began a publishing enterprise. Jakob attended the Hamburg Seminary and was greatly influenced by Baedeker, regularly attended the Blankenburg

---

21. An excellent account of the Mennonite Brethren field in India is in Friesen, 674–87. Also see Peters, *Foundations of Mennonite Brethren Missions*, 37–39, 128–29, and Peters, *The Growth of Foreign Missions in The Mennonite Brethren Church*, 55–69. Also see "Abraham Friesen," ME, 2:404.

22. For the 1904 agreement between the Mennonite Brethren and ABMU, see "Draft of Statutes of the Foreign Missions Committee of the Mennonite Brethren Church of Russia 1904," Dueck, 112–16, and Penner, *Russians, North Americans and Telugus*, 29–31.

Conference, and spoke at Bible conferences. The two published in 1897 an almanac, *Christlicher Familienkalender*. In 1899 they produced a daily devotional booklet that appeared as a wall calendar, *Abreisskalender*, which was also popular among non-Mennonites, and from 1902 to 1904 an annual *Christliches Jahrbuch*.[23]

In 1903 Abraham and his cousin began *Friedensstimme*, an organ for Mennonite Brethren in Russia, the first Mennonite church paper in the Russian Empire. *Friedensstimme* was first published in Berlin, but in 1906 was moved to Halbstadt in Chortitza. It not only covered church and mission news but also included devotional, ecclesiastical, and educational material as well as politics and local issues.[24]

---

23. Lohrenz, "Abraham Jakob Kroeker," ME, 3:245–46. Neff, "Jakob Kroeker," ME, 3:245–46. J. A. Toews, 95–97.

24. "Friedensstimme," ME, 2:400–401.

22

Tolerated Confession

German and Baltic Baptists, 1885–1905

WITH ITS LEGALIZATION IN 1879, German and Baptists became a tolerated body. Even before toleration it organized its first association, Russian-Turkish, in 1872, followed in 1877 by the Russian-Poland Association. In 1884 the Russian-Turkish Association, then called the Russian-Romanian Association, divided into two associations—A South Russian-Romanian Association and a West Russian Association. At the conference of the Russian-Poland Association in June 1884 near Lublin, the delegates agreed to form an association of all associations to include the three associations with the expectation that the Baltic Association, formed earlier in 1879, composed primarily of Latvians, would also join.[1]

In Neudorf in Volhynia in September 1887, the three associations formed the "Union of Baptist Churches of Russia," which would be a separate entity from the German Baptist *Bund* (Union) of Germany. This organization came into existence three years after the Russian Baptist Union. Johann Kargel was present at both organizations. Earlier in August 1885 at the triennial General Conference of the German Baptist Union in Berlin, the German Baptists from Russia had announced their intention of forming their own union. They explained it was necessary due to relations with the Russian government. It was becoming difficult for German Baptists, now a tolerated and legal body, to be part of a foreign organization, but they hoped to continue their ties with the union in Germany.[2]

1. *Der Sendbote*, Aug. 6, 1884, 242–43.
2. *WHZ*, Nov. 15, 1887, 224. *BMM*, July 1886, 303, and July 1888, 312.

PART FIVE—Peril, 1884–1905

In 1888 at the triennial conference of the German Baptist Union in Königsberg, Gottfried Alf, the champion of Baptist work in Poland but now president of the new union in Russia, spoke justifying the move. He pointed out that the great distances were burdensome for delegates from Russia to attend German conferences and the difficulty for Russian subjects to gain passes, which may be denied, and their great cost. He also wanted a better missions program in the country. He hoped for a continuing intimate relationship with the German Union with exchange of visitors. The conference approved the recommendation of Alf that the mission treasury be separated but that churches of the new union would maintain their rights to special funds. The German conference also affirmed the new union's continuing relationship with the seminary in Hamburg and the publishing house.[3]

The Union of Baptist Churches of Russia was patterned after the German Union but with its own mission treasury. It also met triennially. In 1900 it reported an income of 17,600 rubels during the last three years. In 1889 it formed a treasury for widows of mission workers. Each participating member was to pay a gift of ten rules on the death of a mission worker. Unlike the Mennonite Brethren, it could look to co-religionists abroad, especially to Germany and the USA, for financial assistance and theological training. Especially valuable for English readers for news and the needs of Baptist work abroad, including Russia, was the periodical in London, the *Quarterly Reporter of the German Baptist Mission,* published from 1858 to 1914. The new union now received funds directly through the English-German Committee and the American-German Committee, money that formerly had been funneled through the German Union. The new union developed an auxiliary relationship with the American Baptist Missionary Union (ABMU), which for years supplied support for the pastor of the German Baptist church in St. Petersburg. It paid Johann Kargel $400 a year, then A. R. Schiewe, raising his salary between 1880 and 1895 from $400 to $2,000 annually, but then after 1895 with reduced appropriations from $1,800 to $1,200. In 1900–1901 funds from the ABMU helped twenty-two congregations and in 1901–1902 thirty-three workers.[4]

The German Baptists in Russia also appealed directly to their German brethren in the USA. In 1884 and again in 1892 Severin Lehmann went to the USA to gain ministerial assistance for the Volga. Schiewe went to the USA in 1887. In the same year Lehmann with Alf met with the American-German Committee in Hamburg and then continued on to America. These visits from Russia caused the German Baptist leadership in America great irritation and strong condemnation from *Der Sendbote* as encroaching on its mission work. In 1891 Lehmann addressed the German General

3. German Baptist Union, *Bundes-Konferenz*, 1888, 70–72.

4. *WHZ*, Feb. 23, 1901, 62. For financial appropriations of the ABMU, see the July issues of the *Baptist Missionary Magazine* as well as the letters of Kessler in this periodical, Oct. 1891, 450, and July 1893, 358, as well as his letters in ABMU/ABFMS, *Correspondence*, Russian Mission, 1900–1919, Oct. 12, 1901, and Oct. 11, 1902.

Conference in Hamburg for the union in Russia where he was received with sympathetic interest.[5]

In 1888 the Union of Baptist Churches of Russia recorded forty-four congregations with a membership of 11,384. It had 67 chapels and 177 Sunday schools with 3,694 pupils. The union, however, experienced schism in its Baltic Association when Jekabs Rumbergs (Jacob Rumberg), an alumnus of the Hamburg Seminary, left in 1884 with 2,500 members because of resentment by Latvian Baptists of German domination and Rumberg's exclusion from his own church in Riga. Including the schism, membership of the German Baptist work was around 14,000.[6]

The constituency of the union was widely scattered with no one center with islands of strength far distant from each other. The strongest area of concentration was the West Russian Association of 4,200 members consisting of thirty percent of the membership. Except in Kovno, its churches were in Volhynia in northwest Ukraine and included the strong Neudorf church of 857 members whose pastor was Severin Lehmann. A comparable center of strength was in Courland and Livonia, where the two Baltic associations totaled 4,700 members, who were primarily Latvian. The other associations were much smaller—the Polish Association, composed primarily of Germans with thirteen congregations and 2,705 members, and the South Russian Association with eleven congregations and 1,634 members, widely scattered in Kherson Province in southwest Ukraine around Odessa to near Elisabetgrad and also in the Don region and Crimea. In addition, German congregations existed in St. Petersburg (with six mission stations), numbering 314 members, and Riga with 304 members. The membership, as many Mennonite Brethren, was not confined to self-contained villages but interspersed in other village populations and also in various towns. The German Baptists continued their pattern of central churches with numerous mission stations, which helped to spread the Baptist witness over a wide area.

City Congregations

St. Petersburg

It was a challenge for German Baptists to establish a congregation in St. Petersburg, the capital of the Russian Empire. It was not only a center of many Orthodox churches but also a well-established Lutheran constituency of nine churches. Separate congregations also existed for German Reformed, French Reformed, Church of England, British and American Congregationalists, and Moravians. With their sacramental view of infant baptism, Lutherans and Reformed regarded Baptists as a sectarian

---

5. *Der Sendbote*, Apr. 22, 1885, 130, and Feb. 29, 1888, 4. *WHZ*, Dec. 1, 1887, 230. *BMM*, Apr. 1892, 94. Val'kevich, 57.

6. German Baptist Union, *Statistik*, 1888, 18–19, 29. Ekelmann, 86. *Istoriya*, 354. *BMM*, July 1886, 303.

threat. Hermann Dalton, pastor of the German Reformed Church and member of the Evangelical Alliance, was very critical of German Baptists and its pastor, A. Reinhold Schiewe. In 1885 the *St. Petersburg Zeitung* printed Dalton's article, "Sieh' dich vor!" (Be Careful!), a warning against Baptists for considering everything outside Baptists a mission field. He was critical of Schiewe for baptizing Swedes and noted that the latter "also directs his greedy eyes to Estonia."[7]

F. Kiefer, from America on a visit in 1884 to St. Petersburg, wrote to the American Baptist Missionary Union a lengthy but very frank letter, no doubt reflecting Schiewe's views, on the opposition and problems Baptists faced in the city.[8] He referred to "deluded people" who sent to the Minister of Foreign Religions "fearful denunciations against the Baptists." He continued to write: "And at least twice a week since I am here has bro. Schiewe been required to go before the Minister and explain, and has so far succeeded in satisfying the authorities, that we Baptists are not responsible for these things." "But men in high authority tell us plainly, that the government blundered when the religious freedom was granted to the Baptists, that they are such an *aggressive sect*, that they threaten the peace yea even the existence of the Greek Church, and anything like a fair excuse would be hailed with pleasure, to call in the privileges that have been granted us. The Lutheran Clergy far beyond the Russian Clergy are the bitter enemies of the Baptists."

In reference to the Pashkov movement, he wrote:

> The question of baptism is agitating them. They are not willing to call themselves Baptists and as "Plymouth brethren" they have, and cannot obtain recognition. All the Pashkoff influence is against us Baptists because of strict communion. Now think of our little band, standing alone in poverty among the various religious elements all hostile to them. Again and again inducements have been held out of support, the furnishing of a suitable chappel [sic], if we would only introduce open communion, and insinuations made, that it is a shame that we cannot be as liberal as Spurgeon.

He also noted evangelists from abroad and lack of support from Germany:

> Every winter some sort of an Immersionist (secretly) has labored in St. Petersburg as evangelist, but their influence has been against the Baptists. Lord Radstock, George Müller, (whom it may be said is Prince among them who can fervently dispise [sic] and ignore Baptists) excepting when he cannot get any other place in any city to preach in, and Dr Baedicker [sic] of London who is to be here again in 2 weeks.

---

7. *Der Sendbote*, May 21, 1884, 163. *St. Petersburger Zeitung*, March 15/27, 1885, 2.

8. Letter of Kiefer, Jan. 23, 1884, ABMU, *Correspondence*, Russia, 1814–1900. For Shiewe's antipathy toward Pashkovite views on the ordinances, see *Der Sendbote*, May 28, 1884, 171.

> It is also generally known that the brethren in Hamburg have not the heart for Russia, that the now sainted Bro Oncken had. Not a dollar will they even appropriate for Russian Missions that has not expressly been so directed or so stippulated [sic] by you.

Kiefer found opposition on every hand for the struggling band, and, as noted, even indifference from the Baptists in Germany for support of the Baptist cause in Russia. As has already been noted, the letter also reveals, unlike the views of Kargel, Schiewe's antipathy toward Pashkovite views on church ordinances. But the internal problems of the St. Petersburg congregation were even more serious.

A. Reinhold Schiewe (1846–1930) became the pastor of the church in September 1880, succeeding Johann Kargel, arriving with a wife and five small children. He was thirty-four years of age and fluent in German and Russian. The Russian authorities had expelled him from his pastorate in Volhynia in 1877, but remarkably the authorities did not prohibit his taking this new charge. Later in the month, the congregation became an independent church, no longer a mission of the church in Memel, Germany. Writing years later, Schiewe claimed the church had only sixty-three members, seven men and fifty-six women, but seventeen moved away, others fell back into the world, leaving only thirty-five.[9] Schiewe found it difficult to take his oath since Kargel had not yet resigned as pastor as well as facing charges brought to the Minister of the Interior against him by Schwan, who in 1864 had been secretly baptized in St. Petersburg by Oncken but had been excluded five years before. Schwan, who desired to supplant Schiewe, pointed out Schiewe's earlier exile and accused him of being an exporter and thus barred from holding a spiritual office. Under suspense and many sleepless nights for ten months, the regime finally confirmed Schiewe in his office.[10]

In 1881 Schiewe began baptizing within St. Petersburg itself instead outside the city. He obtained permission to use the bathing house on the bank of the river, which two police protected to keep order. He noted the contrast years before when Alf had baptized him and eight others in the middle of the night to avoid opposition from enemies.[11]

In a city where eleven languages were spoken, Schiewe found it difficult to minister when in the congregation German, Swedish, Latvian, Estonian, and Russian were used. On Sunday the church's program was an all-day affair from 10:30 in the morning to 10:00 at night. It began with a prayer meeting at 10:30, a German service at 11:30, Sunday school at 1:00, a Swedish service at 3:30 that lasted two hours, another German service at 5:00, and then another Swedish service at 8:00. On Wednesday

---

9. *WHZ*, Nov. 2, 1880, 166–67. *QR*, Jan. 1881, 6–8. *Der Sendbote*, June 14, 1882, 186. *Texas Baptist*, Mar. 6, 1884, 1. Letter of Schiewe, Sep. 1893, ABMU, *Correspondence*, Russia, 1814–1900.

10. *BMM*, Jan. 1882, 19. *WHZ*, Sep. 1881, 169. Letter of Schiewe, Sep. 1893.

11. *BMM*, 1882, 19. *Der Sendbote*, Jan. 17, 1883, 18.

the church held a German service, on Thursday a Swedish service, and on Friday an Estonian service.[12]

Schiewe found St. Petersburg "bitterly expensive." Because of the high rent of 1,200 rubles, it was necessary to find another meeting place. In 1883 he finally found a more suitable location. In his letter, Kiefer wrote that the small church must raise 1,000 rubles a year for rent, fuel, lights, and the like.[13]

The Schiewe family shared the church's accommodations. He wrote that the health of his family was being affected with the inability to open the windows during the winter because of the cold. His wife's health was particularly affected when she had to care for the eight children, fourteen years to five months, and also quiet them during the services. In respect to Shiewe's wife, F. Kiefer wrote: "I have seen that mother work till 3 and 4 o clock in the morning and then have but little rest when she did get to ly (*sic*) down. Yet she is not able to keep a servant, and thus they toil, endure and pray, and am thankful that the sheriff does not come and take their furniture."[14]

Shortly before Christmas in 1885 the authorities threatened to expel the church from its rented premises because of the absence of two wall ventilators, the lack of drains, and the need of the house door to open to the outside instead to the inside. Although the hall had 100 place sittings, the order limited sixty persons in the hall at any one time. The authorities gave Schiewe only ten days to make the changes, but they extended the time to April. With great difficulty Schiewe will eventually find in 1889 a very suitable place, which, however, the congregation could ill afford, but at least it was not cast out on the street.[15]

Schiewe's pleas for a meeting house were never met; a new building would cost at least $40,000, an impossible sum. He went to Sweden to get assistance and made appeals overseas. In 1889 he wrote that the congregation was unable to pay the required rent and needed additional help from abroad. At the same time he asked the ABMU for $200 more in salary for himself and large family, which was then raised to 700 rubles.[16]

Because of small numbers and poverty, the St. Petersburg congregation itself could do little to alleviate the financial burdens. In one of his letters, Schiewe wrote: "The members here are poor workmen and servants, who scarsly (*sic*) have sufficient means to live, not one has any means." In another letter he stated that "seldom more than one-half can attend our meetings. Some attend only once on the Sabbath, because

---

12. *Der Sendbote*, July 8, 1885, 210. *BMM*, Oct. 1885, 405.
13. *Der Sendbote*, June 14, 1882, 186. *BMM*, Jan. 1884, 18. Letter of Kiefer, Jan. 23, 1884.
14. *Der Sendbote*, July 8, 1885, 210. Letter of Kiefer, Jan. 23, 1884.
15. *Der Sendbote*. April 7, 1886, 114. Letter of Schiewe, Sep. 1893.
16. *Der Sendbote*, May 28, 1884, 171; July 8, 201, 1884. *BMM*, Oct. 1885, 405. Letter of Schiewe, Nov. 1, 1889, ABMU, *Correspondence*, Russia, 1814–1900.

they live so far away; others can come only once in two or three weeks, because of their positions."[17]

Schiewe's work was sustained not only from the provision for his salary from America and contributions from others sources but also literature sent to him. In 1885 Schiewe received the news from Lord Shaftesbury that he would receive for free distribution as much literature from the Bible Depot in German, Russian, and Estonian that he could use. In 1887 the Religious Tract Society reported that Schiewe had received a grant for tracts. As already noted, Schiewe conducted a multi-lingual ministry. One report listed German, Latvian, Lithuanian, and Finnish, which could have also included Estonian and Swedish with also possibly confusing Finnish with Estonian. In the summer of 1882, Schiewe baptized twenty-three Swedes. The Swedes apparently in 1886 formed their own congregation but in 1889 organized as a church, continuing, however, their relationship with the German congregation. Oscar Elof Signeul (1858–1925), ordained in 1889, became pastor and also ministered among Swedes in Estonia.[18] The St. Petersburg church also had stations outside the city. One was a small German congregation in Moscow, which Schiewe visited in 1882. W. E. Galling, a colporterur of the BFBS, reported in that year it numbered only seven. It received such visitors as Severin Lehmann from Volhynia, who came several times; Gottfried Alf from Russian Poland in June, 1881; Johann Wieler and Peter M. Friesen from the Molochna in 1881–1882; and Frederick Baedeker in April 1882, who had difficulty holding a public meeting and will return. Beginning in 1884 Schiewe's most remarkable work outside St. Petersburg was in Estonia where he established a Baptist work, baptizing many converts and establishing numerous mission stations, an enterprise that will be later discussed in the chapter.[19]

In his letter in September 1893 to the ABMU, Schiewe wrote, "I meet with no difficulty from the Authorities but on the contrary enjoy their protection." But little did he know how soon his service will be terminated. A growing faction in the congregation sought his ouster, fueled by Hermann Fast, who as has been noted, was a leading evangelical with Pashkovite ties. Fast wrote at the end of 1893 to the ABMU, "It is clear beyond all question that the preacher and his family cause the trouble which hinders all progress." Dissidents also appealed to the German Union in Russia as well as to the editor of *Der Wahrheitszeuge,* the Baptist paper in Hamburg. In a second letter to the ABMU in October 1894, Fast mentioned again sending a letter again to the editor of *Der Wahrhetiszeuge* as well as one to the editor of *Der Sendbote.* Fast also wrote that earlier in the year the police had searched his home and taken his written materials. Although not charging Schiewe with implication in his case, he nevertheless charged

---

17. Letter of Schiewe, Sep. 1893. *BMM,* Oct. 1886, 403.

18. *WHZ,* Mar. 1, 1885, 56. RTS, *Report,* 1887, 89. QR, Jan. 1886, 8. For the Swedish congregation in St. Petersburg, see *Der Sendbote,* Jan. 17, 1883, 18; *WHZ,* Apr.15, 1886, 85; *BMM,* Aug. 1889, 348; and Modén, *Vittnen och Troshjältar,* 97–103.

19. *Der Sendbote,* Jan. 17, 1883, 18. *WHZ,* Sep. 1, 1881, 168, and Jan. 1, 1883, 6.

Schiewe from an allegation of a "reliable source" (not, however, backed by proof) of his being a police informer some months back in the summer. Fast suggested that either Johann Kargel or Peter M. Friesen, the Mennonite Brethren, should replace Schiewe.[20]

Schiewe's termination, however, did not come from the intrigue of Baptist politics but from the Russian regime itself. On March 19, 1895, Schiewe wrote to the ABMU that on Monday night he has to leave St. Petersburg and Russia forever, otherwise he will be sent to Siberia. He left for Germany, leaving his wfe and children and also a debt of 1,100 rubles to pay for rent and other items. On June 26 he wrote that for nearly two months he had wandered around Germany homeless; his wife and children were still in St. Petersburg with his wife sending a petition to the Tsar. On August lst his son was with him, who also had to flee, and noted his wife with the other children would soon arrive. On October 16 he wrote that his wife with the children arrived on September 20, a separation of almost six months; in the meantime he took a pastorate in Templin, Germany. He said he probably would be unhappy in Germany since he was born in Russia and spent forty-six yeas of his life there. Schiewe next served in Landsberg an der Warthe where he retired in 1910 and will die in December 1930 at the age of eighty-four.[21] On writing in 1896 on his trip to Russia, E. Petrick, regarding cities important and particularly model congregations, felt, in contrast to the very successful German Baptist congregation in Lodz, Russian Poland, that the church in St. Petersburg was a hindrance to the cause since it did not impress the authorities as a blessing to the country.[22] When one considers that Schiewe under the most adverse circumstances maintained a multi-lingual ministry for fourteen and a half years in St. Petersburg while at the same time, as we shall see, begin a very successful ministry in Estonia, his service was far from unsuccessful. This was a time of governmental fears of Baptist work, which brought him two exiles, and at a time when also many co-religionists severely suffered.

Although the church now ceased for four years, it will be revived in 1900 under F. A. Arndt, a graduate of Hamburg Seminary. In 1905 the work included the German congregation of 95 members; a Swedish congregation under O. E. Signeul of 53 members, founded in 1889; a Latvian congregation under A. Podin, formed in 1901; and an Estonian congregation established in 1903 for a total of 240. On July 6, 1903, the congregation consecrated a new location, a hall, which it now held for five years under contract. It was allowed to build its own baptistry. After the toleration act of 1905 it began instructing in Russian a small group of children and even baptized two

---

20. Letters of Fast, Nov. 14, 1893, and Oct. 5, 1894, ABMU, *Correspondence*, Russia, 1814–1900.

21. Letters of Shiewe, Mar. 1895; June 16, 1895; Aug. 1, 1895; and Oct. 16, 1895, ABMU, *Correspondence*, Russia, 1814–1900.

22. *WHZ*, Sep. 5, 1896, 27.

candidates from Orthodoxy. The church survived under Arndt until the outbreak of the First World War in 1914.[23]

Riga

Riga was a city in Livonia (today in Latvia) with a large German population, possibly 120,000 or more than three-fourths of the population. In 1865 August Meyer from Libau formed a mission circle here. In the 1870s Riga gained the services of two young and aggressive pastors. In 1874 the Latvians took the lead under Jekabs Rumbergs (Jacob Rumberg), who, returning from the Hamburg Mission School, formed an independent church in 1876 and consecrated a chapel at the end of 1877. Rumberg knew both Latvian and German. A gifted German leader, Julius Herrmann from Königsberg, East Prussia, arrived in 1878, to lead the German work in the city, a mission of the Königsberg church. He dedicated a chapel in 1878, seating 200, built at his own expense. In 1881 his work became an independent congregation. There is no evidence that he knew either Latvian or Russian.[24] Unfortunately the two growing Baptist congregations in the city were at odds with each other, reflecting the feuding between German and Latvians in the city. H. Berneike and C. A. Kemnitz from Germany arrived in Riga to effect reconciliation at a conference of delegates from both congregations. The two sides agreed that the church that had excluded a member be the only one responsible for his or her restoration. After settling other differences both congregations met in the large Latvian chapel in celebration of peace and reconciliation.[25]

In 1882 Herrmann wrote to the ABMU in Boston, requesting the Union to adopt the German Baptist work in St. Petersburg and Riga as mission stations. He charged that the Baptists in Germany nor the German-American Committee seem to care for the two cities. Herrmann stated that the $500 that Schiewe was receiving in St. Petersburg was inadequate, and he has been serving in Riga without salary.[26]

In 1885 Herrmann suffered a severe setback. After selling the chapel and his home and accepting for payment shares in a company that went bankrupt, the congregation was left without a place of meeting. In visiting England he appealed to the German Baptist mission in London, which set up a fund. With money from abroad and receiving from the city without charge a site worth 8,000 rubles and obtaining a legacy of 4,000 rubles left by a female member of the church, Herrmann in 1887 laid

---

23. *BMM*, Mar. 1901, 86. *Der Sendbote*, Sep. 4, 1901, 550, and Dec. 20, 1905, 809. *WHZ*, Apr. 11, 1903, 119, and Aug. 29, 1903, 271. *Unions-Statistik der Baptisten-Gemeinden in Russland*, 1906, 2. Donat, *Das wachsende Werk*, 140, 183.

24. Ekelmann, 85–86. *Missionsblatt*, May 1878, 85–86. QR, Apr. 1885, 15. Letter from Herrmann, Feb. 8, 1882, ABMU, *Correspondence*, Russia, 1814–1900. *WHZ*, Feb. 25, 1934, 57–58.

25. *QR*, Jan. 1880, 9.

26. Letter of Herrmann, Feb. 8, 1882, ABMU, *Correspondence*, Russia, 1814–1900.

the cornerstone for the large and beautiful Zions-kirche. The new building, which included accommodations for the pastor and his family, was dedicated in 1888. Because of disruption among members of the Latvian church, which numbered over 1,000 members, the authorities closed its house of worship, forcing the Latvians to attend the German church. W. Haupt, who visited the church in January 1889, noted the church, which had over 800 members, held two German services, a Latvian service, and one for Estonians. He wrote that the church carried a heavy mortgage and was ashamed that the Baptists in Germany contributed so little toward the building.[27]

In 1884, as will later be noted, Herrmann introduced at Pernau (Pärnu) a Baptist work in southern Estonia. In 1889 he began a monthly German Baptist periodical, *Der Hausfreund,* the first in Russia. At the end of November 1893, after sixteen years, Herrmann completed his service at the church. He migrated to Danzig in Germany, where *Der Hausfreund* was now published and where in 1896 he became pastor of the German Baptist Church. With the emigration of the pastor and other members, the church was left with a heavy debt.[28]

The German Baptist Union in Russia became very concerned about the church. A new mission committee, after visiting the church, asked Severin Lehmann from the Neudorf Church in Volhynia to assume the pastorate, where he will serve until 1915. Lehmann was forced to take frequent month-long trips to raise money to meet the debt and obtain mission support. The Latvian church, under the capable leadership of Janis (John) A. Frey and Janis Inkis (Inke), continued to meet in the German Baptist structure, causing a great strain with the scheduling of services, Sunday schools, and societies of both congregations. The Latvian Baptists dedicated in 1902 their own building in Roman style with 700 places on Mäthai Street.[29]

Libau

Libau in Courland, today in Latvia, was a mixed town of 30,000 of Jews, Russian, Germans, Latvians, and Poles. August Meyer began a German work here in 1860. The Latvian work thrived and divided into two congregations. With poor relations with the Latvian First Church, four German families formed their own congregation and became a mission of the Riga German church. The Latvian First Church, however, held divine services alternately with German brethren four times each Sunday, twice in Latvian and twice in German. The small German mission will become an independent congregation in 1908.[30]

27. QR, Apr. 1885, 15; July 1886, 6; and Oct. 1887, 6–7. WHZ, Feb. 1, 1889, 27, and Feb. 15, 1889, 37.

28. Wardin, *Evangelical Sectarianism,* 217–18, nos. 1898–1899. WHZ, Jan. 6, 1894, 6–7. Donat, *Das wachsende Werk,* 349.

29. *Der Sendbote,* Sep. 4, 1901, 550. Čukers, *et. al.,* eds. Dzīvības Ceļš, 39.

30. *Der Sendbote,* Jan. 12, 1887, 2; Nov. 14, 1888, 2; Feb. 10, 1892, 2; and Dec. 7, 1892, 2. WHZ, Nov. 19, 1892, 359, and Feb. 25, 1934, 57.

Kovno [Kaunas]

In Kovno in Kovno Province, today Lithuania, a German Baptist work began in 1886 when August H. Stoltenhoff from Volmarstein in Germany arrived as manager of a department of a lock factory. In December 1887 J. Marks arrived on the field as pastor, who formerly served in the Volga. The church organized in February 1889 and in 1896 constructed a chapel. During the First World War most members were exiled to Russia and its building was left in ruins, but it survived the war.[31]

Odessa

The German Baptist congregation in the port city of Odessa on the Black Sea in Kherson Province was formed in 1870. It faced difficult days in its early years until the arrival of August Liebig (1836–1914), who served from 1874 to 1887. Membership grew from 62 to 875 by 1884 with thirty-two mission sites extending into neighboring German colonies. After the formation of three new churches in 1884, the Odessa church was left with 254 members. Peter M. Friesen, the Mennonite Brethren historian, became the next pastor.[32] Karl G. Füllbrandt (1858–1915) followed Friesen. As a boy Füllbrandt moved with his parents from Germany to Yekaterinoslav Province. Abraham Unger, the Mennonite Brethren leader, baptized him. In 1898 Füllbrandt took the Odessa pastorate, and under his leadership the church built a beautiful chapel. Füllbrandt was a writer, publishing in 1896 a book of mediations on biblical texts, *Blätter vom Lebensraum* (Leaves of the Tree of Life), which was translated into Russian in 1913, an editor of hymnbooks, and authored other writings. He entered evangelistic service in 1912, but the First World War forced him to return to Germany where he soon died.[33]

Lodz

The German Baptist church in Lodz, Russian Poland, founded in 1878, became the largest German Baptist church in Russia, reporting in 1905 over 1,500 members and ten mission stations with 1,200 children in its Sunday school. Lodz was a growing industrial center of the cotton textile industry and attracted many Germans. The church was fortunate in 1877 to gain the strong evangelistic ministry of Karl Ondra, who had been exiled from Volhynia. In 1882 it dedicated its house of worship, seating 700, at a cost of 16,000 rubles. Ondra suddenly died in 1887 at the age of forty-seven and was succeeded by August Liebig. Liebig had a short and difficult ministry. As a German

---

31. *WHZ*, Sep. 15, 1886, 185–86, and Feb. 25, 1934, 58. *Der Sendbote*, Jan. 9, 1889, 2.

32. For the career of Liebig, see Wardin, "August G. A. Liebig: German Baptist Missionary and Friend to the Mennonite Brethren," *JMS* 28 (2010), 167–86.

33. German Baptist Union, *Jahrbuch*, 1915, 9.

subject, the government exiled Liebig in 1890 to Germany, who then will settle in South Dakota in the USA. The congregation enlarged its building in 1897 to 1,500 seats at a cost of 20, 000 rubles.[34]

Baltic Peoples: Latvians and Estonians

Latvian Baptists

The most extensive German Baptist work in Russia among non-Germans was among the Latvians in Courland and Livonia, which will later extend to the Estonians. The great majority of Latvians and Estonians were traditionally Lutheran, thus giving German Baptists a greater opportunity of winning converts among them than among other peoples. As members of the German Baptist Union, the Baltic Baptists gained from the toleration act of 1879 the same legal rights as German Baptists.

From the baptisms in 1860 and 1861 of Latvians crossing into East Prussia and the first baptism on Latvian soil in the latter year, Latvian Baptists expanded. In the 1870s the Memel church in East Prussia began to give Latvian congregations their independence, which in turn in 1879 formed their own association. In 1880 Latvian Baptists published their first hymnal. In 1881 Jacob Rumberg of the Latvian Baptist Church in Riga began in 1881 *Ewangelists,* the first Latvian Baptist paper, continuing until 1885. In 1882 Rumberg wrote *Atbilde*, a reply to an anti-Baptist polemical work written a year before by a Lutheran pastor.[35]

After the Baltic Association was established, the issue of accepting it into the German Baptist Union of Germany arose in 1882. Rumberg was president of the association. The antagonism of several years back between the German and Latvian congregations, even with an apparent reconciliation, was continuing to fester. Julius Herrmann, pastor of the German Church of Riga, although stating he was not opposed to acceptance, wanted first the advice of a commission. Herrmann declared that Rumberg stirred up race hatred against the Germans among the Latvian brethren. Herrmann also attacked Rumberg's paper, *Ewangelists*, quoting a friend who claimed the paper "contained no Christian content, engaged in antipathy toward Germans, and had a rationalistic coloring." Rumberg countered such claims. After much discussion the conference appointed a commission of six with Rumberg and Herrmann each selecting three of its members.[36]

Before the German Baptist Union met at its next triennial meeting in 1885, the Latvian Baptist church in Riga in January 1884 excommunicated Rumberg, its

---

34. See Kupsch, 148–64, for the history of the church in Lodz to 1904.

35. An excellent account of Latvian Baptist history is the book by Fridrichs Čukers, *et. al.*, eds., *Dzīvas Ceļš*. For an extensive list of bibliographic sources, see Wardin, *Evangelical Sectarianism*, 247–57.

36. German Baptist Union, *Bundes-Konferenz*, 1882, 6–7.

pastor who was also president of the Baltic Association, on differences over his grandiose publishing program. As a result the association divided. Rumberg continued as president with 2,500 adherents, while those opposing him established their own Baltic Association. The 1885 German triennial conference approved the resolution of a conference of ordained members of the Latvian churches that the exclusion of Rumberg was closed. Upon this, seven members, including Rumberg himself and Andreis Vettlers (Andrew Fetler, father of the later dynamic but controversial revivalist, William A. Fetler), read out a declaration of withdrawal. The conference then resolved that Rumberg was no longer a member of the German *Bund* nor to be regarded as a Baptist minister or member and rejected as "only empty words" his withdrawal from the *Bund*.[37]

As noted earlier, two rising young leaders in Latvian Baptist ranks were Janis (John) Inkis (1872–1958) and Janis Frey (1853–1950). Both became pastors of the Latvian Baptist congregation in Riga (The Matthew Church) and editors. Frey knew Latvian, Russian, German, and English, and served as an interpreter for Baedeker on his visits almost annually to the Baltic. In the late 1880s Frey established a publishing house, which will publish a number of calendars.[38] In 1886 Frey wrote and published in 1887 at Rumberg's printing firm a short work, *Baltijas batisti un Bunde, jeb Baltijas baptistu tagadejs stahwoklis* (The Baltic Baptists and the Union, or the Current Situation of the Baltic Baptists). He was concerned over the issue of German or Latvian affiliation. Frey appreciated the contributions and benefits received from the Germans, but he criticized Latvian pastors who intimidated believers for not belonging to the German *Bund* and excluding those who did not belong to it. He claimed that American and British Baptists sustained the German *Bund*, but it in turn gave nothing to Latvian Baptists. In the *Bund's* listing of pastors and churches, names were "misspelled and messed up." It was also too expensive for Latvians to attend its meetings. He noted that only Germans were elected to administer the funds of the *Bund*. In addition, the *Bund* had not sent out one missionary to work among Latvians nor ever published any Latvian tracts. Some support had come from Germans independently of the *Bund* but far less than what Latvians themselves contributed. Frey called for a united Baptist Latvian work by and for Latvians.

Finally in 1893 the two estranged Baltic Associations united with Frey as president, who was just under thirty years of age. In 1899 Frey published, *Zakon-opolozheniya, kasayushchiyasya baptistskago veroucheniya v Rossii*, a booklet on statutes relating to Baptists in Russian, German, and Latvian. It was republished in 1913 with a bit more material. Latvian Baptists increased by 1905 to a little over 7,000 members in seventy-seven congregations and twenty-five stations. In 1905 they had

---

37. For the division, see Čukers, 38–39, and *BMM*, July 1886, 303. German Baptist Union, *Bundes-Konferenz*, 1885, 46.

38. Čukers, 39. For Frey's career, see Kweetin, *A Hidden Jewel*; Riss, "Brat. Ya. A. Freï," *BV*, 1947, no. 7, 39–42; and Kronlins, *Gaisā celā. Der Sendbote*, Nov. 2, 1888, 2.

forty-six chapels and ninety-three Sunday schools with around 4,000 pupils. Beginning in 1890, some Latvian Baptists began to migrate to Brazil for economic reasons. They formed their first church in Rio Novo in Santa Caterina State in March 1895 with seventy-five members.[39]

Estonian Baptists

Baptist work among Estonian Baptists commenced almost twenty-five years after the beginnings among Latvian Baptists. It began simultaneously in 1884 in northern and southern Estonian. It started under the initiative of two German Baptist pastors who baptized the first converts, A. R. Schiewe from St. Petersburg and Julius Herrmann from Riga.

In the 1870s a free church movement began in Estonia, which was sparked by missionaries of the Mission Covenant from Sweden. Some of its adherents began to observe the Lord's Supper and started to baptize each other by sprinkling. Some in the group, disturbed with unorthodox practices and disorderly behavior, sent a delegation of three men to St. Petersburg in 1883 to find a group with which it could unite. They were led to Schiewe who explained for them Baptist principles.[40]

After some correspondence, Schiewe agreed to help establish church order and baptize. He left on February 20, 1884, and after a journey, in part by sleigh, he arrived in Hapsal (Haapsalu) on the western coast where he found spiritual chaos. After examination of the candidates and breaking ice, he baptized on February 23 in the evening fourteen candidates. On the following day, a Sunday, he preached in German on John 3:16, then spoke, possibly in Russian, through an interpreter to the Estonians, and then preached again in German. The assembly then traveled five kilometers with sled to the Baltic Sea, and in spite of threats from opponents who threatened harm Schiewe baptized thirteen more. On return, the assembly celebrated the Lord' Supper. On Tuesday Schiewe baptized two more for a total of twenty-nine and preached four times twice in German and twice though an interpreter who spoke in Estonian.

On a second trip in April, he stopped in Reval (Tallinn) where the governor gave him permission to work unhindered in all Estonia. He baptized seven in the city. In Hapsal the magistrate, with whom the Lutheran pastor had conferred, tried to stop Schiewe, but by telegraphing the governor Schiewe was able to remove the obstacle. Schiewe baptized candidates in Hapsal, on the island of Dago (Dagö), and on the island of Worms (Vormsi), where a woman interpreted for him in Swedish. Upon

---

39. *Unions-Statistik der Baptisten-Gemeinden in Russland*, 1906, 2–5. Ronis, *Uma Epopéia de Fé*, 106.

40. For the beginnings of Estonian Baptist work by Schiewe, see *Der Sendbote*, Jan. 14, 1885, 14–15; Jan. 21, 1885, 26–27; and July 8, 1885, 210; *WHZ*, Apr. 15, 1884, 85; May 1, 1884, 96; Aug. 1, 1884, 161; Oct. 15, 1884, 210–11; and Dec. 15, 1884, 253; *QR*, Oct. 1884, 12–14, and Jan. 1885, 8–11; *BMM*, Feb. 1885, 46; and Oct. 1885, 404–6.

urgent appeals he returned in October a third time. His baptisms in Estonia in 1884 totaled 202. He again returned in 1885. If he could, he would have withdrawn from the mission because of his responsibilities in St. Petersburg. He felt, however, that he must continue to combat what he felt were chaotic errors, and others told him his withdrawal would bring disintegration.

The gains, however, came in the face of strong opposition from officials, belligerent crowds, and lords of the manor, causing much trouble and costs. In Hapsal the magistrate sent police to harass, and a crowd threw stones and broke locks. On Dago a judge forbade meetings, and a crowd headed by the Lutheran teacher and village magistrate besieged the believers. In one locality, the lord of the manor evicted several families for their beliefs. One Estonian paper made a scurrilous attack, declaring a German had introduced a new baptism at three rubles a head with the assurance of gaining heaven. It also stated candidates were baptized through the ice and got sick and died, and others were tested running naked through fire to prove they were not of the devil. The *St. Petersburg Herold,* however, answered the attack.[41]

Schiewe was interested in providing literature in Estonian and found a native to translate some tracts in Estonian-Reval; 10,000 of them were published in Danzig. He hoped that outside help would assist in the expense. He later reported that of the 10,000 he had printed, half were retained by the censor, and he dared not send the others until he saw his way clear.[42]

While Schiewe was engaged in his mission in northern Estonia, Julius Herrmann in Riga entered at the same time into a mission at Pernau (Pärnu) in the south. A group of "praying brethren," the result of a spiritual awakening, were meeting privately. Someone who attended the German services in Riga returned with German tracts and *Der Wahrheitszeuge,* translated some of the tracts, and shared them with the brethren. Upon a division between those who held to baptismal regeneration and those who supported believer's baptism, two of the brethren traveled to Riga for more instruction where they were immersed. Herrmann then came to Pärnu and secretly at midnight on August 31, 1884, baptized seven candidates. The small group, now led by a brother named Mill, who had been baptized in July, soon had a Sunday school and a choral group.[43]

In February 1888, J. Stadling from Stockholm undertook a very cold mission trip to Estonia, including Hapsal, Reval, Worms, and Dago. Stadling preached some in Swedish. In Reval, a former student of The Lutheran Mission School in the city led the work. Because of Seventh-day Adventism, the congregation in Reval excluded six members.[44]

41. For the scurrilous attack, see *WHZ*, Dec. 1, 1884, and Dec. 14, 1884, 253.
42. *QR*, Jan. 1886, 7. *BMM*, Oct. 1886, 403.
43. *WHZ*, Sep. 15, 1884, 190–91; Feb. 15, 1885, 37; and July 8, 1934, 235. *QR*, July 1885, 9–10.
44. *Der Sendbote*, Oct. 3, 1884, 2.

In 1890 in Hapsal for a month, Schiewe led a mission school with ten brethren. Here he also preached almost every evening, resulting in 120 converts. In March 1893 through ice and snow he visited the various mission stations, holding a conference on the island of Dago. On this trip he visited the estate of Baron Woldemar Üxküll, converted in 1890. He was an exceptional convert for his social class and will become a preacher and leader in the German Baptist Union of Russia. Schiewe's forced exile from St. Petersburg in early 1895 will also terminate his ministry of ten years in Estonia.[45]

In 1894 Estonian Baptists formed their first three congregations at Hapsal, Dago, and Reval (Tallinn). In 1896 they established an association that belonged to the Union of Baptist Churches (or German Union) in Russia. In 1904 Andres Tetermann began editing a paper, *Teekäija* (The Pilgrim). In 1905 the Estonian Association included twenty congregations and fifteen stations, 2,169 members, 648 children in twenty Sunday schools, and eighteen chapels.[46]

The Volga

As a result of the manifesto in 1763 of Empress Catherine II of Russia, with promise of religious freedom, self-government, and exemption from military service, Germans from western Europe began to settle along the lower Volga River. Some settled in the provinces of Saratov and Samara on the right bank or *Bergseite* (hill side) on the west, while others on the left bank or *Wiesenseite* (grassland side) on the east. The 104 original settlements expanded to 192 villages and towns. In the 1880s the Volga Germans numbered probably between 250 and 300,000. The 1897 census recorded around 390,000. About 78% were Protestant and 22% Roman Catholic. Sixty-five of the mother colonies were Lutheran and Reformed, served by a limited number of pastors, while the rest were Roman Catholic. It appeared to be a potentially lucrative field for German Baptists, but in contrast to their advance in the Baltic area the field proved to be difficult with limited returns.[47]

In 1880 Severin Lehmann (1847–1918) from Volhynia and Martin Lasch from Russian Poland visited the Volga region on an inspection trip, responding to frequent calls of "Come over and help us." Lehmann was born of Roman Catholic parentage in Baden, Germany, and studied for a short time in Hamburg with Oncken. At the age

---

45. Ibid., Oct. 29, 1890, 2–3, and May 31, 1893, 3. For Üxküll's conversion, see Prestridge, 137–46.

46. *Unions-Statistic der Baptisten-Gemeinden in Russland*, 1906, 6–7.

47. For an excellent account of the Volga Germans in English, see Koch, *The Volga Germans in Russia and the Americas*. For its religious composition, see Stumpp, *German-Russians: Two Centuries of Pioneering*, 20. For population see Lehmann's and Fetzer's estimates in *Der Sendbote*, Jan. 18, 1888, 3, and Sep. 2, 1903, 10. Also see Roland, "The Population of Volga-German Settlements in Late Nineteenth Century Russia," *JAHSGR* 13/4 (Winter 1990), 10–24.

of thirty in 1877 he became pastor of the strong German Baptist church in Neudorf in Volhynia, succeeding Ondra on the latter's expulsion.[48]

Lehmann and Lasch visited areas near Samara (Kuibyshev) and Sarepta, near Tsaritsyn (Volgograd), a Moravian settlement among the Kalmucks, established in 1765. They found open doors and receptive listeners as well as Baptist believers, but the field lacked missionaries to serve them. Even though it was a long journey by way of Kiev, Moscow, and Kazan or by Odessa, Chortitza, and the Don and entailed extended absences from his own church, yet through regular visits (seven by 1887) and recruitment of missionaries and support, Lehmann became the father of the Volga mission.[49]

In June 1881 Lehmann and Gottfried Alf from Russian Poland traveled to the Volga. On Lehmann's trip in October 1881 with Johann Marks from Lucinow, also from Volhynia, a visit was made to a conference of Mennonite Brethren to establish a united mission effort in the Volga. On his first trip, Lehmann had met Mennonite Brethren who were helpful in accommodations and travel. The Mennonite Brethren hesitated to join in united work, stating they feared that union would lead to their giving up footwashing, the kiss of peace (*Gruss* or greeting), and rejection of oaths. Lehmann assured them that he wished no constraints and desired only a union not contrary to the Word of God. Mennonite Brethren continued to have doubts, stating that the Baptist missionary would be the one who would determine what was in accord with God's Word. Although there was no formal union, Mennonite Brethren, however, provided financial support and relief during the Great Famine of 1891–1892.[50]

Lehmann presided at the formation of the first two German Baptist churches in the Volga. The first was at Brunnenthal on the left bank, February 4, 1885 (o.s.) with 110 members, and the second was at Moor on the right bank on Oct. 21, 1885 (o.s.) with 114 members. German Baptists formed two more before the end of 1886—Galka (Ust-Kulalinka) on the right bank (possibly formally organized or reorganized in 1890) and Strassburg on the left bank. The four congregations had fifty-two stations and almost 450 members.[51]

It was difficult to obtain an adequate mission force, and the field depended on mission trips from outsiders and outside support. Johann Marks served from 1883 to 1886 but left for the German Baptist church in Kovno. On a trip to the USA in 1884, Lehmann visited the German Baptist Missionary Society for financial support and recruits for the Volga field. He gained Harm Husmann (1849–1916), a student at the German Department of Rochester Seminary, who graduated in 1885, ordained in 1886

48. Miller, *In the Midst of Wolves*, 20–23.
49. *WHZ*, Mar. 15, 1881, 61. *QR*, Apr. 1881, 9. *Der Sendbote*, Jan. 18, 1888, 3.
50. *WHZ*, Sep. 1, 1881, 168. *Der Sendbote*, Apr. 26, 1883, 2; Feb. 13, 1884, 50–51; and Jan.18, 1888. 3.
51. *Der Sendbote*, Dec. 1, 1885, 235; Jan. 19, 1887, 2; and Jan. 28, 1891, 2. *WHZ*, Apr. 1, 1886, 78. *Der Familienfreund*, Dec. 1926, 5–6.

at the Neudorf church, and began serving in March 1886 at Galka, receiving mission support from Baptists in America. He served thirty years, noted as an earnest pastor who faithfully visited members of his flock. He was pastor in Galka to 1907, then Tsaritsyn one year, and then in Norka until his death in 1916. Further help came from Friedrich Hammer in 1888, who had served a Masurian (Polish-speaking) church in Volhynia, and by 1891 the arrival of two others, Just Lorenz and A. Schleuning.[52]

The field was beset with a number of problems. In a letter to August Rauschenbusch in Rochester, Husmann, the newly arrived missionary from America, noted that many of the converts who had come out of Lutheran pietism had no experience in providing pastoral support. He wrote that the Volga was a "grinding" field, requiring four to five months to cover the whole area. One could not walk it but needed to travel by wagon, without bench or seat, sitting on a bit of straw covered by a pelt. In 1880–1881 Lehmann had found the territory beset by drought and bad harvests. He was concerned about the many unbiblical views of believers and the difficulty to gain property because of restrictive laws within the settlements.[53]

Outside sources heavily subsidized the mission. Lehmann recorded that at the end of 1887 it had received over the previous six to seven years almost 5,800 rubles with over 2,300 from churches in Russian Poland and elsewhere in Russia, 1,000 from a mission friend in Russia, and almost 2,400 from America. Around 1894 Mennonite Brethren in Volhynia contributed money collected by Lehmann that extinguished the debt of about 939 rubles on two Baptist chapels. In addition, the Volga missionaries appreciated receiving from German Baptists in America copies of *Der Sendbote* as well as Sunday school periodicals, *Der muntere Säemann* (The Happy Sower) and *Unsere Kleinen* (Our Little Ones).[54]

The Volga region faced a serious calamity from the Great Famine of 1891–1892 and the following outbreak of a cholera epidemic. Before the end of 1891 German Baptists in America sent sums of money to Husmann, purportedly located in the most affected area. Other funds came from a relief society formed in the English-speaking Baptist church in Newton, Kansas, attracting both Baptist and Mennonite Brethren support. The American Baptist Missionary Union made an appeal.[55]

About the first of 1892 Husmann wrote that "the need increases with each day and help becomes less." He also stated that for many bread and "steppe tea" from the weeds in the field are the only nourishment. Hammer wrote of members growing increasingly weak and could scarcely move. Although he and Husmann received 100 rubles from two German Baptist churches in Volhynia, they found themselves unable

---

52. *WHZ*, May 15, 1884, 64. *Der Sendbote*, Apr. 22, 1885, 13; Sep. 29, 1886, 306; Jan. 11, 1888, 2; Mar. 5, 1890, 2; and Jan. 27, 1892, 2. Colgate-Rochester Divinity School, *Bulletin*, 1819–1930, 255.

53. *Der Sendbote*, Jan. 19, 1887, 2, and Jan. 18, 1888, 3. *QR*, July 1885, 8–9.

54. *Der Sendbote*, Jan. 18, 1888, 3; Jan. 21, 1890, 2; Dec. 23, 1891, 2; and Mar. 14, 1894, 3.

55. Ibid., Jan. 6, 1892, 4–5. *BMM*, Feb. 1892, 31.

to give money to beggars who came to them. In the cholera epidemic Hammer lost two sons.[56] In the spring of 1892 Johann Kessler, treasurer of the German Baptist Union of Russia, met with the local relief committee composed of the four mission pastors, giving 1,400 rubles that he had received from the ABMU. Kessler claimed that by May 1 8,000 rubles for relief had come from America. Hammer noted that he had received at the end of 1892 for relief 5,870 rubles: 791 from local Baptists; 1,300 through Husmann; 1,600 from Kessler; 445 directly from America; and 1,734 from Mennonite Brethren. In a letter of January 1893, Husmann expressed thanks for assistance from abroad. Severin Lehmann, who made trips collecting funds, expressed special thanks to German Baptists and Mennonite Brethren in America as well as Johannes Lübeck in Lodz, Russian Poland, and Philipp Bickel, editor in the Baptist Union in Germany.[57]

In 1893 J. G. Fetzer, professor from the Hamburg Seminary, visited the Volga. He found only four congregations, which showed little expansion. The field continued to be handicapped by lack of workers.[58]

Other Regions

In the Crimea in 1896 Carl Füllbrandt founded at Eupatoria a German Baptist congregation. It remained a small congregation with members distributed over much of the peninsula. In the first years of the twentieth century, the Adventists, who at the time made this area a mid-point of their mission, won over many of its members.[59]

In the fall of 1884 and spring of 1885 Baptists from Kherson Province established in the Caucasus the village of Friedrichsfeld and a few years later the neighboring village of Blumenfeld. Mennonite Brethren from their church in Woldemfürst served their congregation, a number of whom were Mennonites, and also from visiting Baptist pastors. Christian Fischer settled there, and the German Baptist Union of Russia sent a missionary, Busse, to serve. The Friedrichsfeld congregation in 1905 became an independent church. In the same year a congregation was formed at Kronental, about seventy-four kilometers distant, whose first converts were pietistic brethren who accepted believer's baptism. In 1905 *Der Sendbote* reported German Baptists in the Caucasus had 640 members and had constructed new prayer houses, including one in Friedrichsfeld that seated 500.[60]

Two congregations in the Don area, Belagwesch (Bilachwesch) and Kleinliebenthal, were originally composed of Mennonite Brethren members. The majority of

56. *Der Sendbote*, Feb. 3, 1892, 2, and Mar. 9, 1892, 3.
57. Ibid., Aug. 3, 1892, 2, and Feb. 22, 1893, 2–3. *WHZ*, Mar. 4, 1893, 71.
58. *Der Sendbote*, Sep. 2, 1903, 10.
59. For a history of the Eupatoria Church, see Pritzkau, 121–23.
60. For the congregations at Friedrichsfeld and Kronental, see Pritzkau 131–160, noting particularly 142, 146–48, and 152–53. *Der Sendbote*, May 10, 1905, 298.

the members had been Lutheran with some Roman Catholics. As it was illegal for non-Mennonites to become Mennonites, their status as Mennonites could not be sustained. Thereupon they became German Baptist congregations in 1888. Mennonite Brethren who refused to become Baptists migrated to America. Unfortunately the transfer of the Mennonite Brethren to Baptists caused for a time estranged relations between the two bodies, a rift, however, that was later overcome.[61]

German Baptists began to migrate to western Siberia. In commission from the West-Russian Association, Hermann Klempel from Volhynia and a companion traveled by railroad, ship, and wagon to this area where they found 187 members and 423 other adherents. They located a small flock in Omsk with the greatest number, however, at Thora, around 850 kilometers from Omsk. The two brethren baptized thirty-two converts and returned with the plea, "Come and help us."[62]

Publications

Julius Herrmann, after establishing *DerHausfreund*, the first German Baptist paper, a monthly in the Russian Empire in Riga in 1889, continued publishing it after his move to Danzig in 1893. It could not be published in Russia until after the Edict of Toleration in 1905. In 1906 it appeared again in Riga as a weekly under the editorship of Woldemar Üxküll. The German Baptist press in Germany and in the USA supplied printed material for Russia. From the USA not only came *Der Sendbote* but also *Wegweiser* (Signpost), an inspirational leaflet, and Sunday school literature. F. Rosenau, pastor of the church in Cholossna in Volhynia wrote in 1887 to *Der Sendbote*, "Sendbote has become so loved by me that I always read it through with great interest, and when I have scarcely finished with it then I let it travel about among the hungry and thirsty for these also to refresh and revive." *Der Sendbote* carried a surprising amount of material on Baptists in Russia.[63]

Because of expense, some asked or expected to receive literature gratis. Delivery was not always dependable, and periodicals and other literature were subject to the censor who could stop or block out material. In 1886 Herrmann in Riga wrote that the censor there was not as strict as elsewhere but noticed that for the first time the censor had marked out items in black in some issues. In 1887 Frey wrote that the Latvians wanted to publish a booklet in Latvian translation on religious instruction by Christian Rode, but the work was lying at the censor who had not given permission for publication. Frey stated, "Here is seen what difficulties with which we have to struggle."[64]

61. Friesen, 512–13.
62. *Der Sendbote*, Sep. 2, 1903, 552–54.
63. *MO*, Dec. (1) 1904, 1327. *Der Hausfreund*, June 3 (16), 1907, 8, and Nov. 18/Dec. 1, 1909, 368–69. *Der Sendbote*, Oct. 26, 1887, 2; Dec. 14, 1887, 2; Jan. 27, 1892, 2; and Feb. 1, 1893, 3.
64. *Der Sendbote*, June 23, 1880, 202; Jan. 12, 1887, 2; Oct. 26, 1887, 2; and Nov. 2, 1887, 2.

The *Baptist Missionary Magazine* in America printed in 1894 a letter from Russia reporting that the authorities forbade delivery of *Der Wahrheitszeuge* and *Der Sendbote*. The Baptist publishing house in Germany at the time was also publishing *Christlicher Botschafter* (Christian Messenger) especially for Russia, quoting its price in rubles. After the ban, the publishers in Germany attempted, apparently unsuccessfully, to continue publishing *Christslicher Botschafter* under the name *Familien-Altar* (The Family Altar) in Breslau under a dummy editor, a pastor in Frankfort am Main. In 1901 J. G. Fetzer reported that individuals were now receiving as before from Germany *Der Wahrheitszeuge* and *Christlicher Botschafter* but not *Der Sendbote* from the USA.[65]

Education

Only a comparatively few pastors from Russia were able to acquire theological training. Some, however, were able to attend the Mission School or Seminary at Hamburg. These included G. Alf, E. Aschendorf, and J. Vogel from Russian Poland; V. Pavlov from the Russian Baptists; J. Kargel, J. Pritzkau, A. Liebig, K. Ondra, S. Lehmann, J. Harmon, F. A. Müller, E. Mohr, and P. Brandt from the German Baptists; J. Rumberg and J.Riess from Latvia; and probably others. E. Wurch and H. Husmann received training at the German Department of the Rochester Seminary in the USA.[66]

Most German Baptists pastors were farmer preachers who possibly might occupy land on church property. Vasil Martschoff (Marcheff), who attended Hamburg Seminary for four years and then became a pastor in Bulgaria, noted in 1888 that the German Baptist pastors in Volhynia, although "full of the Holy Spirit and wisdom" lacked education. With little time for Bible study and carrying a heavy preaching load that could include six or eight sermons a week, he said they "often stand back from many farmers in Bible knowledge, in religious faith, in freshness of prayer and speech."[67]

The South-Russian Association, organized in 1872, passed a resolution for the need of annual one-month Bible courses. The first one was at Annenthal; others followed at this location and elsewhere. Sessions were later shortened to one week. August Liebig, Karl Ondra, Johann Kessler, Jacob W. Reimer, who was Mennonite Brethren, and even a Methodist, Professor Ströter, who was engaged in Jewish missions, taught. In 1901 in Neu-Danzig, the German conference passed a resolution that churches should establish more elementary schools.[68]

---

65. *BMM*, Oct. 1894, 465. *Der Sendbote*, Feb. 6, 1895, 3, and Sep. 4, 1901, 7. Val'kevich, App. 3, 81, ft. 3, and 117, ft. 3.

66. For students at the Hamburg Mission School before 1880, see Donat, *Das wachsende Werk*, 257–59. *Der Sendbote*, Sep. 2, 1903, 10.

67. *WHZ*, Oct. 1, 1888, 192–93.

68. Prizkau, "Die Gründung der Bibelkurse," 83–91. *WHZ*, Feb. 23, 1901, 62.

PART FIVE—Peril, 1884–1905

Relations with the State

German Baptists were more in alignment with governmental obligations than Mennonites in such matters as participating in civil office, military service, and the oath. On the accession of Alexander III in 1881, Severin Lehmann, then pastor of the Neudorf Church in Volhynia, administered the oath of allegiance to his members. He administered it several times since numbers of members came from great distances.[69]

The gaining of toleration from the state in 1879 brought certain obligations, such as the registration of births, marriages, and deaths, and also bureaucratic restrictions. At the triennial conference of the German Baptist Union in 1888 at Königsberg, Julius Herrmann was critical of the edict for giving the government the right to determine the legality of gatherings and the right to dismiss pastors as well as prohibiting evangelization among ethnic Russians.[70]

In his report from his travel in Russia in 1896, E. Petrick, who served as a Baptist missionary in Assam, India, felt German Baptists were in a rather tolerable if not positive situation. In his preaching, he found no problems. He wrote that the laws were friendlier than their exception. Everything depended on the officials. The Tsar, who has the best intentions, needed to do better to curb officials who fail to function without a bribe. German Baptists did not suffer persecution as the stundists, and converted Lutherans and Roman Catholics may become Baptists without hindrance. He admitted, however, German Baptists faced some limitations such as the need for confirmation of preachers by the provincial governor and permission to build a chapel, but, however, such requests were generally granted. A preacher may preach only in places confirmed by the government, but a regulation not strictly enforced.[71]

In rebuttal to Petrick's statements, *Der Wahrheitszeuge* printed a lengthy article from a certain "R," who had lived in Volhynia, who related from first-hand knowledge cases of undue restriction or suppression. For one thing, the regime, believing the stundists arose out of the German Baptist work, were open to charges and slander against German Baptists. Those who witnessed to a Russian faced punishment and even exile. For permission to build a chapel, the authorities would first ask the local police and priest if they had any objection, and refusal was often given without any reason. Over a year or more a second and third petition might go back and forth with the same result. It was the exception that permission was given without long and many trips and expenditure costing more than the building itself. The same problems also existed in gaining confirmation for a preacher, who may not preach until he received permission.[72]

---

69. *WHZ*, Aug. 15, 1881, 159.
70. German Baptist Union, *Bundes-Konferenz*, 1888, 71.
71. *WHZ*, Sep. 5, 1896, 271, and Oct. 17, 1896, 310–11.
72. Ibid., Dec. 5, 1896, 364.

Writer "R" told of a chapel at a mission station where a chapel had stood empty three years at the time of his exit from Volhynia. At another location, a chapel had burned down and a new chapel bult, but no permission came while the congregation met for three years in summer in barns and in winter in small living quarters, and as far as "R" knew may still be the case. In Kiev Province a mission station received no confirmation for its chapel, but upon a celebration in the building the police sealed it up and left it with smashed windows and decaying walls. At another location, where both the chapel and preacher were not confirmed, the officials sealed up the chapel; after failure of many efforts to open it, it was finally sold. In the Baltic area a congregation waited three years for permission to build, but just shortly before the dedication the governor without any reason issued orders forbidding entrance into the building.[73]

Writer "R" was not the only one with similar cases. Three weeks after the founding of the Ivanovitch church, because of failure of receiving confirmation the authorities sealed the chapel and forbade the pastor, J. Tiedtke, from preaching. After about a year and five months with "many prayers, tears, petitions, trips and money," the authorities opened the chapel and the minister could "now also again freely open his mouth to proclaim the gospel." F. Rosenau, pastor of the church in Colossna, wrote around 1888 that it often took one to two and even three years with the cost of up to 100 rubles to gain confirmation for chapels, preachers, and teachers. He wrote that the chapels of two mission stations of the church were sealed.[74]

H. Husmann in the Volga reported that he could not hold meetings in villages without a confirmed place of meeting. Husmann also stated that an attempt to build a meeting house was not feasible since it would arouse a great community protest. At one time he preached under police surveillance and in the evening faced a four-hour hearing but was released. F. Hammer in the Volga reported in 1892 that the authorities had charged him for fomenting discord for his attacks on infant baptism with even a threat of exile.[75]

In his report of 1903, Fetzer wrote that there were congregations who had petitioned for years to build but have waited in vain. He noted that Eugen W. Mohr, a native of Russian Poland and a graduate of Hamburg Seminary who became pastor of the Neudorf Church in 1897, had not as yet been confirmed after six years in spite of numerous petitions and outlays of money. He pointed out, however, it was not the same everywhere in Russia. Approval of petitions depended on the governors of the various provinces and whether complaints were brought to the authorities from malicious or excluded members or at times Lutheran pastors.[76]

In this period a number of notable German Baptist pastors were exiled. As already noted, two of them were August Liebig from Lodz (1890) and A. R. Shiewe from

73. Ibid., Dec. 5, 1896, 365–66.
74. *Der Sendbote*, Jan. 26, 1882, 2, and Mar. 21, 1888, 2.
75. Ibid., Sep. 29, 1886, 306; Apr. 16, 1890, 2; Mar. 23, 1892, 2; and Sep. 6, 1892, 2.
76. Ibid., Sep. 2, 1903, 10.

St. Petersburg (1895). In 1891 the authorities will force Gottfried Alf, the pioneer in Russian Poland, to terminate his thirty years as pastor of the Kicin church in Plock Province. He will then move to Lublin Province in 1896 where he will die from an accident two years later.[77]

A fourth pastor was Johann Albrecht, born in Russian Poland who became pastor of the church at Rozhishche in 1882. During his ministry he baptized 445 persons and his church reached a membership of 469. In two secret charges, his enemies reported he traveled over the whole region, holding meetings, propagandizing everywhere, and baptizing people whom he seduced from other churches. In 1889 authorities placed Albrecht under surveillance and ordered him to leave Volhynia in eight days. The congregation also lost the right of the use of its building, which was closed.[78]

A fifth pastor was Friedrich A. Müller (1856–1940), born in Prussia, who attended the Hamburg Seminary from 1889–1890 and served the German Baptist church in Lucinow in Volhynia from 1884 to 1892. In this period he baptized 806 persons. By July 1891 his church had grown to 771 members. He distributed Bibles, Testaments, and tracts, and held meetings in private homes, all illegal, and aroused the opposition of Lutheran pastors and Orthodox priests. The authorities sealed two newly built chapels, forcing the people to meet in the woods, but the larger chapel was opened in November 1891. The regime became cognizant of his proselyting among Russians. On one occasion, he baptized under darkness candidates that included several Russians. The authorities ordered his expulsion in 1892; he and his wife crossed on foot into Germany. He migrated to the USA but after a short stay moved to Alberta, Canada.[79]

Although the limitations were often onerous and costly, German Baptists, however, erected and gained confirmation of numerous chapels as well as confirmation for preachers. In the statistics for 1905–1906, German and Baltic Baptists had 145 chapels and 103 ministers. In his report in 1903, J. G. Fetzer wrote that, although German Baptist brethren had to work under certain restrictions, he felt they were not more heavy than they once were and believed better times were coming. And they did in 1905.

German Baptists and Other Christians

As a religious body with German antecedents, it is not surprising that others called German Baptists the "German religion." As F. Kiefer wrote upon his visit to St. Petersburg in 1884, many high officials believed the regime had "blundered" in granting toleration to German Baptists, noted for their aggressive behavior and even threat to

---

77. Wardin, *Gottfried F. Alf*, 85–86.

78. *Der Hausfreund*, Jan. 17, 1926, 27–28. Kupsch, 374–75.

79. *WHZ*, July 15, 1889, 138; and Feb. 17, 1892, 71. *Der Sendbote*, Sep. 9, 1891, 2, and Aug. 31, 1892, 2–3. Val'kevich, 57. Miller, *In the Midst of Wolves*, 218–22, 281–82. Müller's son, Frederick, baptized the author in Portland, Oregon, in 1939.

the Orthodox Church. Many believed that Russian stundism, labeled by the regime a pernicious sect, descended from German Baptists; they were ready to accept accusations and slander against German Baptists for alleged relations to this movement.[80]

Many Russian stundists were claiming to be Baptists in part to gain legal protection under the 1879 act that granted toleration to German Baptists. A. R. Schiewe in St. Petersburg was forced to go to the authorities to deny that certain fanatical groups claiming to be Baptists were not such. On the other hand, German Baptists in Russia and Germany and elsewhere claimed Russian stundists who accepted Baptist views on faith and doctrine, including believer's baptism by immersion, as most were now doing, as essentially Baptists. As the *Baptist Missionary Magazine* in America wrote in 1896, Russian Baptists were "practically a Baptist body." Pavlov wrote in a letter to the ABMU in 1906 that Russian Baptists were as loyal to Baptist tenets as Regular Baptists in America.[81]

A book in 1897 by Mikhail Kal'nev on Germans and Stundo-Baptism or the Orthodox periodical *Missionerskoe obozrenie* in 1896 in its section on the foreign sectarian world claimed the links between German Baptists and Russian stundists were extremely close. But now the time came when it was important for Russian authorities to claim that the two groups were fundamentally distinct to stop stundists from gaining immunity under the 1879 edict. A prime example of the latter view appeared in an article by N. Belogorskiĭ in 1900 in *Missionerskoe obozrenie*, claiming the two groups had only an outer similarity but no true identity. He asserted stundists, gaining their creed from various sources, differed among other things over justification by faith and in worship and church structure.[82]

Although German Baptists needed to take care in witnessing among the Russian population, yet their witness continued through personal contact and even in German services. Authorities were concerned when Russian was used in German Baptist services that attracted Russians. On his trip to Russia in 1884, G. G. Kliewer reported holding a meeting in the Volga in which both Germans and Russians were present. Kliewer spoke in German, which was interpreted into Russian, and both Russian and German hymns were sung. German Baptists sometimes served as experts in stundist trials.[83]

Except for Mennonite Brethren whom German Baptists considered one in faith and practice, relations with other bodies were often strained or even hostile, such as with Orthodox and Lutherans, who feared aggressive Baptist proselytism. In 1892

---

80. Letter of Kiefer, Jan. 23, 1884. *WHZ*, Oct. 17, 1896, 311, and Dec. 5, 1896, 364.

81. *BMM*, Nov. 1896, 531–32. Letter of Pavlov, Aug. 7, 1906.

82. Kal'nev, *Nemtsy i stundobaptizm*, *MO*, May–June (1) 1896, 63–84, and Nov. 1900, 481–501. For other articles on the relations of German Baptists and stundists, see Wardin, *Evangelical Sectarianism*, 226.

83. *MO*, June (1), 1897, 531–32; Jan. 1900, 136–37; and Sep. (1) 1903, 396. *Der Sendbote*, Apr. 16, 1884, 122. Latimer, *Under Three Tsars*, 104.

Harm Husmann in the Volga wrote that Lutheran pastors sought most anything to hinder them. In the same year Johann Kessler wrote that Lutheran pastors sought not only to hinder but gladly use the arm of the civil authority to inflict injury.[84]

Even with groups with the same evangelical or pietistic faith, relations that may have been mutually beneficial became uncharitable or antagonistic. German Baptists with their aggressive evangelism and strict close communion created barriers. They rejected Pashkovites who held to open communion and infant baptism. Plymouth Brethren, who accepted believer's baptism by immersion, were nevertheless rivals with differences over polity, including open communion. E. H. Broadbent, a leading Plymouth Brethren evangelist, criticized Baptists for imposing on Russian stundism a denominational structure with senior pastors instead of a plurality of elders.[85]

German stundists or pietists, called Church Brethren, who remained members of their Lutheran or Reformed churches and held to infant baptism, resented German Baptist intrusions. In 1884 a certain "Kl." (probably Kludt who served with Liebig in the Odessa region) wrote that the Church Brethren regarded Baptists as stepbrethren or even seducers. In many places they drew up resolutions to terminate all relations with Baptists including the holy kiss and warned their members to refrain from going to Baptist meetings. Church Brethren held their first conference in 1871 in the Volga, insisting that members maintain their membership in the established Lutheran or Reformed churches.[86]

German Baptists expressed hostility toward Seventh-day Adventists for their proselytism in the same way others felt toward Baptists in their evangelism. In 1887 a co-worker with Liebig in the Odessa region wrote that the Adventists were causing much trouble and he hoped "that the members in question will soon sober down again." In 1886 Husmann noted that Adventist literature circulated from North America and indicated appreciation for the article in German by August Rauschenbusch, "Should We Celebrate Saturday or Sunday?" In 1900–1902, as already noted, Adventists gained members from the German Baptist church in Eupatoria in Crimea. Kessler in 1901 stated that Adventists were having success among German Baptists but claimed some had been reclaimed.[87]

Statistics

In 1880 German Baptists, including their Latvian members, claimed 8,000 members with concentration in the border regions of Russian Poland and the Baltic as well as Volhynia, a frontier region for Germans, and near Odessa. In spite of emigration to

---

84. *Der Sendbote*, Mar. 23, 1892, 2, and Aug. 3, 1892, 2.
85. Broadbent, *The Pilgrim Church*, 34–42.
86. *WHZ*, Apr. 15, 1884, 85.
87. *BMM*, May 1887, 140, and July 1902, 230. *Der Sendbote*, Sep. 29, 1886, 306. Pritzkau, 123.

America, their numbers continued to grow with 17,041 in 1893 in 99 churches and 320 mission stations and a bit over 24,000 in 1905.[88]

In 1905 the greatest concentration was the same as it was in 1880. Only sixty percent in the Union were German. The Latvian Association numbered 7,100 with 77 congregations. The Estonian Association, beginning as recently as 1884, had grown to 2,200 members and 20 congregations.

German Baptists were comparatively weak in St. Petersburg and Riga, port cities with large German populations. The church in Lodz, however, had over 1,500 members, The Volga field possessed only four churches and around 600 members in the midst of a large German population. German Baptists also continued to be very weak in central Ukraine, the traditional heartland of Mennonite settlements. They were beginning to enter a new field in Ufa and Siberia, claiming around 200 members.

---

88. MO, Dec. (1), 1904, 1328. *Unons-Statistik der Baptisten-Gemeinden in Russland*, 1906, 10.

PART SIX

*Possibilities and Uncertainties,
1905–1917*

23

The Russian Baptist Union

The New Era, 1905–1908

ON EASTER SUNDAY MORNING, April 17, 1905, in the "Red Hall" of the Lieven Mansion in St. Petersburg, Princess Nathalie Lieven with "joyful countenance" announced that one of the brethren would bring joyful news. The brother then read the manifesto Tsar Nicholas II had issued that day granting religious freedom to Religious dissenters, including the evangelicals that Pobedonostsev had suppressed so long. After the reading, the assembly knelt in prayer with thanksgiving and praise. Jakob Kroeker later wrote that evangelicals had been called to St. Petersburg for a conference on Easter but on the evening before Easter received an invitation to meet in the morning for news of a "joyous surprise" but no information as to its content.[1]

The Edict of Toleration of 1905 was sweeping. It granted dissenters legalization, which religious bodies of foreign origin, such as Mennonites and German Baptists, had enjoyed for years. It fulfilled the promise of toleration of the manifesto issued December 12. It specifically rescinded the Edict of July 4, 1894, which had outlawed stundism. Free church evangelicals could now legally conduct worship services, own property, construct buildings, establish charitable institutions and elementary schools, publish religious literature, and import religious books. The government also exempted their pastors from military service. As other religious bodies, evangelicals would now be responsible for recording births, marriages, and deaths. Members of the Orthodox Church were granted the right of transfer to another faith without loss of

---

1. See Sophie Lieven, 92, for the announcement of the Manifesto. For Kroeker's description, see *The Friend of Russia*, May 1920, 42.

civil rights. On June 25 a further manifesto freed individuals imprisoned or exiled for religious violations. A year and a half later on October 1906 another manifesto issued regulations to implement the April 1905 manifesto. Neither manifesto granted the right of proselyting, a right reserved to the Orthodox Church.[2]

The manifestos did not appear in a political or social vacuum but in a period of revolutionary change. With a growing proletariat, the demands of liberal and socialist groups for democratic reform, the lack of success in the Russo-Japanaese War, the massacre of "Bloody Sunday" on January 9, 1905, and strikes, the Tsar was forced in February to promise a consultative Duma or assembly. The revolutionary tide, however, was so strong that on October 17 he issued a manifesto that transformed Russia into a constitutional monarchy, guaranteeing personal rights and a representative Duma or assembly with legislative powers. On October 19 Pobedonostsev, whose influence had been on the wane for some time, lost his position as procurator of the Holy Synod and will die in 1907.[3]

Baptists and other evangelicals not only celebrated their new freedoms but immediately took advantage of evangelistic opportunities. At the European Congress in Berlin in 1908, V. G. Pavlov stated that Baptists immediately undertook an aggressive evangelistic effort, holding meetings in lecture halls, theaters, and homes. Baron Üxküll reported in September 1905 that in Odessa he had preached in an unoccupied Orthodox Church that had been given to Baptists. The German Baptist paper, *Der Hausfreund*, and the Mennonite Brethren paper, *Friedensstimme*, both published abroad, began publishing in Russia itself in 1906. A new periodical, *Khristianin*, appeared at the same time published by Ivan S. Prokhanov, who had formerly published the underground paper, *Beseda*. In 1906 Pavlov wrote that the persecution that was still continuing here and there was not from the government; in fact, the police were now protecting the large religious gatherings in theaters and club houses in various cities. In 1908 *Der Hausfreund* wrote that the terrible time of persecution of Russian evangelicals was now only a historical fact and new mission opportunities beckoned. In the same year Commissioner Railton of the Salvation Army noted with astonishment the large Baptist churches on major thoroughfares with announcements on front.[4]

Only one month after the Manifesto of 1905, the Russian Baptist Union met in its annual congress in May in Rostov-on-Don, with Deï Mazaev president as before. Over one hundred representatives attended. The old veteran and first native Russian baptized in 1867, Nikita I. Voronin, after arriving at the congress, suddenly took ill

---

2. For a description of the 1905 Manifesto and for its first two sections in English translation followed by a short decription of the remaining sections, see Blane, 41–42, 265–67.

3. For the revolutionary changes in 1904–1905, see Florinsky, 1168–83. For Pobedonostsev's last years, see Byrnes, 358–68.

4. European Baptist Congress, *Proceedings*, 1908, 158. *BMM*, Feb. 1906, 279. Letter of Pavloff, Aug. 7, 1906. *Der Hausfreund*, April 2/15, 1908, 109. *The War Cry*, May 30, 1908. 1.

and died. In light of the manifesto, the congress wrestled over several issues. It resolved to purchase property in towns to erect prayer houses but believers in villages were to gather in private homes. In the lack of means to erect schools, children of believers were to obtain instruction in Orthodox schools. The congress wanted pastors to be exempt from registering births, marriages, and deaths and be replaced by an elected official of the church for the task. It also wished pastors to be exempt as village officials, although lay persons were admonished to serve conscientiously in such posts. With a continuing concern for evangelism, the congress resolved to send out four missionaries to serve a year in outlying districts and thirteen others for a half year itinerating in adjoining settlements.[5]

The Russian Baptist Union, however, did not represent all evangelicals. In a letter in August 1906, Pavlov noted that the Russian Baptist Union included possibly 20,000 members, the German Baptist Union, 25,000, the Mennonite Brethren almost 10,000, and the Pashkovites with possibly three to five thousand. Pavlov observed that the Pashkovites were still "fluctuating" but were beginning to form churches with many of them, however, not accepting the Baptist name. The congress was particularly glad to include Pashkovites from St. Petersburg, now calling themselves Evangelical Christians. In writing some years later in 1911, Mazaev recalled rapturously that the Baptists "almost began to forget that they were Baptists" and "our hearts were filled with joy and our mouths merriment, and we awaited great expectations."[6] The Baptist World Alliance (BWA) held its first congress in London in July 1905. Its inaugural congress came at a most propitious time for Russian Baptists. The BWA will play an important role in Russian Baptist affairs, eclipsing somewhat the Evangelical Alliance in financial support and advocacy of religious liberty in Russia. This organization gave Russian Baptists solidarity in a world movement of six million that included strong constituencies in Germany, Sweden, England, and the USA.

The Russian Union elected Vasiliĭ G. Pavlov, Vasiliĭ V. Ivanov, and Deĭ Mazaev as delegates to the Baptist meeting in London. Baron Üxküll was also present representing the German Baptist Union of Russia. Ivan (Johann) Kargel, now identified with the Pashkovites in St. Petersburg and no longer a Baptist, was seen by Pavlov at the congress. In the roll call of nations, Pavlov was unexpectedly taken by surprise to bring the welcome from Russia although the Russian Baptist Union was not listed as an official member. Pavlov, speaking publicly for the first time in English, apologized for his broken English, spoke of the past suppression, including his own exile, and noted the increased although not yet complete freedom in Russia. Baron Üxküll followed with a few words. Later in the congress Üxküll spoke at great length narrating past history and the present status of Baptists, followed by Mazaev, interpreted by Üxküll, who also spoke of the past suppression. Üxküll will receive criticism from

5. *MO*, Aug. 1905, 291–95. *Istoriya*, 141–42, 522.

6. Letter of Pavloff, Aug. 7, 1906. Deï Mazaev, "Ne ta doroga," *Baptist*, 1911, no. 34, 268. *Istoriya*, 141–42.

PART SIX—Possibilities and Uncertainties, 1905–1917

some delegates from the South in the USA for his entertaining at a luncheon black Baptists with other Russian delegates.[7]

The 1906 Russian Baptist Congress again met in May with over 100 present from twenty-two provinces and *oblasti* (regions). Eighty-seven were representatives from the churches with seventeen on invitation from Mazaev, the president. I. F. Izaak from the Rückenau Mennonite Brethren Church was also enrolled. Besides Ukraine, Caucasus, the Don, and Lower Volga, St. Petersburg was again represented. Pavlov with others who had separated from the Tiflis church in support of two excluded members who allegedly had married unlawfully were not present. The congress, supporting the Tiflis church, admonished Pavlov and his adherents to repent and accept the church's decision. It was reported that twenty paid evangelists and seven unpaid volunteers served the field. The congress thanked the American Baptist Missionary Union in the USA for its gifts, which sent 400 rubles during the first half of the year, and Gavriil Vasil'evich Mazaev (not Deï's brother) who contributed 1,000 rubles.[8]

Deï Mazaev and V. V. Ivanov gave reports on the 1905 congress of the Baptist World Alliance with the congress charging them to produce a printed account of the trip. It also thanked William A. Fetler, then a student from Latvia at Spurgeon's College in London, for serving free of charge as an interpreter at the congress. It also thanked Ivan P. Kushnerov for his judicial work since 1894, an effort that included gathering statistical information and extensive correspondence. Besides compensating him with an annual allowance, it gave him a special reward of 250 rubles. The congress suggested the need of a congress in Omsk, Siberia, and proposed sending I. K. Savel'ev and N. V. Odintsov for assistance. In a footnote to the minutes, the Orthodox editor noted that strangely the congress expressed no gratitude for the freedom granted to it in the Manifesto of 1905.

Evangelical leaders, although enjoying the freedom they now had been granted, wanted, however, changes in the law that would benefit them even more. Soon after the Manifesto of October 17, 1906, a regional preliminary consultative congress of "Christians-Baptists of the Evangelical Faith and Evangelical Christians" met in December in Kiev. Seventy-six delegates from Kiev and neighboring provinces attended. Delegates included two German Baptists—-Johann Pritzkau and F. M. Brauer—and three Mennonite Brethren—Jakob Kroeker, A. A. Reimer, and P. P. Ediger. Russian Baptists predominated. The two German Baptists and Kroeker with Reimer as an interpreter in Russian brought messages. The congress chose Kushnerov as presiding officer.[9]

---

7. For accounts of the participation of Baptists from Russia at the congress, see BWA, Congress, *Proceedings*, 1905, 7–8, 182–85; *Baptist Times and Freeman*, July 14, 1905, supplement, vi, viii, ix, xvii, xxi; *Bratskii listok*, 1906, no. 5, 29–30, and 1906, no. 6, 10. Pavlov, "Diary" (mns.), June 24–29, 1905 (o.s.) for his visit in London. Pius, *An Outline of Baptist History*, 54.

8. For the 1906 congress, see *MO*, Oct. 1906, 459–69.

9. For minutes of the preliminary congress, see *Bratskii listok*, 1907, no. 1, 12–14. Also see the account of Brauer, "Unser Besuch in Kijew," *Der Hausfreund*, Feb.7/20, 1907, 41–43.

A united congress of evangelical rights that quickly followed in January 1907 in St. Petersburg was reminiscent of the St. Petersburg Congress of 1884. It numbered seventy delegates. It included not only Russian Baptists, the dominant group led by Deï Mazaev, but also Pashkovites/Evangelical Christians, and Christians of the Evangelical Faith (New Molokans). It also included again Brauer and Reimer as well as Janis Inkis, a Latvian Baptist. N. F. Höijer and Johannes Svensson, missionaries of the Swedish Mission Covenant, and Walter L. Jack, who worked with the Deutsche Orient Mission. It elected Johann Kargel, the old veteran, as presiding officer, but because of physical weakness much of the leadership fell to Mazaev, the vice-president. In some respects it was a unity congress of evangelicals, but with Baptists rejecting the concept of baptized infants as members of the church, the New Molokans, who practiced infant baptism, left before the conference ended. After the conference, Johannes Svensson and Walter L. Jack, supporters of infant baptism, wrote scathing accounts of the conference for the intransigence of the Baptists under Mazaev.[10]

The congress suggested changes in over half of the fifty-seven articles in the Manifesto of October 17, 1906. The congress wanted to expand the first article to include the right to engage in "personal conversation, preaching and the printed word." Other desired changes included expanding the right to hold prayer meetings in places designated for the purpose in private homes and quarters; to lower the requirement of a minimum of fifty signatures to twenty-five from both sexes in requesting the formation of a congregation; to lower the minimum age of twenty-five to twenty-one, the age of civil majority, for congregational voting; the right to acquire property without imperial approval and unlimited in monetary value; the right to appeal to the circuit court of the decision of a governor suspending a congregation; and rejecting the need of confirmation by a governor for its spiritual leaders. The congress also wished to relieve pastors of the responsibility of keeping a civil registry and to allow the church to elect an individual for this responsibility. Besides freed from military service, the congress also wished pastors be freed from other public obligations. The congress felt the Manifesto gave too much discretion to the administration, but if a better law was not forthcoming it was prepared to utilize the present law as it was.[11]

Even though evangelicals did not gain the modifications they sought, they nevertheless, in spite of some church closings, operated in a time of comparative freedom. One church that was closed in 1908 was an evangelical congregation in Kiev on whose council Kushnerov served, apparently for allowing a Jewish convert to preach.

---

10. See *Bratskiĭ listok*, 1907, no. 2, 7–24, for a full account of the congress, including suggested changes and reasons for changes. Also see Alexandr I. Vvdenskiĭ, *Deĭstvuyushchiya zaknopolozheniya kasatel'no staroobryadtsev i sektantov*, 176–92. For a short account, see *Baptist*, Aug. 1907, 13–15. For two accounts of the conference, strongly criticizing Baptist intransigence, see Jack, "Zwei Konferenzen in Petersburg," *Der christliche Orient*, Mar. 1907, 36–41, and Svensson, *De ewangeliska kristnas konferens i St. Petersburg den 28. Jan.–5 febr. 1907*.

11. For an Orthodox reaction to the congress's proposals, see "Domogatel'stva sektantstva," *MO*, July–Aug. 1907, 969–71.

PART SIX—Possibilities and Uncertainties, 1905–1917

In Elisabetgrad the provincial administration refused to recognize a congregation of Evangelical Christians-Baptists since, as a Russian congregation, it could not establish a relationship with the German Baptists. Censors might still block importation of religious material. A package sent to Riga in 1908 containing a hymnal, a manual for Sunday school teachers, and a biography of Charles Spurgeon, was returned to the sender stamped with the words, "Circulation Prohibited."[12]

On the other hand, the Ministry of Interior Affairs at this time served as a protector of sectarian rights. On the basis of many complaints, it declared closures of churches illegal based on the Manifesto of October 1906. When the Holy Synod closed Baptist prayer houses in St. Petersburg, evangelicals reacted with indignation and were determined to meet in private homes if necessary, appealing to the Manifesto of 1905. The Ministry of Interior Affairs countermanded the orders of the Holy Synod.[13]

In January 1908, as reported in *Missionerskoe obozrenie*, the Orthodox journal, the governor of Kherson Province granted to T. P. Balikhin, affectionately called by his followers, "Teodor Prokhorovich," to hold a meeting in Elisabetgrad from January 20 to 25, 1908. At one of the services, Balikhin spoke of "the gift of freedom of religion to Russian citizens" and "a miracle of the grace of God" while at the same time shedding tears in remembrance of the Stundo-Baptist leader Ryaboshapka who was persecuted and died abroad. The service of over two hours concluded with three hurrahs for the Tsar.[14]

In a trip to Russia in 1908, J. B. Kilburn from the Evangelical Alliance reported finding that religious freedom was a reality and in St. Petersburg Christian meetings were conduced openly in twenty centers. In an article entitled, "Actual Religious Conditions in Russia," in *Missionary Review of the World* in January 1909, Baron Üxküll declared that Russia now had religious liberty, while noting that police may, however, illegally cause difficulties at the instigation of the Orthodox clergy. He was very critical of the Duma, claiming that this body had in it only two genuine evangelicals, Zakharov and Bergman. At the First European Baptist Congress in Berlin in 1908, Pavlov gave perhaps a realistic picture but with some possible exaggeration when he stated that Baptists do not as yet have full liberty. He stated that all meetings are held "only by permission of either the Minister of the Interior or the governor of the province, and the local authorities, co-operating with the clergy, have often endeavored by every possible means to prevent our people from assembling." He also noted that in

---

12. *Bratskiï listok*, 1908, no. 11, 12–14. Yasevich-Borodaevskaya, 622–24. *Baptist Times and Freeman*, Sep. 4, 1908, 619.

13. *Baptist*, 1908, no. 11, 39. *Der Hausfreund*, Nov. 19/Dec 2, 1908, 371. BWA, *Minute Books*, 1904–1931, Continental Committee, Jan. 28, 1909. Nesdoly, 313, 324, quoting Prugavin, *Raskol vverkhu*, 260–61.

14. *MO*, May 1908, 788–93.

numerous villages the police break up meetings, and Baptists were also subject to ill treatment from mobs.[15]

The 1907 congress again met in Rostov-on-Don. Because of the delay in receiving governmental permission for the congress, invitations were delayed, which in part probably explains the low attendance of around fifty representatives. Also representatives were lacking from Moscow and St. Petersburg. Nevertheless the congress undertook some notable actions. It brought reconciliaton with the dissidents of the Tiflis church by accepting back into the Union V. G. Pavlov, who will now play a leading role in its affairs, and A. M. Mazaev. The congress approved *Baptist*, its new journal, as well *as* Deï. Mazaev as editor along with a publication committee of Pavlov and I. K. Savel'ev. It also guaranteed 1,000 rubles in case of financial loss. *Baptist* began publishing as a monthly in 1907 in Rostov-on-Don. It also accepted with some modification the draft of the constitution of a new Baptist Missionary Society, formed earlier in the month, with Pavlov as president. The supporters of the new society argued that for the cause of missions it was necessary to form a self-sustaining organization with its own administration. Support would come from dues of the members of the society. For those who feared that the Union would now be left with little or no responsibility, Pavlov pointed out the Union nurtured the unity and prosperity of the churches, established a publishing society, formed a fund for disabled preachers, including their widows and orphans, provided loans for construction of prayer houses, and looked to establishing a seminary for preachers. The congress elected a commission to consider establishing a missionary school.[16]

The Russian Baptist Union met in May 1908 in Kiev. Its meeting in this city, a major center of Russian Orthodoxy, showed a growing energy and confidence of the Union after being marginalizied so long in meeting in the Lower Volga, Don, and Caucasus regions. Fifty-six with the right to vote were in attendance. In the absence of Deï Mazaev, the president of the Union, the congress elected I. K. Savel'ev as presiding officer. The congress included not only representatives from Russian Baptist churches but also three representatives from the German Baptist Union of Russia—Johann Pritzkau from Alt-Danzig, O. G. Truderung, representing the Lodz Seminary, and A. E. Wuerch from Volhynia—as well as O. F. Lentz, a German Baptist pastor from Kovno. Other guests with the right of voting included L. L. Rosenberg, missionary to the Jews in Odessa, and P. P. Perk, a Mennonite Brethren. All four German Baptists preached at missionary meetings held in the evening apart from conference sessions or at the Sunday services. On the Sabbath L. L. Rosenberg lectured in "classical Hebrew" on Psalm 41 in a hall filled with Jewish listeners. He also spoke in German with Pavlov as interpreter. William Fetler, the young pastor

---

15. *EC*, Nov.–Dec. 1908, 140. *MRW*, Jan. 1909, 35–38. European Baptist Congress, *Proceedings*, 1908, 158.

16. For minutes of the 1907 congress and formation and first meeting of the Baptist Missionary Society, see *Baptist*, 1907, no. 2, 15, 16, 19–24.

from the Russian-Latvian congregation in St. Petersburg, a rising star in Baptist ranks, preached Sunday morning with others at which time the Lord's Supper was observed. P. P. Perk offered to send A. G. Raevskiĭ, a director, to assist churches in their choirs, an offer that the congress accepted with thanks.

The congress resolved to begin in January 1909 publishing *Baptist* each week. The congress, although approving a committee for donations for building a Russian Baptist seminary, approved in the meantime the sending of young men to the Lodz German Baptist Seminary with the request to the churches for funds for their support. The congress accepted Fetler's proposal of building a home for the Union in St. Petersburg and appointed a committee to accept contributions for it. It also approved collecting money from the churches for constructing an almshouse or workhouse, the place to be later determined. The congress voted to send Deĭ Mazaev to the first European Baptist Congress in Berlin in August. It voted to send a telegram to Martin Kalweit, the veteran Baptist in the Caucasus, on the fiftieth anniversary of his conversion and fifty rubles each to the widows of Nikita Voronin and Ivan Ryaboshapka.[17]

Russian Baptists held a Youth and Sunday School Congress in Moscow in 1908. In the following year at Rostov-on-Don it held its First All-Russian Congress of Youth Circles and Sunday Schools.[18] In 1908 the first European Baptist Congress was held from August 29 to September 3 (n.s.) in Berlin. It drew 1,800 delegates from much of Europe. From Russia ninety-eight attended that included Russians (with fifteen from the Russian Baptist Union), Germans, Finns, Estonians, and other nationalities. V. G. Pavlov was the most prominent with a major address but also other leaders, including Martin Kalweit from Tiflis, V. V. Ivanov from Baku, T. P. Balikhin from Astrakhanka, N. V. Odintsov from Balashov, and William Fetler from St. Petersburg were present. Mazaev did not attend because of ill health. Many of the Russians knew neither German nor English, the official languages of the congress, but interpreters, including Fetler and Pavlov and others, whispered an interpretation in their ears. In his review of the congress, Pavlov wrote that the Russian brethren could see with their own eyes "how great is our church, broadcasting to all the world also that Baptists are not a despised sect but are composed of great power in the hands of Christ to spread His kingdom and for us there are no reasons to be ashamed of our name Baptist and replace it with another."[19]

In his message to the congress, "The Rise, Growth and Present Position of the Baptist Body in Russia," read in German, Pavlov first described the two origins of Baptists in Russia, the stundists in Ukraine and the Molokans in the Caucasus, but

17. For the Kiev conference and missionary meetings, see *Baptist*, July 1908, 17–19, and Aug. 1908, 16–18.

18. *Baptist*. 1908, no. 10, 12; 1909, no. 23, 8–21; and no. 24, 6–14. *Pervyĭ vserossiĭskiĭ s"ezd kruzhkov baptistskoĭ molodezhi yunosheĭ i devits.*

19. For the congress in Berlin, see European Baptist Congress, *Proceedings*, 1908; Pavlov "Evropeĭskiĭ congress baptistov v Berline," *Baptist*, 1908, no. 11, 24–35; and *Baptist Times and Freeman*, Sep. 4, 1908, 614, and Sep. 11, 1908, 629.

leaving out the Pashkovites. He then described Baptist growth but also persecution under Pobedonostsev, including his own exile, which was followed by the present era of freedom but, as previously noted, still beset by restriction and some persecution. He noted that Baptists have grown across the nation and now produced five publications, four of which were for general edification. In conclusion he declared the necessity for theologically trained ministers, the need for a theological college, production of "a healthy literature," and a Building Society for the erection of chapels, along with an appeal for financial support from England and America.[20]

In spite of the current freedom, the congress continued to dwell on past suppressions. After the evening services, social times with conversation and refreshments were devoted to "Heroes of the Faith." After the Sunday evening service at one of the social times, Pavlov and Kalweit spoke in German and Odintsov in Russian, interpreted into German by Kalweit, about persecution and exile. In his speech at the congress, "Baptists as Champions of Liberty of Conscience," Pastor Saillens from Paris hailed the revolutionary changes in Russia for liberty of conscience but also dwelt on the past sufferings of believers. In his inaugural address, John Clifford, president of the Baptist World Alliance, in light of the Missionary Congress of the Orthodox Church in Kiev in 1908, condemned the Russian Orthodox Church by stating, "It is not only non-progressive, it is most reactionary, so far as I can see, the persecution of our friends in Russia by the authorities of the State Church is likely to be fiercer than ever." He also added, the prelates of this church "misrepresent the Christ in whose name they profess to preach, and sap the sources of moral and spiritual progress."[21] The Congress passed a resolution on international peace. It approved a resolution on liberty of conscience, stating that Baptist churches are not political and not allied with any revolutionary party or program and regretted that in much of Europe restrictions continue for freedom of conscience.

The vitality and strength of the Russian Baptist Union were evident in its continuing spread and the appearance of regional congresses. In July 1907 the Siberian Department of the Russian Baptist Union met in Omsk, Siberia, with representatives from twelve congregations and two guests. Gavriil I. Mazaev, the brother of Deï Mazaev, was president and A. L. Evstratenko, who had been exiled to Siberia, was vice-president. Gavriil began serving the Omsk congregation in 1905 where at his own expense he built a large meeting house seating 2,000. The congress in Omsk heard mission reports from the two officers and six others on their mission work in 1906. It also formed its own missionary society. A regional congress in Stavropol Region in April 1909 with eighty-three representatives formed a Caucasus Department of the Russian Union. In 1907 a number of regional congresses were held in Kharkov, Odessa, Kiev, Rostov-on-Don, and Novouzensk.[22]

20. For Pavlov's speech in English, see European Baptist Congress, *Proceedings*, 1908, 152–60.
21. *Baptist*, 1911, no. 11, 27. European Baptist Congress, *Proceedings*, 1908, 53, 114.
22. *Baptist*, Oct. 1907, 8–17, and Apr. 1909, 17–20. *Istoriya*, 140.

24

Russian Baptist Union

The Era of Reaction, 1909–1914

IN CONTRAST TO THE previous era, the Era of Reaction will prove to be one of the most complex periods for Russian Baptists in the Tsarist period. External and internal relations become more intense and antagonistic, and more players enter the field. The Tsarist regime, never truly accepting democratic reform, and the Orthodox Church, attempting to regain its lost position, became increasingly reactionary and hostile toward evangelicals. Evangelicals themselves heightened the tension by their aggressiveness and growth.

The Russian Baptist Union itself will experience strain within its own leadership. Evangelical Christians, emerging from the Pashkovite movement, will become a strong competitor that will lead to acrimonious charge and countercharge. In theological education, competing parties, including the government, will attempt to further their own agendas, leading to difficult relations and unsatisfactory results. The Baptist World Alliance, a new organization in Russian Baptist affairs, will be both a strength and a stumbling block. A new dynamic evangelical movement, Pentecostalism, will suddenly appear on the horizon, causing concern. Yet through all the difficulties, Baptists and other evangelicals will continue to grow while experiencing both triumph and defeat.

Church Relations

With democratic reform, the relations between evangelicals and the Orthodox Church did not improve and were as bad as ever if not worse. The Orthodox Church no longer held the legal and judicial powers it possessed under Pobedonostsev to suppress dissidents, but it did not make it any less antagonistic. With their new freedoms, evangelicals were now even more of a threat, disregarding as before the laws against proselytism.

In noting the growth of evangelicals, the Orthodox falsely claimed that foreign missionaries were pouring in. The growth, however, was indigenous. In 1910 the procurator of the Holy Synod noted the "unusual intensity" of the propaganda of sectarians, including Baptists and Evangelical Christians, in all dioceses in Russia. He noted that Baptists furthered their goals with mixed choirs, practicing baptisms publicly accompanied by choirs with moving melodies. He complained that in conversation with sectarians the ill-informed Orthodox finds himself "in the clutches of the texts of the Holy Scripture ably juggling before him with a solution of this or other debatable question." Their propaganda as well is persistent and reaches into locations where sectarian prayer houses are not legalized. They spread their literature even in purely Orthodox areas and in youth circles. In their Sunday schools and youth work, Baptists have also now turned special attention to the moral and mental education of youth.[1]

In an article in 1911 in *Missionerskoe obozrenie*, "In the Depths of Sectarianism," the author stated that in all mission reports "the Orthodox Church had never yet been subjected to such a frightful onslaught from the propagandists-sectarians, as now." He also declared, "Not one of our rationalistic and mystical sects has so quickly and broadly spread in Russia as the sect of the Stundo-Baptists." The author pointed to "its wild fanaticism" and the bellicosity and danger of its missionary organizations.[2]

Another article in the same periodical, "Chief Center. Means and Ways. Publications," noted that Evangelical Christians, whose center had been St. Petersburg and Moscow, like the Baptists, whose center had been Rostov-on-Don, now publish in Odessa. It recognized also the importance of aggressive young leadership within both the Evangelical Christians and Baptists. It noted that in Prokhanov, the leader of the former, one could not deny his energy and impertinence and also his organizational talent. For Fetler, a leader in the latter, it stated that he had been able to install the main headquarters of Russian Baptists in his congregation in the capital.[3]

The hostility was not only fueled by the aggressive evangelism of the sectarians but also from attacks by each other on doctrine, rites, church polity, and ecclesiastical leadership. The Orthodox, maintaining it was the one true church, holy and apostolic,

---

1. Procurator of the Holy Synod, *Report*, 1905–1907, 150, and 1910, 170–74.
2. *MO*, Apr. 1911, 931–36.
3. Ibid., Jan. 1911, 189–90.

labeled sectarian dissidents as vile heretics. Baptists and Evangelical Christians were not content, as some dissidents, to meet quietly in their own conventicles for Bible study and worship and even maintain a nominal allegiance to the established church. They claimed to be a true New Testament church, feeling it incumbent to attack what it considered were the false teaching and practices of the spiritually dead and apostate Orthodox Church.

S. P. Bondar, a careful Orthodox researcher who dispassionately in 1911 described the strengths of the Baptist movement, noted that Baptists portrayed Orthodoxy as only outwardly Christian and inwardly devoid of Scripture, leading a life of "servitude to sin." Bondar pointed out that the Baptist journal, *Baptist*, a periodical he called "an organ of anti-Orthodox polemics," began in 1908 a series of articles attacking the dogmas and institution of the Orthodox Church, attempting to show it lacked a basis for church rites, including infant baptism, relics, and the priestly claim of forgiving sins. Baptist pastors maintained they were the only "true believers," calling themselves "saints" and "born again," and composed the "living church."[4]

An article in *Tserkovnyï vestnik* in 1913 claimed Baptists and other evangelicals openly mocked Orthodox practices and called Orthodox priests "scribes and pharisees." The author took offence of charges in sectarian publications that the Orthodox Church was "very reactionary," its high officials persecuted dissidents, and they were angry over religious freedom in the country. In an article in *Missionerskoe obozrenie* in 1915, the author claimed that each Baptist member possessed the goal of subverting the Orthodox into the sect. He declared that Baptists began their preaching by blaspheming the Orthodox priests, holy ikons, the holy cross, temple, and even the mysteries.[5]

To counteract the sectarian and Roman Catholic threat and revive church life after the revolutionary shocks of 1904–1905, the Orthodox Church held in July 1908 its Fourth All-Russian Missionary Congress in Kiev where the Russian Baptist Congress met earlier in the year. Over 600 delegates attended, including three metropolitans and thirty-four diocesan archbishops and other higher clergy. Even earlier, before the missionary congress assembled, the Holy Synod had already suggested measures against evangelical sectarians. The missionary conference, besides spending an inordinate amount of time in trying to describe the various parties among evangelicals, considered numerous strategies that not only tried to counter the evangelical sectarians but also to meet the religious needs of the Orthodox population.[6]

One measure was to establish extra theological conversations with sectarians as well as teaching the word of God with preaching, singing of Psalms and spiritual

---

4. Bondar, *Sovremennoe sostoyanie russkago baptizma*, 64–66, and "Sovremennyï baptizm v Rossii," *MO*, 1911, no. 10, 302–18; see 317–18.

5. *TsV*, 1913, no. 49, 1528–29. *MO*, Jan. 1915, 107.

6. Maevskiï, *Vnutrennyaya missiya*, 197–98. Procurator of the Holy Synod, *Report*, 1908–1909, 199–202. "Voprosy o sektakh i sektantakh," *MO*, 1908, no. 9, 1234–46.

songs, and undertake conversations with the Orthodox population itself. The congress proposed in areas populated by sectarians and distant from parish churches the construction of prayer houses and the need to improve church discipline. There was also the necessity to form missionary and religious-philosophical courses and sessions for candidates to the priesthood as well as form an institute of evangelists at parish churches. To "paralyze" the influence of Baptist "invitational meetings," it was felt the missionaries or their helpers needed to visit these meetings to refute attacks on the Orthodox Church; if this was impossible, then distribute anti-sectarian brochures and leaflets. The Orthodox also needed to produce wall calendars with missionary citations from the Bible, the church fathers, and missionary publications to counter the sectarian calendars. The congress passed resolutions to forbid entry of foreign missionaries and to prohibit Orthodox attending sectarian meetings.

STATE RELATIONS

The reactionary developments in the nation after 1908 seriously affected the rights and privileges of evangelical sectarians. The Manifestos of 1905 and 1906 provided a legal basis for freedom of conscience, yet the Duma, the legislative body, which became more conservative, never enacted the necessary legislation to make them operational. Prokhanov, editor of *Khristianin,* would go with complaints of abuses to the Commission on Religious Cults in the Duma, whose president was sympathetic toward the evangelical cause and who then could appeal to the Minister of the Interior for rectification. Prokhanov also found P. N. Miliukov, leader of the Constitutional Democratic Party in the Duma, a sympathetic supporter as well as members in the Octobrist Party. Prokhanov published in his paper, *Bratskii listok*, the addresses of such men in the Duma as Peter. A. Stolypin, president of the Council of Ministers and Minister of Internal Affairs, and Z. D. Zakharov, leader of the New Molokans. The Ministry of Internal Affairs introduced a bill into the Duma in 1909 to enact into legislation the Manifesto of 1906, a bill that the Duma even liberalized, but it failed to be enacted for lack of agreement between the Duma and the Council of State.[7]

The government began to issue decrees, which, beyond those of a technical nature or eliminating administrative abuses, had a negative impact on the legal status of the Old Believers and sectarians. Decrees in 1909 directed authorities to investigate whether sectarians were engaged in activity outside religion, made officials conscious of the law that prohibited sectarian propaganda among the Orthodox, and prohibited sectarians issuing printed invitations and announcements. The decrees also forbade their distributing religious books and required permission from the Minister of Internal Affairs for baptism in the open air.

---

7. For church-state relations in the period of reaction, see Blane, 73–87, and Curtiss, 322–32. Prokhanov, *In the Cauldron*, 141–42. *Bratskii listok*, 1909, no. 6, 1–4; no. 7, 1–3; no. 8, 1–14.

In 1910 a decree provided for legal action against sectarian meetings where Orthodox were present that attacked the Orthodox Church or appealed to them to join the sect. The Minister of Internal Affairs issued a circular in 1910 that granted to authorized individuals, who represented at least twelve communities of the sect, one religious and one business conference per year, neither of which were permitted to meet concurrently. Conferences were limited to ten days. Aliens in the country were barred participation unless granted special permission, and no financial collections were allowed. The Minister of Internal Affairs approved the agenda and the officiating personnel of the conferences. A representative of the Minister must be present.[8]

A second circular in 1910 regulated religious services. Services outside registered buildings must gain permission from the authorities. It was forbidden to hold meetings of a non-religious nature, youth meetings unauthorized by the authorities, and all meetings for the evangelization of minors. An official, appointed by the local police department, was to be present and given a proper place in the meeting. No attacks on the Orthodox Church were allowed or appeals to leave it.[9]

Although evangelical sectarians still possessed some basic freedoms, including the right of assembly and worship, clearly a new period had arrived. The new restrictive regulations, the increasing closure of churches, censorship, the stopping of institutional development, the disruption of the Russian Congress of 1909 in Odessa, disturbances and restrictions of later congresses, and the final ending of all conferences clearly portrayed the developing suppression. The evangelical press reported numerous cases of restrictions and harassment. Foreigners from abroad faced prohibitions or challenges in attempting to speak in evangelical meetings. Archibald McCaig, principal emeritus of Spurgeon's College, who in earlier days had spoken freely in Russia now in 1910 was denied permission to speak. C. T. Byford, Commissioner of the Baptist World Alliance for Europe, spoke several times in the congress of the Russian Baptist Union in St. Petersburg in 1910 but was challenged in doing it. Johannes Warns, Plymouth Brethren from Germany, in 1911 was forbidden to speak at the congress of Evangelical Christians in St. Petersburg. Authorities put pressure on Fetler in St. Petersburg and Moscow not to allow Orthodox children to attend his Sunday schools, but Fetler resisted. Karl Füllbrandt, pastor of the German Baptist church in Odessa, wrote in 1911 that a ban on Sunday schools was carried out almost everywhere, even somewhat affecting the German churches, along with pressure on parents not to take their children to divine services.[10]

Officials sometimes used administrative exile, although they might be of limited duration. Pavlov wrote a letter in 1909 on the exile of Daniel Timoshenko (who had earlier once before been exiled in the 1890s) and his son, Mikhail. For an unauthorized

8. Blane, Appendix D, 270–71.

9. Ibid., Appendix E, 272–74.

10. McCaig, *Wonders of Grace in Russia*, 65, 122–23. *Baptist Times and Freeman*, Sep. 30, 1910, 637. Warns, 137. *Der Sendbote*, Apr. 19, 1911, 244.

financial appeal in the *Baptist* for a poor widow, Pavlov, then editor of the paper, was brought to court with the threat of a fine of fifty rubles or eight days in prison. Pavlov was also fined fifty rubles for exposing a priest who had beaten a Baptist woman and 300 rubles for printing a letter from a church asking for assistance in paying the expenses of its prayer house. The Continental Committee of the Baptist World Alliance in January 23, 1911, voted to send Pavlov £25 to recover his "heavy legal expenses" from prosecution by the police. At the Moscow Conference of Russian Baptists in 1911, it was reported that Pavlov as editor of *Baptist* was fined 300 rubles and the periodical was confiscated twice during the year. One issue was returned but the other was still in court. Prokhanov wrote that in 1912 he was taken to court and fined for an article in one of his periodicals. In an attempt to stop the itineration of missionaries and preachers, the State Senate in 1913 permitted only ministers of registered congregations to preach. In the same year the Minister of Internal Affairs forbade the sale of gramophone records of sectarian preaching.[11]

In this period Ivan P. Kushnerov of Kiev, the advocate for sectarian rights, felt the pressure of cases as well as facing personal difficulties. In 1910 Kushnerov showed to John R. Kliburn of the Evangelical Alliance his correspondence, which included 637 letters for 1909, all filed. He claimed that he received almost each day two new cases to defend. In 1911 Abraham Regier visited Kushnerov, noting that he had a family of "ten heads" to support, a difficult task since his numerous clients were unable to pay him, including travel costs. Because of a nervous condition, he could not bear the pounding of his typewriter, but he could not afford a secretary. In 1911 the congress of the Russian Baptist Union in Moscow, noting that Kushnerov was undergoing medical treatment "from wounds inflicted on him," sent 100 rubles. An article in 1913 noted, however, that Kushernov was still busy at work; in this case he was defending a father who had been fined and imprisoned for burying his child without the rites of the Orthodox Church.[12]

As in earlier times, a period of growing restriction did not automatically turn into full suppression. The situation might be dirty gray rather than simply black and white. Füllbrandt wrote in 1910 that the laws were handled differently by different officials, especially those who wish to please the priesthood. Later in the year he wrote that the regime earnestly was trying to provide freedom, but he noted that it was not easy to resist against the old regime and the priesthood as well as confronting pliant police officials and the fanaticism of the people. He also pointed out that sectarians themselves may cause unnecessary difficulties through imprudent words and conduct

---

11. *Der Hausfreund*, Sep. 8/20, 1910, 287. BWA, Continental Committee, *Minutes*, April 23, 1909, and Jan. 23, 1911. Byford, *Peasants and Prophets*, 84. *Der Sendbote*, Aug. 31, 1910, 549. *MO*, Nov. 1911, 644. Prokhanov, *In the Cauldron*, 165. Blane, 84.

12. *EC*, Sep.–Oct. 1910, 112–14. *Offene Türen*, 1911, no. 9, 3–4. *Baptist*, no. 47, 1911, 375. *Christian Standard*, Apr. 16, 1913, 8.

and a challenging attitude.[13] In reviewing the religious situation at the Baptist World Alliance in 1911, Pavlov presented a mixed but rather negative assessment:[14]

> Concerning the religious liberty, I have to say that it is yet very limited, though we are in better condition than before the revolution. We can now print our own literature and permitted services are not dissolved. But the Minister of Interior defends very carefully the established church and enacts circulars that do very considerably limit our rights. . . . Sunday-schools and young men's associations are forbidden without special permission. . . . In many places our members are beaten and their gatherings are dissolved by mob.

During the issuing of its first regulations, the regime was seemingly giving mixed signals. Fetler recorded that in 1910 he had a long conversation with Pyotr A. Stolypin in which he was informed that the Department of Spiritual Affairs would immediately investigate complaints of abuses. Stolypin became Minister of Interior in April 1906 and in June of the same year President of the Council of Ministers. C. T. Byford later wrote that the regulations of October 1910 issued under Stolypin, although declaring sectarians may freely assemble, yet placed their meetings under the discretionary control of the police. In noting cases of abuse, Byford also accused the Ministry of Interior of "double-dealing" in the administration of the law. But on the other hand, Byford, upon the assassination of Stolypin then in September 1911, wrote, although "he ruled with an iron hand" in suppressing revolutionary disruption, claimed he was a friend of Baptists and other dissenters. Byford quoted him as saying that he favored full liberty for all recognized religions that did not seek the overthrow of the regime and declared he would not oppose Baptist propaganda by "purely Russian Baptists" and if they were persecuted should appeal to him. Byford pointed out Stolypin's removal of any difficulties for the cornerstone laying of Fetler's *Dom Evangeliya* and, while earlier he was governor in Saratov, Baptists built in Balashev a very fine church structure. On the second day of the congress of the Russian Baptist congress in September, Deï Mazaev, after referring to Stolypin as "one of eminent sons of Russia" who "took much pains for the benefit of all," proposed that all rise in honor of his memory. Everyone stood.[15]

After Stolypin's death, religious conditions continued to worsen for sectarians. George A. Simons, the superintendent of Methodist work in Russia, stated in 1913 in his article, "Awakening in Russia": "During the past two years there has been a strong political reaction and religious repression under which practically all Free Church bodies have had to suffer more or less." In 1912 the regime closed many prayer houses in Kherson Province for failure to produce a copy of their confirmation. The

---

13. *Der Sendbote*, June 1, 1910, 345, and Aug. 31, 1910, 549.

14. BWA, Congress, Proceedings, 1911, 233.

15. *WHZ*, June 18, 1910, 198. *Baptist Times and Freeman*, Jan. 20, 1911, supp. 2, and Sep. 19, 1911, 615. Byford, *Peasants and Prophets*, 142–48. *Baptist*, 1911, no. 43, 343. For a recent appraisal of Stolypin, see "Pyotr Stolypin," *Russian Life*, Sep.–Oct. 2011, 24–25.

government preserved such copies only ten years, and thus new plans must then be submitted. In January 1913 the Prefect of Odessa ordered two Baptist chapels closed but were later reopened. Pavlov, continuing as pastor in Odessa, faced a particularly difficult time along with Mikhail Timoshenko, who was his co-editor of the paper *Slovo istiny*. With their animosity, the Orthodox clergy took Pavlov to court on six occasions in a year's time. In the last case the court charged Pavlov and two or three other pastors with blasphemy against Christ and the Orthodox Church. The charge of blasphemy was withdrawn but a new charge of proselytism was then brought forward that resulted in a sentence of imprisonment for one month. On appeal the Senate confirmed the sentence but it was reduced to twenty days. In the meantime Pavlov with his wife had gone in September 1913 on a five-month mission trip to Blagoveshchensk in the Far East where in February he was imprisoned for twenty days for the charges against him in Odessa. Upon his return to Odessa in 1914 his case was reopened, and he was imprisoned for two months. In 1913 Timoshenko was charged for preaching illegally in June to a small group of Baptists adjoining the Odessa church, but the case was dismissed. In April 1914 Timoshenko was indicted for publishing an article by N. Ivanov on Lent that reflected on the Orthodox Church. The case, however, was set then for a new hearing. After the outbreak of the First World War in 1914, officials sought the exile of both Pavlov and Timoshenko. Fetler continued to face problems. While Fetler was in the Caucasus in 1913, the authorities closed *Dom Evangeliya* for ostensibly not conforming to original specifications by the authorities, but Fetler soon got it reopened. In 1913–1914 the authorities brought against Fetler three cases of a trivial nature, but he was acquitted in two of them and in the third case appealed the fine of five rubles.[16]

In this period both Fetler and Prokhanov personally approached officials on behalf of sectarian rights and issued in 1910 books on the subject. Fetler's volume, *Svoboda sovesti i veroterpimost'* (Freedom of Conscience and Toleration) whose cover sported a portrait of Nicholas II, contained imperial manifestos, ministerial decrees, instructions on registration of churches and confirmation of pastors, and speeches in the Duma on religious rights. Prokhanov's work, *Zakon i vera* (The Law and Faith) was a legal guide to the formation and administration of congregations. A third edition appeared in 1917. Prokhanov also issued in 1913 a memorandum on the legal position of Evangelical Christians, Baptists, and related Christians. J. A. Frey's earlier booklet of 1899 on religious statutes relating to Baptists was reissued in 1913 with limited additional material.[17]

16. *EC*, Sep.–Oct., 1913, 170. *WHZ*, Dec. 21, 1912, 407, and Mar. 26, 1922, 95, *Der Hausfreund*, Jan. 23/Feb. 5, 1913, 27–28. *Baptist Times and Freeman*, Apr. 4, 1913, 253; Feb. 27. 1914, 172; and Mar. 6, 1914, 196. *Slovo istiny*, 1913, no. 11, 135; no. 14, 169; and no. 18, 200, 220–21; 1914, no. 22, 261, no. 27, 323–24, and no. 39, 458. *The Gospel in Russia*, Jan. 1914, 8–9. *The Weekly Evangel*, July 11, 1916, 4–5.

17. See Wardin, *Evangelical Sectarianism*, 390, for a description of evangelical publications on the law. Also see *Der Hausfreund*, July 7/20, 1910, 215, and *Pacific Baptist*, July 7, 1910, 10, on Fetler's book.

Evangelicals were not hesitant in voicing their complaints or to petition. In 1909 *Bratskiĭ listok* reported that a deputation from the Evangelical Christian congregation in St. Petersburg went to lobby the Duma. The congress of Evangelical Christians in 1911 voted to send a petition from its council to the Minister of Internal Affairs. In January 1913, Prokhanov and his associate, G. M. Matveev, petitioned the chairman of the Council of Ministers. A deputation of Russian Baptists also approached the president of the Council of Ministers with their complaints.[18]

Congresses of the Russian Baptist Union, 1909–1911

In the period of reaction, Russian Baptists found it hard to maintain national congresses or national institutions. The hostility of the Orthodox Church to Baptists made it difficult to convene national congresses in major centers without attack. In addition, the state extended its control over the agenda and participants of congresses and then finally forbade their convening at all. The last congress of the Russian Baptist Union in the Tsarist period was in Moscow in 1911, even though Baptists continued to ask permission to assemble. In 1913 a delegation of Baptists complained to the President of the Council of Ministers that a proposed congress had been denied three times.[19] The government also forced the Baptist Missionary Society to terminate after three years of existence. From lack of reports, youth and Sunday school congresses apparently were unable to meet. Russian Baptists could never get approval for a theological institution. Even though in theory the principle of liberty of conscience still existed, the regime was determined to limit as much as possible the collective and institutional efforts of Baptists and other sectarians.

On a petition of William Fetler in St. Petersburg, the authorities approved the meeting of the annual congress of the Russian Baptist Union in Odessa from May 6 to 10 in 1909. The Orthodox authorities, however, were very concerned. Mikhail A. Kal'nev, expert in the anti-sectarian mission, felt that the congress, besides the business of the Union, would be a staging ground for evangelization among the Orthodox population. In preparation for the coming of the Baptists, the Odessa Brotherhood of St. Andrew called a special meeting with participation of diocesan anti-sectarian missionaries and clergy from Odessa. It was decided to arrange preaching in all Orthodox churches each day during the congress, undertake special missionary conversations, reading, and debates, and distribute anti-sectarian brochures and leaflets.

On Wednesday May 6, V. G. Pavlov, vice-president of the Union and presiding officer, gave the presidential address based on the words from the *Song of Solomon* 2:11, "For lo, the winter is past." Little did he know at the time how inappropriate these words were as a prophecy for Russian Baptists. The agenda included such matters as

---

18. *Bratskiĭ listok*, 1909, no. 6, 1–4; no. 7, 1–3; no. 8, 1–14; and 1911, no. 3, 43. *Christian Standard*, Apr. 26, 1913, 8. *Baptist Times and Freeman*, Apr. 4, 1913, 253.

19. *Baptist Times and Freeman*, Apr. 4, 1913, 253.

the constitution of the Union, organization of youth and children's circles and Sunday schools, the legalization of congregations, and formation of mission stations.[20]

Pavlov invited the assembly to gather on the next day, May 7, on Ascension Day, for a public meeting on Zhevakov Mountain in a suburb of Odessa with a magnificent view of the harbor and the sea, requesting people to bring samovars, tea kettles, and refreshments for a picnic. A number of months before in August 1908 on the Day of Transfiguration, after baptizing four candidates in the Black Sea, Pavlov with those in attendance had gone without incident to the mountain for a love feast with F. Brauer, president of the German Baptist Union, as guest speaker.[21] With Fetler's bold appeal for evangelizing everywhere in the city and also allowing Jews to attend the meeting on the mountain, the authorities sent the police to disrupt the gathering, maintaining the Baptists were breaking the law for an unauthorized public meeting. The police arrested 206 persons, with Pavlov sentenced for two months, one other leader for one month, and the remainder for seven days.

According to Kal'nev, the Baptists were still not ready to calm down. At a meeting place on Kherson Street, a place approved for their meetings in the city, Fetler, who escaped arrest, and Balikhin held meetings. Here prayer was raised "for the innocent victims" and for the chief of the city that the Lord would "enlighten his mind and to induce his heart to free them who suffer for the path of Christ." With evident satisfaction, Kal'nev claimed that God did not hear them.

On Sunday, May 10, when Baptists at four in the morning attempted to baptize twenty-five men and women, the service was stopped and those in attendance taken to the police station. Thirty-eight were subjected to one week of arrest, while the leader, K. I. Kravchenko, was given two months. Another believer, noted for his defense of fellow believers and alleged coarseness, was given three months and loss of employment. Finally on May 15, Fetler and other members of the congress were deported to Rostov-on-Don and from there Fetler returned to St. Petersburg. The congress, what remained of it, was ended. Before the end, however, the Missionary Society met on the thirteenth, where Gavriil V. Mazaev was elected treasurer for one year.[22]

With its success in helping to disrupt the congress in Odessa, the Orthodox Church again marshaled its mission forces before and during the next Russian Baptist congress, which was rescheduled to meet from September 27 to October 7 in Rostov-on-Don, back in the traditional Baptist territory for congresses. The congress included 112 representatives and 134 guests, who it was reported "joyfully welcomed each other." Church representatives included three Mennonite Brethren, including P. P. Perk

20. See *MO*, 1909, no. 7, 1041–49, for Kal'nev's account of the congress, the most detailed and accurate of any. For Pavlov's speech, see Packer, *Among the Heretics in Europe*, 44. For the agenda of the congress, see *Baptist*. 1909, no. 10, 18–20.

21. *Baptist*, 1909, no. 5, 14.

22. For evangelical responses to the congress, see *MRW*, Aug. 1909, 561–62; *Baptist*, 1909, no. 23, 21; and *Der Sendbote*, July 28, 1909, 10–11. For minutes of the Baptist Missionary Society, see *Baptist*, 1909, no. 10, 18.

from Halbstadt, in addition to Peter M. Friesen, now in Sevastopol, who was given the right to vote. Also present were L. L. Rosenberg from the Hebrew congregation in Odessa; I . P Kushnerov, the advocate of sectarian rights; a woman, Melanie Fetler, the sister of William Fetler from St. Petersburg; and Ya. P. Kurtsit from Latvia, for whom Fetler interpreted when he preached. In the evening, public meetings were held that included preaching in Russian, Latvian, German, English, and Hebrew. Police were present at all business sessions of the congress, verifying the tickets of entry of the representatives.[23]

The first item on the printed program was for the election of a deputation of top leaders to be sent to the Tsar for "gratitude for the gift of religious freedom." O. Truderung, president of the school committee of the German Baptist Union in Russia, urged Russian Baptists to contribute to the support of Russian students at the German Baptist seminary in Lodz. The congress approved an annual collection in December for the school. The congress, however, approved establishing its own seminary in Moscow and approved a committee to form a school society for the purpose. Since Baptists could only legally establish elementary schools, the congress expressed its desire to form a "Russian Baptist School Society" to form schools of secondary and higher education. With the refusal of Deï Mazaev to serve as president of the Union, the congress elected Pavlov for the next year. During the time of the congress, Fetler directed the First All-Russian Congress of Youth Circles and Sunday Schools. After the congress on October 13, Margaret M. Mazaev organized a woman's meeting where Pavlov, Fetler, and Maria Yasnovskiï spoke.

The next Russian Baptist congress met in the capital city, St. Petersburg, from September 1 to 8, 1910. The roll call of delegates included eighty-six Russians, eighteen Germans, five Latvians, five Estonians, four Poles, two Finns, and one Jew for a total of 121. Most delegates were poor and could not afford hotel rooms in expensive St. Petersburg but slept on the floor on rough mattresses in the half finished mission house. Deï Mazaev informed the congress by telegram that he could not attend because of illness. The congress was also informed that O. Truderung had died. Two foreign guests attended.—Charles. T. Byford, an Englishman and European Commissioner of the Baptist World Alliance, and J. A. Packer (1863–1941), a journalist from Australia and later editor of *The Australian Baptist*. Both will later write works incorporating material on Baptists in Russia—Byford in his *Peasants and Prophets* (1911) and Packer in his *Among the Heretics of Europe* (1912). When Byford requested delegates to stand who were either exiled or imprisoned, over one-third responded, thirty-two men and two women. The government approved the agenda of the congress, and a representative of the Minister of Internal Affairs was present at all sessions. The police allowed only delegates, who were issued entry tickets, and approved

23. *Baptist* provided extensive coverage of the congress in 1909, no. 18, 2; no. 19, 2; no. 22, 15–18; and no. 23, 21–24. Also see *MO*, Nov. 1909, 1765–76. See Bogolyubov, "Mechty i deïstvitel'nost' v russkom baptizme," *TsV*, 1910, no. 1, 15–19, for an Orthodox review of Russian Baptists after the congress.

guests to attend the official sessions of the congress, but public meetings were open to the public. On three occasions the police attempted but unsuccessfully to stop Byford from addressing the delegates.[24]

Packer will write that authorities in the Orthodox Church attempted to stop the government from allowing the congress at all and also used priests to counter as much as possible the influence of the congress. At midnight the hall was filled with believers bringing derelicts from the streets of the city. The priests also came who attempted to begin an uproar, but the police stopped such further tactics. The priests, however, continued to attend and took copious notes.

On the first day of the congress, Pavlov, president of the Union, reported that itinerant evangelists were twelve during the year and 7,756 rubles had been collected for their support. In a speech at the Baptist World Alliance later in 1911, Pavlov reported that the Baptist Missionary Society, formed in 1907 but ceased in 1910 due to its failure to gain legalization, had engaged twenty to twenty-six missionaries each year and raised over $4,000. Nevertheless the Union itself would now continue to carry on the mission commitment. In his report to the congress, Pavlov noted that the journal, *Baptist,* had around 600 subscribers but was expecting a loss of about 1,000 rubles. At the end of his report, he said that Baptists were not a sect but was carrying the gospel to the Russian people. For this it was necessary "to show practical Christianity, that is, to be engaged in the construction of schools, shelters (asylums), prayer houses, etc." Byford and Packer then spoke. That evening at seven in the large Tenishevskiĭ Hall a supper was provided for most of the participants of the congress followed at eight by a public meeting.

On the second day of the congress, Pavlov, president of the Union, was elected to preside by a divided vote of 53 to 41 and 22 abstentions. The congress voted to send by telegram its "loyal greetings" to the Tsar. Pavlov prayed for the Tsar and his family, the ministers of state, and members of the Duma, thanking the Lord for liberty. The congress then sang the national anthem, however, substituting, "You our glorious Tsar" for "Tsar of the Orthodox" and "Death to sin" for "Death to his enemies." An official from the Minister of Internal Affairs stood and demanded the singing stop but was ignored. After the session, the official irately declared to Fetler that the government cannot allow anyone composing the national anthem for himself.[25]

The congress approved a committee of fifteen, including seven Russians, three Germans, three Latvians, and two Estonians, to present a memorandum on Baptist concerns on the proposed bill in the Duma on freedom of conscience. The congress rejected the proposal of V. V. Ivanov to add representation from the Evangelical

---

24. For accounts of the congress, see *Baptist*, 1910, no. 38, 301–304; no. 39, 309–10; no. 43, 341–43; and no. 46, 365–68; *Bratskiĭ listok*, 1910, no. 9, 11–18, and no. 10, 5–24; and Byford in *Baptist Times and Freeman*, Sep. 23, 1910, 621, and Sep. 30, 1910, 637. Also see Packer, 43–57. *Der Hausfreund*, Sep. 29/Oct, 12, 1910, 308.

25. *Bratskiĭ listok*, 1910, no. 9, 15–16. Coleman, 106. Packer, 49.

Christians. The congress expressed support for Elena V. Beklemisheva, an educator for twenty-seven years and a member of the university in St. Petersburg, for her appeal to Baptists to establish nurseries and schools because of the inadequacy of public education. The congress discussed the need for a committee to draw up a report to the Minister of Internal Affairs on a bill in the Duma for a theological school. The congress resolved to establish an institution for the aged and orphans and support the church in Balashev, which would assume responsibility for its construction. It approved a treasury for invalids, preachers, and their widows.

Although Pavlov wished to resign as editor of *Baptist*, he was prevailed to continue and was designated 600 rubles for a helper. Although Fetler was publishing his own literature, the congress voted, however, to establish a Baptist publishing house. It also chose a committee to compile a collection of hymns. After a long debate, the majority, fifty-six to twenty-six, resolved to call the Union the "Union of Evangelical Christians-Baptists." Pavlov and Fetler especially wanted "Baptist" only. The question was raised whether it was necessary to have a confession of faith apart from the Word of God. Beginning in its first issue in 1907, *Baptist* had begun publishing in installments the German Baptist confession of 1847 that had circulated for some time under the name, "Kratkoe verouchenie baptistov." By a vote of 46 to 35 the congress voted for the need for a confession, but no committee was chosen to form it. The congress elected for the next year Il'ya A. Golyaev for president, William Fetler for vice-president, and V. P. Stepanov for secretary of the Union.

On the seventh day, the congregation of Evangelical Christians in St. Petersburg invited all delegates to a love feast. The congress responded with thanks. On the eighth day, members of the administration of the Baptist Union, some delegates of the congress, Prokhanov and Kargel of the Evangelical Christians, and others attended the laying of the cornerstone (foundation stone) of the *Dom Evangeliya*, Fetler's large meeting house. Both Prokhanov and Kargel spoke along with many others. On the final day of the congress, it resolved to collect money for six funds: (1) The Union asylum at Balashev Church; (2) literature and the publishing house; (3) itinerant missionaries; (4) the school of Beklemisheva; (5) the building fund; and (6) the general expenses of the Union. It also approved sending thirty-two delegates to the Baptist World Alliance congress in Philadelphia in 1911, of which four would be sisters and two youth, while the remaining would be venerable elders who had experienced persecution and exile.

The next congress of the Russian Baptist Union was in Moscow in 1911 from September 25 to October 1. Seventy representatives from the churches and over thirty guests were present with each representative receiving a membership ticket. Deï Mazaev was present, who was elected presiding officer. Two officials from the Department of Spiritual Affairs and the president of the local police were also in attendance. Again public meetings were also held. On the first evening over 1,000 persons packed full the auditorium of the Polytechnic Museum. The crowd sang "Our Father" and

"God Save the Tsar," and Pavlov prayed for the Tsar. At the same time the Orthodox held their own meeting in an adjoining room with the Archpriest Ioann Vostorgov giving an anti-sectarian lecture. Also the right-wing press attacked Baptists for using the Polytechnic Museum, a center of secular culture, for their heretical views.[26]

On the second day, the congress received telegrams from the Council of the Evangelical Christians expressing God's blessing on its work and from L. L. Rosenberg, pastor of the Hebrew Baptist Church in Odessa. The congress sent a telegram to the Tsar, and V. V. Ivanov expressed prayer for him. Upon the recent assassination of P. A. Stolypin on September 1, who died five days later, the congress stood in his honor. In his report, a police agent wrote that the congress "draws attention to itself by the demonstrative emphasis of its patriotism and nationalist aspirations."[27]

Pavlov reported that subscribers of *Baptist* had reached 2,200 but its deficit at the end of the year was around 600 rubles. He complained of clashes with censors— "fraternal," evidently from fellow believers, and "administrative," from the state. He was forced to pay fines and even one number was confiscated. Upon Pavlov's resignation as editor, the congress elected a committee of eleven to take charge of the paper. It also chose three persons to investigate the possibility of establishing its own letterpress for publication. It was reported that the Union had sent out twenty-nine missionaries and expended over 2,000 rubles. Some missionaries faced serious opposition. For example, in Poltava the authorities prohibited Balikhin for holding a meeting; Bronshtein was arrested and transported to Kiev where he was freed; and Savel'ev was oppressed in Nizhnii Novgorod Province.

In the evening of the second day, Orthodox distributed at the entrance of the museum leaflets attacking the Baptists. During the meeting some hecklers began to shout out and some were removed. The Moscow city governor invited Mazaev and Semen P. Stepanov to explain the problem in the museum and advised them not to continue meeting there. On the fourth night, the city governor closed the museum to the Baptists, and police dispersed the crowd before it. Orthodox also arrived to distribute brochures attacking the Baptists. The city governor himself was strongly chastised for allowing the meetings at all in the Polytechnic Museum, which also permitted attacks on Orthodox, and for permitting general religious meetings when the law specifically forbade such meetings simultaneously with business meetings of a sectarian body. Baptists moved their public meetings to one of their prayer halls. Here some Orthodox youth and monks and a priest attempted to be disruptive, talking and laughing or even singing Orthodox hymns, but the meetings continued. The city governor, however, forbade public evening meetings on Saturday and Sunday, October 1 and 2.[28]

26. Sources for the congress are in *Baptist*, 1911, nos. 42–47, and in *MO*, Nov. 19, 1911, 641–57. Also see Coleman, 113, for attacks from the Orthodox and the right-wing press.

27. For the quotation from the police agent, see Coleman, 113.

28. *Baptist*, 1911, no. 44, 351–52. Coleman, 114, and 250, ft. 16.

Mazaev again declined the presidency of the Union and Il'ya Golyaev (1859–1942) was elected for the next year. Mazaev, however, was elected vice-president. Mazaev also declined the editorship of the *Baptist* but will become its editor again in 1912. The congress voted to meet in Kharkov in September 1912, but it never met since the Tsarist regime never again permitted another Russian Baptist congress. Nevertheless the Union continued, and Mazaev will assume the leadership.

Congresses of the Baptist World Alliance

The second congress of the Baptist World Alliance met earlier in 1911 in June in Philadelphia. For some time Russian Baptists looked forward to the congress; in September 1910 they had already authorized sending a full delegation. The congress will help to put Russian Baptists on the world stage and will have repercussions within the Alliance itself as well as with the Russian government. Relations between the Baptist World Alliance and Russian Baptists had been growing. Officials of the Baptist World Alliance had earlier tried to use their good offices in 1909 upon the fiasco of the Odessa congress by attempting to obtain the release of Pavlov and other Baptists who had been imprisoned. John Clifford, President of the Baptist World Alliance as well as a secretary of the Continental Committee of the Alliance, interviewed the Russian ambassador to Great Britain who had intervened for their release. J. H. Shakespeare, the British secretary of the Baptist World Alliance, wrote Robert S. MacArthur of New York, who in turn met with President Taft of the USA on the issue. Clifford and the secretary also sent a memorial to the Tsar. As already noted, Charles T. Byford, Commissioner for Europe from the Alliance, attended the Russian congress in St. Petersburg in 1910.[29]

A couple of months before the congress, Prokhanov from the Evangelical Christians in St. Petersburg, had written earlier that because of "unforeseen circumstances" it would not be possible for a "Russo-German" delegation to attend. Difficulties did arise, and because of them the Alliance sent Byford to Russia. He went to Balashev in Saratov Province in the Lower Volga to work with Il'ya Golyaev, pastor of the Baptist church there and president of the Russian Baptist Union. Byford with Golyaev and Andreï Evstratenko and possibly four others left Balashev and in Moscow were joined by Vasiliï P. Stepanov. By the time the party reached the border, more had joined for a total of twenty-eight. The party sailed from Hamburg and then from South Hampton to York on the *President Lincoln*. With most Russians pastors earning little income, funds for their passage were raised through the efforts of J. H. Shakespeare and contributions from America.[30]

---

29. Jowers, "The Promotion of Religious Liberty by the Baptist World Alliance," 44–45. BWA, Continental Committee, *Minutes*, Oct. 14, 1909.

30. For detailed references to Russian Baptists at the BWA congress in Philadelphia, see BWA, Congress, *Proceedings*, 1911; *Baptist Times and Freeman;* and other sources in Wardin, *Evangelical*

The Russian delegation on the ship included a veritable "who's who" of the Russian Baptist Union. Besides Golyaev, Evstratenko, and V. P. Stepanov, the group included Pavlov and his wife, V. V. Ivanov, Semen P. Stepanov, Fedor P. Balikhin, Jakob Vins (Wiens), Ivan P. Kushnerov, and Melanie Fetler. Also included were two German Baptists, Carl Füllbrandt from Odessa and F. A. Arndt from St. Petersburg, and Adam K. Podin from Estonia. Also in the group were Martin Schmidt, a teacher from the German Baptist seminary in Lodz, now closed, and six of its students. Services on board were conducted in Russian, German, and English with generally from 100 to 120 passengers in attendance. William Fetler and Maria Yasnovskiĭ, the treasurer of Fetler's congregation, arrived apart from the delegation on the *President Lincoln*. Others in the roll-call of nations but from the empire included from Finland Eric Jansson of the Finnish Conference and a Mr. Ingar of the Swedish Conference; Janis Inkis from Latvia; F. Brauer, president of the German Baptist Union in Russia; and E. Mohr, from the German Baptists of Russian Poland.[31] Fetler almost failed to attend because of charges against him for his activity in Moscow, where the regime alleged he had illegally preached, and work in Grodno. Shortly before leaving, he had received a police order that he was under police surveillance until his trial in Moscow in the fall, but with an appeal to Shakespeare the Baptist World Alliance advanced $2,750 for bail that enabled him to leave the country and crossed the border just in time before the arrival of a second charge. On his return to Russia, Fetler was acquitted and repaid the bail. The authorities brought an old charge against Andreas Levuchkin of several years back when they discovered he was planning to go to Philadelphia, but he had already crossed the border before he could be stopped although he feared standing trial upon his return. Ivan Savel'ev also left with a change pending against him and also feared arrest on his return. Jakob Vins was introduced at the congress as one facing a fine or imprisonment on his return for baptizing eight believers. He chose, however, not to return and stayed in the West. Prokhanov did not attend but sent a message that was printed in the proceedings of the congress.[32]

At the opening in the Baptist Temple of Philadelphia, Russell Conwell, its pastor, spoke and also served as presiding officer. Conwell was widely known for his famous sermon, "Acres of Diamonds," published in 1892, and founder of Temple College in 1886. After a number of other addresses, Fetler, after a parade of notables, presented the last message of the afternoon. Fetler's message, spoken in English, portrayed his

---

Sectarianism, 194–95. See BWA, Continental Committee, *Minutes*, May 22, 1911, for Prokhanov's statement and the sending of Byford to Russia.

31. For a list of the delegates and picture on the *President Lincoln*, see *Baptist Times and Freeman*, Sep. 7, 1911, supp. 2. For the names of the students formerly at the Lodz Seminary, see *Baptist*, 1911, no. 26, 207. For other delegates from Russia, see BWA, Congress, *Proceedings*, 1911, 19, 171, and the roll call of nations.

32. *Baptist Times and Freeman*, May 19, 1911, 308. BWA, Congress, *Proceedings*, 1911, 21, 237, 439–41. Prestridge, *Modern Baptist Heroes and Martyrs*, 43–44, 47–48. Wardin, "Jacob J. Wiens: Mission Champion in Freedom and Repression," *Journal of Church and State* 28/3 (1986), 498.

PART SIX—Possibilities and Uncertainties, 1905–1917

oratorical gift as a great revivalist, pulling at mind, heart, and soul. With telling anecdotes, he spoke of continuing incidents of oppression. He told of the high official who refused to come to the cornerstone laying of the new *Dom Evangeliya*, contemptuously referring to Baptists as an insignificant body in Russia. Fetler then predicted that Russia would become the "first nation in Europe for Baptist work"—a prediction today that is true if one includes all nations of the former Soviet Union. Fetler also declared he was glad for the liberty now in Russia but admitted Baptists did not have all they want, but at a time when in Russia Baptists received "only dry crusts of bread" he suggested "we are enjoying tremendously our black bread after the crusts, and when we get the white bread you have here in America, well, we shall be more glad still." He declared that Russian Baptists will get butter and cheese with their bread in due time, and the Baptist World Alliance will help to obtain it. He thanked the assembly for the financial support he and other delegates from Russia received. He also appealed to American Baptists as "a big brother," who have so many educational institutions while Russia has not one, for a European college for the training of ministers.[33]

Fetler was not the only Russian delegate to speak at the Congress. Pavlov spoke on "The Christianizing of the world—Russia," the third time before an international Baptist congress. He provided a historical resume of Baptist work in the Caucasus, the home of his own Baptist beginnings, the coming of suppression with his exile and his successful work in Odessa. He declared that religious liberty in Russia is "yet very limited," but better before the revolution in 1905. He, however, accused the Minister of the Interior, that is, Stolypin, for issuing circulars that curtailed Baptist rights. He appealed for funds for a theological school, the erection of prayer houses, and a publication society. Before Pavlov spoke, Byford told of the spread of the Baptist witness in Central and Southeastern Europe and how persecution of Baptists in Russia helped spread the Baptist movement to Siberia in the east and in the Balkans to the west. Madame Maria Yasnovskiĭ and Miss Melanie Fetler spoke on women's work.[34]

After Pavlov's message, Shakespeare introduced individually twenty-two representatives from Russia, including Podin from Estonia and two women. He frequently made comments on their suffering and included five others from Central and Eastern Europe as representatives of the "Baptist suffering church." In this exhibition of the "heroes of the faith," the assembly greeted them with "the greatest enthusiasm."

After the presentation, A. J. Vining, pastor from Ontario, Canada, noted for his oratorical skills, spoke passionately for the need of a Baptist training school. He played to the limit the pleading of "scarred and battered old men" for millions of people "who wait for the coming of the trained evangelist, and the pastor who is 'apt to teach.' Must these men call in vain?" After Vining's plea, F. B. Meyer, the presiding chairman, appealed to the audience to raise $100,000 that very morning for a Baptist university to be it was hoped either in Moscow or St. Petersburg. The response was enthusiastic;

33. For Fetler's message, see BWA, Congress, *Proceedings*, 1911, 20–25.
34. BWA, Congress, *Proceedings*, 1911, 171–77, 228–34.

delegates all over began to promise various sums. The rest of the morning was devoted to solicitation and by one o'clock $66,000 had been pledged.[35]

The presentation of the Russians as suffering martyrs together with the raising a vast sum for a school in Russia will have unforeseen problems and consequences. The fate of the theological fund will be discussed in a succeeding chapter, but the presentation of the Russian representatives will have negative repercussions among officials in Russia and in the Russian embassy in Washington, D.C. After the congress, the Russian delegates were taken to Washington where at the White House they visited President Taft, who shook hands with each of them. Fetler gave Taft R. S. Latimer's book, *With Christ in Russia*. In the capitol they met Speaker Cannon and observed the proceedings of the House of Representatives. At the Russian Embassy the deputy graciously received them, asking about the purpose of their trip, but also whether it was true, as reported in the papers, they had come to complain about their government in another land. The Russian delegates explained that for the most part what they told was mainly in the past and persecution today has ceased. Before leaving, the Russian delegates sang the national hymn, gave a triple hurrah for the Tsar, and prayed for the health and prosperity of the royal house.[36]

Soon after the congress in Philadelphia, Ioann I. Vostorgov published in Russian a booklet of twenty-nine pages in Moscow, "How Did the Russian Baptists, Headed by Fetler, Lie in America on the Orthodox Church and on the Russian Government?" In it he included articles printed in Russian translation from the *Philadelphia Press* with comments and a conclusion. He labeled the assertion of the phenomenal growth of Baptists in Russia as boasting, the claim of the Russian delegates as "the greatest martyrs for the faith of the present century" a lie, and ridiculed their "huge endurance" as "liberators of Russia" to obtain religious rights. He wrote that nobody in Russia heard of chains or prisons for Baptists, and the stories of their suffering a farce. He criticized Fetler for his boast of converting large numbers in his ministry of three and a half years. Vostorgov was correct that the *Philadelphia Press* was in error in reporting that Fetler came out of Russian Orthodoxy (how did he become William?) and attended Oxford University.[37]

After the congress, Shakespeare sent a letter to the editor of the *Philadelphia Ledger*, claiming he was misrepresented in his remarks about the suffering of Russian Baptists, stating "While we cannot forget the past we have no wish to promote resentment" and believed the Tsar and his officials have no sympathy with the persecution. When James H. Franklin, the secretary of the American Baptist Foreign Mission Society interviewed Fetler in St. Petersburg in 1913, Fetler stated the reports in Russia of the congress in Philadelphia hurt the evangelical cause. He claimed the message of

---

35. For Vining's speech and the response for a Baptist university, see BWA, Congress, *Proceedings*, 1911, 239–42, and *Baptist Times and Freeman*, July 7, 1911, 421.

36. *Baptist Times and Freeman*, July 14, 1911, 436–37. *Baptist*, no. 35 (August 24, 1911), 278.

37. Vostorgov's booklet was also printed in *MO*, Jan. 1912, 208–15.

Walter Rauschenbusch, "The Church and Social Crises," in addition to the message of John Clifford at the Berlin Congress made Baptists appear at heart socialists. He admitted that relating the severe suppression in Russia before 1905 gave the wrong impression that such conditions exist at present.[38]

The next and final congress of the Baptist World Alliance in the Tsarist period was the Second European Baptist Congress in Stockholm, Sweden, in July 1913. The delegation from Russia was far smaller than in Philadelphia. Sixteen were present, including Russian, German, Latvian, and Estonian Baptists as well as two Evangelical Christians. Prokhanov was not present because of the illness of a son. Semen P. Stepanov, pastor of the Moscow church, brought greetings from the Russian Baptist Union. Latvian Baptists had a delegation of four that was represented by J. A. Frey, who also brought a devotional.

E. Mohr from Lodz brought greetings from the German Baptist Union of Russia, while F. Arndt, German Baptist pastor from St.Petersburg, brought one of the devotionals. In the absence of Prokhanov, A. Persianov brought greetings from the Evangelical Christians and presented a paper, "Fellowship with God." The other Evangelical Christian, Martin Schmidt, formerly a teacher at the Lodz Seminary but now at Prokhanov's Bible School, read a paper, "Liberty of Conscience in Russia."[39]

On the Sunday evening before the congress, Fetler spoke on evangelistic work in Russia, ending his message by reading a hymn in Swedish and leading the congregation in singing, "A Mighty Fortress." On Thursday morning he read a paper on "Our Spiritual Resources: the Redemption which is in Christ." Fetler also played an important role as interpreter. On Monday afternoon in the Bethel Chapel at a special conference on the Russian mission field, L. Luther, an Estonian from Narva, Frey, Mohr, and Persianov all presented reports. In addition, F. P. Balikhin and Fetler spoke. Besides Fetler, other members of *Dom Evangeliya* spoke at the congress, including Maria Yasnovskiï, who addressed a women's meeting and an open-air service, as well as Ivan Neprash and Johann Urlaub.

The reports from Baptist and Evangelical Christian representatives on religious conditions in Russians were not as positive as earlier. Persianov reported, "We have nominal freedom, but our Sunday-schools have been closed, our assemblies hindered and prohibited." Fetler said the door of freedom was "thrown open," and then in 1910 became "half shut," and now "barred and "bolted." He also said that Baptists were protesting against the recent regulation that a pastor's ministry must be confined to his own congregation. In his paper, Schmidt noted that in 1905 and 1906 Baptists rejoiced with the promised freedom and hopes for even more, but the regime did not abrogate

---

38. Extracts of Notes of Franklin in St. Petersburg, April, 1913, ABMU/ABFMS, *Correspondence*, Russian Mission, 1900–1919.

39. For the conference in Stockholm, see *Baptist Times and Freeman*, 1913, July 25, 572, 577; Aug. 1, 590–91; Aug. 8, 602–603; and Aug. 13, 620; *Slovo istiny*, 1913, no. 12, 146; no. 13, 158–59; no. 14, 170–71; no. 15, 182–83; no. 16, 193–94; and no. 17, 201–3. McCaig, *Wonders of Grace*, 121–46.

Russian Baptist Union

the old restrictions. Evangelicals still faced problems in burials, marriages, and in the education of their children. He nevertheless ended positively with the words that eventually "religious freedom will come to Russia."

The congress passed a resolution on religious freedom that stressed the Lordship of Christ with rulers and his ministers for righteous government. It noted that Christ commanded to make disciples and baptize and teach them. It concluded,"This Congress trusts that the day will soon arrive when no attempt will be made to restrict liberty of conscience, and when every believer will be left responsible in matters of religion to Christ as the only Lord."[40]

Internal Tensions

In addition to the worsening conditions for Baptists and other evangelicals, the Russian Baptist Union also experienced other strains, such as its relations with the growing Evangelical Christian Union and the problem of theological education that will be treated in a following chapter. In addition, it had its own internal difficulties. It was fortunate to have strong leaders, such as Deï Mazaev, Il'ya A. Golyaev of the Balashev Church, Semen P. Stepanov of the Moscow Church, William Fetler of St. Petersburg, F. P. Balikhin, a leading evangelist, V. V. Ivanov in Baku, and V. G. Pavlov in Odessa. Deï Mazaev with his gifts of leadership and financial resources continued to provide much of the leadership, but it faltered and at one time was practically non-existent and was even challenged. Some Baptists resented his great wealth and his autocratic ways. He was also beginning to be beset by poor health. He did not attend in 1908 the Russian Baptist Congress in Kiev nor the Baptist congress in Berlin. As vice-president, Pavlov, then also president of the Baptist Missionary Society, led the Odessa Congress in 1909, that was a disaster, and later the congress in Rostov-on-Don in the same year. Mazaev did not seek the presidency of the Union for 1910 that allowed Pavlov then to serve as president nor in 1911 with Golyaev becoming president. Pavlov became editor of *Baptist* in 1910–1911, a journal that Mazaev had started. But Mazaev and Pavlov became estranged. In 1911, evidently with assistance of the Baptist World Alliance, an agreement was forged between Pavlov and Mazaev and other leaders of the Russian Baptist Union. Evidently it did not last. In 1912 Mazaev will again become editor of *Baptist*, but in 1913 Pavlov with Mikhael. D. Timoshenko will establish in Odessa a rival paper, *Slovo istiny*. A. E. Leushkin and others in Tiflis, no friends of the Mazaev leadership, wrote in a letter printed in 1916 that referred to "the exclusion from the Union three years ago of their old preacher, V. G. Pavlov." With their Marxist ideology of economic determinism and class struggle, Marxists, such as A. I. Klibanov and G. S. Lyalina, have attempted to interpret the differences between Mazaev and Pavlov as a struggle between the authoritarianism of Mazaev and his supporters over

---

40. Jowers, 56–57. BWA, Continental Committee, *Minutes*, Sep. 18, 1913, 10–11.

a more democratic liberal-bourgeois orientation of Pavlov. Whatever political or even economic differences might have existed between Mazaev and Pavlov, they both held common evangelical principles. It should be sufficient enough to believe that the fundamental differences between these two leaders arose more over personal ambitions and authority and differences over religious policy.[41]

Without a fully coordinated denominational structure and the independence of congregations, other centers of power would naturally arise within Baptist ranks. Gavriil Mazaev, Deï's brother, moved to Omsk in Western Siberia at the beginning of this period where he became the leader and built an imposing church, seating 2,000. William Fetler, a Latvian and Baltic German, arriving in 1907, soon became a leader in the Russian Baptist Union. Because he was able to develop far from other Russian Baptists a large following in St. Petersburg and build *Dom Evangeliya*, also seating 2,000, and counter the influence of Evangelical Christians under Prokhanov, he was able to operate independently with the support of Mazaev and other Baptist leaders.

Political Issues

As a persecuted minority, Russian Baptists and other evangelical sectarians looked forward to a time of toleration and democratic reform but not revolution. In their attempt to discredit evangelical sectarians, opponents nevertheless accused them of being revolutionary socialists. In return, Baptists took the opportunity on numerous occasions to express their loyalty to the Tsar and denied the charge. In 1901 Pavlov wrote in a letter that he was against "all forced revolutions and I stand for the peaceful development of our fatherland and all mankind." In the next year Balikhin wrote that as Jude wrote in his epistle of the destruction of dreamers who despise dominion so will also be the fate of individuals with similar thoughts, and God directs the hearts of the Tsars. In 1903 the Russian Baptist Union in Tsaritsyn condemned one of its members circulating anti-government brochures. A Baptist preacher who had been able to evade the police on his many trips told Ernst-Ferdinand Klein, a German pastor, that in 1904 revolutionaries from abroad approached him to distribute revolutionary publications. He replied to them that on the Word of God the salvation of the people would not come by brutal power with bombs and dynamite but through spiritual conversion.[42]

---

41. BWA, Continental Sub-Committee, *Minutes*, Jan. 12, 1912 (p. 148). *Pis'mo vsem baptistskim obshchinam i otdel'nym bryat'yam baptistam v Rossii*, 30. Klibanov, 298–300, who built on the work of G. S. Lyalina, "Liberal'no-buzhuaznoe techenie v baptisme (1905–1917 gg.)," *Voprosy nauchnogo ateizma* 1 (1966), 312–40.

42. Detailed surveys of the political and social views of Baptists and other evangelicals may be found in Klibanov, 293–332, for a Marxist interpretation, and in Nesdoly, "Evangelical Sectarianism in Russia," 307–434, for an evangelical perspective. Also see Putintsev, *Politicheskaya rol' i taktika sekt*, 27–28, as quoted in Mitrokin, *Baptizm*, 66–67. Klein, *Russische Reisetage*, 6–8.

Vladimir Bonch-Bruevch, the Bolshevik researcher who attempted to attract evangelical sectarians for the revolutionary cause, wrote in 1902 that well-to-do Baptists were completely unaffected by economic questions although poorer Baptists exhibited more concern. In Bonch-Breuevich's short-lived periodical, *Razsvet*, in 1904, B. Pravdin noted that, although their persecution broadened their views on public issues, stundists rarely discussed questions of a social character and were "far from a class point of view." He nevertheless maintained that they were good ground for sowing socialist seeds. At the end of his article in 1910 on the persecution of Baptists in Russia, Bonch-Bruevich wrote that with their religious success the position of Baptists had changed since 1905. He claimed they were now passive, but he felt that "the many fallen asleep will awaken in the following years."[43]

F. M. Putintsev, the Marxist researcher, who wrote after the Bolshevik revolution, attempted to portray evangelical sectarians as a reactionary force after the Revolution of 1905, supporting the autocratic regime of Nicholas II. He claimed that Baptists and other evangelicals were under the leadership of the merchant class that feared revolution although their followers wanted revolutionary change. In his 1928 volume, Putintsev tarred Mazaev, Pavlov, and Baron Üxküll, delegates to the Baptist World Congress in London in 1905, as monarchist supporters for not objecting to the sending of a telegram by the congress to Edward VII of England, the monarch of the nation where the congress was meeting. Putintsev, of course, did not note, on the other hand, the criticisms from the Russian delegates of persecution or the remarks of Üxküll on the Russo-Japanese war of the time, "We Christians recognize the justice of God in using the heroic and wonderful Japanese people as his instruments to destroy the bureaucracy of Russia."[44]

Putintsev will use excerpts from the letters of Baptist leaders and resolutions of the Russian Baptist Union opposing violent revolution as expression of support for the autocratic regime. With his own advocacy of social revolution, his economic derminism, and atheism, he gives no room for religious sentiment that counsels respect for political authority, the rejection of bloodshed and terror, and the primacy of the inner religious life over social goals. Evangelical sectarians would naturally be grateful to the regime for any freedom granted to them with the hope for more to come.

Baptists and most other evangelicals, aside from Mennonites, did not oppose participation in government or service in the military. Z. D. Zakharov, head of the New Molokans, served in the Duma, where he was a strong advocate for sectarian rights, as also I. T. Losev, an Evangelical Christian from Tambov Province. In his article on Deï Mazaev, N. A. Levindanto claimed that Mazaev ran for a seat in the

---

43. Bonch-Bruevich, "Znachenie sektantstva dlya sovremennoï Rossii," *Zhizn'*, 1902, no. 1, 302. *Razsvet*, 1904, no. 2, 44. Bonch-Bruevich, "Presledovanie Baptistov v Rossii," *Vestnik evropy*, June 1910, 183.

44. Putintsev, *Politicheskaya rol' i taktika sect*, 12–13. Putintsev, *Politicheskaya rol' sektantsva*, 7–10. Ivanov and. Mazaev, *Vsemirnyï kongress baptistov v Londone v 1905 godu*, 40–42.

Duma and won from Northern Caucasus but was stopped by a higher authority for fear that he might assume too much political power. Mazaev might possibly have been an Octobrist, a party that represented the right wing of liberal politics. A new party, "The Union of Freedom, Truth and Peace," led by P. M. Friesen, Mennonite Brethren, advocated democratic reforms and was closely aligned with the Constitutional-Democratic Party or Kadets, the left wing of liberal politics. It received some Baptist support along with other evangelicals but was short-lived. Baptist leaders appeared to be in general agreement with the Kadets.[45]

The views of Pavlov are a good indication of the general political mood of Baptists. In 1908 at the First European Baptist Congress in Berlin in 1908, Pavlov stated: "The revolution shook the Russian nation, both as regards politics and religions, to its very foundations. At the same time it showed clearly how false had been the accusations of hostility to the Government, brought against the sectarians by the clergy of the established Church—since with a few exceptions our brethren remained neutral throughout the Reign of Terror." In his article in *Baptist*, "Who Is My Neighbor," Pavlov wrote that the principle of love for one another "is able to resolve all our social questions and there is no other outcome for the increasingly strained class and economic questions."[46]

In his series, "The Truth Concerning Baptists," in *Baptist* in 1911, Pavlov wrote:

> The principle of mutual relations of people given by Christ is in his command, 'Love your neighbor as yourself.' On the basis of this command the proprietor ought to love his workers as himself, and the workers mutually the employers. . . . The method of Christianity in this relation is not the method of scientific socialism which has in view to take in its hand by the state authority and afterwards reorganize society by means of direct legislation.

Pavlov condemned all revolutionary activity to redistribute property as an unending process. He maintained that socialists "forget that moral evil is the root of all social injustice."[47] Pavlov also translated from English two articles on socialism, both printed in *Baptist*. In the first, "Socialism as a Religion," by John Carlyle, Pavlov rejects the idea that socialism is another religion. He declared that "as long as it remains the object of political economy it is from the earth and earthly." In its love for the land, it "does not reach heaven." In the second article, "Socialism and Individualism," by E. M. Martinson, he admitted that socialists may have high ideals in meeting social injustice but is lacking on other counts. It causes the brotherly love of man by compulsion and undertakes "a deadly attack on individualism."[48]

45. Nesdoly, 225–26. *Bratskiï listok*, 1907, no. 7, 3. Levindanto, "Pamyati Deya Ivanovicha Mazaeva," *BV*, 1953, nos. 2–3, 98. Steeves, *The Russian Baptist Union, 1917–1935*, 492–93. Klibanov, 317–21.

46. European Baptist Congress, *Proceedings*, 1908, 158. *Baptist*, 1908, no. 4, 3. Nesdoly, 409–10.

47. *Baptist*, 1911, no. 46, 363.

48. Ibid., 1908, no. 8, 9–11, and 1909, no. 18, 13–15. Nesdoly, 337.

Vasilii V. Ivanov, Pavlov's contemporary, also discussed social and political issues. In an article in *Baptist* in 1909, he wrote that, although political measures may bring some benefit, they cannot bring peace or heal old wounds. Also, "The improvement of the life of the people is not a matter of wise politics but a matter of the church that performs its mission in the name of Christ and the power of Christ." For Ivanov religion provided the ultimate solution for social problems, but he with other Baptists were not simply reactionaries satisfied with the status quo. In his article, "The Position of the Baptists," in 1911, Ivanov wrote that the gospel needed to transform the life of the people both spiritually and in economic relations. In the economic realm he leaned toward a democratic socialism in which believers should have large communal workshops or factories or land conformable to local conditions with distribution of the returns justly distributed "conforming to the investment of work and the extent of the needs." In education each congregation should establish its own schools and should encourage children to aspire for higher education and also provide evening courses for adult members.[49]

Internal Organization

The most balanced and dispassionate evaluation of Russian Baptists in this period from an Orthodox researcher is S. P. Bondar's publication in 1911 of an article in *Missionerskoe obozrenie*, "Sovremennyï baptizm v Rossii," and his booklet, *Sovremennoe sostoyanie russkago baptizma*. Bondar was an official in the Department of Spiritual Affairs of the Ministry of Internal Affairs. He attempted to use reliable sources, which included evangelical materials. He was personally acquainted with Baptists, probably attending their congresses in 1910 and 1911. Bondar surveyed the history, beliefs, worship, and polity of Russia Baptists. Forty percent of his booklet was devoted to the Russian Baptist congress in St. Petersburg in 1910.[50]

In the section in Bondar's article on the character of Russian Baptists, he noted first that the movement had extended to almost all the provinces in Europe and Asiatic Russia, spreading not only among Orthodox but also various sects. Its mission was conducted "systematically" with the entire organization, including congregations, unions, and circles and the like, directed toward missionary goals. The Baptist churches with "their inner autonomy" were a basic unit in Baptist organization. Here members freely deliberated and "the most mature resolutions" were quickly executed. The ministers of the churches, traveling missionaries, youth circles, and all members of the congregation ascribed to the mandate of Oncken, "Every Baptist a missionary." A chief means of evangelization were the "invitational" meetings held in a majority

---

49. *Baptist*, 1909, no. 17, 4, and 1911, no. 9, 69–71. Nesdoly, 331, 401–3.

50. Bondar, "Sovremennyï baptizm v Rossii," *MO*, Oct. 1911, 302–18. Bondar, *Sovremennoe sostoyanie russkago baptizma*. For a reference of Bondar's attendance at the congress in Moscow in 1911, see *Baptist*, no. 42, 335.

of the congregations and conducted as well in public buildings, halls, and homes. Another evangelistic means were Sunday schools for children (or called children's meetings in Russia) where the Bible was taught, sectarian hymns sung, and the plan of salvation presented. Bondar claimed in St. Petersburg in 1909–1910 by far the greatest number of pupils in these schools came from Orthodox families. Bonder also noted another tool in evangelism in the production of thousands of cheap books, brochures, and leaflets. Bondar pointed out that the journal *Baptist* not only fulfilled the spiritual needs of its readers but also provided the dogmatic basis of the Baptist movement and published polemical articles against the Orthodox Church. In an article in 1910 in *Der Sendbote,* Carl Füllbrandt of the German Baptist Church in Odessa reported that there were now not less than seven weekly journals in addition to six or seven hymnals with texts and notes. Fetler's journal *Gost'* in January 1915 published a list of "Useful Literature" that included 164 titles, mostly tracts, some written by Fetler, but also books from Füllbrandt, Kargel, and Frey, and commentaries on the Pentateuch.[51] In his study, Bondar took special note of youth circles as an important adjunct to the work of the local church. They were a means of spiritual development and mission work. Their program included prayer, study of the Bible, and perusal of Christian literature. Members had the opportunity to practice preaching and prepare for teaching in Sunday schools. The All-Russian Union of Baptist Circles had its own treasury and supported its own missionary. Finances came from dues, collections, and donations. An article in *Missionerskoe obozrenie* on sectarians in 1914 noted that urban congregations, if not elsewhere, were as organized as in Western Europe and America. Sectarians were also elevating pulpits and providing chairs and benches for worshipers. It also stated that Baptists gave special attention to both choral and general singing. As Bondar, the article noted their publication of cheap popular literature with distribution among railroad passengers and in large railroad stations, fairs, and markets. It was legal to sell literature but illegal to distribute it freely but it was nevertheless done.[52]

Worship

One of the greatest strengths of the Baptist movement and other evangelicals was the intensity of their worship. The services were well balanced with preaching, prayer, and music. Services preserved the stundist and pietistic heritage of prayer or personal devotions equally with other elements of worship. The designation of "prayer house" was not just simply because sectarians could not claim they had churches but more so an indication of the importance of prayer in their services. In his attendance in 1910 for the Russian Baptist congress in St. Petersburg, Packer from Australia noted how worshipers went forward before seated with written messages of requests for prayer.

51. *Der Sendbote*, Mar. 13, 1910, 231. *Gost'*, Jan. 1915, 22–24.
52. "Sektantstvo v 1914-m godu," *MO*, Jan. 1915, 107–10.

The whole congregation participated in periods of prayer when all knelt and participated in a quiet undertone with possibly one or more praying simultaneously aloud. R. S. Latimer from England wrote, "The tones are so tender and so pathetic, and there is such a persistent gentle undertone, a wail of yearning desire rising almost to a sob, that the heart would be hard indeed that was not deeply moved."[53]

The services also attracted people who were hungry for preaching, and crowds often filled the places of meeting. In his remarks at the Baptist World Alliance in 1905, Üxküll reported that he had seen meetings so crowded that the candles could not burn because the room was so full. Preaching emphasized sin and salvation and stressed the blood of Christ that cleansed from all sin. Orthodox criticized Baptist speakers for their attacks on Orthodox priests and rites.[54]

Music was a third component that not only appealed to the worshiper but was also an important attraction to outsiders. Worshipers in St. Petersburg often carried both a Bible and hymnbook to the service. In the stundist period, Ukrainian tunes and words were used, while in St. Petersburg among the Pashkovites evangelical hymnody was an early element along with the use of a piano or organ. Pavel Pavlov, the son of Vasilii Pavlov, found it difficult to introduce a choir in the Tiflis church against the resistance of members with a traditional Molokan heritage that lacked choral singing and instrumental accompaniment. When he with some older brethren favored introducing a harmonium, some members threatened to leave and the controversy was not resolved until the return of Vasilii from Romania in 1901. In one of his sermons, Vasilii preached that in the Bible instruments were suitable in worship. Pavel used the harmonium in conducting both the congregational singing and the choir. As already noted, Ivan Prokhanov published many hymnals and his periodical, *Khristianin*, included issues with one or more new hymns with notes. Choirs grew in importance, noted already through the efforts of P. P. Perk, and the choir in the church in Samara grew by 1910 to sixty-five members, the largest choir in the Russian Union at the time. Choir directors served various churches, and some choirs accompanied itinerant missionaries.[55]

The music was diverse, drawing from both Russian roots and western evangelicalism. An Orthodox who reported on the music in Kharkov Province spoke of "simple melancholy melodious melodies" portraying a "misty and formless mysticism" but which worshipers sang with great fervor with trembling voice and tears in their eyes. In his message at the Baptist World Alliance in 1928, Pavel V. Ivanov-Klyshnikov stated, "Although in our songs may often be heard notes of tears and sadness, like the

---

53. Latimer, *With Christ in Russia*, 29–30. Packer, 37–38. McCaig, 175.

54. BWA, Congress, *Proceedings*, 1905, 184. McCaig, 62, 236–40. *TsV*, 1900, no. 12, 1328. Rennikov, *Zoloto Reina. O Nemtsakh v Rossii*, 386–88.

55. Grachev, "Iz istorii pesnopenii nashnego bratsva," *BV*, 1973, no. 4, 65. Packer, 36. *Istoriya*, 169–70. *BV*, 1967, no. 4, 28. *MO*, Jan. 1915, 107–10. Goncharenko, "Perfect Future in Past Traditions," *REE* 31/4 (Nov. 2011), 15–19.

sighs of snowdrifts on the boundless Russian plains, nevertheless, there is always in them the note of thanksgiving and a double joy or rest and labour:—rest in God and Labour for God!"[56]

In 1910 at the Russian Baptist Congress in St. Petersburg, a discussion arose over music. One speaker, Vyasovskiĭ, said he was dissatisfied with music in the Baptist church that had too many hymns "of a merry character" and lacked the prayerful mood of singing in Orthodox and Catholic churches. Semen Stepanov, however, countered by declaring that melodies needed to be "militant." S. V. Belousov quoted from an Orthodox priest who said that the major deficiency in singing in the Orthodox Church was its lack of popular melodies, which sectarians use and thus attract people to their meetings. Jakob Vins said that the solemn melodies in the Orthodox Church are without power as they are sung by specialists who are prepared for this task since childhood and to introduce such singing in Baptist churches would cause a disturbance.[57]

In their services Russian Baptists incorporated various Biblical customs such as the Love feast, which was a time of fellowship and devotion with refreshments, and the kiss of peace. In St. Petersburg men and women sat together, but in Ukraine they sat separately. Married women often covered their heads even if it was just a lace kerchief. In St. Petersburg, however, women often attended hatless but some wore a simple head covering but then removed it in the vestibule.[58]

Church Leadership

An article in *Baptist* in 1907, "Nashi presvitery" (Our Elders), stated that the elder, who may be called a pastor, or bishop, or some other term, is "the chief manager and first person of responsibility before the church and Christ Jesus." It also noted that ordination was only a blessing that gave him "a certain preference." Teachers assisted the elders in teaching, and the deacons cared for the poor and were responsible for the business needs of the church.[59]

The article also recorded a succession of ordinations beginning with Oncken in Germany in 1834 who in turn ordained Pavlov and Unger in 1869, the latter ordaining Johannes Wieler in 1872 who in turn ordained Balikhin in 1886 who in turn ordained others, listing nine men from 1898 to 1905. A further account listed V. V. Ivanov, ordained by Pavlov, who ordained eleven, and a final account listed Deï Mazaev who between 1893 and 1907 ordained eight.[60]

---

56. *TsV*, 1909, no. 12, 372. BWA, Congress, *Proceedings*, 1928, 76.
57. *Bratskiĭ listok*, 1910, no. 10, 12–13.
58. Packer, 35–37. McCaig. 55, 71. BWA, Congress, *Proceedings*, 1911, 176–77.
59. *Baptist*, 1907, no. 1, 20–21.
60. Ibid., no. 1; 20–21, no. 4, 17–18; no. 5, 12.

Pastors received little financial remuneration, providing their own support from their farms or other employment. Missionaries were generally employed six months or less for missionary service and must support themselves for the rest of the year. Missionaries were assured room and board but gained little money from the people themselves who were generally poor. In 1906 Pavlov claimed that when he was at the church in Tiflis he received a small salary, the only self-sufficient church at the time. When he moved to Odessa, the church also paid him a salary, providing in 1911 about $250 for the year. At the same time William Fetler was receiving at least $300 if not more. A few pastors received training in Germany or at the German Baptist seminary in Lodz when it was operating but generally had to be satisfied with short-term Bible courses if they received any training at all.[61]

Women

In his description of Baptists in 1911 at the Baptist World Alliance, Pavlov stated that in the church women have equal rights, including the right to vote, but may not occupy the office of minister or teacher. In the same year, an article appeared in *Baptist*, entitled with the German words, "Kinder, Kirche und Küche," describing the traditional role of women as confined to children, the church, and the kitchen. The author declared that God had mandated separate roles for men and women. He noted the Scripture admonished women to be silent in the church but yet women might preach if no men were available and also exhort in the home if she filled her traditional role within the family. Women might work with other women or serve in the medical profession if she had no family.[62]

At the Baptist World Alliance in 1911, Madame Yasnovskiï, who served as treasurer of Fetler's *Dom Evangeliya*, noted that women in St. Petersburg conducted sewing meetings, whose items were sold to raise money for their causes. Her circle gave money for construction of the church building and supported a missionary. Women who knew a foreign language translated tracts into Russian. At the same congress, Melanie Fetler said that in Russia women were "still very far behind the men," with few workers among women. She stated that many women were attempting some mission work but not openly. She noted that in the south of Russia one woman held meetings and gained a large number of converts.[63]

Young women in the youth circles were far more engaged in mission activity than women of an older generation, especially outside of St. Petersburg. Women also had their own women's meetings, but according to V. V. Ivanov proved unsatisfactory for a number of women who preferred powerful preaching. As previously noted, Elena V.

61. Letter from Pavlov, Aug. 7, 1906. Packer, 31–32. BWA, Congress, *Proceedings*, 1911, 21. Bondar, *Sovremennoe sostoyanie russkago baptizma*, 64.

62. *Baptist*, 1911, no. 31, 145–46, and no. 46, 361.

63. BWA, Congress, *Proceedings*, 1911, 174, 176.

Beklemisheva, an educator, took the floor at congresses of the Russian Baptist Union. Generally only educated women as Beklemisheva and the aristocratic women from the Pashovite movement could play any leadership roles, but they were comparatively few in number.[64]

Statistics

Because of the independence of local congregations, it has often been difficult to obtain a satisfactory and complete accounting of Baptist statistics. Pavlov in 1905 estimated that Russian Baptists numbered 20,000, but the Russian Baptist Union wanted an exact compilation. But it was a struggle. In April 1909 *Baptist* published statistics from Pavlov of Russian Baptist congregations for 1907, recording 160 congregations and 11,256 members. Pavlov readily admitted the report was incomplete. He was unable to get memberships from all congregations and could not obtain locations of others. In 1910 Fetler issued a work on Baptist statistics for 1909, listing 10,935 Russian Baptists in 149 churches, 26,126 German and Baltic Baptists in 147 churches, and 2,470 in 57 churches in the Duchy of Finland. Including children, Fetler arrived at the figure of 49,690. For 1910 he listed only 9,186 Russian members in 146 churches out of 420. Although his statistics for German and Baltic peoples appear accurate, the statistics for Russian Baptists were clearly inadequate.[65]

With the rapid number of baptisms, Baptists were claiming higher figures. Madame Yasnovskiï stated in London on her way to the Baptist World Alliance in Philadelphia 1911 that Baptists were baptizing converts by the hundreds and were making "astonishing progress" in all parts of Russia. Dr. William Kean at the depot of the British and Foreign bible Society in St. Petersburg told George Macalpine in a delegation of the Baptist World Alliance "that the evangelical movement had fallen into the hands of the Baptists all over Russia" and was threatening "the very existence of the Orthodox church." At the Baptist World Alliance meeting in Philadelphia in 1911, I. A. Golyaev claimed more than 500 Russian Baptist communities with 50,000 members. At the congress in Stockholm in 1913, Semen Stepanov greeted the assembly from 100,000 Baptists in Russia, probably including the entire Baptist constituency in the country. The Orthodox writer, V. Fedorov declared in his article in 1912 that such a figure showed that Baptist success in Russia was "phenomenal."[66]

---

64. *Baptist*, 1909, no. 22, 17–18; 1910, no. 43, 352; and 1912, no. 20, 5. Nesdoly, 355–57. *Baptist Times and Freeman*, Sep. 23, 1910, 621. *Bratskiï listok*, 1910, no. 10, 5–6.

65. *Baptist*, 1909, no. 8, 17–19. V. A. Fetler, *Statistika russkikh baptistov za 1909 god* and *Statistika Russkikh Evangel'skikh Khristian Baptistov za 1910 god*. Klibanov, 175. *Missionerskiï sbornik*, 1913, no.12, 1050.

66. *Baptist Times and Freeman*, July 6, 1911, 1, and July 25, 1913, 577. Mcalpine, "Report of a Delegation to St. Petersburg from the Baptist World Alliance," BWA, Continental Committee, *Minutes*, Sep. 18, 1911, 130. BWA, Congress, *Proceedings*, 1911, 42. Fedorov, "Sredi baptistov," *Missionerskiï sbornik*. 1913, no. 12, 1050.

Russian Baptist Union

Government statistics also were supporting the Baptist claims of growth. The Department of Spiritual Affairs in the Department of Internal Affairs reported that on January 1, 1912, Baptists numbered 114,642. Of these about 67,000 were of Russian nationality and about 48,000 non-Russian. It noted that in seven years from 1905 through 1911, about 28,000 left Orthodoxy for the Baptists, significantly increasing the number of Baptists of Russian nationality.[67]

One, however, needs to question the figures of the Department of Spiritual Affairs whether they reflect the baptized membership or figures of a community. The German Baptist Union in Russia, which included the German and Baltic peoples, reported in 1912 with its usual careful calculation 27,913 baptized members but a community of adherents of almost 58,000,[68] One is then led to consider the government's figures of 48,000 for non-Russians as figures for a community of adherents rather than church membership. For Orthodox to include infants and children as members was normal but not for Baptists who upheld believer's baptism. The figure of 67.000 for Russian Baptists is then probably approximately correct for the Russian Baptist community. Usually in a comparatively young and vigorous movement, adherents often significantly outnumber members and thus the grand total for the entire Baptist community but not baptized membership may very well have been over 100,000. In any case, Baptist growth was significant in spite of the obstacles Baptists faced from both church and state.

---

67. Klibanov, 274–76. *Slovo istiny*, July, 1914, 566.
68. *Der Hausfreund*, Aug. 29/Sep. 11, 1912, 286.

25

The Rivals

Baptists and Evangelical Christians

IN THE PREVIOUS CHAPTER of this work, "Survival," Ivan S. Prokhanov (1869–1935) emerged in the last decade the nineteenth century as an evangelical leader with his production of the underground paper, *Beseda*. He came from a Molokan family, but his parents became Baptists. He was converted and joined the Baptist church in Vladikavkaz by baptism in January 1887. Upon his entry at the St. Petersburg Technological Institute in 1888, he associated with the Pashkovites, the only Russian evangelical body in the city at the time. He already, however, showed his independence by rarely attending the regular Pashkovite meetings in the Lieven mansion and rather preached in secret to small groups. In 1895 he fled Russia, fearing arrest, and for three and a half years he was in England, Germany, and France, attending various educational institutions and acquiring English, German, and French.

He returned in 1898 to Russia with the determination to spread the evangelical faith through publication. Although he preached, he was still a layman. With his training as an engineer, he gained in 1901 employment with the Westinghouse Electric Company in St. Petersburg. In 1902 he was able to get past the censor the publication of *Gusli,* a collection of 571 hymns, some his own compositions or translations of other hymns, which became a standard hymnal for evangelicals. Upon the 1905 Manifesto granting religious freedom, he took the lead in Russian evangelical publishing by launching and editing in 1906 *Khristianin* (The Christian), patterned after the English periodical of the same name, which became a leading journal of evangelical faith and work. The first issue of fifty-eight pages with a supplement of sixteen pages included poetry; a sermon by Spurgeon; articles on the unity of the church, prayer, the crucified Christ, and faith for young readers; and news. Russian Baptists did not publish their own journal until the following year.[1] Prokhanov's publishing interests rapidly expanded. As a supplement to *Khristianin*, he issued *Bratskiï listok*, (The Fraternal Leaflet), a periodical of the denominational affairs of evangelical bodies. At first it was a separate publication but with issue no. 8 in 1908 and beginning in 1911 its issues were incorporated with *Khristianin*. Further supplements included *Yunyï khristianin* (The Young Christian), which was superseded by *Molodoï vinogradnik* (The Young Vineyard), published from 1909 to 1917, and *Detskiï drug* (The Children's Friend). He also published a monthly, *Detskaya biblioteka* (The Children's Library). In 1908 he began editing a weekly tract, *Seyatel'* (The Sower), but in 1909 its editorship was assumed by G. G. Rodd. Prokhanov also edited *Utrennyaya zvezda* (The Morning Star), a weekly religious periodical of progressive thought that dealt with political and social issues. It began with a trial issue in December 1909 and was published from 1910 to 1922.[2] Prokhanov expanded his musical ministry after *Gusli* by including hymns with notes in *Khristianin*, the publishing of a monthly musical magazine, *Novaya Melodiya*, and the publication of hymnals with a special purpose. By the early 1930s Prokhanov had published ten hymnals, most published before 1917 but with plans for two more.[3]

With his growing publishing enterprise and other Christian work while still maintaining his position as an engineer with Westinghouse, Prokhanov turned for help in 1908 to the Mennonite Brethren, which had a printing firm in Halbstadt, Molochna, that published, *Friedensstimme*. On his suggestion, he proposed forming a publishing company, *Raduga* (The Rainbow), representing peace after the storm of 1905. Beside himself, it included five Mennonite Brethren—Heinrch Braun, Isaak Regier, Abraham Kroeker, David Isaak, and Peter P. Perk. Prokhanov was now relieved of publishing to concentrate on his editorial work and his responsibilities for the Russian literature of *Raduga*. Kroeker would be responsible for German literature. The new company opened a Christian bookstore in St. Petersburg that carried a wide range of evangelical literature, offering Scripture, Christian books, hymnals, tracts, periodicals, and gramaphone records.[4]

As previously noted, he published in 1910 and 1912 works on the legal position of evangelicals. In 1911 he issued four small booklets on the laying on of hands and ordination, Sunday, the service of women, and marriage and divorce. In September 1911 he began publishing in *Bratskiï listok* four lectures on homiletics, "Kratkoe uchenie o

---

1. Prokhanov, *In the Cauldron*, 121–23, 137–139. MO, June 1903, 1347–51. Fast, "Nachrichten aus Russland," *Der Sendbote*, Feb. 21, 1906. 122–23.

2. Prokhanov, *In the Cauldron*, 157–58. Puzynin, *Gospel Christians*, 136–38. Wardin, *Evangelical Sectarianism*, 330.

3. Prokhanov, *In the Cauldron*, 143–47. Wardin, *Evangelical Sectarianism*, 330–31.

4. Prokhanov, *In the Cauldron*. 148–49. *Khristianin*, Dec. 1908. *Utrennyaya zvezda*, Jan. 27, 1912, 6.

propevedi," which appeared in 1911 as a book. It was the first work on homiletics in the Russian language.[5]

Prokhanov was not content, however, to be simply a publisher and editor of evangelical material but with the new era of freedom sought to be the head of a congregation of his own. In St. Petersburg, however, Ivan Kargel, since his return to St. Petersburg, in 1898, had become the pastor of the Pashkovite body in the Lieven Mansion. Under Kargel Pashkovites had divided when under his direction they began to elect elders and deacons. Pashkovites were also increasingly accepting believer's baptism by immersion. As Pashkovites under Pashkov, Kargel also practiced open communion, not requiring believer's baptism for either communion or membership. This was very satisfactory for the aristocratic Pashkovite women who did not favor a separatist Baptist position that would bring a formal break with the Orthodox Church. With his views of Christian unity, sanctification, and open communion, Kargel had traveled far from his original German Baptist position of close communion and close membership. He attended the Baptist World Alliance in London in 1905, but according to Yakov Zhidkov he reported regretting he had attended the congress since he found "little that was spiritual, and for the most part was done and decided there in the flesh."[6] Prokhanov, however, will find an opening in a growing dissatisfaction with Kargel's leadership. V. P. Stepanov (1874–1938), who began associating with Pashkovites in coming in 1897 to St. Petersburg during his military service, claimed that a leader of Pashkovite youth who were dissatisfied with Kargel approached him for leadership. Stepanov, who was now an ordained Baptist minister and outside St. Petersburg, however, refused. Consequently the youth now turned to Prokhanov who, according to Stepanov, now took over two-thirds of Kargel's congregation while Kargel was away from the city. Upon his return, Kargel, again according to Stepanov, called Prokhanov a "*plotskioïchelovek*" (a carnal man). Prokhanov's congregation took the name of First Evangelical Christian Church, while Kargel's group will be called the Second Evangelical Christian Church. Whatever Kargel's true feelings, with his disgust with Baptists he will nevertheless find it more compatible to be associated with the Evangelical Christian movement.[7]

For Prokhanov a publishing career and pastor of a church in St. Petersburg will still not be enough for his calling. He sought now an even broader platform. He always tended to be an independent operator, not seeking collegiality but to play a leading if not dominating role. In the 1890s he was successsful in publishing his own independent underground paper, *Beseda,* already making a name for himself in evangelical

---

5. Wardin, *Evangelical Sectarianism*, 328–29, 390. For a review by Archimandrite Arsenii of the first installment of the work on homiletics, see "Sektantskii professor gomiletiki," *Vera i razum*, Jan. 1912, 115–24, and which appeared as a pamphlet in Kharkov in 1912.

6. *BV*, 1957, no. 3, 61.

7. See the speech of Stepanov and the speech of Odintsov, two Baptists opposed to Prokhanov, on his splitting the Pashkovite congregation in *Baptist*, 1925, nos. 6–7, 38–39, and 1927, no. 1, 20–21.

circles both in Russia and abroad. When in St. Petersburg in the 1890s and again in the early years of the twentieth century, he followed largely his own independent path away from the old-time Pashkovites, even to the extent of splitting the Pashkovite congregation. He will now find opportunity for further advancement among evangelicals disgruntled with the leadership of the Russian Baptist Union and develop a competing evangelical body, the Evangelical Christian Union.

The period from 1908 to the outbreak of the First World War in 1914 will not only be a time of increased pressure against Baptists and other evangelicals but will also be further complicated by the rivalry of two competing unions. In the growing hostility, their relations, however, will be punctuated by flashes of cooperation and even overtures for unity. In addition, in St. Petersburg the careers of Prokhanov and William Fetler, two remarkable men, will intersect.

Prokhanov and Fetler

In an article in January 1911 in *Missionerskoe obozrenie*, the Orthodox author recognized the importance of both Prokhanov and Fetler for the evangelical cause. He wrote concerning Prokhanov, "it is impossible to deny (him) not only in energy, in persistence, but also in organizational talent." He also does not "cool down" his devotion to student work. The author recognized Fetler for "placing in prominence the main headquarters of the sect in the community of the capital." He also noted that Fetler considered himself "an apostle to Russia," and was forming in his church the "Brotherhood of the Acts of the Apostles," individuals, as the first apostles, placing all on the altar for Christ.[8]

At the final session of the Congress of Sectarian Rights in St. Petersburg in January 1907, Deï Mazaev preached a sermon based on Moses, who after fleeing Egypt defended the daughters of Jethro, the Midianite priest, whom shepherds had blocked in drawing water for their sheep. Mazaev went on to say that in their sessions at the congress believers had been limited in being forced to meet in small meeting spaces when they needed a large prayer house in the city for all believers and others. He then predicted if the believers in St. Petersburg would not do it, then an Egyptian, such as Moses, will come and do it for them.[9]

As Paul Steeves noted in his dissertation, Mazaev's Egyptian did arrive a short time later in the person of Fetler. As already indicated, Fetler built in St. Petersburg the large *Dom Evangeliya*, seventy feet high, seating 2,000 in its sanctuary on an upper level with its two galleries and smaller rooms on its first level. It opened on December 25, 1911, four and a half years after Fetler's arrival. For Mazaev Fetler was a Moses

---

8. *MO*, Jan. 1911, 189–92.
9. *Bratskiï listok*, Jan. 1907, 7–8.

who established in the capital a thriving Russian Baptist presence that could meet Prokhanov on his own ground.[10]

Fetler and Prokhanaov were similar in a number of respects but also opposites. Both men were preachers, editors, publishers, authors, and poets. Both were charismatic, developed large congregations, and drew devoted followings. In publication Fetler and Prokhanov were in tandem with the former even maintaining his own printery and bookstore. Both were committed evangelicals with the belief, an almost messianic complex, that they were God's instrument to enter Russia with the transforming work of the gospel. Both were young—Fetler only twenty-four and Prokkhanov in his thirties, when they began their pastoral work in the city. Both men were most energetic, extremely devoted to their tasks. Prokhanov was a hard worker; toward the end of the period with increasing responsibilities he was even working until two in the morning or even all night.[11] In addition he continued his position as engineer. Fetler appeared constantly on the move, putting his mission calling first, even in later years with a growing family. Both Prokhanov and Fetler had studied abroad and came with Western ideals. Both wrote and spoke out on sectarian rights. They were outstanding linguists; both knew Russian, English, and German, while Fetler also spoke Latvian and Prokhanov was familiar with French. Both were strong advocates of Christian education, providing Sunday schools for children, training for youth, and theological education for pastors. In September 1907 in the mansion of Nathalie Lieven, both Prokhanov and Fetler participated in a session devoted to the education of children. In his article in early 1908, "A Call for a Holy Cause—Sunday Schools for Children," Fetler reported that he with others had already started a Sunday school in the Lieven home with 200 children in thirty classes. He also stated that lessons for Bible teachers produced by the World International Union of Bible Teachers, now printed in Russian, may be obtained from Prokhanov. Fetler was able to gain the hall of the city Duma, seating 2,000, for an Easter festival of evangelical Sunday schools in 1908. Eight Sunday schools cooperated including Russian, Latvian, and German Baptists as well as Evangelical Christians. Fetler, Prokhanov, Kargel and others spoke at the festival. A congress for all evangelical youth was held in Moscow in 1908. In 1909 Prokhanov began in St. Petersburg the first Christian school for children from seven to fifteen, open to all children of evangelical believers.[12]

Although Fetler and Prokhanov were church builders in the same evangelical cause, they became rivals and both had reservations about the other. Prokhanov disapproved Fetler's emotionalism, and Fetler questioned Prokhanov's theology. On the other hand, even with the growing hostility of the leaders of the Russian Baptists toward Evangelical Christians, Fetler and Prokhanov never severed their ties while both

---

10. Steeves, 64–65. For a description of *Dom Evangeliya*, see *Missions*, Mar. 1912, 186–88.

11. Prokhanov, *In the Cauldron*, 168.

12. *Bratskii(listok*, 1907, no. 9, 1–3, and 1909, no. 9, 2. *Baptist*, 1908, no. 2, 12–23, and no. 10, 12. Latimer, *With Christ in Russia*, 17–18, 47–54. *Baptist Times and Freeman*, March 19, 1909, 213.

were in St. Petersburg. Robert Latimer from England noted in 1910 at an evangelistic service led by Fetler in Nobel Hall that the choirs of both Fetler's and Prokhanov's churches participated. After the First All-Russian Congress of Evangelical Christians in September 1910, Fetler spoke at the Spiritual Congress that followed. At the laying of the granite cornerstone and bricks of Fetler's *Dom Evangeliya* in September 1910, both Prokhanov and Kargel spoke and also laid bricks. Before calling on Prokhanov to speak, Fetler read Psalm 133 with the words, "How good and pleasant a thing it is for brethren to dwell together in unity." Prokhanov then brought greetings from the Evangelical Christian churches and expressed the hope that the laying of bricks for the new prayer house will also be the laying of a spiritual union for all believers. On the day following the opening of *Dom Evangeliya* in December 1911, Kargel, representing the Evangelical Christians, spoke. At the opening of Prokhanov's Bible school in 1913, Fetler gave a rousing speech, congratulated Prokhanov, and extended his best wishes to the students.[13]

Along with common traits and shared civility, both Prokhanov and Fetler, however, also shared negative qualities. Both men gained access to their preaching positions in St. Petersburg by certain questionable means. As noted, Prokhanov, apparently surreptitiously, helped to split the Pashkovite congregation for his own ends. In addition, Baptist hostility toward Prokhanov was often fueled by the belief that his movement accepted members whom Baptists had excluded, thereby destroying the discipline of their churches. In Fetler's case, the Latvian Baptists in his congregation accused him for using them and their contributions in developing his Russian congregation at their expense. In addition, Pashkovites accused Fetler of bringing discord in their ranks in St. Petersburg. In entering Moscow, Fetler divided the Pashkovite work there and his entry into Riga with a new Baptist work upset the Latvian Baptists already established in the city.[14]

Both Prokhanov and Fetler were autocratic and self-centered. Both were their own persons and neither exercised a shared collegiality with their peers. Before his retirement, Prokhanov always held the chief position of his union and directed its affairs. He was also president of the youth organization and headed his congregation's church council. Abraham Friesen, a Mennonite and a professor of history wrote, "from reading Prokhanov's autobiography one could be misled in thinking that he did everything." Fetler became known as dictatorial and shunned the advice of others. Fetler arrived in Russia with the support of the Pioneer Mission, formed in 1889 with

13. Interview of Wardin with Mrs. I. V. Neprash, Aug. 17, 1970. Interview of Franklin with Fetler, ABMU/ABFMS, *Correspondence*, Russian Mission, 1900–1919. Latimer, *With Christ in Russia*, 84–85. *Bratskii listok*, 1910, no. 10, 19–20. *MRW*, Dec. 1910, 946. *Baptist Times and Freeman*, Sep. 30, 1910, 637. *Baptist*, Dec. 31, 1911, 394. *Christian Standard*, Mar. 22, 1913, 10–11.

14. For Paskovite charges of Fetler's disruptive activity in St. Petersburg and Moscow, see *Pis'mo vsem baptistskim obshchinam*, 25–26, 79, 87–88. For Latvian Baptist charges against Fetler, see letter of William S. Oncken to Philcox, July 11, 1911, and letter of Inke and Frey to the American Baptist Foreign Mission Society, Dec. 17, 1912, ABMU/ABFMS, *Correspondence*, Russian Mission, 1900–1919.

work in the British Isles and France, and grateful to Fetler for opening a new field. But later in 1911 with his supporters in England, he formed the Russian Evangelization Society, which he headed as "Superintendent to Russia." After the First World War he established in America the Russian Missionary Society, which he himself led, and made the Russian Evangelization Society a British section of the new society. In America Fetler had a very disruptive relationship with his boards. While he was still in Russia, he and the Russian Baptist Union, however, were able to work cooperatively only because of mutual interests and in territory where he could work independently far from the interests of other Russian Baptists. He could operate here without the supervisory role of an outside mission agency.[15]

Although both were Russian subjects and came from Baptist families and embarked on similar mission enterprises, they also had markedly different characteristics. Prokhanov was of Russian nationality while Fetler had a Latvian father and a German Baltic mother. Prokhanov possessed an analytic and calculating mind with an ability to shade appearances. For him, relationships outside his organization were only tentative and only maintained if they suited his purposes. He was circumspect in his relations with the government. Although a conservative evangelical, Prokhanov with a rather broad educational background and travel was not a traditional fundamentalist. He had a broad interest in political and social issues and an ecumenical concern for the unity of evangelical believers. Fetler, although also possessing a fertile mind, was above all the consummate revivalist. His services were exuberant with brass bands and singing brigades. He was not duplicitous but bluntly forthright in his beliefs and feelings. He was impulsive, often lacking balance. Although he was adept at raising funds, such as for *Dom Evangeliya*, he was a poor financial administrator. Fetler was far more confrontational than Prokhanov with government and repeatedly faced legal challenges. Some evangelicals felt he was too bold if not fanatical. Fetler was a dogmatic fundamentalist in doctrine and outside the realm of relations between church and state and traditional morality, such as reclaiming drunkards and street women, showed little interest in social and political problems. As many evangelicals of the time, he preached living the victorious Christian life. With his emotionalism and apparent attraction to Pentecostalism, he was accused of Pentecostalism but denied it and always remained a Baptist.[16]

---

15. Friesen, *In Defense of Privilege*, 416, ft. 10. For Fetler's shift to an independent missionary and his lack of ability to work with his own boards, see Wardin, "William Fetler," 238–42, as well as the letter of William S. Oncken to Philcox, July 11, 1911, ABMU/ABFMS, *Correspondence*, Russian Mission, 1900–1919; letter of Rushbrooke to the secretaries of the cooperating boards, June 9, 1922, W. O. Lewis Papers; and Craig, *Wonders of Grace*, 57.

16. For Fetlers' use of rousing music, see Larsson, "10 Years in Russia," *The War Cry*, July 19, 1969, 13. Letter of William S. Oncken to Philcox, July 11, 1911. Unsigned mns., c. Dec. 1912, of a visit of an American to St. Petersburg, and Franklin, "Extracts from Notes," 1913, ABMU/ABFMS, *Correspondence*, Russian Mission, 1900–1919. For charges of Pentecostalism against Fetler, see *Pis'mo vsem baptistkim obshchinam*, 13–15, 95–96.

The Evangelical Christian Division

With his church in St. Petersburg and publication enterprise, Prokhanov had a firm base for further expansion of his work. Prokhanov's First Evangelical Christian Church in St. Petersburg, as was Fetler's congregation, a prominent congregation. Prokhanov wrote that he generally preached on Sundays in the large Terishevsky Hall in the city center that held up to 1,000 persons, claiming it was almost always filled. In August 1908 Prokhanov led in formally organizing his church, which was headed by a church council and included numerous committees. The congregation received legalization on November 16, 1908, the first, Prokhanov claimed, in St. Petersburg. By 1911 the church had 860 members and eleven places of worship.[17]

The Prokhanov and Kargel churches were not the only Evangelical Christian congregations. Earlier stundist and Pashkovite influences with their rejection of centralization and strict confessional statements, as advocated by Baptists, played a role in producing congregations resistant to the Baptist name and polity. Congregations of Evangelical Christians appeared in Kiev, Konotop, Sevastopol, Odessa, and Yekatarinoslav. With his great influence and leadership skills, Prokhanov, now found a constituency that would follow his lead independent of the Russian Baptist Union.[18]

A congress of Evangelical Christians met in Odessa in 1908 with fourteen representatives from ten churches. It appointed A. A. Persianov as evangelist, which indicated a desire for expansion. A second regional conference met at Yekaterinoslav in April 1909 and resolved to meet again here in September but with the approval of the authorities met instead in St. Petersburg as the first All-Russian Evangelical Christian Congress.[19]

In his autobiography, Prokhanov justified his formation of an Evangelical Christian Union as an effort to organize the entire Evangelical movement. He further explained, "At that time the Evangelical churches and groups in Russia were not united with each other in any way, and besides there was a lack of organization inside the individual churches." He wrote to Odessa and Sevatopol and other places explaining his views. Prokhanov's statements are ambiguous and false, deliberately leaving out any mention of the Baptists and their organizations. In their letter to the Russian Baptist Union in 1911, Prokhanov and other Evangelical Christian leaders will maintain, again clouding the facts, that the St. Petersburg Evangelical Christian Church was

17. Prokhanov, *In the Cauldron*, 150, 158. Bratskiï *listok/Khristianin*, 1908, no, 8, 9–12. BWA, Congress, *Proceedings*, 1911, 439. Byford, *Peasants and Prophets*, 99.

18. For Sevastopol, see Latimer, *Under Three Czars*, 109, and Warns, 127. For Kiev, Konotop, and Sevastopol, see *Baptist*, 1925, nos. 6–7, 39. For Odessa, see *Evangelical Christendom*, July–Aug. 1910, 85–86, and *Der Sendbote*, Aug. 31, 1910, 549.

19. For places and dates of the first two Evangelical Christian congresses, see the letter of the Evangelical Christian Union to the Russian Baptist Union in 1911 in Chepurin, *Obzor sektantskoï literatury: Religioznyya razdeleniya v sektantstve*, 22–24. Stepanov in *Baptist*, 1925, nos. 6–7, 39, and Odintsov in *Baptist*, 1927, no. 1, 20, make no mention of the Odessa congress but claim the congress in Yekaterinoslav met in 1908, which is in error.

only a guest at the Russian Baptist congresses in 1904, 1905, and 1906 and did not seek union. In a letter to Deï Mazaev from A. E. Leushkin, now with others in the Tiflis church rejecting Baptist leadership, Leushkin took the same line as other Evangelical Christians. He declared that Evangelical Christians did not arise from Baptists but were an independent movement of Evangelical Christians with Pashkovite roots, such as in St. Petersburg, pointing out that neither Radstock nor Pashkov were ever Baptists.[20]

Baptists, however, saw the Evangelical Christians as a movement bringing division in the Baptist Union that in the first years of the twentieth century was witnessing a union of Pashkovites/ Evangelical Christians. In his article, "Ne ta doroga" ("Not This Way"), Deï Mazaev wrote that at the "memorable meeting" in 1905 Baptists welcomed the St. Petersburg church and other evangelical congregations with the congress taking the name "Evangelical Christians-Baptists." Mazaev was so delighted that he wrote "as if we stopped being Baptists and almost began to forget that we were Baptists. Our hearts were full of joy and our minds—merry and we expected great after-effects." In a speech delivered much later, V. P. Stepanov noted in the period from 1904 to 1906 Evangelical Christians from Kiev, Konotop, and Sevastopol joined with the St. Petersburg church contributing as well 500 rubles. In his letter to Leuschkin, I. K. Savel'ev claimed that when the Pashkovites rejected infant baptism Baptists accepted them in communion and the two worked together at a time Prokhanov had not as yet settled in St. Petersburg. He also declared that Prokhanov "conducted a competition and began to undertake hunting for Baptists and desired to increase the number of his party."[21]

After his criticism in *Baptist* in October 1908 of the Odessa congress of Evangelical Christians, Mazaev wrote another article two months later, "Ot redaktsii" (From the Editor). Although he wrote that he didn't wish to write against other fraternal journals that included edifying Christian material, yet he found *Khristianin* to be an anti-Baptist periodical. He did not object to its teaching but its appeal for contributions to a *Khristianin* fund that would divert money away from the Baptist mission fund. He objected to the six-week courses that Prokhanov organized that attracted excluded members of Baptist churches, thereby subsidizing with funds, which should come to Baptists, a hostile institute that supported these members. In the following year in June he wrote an article "O Peterburgskoï 'svobode'" (On Petersburg "Freedom"). He said that ever since the conference in Rückenau in 1882, Baptists have rejected the appeal of Pashkov to accept in the church infants equally with immersed believers. He now claimed that the Evangelical Christian Union in St. Petersburg, based on a platform of enlisting all Christians but allowing them to remain in their respective congregations,

---

20. Prokhanov, *In the Cauldron*, 149–50. Fourth letter of Leushkin to Deï Mazaev, *Pis'ma k brat'yam*, 80–82.

21. *Baptist*, 1911, no. 34, 268, and 1925, nos. 6–7, 39. Letter of Savel'ev to Leushkin, *Pisma k brat'yam evangel'skim khristianam baptistam*, 73.

as creating a "half gospel" as over against the "full gospel" of the Baptists. Mazaev, however, was unfairly overreaching. Although Prokhanov wished to unite all evangelicals, he clearly drew the line as Baptists in rejecting infant baptism and accepted only immersed believers as members of his organization. Unlike Baptists, however, he observed a semi-open communion, restricting it to the regenerated.[22]

Were there any fundamental differences between Baptists and Evangelical Christians? Both groups were evangelical, preached the new birth, and required baptism by immersion for membership. Prokhanov himself had been a Baptist and never repudiated basic Baptist principles of polity or the symbolic nature of baptism even when he sought later support from the Disciples of Christ. One problem was leadership, which was a problem on both sides. As noted, Prokhanov was his own man, even taking an independent course from traditional Pashkovites in church government. With his gifts he felt he was equal if not superior to any Baptist leadership and must mark out for himself a course of leadership if not dominance. Although he advocated a joint operation with Baptists and other evangelicals on a common front, it must be done on his terms without genuine copartnership.

It was almost the same for Deï Mazaev, who as noted, was regarded even by Baptist colleagues as autocratic. He was noted for his leadership skills, knowledge, and his financial prowess. He carried the Russian Baptist Union through the period of suppression from the 1880s to 1905. The Baptist movement grew at least in part because of the centralized authority of Mazaev and the Baptist program. Leushkin's fourth letter to Mazaev, although with an ax to grind because of his excommunication, indicted him with some truth by stating, "that all your activity was without love, without guardianship and spiritual guidance of the congregations, and was based on 'the scourges' of sharp expressions and 'the scorpion of excommunication.'" Leushkin also accused Mazaev thinking only "to preserve your power and position in the Union." As previously noted, opponents of Mazaev's rejection of infants in church membership at the Sectarian Rights Conference in 1907 charged him with dominating control.[23]

Evangelical Christians also objected to the name "Baptist," preferring "Evangelical Christian" or "Gospel Christian." As early as 1895 in an article, "Kto my?" (Who Are We?) in his periodical, *Beseda*, Prokhanov wrestled over a proper designation for evangelicals, recognizing they were called many different names. He rejected "sectarian," "rationalist," "stundist," as not representing the true nature of evangelicals. The name "Pashkovite" was objectionable as suggesting a foreign origin. "Baptist," although euphonius and indicating baptism, yet a word that only reflected its outward character but not its true nature. He opted for "Evangelicals" and "Gospel Christians," since evangelicals are "Bible Christians," based on the Gospels. In his interview with J. H. Franklin in St. Petersburg in April 1913, Prokhanov maintained that people in Russia

---

22. *Baptist*, 1908, no. 10, 13–16, and no. 12, 1–3; 1909, no. 11, 14–15.

23. Fourth Letter of Leushkin to Mazaev, *Pis'ma k brat'yam*, 83–84, with Leushkin's words translated in Klibanov, 299–300.

generally do not understand the name "Baptist," but "Evangelical Christian," meaning "Gospel Christian," sounds beautiful in Russian. He also argued that using "Baptist" is an affront to the Orthodox Church in declaring their baptism is no baptism. It also called attention to the form of the ordinance, which was not the essential difference between Baptists and the Orthodox. Elsewhere he noted that "Gospel (*evangel'skie*) Christians" is a more accurate translation than "Evangelical Christians," but the latter has been generally adopted in the West and is therefore convenient to use.[24]

In the 1906 congress of the Russian Baptist Union, the issue arose whether the name "Baptist" was obligatory for congregations who wished to join but objected to "Baptist" as neither biblical nor Russian. Mazaev responded that Baptists carried under their name the true gospel teaching. At the preliminary consultative conference on sectarian rights at the end of the year in December in Kiev that included Baptists, Evangelical Christians, and Mennonites, the minutes always designated those present as "Evangelical Christians." F. Brauer, president of the German Baptist Union of Russia, noting some tension over a proper name, took the matter to the leadership but was always brushed aside. Brauer then went to I. P. Kushnerov, the respected advocate of sectarian rights, who told him that the name "Baptist" was a stumbling block for many and was strenuously objected to by Evangelical Christians. When the opportunity presented itself, Brauer requested a vote on the name; out of seventy-nine only six or seven rejected the name "Baptist." At the Congress of Sectarian Rights in 1907, Mazaev insisted on the name "Baptist," while others contended for "Evangelical Christian." It was agreed that the name should be "Baptists and Evangelical Christians" but strangely in the reading of the minutes the name "Baptist" did not appear.[25]

In the following year, the very first issue of the new journal, *Baptist*, edited by Mazaev, included a picture on the front page of John immersing Christ in the Jordan, and an article, "Nazvanie 'Baptists'" (The name "Baptists"). The article pointed out that both "Christian" and "Baptism" were Greek and not Russian. Baptists do not rest on any other denomination but as with the apostles "the one same Lord, the one same faith, and namely the same one baptism itself, which you do not come across once or anywhere in any other Christian church. Another name other than Baptist would destroy our unity with ten million Baptists abroad." Several years later V. V. Ivanov wrote in his article, "Who Are the Baptists and Their Union," that the Baptists received their name since they were known as baptizing believers only. "Baptist" he admitted may be a Greek word but also were such words as Christ, Jesus, gospel, and Christian, and the New Testament itself was written in Greek.[26]

---

24. *Beseda*, Aug. 1895, 122–25. "Interview with Rev. I. S. Prokhanov," ABMU/ABFMS, *Correspondence*, Russian Mission, 1900–1919. *The Gospel in Russia*, Nov. 1926, 8.

25. *MO*, Oct. 1906, 461. *Der Hausfreund*, Feb. 7/20, 1907, 41–42. Svensson, *De ewangeliska kristnas konferens*, 25–26.

26. *Baptist*, 1907, no. 1, 2–4, and 1909, no. 16, 1–3.

At the St. Petersburg congress of Russian Baptists in 1910, the question of the name for the Russian Baptist Union was raised when Fetler proposed that only "Baptist" be used for its constitution. After a long debate the congress by a vote of 56 to 26 resolved to retain the full name, "The Union of Evangelical Christians-Baptists."[27]

Probably the most divisive issue was the charge against Evangelical Christians of their causing division within Baptist churches and accepting Baptists who had been excluded from their churches. For Baptists it was not only a means of Evangelical Christians gaining disaffected Baptists for their party but also destroying church discipline, which theoretically should lead to repentance and restoration into the church that excluded them. In his article in 1911, "Ne ta doroga," Mazaev accused Evangelical Christians sending out their own evangelists who agitated among the Baptists and in places "where they either accepted our 'grumblers,' the somewhat dissatisfied, or picked up our excluded." After the First World War, V. P. Stepanov will follow the same line of argument, claiming the Evangelical Christians did not find it difficult with their evangelists, whom Stepanov called "agents," to form churches since they found them among dissatisfied Baptists.[28]

In 1909 the Evangelical Christian Union sent to the Russian Baptist Union congress in Rostov-on-Don a reply to a letter that V. V. Ivanov had sent on the issue of accepting excluded members from Baptist churches. It stated that its churches would provide certificates to any who wished to transfer elsewhere and require a certificate from fellow Baptists or Mennonite Brethren who wished to join. Excluded Baptist and Mennonite Brethren members must explain their reasons for their exclusion and would not be accepted if they remained excluded. But for Baptists, even with discussions of unity, this issue was never finally resolved.[29]

On his side, Prokhanov, could not but note the aggressive nature of Fetler's activity, even with the outward cordiality between the two of them. Russian Baptists were more than supportive of Fetler's *Dom Evangeliya* in Prokhanov's own home territory of St. Petersburg. Fetler was able to draw to his cause such outstanding Pashkovite aristocrats as Elizaveta Chertkova and Maria Yasnovsky. A. E. Leushkin, the Prokhanov supporter, accused Mazaev and his board both knowing and approving Fetler's activity "to settle a Russian congregation in the capital with the name 'Baptist' and by this to remove the name Evangelical Christian." Leushkin quoted F. A. Arndt, pastor of the German Baptist Church in St. Petersburg, that before Fetler's arrival all the congregations lived in peace but Fetler brought division and grief. But Baptists saw another side. In a letter to *Baptist* in 1909 M. F. Popov, in his return to St. Petersburg, noted evangelicals were divided into three congregations and their mutual hostility. He reported reading in the paper where members of Prokhanov's church tore down posters and snatched from strangers the same that advertised meetings in the City

27. Ibid., 1910, no. 38, 304.
28. Ibid., 1911, no. 34, 269, and 1925, nos. 6–7, 39.
29. Ibid., 1909, no. 2, 13–14.

Duma. In the next issue, N. V. Churzin wrote regretting the stand of Evangelical Christians who refused to cooperate with those with the odious name "Baptist" and that *Khristianin* gave nothing to its constituency to rejoice in the success of Baptists in St. Petersburg and the provinces.[30]

Fetler proved to be disruptive in Moscow where already an Evangelical Christian church existed. In Moscow a congregation with Pashkovite ties had developed as early as 1882. It took a turn toward Baptists when two brethren from St. Petersburg came at the request for help from Teodor S. Savel'ev, a leader of the Moscow congregation. One of the brethren will immerse Savel'ev in 1903. In 1908 the Moscow congregation denied communion to those not immersed as believers, which led to a division of its Lutheran supporters. In 1909 the Moscow congregation was legalized as an Evangelical Christian congregation. In 1909 Fetler arrived on the scene, held the first public baptism in January of the following year, and upset both Evangelical Christians and the Orthodox. The latter looked upon his coming as an invasion of "Holy Moscow" and will bring a court case against him. A. E. Leushkin will accuse Fetler of evasively enrolling Evangelical Christians to gain legalization for his church. After Fetler, S. P. Stepanov will carry on the work of the Moscow Baptist congregation.[31]

One of Prokhanov's visions was for the unity of evangelicals as expressed in the program of the Evangelical Alliance. As noted earlier, he spoke at the World Evangelical Alliance in London in 1896. In a letter to Pashkov in 1898 he stated that not dogma but the "requirements of Christ's love" should be the foundation. His publication of *Khristianin* sought to further basic evangelical principles apart from doctrinal differences that divided denominations. He with others advocated unity in essentials, liberty in non-essentials, but in everything love. In 1906 Prokhanov with Kargel, Baron Nikolay, and several others formed a Russian Evangelical Alliance. For this organization Prokhanov published a paper, *Drug* (The Friend), but without Baptist support the Alliance was a failure. In 1908 he began to form his own structured organization but placed a strong Baptist imprint on it. Both Wilhelm Kahle in his biography of Prokhanov and Andrew Puzynin in his work on Gospel Christians noted Prokhanov found it necessary to move toward a Baptist position if he were to be successful in developing a viable presence among evangelicals. Unlike earlier Pashkovites, only individuals baptized as believers were accepted as members in his church, although unlike Baptists he observed open communions with evangelicals of other traditions. At the Baptist World Congress in 1911, S. P. Stepanov noted that Evangelical Christians had even accepted the Baptist position on presbyters.[32]

30. *Pis'ma k brat'yam*, 25, 79–80, 87–88. *Baptist*, 1909, no. 8, 20–21, and no. 9, 21–22.

31. For history of the Moscow congregations, see Val'kevich, App. 4:7, ft. 2; *BV*, 1966, no. 4, 65–68; and Kahle, *Kirche im Osten* 31 (1988), 23–68. For Fetler and the Baptist congregation, see "The First Baptismal Service in Moscow," *Baptist Times and Freeman*, Mar. 11, 1910, 135, and "The Defilement of Holy Moscow," in Latimer, *With Christ in Russia*, 101–16. For Leushkin's charges, see *Pis'ma k brat'yam*, 26.

32. For the Russian Evangelical Alliance, see *EC*, Jan.–Feb. 1907, 7–8; *Bratskii listok*, 1908, no. 10,

As early stundists and Pashkovites, Prokhanov rejected the necessity of ordination or the laying on of hands for pastoral leadership or the administration of the ordinances. On the other hand, in his brochure in 1911 on the subject, he recognized its use for recognition of service in the church if authorized by the entire church and limited the term of service. In England Prokhanov noticed that English Baptists did not observe the laying on of hands on the baptized and thus did not introduce it among the Evangelical Christian churches, a practice observed by Baptists in the southern part of the country. Prokhanov himself continued unordained throughout the period, although in 1924 he finally was ordained in the Baptist church in Prague by Czech Baptists and Bohemian Brethren (Moravians). In his letter to the Disciples of Christ in 1914, he clamed that Evangelical Christians observed communion weekly. There is evidence, however, that his church St. Petersburg observed it monthly on the first day of the month as Baptists and a lack of evidence of its weekly observance among Evanglical Christians elsewhere.[33]

Whatever the issues in contention and minor differences in church practice, Orthodox observers at the time concluded that Baptists and Evangelical Christians were one. When asked in a letter from a priest, what was the difference between the two groups, Aleksandr I. Vvedenskiĭ replied in 1912 in his article "Khitrost' sektantov": "In our deep conviction based on documentary data, all of our above cited designations (i.e., of various evangelical groups) present none other than different names of one and the same sectarian church." An Orthodox missionary N. Chepurin in his work in 1914, "Religious Divisions in Sectarianism," published as a series in *Missionerskoe obozrenie* and also in a separate volume, found the differences between them insignificant with no doctrinal differences but "amongst them seethes a very embittered struggle. A struggle with all its excesses."[34]

In an article in *Tserkovnyi vestnik*, D. I. Bogolyubov, an Orthodox missionary and debater with sectarians, asked why the need for an Evangelical Congress in 1909 while Baptists were meeting about the same time in Rostov-on-Don? He concluded that Pashkovites wanted their own congress in St. Petersburg to "stress that they do not want their story to drive into the channel of Baptism," whose members they considered fanatical on baptism. He also wrote they regarded themselves more spiritual than Baptists who made organization and order ends in themselves. They appealed for respect and toleration of other churches, except, of course, the Orthodox Church and fanatical Baptists. Vasiliĭ Skvortsov, the Orthodox sectarian authority who attended the Evangelical Christian Congress in 1909, noted in his article in 1911 on

---

1–10; and *MRW*, June 1908, 472. Puzynin, 131–32, 137, 151. Kahle, *Evangelische Christen*, 140–41. Klibanov, 290.

33. Prokhanov, *O vozlozhenii ruk i rukopolozhenii*, and reprinted in *Khristianin*, 1924, no. 6, 75–87. Kahle, *Evangelische Christen in Russland*, 203–205. *Die Gemeinde*, Dec. 5, 1965, 12. *Utrennyaya zvezda*, 1914, no. 31, 6.

34. Vvedenskiĭ, "Khitrost' sektantov," *Rukovodstvo dlya sel'skikh pastyreĭ*, Jan. 29, 1912, 227–32. Chepurin, "Religioznyya razdeleniya v sektantstve," *MO*, April 1914, 685.

"Rationalistic Sectarianism," that Evangelical Christians with their open communion and lack of ordination were more democratic and tolerant than Baptists, whom he claimed were beset by "German stiffness" and "Puritanism." He thought Prokhanov's movement carried "more Russian traces" while Baptists were more influenced by German and Anglo-Masonic influences from the West.[35]

During a time Prokhanov approached Russian Baptists for united action, he published in *Utrennyaya zvezda* at the end of August 1910, shortly before the convening of the Russian Baptist congress in St. Petersburg, a statement "To the Congress of Baptists," in which he attempted to define both bodies. He stated that Evangelical Christians and Baptists were "two branches of the same evangelical movement." He pointed out that they both differed from the Orthodox, not on the basic dogmas of the Christian faith, but their insistence that only converted individuals may be baptized and join the church. On the other hand, he pointed to different origins with his movement originating in St. Petersburg from the Pashkov movement while Baptists appeared in the 1860s in the Caucasus and Ukraine. He said his movement respected more the autonomy of the local church and its democratic structure than Baptists. In his interview with J. H. Franklin from the American Baptist Foreign Mission Society in 1913, he noted the different origins of Baptists in the South and Pashkovites in St. Petersburg. He admitted that the Pashkovites "gradually became known as Baptists" with the major difference that they object to the name "Baptist."[36] How relevant is Prokhanov's stress on the origins of the evangelical movement in three different areas with the Pashkovite movement beginning with Radstock and Pashkov? It is, of course, historically important but twenty-five years later, as Prokhanov himself admits, the Pashkovites were becoming Baptists. A number of years ago Paul Steeves in his dissertation challenged the view of such historians as Blane, Durasoff, and Nesdoly, who in following Evangelical Christians sources, that the Evangelical Christians were directly descended from the Pashkovites. Although admitting that former Pashkovites were more at home with Evangelical Christians, Steeves pointed out that not all of them followed Prokhanov and that Prokhanov also drew numbers of Baptists. On the other side, Fetler, the Baptist, drew some notable Pashkovites. It should be added that Prokhanov, himself originally a Baptist, never identified closely with the original Pashkovties and took his own course. His affinity with Baptists, although accepting open communion, is shown in his insistence of believer's baptism for membership, contrary to Pashkov's views.[37]

---

35. Boglyubov, "O s"ezd sektantov v S.-Peterburge," *TsV*, 1909, no. 38, 1188. Vasiliĭ Skvortsov, "Ratsionalisticheskoe sektantstvo," *MO*, Jan. 1911, 186–89.

36. "K s"zedu baptistov," *Utrennyaya zvezda*, 1910, no. 35, 1. See Puzynin, 152, for a translation into English of a portion of the article. "Interview with Rev. I. S. Prokhanoff," ABMU/ABFMS, *Correspondence*, Russian Mission, 1900–1919.

37. For Steeve's views on Evangelical Christian origins, see his, *The Russian Baptist Union, 1917–1935*, 87–89, and particularly, 89, ft. 4.

The Rivals

In comparison to Mazaev's autocratic rule and the Baptist position on communion, Prokhanov appeared more flexible and tolerant, such as his advocacy of open communion and support of ecumenism, even though his later denunciations of Baptists for his own purposes raises the question of its depth. His claim of church autonomy and democracy in his own union was also overplayed. As already noted, his presidency of the union with his full control proved to be a position practically for life. The St. Petersburg church adopted a church council, which Prokhanov dominated. Ya. Demikhovich, one of the members of the Kiev Evangelical Christian congregation, wrote in 1914 that the domination of the church council in his church also brought division. He also claimed that the organization by Prokhanov of an Evangelical Christian Union similar to Baptists brought division within Evangelical Christian ranks with some congregations refusing to enter the union to "preserve their former autonomy."[38]

How fundamental were the differences between Baptists and Evangelical Christians? A few differences, of course, were present but fundamentally because of Prokhanov's own personality and dominance the differences practically dissolve into a power struggle that gave no credit to either side.

ALL-RUSSIAN CONGRESSES OF THE EVANGELICAL CHRISTIAN UNION, 1909–1912

During the Tsarist period, Prokhanov was able to hold three All-Russian congresses of the Evangelical Christian Union with the first in September 1909 and the last in December, 1911–January 1912. All of them were held in St. Petersburg, the center of Prokhanov's church and work. As with the Baptists, the regime stopped further congresses, which could not be revived until 1917 after the overthrow of the regime.

In 1909 twenty-three representatives from eighteen churches with ten of them from the St. Petersburg church were in attendance. In addition about sixty others from local churches were also present. Letters or telegrams of greeting came from Janis Inkis, the president of the Latvian Baptist Union; I. F. Isaak and P.M. Friesen from the Mennonite Brethren; the German Baptist church in St. Petersburg; two evangelical Armenians; V. V. Ivanov, the old Baptist pioneer from Baku; and I. V. Kargel. A representative of the city governor was also present. If government permission for the congress had not come just shortly before its opening, attendance may have been larger from the provinces.[39]

Prokhanov presided. The congress sent to the Tsar an address of thanksgiving for the Manifestos of 1905 and 1906 that granted freedom of conscience. At the opening

---

38. Klibanov, 301–2.

39. For the business sessions and the program of the spiritual session of the Evangelical Christian congress of 1909, see *Bratskii listok*, 1909, no. 11, 1–24, and no. 12, 1–17, for the spiritual sessions. Also see *Der christliche Orient*, Dec., 1909, 183–84, and Prokhanov's evaluation of the congress, *In the Cauldron*, 150–51.

prayer meeting, Prokhanov read Ephesians 4:1–7 with an exposition of the significance of the word "unity." After which he feverntly prayed thanking the Lord for giving freedom and calling for a blessing from the Lord on the sovereign and his home as well as on the congress and its work.

After one of the sessions, a large meeting was held for the unification of the evangelical churches in Russia under the name of "The All-Russian Evangelical Christian Union." Prokhanov's grand vision was far more than a union of his own group but an organization for all evangelicals. It proposed that the next congress develop a draft for a Bible institute but resolved also in the meantime to create a six-week course beginning in December.

The second week was a spiritual congress, drawing on the preaching of a broad range of evangelicals. It included the Baptist champion Fetler; Jakob Vins (Wiens) from Samara; G. J. Braun, Mennonite Brethren; Neuman, pastor of the Swedish-Finnish Baptist Church; Gruenfeldt of the German Baptist Church; and George Simons, superintendent of the Methodists in Russia.[40]

The second All-Russian Congress of the Evangelical Christian Union met from December 28, 1910 to January 4, 1911, with sixty-two representatives. Among others the president and vice-president of the Latvian Baptist Union and Z. D. Zakharov, president of the New Molokans (or Evangelicals of the Christian Faith) and member of the State Duma, sent greetings. A representative of the Ministry of the Interior as well as V. M. Skvortsov, head of the anti-sectarian mission of the Orthodox Church, also attended. An article on the conference in the *Baptist Times and Freeman*, the journal of the British Baptist Union, was headlined, "The Russian Open Baptist Conference in St. Petersburg," evidently a name that Prokhanov in spite of his criticism of the name "Baptist" accepted if not cultivated among his British Baptist friends.[41]

The congress adopted statutes of the union and also a confession of faith. According to the statute of the union, its goal was to further the union of the churches of Evangelical Christians for purposes common to any evangelical. It was designed for a specific body, not a general alliance, with headquarters in St. Petersburg, bound by a common doctrinal statement, and contributing to a common treasury. The union included congresses and a union council, composed of six officers living in St. Petersburg, two other members from St. Petersburg, and four from elsewhere. It was clear that the center of power would be in the hands of Prokhanov and his own church in St. Petersburg. The doctrinal statement of eighteen articles with numerous scripture references incorporated classical Protestantism on God, Scripture, and salvation, and Baptist positions on church officers, the ordinances, including believer's baptism by immersion, and separation of church and state. In comparing the statement with the doctrinal statement of the German Baptist Union in 1847 and affirmed by the Russian

40. *Bratskiï listok*, 1909, no. 11, 16.

41. For the congress, see *Protokoly*; *Bratskiï listok*, no. 1, 42–46, no. 2:41–47, and no. 3:35–45; and *Baptist Times and Freeman*, Feb. 17, 1911, supp., ii.

Baptist Union in 1906, at least two significant differences emerge. The doctrinal statement of 1847 affirmed God's sovereignty in salvation while the Evangelical Christian statement stated that God's grace did not inhibit man's freedom and was not irresistible. It also included descriptions of both the local church and the universal church.[42]

The congress endorsed the opening of a Bible institute upon receiving governmental permission. It recommended to the churches the opening of schools where possible. In its concern for religious rights, it voted to send a memorandum to the Minister of Internal Affairs on such issues as closing meetings, preventing burials, and expulsion of children from school. It admonished its members to avoid alcoholic drinks, tobacco, and playing cards. It also resolved to petition the Holy Synod to print Bibles without the Apocrypha, provide smaller copies, use black-face type, separate verses from each other, and produce paper of better quality. Well-attended public meetings were held in the evening.

The third congress from December 18, 1911 to January 4, 1912 included 167 persons of which 91 were representatives of the congregations, ranging across Russia from Finland to Siberia. Among the guests was M. T. Ratushnyĭ, the old Stundo-Baptist leader from Kherson Province, but now from Perm Province. In a translation in *The Christian Standard* from *Utrennyaya zvezda,* he was described as eighty years old of medium size with a small white beard and "intelligent-looking gray eyes." Prokhanov was again elected president and vice-presidents included I. V. Kargel and F. F. Sheneman. The congress approved sending a telegram to the Tsar through the Minster of Internal Affairs and offered prayer for his and his family's health and prosperity.[43]

The congress resolved to engage in the development of youth circles and encouraged churches to pay special attention to the spiritual instruction of children through the Sunday school. In the face of obstacles in admission of their children in parish and government schools, the congress authorized the council of the union to petition removing the obstacles but also recommended churches to utilize the Manifesto of October 1906 to open their own schools. After a discussion of the great number of obstacles congregations faced in meeting and gaining legalization and the right of burial, the congress authorized the union council when finding it suitable to petition to remove the obstacles.

At the congress four brochures written by Prokhanov were introduced—on the laying on of Hands and Ordination, on Sunday, on the service of the women in the churches, and on marriage and divorce. The congress did not adopt them as resolutions but suggested they be used in the spirit of Philippians 3:15–16 in which Paul admonishes Christians to be of one mind. The congress heard Sister Kapranova on the service of women in the churches, after which the congress expressed its desire

---

42. See *Bratskiĭ listok*, 1910. No. 2, for the proposed statement of faith and the statute of the Evangelical Christian Union, which the second congress of 1910–1911 adopted almost in their entirety. Two further members living in St. Petersburg were added to the council.

43. For the congress, see *Bratskiĭ listok*, 1912, no. 1, 40–48. *Christian Standard*, April 26, 1913, 8.

for churches to give special attention to women's meetings and their service, including needlework and evangelism among women. In his brochure on women's service, although restricting their roles as elders or teachers, Prokhanov maintained, under the direction of the brethren the right of women to prophesy, pray, evangelize, and engage in benevolent work with the deacons. In his autobiography, Prokhanov noted that in their producing and selling their needlework and toys they helped to provide funds for mission work.[44]

Efforts at Reconciliation

Although the antagonism between Baptists and Evangelical Christians was deep, Prokhanov sought cooperation and even reconciliation. With failure of Baptist cooperation, Prokhanov's attempt in forming a Russian Evangelical Alliance in 1906 proved, as already noted, a failure. In April 1908 twenty representatives met in Moscow for a youth congress at the invitation of the youth circles of the Evangelical Christian Church in St. Petersburg. Besides Evangelical Christians, V.G. Pavlov and M. D. Timohshsenko from the Baptists were also present, but no united youth congress was formed. In the following year in September 1909, the Evangelical Christian congress proposed the formation of a Union of Christian Youth of the Evangelical Faith. In an effort to reach youth, the congress proposed to the "Baptist brethren" that they cooperate in an annual day of prayer, Bible courses, and a publication. In October at their own annual union congress at Rostov-on-Don, Baptists under the leadership of William Fetler, who was elected president, held their first congress of youth circles and Sunday schools without any response to the Evangelical Christian overtures.[45]

The Evangelical Christian congress of 1909 also took additional steps in developing other relationships. It proposed during Holy Week an annual day of prayer and fasting for Christian unity. Along with this emphasis Prokhanov promoted unity meetings, which gained the participation of some Baptists along with other evangelicals.[46] In a letter that the congress sent to the Russian Baptist Congress in Rostov-on-Don in 1909, it stated its position on certificates of good standing and also went further in suggesting a unity committee for rapprochement and joint work.[47] In 1910 Evangelical Christians sent two letters to the Russian Baptist Union, which was meeting from September 1 to 9 in St. Petersburg. The first letter from the Council of the Evangelical Christian Union referred to the communication from the Evangelical Christians the year before through Jakob Vins of Samara to the Russian Baptist Congress at Rostov-on-Don. The message at that time proposed a committee of unity of ten members

---

44. Prokhanov, *O sluzhenii zhenshchin v tserkvakh*. Prokhanov, *In the Cauldron*, 156–57.

45. *Baptist*, 1908, no. 10, 12. *Bratskii vestnik*, 1970, no. 3, 55. *Bratskii listok*, 1909, no. 11, 6–7.

46. *Bratskii listok*, 1909, no. 11, 6; Jan. 1911, 36–41; May 1911, 36–39. Prokhanov, *In the Cauldron*. 158. *Khristianskii pobornik*. 1910, 42–43. *The Christian-Evangelist*, July 16, 1914, 922.

47. *Bratskii listok*, 1909, no. 11, 7. *Baptist*, 1909, no. 2, 13–14.

with two each from Evangelical Christians, Russian Baptists, German Baptists, Latvian Baptists, and Mennonite Brethren. It was to deal with inter-union matters such as representation before the government, regulations concerning excluded members, obstacles to a Bible institute, and removal of misunderstandings. In its proposals on cooperation, it claimed two were already now in existence—the annual day of prayer on unity and the existence of a periodical, *Utrennyaya zvezda,* which represents the social and political interests of evangelicals. The letter suggested the Baptist Union should pass resolutions supporting the Day of Prayer and also *Utrennyaya zvezda.* It also looked for support for establishing a Bible institute in St. Petersburg for Evangelical Christians, Baptists, and Mennonite Brethren with special German and Latvian departments like Rochester Seminary in the USA with its English and German departments. It also requested a resolution from the Baptist Union to form a united youth congress.[48] The second letter from the St. Petersburg Evangelical Christian Church dealt again with the problem of excluded members, noting that some churches simply without justification exclude a member who desires to join another evangelical group and refuse a certificate of standing. The letter felt such action was unjustified since the Manifesto of 1905 allowed change of denominations and Christ Himself did not force followers who had left to stay with him.

The Russian Baptists Union found it necessary, now meeting in the same territory of the Evangelical Christians, to respond to their overtures. Before agreeing to a response, several other events occurred earlier that showed some attempts of reaching out from both sides. On the sixth day of congress, the representatives by a vote of 56 to 26, over the objections of Fetler and Pavlov, kept the full name "Evangelical Christians-Baptists" in the name of the constitution of the union. On the seventh day the Evangelical Christian Church of St. Petersburg invited the representatives to a love feast at the church to which the congress resounded with thanks. At the love feast some Baptists spoke, including S. V. Belousov, secretary of the Russian Baptist Union. On the eighth day at the laying of the foundation stone of Fetler's *Dom Evangeliya,* as previously noted, both Prokhanov and Kargel participated.[49] Finally on the ninth, the final day, the congress took up the question of responding to the two letters from the Evangelical Christians. The discussion and debates were long. S. P. Stepanov took the Baptist line that unity with Evangelical Christians had already been achieved in previous congresses at Tsaritsyn and Rostov-on-Don, and Baptists were not at fault for any disuntiy. He charged Evangelical Christians for forming their own union and then accepting excluded Baptists. He reminded the congress that when he came to St. Petersburg to preach in 1909 he met with no sympathy from the Evangelical Christians and advertisements of his meeting were torn to shreds. In his speech, Fetler said the Evangelical Christians had come by way of Lord Radstock, who associated with the Plymouth Brethren, and the two sides "follow completely different goals." He said that

48. *Bratskiï listok,* 1910, no. 9, 18–23.
49. Ibid., 1910, no. 9, 15, 18, 19–20, 24.

Baptists were able to achieve at most spiritual relations with Evangelical Christians but not "practical union." To the letter from the St. Petersburg church of Evangelical Christians, the congress decided to accept the response of Pavlov with some excerpts from Stepanov. This response made the point that Baptists, unlike Evangelical Christians, did not grant letters of dismissal to churches of other denominations. To the letter from the Evangelical Christian Union, the congress agreed to use Stepanov's response but to eliminate some "course and abusive expressions." When the *Baptist* printed the responses, the one to the Council of Evangelical Christians followed Stepanov's reasoning, although signed by V. G. Pavlov, president, and S. Belousov, secretary of the Baptist congress.[50]

After all was said and done, how strange it was that Deï Mazaev himself, too ill to attend the Baptist congress in September, attended a service at Prokhanov's church on December 10 with Z. D. Zakharov, president of the New Molokans, as guest speakers. Mazaev took the text of the angels at Christ's birth, "peace on earth and good will to men" and stated "this peace touches relations of people in general and Christians in particular for enmity is an anti-Christian affair."[51]

Prokhanov's Election

The indicators of good will between Baptists and Evangelical Christians in 1910 were, however, obliterated the next year at the congress of the Baptist World Alliance in June 1911 in Philadelphia. For some time the Baptist World Alliance had wanted to bring Baptists and Evangelical Christians together but with the nominating committee of the Alliance proposing Prokhanov, president of the Evangelical Christian Union, as a vice-president of the Alliance raised troubling questions. Writers on Russian Baptist history have speculated over this event without coming to a final answer. Wilhelm Kahle in his biography of Prokhanov speculated that the Alliance, unable to decide on a Russian Baptist leader without causing a problem within the Baptist Union itself, now found a way of giving recognition to an outstanding evangelical leader in Russia and noted Prokhanov' earlier ties with Baptists and travel abroad. In his dissertation, Paul Steeves speculated Prokhanov was chosen possibly because of his impressive personality, his more open views, or even the desire of Baptists to cause him to be less divisive in respect to the Baptist cause. A. I. Klibanov supported the view that Prokhanov had closer personal ties with British and American Baptists and was more closely aligned with them politically.[52]

---

50. Bondar, *Sovremennoe sostoyanie russkago baptizma*, 56–58. Chepurin, "Religioznyya razdelenliya v sektantstve," *MO*, May 1914, 109–11. *Bratskiï listok*, 1910, no. 10, 23–24. *Baptist*, 1910, no. 46, 368.

51. *Bratskiï listok*, 1910, no. 12, 12.

52. Kahle, *Evangelische Christen in Russland*, 135–36. Steeves, 85, ft. 2. Klibanov, 291.

Prokhanov's election affirmed the acceptance into the Alliance of a Russian body calling itself "Evangelical Christian" but opposing the name "Baptist" into an organization whose constitution limited membership to Baptist bodies. For acceptance into the world body, the Evangelical Christian Union used "Open Baptist," as seen in Prokhanov's message to the Alliance and in the nominating committee's report. Some months before the Philadelphia meeting, the *Baptist Times and Freeman* in London highlighted the name "Open Baptist" in an article on the annual meeting of the Evangelical Christian Union. At least for British Baptists, the Evangelical Christians were essentially Baptist and were like them far more "open" in their relations with other denominations than those in the Russian Baptist Union.[53]

In his account in *Utrennyaya Zvezda* on the Baptist World Alliance, which he called "The World Congress of Christians (Baptists) Baptized on Faith," Prokhanov stated that Evangelical Christians had received an invitation to the congress from J. H. Shakespeare, the European secretary of the Alliance. As president of the Evangelical Union, Prokhanov himself received two invitations—one from the Continental Committee of the Alliance and one from Philadelphia itself. Prokhanov and three other Evangelical Christians planned to attend but did not go because of personal circumstances or in the case of Prokhanov and G. M. Matveev six weeks for the trip could not be spared. On the other hand, Prokhanov was able to go to London on May 9 for a preparatory meeting led by F. B. Meyer, noted Baptist preacher and writer, where Pavlov was also present. Here Prokhanov, speaking in English, declared that the Evangelical Christian Union, although desiring to keep its "full spiritual independence, nonetheless was gladly conscious of unity with all Christians baptized by faith." With his British Baptist ties, going back as far as the 1890s, his ideological affinity with Anglo-American Baptists, his recognition as a leading Russian leader, his adroit use of "Open Baptist" and "unity with all Christians baptized by faith," and the desire of the Alliance to draw him into full cooperation, it is not all that surprising that the Baptist World Alliance elected him as one of its vice-presidents.[54]

The leaders of the Russian Baptist Union, however, were very upset with the election of Prokhanov, who was even absent at the Baptist world body, which gave recognition to a body who derided the Baptist name in Russia and was considered divisive and competitive. Although each contributing union, including the Russians Baptist Union had the right to nominate its own vice-president, but Prokhanov was, however, elected with nine others as a vice-president by the congress itself and listed as one of the officers of the Alliance. The administration of the Russian Baptist Union sent a written protest, but the Alliance leaders in London refused to change the election.[55]

---

53. BWA, Congress, *Proceedings*, 1911, 245, 440. *Baptist Times and Freeman*, Feb. 17, 1911, supp., ii.

54. *Utrennyaya zvezda*, July 8, 1911, 1–2.

55. Fourth letter of Leushkin to Mazaev, *Pis'ma k brat'yam*, 87–91. BWA, *Minute Books*, Sep. 18, 1911, 27.

PART SIX—Possibilities and Uncertainties, 1905–1917

The Alliance bypassed such notable Baptist leaders as Pavlov, Mazaev, and Fetler for any office except that Fetler was placed as a member on two committees—the one on peace and the one on young people. Pavlov and Mazaev lacked the British ties, Mazaev and Fetler were domineering personalities and critics of Evangelical Christians, and Fetler himself was an alumnus of Spurgeon's College, which was founded by Spurgeon who himself broke with the British Baptist Union for its alleged toleration of theological liberalism. On the other hand, the 1911 congress of the BWA listed as officers of the Executive Committee of the Alliance Il'ya Golyaev, president of the Russian Baptist Union, J. A. Frey, president of the Latvian Baptist Association, and F. Brauer, president of the German Baptist Union in Russia. According to its constitution, the BWA was to elect eight officers of the Executive Committee residing in countries outside Britain, USA and Canada. The minutes record only the election of Brauer but not Golyaev nor Frey. Were the latter two added later to heal wounds?[56]

Shortly after the congress, Mazaev wrote a lengthy article, "Nebyvalyĭ kongress" (An Unprecedented Congress), which severely condemned the Evangelical Christians for joining an alliance of Baptists alleging it was a union of "Christians baptized by faith." In early 1912 Mazaev wrote an article "Nachlo i konets" (The Beginning and the End) charging that Evangelical Christian advocacy for an annual day of fasting and prayer for Christian unity and entry into the Baptist World Alliance have changed "not an iota" their hostile relations with Baptists. Mazaev declared that Russian unity cannot be achieved except in Russia itself and cannot be achieved by special committees or commissions but only directly by congregations.[57]

In his letter to A E. Leushkin, I. K. Savel'ev showed his rancor in charging that Prokhanov was able to "worm himself" into membership into the Baptist World Alliance, adding that the "sons of the age are wiser than the sons of light." He claimed Prokhanov in London portrayed himself as president of a northern Baptist union. Leushkin, a strong Prokhanov supporter, rejected such allegations and also asserted that Evangelical Christians did not disguise their name at the congress.[58]

At the session of the Russian Baptist Congress in Moscow from September 25 to October 1 in 1911, some delegates complained of the divisive activity of Evangelical Christians. The congress finally resolved to enter relations with all churches that wished mutual relations, even though they rejected the name "Baptist," and to reject accepting any excluded members from these churches. V. V. Ivanov said that Evangelical Christians were divided into two parts—one part that arose independently with which one could have relations and a second part, which V. P. Stepanov claimed Prokhanov supported, that was divisive and irreconcilable.[59]

---

56. BWA, Congress, *Proceedings*, 1911, xiv–xvi, 245–46.
57. *Baptist*, 1911, no. 30, 234–36, and 1912, no. 2, 4–6.
58. Letter of Savel'ev to Leushkin and letter of Leushkin et al., *Pis'ma k brat'yam*, 32, 74.
59. *Baptist*, 1911, no. 46, 367.

In addition, the board of the Russian Baptist Union responded to two letters that the Evangelical Christians sent to the Moscow congress. It flatly rejected the idea of a unity committee with Evangelical Christians that included Russian, German, and Latvian Baptists and Mennonite Brethren. It claimed that no differences existed between various Baptist groups and the Mennonite Brethren and therefore such a committee was unnecessary. On the question of a unity committee of Baptists with Evangelical Christians, the board stated it was first necessary to establish relations between their churches; since, however, Evangelical Christians were destroying such relations, a unity committee would be a reproach. In response to the second letter from Evangelical Christians, the board rejected the assertion that the journal, *Baptist*, published "untrue information" on them during the last four years.[60]

Further Negotiations

In spite of the recriminations, eight Baptists led by Mazaev and Prokhanov and T. F. Dadianov for the Evangelical Christians met in Vladikazkaz on July 19, 1912, and signed what is known as the Valdikavkaz Agreement. First, the Baptists accepted the proposal of the Evangelical Christians for a joint committee on the condition that the excluded Baptists in Evangelical Christian churches come to repentance and are reconciled and return to their former churches. Secondly, the Evangelical Christians were to present this proposal before their council and congress, and if accepted Baptists then would elect persons to serve on the joint committee. The agreement will lose its force if not accepted by the administrative boards or congresses of the two unions. Thirdly, excommunicated Baptists who refuse to repent will also be considered excommunicated by Evangelical Christians.[61]

In March 1913 in St. Petersburg, the administrative board of the Russian Baptist Union, including Mazaev, Fetler, Golyaev, and others met with the council of Evangelical Christians, including Prokhanov on discussing the lack of implementation of the agreement. Prokhanov had pulled back from the agreement; both his council and board rejected it in 1913. Baptists also did not follow through. One stumbling block appeared to be the Baptist insistence on Evangelical Christians cleansing first their churches of excluded Baptists rather than both bodies simultaneously cleansing their ranks.[62]

During the European Baptist Congress in Stockholm in July 1913, John Clifford, past president of the Baptist World Alliance, called a special meeting of Russian Baptists and Evangelical Christians with English and American participants to discuss these problems between the two bodies and ways of removing them. An attempt was

---

60. Ibid., 1911, no. 45, 358.

61. For the Vladikavkaz Agreement, see Steeves, 85–86, and *Pis'ma k brat'yam*, 76.

62. Fourth All-Russian Congress of Evangelical Christians, 1917, 57–58. Letter of Leushkin, *at al.*; letter of Savel'ev to Leushkin; and fourth letter of Leushkin to Mazaev, *Pis'ma k brat'yam*, 21, 72, 86.

made to form a unity committee to meet in Berlin in 1914, but it did not meet because of the refusal of Prokhanov and the Evangelical Christians to attend. By this time, as will be noted in the next chapter, Prokhanov's status will be notably strengthened and his relations with Baptists abroad will be altered. In addition, Europe will soon be engulfed in war and further attempts at unity will not be made until after the demise of the Tsarist regime in 1917.[63]

STATISTICS

J. C. Heinrichs, the Baptist missionary from India, who visited Russia in 1909, reported that Evangelical Christians numbered around 5,000. In Stockholm at the European Baptist Congress, Percy Arnov, an Evangelical Christian delegate, reported 7,000 members. The ABFMS, *Annual,* 1914, stated that the Evangelical Christian Union had around 8,000 members. The Department of Spiritual Affairs reported that on January 1, 1912, that Evangelical Christians numbered 30,716, but as with their Baptist figures these numbers indicate community rather than actual membership. As with Baptists, Evangelical Christians, although decidedly smaller, showed they too were able to expand.[64]

---

63. *Der Hausfreund*, Oct. 30/Nov. 12, 1913, 352. Letter of Prokhanov to Franklin, June 20/July 3, 1914, ABMU/ABFMS, *Correspondence*, Russian Mission, 1900–1919.

64. *Der Sendbote*, Aug. 11, 1909, 501. *Baptist Times and Freeman*, Aug. 1, 1913, 590. ABFMS, *Report*, 1914, 161. *Slovo istiny*, 1914, no. 48, 566.

26

Theological Education
The Problems

ALTHOUGH A DISCUSSION OF the development of theological education might have been integrated with earlier chapters, the complexity of the subject, however, merits its own chapter. So many groups were involved with their own agendas for establishing a program of theological instruction. It was difficult to reach solutions related to sponsorship, support, control, relationships, and students. The problems were never finally resolved.

The opportunity for a theological education was very limited. Some Russian Baptists along with German Baptists from Russia attended the German Baptist seminary in Hamburg, but these were few in numbers. In its annual report in 1904, the American Baptist Missionary Union wrote that a theological school was needed in Russia since the Hamburg school was far distant and costs were difficult to meet. Theological training in a foreign land was also likely to arouse suspicions from the authorities.[1]

Both Russian Baptists and Evangelical Christians recognized the need for theological and missionary training and with the Manifesto of 1905 looked forward to establishing a theological institute, if not college or seminary. In the meantime they provided theological courses and night classes. Evangelical Christians took the lead. From December 1, 1906 to January 15, 1907, *Bratskiï* listok advertised the opening of a six-week evangelical course on sin and sanctification and an interpretation of *Revelation* taught by Kargel. In 1907 *Bratskiï listok* announced six-week courses from November 15 to November 31 taught by Kargel, Prokhanov, Baron Nicolay, and a

---

1. *BMM*, July 1904, 527–28.

certain "A.M.M.," who lectured on interpretation of Scripture, history of the Christian church, and spiritual problems. The 1908 session expanded the courses and number of instructors.[2]

Russian Baptists also provided courses. Fetler offered weekly classes for pastors in St. Petersburg. *Tserkovnï vestnik*, the Orthodox journal, reported in 1909 that Baptists in cultural centers opened schools of general education with theological courses and night classes in the Bible. In Kharkov they offered missionary courses. In his survey of Baptists in 1911, Bondar claimed that many congregations provided short courses for pastors, Sunday school teachers, and youth, including Bible and discussion sessions and reports on religious themes.[3]

ALTERNATIVE SCHOOLS

The Alliance Bible School

Beside the Hamburg Baptist Seminary in Germany, an Alliance Bible School appeared in Berlin, Germany, as an alternative. In March 1905 three Russian men followed by others visited Karl Mascher (1864–1922), mission inspector of the German Baptist Mission in the Cameroons in Africa, with pleas for assistance. On April 11, 1905, a group of evangelicals met on the premises of the Blücher Mission of Fräulein Toni von Blücher, a pietist, and formed The Alliance Bible School. The group included Mascher, a strong Alliance supporter who worked with the Blankenburg conference, Friedrich W. Simoleit (1873–1961), a German Baptist pastor who became president of the German Baptist mission in 1905, George von Viebann from the Elberfelder Brethren, and Frederick Baedeker, the veteran missionary to prisons in Russia and a Plymouth or Open Brethren. The school opened in September in Berlin-Steglitz, where the German Baptists possessed a mission house, but will move the next year to the Blücher mission in Berlin proper.[4]

As its name implies, the school was founded on Alliance/Brethren principles, appealing to all evangelicals, disregarding denominational differences, and based on the all-sufficiency of Scripture. Its purpose was to train evangelists for Eastern Europe, particularly Russia. The school accepted evangelicals regardless of denominational affiliation or nationality. Its two teachers were Christopher Köhler (1860–1922), who also served as director, and his son-in-law, Johannes Warns (1874–1937). Both of them had left the Lutheran state church for Brethren principles. The first committee

---

2. *Bratskii listok*, 1906, no. 10, 12–13; 1907, no. 7, 24; and no. 12, 3. Prokhanov, *In the Cauldon*, 139.

3. *TsV*, 1909, no. 12, 372. Bondar, "Sovremennyï baptizm v Russii," *MO*, 1911, no. 10, 317.

4. *Evangelical Alliance Quarterly*, Oct. 1905, 121–24. *EC*, Oct. 1906, 123. Jordy, *Die Brüderbewegung in Deutschland*, 2:143–46. Coad, *History of the Brethren Movement*, 196. See Balders, *Ein Herr, ein Glaube, eine Taufe*, for short biographical accounts of Mascher, 353–54, and Simoleit, 361–62.

of the school included Baedeker, Mascher, Baron Nicolay, and Baron Üxküll. Nicolay had attended the meeting of the Evangelical Alliance in England in May 1905 where he appealed to British Baptists for support of dedicated teachers for Russia. The Alliance in England became a major financial supporter.[5]

In 1905 eight students from Russia were in attendance, but four returned home in 1906 and were replaced by others taking their place. In September 1906 the school enrolled twenty-one with two more expected by October 1st. In 1910 twenty-five were in attendance with ten from Russia. The school continued in Berlin until 1919 when it moved to Wiedenest.[6]

Seminary in Astrakhanka

Another alternative school was the seminary in Astrakhanka in Taurida Province in Ukraine. An evangelical body, the New Molokans or Christians of the Evangelical Faith, who unlike most Russian evangelicals observed infant baptism, appealed to the Deutsche Orient Mission to establish a seminary for them. The Deutsche Orient Mission was founded by Johannes Lepsius (1858–1926), a German Lutheran pastor. Lepsius had become closely identified with a relief ministry to Armenians whom the Turks were massacring. While on a trip to Bulgaria where Armenian refugees had fled, Lepsius met in 1897 Andreï Stefanovich, son of a Russian priest. Lepsius engaged Stefanovich to serve with the Deutsche Orient Mission; for several years Stefanovich visited stundist congregations but died in December 1905.[7]

In its desire to provide theological instruction for stundists, the Deutsche Orient Mission opened in July 1904 under the leadership of Pastor Jellinghaus a stundist seminary in Germany in Lichtenrade, a school that moved to Lichterfeld on January 1, 1905. From the start the school faced difficulties when two Russian students were baptized in the Baptist church at Steglitz. The seminary, supported by the established Protestant churches in Germany and Switzerland, could not approve baptism of any of its students by a "German sect." The two students, now joined by a third student, then joined the new Alliance Bible School in Steglitz. Although the school now forbade any intercourse with Steglitz, at the end of May 1905 three more suddenly declared they were Baptists and went to the Alliance school, leaving only one student. The first year of the school was an entire loss. One of the students in Lichtenrade was Jakob Vins (Wiens), who may possibly have been involved with the Baptist difficulties. He will

---

5. *Evangelical Alliance Quarterly*, Oct. 1905, 123. Coad, 196. *EC*, May 1906, 76.

6. *EC*, October 1906, 123. *Echoes of Service*, Mar. 1910, 107–8.

7. For the beginnings of the Deutsche Orient Mission and its initial relationship with Russia, see Schäfer, *Geschichte der Deutschen Orient-Mission*, and *Der christliche Orient*, Jan. 1905, 4. Also see Diedrich, "Johannes Lepsius und die südrussischen Stundisten," *Akten des Internationalen Dr. Johannes- Lepsius-Symposiums* 1986, 230–36, which also includes a listing of the literature written by Lepsius and Stefanovich (under the pseudonym "St." or "Christophilus").

PART SIX—Possibilities and Uncertainties, 1905-1917

return to Russia and, as earlier noted, in 1905 became pastor of an evangelical church in Samara and attended the congress of the Baptist World Alliance in Philadelphia in 1911.[8]

The seminary began anew with a few students but with no more problems with Baptists. Instruction was difficult, however, since students had first to be taught German. The Manifesto of October 1906 and the invitation of the New Molokans now opened the opportunity of moving the seminary into Russia itself. In 1906 the mission sent Walter L. Jack, a German subject, to Russia, who opened on February 19, 1907, the Astrakhanka Teacher and Pastor's Seminary with eleven pupils in a preparatory class. The governor of Taurida had not given permission but allowed it to begin until it received official recognition. During the school's first vacation, from June 12 to July 6, Jack conducted a Bible course in Moscow. In September the preparatory students entered the first class while twelve new students entered the preparatory class.[9]

The authorities now closed the school. Through Zinovii D. Zakharov, president of the New Molokans and member of the State Duma and member of its committee for religious freedom and agricultural questions, the governor lifted the ban. Shortly before Christmas the police again closed the school, this time for three months. One charge was that Jack was in the pay of German propagandists who were out to Germanize southern Russia. The governor, who sympathized with Jack's efforts but otherwise with hands tied, was nevertheless able to protect Jack from deportation. Zakharov now persuaded the Ministry of Spiritual Affairs to authorize the school as an evangelical teacher's training school but not a theological seminary. The regional educational ministry would confirm the manager and the teachers who must have received their higher education in Russia. Its teaching must conform to New Mololkan belief.[10]

In the summer of 1908 Zakharov gave land in Astrakhanka for the construction of a two-story building and a teacher's residence. Through him the school received an initial contribution of around 5,000 rubles (10,000 marks). The building provided for 120 students, a library, a laboratory, and a room for the director. At the cornerstone laying Deï Mazaev, president of the Russian Baptist Union, spoke. Only a year and a half before Grigor Zakharov, the son of Zinovii, who headed a delegation of five New Molokans, walked out of the Conference of Sectarian Rights in January 1907 in St. Petersburg because of the intransigence of Mazaev and other Baptists who refused

---

8. *Der christliche Orient*, Jan. 1905, 3-4, and Dec. 1905, 187-89. For the career of Vins, the grandfather of Georgi Vins, who may possibly have been involved with the Baptist difficulties in Lichtenrade, see Wardin, "Jacob J. Wiens: Mission Champion in Freedom and Repression," *Journal of Church and State* 28 (Autumn 1986), 495-514.

9. *Der christliche Orient*, Dec. 1905, 188-89, and Apr. 1907, 51-58. Schäfer, 50-57.

10. *Der christliche Orient*, May 1908, 73-77. *Baptist*, 1908, no. 8, 22.

recognition of baptized infants as church members. Jack who was also present wrote at the time a very critical review of Mazaev's domineering leadership.[11]

In September 1909 the building was opened, financed by the New Molokans themselves. Jack continued as director and was assisted by a couple of teachers. The Deutsche Orient Mission paid for the director and for a teacher of religion. One of the teachers was Ivan V. Neprash, who will later become a co-pastor with William Fetler at his *Dom Evangeliya*. To protect its existence because of the fear in Russia of foreign religious influences, the school maintained only a very loose relationship with the Deutsche Orient Mission. After an investigation in March 1910 of sectarian influences at Halbstadt in the neighboring Molochna Mennonite colony by the vice-governor of Taurida Province, the governor wrote to Stolypin that he had closed the school on March 25, but it continued illegally. In 1912 the Deutsche Orient Mission was not allowed to provide any support, and the school was required to rely on Russian resources. At the end of 1912, N. Bortovskiĭ, diocesan missionary in Taurida, lamented the missionary courses provided by sectarians in St. Petersburg, Moscow, Kharkov, Odessa, and elsewhere. He then turned his attention to the school in Astrakhanka, claiming it was officially closed but continued unofficially and was producing next year "totally energetic fanatical preachers." Wilhelm Kahle claimed the school closed in 1911 but evidently continued into 1913 but probably no longer than after the outbreak of the First World War. Walter Jack learned Russian, married a daughter of a Mennonite landowner, and acquired a small estate on which he illegally held Bible studies. With the outbreak of the First World War in 1914, he, as a German national, and his family were exiled to Vologda.[12]

The German Baptist Seminary in Lodz

The German Baptist Union in Russia was the first body to take the initiative in establishing a Baptist seminary in Russia. Baron Woldemar Üxküll, treasurer of the Union, spearheaded the effort. Üxküll, a Baltic German noble from Estonia, was baptized in 1891, founded and pastored the Laitse Baptist congregation on his estate located in the area of Kegel (today Keila), a few miles west of Reval (Tallinn). He was of large size, blond complexion, balding head and goatee, well mannered, and spoke German, French, Russian, and broken English. He spoke at the Baptist World Alliance in London in 1905 and was elected one of its vice-presidents.[13]

---

11. *Der christliche Orient*, May 1908, 77–78. *Bratskiĭ listok*, 1909, no. 2, 11–12. Schäfer, 58. *Baptist*, 1908, 22–23.

12. *MRW*, Jan. 1909, 69, and Jan. 1910, 66. Schäfer, 76–77. Friesen, *In Defense of Privilege*, 155–56. *MO*, Dec. 1912, 916. Kahle, 472. Brandenburg, *The Meek and the Mighty*, 149–50.

13. Dahl, "Laitse Kodudus," in Kaups, *Viiskümmend aastate apostlite radadel*, 1884-1934, 89–92. Prestridge, 137–46. *MRW*, June 1906, 471. BWA, Congress, *Proceedings*, 1905, 182–84.

PART SIX—Possibilities and Uncertainties, 1905–1917

At its triennial conference in September 1906 in Radawczyk, Russian Poland, the German Baptist Union approved the establishment of a seminary. Its executive committee appointed Üxküll, who had already accepted the invitation of the American Baptist Missionary Union to speak on the needs of Russia at the May Meeting of Northern Baptists. In 1907 Üxküll traveled to America to raise $100,000 to acquire property and equipment for such an institution. He received a hearing among Northern, Southern, and Negro Baptists as well as Baptists in Canada. The Southern Baptist Convention in Richmond, Virginia, in 1907, where he spoke briefly, passed a resolution of support. Influential Baptists from the Baptist bodies formed a committee to further the effort. In Washington, DC, Üxküll discussed religious conditions in Russia for half an hour with President Theodore Roosevelt, who had received in 1905 the Nobel Peace Prize for his work in negotiating the peace that ended the Russo-Japanese War. In the name of many Russian Christians, Üxküll expressed his gratitude to Roosevelt for his role.[14] The German Baptist executive committee voted to obtain an option to purchase a house in the heart of Reval for the proposed school. In an article in June 1907 in the *Baptist Missionary Magazine,* Üxküll explained that the school would use both German and Russian. He returned home in 1908, reporting he had collected almost $23,400 and subscriptions of $7,900. The question of the final location of the seminary, however, was not settled. The executive committee in Neudorf in September 1907, although willing to receive Üxküll's gift of a house in Reval and rent it for school purposes, decided to wait until the next triennial convention in 1909 to decide on a permanent location. Earlier in the spring of 1907, the school committee of the German Baptist Union, while waiting for funds, decided in the meantime to open in the fall a school either in Pulin in Volhynia or Lodz in Russian Poland. It accepted the offer of the large Lodz church, which would provide two large teaching halls, a kitchen, dining hall, rooms for students, and a house mother. The school opened on October 14, 1907, offering a two-year course. The school had two professors—Eugen W. Mohr (1868–1917), a graduate of Hamburg Seminary who left now his pastorate at the Neudorf church, and Martin Schmidt from Königsberg, Germany, but who knew Russian. By the end of the year, it had enrolled thirteen students. The school was open to all nationalities, but instruction was in German.[15]

In an appeal for Russian Baptist students, Oskar Truderung (1876–1910), president of the school committee of the German Union who lived in Warsaw, published in March 1908 in the Russian Baptist periodical, *Baptist*, that the school would open a preparatory class on April 15 before the opening of the new school year in August for students not proficient in German. *The Missionary Review of the World* reported

14. *BMM*, Feb. 1906, 67; July 1906, 279; Mar. 1907, 98; and June 1907, 108–9. *Baptist*, 1908, no. 2, 23–24. *Baptist and Reflector*, May 30, 3; June 17, 6; and July 4, 7; July 18, 1907, 15. *Der Sendbote*, June 19, 1907, 12. *Der Hausfreund*, Sep. 16/30, 1908, 302.

15. *MRW*, June 1908, 472. *BMM*, Nov. 1907, 440. *Der Hausfreund*, Mar. 21/Apr. 3, 1907, 95; Aug. 1/14, 1907, 246; Sep. 26/Oct. 9, 1907, 308–9; Oct. 24/Nov. 6, 1907, 340; Dec. 26/Jan. 8, 1908, 414–15; and Jan. 9/22, 1908, 14. Eighth Union Conference, 1909, *Minutes*, 31–32.

in June that the seminary, besides its German-Russian students, had one Estonian and two Russians. Truderung attended the Russian Baptist congress in Rostov-on-Don in the fall of 1909 and stated the school was willing to accept Russian students but that it was necessary for the Russian churches to provide their support. Although the Russian congress authorized appealing for funds for the school and chose a school committee to approve students who wished to attend, it nevertheless expressed a desire for a school of its own.[16]

Upon his return to Russia in 1908, Üxküll transmitted for the capital of the school $20,750 in American bonds, guaranteed to pay out with cash. But Üxküll will drop out of the picture. Already in 1907 he had resigned as editor of the German Baptist paper, *Der Hausfreund,* and will relinquish his position as treasurer of the German Union. In his report on his trip to Russia in May and June, 1909, J. C. Heinrichs, Baptist missionary from India, reported that Üxküll was now relating more to the Evangelical Alliance than to Baptists and refused to go to Baptist conferences in Odessa or Lodz. He did not attend the Baptist World Alliance in Philadelphia in 1911, claiming poor health with a painful foot. In the meantime the seminary faced financial problems. In January 1908 the Continental Committee of the Baptist World Alliance sent the school £20 "to assist it in its present difficulties."[17]

In September 3–5, 1909, the German Baptist Union met in its triennial congress in Neudorf with around 154 delegates. Although the police authorities had granted authorization, the school had not yet received approval of its statutes, which was proving to be a slow process. Mohr reported he had collected from Mennonite Brethren only 300 rubles with another 400 promised. The question of the permanent location of the seminary was high on the agenda of the conference. V. G. Pavlov from the Russian Baptist Union actively participated. Pavlov stated that the delegates should determine whether the school should be a German school without consideration for Russians but reminded them that Üxküll collected money from donors who particularly wanted their money to train Russians. He also said the seminary should be located where Russians lived, which would also be advantageous for German students to learn the native language. Riga would be suitable but Odessa (where, by the way, Pavlov was pastor) would be far better where a mix of Russian and German congregations existed and a site that Russians could support.[18]

F. Brauer, president of the German Union, also supported Odessa if the purpose was to evangelize all of Russia. Others, however, felt that the primary purpose of the school should be for Germans. Mohr, one of the professors, stated that the Union

16. *Baptist,* Mar. 1908, 14, and Oct. 1909, 17. *Der Hausfreund,* Oct. 21/Nov. 3, 1909, 337.

17. Eighth Union Conference, 1909, *Minutes,* 12. Heinrichs, "Abstract of Report," ABMU/ABFMS, *Correpondence,* Russian Mission, 1900–1919, 618. Prestridge, 141. BWA, *Minute Books,* 1904–1931, Continental Committee, Jan. 28, 1909, 80.

18. For a description of the seminary and the debate on its permanent location, see Eighth Union Conference, 1909, *Minutes,* 12–23, 31–32, 38, 40–47, 59. Also see *Der Hausfreund,* Sep. 23/Oct. 6, 1909, 305–7, and *Baptist,* 1909, no. 23, 21–24.

should not support Russians at the cost of the German work and provide for Russians only if funds to spare were available. He pointed out the Russian brethren have provided almost nothing for their students. In the first round of voting, 159 votes were cast from 154 accredited delegates; with these questionable results the vote had to be redone. Zhitomir in Volhynia, supported by a voting block formed at a previous meeting, led with 70, followed by Odessa with 58, Riga with 22, Lodz with 3, and St. Petersburg with 2. Vote on the top two resulted in Zhitomir with 79 and Odessa with 76. In his disappointment, Brauer wrote that only the future will show whether one could say "amen" to the decision. By a close vote, regional and national self-interest prevailed. In August 1910, almost a year later, German Baptists learned that the authorities closed the school in Lodz for not being authorized. They charged the school for being propagandist, and reports had circulated that the school was training students who had earlier been members of the Orthodox Church. All appeals to keep the school open were fruitless. The highest number of students during its existence of three years was twenty-two. In its first year it had ten German-Russians, one Latvian, and one Russian. Schmidt claimed that at one time there were ten brethren from the Russian churches. Some Russian students failed to gain calls from Russian congregations, and German Baptists appointed few of them for Russian work.[19]

No school was ever established in Zhitomir. German Baptists now transferred fourteen students to Riga, where Severin Lehmann was pastor of the German Baptist church. It proved to be a stopgap measure with provision for no systematic but only informal instruction. The German Union defrayed expenses from the interest of the fund that Üxküll had collected, but it also used money from the fund to loan 15,000 rubles to the German Baptist church in St. Petersburg. Mohr, who could not get residency in Riga, became pastor of the large German Baptist church in Lodz, but Schmidt was able to go with the students. Schmidt with six students attended the Baptist World Alliance congress in Philadelphia in 1911. In January 1912 the school committee of the German Union arranged to send twelve students to the German Baptist Seminary in Hamburg. The Hamburg Seminary charged only 400 rubles a year for each student even though it cost the school 500 rubles. J. H. Rushbrooke of the Baptist World Alliance reported in 1913 that twenty students from Russia were at the Hamburg Seminary but only two were of Russian stock. In 1914 around twenty students from Russia were in Hamburg, but the First World War will cut off the supply.[20]

---

19. *Der Hausfreund*, Nov. 30/Dec. 13, 1911, 381. ABFMS, *Report*, 1911, 117. *Der Sendbote*, Mar. 11, 1914, 152. Letter from F. Schweiger, Nov. 2/15, 1912, in "The Present Baptist Situation in Russia," in ABMU/ABFMS, *Correspondence*, Russian Mission, 1900–1919.

20. *Der Sendbote*, Mar. 11, 1914, 152. *Der Hausfreund*, Nov. 30/Dec. 13, 1911, 381; Jan 18/31, 1912, 14; Mar. 28/Apr.10, 1912, 106; and Dec. 5/18, 1912, 402. Prestridge, 138. "Extracts of Notes Made by Rushbrooke," in an interview with Arndt, ABMU/ABFMS, *Correspondence*, Russian Mission, 1900–1919. *Baptist Times and Freeman*, Aug. 15, 1913, 620. ABFMS, *Report*, 1914, 161.

The Baptist World Alliance: A Thwarted Hope

Even though some Russian Baptists attended the Baptist seminary in Lodz, Russians wanted their own school. Deï Mazaev wrote an article in *Baptist* in January 1909, "On Religious Seminaries," appealing for such an institution. Even though the Russian Baptists at their congress in the fall of 1909 supported an appeal for funds for Russian students at the Lodz school, at the same time they voted to establish a seminary in Moscow "common for all Russian Baptists." At its congress in St. Petersburg in the fall of 1910, Russian Baptists authorized a commission to draw up a curriculum and to submit a suitable petition to the Minister of Interior to open a three-year theological institution. In a private session with representatives from the German Baptist Union at the congress, Russian Baptists expressed their intention to establish a Russian school with a German department. As noted at the German Baptist triennial congress in 1909, a joint enterprise of the German Baptist Union with the Russian Baptist Union was entirely unacceptable. On a trip to Russia, Jacob Heinrichs, missionary and president of a Baptist seminary in India, was also unable to interest Mennonites to support a Russian Baptist seminary.[21]

Russian Baptists looked to Baptists abroad for financial assistance in establishing a seminary. At the First European Baptist Congress in Berlin in 1908, Pavlov pointed out, besides the need for literature and a building society, the need for a school to train pastors and proposed Odessa, as he did a year later before the German Baptists in Russia. At the end of his speech he appealed to the Baptists of England and America for assistance in fulfilling these needs. He declared, "There are over a hundred tribes in Russia stretching out their hands to us for the Bread of Life, and crying to us, 'Give us to eat!' And our Master's command is, 'Give ye them to eat!' Up then, brethren! Up, and to the work." The congress appealed to the Executive Committee of the Baptist World Alliance to form a Special Committee that among its tasks was to form in a central location "an international European Baptist University College."[22] There were competing interests for the location for a central European college. For Hungarians it was Budapest, but the Russian Baptists with a reputation of heroism under suppression and personal appeals focused the attention of the Baptist world community toward Russia. At the Philadelphia Baptist Congress in Philadelphia in 1911, Fetler, in his rousing speech, appealed to American Baptists, whom he claimed had so many educational institutions while Russian had none, to support a European Baptist college. In his speech at the congress, Pavlov also presented the need for a theological school. After a presentation of the Russian delegates who spoke of their past suffering, A. J. Vining, pastor from Ontario, Canada, and noted for his oratorical skills, spoke

---

21. *Baptist*, 1909, no. 23, 24, and 1910, no. 43, 342. *Der Hausfreund*, Sep. 29/Oct. 12, 1910, 308. Heinrichs, "Abstract of Report," ABMU/ABFMS, *Correspondence*, Russian Mission, 1900–1919.

22. European Baptist Congress, *Proceedings*, 1908, 160. *Baptist Times and Freeman*, Sep. 11, 1908, 630.

PART SIX—Possibilities and Uncertainties, 1905–1917

passionately for a Baptist theological school in Russia. After his plea, F. B. Meyer, the presiding chairman, appealed to the assembly to raise $100,000 that very morning for a Baptist university to be built either in Moscow or St. Petersburg. The response was enthusiastic and by one o'clock $66,000 had been pledged.[23]

On the day before on June 21, the Executive Committee of the BWA met at the Baptist Temple. It knew that earlier in May the European Executive in London had already recommended the establishment of a European Baptist college. With this in mind, the Executive Committee passed resolutions that looked to the forming of a college, if possible in St. Petersburg, erecting a building and holding property by trustees nominated by the Northern and Southern Baptist Conventions in the USA subject to requirements of the Russian government. It stipulated that for the first year the Executive Committee of the BWA approve the president and the European Committee of the BWA a Russian tutor and approved an appeal to raise not more than $125,00 in the USA and Canada. It also agreed to send a deputation to Russia to gain authorization.[24]

Immediately attacks appeared in the Russian press opposing the establishment of a Baptist college in Russia. The press attacked the pernicious influence of the Baptists and alleged the purpose of such an institution was to educate evangelists who would seek to proselyte Orthodox members.[25]

With support of the American ambassador and letter from Theodore Roosevelt, now a former president of the USA, Sir George Macalpine, a vice-president of the BWA and former president of the Baptist Union of Great Britain and Ireland, planned a trip to Russia but received rejection from the Ministry of Internal Affairs as importing an organization that was too "cosmopolitan" and "socialist." Nevertheless in November he was able to head a delegation to St. Petersburg to meet with Russian officials. The delegation met with the American ambassador, who warned that it would be impossible to have American trustees for such an institution, the head of the institution must reside in Russia, and a supporting committee must have no official relationship to the institution. Macalpine met with the President of the Council of Ministers, the Minister of the Interior, and the Minister of Education. Macalpine believed they were all favorable toward the project. He stressed to them that he was not coming from an outside body but one that included Russian Baptists. He assured them that the school was designed to provide only a theological education for pastors and would exclude all political propaganda.[26]

---

23. BWA, Congress, *Proceedings*, 1911, 24–25, 233, 239–242.

24. BWA, *Minute Books*, 1904–1931, Executive Committee, June 21, 1911.

25. *Der Hausfreund*, Aug. 24/Sep. 6, 1911, 269–70. BWA, *Minute Books*, 1904–1931, Continental Committee, Dec. 26, 1911, 138–39.

26. Ivanov, "The Making of a Conspiracy: Russian Evangelicals During the First World War," *REE* 22/5 (Oct. 2002), 37. BWA, *Minute Books*, 1904–1931, Continental Committee, Nov. 21, 1911, 129–36, and Dec. 20, 1911, 138–39.

Robert S. MacArthur, president of the BWA, now went to St. Petersburg, carrying from America letters from President Taft and the Secretary of State and other credentials. He spoke at the opening of Fetler's *Dom Evangeliya* in December (o.s.) and met with the American ambassador and the Minister of the Interior. From the latter he felt he got under certain circumstances approval for the project.[27]

At a meeting of the Continental Committee of the BWA, April 25, 1912, it was revealed that a letter from the Imperial Russian Consulate General reported that the Minister of the Interior had given his consent to the college. The committee then asked Johann Urlaub, an optician who was a member of Fetler's church and a German subject, to purchase in his name the site for the college in Lesnoy (the Woods), a summer suburb of St. Petersburg. The property contained two and three quarter acres with six rental wooden houses. It cost $13,500 with funds coming from British donors. The sum of $125,000 was now needed from the USA and Canada for equipment and finishing the buildings. At this point the treasurer had collected only $14,242 with another $5,000 check ready to be cashed when needed. On June 25, 1912, the American Executive Committee of the BWA at the University of Chicago assured its constituency that it would provide full information on the procuring of funds. It also stated that, although Russian trustees must hold the property, yet twenty-one American and British directors will have oversight of the school and select its faculty.[28]

In July the Continental Committee received the news from Macalpine that the Minster of Public Instruction had declined to authorize the school. At the very same time, I. S. Prokhanov, head of the Evangelical Christians, received permission to open his own institute. What a surprise. How could the Baptist World Alliance be denied opening a school while Prokhanov, a vice-president of the Alliance, could open his? It was also a blow to the Russian Baptist Union that its rival again had come out on top.[29] In the eyes of Russian officials, the Baptist World Alliance was not looked on with much favor. The accounts of suppression before 1905 at the congress in Philadelphia did not set well. In addition, the regime feared the aggressive behavior of Russian Baptists, who were now greatly strengthened by their association with a world Baptist body that could provide large amounts of money for a theological school under foreign control on Russian soil. Besides, the regime was bent on limiting sectarian inroads by closing or limiting theological institutions, particularly those with foreign ties. As a slap to the Baptist World Alliance and possibly to stir up more controversy in sectarian ranks and at the same time to show the world that Russia was not intrinsically against sectarians, why not grant Prokhanov his school? Prokhanov would be far

---

27. *Baptist Times and Freeman*, Jan. 26, 1912, 67. *Baptist and Reflector*, Feb. 8, 1912, 8.

28. BWA, *Minute Books*, 1904–1931, Continental Committee, April 25, 1912, 561. McCaig, *Wonders of Grace*, 31. *Baptist and Reflector*, Apr. 18, 1912, 8; May 16, 1912, 12; and July 25, 1912, 3–4.

29. BWA, *Minute Books*, 1904–1931, Continental Committee, July 17, 1912. Prokhanov, *In the Cauldron*, 167.

less a threat as a native Russian, living in St. Petersburg, and far less confrontational than a Fetler or a Pavlov. Also his institute was not the creation of a foreign body.

The situation now raised a host of serious questions. To what extent should the Baptist World Alliance attempt to continue its project of a college in St. Petersburg where it now had property? What about the collection of the Philadelphia Fund and its use? Should it provide any support to Prokhanov's new Bible institute? What help was needed for students from Russia at Hamburg Seminary?

In September Martin Schmidt, who had taught at the Lodz seminary from 1907 to 1910 and then went to Riga, was now working with Prokhanov. Schmidt went to London in September 1912 to obtain funds for the proposed Bible institute. The Continental Committee of the BWA responded to the Schmidt visit by writing to Prokhanov that, although it was in sympathy with his efforts and remaining open to his appeal, it was now engaged in its own enterprise in establishing a school in St. Petersburg and had no funds for him. In a letter of September 22, Prokhanov wrote to the committee that he hoped the various Russian unions would endorse his project and requested the use of some of the property at Lesnoy purchased by the BWA. In a meeting on November 7, the committee received word that the Latvian Baptist Union had approved but at the same time received information that the Russian Baptist Union would probably oppose. In February 1913 if not earlier, the committee had received another letter from Prokhanov, stating he believed the Latvian and Estonian Unions had approved the school and asked if Schmidt could solicit funds in England. The committee refused.[30]

The BWA could scarcely provide Prokhanov support since its money was for a European Baptist college in Russia and not for a small Evangelical Christian (Open Baptist) Bible school entirely under Prokhanov's control. Also the Russian Baptist Union strongly opposed. The failure of Baptist support for Prokhanov's school, except for possible support of Baptist students in his school, will, as to be seen later, seriously strain Prokhanov's ties to Baptists and will push him to look elsewhere for support.

Fetler wrote to the Continental Committee suggesting that it should start the school on a small scale on a site in the city rather than the outside, possibly using rooms in *Dom Evangeliya*. Instead of cutting its losses and stop the project or look elsewhere, the committee resolved in February 1913 to begin to use the Lesnoy property "on a small and unobtrusive scale." A letter from J. N. Prestridge in America was read that contributions would not continue with uncertainty over the school.[31]

Baptist officials were now floundering as to what measures should be undertaken. J. H. Shakespeare in England wrote in May 1913 suggesting to W. C. Bitting, corresponding secretary of the Northern Baptist Convention, that it might be possible

---

30. BWA, *Minute Books*, 1904–1931, Continental Committee, Sep. 16, 1912; Nov. 7, 1912; and Feb. 13, 1913. *Der Sendbote*, Mar. 11, 1914, 152–53.

31. BWA, *Minute Books*, 1904–1931, Continental Committee, Nov. 17, 1912, and February 13, 1913.

Theological Education

to send privately to St. Petersburg Dr. W. J. Whitley, who knew German, to gather three or four students in a house at Lesnoy, learn Russian in twelve months, and then apply for temporary statutes. Three months before, Shakespeare had sent a letter to a Mr. Huntington that it would not be the time now to approach any Russian officials, pointing out that among various circumstances MacArthur, president of the Baptist World Alliance, was looked on with disfavor for participating in a protest against Russian treatment of Jews. In April in his visit to St. Petersburg, J. H. Franklin, secretary of the ABFMS, interviewed Fetler who reiterated his view that work should begin in a local church or perhaps rent a hall. Franklin also was able to get Fetler and Prokhanov together with leaders of the German and Latvian Baptists in Russia to attempt to form a committee of cooperation, but this proved to be an illusion. In Franklin's letter to Shakespeare in May, Franklin advised caution and the need to get the endorsement of Baptists in Russia. He maintained the effort should appear to originate from the Russians and not as a foreign effort.[32]

During the European Baptist Congress in Stockholm in July 1913, a meeting of the Committee on College Questions was held in the Emanuel church on July 22. On the following day a committee of representatives of the Baptist unions in Russia and the Evangelical Christian Union with representatives of the BWA from America and Europe also met. Representatives of the Russian Baptist Union declared Prokhanov's school was not suitable, while Schmidt said Prokhanov'school was open to all nationalities and all Baptist groups. After hearing proposals, the following policy was approved: (1) To continue to form a college in St. Petersburg by sending a tutor to serve quietly until temporary statutes can be applied. (2) Assist students from Russia to attend either the Hamburg Seminary or Prokhanov's Bible School upon the approval of the student's respective union. (3) Assist students from other non-German Unions to attend Hamburg Seminary or other Baptist seminaries. (4) To request the ABFMS, the Foreign Board of the Southern Baptist Convention, and the British Section of the BWA each to furnish one-third of the funds for support of such students. In September the Continental Committee endorsed the policy statement. In December the Continental Committee reported the reception of a letter from the American Executive Committee, although it approved other policy statements strongly rejected the recommendation of engaging a tutor without the approval of the Russian authorities. In March 1914 the Continental Committee resolved to write to Prokhanov it was "entirely sympathetic towards his work" but was unable to provide financial support for the St. Petersburg institute except for Baptist students who entered with the approval of their unions.[33]

32. Letter of Shakespeare to Bitting, May 19, 1913; letter of Shakespeare to Huntington, Feb. 21, 1913; letter of Franklin to Shakespeare, May 10, 1913; and Extracts of Notes Made by Franklin, April 1913, ABMU/ABFMS, *Correspondence*, Russian Mission, 1900–1919.

33. BWA, *Minute Books*, 1904–1931, Committee on College Questions and Committee of Russian Delegates, July 22–23, 1913, 19–24; Continental Committee, Sep. 18, 1913, 193; Dec. 18, 1913, 199; and Mar. 23, 1914, 205.

PART SIX—Possibilities and Uncertainties, 1905–1917

The Baptist World Alliance held property and a seminary fund but had no school. The German Baptist Union in Russia had a fund but neither property nor a school. Prokhanov had a school but no property and no Baptist support. The Mennonite Brethren had no school, property, or a fund. The outbreak of the First World War in 1914 terminated further efforts of establishing a Baptist college in St. Petersburg. The war also stopped students from Russia attending the Baptist seminary in Hamburg. The Baptist World Alliance continued to hold the property in Lesnoy, and the fund, started in Philadelphia, had reached by July 1913 $35,000, bearing interest in a bank in Columbia, Missouri. In the midst of the war in 1916, the Continental Committee resolved that "it would be contrary, both to the letter and spirit of the fund in question, if it were other than for the establishment of a College in Russia, or, if that proved impossible, in some other country in Europe."[34]

In 1922 it was reported to the Executive Committee of the BWA that the fund for the school had reached $42,757 in the U.SA., $12,532 in Canada, and £1,427 in England. In 1922–1923 around $44,500 was contributed to a joint Bible school of Evangelical Christians and Baptists in Petrograd that failed to materialize and $24,000 in 1928 to a Baptist school in Moscow that closed the following year. But what happened to the property in Lesnoy in Russia? At the outbreak of the war, Urlaub, who was not a Russian subject transferred the deed of the property to another member of his family for safety but the latter died. As a result of rioting in 1918, the houses on the property were burned. The communist regime nationalized the property, and it was reported in 1925 another party was renting it temporarily. In the previous year the Continental Committee learned that Urlaub, still living, submitted a claim of £1,200 for legal and adminstrative expenses, which the committee acknowledged. The committee voted to inform the British government of the history of the property held by the BWA, but the $13,500 originally paid was never recovered.[35]

At the meeting of the Administrative Committee of the BWA in November 1965, it was reported that the fund had increased to $159,732.63. In the meantime the BWA had borrowed from the fund for its own real estate transactions at 4 1/2% interest, which by this time, although unpaid, had grown to $12,956.40. The Committee voted that due to the services the BWA had rendered to the fund this amount be canceled and not be paid. In 1977 the fund was only $110, 251. The General Council of the BWA voted to reserve $50,000 of it for a future institution of theological training in Moscow and the balance to provide funds for Slavic-speaking ministerial students outside the USSR in Eastern Europe. When finally, eighty years later in 1991, a Baptist seminary was planned for Moscow but with classes in Odessa, a Baptist seminary seemed possible in that city. Finally the Moscow Baptist Theological Seminary opened

---

34. *Baptist Times and Freeman*, Aug. 15, 1913, 620. *Baptist and Reflector*, Apr. 17, 1913, 4. BWA, *Minute Books*, 1904–1931, Continental Committee, Nov. 2, 1916, 21.

35. BWA, *Minute Books*, 1904–1931, Executive Committee, July 31 to Aug. 2, 1922, Feb. 25–26, 1925, and Appendix A. Continental Committee, June 1, 1923, 25, and Sep. 15, 1924, 64.

in 1993. Baptists in the West showed again their support for theological education in Russia. One major example was the commitment in 1991 of the Foreign Mission Board of the Southern Baptist Convention to commit $200,000 from its Lottie Moon Offering to the new school. In 1993 the BWA donated $178,000. In subsequent years additional funds from the BWA and others have come to the school.[36]

St. Petersburg Bible Institute

After years of refusal from the authorities, Prokhanov received in July 1912 the right to open a Bible institute. Prokhanov, fearing the government might withdraw its permission, hurried to open his school. It began on February 14, 1913, with nine students on the premises of Prokhanov's Evangelical Christian Church. Prokhanov was the principal and taught interpretation of the New Testament, dogmatics, apologetics, and homiletics. A. A. Reimer, a Mennonite Brethren, taught interpretation of the Old Testament and church history, and K. G. Inkis, a Latvian Baptist, music. Martin Schmidt, a German Baptist and former teacher at Lodz Seminary who was working with Prokhanov, will in time also teach. All teachers were part-time. The school began with a two-year program. Prokhanov provided on Monday nights special instruction for about fifty preachers.[37]

Prokhanov reported that for the 1913–1914 academic year the school accepted ten new students for a total of eighteen. Among them were Evangelical Christians, Russian Baptists, Latvian Baptists, two Mennonites, and others. In the spring of 1914, the school had five part-time teachers and sixteen students, eight Evangelical Christians and eight Baptists. Of the latter probably only three were Russian. The nationalities for both denominational bodies included ten Russians, five Latvians, and one Karelian. For the fall Prokhanov hoped for fourteen or fifteen new students to bring the student body to thirty. He looked forward to adding a third year and then a fourth, thereby creating a regular theological institution.[38]

Prokhanov was facing financial difficulties with his mission program and the establishment of his institute. Foreign Baptists promised no aid, and Russian Baptists refused cooperation. Fortunately for Prokhnov the Disciples of Christ in the USA, which incorporated a number of Baptist principles as believer's baptism and the independence of the local church, made contact with Prokhanov in looking to Russia as a possible mission field. Joseph Keevil of the Disciples of Christ Missionary Union of New York City and I. N. McCash, secretary of the American Christian Missionary

---

36. BWA, *Minute Books*, 1904–1931, Administrative Committee, Nov. 22–23. 1965. *Baptist World*, Sep. 1977, 4, and Mar. 1978, 6. *BWA News*, Jan.–Mar.1991, 12–13, and Apr.–June, 1991, 9. International Mission Board of the Southern Baptist Convention, Archives and Records, Accession numbers 572 and 623. Pierard, *Baptists Together in Christ*, 1905–2005, 266, 291–92. E-mail message of Neville Callam, General Secretary of the BWA, to Wardin, July 22, 2011.

37. *Utrennyaya zvezda*, Feb. 15, 1913, 2, and Sep. 13, 1913, 5–6. *Christian Standard*, Mar. 22, 1913, 10–11. Prokhanov, *In the Cauldron*, 167–68. *Der Sendbote*, Mar. 11, 1914, 152–53.

38. *Der Sendbote*, Mar. 11, 1914, 152–53. *The Christian-Evangelist*, June 4, 1914, 731.

Society (ACMS), sent a cable, greeting the Evangelical Christian Union congress in St. Petersburg in 1911–1912. Keevil quickly followed the cable with a letter to Prokhanov asking about the origin, size, beliefs, and polity of his movement. Both the Missionary Union and ACMS had become acquainted with the Prokhanov movement largely through John Johnson, a migrant from Russia who had formed in New York City a Russian Christian Church that joined the Disciples of Christ.[39]

In the fall of 1912 Martin Schmidt and Aleksandr Persianov, an Evangelical Christian missionary, traveled to America and attended the annual meeting of the ACMS and appealed for financial support for the Bible institute. The Disciples formed a Special Russian Emergency Committee, chaired by Z. T. Sweeney, to raise funds. The *Christian Standard* and *The Christian-Evangelist*, two national periodicals of the Disciples, strongly supported the effort. By December 1913 the Emergency Committee had raised about $5,500 of which over $4,300 had been distributed. In 1913 and 1914 Sweeney and other Disciples visited Prokhanov. The Disciples felt they were in essential agreement with Evangelical Christians by the latter designating themselves "Gospel Christians," their emphasis on Christian unity, independent congregations, believer's baptism, and open communion, although insisting communicants must indicate regeneration. The biggest difference was over baptism—Prokhanov, following the Baptist view, rejected any suggestion that baptism was for "remission of sins," a Disciples position.

In a lengthy letter in 1914, which was printed in *Christian Standard*, Prokhanov showed to what lengths he would go to appeal to the expectations and practices of the Disciples, who themselves historically were rivals to Baptists, and at the same time disparage fellow Russian Baptists. He played up his position on open communion, claimed the practice of weekly communion, and approved baptism without delay if weather permitted, all positions conformable to the practice of the Disciples. He stated his Union council was only consultative and his movement had a separate origin from Baptists. He declared his passion for Christian unity. He endorsed the views of the Disciples that the church must be "apostolic" or restorationist, and accepted the words, "He that believeth and is baptized shall be saved" (but not as Disciples interpreted them), and was publishing and commending the book by T. W. Phillips, *The Church of Christ*.

He claimed Russian Baptists opposed Gospel Christians for their great success and the "spiritual and intellectual superiority" of their leaders and institutions. He condemned Baptists for their rigid practice of excommunication, their calumnies both verbally and in almost every issue of the *Baptist*, giving at times false reports to the police, the control of their Union council over the churches, and their rejection of the union proposals of Gospel Christians. He downplayed the membership of the

---

39. For Prokhanov's relations with the Disciples of Christ and bibliographic sources, see Wardin, "The Disciples of Christ and Ties with Russia," *Discipliana* 52 (1991), no. 3, 33, 35–41. *The Christian-Evangelist*, Apr. 11, 1912, 530.

Evangelical Christians in the Baptist World Alliance by stating it did not compromise their freedom and only meant participating in their congresses every five years.

Prokhanov also emphatically rejected in his letter the recommendation from the Disciples that Gospel Christians ought to cooperate with Baptists in a union committee, which had been scheduled in Berlin in 1914, and their Bible school should be a union school. He claimed it was now too late and conditions had changed for a union committee. He declared that after obtaining the charter for his school he was determined to keep full control. He suggested the entry of Baptists into a union school would introduce sectarianism, a practice Disciples claimed as over against other church groups to have effaced.

Whatever elements of truth the letter contained, it displayed only one side and distorted the picture of relations between Evangelical Christians and Baptists. It also showed his adroit ability to play up or play down facts that he believed supported his own views. It also showed an arrogance and determination that he must be on top, even if it contradicted his own beliefs on Christian unity.

Prokhanov hoped to open the Bible institute in September 1914 for the new school year. But the First World War began in July. He could not open the school since four students were forced to serve in the army and no financial assistance could be received from abroad.[40] The school could not open until eight years later in 1922. The communist regime will terminate it in 1929 about the time it closed a short-lived Russian Baptist Preacher's School.

---

40. *The Christian-Evangelist*, Dec. 3, 1914, 1571.

27

Mennonite Brethren

Prosperous and Challenged, 1905–1914

IN A MENNONITE POPULATION of around 100,000 in the early twentieth century, Mennonite Brethren with a community of twenty to twenty-five percent of the total was a prosperous religious community. The settlements of the Mennonite commonwealth, particularly in southern Ukraine, were islands of prosperity with a far higher standard of living than their Russian neighbors. Instead of clay and straw, their homes were now built with burned decorative bricks and tile roofs. Home furnishings and clothing reflected bourgeois tastes. Mennonites, by and large, continued to live in farm communities with economic stratification reflected in a small but very wealthy class of estate owners on the top, followed by industrialists and professionals, and then by a lower class with little or no capital.[1] Mennonite Brethren participated with other Mennonites in providing a significant network of educational and benevolent institutions. In his massive history of the Mennonite Brotherhood, Peter M. Friesen recorded in 1911 that Mennonites had established at least 400 village and estate schools with 500 teachers in educational institutions. The system included boys' and girls' high schools, pedagogical schools in Chortitza and Halbstadt, and a business school in the latter center.[2]

---

1. For the economic status of Mennonites in late Imperial Russia, see Urry, "Through the Eye of a Needle," Conference on "Images of Imperial Russia," Conrad Grebel College, University of Waterloo, Canada, May 9–10, 1984. For buildings see Friesen with Shmakin, *Into the Past: Buildings of the Mennonite Commonwealth*.

2. Friesen, 787–88. Urry, "The Cost of Community," *JMS* 10 (1992), 28–31.

At the end of the nineteenth century, Mennonites began to organize public benevolent institutions. They included the Maria School for Deaf Mutes (1885); hospitals in Muntau (1887), Ohrloff (1908), and Waldheim (1908); an orphanage at Grossweide (1906); a home for the aged in Kuruschan (1904); and a deaconess home in Neu-Halbstadt (1909). Their most ambitious project was Bethania, the psychiatric institution at Alt-Kronsweide (1910/1911). Institutions, including hospitals, often charged fees, but hospital beds were reserved without cost for poor patients. Mennonties were also generous in providing public charity such as funds for wounded and sick soldiers during the Russo-Japanese War and during the years of famine from 1906 to 1908.[3]

The Challenges

The years from 1905 to 1914 were a golden age for Mennonites. In spite of the Russification of their schools and the increased bureaucratic environment of Russian civil society, Mennonites still maintained their traditional closed ethnic society with religious and social privileges. Nevertheless the age presented a number of threats. The revolutionary years of 1904–1905 that accompanied the Russo-Japnese War were unsettling for political stability and the protection of property. The imperial manifestos of 1905–1906 promised civil liberties and guarantees of freedom of conscience, but their implementation at times appeared problematic. With the continuing growth of anti-German sentiment with charges of a German menace to Russian economic and political interests, Mennonites faced uncertainty in maintaining their special privileges, particularly the one that granted military exemption. Although the Old Mennonite Church and Mennonite Brethren cooperated in district and local administration, the Mennonite school system, the Forestry Service for Mennonite men of military age, and in benevolent contributions, they now felt pressure to present a common front before the government. In 1910 Mennonite Brethren began to cooperate in an All-Mennonite Conference.

The promise of religious liberty beckoned a number of Mennonite Brethren in an outreach to their Russian neighbors. They soon, however, had to face the reality of opposition from entrenched reactionary forces in church and state. Their mission zeal increased the suspicions of the regime, and they needed to defend themselves that they were truly Mennonite and not Baptist and were a tolerated confession and not a sect. The question of their status also brought tensions with the Old Mennonite Church in whose ranks some wanted to repudiate cooperation with the Mennonite Brethren for fear of losing their own privileges.

3. P. M. Friesen, 809–31. Urry, "The Cost of Community," 31–38.

PART SIX—Possibilities and Uncertainties, 1905-1917

The Political Scene

In May 1904 Mennonite Brethren met in annual conference at Reinfeld. Several prayed "fervently and earnestly" for Tsar Nichols and his family. They also prayed for ending the Russo-Japanese War that had begun in January. With growing discontent and the massacre of "Bloody Sunday" on January 9, 1905, revolution broke out that led the regime under great pressure to issue manifestos guaranteeing religious and civil liberties. The Manifesto of April 17 promised freedom of conscience and the one on October 17 promised the establishment of a constitutional monarchy with civil liberties and a State Duma with full legislative authority.

Abraham Kroeker, who edited *Die Friedensstimme* and *Christlicher Familienkalender,* in a review of the year from July 1905 to August 1906, wrote that "The future lies dark before us," but along with submission to the authorities he requested prayer for a spiritual awakening that will also settle the social question. Heinrich Dirks, editor of the *Mennonitisches Jahrbuch*, an Old Church Mennonite publication, wrote in a review of 1905 that the various manifestos brought economic relief in land purchase and above all a new guarantee of religious liberty. He noted that the Manifesto of October 17 did not shut out Mennonite peculiarities in faith and practice. He continued to say, however, that only time would tell what the new relations would bring Mennonites, but he hoped for the best.[4]

Unlike their Anabaptist ancestors who rejected participation in government, Russian Mennonites, now with the legalization of political parties, identified with party politics and participated in the election of representatives to the State Duma. In the election for representatives to the first Duma in 1906, *Die Friedensstimme* described the concern of the German minority in South Russia to maintain German culture and education with the use of German in the school system and protection of religious freedom. *Der Botschafter*, the Old Church Mennonite journal, rejected the social revolutionary parties of the left and the reactionary parties of the right as well as the Constitutional Democrats (Kadets) of the middle for not guaranteeing private property and support for the franchise of women. Instead it favored the party of October 17 (the Octobrists), the middle party of the right, and printed its party platform. As a whole Mennonites tended to support the Octobrists. Mennonites wanted a party that would support the monarchy and protection for their cultural, religious, and economic interests.[5]

A short-lived party of evangelicals, "The Union of Freedom, Truth and Peace," was led by the Mennonite Brethren historian, Peter Martin Friesen. It included Baptists, such as N. V. Odintsov, and the Evangelical Christian leader, Ivan S. Prokhanov. Because of his leadership and Mennonite participation, it became known as "The

---

4. *Christlicher Familienkalender*, 1907, 123. *Mennonitisches Jahrbuch*, 1905-1906, 12-13.

5. *Die Friedensstimme*, April 15, 1906, 153. *Der Botschafter*, March 15/28, 1906, 1-2. P. M. Friesen, 627-29.

Friesen Party." Its initial program opposed violence, supported the stability of the monarchy with both Tsar and State Duma exercising a legislative initiative, judicial reform, universal suffrage, free compulsory education, individual freedoms, and access of peasants to land at just prices. The party was closely aligned with the Kadets, but it disintegrated in 1906. Friesen claimed Mennonites became disillusioned with the Kadets for their failure to be explicit on the monarchy and the language question.[6]

With concern in preserving their privilege of military exemption, elders in Halbstadt in May 1906 sent Isaak Dück from Chortiza and Abraham Görz from Molochna to St. Petersburg to meet with the Council of Ministers and possibly members of the State Duma. Because of limited contacts, the mission largely failed.[7]

Congregations

With the Manifestos of April and October 1905, Mennonite Brethren looked forward to less restrictions and greater mission opportunities. At the close of 1906 Mennontie Brethren numbered 5,700 in forty-five congregations, including affiliates. The concentration of congregations was in southern Ukraine, the area of first settlement. Other congregations were widely scattered with one in Russian Poland, one in the Crimea, three in Kuban, four in the Volga region, and one in Turkmenistan. After the turn of the century, a new area opened in western Siberia as Mennonites began to settle the area. Congregations appeared in the Omsk area, Pavlodar, and Barnaul with Jakob Wiens as leader. In his travels, E. H. Broadbent, the Plymouth Brethren itinerant, made particular note in 1914 of the influx of Mennonite settlers, including Menonite Brethren, in the area from Pavlodar to Barnaul.[8]

Mennonite Brethren pastors continued to be unpaid except possibly for expenses. They were also generally untrained. Some, however, attended the Hamburg Baptist Seminary, such as Heinrich J. Braun (1873-1946), pastor of the large Rückenau Mennonite Brethren Church, wealthy landowner, and Mennonite Brethren leader. Although discussed, neither the Mennonite Brethren nor the Old Mennonite Church or collectively were able to establish a theological school of otheir own. At Tiege in 1910, the Mennonite Brethren conference elected Heinrich Braun, Wilhelm Dück, and Peter Thielmann to petition the government to establish Bible courses for pastors. A number of Mennonite Brethren attended the Alliance Bible School in Berlin. Abraham Braun, secretary of the Bible School and a younger brother of Heinrich Braun,

---

6. Klibanov, 317-20. P. M. Friesen, 1029, ft. 3.

7. *Die Friedensstimme*, June 3, 1906, 234, and June 24, 1906, 262-63. Toews, *Czars, Soviets & Mennonites*, 49.

8. Abraham Friesen, *In Defense of Privilege*, 121. Dueck, 24-33. Toews, *History of the Mennonite Brethren Church*, 92-93. *Echoes of Service*, Feb. 1914, 1:71.

wrote in 1912, from a student enrollment of about 160 beginning in 1905 to the present, 66 were from Russia.⁹

Except for the Rückenau church and its affiliates, the Mennonite Brethren, by and large, continued to observe close communion. The Alliance movement, however, continued to have an impact among Mennonite Brethren. The annual meetings of the Blankenburg Alliance in Germany stressed the inner spiritual life and the unity of all evangelicals. Peter P. Schmidt (1860–1910) of Steinbach, who attended conferences at Blankenburg, and his brother-in-law David J. Dick (1816–1919) of Apanlee conducted meetings on their estates for worship and observed open communion. In 1902 at Steinbach a conference led by Ernst Ströter attracted sixty evangelical believers including Mennonite Brethren and Old Mennonites. The guest books of Peter Schmidt and his brother Nicolaï included many of the top leaders of the evangelical movement, including Mennonite Brethren, German Baptists, Plymouth Brethren, and evangelical Armenians as well as Paul Lieven, son of Princess Nathalie Lieven, and Johannes Lepsius of the Deutsche Orient Mission.¹⁰ In 1905 in Lichtfelder in the Molochna, Peter Schmidt led in the formation of the Evangelical Mennonite Brethren Church, an Alliance church that observed open communion. A council of elders led the church. It elected three Mennonite Brethren pastors as associate elders, Jakob Kroeker, Peter Unruh, and Jakob W. Reimer, although not members of the congregation. A second church of similar belief arose in 1907 in Altonau, Sagradowka settlement.¹¹

Foreign Missions

The Mennonite Brethren continued support of the Telugu field in South India in cooperation with the American Baptist Missionary Union (ABMU) or American Baptist Foreign Mission Society (ABFMS) as it was later called. Mennonite Brethren from America also established their own Telugu field, looking to the Russian Mennonite Brethren for assistance and fellowship. In 1906 both fields experienced revival that resulted in an increase of conversions and baptisms. In 1907 at the Mennonite Brethren conference in Nikolayevka, Jacob C. Heinrichs (1860–1947), who was born in Germany, a graduate of Rochester Theological Baptist Seminary, missionary of the ABMU, and president of the Baptist theological seminary at Ramapatam on the Telugu field, was a guest speaker. He worked with the Mennonite Brethren missionaries on their field and could communicate with them in German. Another guest speaker was Karl Mascher, mission inspector of the German Baptist field in the Cameroons in Africa. The two had just been guests at the South Russian Association of German Baptists

---

9. Dueck, 72. *Die Friedensstimme*, Sep. 18, 1912, 2–3.

10. Dueck, 164. Toews, "The Calm Before the Storm," *Direction* 31/1 (Spring 2002), 78–80. Toews, *Perilous Journey*, 58–59. Sudermann, "*Allianz* in Ukraine," *Mennonite Historian* 23/1 (Mar. 1997), 1–2 and 23/2 (June 1997), 6–7.

11. P. M. Friesen, 918–25. Toews, *History of the Mennonite Brethren Church*, 103–4.

at Neu-Danzig, where Heinrich Braun had gone to get them and pay their expenses. In addition, the Mennonite Brethren conference agreed to pay the expenses to send Braun, who was competent in Russian, to accompany Heinrichs on an inspection trip to Persia for the possibility of opening a Baptist field there. The two successfully completed the trip.[12]

In 1910 the Russian Telugu field had seven mission workers, including wives, located on three stations with 3,000 baptized members. The veteran missionary Abraham Friesen and his wife were now in retirement, returning home to Russia in 1908. Heinrich Unruh and his wife returned from their furlough in 1911, but unfortunately Heinrich died of typhus in 1912 and his wife left the following year. Johann Wiens and his wife left in 1911 because of the illness of their daughter. With resentment over control by the Baptist society, Franz Wiens, the son of Jakob Wiens, Mennonite Brethren leader in Siberia, resigned in 1913 and left with his family in 1914.[13]

One of the missionaries, Kornelius Unruh (1873–1941), who was on furlough when his brother Heinrich died, wrote a letter in 1914 to *Das Erntefeld*, the mission publication, "Our Ranks Are Thinning Out." It was a heart cry of mission reality without the romance. He wrote:

> Whereas every disciple of Christ needs to carry his cross. Those in foreign mission work have more than their fair share of distressful and thornfilled situations: deadly climates, persecution, ridicule and slander at the hands of our neighbors, travel hazards, a sacrificial existence, separation from children, disappointments and trials of all kinds.

Kornelius will serve four terms on the field from 1904 to 1939 and will die two years later.[14] Abraham Friesen will return to the field in 1913–1914 and bring with him three new missionaries, Johann and Anna Penner and Aganetha Neufeld. Upon the outbreak of the First World War in 1914, funds from Russia were cut off and the missionaries were forced to ask the American Baptist Foreign Mission Society to take them as their missionaries. Because of war and the Communist revolution, the field was aborbed into the American Baptist work, and Russian Mennonite Brethren were unable to regain it. In their twenty-five years of support, the Mennonite Brethren contributed over $150,000.[15]

The Mennonite Brethren mission to India presented a remarkable confluence of denominational and national currents. Not only was there a cooperative endeavor of Mennonite Brethren and Baptists, not entirely unusual, but even more it brought together a German-Russian Mennonite body partnering with a Baptist mission society

---

12. Penner, *Russians, North Americans and Telugus*, 33, 45–46. Dueck, 61–65. *BMM*, Jan. 1908, 23–26, and Feb. 1908, 61–65.

13. P. M. Friesen, 686–87. Penner, 35–36, 55–60.

14. Penner, 57, 291.

15. Ibid., 62–64.

in the USA that worked on an Asiatic field with almost all of its male missionaries receiving their theological training in Germany. Abraham Friesen, Heinrich and Kornelius Unruh, Abram Huebert, Johann Wiens, and Johann Penner were all students at the Baptist seminary in Hamburg.[16]

Mission to Russians

In 1882 Johann Wieler, the Mennonite Brethren leader, as already noted, arranged a joint meeting of Mennonite Brethren and Russian Baptists at the time of the former's annual conference at Rückenau. In the following year, however, the Mennonite Brethren Conference rejected Wieler's proposal for a continuing mission with Russian Baptists. Mennonite Brethren feared that a charge from the Russian regime of proselyting would seriously jeopardize their status in the empire. In 1905 many Mennonite Brethren, such as Jakob Kroeker, felt, however, a new day of mission opportunity had now arrived with the Manifesto of April 17. He recorded that those who first heard the Manifesto felt it would have significance for thousands, including the many who had suffered for their faith. Years later, Abraham Braun, brother of Heinrich Braun, wrote that the October 17 Manifesto with its promise of religious liberty made Mennonite Brethren believe that the old barriers were gone. In 1908 Abraham Kroeker wrote to *Der Wahrheitszeuge* about the generosity in Halbstadt of Mennonites providing money, food, and clothes to starving Russians and declared that war and revolution in 1904–1905 had opened Russia to the gospel. He admitted that full liberty had not been attained but was thankful for the level of freedom now available.[17]

To what extent did Mennonite Brethren take advantage of the new situation? Peter Riediger, who himself participated in Russian evangelization, in his paper, "Mennonite Missions Among the Russians," gave examples of mission initiatives of individual Mennonite Brethren but stated that both the Old Mennonite (or *Kirchliche*) and Mennonite Brethren conferences were inactive. It was true for the former conference, but not the full truth for Mennonite Brethren. In this period the Mennonite Brethren supported for a time a Russian mission committee in addition to the mission engagement of individual Mennonite Brethren and a fruitful publishing partnership with a Russian evangelical body.[18]

At its conference in 1906, Mennonite Brethren appointed a committee for evangelizing Russians. Heinrich J. Braun, pastor of the Rückenau church, was appointed treasurer of the committee besides treasurer for the committee on foreign missions and a committee on Bulgarian missions. With such a heavy responsibility, Braun

---

16. Ibid., 2, 7, 9, 21–22, 34–35, 47, 58.

17. Kroeker, *Die Sehnsucht des Ostens*, 19. Abraham Friesen, 121. *WHZ*, Apr. 25, 1908, 136.

18. Riediger, "Mission der Mennoniten in Russland unter den Russen." In Eng. tr., "Mennonite Missions Among the Russians," mns., B. B. Janz Papers, Centre for Mennonite Brethren Studies, Winnipeg, Manitoba.

asked Gerhard P. Froese to serve as treasurer of the Russian Evangelization Committee, who evidently was elected in 1908 at the conference in Memrik for the position. Within two years the committee engaged nine Russian brethren for the work.[19]

A year previously in 1907 the conference in Nikolayevka was a high point of mission enthusiasm with around a thousand in attendance. Here Heinrichs from India, Mascher, mission inspector for the Cameroons, Rosenberg, missionary to the Jews in Odessa, gave reports, and others spoke on the Russian mission. Peter Isaak appealed for its support. Adolph A. Reimer gave his testimony of his entry into work among the Russian people and appealed for more workers for the work. C. Reimer spoke of visiting about 138 villages and urged prayer and work for the mission, and Jakob J. Vins (Wiens) from Samara told of his identification with it.[20] In July 1907 Adolph Reimer pariciparted in Berdyansk in Russian meetings with the Russian evangelist, Fedor P. Balikhin. In fifteen general gatherings and eleven biblical meeetings on Philippians in October and November 1908 in the villages of Timoshevka, Astrakhanka, Novovasil'evka, and Novospasskoe, Johann Isaak, Adolph Reimer, Jakob W. Reimer, Peter V. Unruh and others served with Balikhin. In 1908 Jakob W. Reimer, Peter V. Unruh, and Johannes Haak participated in Bible conferences with three Russian congregations in the Odessa region. Haak also led evangelistic meetings in Russian prayer halls.[21]

Two businessmen who were involved in Russian evangelistic activity were Gerhard P. Froese (Fröse) (b. 1867), the treasurer of the Russian Evangelization Committee, and Cornelius Martens. Froese and his wife Anna settled in Barvenkovo in Kharkov Province where he established a mill and ministered at the Naumenkovo Mennonite Brethren Church. Russian services were also held in the church, requiring only prior notice to the authorities for such meetings. The Naumenkovo church collected funds for 2,000 Testaments and provided tracts for distribution. Froese along with three other mill owners, whose businesses were about seventy kilometers along the railroad, arranged on their properties the sale of Testaments at ten kopecks each and also gave Testaments and tracts without charge.[22]

Cornelius Martens (b. 1876) left his Mennonite home as a young man because of his parents' disapproval of his conversion. He finally found work in Kharkov where during his first year of employment formed a Baptist church. In 1905 he and wife moved to the Don district where he and a brother-in-law entered into a business partnership that prospered. He immediately began preaching to Russians, who organized into a church. He became a member of the council of the Russian Baptist Union and

---

19. Abraham Friesen, 121. Froese, "Ein Bericht über die Mission unter den Russen," Unruh, *Die Geschichte der Mennoniten-Bruedergemeinde*, 258.

20. Dueck, 60–63.

21. *Baptist*, 1907, no. 3, 14, and 1909, no. 2, 16. South Russian Association of German Baptists, *Minutes*, 1908, 13.

22. Töws, *Mennonitische Märtyrer* 2 (1954), 357–58. Froese. "Ein Bericht," 259.

spent much time away from his firm as a traveling missionary. He continued his evangelistic ministry after the First World War but in 1927 left the Soviet Union.[23]

There were several men of German-Russian Mennonite Brethren background who pastored or preached in Russian Baptist churches. One was Jakob J. Vins (Wiens) (1874–1944), mentioned earlier, who maintained relations with Baptists, Evangelical Christians, and Mennonite Brethren. He was born in the Molochna. As a young convert in his late teens, he felt a call to ministry and began to minister among Russian nationals. In the late 1890s he was a colporteur for fifteen months at Samara (Kuibyshev). For a short time he attended the seminary of the Deutsche Orient Mission in Berlin but will return to Russia in 1905, where he began as pastor of a Russian church, the Samara Brotherhood of Evangelical Christians. Because of his zeal in evangelism in Samara and elsewhere, he was forced in 1910 into exile in Siberia but was able to attend the meeting of the Baptist World Alliance in Philadelphia in 1911. With the prospect of a fine or imprisonment on his return to Russia, he stayed abroad in Canada and the United States, serving both Mennonite Brethren and German Baptist churches. After the First World War he served as a missionary in the Far East but will again leave Russia in 1928. He was the grandfather of Georgï Vins, a leader in the Reform Baptist movement in the Soviet Union.[24]

Heinrich P. Sukkau (d. 1937) was known among Russians as Andreï P. Sukkau. He was born in a Mennonite village in Yekaterinoslav, but with his family he moved to Neu Samara settlement east of the Volga River. In 1902 he married, but he and his wife lived in the parental home. In 1907 both were immersed and joined the Mennonite Brethren church in Lugovsk. He felt a call to minister among Russians and in his early thirties began to preach among them. He went to the district town of Busuluk (or possibly Samara) to improve his limited Russia where he began preaching in a small Russian congregation. Without support of any mission organization, he went out by faith, living very simply, dressing and eating as a Russian. He received invitations to preach in Orenburg, Samara, Ufa, and Siberia. After the First World War he continued his evangelistic activity, exiled from 1930 to 1935 to Kotlas but freed, but then in 1937 the authorities arrested him and was evidently shot.[25]

A third Mennonite Brethren minister among the Russians was Adolph A. Reimer (1880–1922). He came from a distinguished religious heritage. Jakob Reimer, a founder of the Mennonite Brethren in the 1860s, was his paternal grandfather, and Martin Kalweit, the German Baptist pioneer in the Caucasus, was his maternal grandfather. He was born in Yekaterinoslav Province and began his career as a school teacher.

---

23. For Marten's career, see McCaig, *Grace Astounding in Bolshevik Russia*, and Martens, *Unter dem Kreuz*.

24. For the career of Wiens, see Wardin, "Jacob J. Wiens: Mission Champion in Freedom and Repression," *Journal of Church and State* 28/3 (Autumn 1986), 495–514.

25. For accounts of Sukkau's life, see Riediger, "Mennonite Missions Among the Russians," 7–9; Töews, *Mennonitische Märtyrer* (1949), 123–29; and Plett, *Zdes' terpenie i vera svyatykh*, 2:183–204.

In 1902 he started to witness among Russians workers in his village, and a Russian congregation began meeting in the Mennonite Brethren church in Tiege where he taught. In 1906 he resigned as a teacher to devote his time to preaching among the Russians, preaching in churches and in theaters without any congregation. His report in 1907 in *Friedensstimme*, "Pictures from the Work Among the Russians," described a wide-ranging activity from St. Petersburg and Moscow to the Ukraine. He served in Prokhanov's Bible school in St. Petersburg in 1913–1914. With the outbreak of the First World War he served as a medic in the Red Cross. After the war he continued work among the Russians but died of typhus in 1922.[26]

Another Mennonite Brethren who became interested in reaching Russians was Peter Riediger. After his conversion in 1900 he felt a love for the Russian people. He witnessed to workers and on occasion read Scripture to them. In 1905–1906 fifty Russians came regularly to worship in his home. In 1908 he became a member of the Mennonite Brethren Church in Lugovsk east of the Volga River. In the winter of 1911–1913 he and Cornelius Janzen traveled in Orenburg Province on a preaching mission, but after the First World War his travels became more limited.[27]

In his booklet in 1912, *Konfessison oder Sekte?*, Peter M. Friesen, the Mennonite historian, tried to defend Mennonite Brethren against the charge of illegally proselytizing Russians. He noted that Mennonite Brethren far more than Old Mennonites provided financial support to "authorized Russian evangelical ministers," and their preachers preached far more in "legally authorized Russian evangelical church services." He also noted that three Mennonite Brethren were serving, at least until recently, "legally registered Russian 'evangelical' congregations," naming Jakob Wiens, Adolf Reimer, and a certain Rempel in Kherson. He admitted that individual Mennonite Brethren speak privately, even to Orthodox, of their own personal faith. In earlier years Friesen himself was under suspicion for his ties to Russian evangelicals. In M. A. Kalnev's account of the conference of Mennonite Brethren and Russian Baptists in Rückenau in 1882 but published in 1897, he stated in a footnote that Friesen was very influential among stundists in Kherson Province. Although earlier he had been very bold, he was now more cautious upon the surveillance of the mayor of Odessa, a city where he was pastor of the German Baptist church.[28]

One institution that significantly furthered the spread of evangelicalism was the publishing house of Raduga (The Rainbow). It had its beginnings in 1887 when Peter J. Neufeld established in Halbstadt the first Mennonite printing press in Russia. In 1903 Heinrich Braun with others purchased the press with the firm taking the name

---

26. For Reimer's ministry, see Goossen, *Adolf Reimer*, and Reimer in Töws, *Mennonitische Märtyrer* (1949), 67–72, with different dates for Reimer's birth and death. *Die Friedensstimme* 4 (1907), 128–29, 141–42.

27. See Riediger, "Mennonite Missions Among the Russians," for his own ministry and the ministry of others.

28. Dueck, 46, ft. 97, 150–51. See Unruh, "Anhang," 263–64, for difficulties Friesen faced from the regime for writing a letter in opposition to exiling stundists.

Braun and Company. In 1906 Abraham Kroeker brought to Halbstadt his paper, *Die Friedensstimme*, which had been published in Berlin.[29]

When Braun visited Ivan S. Prokhanov in St. Petersburg, the latter, according to his autobiography, suggested to Braun the forming of a publishing company that would produce not only German but also Russian literature. As a result Raduga was formed with six shareholders. Besides Prokhanov, the other five, all Mennonite Brethren, included Braun, Abraham Kroeker, Isaak P. Regier, David P. Isaak, and Peter P. Perk. The publishing house now entered the Russian market. Prokhanov with his office in St. Petersburg became chief editor of Russian publications while Kroeker was chief editor of German publications. The firm soon opened a bookstore in St. Petersburg besides bookstores already in its possession in Halbstadt and Schönwiese.

In 1908 Abraham Kroeker wrote to *Der Wahrheitszeuge* in 1908 that Raduga has produced thousands of tracts, Testaments, and pull-off calendars. He also noted that mission committees had been formed to support traveling preachers in South Russia but felt that the efforts, however, were much too little for the large mission field. The publications of the press needed to pass the censor, and it was careful not to attack the Orthodox Church. On the other hand, Kroeker later wrote, when he lived in Germany, that the press also published large amounts of Russian tracts beyond the censor's purview.[30]

The operation of Mennonite Brethren and other evangelicals in reaching the Orthodox population was no doubt more extensive than people knew, including the government (even though very suspicious) or people know today. Nevertheless as Abraham Kroeker noted, the effort was far too little for the size of the country. In his eighties, G. P. Fröse, after settling in the West, asked a number of questions. Could Mennonite Brethren and other evangelicals have done more for the spiritual welfare of the Russians? Could more had been done for the cultural improvement of the workers? Could more Christian literature been circulated within the limits of the law? Could Baptists and Evangelical Christians have been more productive with more resources? Could personal workers have strengthened their knowledge of Russian if our schools had fostered more Russian scriptural language? Could the Bible school in St. Petersburg been strengthened through financial resources? For all these questions, Fröse answered with a decided "yes!"[31]

Troubled Waters

The third State Duma (1907–1912), under the control of conservative parties, raised Mennonite concerns over religious legislation. Isaak Dück and Abraham Görtz again went to St. Petersburg to represent Mennonite interests. In 1908 representatives of

---

29. Reddig, "Mennonite Publishing in Russia:" *Mennonite Historian* 13/1 (Mar. 1987), 1–2.
30. *WHZ*, Apr. 25, 1908, 136. Abraham Friesen, 146–47.
31. Unruh, 264.

the three Mennonite bodies met in the Molochna in Alexdanderwohl and issued, "The Position of the Mennonites with Regard to the Question of Freedom of Faith and Propaganda." Mennonites feared they might lose their status as a confession with other Protestants and be listed as a sect, a designation that could lose their special privileges. They stated the right to follow Christ's command to make disciples in all nations but affirmed they did not engage in active propaganda among other Christian bodies nor extolled their faith by defaming others. They submitted the document as soon as possible to Hermann A. Bergmann, Mennonite member in the Duma. The General Mennonite Council (*Gemeinsames Mennonitisches Kirchen Konvent*) adopted an Explanatory Supplement in January 1910 and presented it with the 1908 document to the Department of Religious Affairs in March 1910. The Supplement maintained Mennonites confessed the truths as found among all Christians and recognized the universal Christian church in all bodies who upheld the faith of Christ, the Redeemer. In the strictest sense Mennonites only carry on mission activity among non-Christians.[32] In March 1910 in St. Petersburg, the officials of the Department of Religious Affairs, A. Kharusin, its head, and N. I. Pavlov, a subordinate, assured the Mennonite deputies, Heinrich Braun, David Epp, and Abraham Görz, that Mennonites would not lose their rights nor be denominated a sect. The government officials, however, suggested that it would be advantageous to Mennonites to form a union in their relationship to the government instead of existing simply as independent congregations. In his report to the Mennonite Brethren conference in Tiege in May 1910, Braun stated that the officials had no intention of restricting their rights and practices.[33]

Whatever appeared on the surface did not mean all was calm and placid. Beginning in 1909 Mennonite Brethren were beginning to feel restrictions that the increasingly reactionary regime was imposing upon all evangelicals. The regime continued to be disturbed over the spread of the evangelical faith and had always been suspicious of the Mennonite Bethren for their activism. For failure to give notice to the authorities of a Russian evangelist who spoke of his work among Russians, Gerhard Fröse and the school teacher, Abraham Unruh, whose two brothers Kornelius and Heinrich were missionaries on the Telugu field in India, were arrested for a month. By intervention of two members of the State Duma, they were released after twenty days.[34] But worse was to come. At the same time the local authorities canceled in 1909 the annual Mennonite Brethren conference at Petrovka/Naumenkovo. The authorities had just shortly before disrupted the congress of the Russian Baptist Union in Odessa and had incarcerated Pavlov with others. Police stopped J. C. Heinrichs, the missionary from India, and representatives on their way to the congress who now faced the prospect

---

32. P. M. Friesen, 631–36, 1030, ft. 9. Abraham Friesen, 133–35.

33. Abraham Friesen, 135–37. Dueck, 72–73.

34. Töws, *Mennonitische Martyrer* 2 (1954), 358. P. M. Friesen, 536. *Der Sendbote*, July 28, 1909, 475.

of either returning or going to prison. Heinrichs wrote that the authorities had never before so treated Mennonites.³⁵

The regime was becoming increasingly concerned about the evangelistic activity in Halbstadt in the Mennonite colony of Molochna, the site of Raduga, and a Mennonite Youth Association, a possible cover for training sectarian ministers. In October 1909 Karuzin and Pavlov in the Department of Religious Affairs, whom the Mennonite Brethren representatives will meet in March, 1910, sent a letter with the attachment of a report of S. D. Bondar to the governor of Taurida Province demanding an investigation of Halbstadt. In his report in January 1910, the governor stated he had undertaken an investigation that included secret interviews with both Mennonites and Russian Orthodox. His report noted the existence of a *Vereinshaus* where evangelical meetings were held that attracted Russian seasonal workers. He suggested that although no evidence exited of a training program for sectarian preachers the Youth Association should be terminated for its propagandistic purposes.³⁶

Bondar and Stolypin, the premier and head of the Ministry of the Interior, were dissatisfied with the governor's report, feeling that an illegal school organization existed. Stolypin was also concerned about the New Molokan school in Astrakhanka. He wrote that evangelical teaching was sweeping Russia, particularly in the south, and the authorities need more stringent surveillance of sectarian movements.³⁷

Shortly after the meeting of Heinrich Braun and the other two representatives with the officials of the Ministry of Religious Affairs, the regime launched from March 19 to 22 an investigation of Halbstadt led by the vice-governor of Taurida Province. Its focus was on the *Vereinshaus*, on Raduga, and also on Heinrich Braun himself. Braun was extensively interrogated, a natural target as pastor of the Rückenau Mennonite Brethren Church, head of Raduga, and patron of the *Vereinshaus*. The *Vereinshaus* (an Alliance House) was a building for interconfessional meetings but was used almost entirely by Baptists, such as Balikhin, the Russian Baptist evangelist, and Mennonite Brethren, such as Braun himself. The investigation raised the question whether the Rückenau church was truly Mennonite or Baptist. Although the reports after the investigation did not mention Raduga, Abraham Kroeker, who had been present at the investigation, admitted that the investigation also showed concern about evangelical literature in Russian that sought to win Russians to the evangelical faith. He said, however, that a tract society, later called the Philadelphia society, was not discovered. It worked with Raduga in producing Russian tracts that were distributed without

---

35. P. M. Friesen, 536. *Der Sendbote*, July 28, 1909, 475. "Abstract of Report of Rev. J. Henrich's (sic) Visit to Russia in May and June, 1909," ABMU/ABFMS, *Correspondence*, Russian Mission, 1900–1919.

36. See Abraham Friesen, *In Defense of Privilege*, 141–57, for a detailed and careful use of official documents from the Russian archives in the investigation of Mennonite Brethren operations in Halbstadt.

37. Abraham Friesen, 144–45.

charge. Kroeker admitted later that if the authorities had discovered the operation, he and others would have involuntarily spent time in Siberia.[38]

The investigation left without recommending any judicial charges. It found that Russian Baptists used the *Vereinshaus* for services but were conducted with the permission of the governor. It found no secret program of sectarian instruction. Nevertheless on leaving the vice-governor declared:

> We know that the Rückenauers are not Mennonites but Baptists, and that they are actively trying to convert Russians. Tell your congregations, and especially the Rückenauers, that this is a very dangerous business. . . . Don't send any missionaries out to lead them away from their faith, for she [Orthodox] too wants to be left in peace!! If you do not heed my warning, your congregations could suffer dire consequences.

A few months later in a lengthy report in the German Baptist journal in Russia, *Der Hausfreund,* Philipp Bier noted that the *Vereinshaus* held Bible discussions and in the previous year two foreign preachers were present but most generally on Sundays a Russian Baptist preacher with legal permission conducted a Russian service. He also wrote that the youth association was not functioning in part because of the lack of a leader. He noted as well that the investigation with the warning of the vice-governor left a very strong impression.[39]

On his part, Heinrich Braun stressed that he and others in Halbstadt had been cleared of any illegal activity. He nevertheless sent a long letter to N. I. Pavlov of the Ministry of Religious Affairs justifying his testimony. He made a clear distinction between Mennonite Brethren and Baptists and declared Bible courses were always in German without Orthodox present and Raduga's publications always passed the censor. He also sent to the Mennonite press an article, "Mennonites or Baptists?," that used every possible difference he could find between the former and the latter. He pointed out affinities with fellow Mennonites, with whom, however, most Mennonite Brethren did not commune, but did not recognize any Baptist contributions to the Mennonite Brethren with whom they did commune.[40]

In his report, the vice-governor wrote as he had also expressed on his departure in Halbstadt that Mennonite Brethren in Halbstadt were engaged in proselytizing Russians. He claimed that during the summer months Mennonite Brethren used the *Vereinshaus* for evangelization where its sermons were interpreted into Russian, supported itinerant evangelists, and at Raduga published tracts to reach the Russian population. The vice-governor also launched an attack on the New Molokan school in Astrakhanka as a center for proselytizing. On their side, however, S. D. Bondar and

---

38. Ibid., 145–47.
39. Ibid., 146. *Der Hausfreund,* Aug. 25/ Sep. 7, 1910, 269.
40. *Abraham Friesen,* 147–49. For Braun's article, "Mennonites or Baptists?," see *Der Botschafter,* May 25, 1910, 4, and May 28, 1910, 3, and Dueck, 117–22, for an English translation.

S. Margaritov, supervisor of schools in Taurida, were critical of the vice-governor's investigation, claiming he was incompetent, lacked knowledge of the ties between the various evangelical groups, and conducted only a routine investigation of the Astrakhanka school. Stolypin himself was very upset at the lack adequate state control and the fact that the economically successful Mennonites, who resisted Russification, were transforming Orthodox peasants into German Protestants.[41]

The regime did not close Raduga, which operated even after the First World War began. In 1915 *Missionerskoe obozrenie*, the Orthodox journal, complained that Raduga continued with intensity and was systematically subverting the Russian people with its "leaven" and "putrid teaching." Its publications, it averred, appeared under "various dressings" as wall and desk calendars, booklets, and leaflets and were sold or given without charge as a premium with a purchase or as a reward. Its literature seemingly was everywhere.[42]

With the growing hostility toward Mennonite Brethren for their evangelistic activity and in a climate of reaction expressed against all evangelicals, Mennonites as a whole now faced restrictions as other Russian evangelicals. The investigation of Halbstadt with the warning of the vice-governor rattled Mennonites as to their status and heightened antagonism between the Old Mennonite Church and Mennonite Brethren.

Mennonite Brethren, unlike the Russian Baptists and Evangelical Christians, were, however, able to continue after 1909 and to 1914 their annual spring conferences except that the one in 1911 was canceled. Conferences, however, were closely monitored with one or more official, such as S. D. Bondar, required for attendance. *Mennonitisches Jahrbuch*, published by Old Church Mennonites, reported for the year 1910 that the Mennonite flock was now more or less restricted in its usual religious freedom. Authorities must be notified of meetings of conventions and executive committees with the former under government control. Meetings for Biblical discussion and divine services on school premises were forbidden. It also observed that time will tell whether the zealots will hold back in face of the warning against propaganda. God holds the key whether the door is open for missions, but in Russia "we may not ourselves force open the door." It is not surprising that the committee of the Mennonite Brethren for Russian Evangelization was terminated in 1910.[43]

In the Mennonite periodical in Germany, *Mennonitische Blätter*, an article, "Aus Russland," appeared in August 1910 that noted how the wind was now blowing. The assumption that the new freedom allowed *Vereinshäuser*, youth associations, and conferences for deepening the Christian life was now checked. The article also described the Halbstadt investigation and the warning of the vice-governor. It pointed out that

---

41. Abraham Friesen, 149–51, 154–55.
42. *MO*, May–June, 1915, 188–89.
43. Dueck, 10–12. *Mennonitisches Jahrbuch*, 1910, 9.

Mennonites will need to confront the question of forming a corporate unity and possibly face alteration of their military exemption.[44]

Confession or Sect?

The Mennonite Brethren retained their relationship with German Baptists in intercommunion, acceptance of German Baptist members, and German Baptist preaching.[45] Nevertheless Mennonite Brethren with the government investigation of their proselyting above all wanted to keep their identity as Mennonites and not as Baptists if they were to retain their status as a confession and not be considered a sect and lose their privileges.

By 1909–1910 the relationship between Mennonite Brethren and German Baptists had apparently begun to cool. It is a question whether changing circumstances brought this about or was just a natural course of events. In any case, the days in Baptist relations in 1907 were a thing of the past. In 1907 J. C. Heinrichs, the Baptist missionary from the Telugu field, was warmly received, but in 1909 on a return visit he wrote to the American Baptist Missionary Union, "Indications are that relationship to us is not as intimate and cordial as formerly." L. Horn, a German Baptist missionary, although greatly admiring the economic and educational activity of Mennonites, criticized them in 1910 for living such a "completely separate life." He added that the Mennonite Brethren Church "stands completely isolated and on the whole little is known of our work; in many cases our leading brethren are unknown." On the other hand, Peter M. Friesen, the Mennonite Brethren historian who over the years had been so intimately related to Baptists, wrote in 1911 in his, *The Mennonite Brotherhood in Russia*, that ties were not completely severed. He stated, "The use of Baptist literature, the Hamburg seminary—all missionaries of the M. B. Church of Russia have been students at Hamburg—interchange of visiting ministers between the Mennonite Brethren and Baptists—although all too rare—as well as monetary contributions to the needs of the Baptists—all these things, God be praised, have never ceased entirely." But yet his words reveal the ties were not as before.[46]

As already noted, Heinrich Braun in his article, "Mennoniten oder Baptisten?," defensively highlighted the Mennonite character of Mennonite Brethren after the Halbstadt investigation in which Mennonite Brethren were accused of being Baptists. Braun asked how was it possible that fellow Mennonites, a question repeatedly raised by the vice-governor of Taurida in the investigation, label Mennonite Brethren "Baptist?" Braun received a quick response from David H. Epp (1875–1955), minister of the Chortitza Mennonite Church and co-editor of *Der Botschafter*, in his article, "How

---

44. *Mennonitische Blätter*, Aug. 1910, 62–63.
45. Toews, *Perilous Journey*, 80–81.
46. Heinrichs, "Abstract of Report of Rev. J. Henrich's Visit to Russia," 6. *Der Hausfreund*, July 28/Aug. 10, 1910, 238. P. M. Friesen, 532–33.

is this Possible?"⁴⁷ Epp acknowledged that Mennonite Brethren were Mennonite and not Baptist but pointed out that Mennonite Brethren by calling themselves "brethren" implied that other Mennonites were impure when all Mennonites were regarded as a "brotherhood." He noted that Mennonite Brethren do not invite other Mennonites to their Lord's Supper nor exchange pulpits with them but maintain intimate relations with Baptists. They also insist that immersion is the only correct mode of baptism and rebaptize Old Mennonites who wished to join them. They accuse Old Mennonites as "spiritually dead" and proselytize them. An acrimonious exchange between Abraham Kroeker and Epp over Mennonite relations in 1910 was evidence of the continuing antagonism between the two Mennonite bodies. In spite of differences, representatives of the two Mennonite bodies met in October 1910 in Schönsee in their first general conference. The issue of inter-Mennonite relations, however, was not on the agenda but instead the issue of church records in reference to the state. Always on the alert concerning their religious freedom and special privileges and concern over designation as a sect, a meeting of the general conference at Nikolaipol in October 1912 authorized the publication of a brochure in Russian, *Mennonites in Russia,* to be distributed to members of the State Duma. It included a defense of Mennonites as a confession and their practice of nonresistance.⁴⁸

In April 1914 a consultation at Neu-Halbstadt of Old Church Mennonites and Mennonite Brethren leaders met on finishing an "Evangelical Mennonite Confession of Russia," which was necessary if Mennonites were to petition the regime for recognition as a confession. Immediately after the election of the chair for the meeting, Peter J. Penner, an Old Mennonite from Chortitza, provocatively declared that a united effort with the Mennonite Brethren to petition for confessional status would be "absolutely hopeless." He justified his statement by stating that the Mennonite Brethren, unlike Old Mennonites, have caused great difficulties in its mission activity among other faiths and will be an excuse for the government to deny confessional status. This was a serious allegation. Mennonites recognized that classification as a sect would threaten their privileged status and would possibly require local approval for registration of new congregations. Penner's statement along with his reference to the Halbstadt investigation brought intense debate.⁴⁹ After the consultation, Peter M. Friesen, who had been present and had opposed Penner, wrote a brochure, personally printed, "*Konfession oder Sekte?*"⁵⁰ On completing his, *Alt-Evangelischen Mennonitischen Brüderschaft (Old-EvangelicalMennonite Brotherhood)*, which included the story of all Mennonites, he stated that he was filled with Mennonite pride and felt much of the antagonism between the two Mennonite bodies had abated. But he was soon surprised how much of

---

47. *Die Friedensstimme*, July 21, 1910, 4–5, and July 28, 1910, 3–5. For an English tr., see Dueck, 123–31. See Abraham Friesen, 163–65, for a review of Epp's article.
48. Abraham Friesen, 169–78.
49. Ibid., 179–81.
50. P. M. Friesen, *Konfession oder Sekte?*. See Dueck, 142–57, for an English translation.

it remained on both sides. Although some in the Old Mennonite Church commended the work, others, however, considered Friesen hostile toward them.

In his brochure Friesen, as already noted, defended the Mennonite Brethren against proselytism. He maintained the Halbstadt investigation found no wrong doing, and the publications of Raduga passed the censor. The several Mennonite Brethren who serve in Russian congregations had received authorization from the authorities. In closing he said he would sing "hosanna" if the two bodies would come to an understanding and union, but if not "all who desire to live godly in Christ Jesus must suffer persecution."

In spite of controversy, cooler heads prevailed. The Neu-Halbstadt meeting in April 1914 was able to submit to the churches for their examination, "Constitution of the Evangelical Mennonite Confession in Russia." Congregations were to send the results to D. G. Epp, the chair of the Mennonite Commission for Church Affairs," who would then send the responses to the next General Mennonite Conference in August in Halbstadt. But the First World War broke out in July, and a confession had to wait for approval until after the war in 1917.[51]

---

51. Dueck, 132–36.

28

German and Baltic Baptists

Growth and Stability, 1905–1914

IN THE PERIOD FROM 1905 to 1914, German and Baltic Baptists in the Union of Baptist Churches in Russia increased in strength and numbers. Although as other evangelicals they faced an increasing hostile environment, nevertheless they exhibited stability and avoided internal division. Their growth was steady—17, 000 in 1892 to 24,000 in 1906 to 28,000 in 1912—in spite of strong emigration abroad. The membership included 17,000 Germans, 8,500 Latvians, and 2,500 Estonians, including small numbers of other nationalities. Its constituency of 57,000, including unbaptized family members and attendees, was double the membership.[1]

Unlike Mennonite Brethren who because of their legal status could not incorporate non-Mennonites into their community, German Baptists possessed potentially a wide field in gaining converts from both the German and non-German populations. With admiration for the German Baptist Union (or Union of Baptist Churches in Russia), Vasiliĭ Pavlov, the veteran Russian Baptist leader, stated in a letter to the American Baptist Union in 1906, "The churches of the Union are well organized and many of them have trained pastors whom they support and their own chapels and have been tolerated by the state till now."[2]

Unlike Mennonite Brethren, German Baptists had no need to defend their identity or define their relations with a larger body in the same denominational family. Also unlike Mennonite Brethren they were not required to assume governmental

---

1. *Der Hausfreund*, Aug. 29/Sep. 11, 1912, 286.
2. Letter of Pavloff, Aug. 7, 1906.

responsibilities in their localities or in trying to protect their special privileges as closed communities or military exemption. They avoided severe denominational conflict as beset Russian Baptists and Evangelical Christians.

Except for some minor eschatological differences, German Baptists were theologically united and continued to adhere to the confession of the Baptist Union in Germany. They strictly observed close communion, admitting only fellow Baptists and Mennonite Brethren. German Baptists were also fortunate in being a member of the Baptist World Alliance, which brought them status as part of a world body. Their participation in Baptist world congresses in 1905 and 1911 and European congresses in 1908 and 1913 brought them into personal contact with other Baptist leaders. It also helped them to gain financial support from Baptists abroad.

The Union continued to have strong leadership. Such veterans as Johann J. Pritzkau in Alt-Danzig and Severin Lehmann and John (Janis) Frey in Riga remained, but new leaders appeared. After the deaths of the first two presidents of the Union, Gottfried Alf (d. 1898) and J. Kessler (d. 1904), Friedrich Brauer (b. 1854), pastor of the Baptist church in Lodz but later in Neu-Danzig and Warsaw, became president. He was energetic and committed to a strong mission program. Eugen Mohr (1868–1917) served as pastor in Neudorf and Lodz and was a teacher at the Lodz Seminary. Johannes Lübeck (b.1867) pastored in Lodz and Odessa and served as an editor of *Der Hausfreund,* the organ of the Union. Carl Füllbrandt was an effective pastor in Odessa and an able writer who maintained a close relationship with Pavlov in the same city. Friedrich Arndt carried on a difficult ministry in St. Petersburg. Except for Lübeck and Frey, all these men were graduates of the Baptist seminary in Hamburg.

As in Germany, the churches of the Union were closely knit that provided a strong sense of corporate unity. Unlike other bodies, their statistical reports, exhibiting typical German attention to detail, were complete. The conferences of the Union met triennially and fortunately unlike other evangelical bodies continued to meet throughout the period without prohibition or interruption from the authorities. A Union committee met annually to carry on the work between the conferences. The six associations met annually and looked after regional interests. Its greatest disappointment, as described in a previous chapter, was the forced closing by the authorities of its seminary in Lodz. It was the only free evangelical body in Russia to establish such a school in the period until 1913 when Ivan Prokhanov gained permission to open a Bible school in St. Petersburg.

Geographical and Statistical Distribution

The editor of *Der Hausfreund* attempted to use his poetical gifts to describe the coming of the delegates in 1912 to the triennial conference in Neufeld. He noted their coming from the Baltic Sea coast, Siberia, the country churches of Volhynia, the Weichsel region of Russian Poland, the southern steppes, the wide Volga, the Don, and the Black

Sea. And he summed it up by writing, "*Überall aus Russlands Breiten, Strömt herbei der Heil'gen Heer.*" (Everywhere from Russia's span, Gathers here the holy band).[3]

Churches ranged from Russian Poland in the west to Siberia in the east and from St. Petersburg in the north to Crimea and the Caucasus in the south. The membership was widely distributed over this huge area but yet included some islands of concentration, such as Germans in Volhynia and Russian Poland and Latvians and Estonians in the Baltic Sea provinces. About sixty percent were German and forty percent composed of other nationalities. The Germans held to the typical German pattern of strong central churches with numerous mission stations, while the Latvians and Estonians formed many churches with very small memberships and comparatively few mission stations. Most churches were members of an association except the German and other ethnic congregations in St. Petersburg and the German churches in Riga and Libau on the Baltic coast.

The German Baptist church St. Petersburg, revived by Friedrich Arndt, continued as a struggling congregation with around 100 members and subsidized from abroad. Small Swedish, Latvian, and Estonian congregations existed along with it. After having met over the years in eight different locations, the St. Petersburg church made a bold move in 1912 by purchasing a large tenement house for 126,000 rubles while possessing only 14,000 rubles. The church planned to finance the transaction from the over 12,200 rubles it would receive in annual rental income from the building as well as outside gifts. In February 1913 it dedicated its meeting hall inside the building. Johann Kargel, the first pastor of the church almost forty years before in 1874, spoke first. He was followed by Ivan Prokhanov (Evangelical Christian); Jakob Kroeker (Mennonite Brethren); Mr. Nyman, choir director who represented William Fetler who was absent (Russian Baptist); Severin Lehmann (German Baptist); and Adolph Reimer (Mennonite Brethren). Four choirs sang—German Baptist, Evangelical Christian, Russian Baptist, and Latvian Baptist. The church was saddled with a debt of 120,000 rubles.[4] The Estonians and Latvians farther south on the Baltic coast with their own associations operated practically as independent entities with their own churches, pastors, and publications. In 1912 The Estonian Association had 2,500 members and the Latvian Association, the fastest growing association in the Union, numbered 8,500 members.[5]

A leading member in Estonia was Andres Tettermann (b. 1854), pastor of the First Baptist Church in Reval (Tallinn), who began publishing Teekäija (The Pilgrim) in 1904 with some fear in passing the censor. At first the journal was a monthly and

---

3. *Der Hausfreund*, Nov. 14/27, 1912, 371.

4. "Extract from letter of Schweiger, Nov. 2/15, 1912, ABMU/ABFMS, *Correspondence*, 1900–1919. *Der Hausfreund*, May 30/June 12, 1912, 180; Feb. 20/Mar. 5, 1913, 61; May 8/21, 1913, 147; June 5/18, 1913, 181. *Bratskii listok/Khristianin*, Mar. 1913, 16–17.

5. For 1912 statistics, see *Der Hausfreund*, Aug. 29/Sep. 11, 1912, 28.

then became a semi-monthly. Baron Üxküll contributed 100 rubles to help start it. Tettermann was gifted in music and poetry and began publishing songbooks.[6]

Leading members in the Latvian Association were John (Janis) Frey (1863–1950), a pastor in Hagensberg Church in Riga, publisher, and editor, and John (Janis) Inkis (Inke), a pastor in Matthaus Church in Riga and an editor. Frey edited *Awots* (The Spring) in Riga from 1905–1914 as well as a paper for young people and various Christian calendars. He printed *Der Hausfreund.* from 1902 to 1914 and served on the Union Committee. Inkis edited *Kristigs Draugs* (The Christian Friend) from 1903 to 1905, printed in Memel, and was a coeditor of *Awots* from 1912 to 1915. Another Latvian Baptist periodical was *Kristigs Wehstnesis* (The Christian Messenger), which was published in several locations with a succession of editors.[7]

On behalf of the Union Committee, Carl Füllbrandt, pastor of the Odessa German Baptist Church, attended the Latvian Baptist Association in Weldon in 1908. Everything had to be interpreted for him. He noted the diligence of the members and their support for home and foreign missions. He thought, however, they had too many small churches, some with only sixteen or twenty members, feeling it would be more efficient if they had central churches with more mission stations after the German pattern. The association set a goal of raising 10,000 rubles to establish the Baptist seminary in Riga. Because of their economic status and weakness in stewardship, both the Estonian and Latvian associations were on a far lower level in finances than their German counterparts.[8]

Further to the south was the Weichsel-Gebiet Association in Russian Poland, the oldest association in the Union and where the first German Baptist congregations began. With thirteen churches and 4,881 members in 1912, it also showed growth, largely, however, because of the church in Lodz, located in an industrial center that was drawing people from other areas. Baptists moved here from other parts of Russian Poland and Volynia in Ukraine. The Lodz church grew very rapidly under the pastorate of Friedrich Brauer, who served from 1896 to 1906. In 1897 the church enlarged its sanctuary to 1,500 places that continued to be filled. In 1906 it had 1,563 members with a community of 3,243, the largest Baptist church in Continental Europe, with 10 mission stations (two in Lodz itself), 1,210 children in 13 Sunday schools, and 13 choirs with 270 members. The association also had a Czech church in the small industrial town of Zelów. Moravian Brethren who lived in the Czech colony in the town were attracted to Baptist preaching and formed a church in 1886.[9]

---

6. *Eesti Baptisti koguduste ajaloolik Album*, 83–85. *Der Hausfreund*, Sep. 12/25, 1907, 293. Wardin, *Evangelical Sectarianism*, nos. 2251, 2253, 2274, 2276–77.

7. Wardin, *Evangelical Sectarianism*, nos. 2221–26. Kweetin, *A Hidden Jewel*, 11–12, 19–21. BV, 1947, no. 6, 41.

8. *Der Hausfreund*, July 23/Aug. 5, 1908, 237–39.

9. Kupsch, 162, 164, 400–405.

PART SIX—Possibilities and Uncertainties, 1905–1917

The association in Russian Poland sought to win Poles. Since Poles were non-Orthodox, the authorities placed no obstacles in winning them. With the identification of the Polish people with the Roman Catholic Church and the strong control of the priests of the church over their people, it was a difficult field. Some German Baptist pastors in Russian Poland were able to preach in Polish, including Gottfried Alf, founder of the Baptist work in the area, Oskar Truderung (1876–1910), pastor in Warsaw, and Friedrich Brauer, president of the Union and pastor in Lodz and Warsaw. Around 1880 with support of the association, Josef Antoschewski, a native Pole, served several years but will emigrate to America. The association formed a Society for Polish Missions and placed on the field in 1904 Bernard J. Herb, a German Russian who spoke Polish. Herb lived in Lodz at the time Brauer was pastor who strongly supported the Polish work. Herb translated tracts into Polish and composed a hymnal of 250 songs. He formed in his small congregation in Lodz a choral society. He traveled about speaking to Polish gatherings. After three years he left for a German work in Volhynia.[10]

The next missionary was Karl Strzelez, a Czech and student at Hamburg Baptist Seminary, who had been a pastor of the Czech or Moravian congregation in Lodz. He conducted Polish services in Lodz as well as in Choiny and Zgierz. At this time Oskar Truderung also preached in Polish in Warsaw. In 1907 Trudering began publishing a small monthly paper, *Drogowskaz* (The Signpost) for thirty kopecks a year, which could also be used as a tract. In 1910 the Polish mission suffered a sad loss with the death of Truderung at the age of thirty-three. In 1912 Brauer reported that the mission committee of the association placed in service a second Polish missionary in Warsaw and had called a third one.[11]

The West Russian Association in Volhynia in northwestern Ukraine numbered 6,660 members in 1912. It composed a rather compact community of churches. It also included in 1906 four churches with 591 members in the Volga and 214 members in 12 mission stations in Ufa and Siberia. In 1912 Volga and Siberia reported as separate asssociations with 712 and 1,342 members respectively. The South Russian Association numbered 2,934 members in 1912. The association was very dispersed stretching from Odessa in southern Ukraine to the Crimea (with one church), to the Don region, and to the Caucasus.

---

10. For historical accounts of the Polish Baptist Mission, see Pufahl, "Mission und Evangelisation unter den Polen," *Der Hausfreund*, Sep. 30/Oct. 13, 1909, 310–11, and Oct. 7/20, 1909, 321–22; Kupsch, 388–90; and Brauer, "Fortschritt in der Polenmission," *Der Hausfreund*, Dec. 19/Jan. 1, 1913, 421–22. Also see Miller, *In the Midst of Wolves*, 149–50; WHZ, June 1, 1880, 86; and *Der Hausfreund*, June 27/July 10, 1907, 206, and Oct. 7/20, 1909, 321. Dates in sources may be only approximate and may differ with other sources.

11. *Der Hausfreund*, June 27/July 10, 206–207, 1907; Mar. 14/27, 1909, 88; and Dec. 19/Jan. 1, 1913, 421–22. See Strzelez, "Die Polenmission," *Der Hausfreund*, July 6/19, 1911, 213, and July 13/26, 1911, 222, for his account of the difficulties of the mission among the Poles.

In 1909 Alfons Herb sent to *Der Hausfreund* a comparative study of the statistics of the Union between 1898 and 1908. He pointed out how the Union had thrived in ten years from 20,875 to 25,726 members, from 110 to 279 chapels and prayer halls, from 209 to 331 Sunday schools, and contributions from 70,143 to 124,200 rubles. But four years later in 1913 Ernst Heiter with a different view sent to the periodical a series of articles, "Sturmglocken" (Alarm Bells), which pointed out the net loss among the German membership in the West and South Russian Associations and the three German churches on the Baltic coast. In response Lehmann, the German Baptists pastor in Riga, pointed out the large migration to the Mid-West in America and Canada.[12]

In a second article that soon followed, Heiter came out hitting hard, even comparing German Baptist retreat to the loss by Bulgarians to the Turks at Adrianople in the Second Balkan War. He noted the Sunday school mission had ended and lamented the lack of young people in the youth societies who were willing to give themselves sacrificially for the work. He charged that only three young men applied for pastoral training but only one could be accepted. The Saratov mission, which began with so much support, appeared to have died. In a third article he continued in the same vein. He asked, what does one need to do to sink into the mire? One needs to do nothing at all. He reminded the readers of the recent sinking of the *Titanic,* while the musicians were playing "Nearer my God to Thee." In a fourth article he noted it was not only the pastors but also each member who was to blame, reminding the readers of Oncken's motto, "Every Baptist a missionary." He pointed out that each church had a large mission field in its own midst; for every 100 members at least 125 unsaved also attended.[13]

In an article, "Pessimismus und Optimismus," also written in 1913, Friedrich Brauer, president of the Union, countered Heiter. He chided him for painting such a dark picture without anything positive. He claimed that even without the Latvians and Estonians the German churches baptized in this year more than past years if all the churches had sent in their reports. The Union also collected 150,000 rubles, more than the previous year. He admonished not to call the decline from emigration "a bankruptcy of the work and instill despondency!" He also noted four or five brethren were now in school at their own expense.[14]

In his next article, Heiter proclaimed the need for believers to return to their first love. He wrote, "What was needed in all churches, in every association, in our entire Union,—is a sweeping general awakening and new revival at the head and the members." In his final article he appealed to parents to bring their children to the Lord and the Sunday schools to win the many unconverted children who attended.[15]

Whatever the need for revival, at least the Russian regime continued its concern about Baptist growth and did not seem to notice any slackening of German Baptist

---

12. *Der Hausfreund*, July 1/14, 1909, 209–10, and Aug. 21/Sep. 3, 1913, 271, 276.
13. Ibid., Aug. 28/Sep. 10, 1913, 280; Sep. 11/24, 1913, 295–96; and Sep. 18/Oct. 1, 1913, 303–4.
14. Ibid., Sep. 18/Oct. 1, 1913, 304–5.
15. Ibid., Sep. 25/Oct. 8, 1913, 310–11, and Oct. 16/29, 1913, 337–38.

zeal. Of the free evangelical bodies at this time, the German Baptist churches nevertheless suffered far heavier migration abroad than any other. Numbers went to Germany, America, Canada, Argentina, and Brazil while others moved to Siberia. It was recorded in the 1906 statistics that the Union lost in one year twenty Latvians and one Swede but 473 from the three German associations and the St. Petersburg and Riga German churches.[16] In 1887 in the western regions of Russia, including Volhynia, the regime forbade foreigners to acquire property rights, considering even early German immigrants German subjects. My own maternal great-grandfather, Martin Klemm, a Baptist convert of the revival under Alf, after failing twice to gain property left Volhynia with his wife and two children for America in 1893. For many German-Russians, it was not religious persecution but economic prospects abroad that looked more promising than staying in the Russian homeland.[17]

Church Organization and Pastors

The increase in the number of churches and the growth in property and contributions between 1898 and 1908 showed increased prosperity. In 1898 the Union had 91 congregations and 110 chapels and in 1910 159 congregations and 279 chapels and prayer halls. The worth of their property had grown from 217,178 rubles to a bit over 590,000; contributions rose from 70,173 to 124,200 rubles. According to the 1906 statistical report, all the German churches had chapels except the one in St. Petersburg, three in the West Russian Association (two in the Volga lost their chapels by government action), and five in the South Russian Association. On the other hand, thirty-four out of seventy-eight Latvian congregations lacked chapels as well as four out of twenty-one Estonian congregations. Many congregations and mission stations that lacked chapels met in prayer halls.[18]

Some congregations built very impressives structures. The large church in Lodz in Russian-Poland built in 1881 a large building at a cost of 16,000 rubles, which it enlarged to seat over 1,500 in 1897 for 20,000 rubles. With its Romanesque style, an impressive portal, and outside decoration, it was one of the most beautiful structures in the Union. West of Lodz at Zdunska-Wola, the congregation constructed in 1902 a similar structure with 600 seats at a cost of 16,000 rubles. In Volhynia the church at Neudorf built in 1907 a large red brick building seating 3,000. The church in Rozyszcze, also in Volhynia, constructed in 1908 a beautiful structure seating 1,000 with a parsonage and other buildings at a cost of over 17,000 rubles.[19]

16. Ibid., June 10/23, 1909, 182; Aug. 18/31, 1910, 261–62; and June 12/25, 1913, 191.

17. Ibid., Feb. 16/Mar. 1, 1911, 55.

18. Ibid., July 1/14, 1909, 209–10. *Unions-Statistik der Baptisten-Geminden in Russland*, 1906.

19. Kupsch, 156, 162, 226. Miller, *In the Midst of Wolves*, 25–28, 230–31. For pictures of the Lodz and Zadunska-Wola churches, see Kupsch, 155 and 227. For a picture of the Neudorf church, which has since been restored, see Miller, 49.

In 1914 an article was submitted to *Der Hausfreund*, entitled "Kirchen? Kapellen? oder Versammlungshäuser?," (Churches? Chapels? or Meetinghouses?). The author declared that the task of a Baptist congregation was not to build large churches and cathedrals but to build a spiritual house. He signaled out the structures in Lodz, Zdunska-Wola, and Rozyszcze for extravagant buildings whose sanctuaries he claimed were empty during the week and on Sundays only partially filled. Instead a congregation might build a structure with rooms that could be rented to carry the debt. Otherwise "the members sigh under the burden of debt and send their pastor from place to place, even across the ocean, to gather money for the liquidation of the debt. Is this the will of God?" Perhaps he was thinking of Lehmann in Riga or Brauer in Warsaw who went to America struggling to eliminate the debt resting on their buildings when here they began their pastorates.[20]

Most congregations had one pastor and the support of deacons, but a large congregation often had multiple ministers with a senior pastor in charge. The number of ministers between 1898 and 1908 rose only from 105 to 121. Most German churches contributed to the pastor's support. A few churches paid annually over 1,000 rubles. Füllbrandt in Odessa and Brauer, then in Neu-Danzig, received respectively 1,500 and 1,714 rubles a year. Pastors' salaries generally ranged from 300 to 500 rubles a year, although others paid much less. Estonian pastors received comparatively little or nothing, which was also probably the case for Latvian pastors. Many pastors gained support from their farms or other employment. Churches were not to ordain pastors unless reference was first made to an associational committee. Congregations also ordained deacons.[21]

With reluctance to organize churches until they were well established, the German churches often had multiple mission stations, some with their own chapels or prayer halls. A pastor may visit such stations only once a year or even less. F. Schweiger in Russian Poland wrote in 1914 an article for *Der Hausfreund* in which he responded to a reader in Volhynia on the question of the great lack of ministers in the region. Schweiger noted that a pastor of a widely distributed membership was too often overburdened. He asked, "Is it possible for a man with 500 or 1,000 members can serve twelve or fifteen stations in a circuit of eighty *versty* (53 miles) or more?" He suggested larger churches should be divided, and a country church should have no more than 100 to 300 members. He declared new congregations bring "new life, new spirit, new work, new obligations." On the issue of the scarcity of ministers he suggested the older brethren should bring forward the younger generation who already are in service in the mission stations. He pointed to the words of Christ to pray to the Lord that he would send workers into His harvest field.[22]

---

20. *Der Hausfreund*, July 16/29, 1914, 232–35.

21. *Unions-Statistik der Baptisten-Gemeinden in Russland*, 1906. *Der Hausfreund*, July 1/14, 1909, 209–10; Jan. 26/Feb. 8, 1911, 23; and Dec. 12/25, 1912, 410.

22. *Der Hausfreund*, Aug. 1/14, 1912, 250, and Apr. 16/29, 1914, 129.

As in the West, regularly organized congregations tried to be more than preaching stations and incorporated auxiliary organizations. In statistics for 1906, the churches of the Union reported 313 Sunday schools and around 1,100 teachers and 12,000 children. With their multiple mission stations, German churches often had multiple Sunday schools. At times Sunday school missionaries served, such as A. Johannson who began in March 1907 to serve the whole field.[23] In 1906 the Union had 92 youth societies, almost equally between men and women, and 1,724 members; 996 with 47 societies in the German churches and 45 with 728 members in the Latvian churches. The West Russia and South Russia Associations were poorly represented and none reported in the Estonian Association. The youth conference of the Weichsel-Gebiet Association in Russian Poland approved in 1895 *Der Hausfreund* as its organ, but in January 1907 the youth conference began a monthly youth magazine, *Die Jugend-Warte* (The Youth Watch Tower), edited by Oskar Truderung until his untimely death. In 1909 it was reported that a "Sister Lohrer" was serving as a youth missionary in the association, but in August 1909 Eduard Wenske began serving for one year in this post. In the first months of his ministry, he reported both evangelistic and youth work, giving sermons and addresses in the churches (four in Russian) and in youth meetings giving addresses, Bible hours, and sessions on practical issues. Women's societies were not well developed. Only twenty-one and 350 members were reported in 1906 with the South Russia Association leading with nine.[24]

The churches in South Russia also held harvest festivals. In Volhynia some churches conducted deeper life conferences that included Bible study and prayer. In the church in Iwanowitsch, the pastor, Bernard J. Goetze (1888–1962), a graduate of the seminary in Lodz, developed in 1912 a program that included lectures with themes on church life as well as Bible classes.[25]

Music

Along with Russian Baptists and Mennonite Brethren, German and Baltic Baptists were noted for their music. In 1906 they had 188 choral societies or choirs with 3,630 singers; in 1912 the number of singers had increased to 4,548. The large church in Lodz in 1907 had 13 choral groups and 270 singers, which included two church choirs, a women's choir, a men's chorus, a Polish choir, and a Czech choir. It also had brass, violin, mandolin, and zither groups.[26] From December 7 to 14, 1908, the Alt-Danzig

23. Ibid., Mar. 21/Apr. 3, 1907, 89.

24. *Unions-Statistik der Baptisten Gemeinden in Russland*, 1906. Kupsch, 259, 430. WHZ, Apr. 3, 1909, 112. Eighth Union Conference, 1909, Minutes, final page. *Der Hausfreund*, Mar. 10/23, 1910, 79.

25. *Der Hausfreund.*, Oct. 28/Nov. 10, 1909, 345; Nov. 2/15, 1911, 237; Nov. 28/Dec. 11, 1912, 390; and Mar. 5/18, 1914, 81. See Miller, *In the Midst of Wolves*, 128–34, for the career of Goetze, including in the 1930s his publication of the widely distributed Russian "Goetze Bible."

26. *Unions-Statistik der Baptisten-Gemeinden in Russland*, 1906. *Der Hausfreund*, Mar. 21/Apr. 3, 1907, 92; Sep. 12/25, 1907, 295, and Sep. 16/30, 1908, 298–300.

congregation held a course of instruction with participation of six congregations in a directors' and singers' course in German and Russian that also included preaching and prayer. In early 1909 the Weichsel-Gebiet Association held a course for directors and choirs. In January 1910 in Neudorf a directors' course was conducted with thirty-six brethren. It also held a Bible hour.[27]

Choral and even instrumental festivals were popular and often crossed denominational and cultural barriers. In 1908 in Odessa a choral festival was conducted in the large hall of the Russian congregation with Vasilii Pavlov preaching in Russian followed by Friedrich Brauer also in Russian with the Russian choir participating. In the afternoon in the German chapel six choirs were represented—the Russian and German choirs, a Russian men's chorus, a women' chorus, a brass choir, and a choir from outside the city. In the summer four choirs participated with forty singers from four congregations—the German and Russian Baptist congregations and two that were non-Baptist. In November a choir festival was held at the Russian congregation with over 1,200 in attendance from the Russian, German, and Hebrew congregations. A choir of about sixty sang, accompanied by piano and harmonium, as well as male and women's choirs. The program included a short Russian message, poetry from members of the three congregations, and refreshments. In an annual choir festival in Lodz in January 1909, an association of choirs from fifteen choral groups and over 300 singers participated.[28]

In 1908 on Ascension Day, 5,000 gathered in the large chapel in Neudorf to hear seven brass choirs. In August at Sorotschin eighty-five men from six churches participated in a brass choir festival. In 1908 some individuals considered forming an instrumental association that would include seven string ensembles, three brass choirs, and one mandolin choir.[29]

Church Observances and Relations

Churches began to observe anniversaries of the denomination. In November 1908 *Der Hausfreund* produced an anniversary issue, which celebrated the fiftieth anniversary of the beginning of the German Baptist work in Russian Poland. During the year churches contributed to a jubilee fund that brought in about 4,400 rubles. In 1911 Latvian Baptists celebrated their fiftieth anniversary, commemorating the first baptism on Latvian soil by Adams Gertners. The churches celebrated on different Sundays throughout the year with special jubilee preaching and the singing of jubilee choirs. A notable jubilee year was 1914. In connection with the West Russia Association, the church in Horstschik, the first German Baptist church in Volhynia in Ukraine,

---

27. *Der Hausfreund*, Jan. 14/17, 1909, 10–12; Feb. 25/Mar. 10, 1909, 61; and Feb. 10/23, 1910, 45.
28. Ibid., June 4/17, 1908, 182; June 11/24, 1908, 191; July 30/Aug. 12, 244; Aug. 6/19, 1908, 253; Oct. 15/28, 1908, 335; Dec. 10/23, 1908, 398–99; and Jan. 21/Feb. 3, 1909, 22.
29. Ibid., June 11/24, 1908, 191; Aug. 6/19, 1908, 253; and Oct. 15/28, 1908, 335.

celebrated its fiftieth anniversary. In June the church at Sorotschin, the second church in Ukraine, observed its fiftieth jubilee. The South Russia Association in Johannestal observed the first Baptist baptism in Ukraine in 1864 in Neu-Danzig. In 1914 Johann Pritzkau, the veteran preacher who began his work in the 1860s and still active, produced his history, *Die Geschichte der Baptisten in Süd-Russland*. It was fortunate that the celebrations in 1914 occurred before the outbreak of the First World War in July.[30]

Baptism by immersion was often in a river or lake. The church in Rozycsczce, although incorporating a baptistry in its beautiful new budding, was still more apt to conduct baptism in the open. Churches used the common cup at the Lord's Supper, not the individual cups that Brauer observed on his trip in America. German Baptists, however, did not observe as Mennonite Brethren foot washing at the Lord's Supper. They maintained Christ observed it as an example of service, not instituting it as a church ordinance.[31]

In early 1910 *Der Hausfreund* printed an editorial on the misuse of the holy kiss, a custom observed in many churches of men with men and women with women, especially after the Lord's Supper. In some churches the holy kiss was observed at each meeting on arrival and departure. The editor wrote that a holy kiss should be an expression of a heartfelt and holy love and wanted unfeeling routine kissing to cease. In a letter to the *Der Hausfreund* two months later, E. Mahr supported the editor. He noted that kissing was a custom among Eastern peoples, such as Russians, and declared "A warm German handshake as a greeting says more than many a kiss."[32]

During the Conference on Sectarian Rights in Kiev in December 1906, Friedrich Brauer debated Jakob Kroeker and Adolf Reimer, two Mennonite Brethren who were adherents of the Evangelical Alliance, on the blessings and dangers of the Alliance movement. At the South Russia Association in 1907, Brauer maintained that the Evangelical Alliance's watchword "does not resound with us Baptists: 'One Lord, one Faith, one baptism.'" He claimed the Alliance did not unite believers in obedience to God's word but in loving one another. Later in the year *Der Hausfreund* published an article by Carl Füllbrandt, "Dies und Das über Allianz." Although he wrote that he could work hand in hand with those who are based on the foundation stone "Jesus Christ," but "God is a God of order," and "we fear coming into disharmony with God's word."[33]

The annual conferences of the Blankenburg Alliance in Germany with its advocacy of the union and fellowship of all believers had little practical impact on the

---

30. *Der Hausfreund*, Sep. 16/30, 1908, 302; Nov. 5/18.1908, 353–55, Dec. 12/25, 1912, 410; May 14/27, 1914, 161–62; June 11/24, 1914, 193–95; July 2/15, 1914, 217; and July 16/29, 1914, 235. Eighth Union Conference, 1909, *Minutes*, 16–17.

31. Miller, *In the Midst of Wolves. Der Hausfreund*, May 7/20, 1908, 148; July 30/Aug. 12, 1908, 243; July 1/14, 1909, 206–8; and Dec. 21/Jan. 3, 1912, 410.

32. *Der Hausfreund*, Jan. 20/Feb. 2, 1910, 21, and Mar. 31/Apr. 13, 1910, 98–99.

33. Ibid., Feb. 7 /20, 1907, 42; June 13/26, 1907, 188–89; and Sep. 19/Oct. 2, 1907, 299–302. South Russian Association, *Minutes*, 1907, 32–35.

German Baptists. On his visit to Blankenburg in 1908, Johannes Lübeck, a leading pastor and an editor of *Der Hausfreund*, reported he was especially blessed with the evening sessions, particularly the evening session on evangelisation. On the other hand, he was critical of the conference messages that simply repeated what he had heard in previous years and felt they could have gone deeper into God's word.[34]

Numbers of evangelicals, including members of the Alliance, became adherents of the dispensational views of J. N. Darby that included a rapture of believers before the Great Tribulation. Johann Kargel, the former German Baptist pastor of the German Baptist Church in St. Petersburg, became an adherent of the pretribulation rapture as well as an advocate of open communion and the doctrines of the Deeper Life movement as advocated in Blankenburg. Besides becoming a colleague of Prokhanov in the Evangelical Christian movement, he became an influential Bible teacher and writer. *Der Hausfreund* ran until 1913 a series of articles on Kargel's exposition of the Book of Revelation. Kargel also defended the pretribulation rapture against its attack in the journal. *Der Hausfreund* printed articles from others, either in agreement or in opposition to Kargel's eschatological views.[35]

Personal Morality

German Baptists advocated a strict code of morality, and members who did not follow the standards of the church faced exclusion. The rate of exclusion was high, although there was opportunity for repentance and re-admission. In 1906 the German churches reported 329 exclusions—261 in the German churches and 68 in the others. The Union Committee at the Union conference in 1909 stated in its report that the exclusion of 863 persons during the last triennium was both sad and joyful—sad because it showed how great was the power of sin but joyful that showed the churches were holding fast to the "infallible Word of God" for with no life the spiritually dead will no more be excluded.[36]

In an editorial in 1910 *Der Hausfreund* listed a number of questionable activities that should be avoided. It included attendance at the theater, telling suggestive jokes and stories, reading material that included improper material, playing billiards, dancing, beer drinking, and smoking tobacco. The editor stated that life was too short to dance the polka and did not go well with the "footsteps of Jesus." He pointed out that Herodias danced and the Israelites danced before the golden calf. In 1913 *Der Hausfreund* condemned the lottery and upheld Sunday as a day for rest and worship.[37]

---

34. *Der Hausfreund*, Sep. 16/30, 1908, 302.

35. See Wardin, *Evangelical Sectarianism*, 234–35, for entries of Kargel's articles and the views of others on eschatology appearing in *Der Hausfreund*.

36. *Unions-Statistik der Baptisten-Gemeinden in Russland*, 1906, 2–3, 10. Eighth Union Conference, 1909, *Minutes*, 11.

37. *Der Hausfreund*, Oct. 6/19, 1910, 316–17; Feb. 27/Mar. 12, 1913, 69; and Aug. 14/27, 1913, 263.

The use of tobacco and alcohol, however, could be problematic. In 1888 V. Martsch'off claimed that in South Russia churches excluded members without mercy for smoking. In a rejoinder Carl Füllbrandt stated that he knew of only two congregations that took such action. He maintained that when most became Christians they gave up tobacco as unnecessary and improper. In respect to alcohol, Füllbrandt noted that churches excluded drunken behavior but felt that forbidding the drinking of wine had no support from God's word. In the early twentieth century, however, *Der Hausfreund*, as with other evangelicals elsewhere, took a strong stand against alcohol, condemning it as dangerous for body and soul. In 1914 the journal declared it was the greatest murderer of mankind and one can live well without wine and beer.[38]

In distinction to Mennonite Brethren, German Baptists accepted military service, and their young men served in the Russian army. One solider wrote to *Der Hausfreund* that he was pleased to receive the journal and had the opportunity to share its contents with his comrades. In his listing of differences with German Baptists in 1910, Heinrich Braun, the Mennonite Brethren leader, noted that unlike Mennonite Brethren German Baptists permitted divorce. In their discussion of divorce in 1912 at the Union conference in Neufeld, the delegates noted that divorce until now was more or less unknown in their churches. Nevertheless it was felt according to Scripture that divorce was recognized but marriage with one who had divorced committed adultery.[39]

Missions and Benevolence

With the Manifestos of 1905, German and Baltic Baptists felt as other evangelicals a new era had now dawned for mission efforts. With increased vigor and vision, they extended their mission efforts into new areas and formed new mission and benevolent organizations. The membership contributed to chapel building, debt relief for churches, a jubilee fund in 1908, a new seminary, as well as missions abroad. They continued support for the Union's own home mission program, associational missions, famine relief, funds for widows and retired ministers, and Sunday school work. In the nineteenth century the West Russian Association in Volhynia, led by Severin Lehmann, made an effort to plant mission work in the Volga, and as described earlier the Weichsel-Gebiet Association in Russian Poland appointed missionaries to the Polish people. With the arrival of German Baptist settlers in Siberia in the early twentieth century, a new mission field opened. The first settlers lived at far distances from each other and were unorganized. In 1901 Eugen Mohr visited the area and saw the needs; Semen Lehmann and others followed him. In the statistics of the Union in 1906, Siberia and Ufa reported twelve mission stations and 214 members. On June 22, 1907, a church of fifty-four members with M. A. Krüger was founded in a settlement soon

---

38. *WHZ*, Oct. 1, 1888, 193, and Nov. 15, 1888, 222. *Der Hausfreund*, July 30/Aug. 12, 1908, 242–43; Mar. 5/18, 1914, 79–81; and Mar. 12 /25, 1914, 87.

39. *Der Hausfreund*, Dec. 12/25, 1912, 410.

called Hoffnungstal. In the same year a second congregation was founded in Trubetzskoi. With a loan from an individual, chapels were built in 1908 at Hoffnungstal and Halbstadt, both costing 10,000 rubles. The German Baptist movement spread as settlers took land in Barnaul, Slavgorod, and Pawlodar. In 1918 Siberian Baptists formed a West Siberian Association.[40]

Siberia was not an easy field because of the cold winter climate and distances. In 1908 the meeting of the mission committee of the Union reported that four workers were far too little for the enormously large field. Hermann Klempel in Omsk had a field 14,000 *versty* (9,280 miles) in length, and Krüger's field was 700 *versty* (464 miles) long. In April 1910 *Der Hausfreund* published cries from Siberia for material and spiritual help. Friedrich Brauer wrote to the American Baptist Missionary Union in January 1911 that one pastor who had been scarcely in Omsk for a year lost his voice and finally had to leave. Some settlers who settled far from the railway experienced starvation and were forced to return to their former homes.[41]

As with Mennonite Brethren, German Baptists also entered into a mission program to win native Russians. They felt, as Baron Üxküll in an article in April 1908 in *Der Hausfreund*, which had been published in America in English, the field for missions in Russia was open. Earlier in January 1907 Karl Furmann wrote in *Der Hausfreund* that the opportunity to preach to Russians would be better served to send Russians, who were more apt to trust their fellow countrymen, rather than Germans.[42]

In an article in the following month, Johann J. Pritzkau, told of the formation in the spring of 1906 at the South Russian Association in Alt-Danzig of a Väterlandische Mission (Native Mission). As the Mennonite Brethren mission to Russians, the new society provided support for its missionaries. A committee of four members with Pritzkau as treasurer conducted its affairs. The mission began with fifty supporting members who for at least five years pledged to contribute twenty-five rubles yearly. Support was inter-denominational. Besides Baptists, Mennonites, Lutherans, and even Congregationalists from America participated. The society began supporting three Russian missionaries on the field.[43]

At the beginning of 1908, Pritzkau reported four missionaries with annual support and others placed from time to time during the winter months. He reported the work was blessed with small and large revivals and an increase in converts. He also wrote that the mission's missionaries were not revolutionaries and their work was the best means against the terrors of revolution.[44]

40. Krüger, "Entstehung und Entwicklung der Baptistengemeinden in Westsibirien, *Der Familienfreund*, Nov. 1926, 6–7. *Der Hausfreund*, Apr.25/May 8. 1907. 135.

41. *Der Hausfreund*, Sep. 16/30, 1908, 302; Feb. 10/23, 1910, 43; and Apr. 7/20, 1910, 109–10. Letter of Brauer to Huntington, Jan. 10, 1911, ABMU/ABFMS, *Correspondence*, 1900–1919.

42. *Der Hausfreund*, Jan. 17/30, 1907, 22, and April 2/15, 1908, 109.

43. Ibid., Feb. 7/20, 1907, 43. South Russian Association, *Minutes*, 1906, 18, 32.

44. *Der Hausfreund*, Feb. 6/19, 1908, 45.

PART SIX—Possibilities and Uncertainties, 1905–1917

One of the missionaries was Ivan Nassipaiko, who could speak both Russian and German and had attended the Alliance School in Berlin for three years. In 1908 he reported conducting Bible conferences in Sevastopol, traveling with Alexander Persianov into Crimea where he held meetings at Yalta, and visiting villages out from Odessa where he countered Adventist teaching. In a meeting attended by Germans and Russians where he spoke in both languages, the worshippers sang together their Russian and German songs. He also reported that travel conditions could be most difficult with heavy rain, the snow turning into ice, and the necessity to reach some villages only by foot. Another missionary, W. Skaldin, a deacon in Pavlov's church in Odessa, preached in Annenthal, a German settlement where Germans as well as Russian workers attended his meetings. In another village he was challenged by Mikhail A. Kal'nev, an Orthodox missionary, to participate in a religious debate in the village church that drew a mixed crowd of around 2,000 Russians, Germans, and Jews. On the basis of John 3:14–18, Skaldin maintained salvation came by faith alone while Kal'nev countered with the need for good works. In another village, Skaldin and a companion were arrested but released with an order to leave the area.[45]

At the end of 1909 Pritzkau reported that the mission had placed on the field three men for a full year, three for a half year, and three monthly workers, besides providing assistance for students at the Lodz Seminary. It also distributed Russian tracts. By the end of 1912, however, some were asking whether the mission still existed. Pritzkau responded that it continued without much stir and clamor but admitted the mission lacked funds since many brethren were not maintaining their former interest. The mission evidently simply faded away.[46]

German support for Russian missions sometimes occurred outside the efforts of the Väterlandische Mission. It was reported in 1910 that Carl Füllbrandt of the German Baptist church in Odessa sent out several brethren who preached the gospel to Russians. In 1910 a Russian, Josef Rotaryuk, came to the village of Friedenfeld where Germans and Russians of the area decided to support him with each group choosing its own treasurer.[47] The German Baptist church in St. Petersburg also attempted some outreach to Russians. In 1906 the church began conducting a Russian Sunday school. The parents were Russian, Estonian, Polish, and Jewish. It was reported in February 1909 that within the space of a year Russian services had been regularly held on Saturday and Sunday evenings at the church. A small Russian choir of youth had existed since the fall.[48]

In 1909 in Kronenthal in the Caucasus a number of Russians attended a Bible course for two weeks in which Friedrich Brauer spoke in Russian and W. K. Seibel distributed tracts. In 1912 in Omsk Friedrich Hörmann ministered in Russian in five

45. Ibid., May 7/20, 1908, 149–50, and May 21/June 3, 1908, 165–67.
46. Ibid., Nov. 18/Dec. 1, 1909, 370, and Nov. 28/Dec. 11, 1912, 391.
47. Ibid., Mar. 10/23, 1910, 78–79.
48. Ibid., Aug. 6/19, 1908, 254, and Feb. 18/Mar. 3, 1909, 55.

meetings, reporting increasing attendance.[49] German Baptists also developed special relations with leaders of the Russian Baptist Union.

In 1906, Deï Mazaev, president of the Russian Union, sent a letter of regrets to the South Russian Association of German Baptists for his inability to accept the invitation to speak because of conflict with his own conference. At the German Baptist congregation at Neufreudenthal, a church conference was held in 1910 with Füllbrandt, Pavlov, at the time president of the mission committee of the Russian Baptist Union, and Johannes Rempel, a Mennonite Brethren from Kherson who was devoting himself as an itinerant missionary among Russians. The latter two spoke in both Russian and German. After the regime refused to grant permission to John Clifford and John Shakespeare of the Baptist World Alliance to participate in a mission consultation in Russia with German and Russian leaders, the Union Committee of the German Union arranged to meet in St. Petersburg in September 1910 during the annual congress of the Russian Union. The leaders of both groups met for three days with sessions stretching into the night.[50]

German Baptists also supported other home missions. The Riga Street Mission, headed by Fritz Junker, was established in 1906 with the purpose of not only bringing the gospel to homeless and destitute men but also provided shelter, such as a home that housed twelve men. Members of the mission also engaged in preaching and singing at a public home. The association in Russian Poland established a tract society, which was followed at the General Conference in 1909 by the formation of a tract society for the entire Union. It produced German, Polish, and Russian tracts. The Union chose seven representatives for each region to further its program. Life members paid a one-time contribution of 100 rubles with others paying annually smaller fees. The society produced new tracts from the contributions of its members and from gifts.[51]

A soldiers' mission was established to send letters, tracts, and Christian publications, such as *Der Hausfreund* and *Jugend-Warte*, to Germans in the military and *Baptist* and *Gost'* to Russian soldiers. A report at the end of 1911 stated that in the past year 240 letters and cards were sent to 81 soldiers, including 69 Baptists (66 German, 1 Polish, and 2 Russians) and 12 Lutherans, besides periodicals and tracts.[52]

As other evangelicals, Baptists in Russia also had an interest in Jewish missions. In 1906 the Latvian Association began to support a colportage ministry among Jews. In an annual report, Immanuel Altmann described his travels in Poland, Volhynia, and South Russia, receiving funds from German Baptist congregations for his travels

---

49. Ibid., Jan. 14/27, 1909, 13, and Feb. 15/28, 1912, 54.

50. South Russian Association, *Minutes*, 1906, 12. *Der Hausfreund*, Aug. 4/17, 1910, 247, and Oct. 6/19, 1910, 318.

51. *Der Hausfreund*, Mar. 21/Apr. 3, 1907, 90; Sep. 5/18, 1907, 286-87; July 2/15, 1908, 213; Feb. 10/23, 1910, 43-44; and Feb. 17/Mar. 2, 1910, 54. Eighth Union Conference, 1909, *Minutes*, 58.

52. *Der Hausfreund.*, Dec. 9/22, 1909, 394; Nov. 23/Dec. 6, 1911, 373-74; and Aug. 28/Sep. 10, 1913, 280-81.

and for publishing tracts. In 1907 a Jewish woman missionary from Odessa spoke at the South Russian Association. The hat collection for the Jewish mission produced 167 rubles.[53]

Both German and Russian Baptists were acquainted with the work of Leon L. Rosenberg, a missionary of the Milday Mission to Jews. In 1903 he settled in Odessa, but his first three years were a time of suffering during a period of revolution and counter-revolution. In 1908 the authorities gave him legal recognition. In an article in *Baptist* in 1910, it was claimed his congregation had grown from only one or two to around 330, but only fifty were active. *Der Hausfreund* published an article of his work in 1913, celebrating his tenth anniversary, in which he claimed that each year perhaps as many as 25,000 Jews attended his meetings with each receiving a New Testament or a mission paper. Rosenberg attended the congresses of the Russian Baptist Union in 1908–1910.[54]

Although German Baptists in Russia unlike the Mennonite Brethren did not establish a foreign mission field, they nevertheless showed interest in missions in Cameroon in West Africa and the Telugu field in South India. The Baptists in Germany established in 1891 a mission field in Cameroon, then a colonial possession of Germany. After 1905 German Baptists in Russia began to make limited contributions to it. At the annual session of the South Russian Association in 1907, Karl Mascher, mission inspector of the Cameroon mission, reported on its work.[55]

In 1909 Heinrich Reimer, a Mennonite Brethren from Schönau in the Sagradowka Settlement who served as a missionary on the Cameroon field, attended the session of the South Russian Association in Alt Danzig. By his speaking and the showing of an enlarged projection of a map of the land and people, Reimer aroused great interest and received a sizable collection. In a report to *Der Hausfreund*, Reimer reported contributions of almost 200 rubles from six churches, the deaconess home, and Oskar Truderung. In 1912 Mascher was again in Russia but was struck with nephritis and after being sick for fourteen days returned to Germany. Even with his medical mishap, the churches in Volhynia and South Russia still benefited from his visit.[56]

J. C. Heinrichs, an American of German birth, who served on the Telugu field in India under the American Bapist Missionary Union, on two trips to Russia created among German Baptists some support for his mission. In 1907 he attended with Mascher the meeting of the South Russian Association in Neu-Danzig where he spoke. As earlier noted, he also visited the annual meeting of the Mennonite Brethren. Heinrichs also visited German Baptist but particularly Mennonite Brethren churches. On

---

53. Ibid., June 13/26, 1907, 191; July 16/29, 1908, 229; and Dec. 12/25, 1908, 397.

54. *Baptist*, Oct. 20, 1910, 341. *Der Hausfreund*, Nov. 6/19, 1913, 362–63.

55. European Baptist Congress, *Proceedings*, 1908, 184. *Der Sendbote*, Aug. 14, 1907, 3.

56. *Der Hausfreund*, Apr. 29/May 12, 1909, 134; June 10/23, 1909, 180–81; and Nov. 14/27, 1912, 372.

his trip in 1909, Heinrichs collected almost 265 rubles from German Baptist churches and individuals.[57]

In 1907, as earlier noted, J. C. Heinrichs with Heinrich J. Braun, Mennonite Brethren leader, undertook an inspection trip to Persia for a possible field for American Baptists. No field, however, was opened. In 1912 *Der Hausfreund* began printing letters from missionaries from the area of Urmia in northwest Persia, an area that had recently come under Russian military protection. One was from M. Permian, an Armenian who was baptized in the Baptist church in Tiflis in 1895 and studied in Germany and Switzerland. Since 1903 he and a coworker from Switzerland, Marie Brennwalder, had been on the field and were now working in Urmia among Armenians, where a small Baptist church existed.[58]

Another missionary who wrote to *Der Hausfreund* was Ruben Joseph, a native of Persia who spoke Syrian and Turkish but also knew German. He had spent a year in Russia and on his return extended greetings from Baptists and Mennonite Brethren. He brought with him a bicycle and a harmonium for which he was forced to pay a high duty at the Persian border. He lived in the village of Ahda near Urmia. He found the work difficult traveling from village to village among the Moslems, preaching and distributing tracts, but reported some baptisms. In one service Syrians, Armenians, Moslem Persians, and Russians were in attendance and sang and prayed in four languages. In 1914 the South Russian Association, which had had the most contact with foreign missions, adopted the Baptist church in Ahda as a mission field. But then the First World War erupted and destroyed this mission opportunity.[59]

German Baptists also engaged in some benevolent activity. In 1889 the Union Conference in 1889 established a Widows' Relief Society whose members paid ten rubles to the widow of one who had served in mission service. It never reached its goal of 1,000 rubles from 100 members. In 1910 the society reported paying half of a promised benefit to a living but suffering mission worker, leaving in the future only half to the widow. In 1906 the Union Conference in Radawczcyk in Russian Poland approved the statutes of a fund for aged and disabled ministers (*Invaliden-Kasse*). For its administration it chose a committee of five members that included Severin Lehmann as treasurer. Churches were requested in March to make special collections for the fund, but the treasurer was forced to make special appeals. In 1911 the fund was supporting three complete invalids, three widows, and two orphans; in 1914 five ministers and three widows with their children. Up to 1914 the fund had received a bit over 10,700 rubles and dispersed 2,819 rubles.[60]

---

57. *Der Sendbote*, Aug. 14, 1907, 3. *Der Hausfreund*, June 24/July 7, 1909, 203.

58. *Der Hausfreund*, Sep. 12/25, 1912, 301–2, and Sep. 4/17, 1913, 290–91.

59. Ibid., Sep. 12/25, 1912, 301; Sep. 4/17, 1913, 290–91; Sep. 11/24, 1913, 298; Jan. 1/14, 1914, 4; June 25/July 8, 1914, 211; and July 2/15, 1914, 217.

60. Kupsch, 452–53. *Der Hausfreund*, Feb. 7/20, 1907, 44; Sept. 10/23, 1908, 294; Oct. 8/21, 1908, 325; Aug. 4/17, 1910, 245; Nov. 30/Dec. 13, 1911, 381; and Feb. 19/Mar. 4, 1914, 66.

PART SIX—Possibilities and Uncertainties, 1905–1917

With their limited resources, German Baptists were far behind Mennonites in establishing benevolent institutions but made some effort. Through the efforts of Friedrich Brauer, a Lodz Deaconess Association, "Tabaea," was founded in 1904 with its own house to serve the sick and needy. The first house mother was Bertha Adam, who had served in Bethel, the deaconess home in Berlin. As early as 1897 she had been engaged in deaconess work from a dwelling provided by the Lodz church. She served until 1914.[61]

In 1908 the Lodz church founded a children's home or orphanage with the Union approving churches in the Union to contribute to it. In 1912 the home held thirty-five children and needed from four to five thousand rubles yearly. Because of the high rent, the home decided to own its own property. The Union agreed to make the home a cause of the Union with the committee in Lodz left with its management. The cost of the building with the land was likely to be 10,000 rubles. Eugen Mohr, then pastor of the Lodz church, appealed for financial assistance. The home moved into its new location in Aleksandov near Lodz in 1913.[62]

The Union had no single mission treasury and local and associational interests initiated societies or missions on their own. The appeals for home missions from the Union and associations, chapel building, foreign missions, and benevolence increased. It is not suprising that an article appeared in *Der Hausfreund* with the title, "Schon wieder eine Kollekte!" (Yet Once Again a Collection!), even as early as 1907 before the full magnitude of requests had peaked. It was no doubt a common cry from pastors and members. The author of the article, however, tried to counteract this cry of exasperation by stating that it was better judgment the contribution be made quickly rather than postponing or canceling it. He quoted a writer who declared that a congregation that repulses a collection becomes over time impoverished.[63]

Even though German and Baltic Baptists financed much of their own needs and mission and benevolent programs, the Union continued to appeal abroad for financial assistance. Baptists in Western and Central Europe and America continued to look upon Russia as a mission field, especially now with the constitutional changes in 1905 mission opportunity even seemed greater. Two committees, an Anglo-German Committee in London and an American-German Committee in Hamburg, served as conduits for funds for Baptist work in Germany and other regions on the European continent, including Russia. Baptists from Germany also established in London a German Mission under the leadership of W. S. Oncken, son of Johann Oncken, as treasurer, and published the *Quarterly Reporter of the German Baptist Mission,* which publicized Baptist work in Germany and elsewhere on the continent. The German Mission worked with the Anglo-German Committee.[64]

61. Kupsch, 457–60. *Der Hausfreund*, Feb. 27/Mar. 11, 1908, 69.
62. Kupsch, 454–55. *Der Hausfreund*, Sep. 16/30, 1908, 302, and Dec. 12/25, 1912, 409.
63. *Der Hausfreund*, Mar. 21/Apr. 3, 1907, 89–90.
64. *Baptist Times and Freeman*, March 30, 1907, 225.

One source of income, although limited, was from the American Baptist Missionary Union (changed to American Baptist Mission Society in 1910), which developed a direct link with the German Union in Russia. In 1906 the ABMU reported it made a comparatively small appropriation with support going only for rent and not salaries except for the churches in St. Petersburg and Warsaw. In addition the ABMU did not aid the Russian Baptist Union as it had no ties with it. In 1908 Friedrich Brauer reported that the ABMU was regularly sending $1,300 with supplementary donations of $200, a total of $1,500 or 3,000 rubles. He, however, called for greater assistance for work in the Caucasus and Siberia, for the native Russian missionaries the Union was supporting, and for the Russian students in the Lodz Seminary. In 1913 he wrote that he was disheartened that the American Baptist Society was reducing its aid of $1,300 to $1,170. In 1914 Brauer was pleased, however, that the society was sending a special appropriation of $400 for a Polish missionary in Russian Poland. In January 1911 Brauer wrote to George Huntington of the ABMU that he had been told that John D. Rockefeller "could let fall of his gigantic wealth some good-sized crumbs from his rich table for the sorely struggling mission in Russia also." But if he tried, nothing apparently came from this source.[65]

The small German Baptist Conference in the USA was also a donor. Contributions to Russia before 1907 were generally limited except for Harm Husmann, missionary in the Volga. From 1906 to 1914 it contributed regularly to Friedrich Arndt, pastor of the German Baptist church in St. Petersburg, and from 1910 to 1914 supported twelve to thirteen pastors, including Husmann and Friedrich Brauer, who beginning in 1911 moved to the church in Warsaw. In 1911–1912 Brauer went from city to city in America raising funds, which retired the debt on the Warsaw church. The German Baptist Conference in 1908 forbade solicitation of pastors from abroad unless they had credentials from the Union Committee in Russia and permission of the Mission Committee of the German Baptist Conference.[66]

A third source of foreign support was from the Baptist Union in Germany. At the German Baptist *Bundes-Konferenz* in Berlin in 1912, it was reported that since 1894 it had supported thirty-one missionary workers in Russia at a cost of almost 40,000 marks. Over the years the Union Committee in Russia sent representatives to the triennial meetings of the *Bundes-Konferenz*, and although not sending an official representative in 1912 nevertheless encouraged brethren from Russia to attend.[67]

---

65. ABMU/ABFMS, *Reports*, 1906, 400; 1907, 206; and 1909, 142. Letters of Brauer to the ABMU/ABFMS, Nov, 4, 1908; Jan. 10, 1911; Sep, 13, 1913; and Apr. 15, 1914, ABMU/ABFMS, *Correspondence*, 1900–1919.

66. See Wardin, *Evangelical Sectarianism*, 244, for reports of contributions from the German Baptist Conference. Kupsch, 126, 259. *Der Hausfreund*, Sep. 16/30, 1908, 301; Aug. 17/30, 1911, 262; and Dec. 7/20, 1911. 388.

67. German *Bundeskonferenz*, 1912, *Minutes*, 139. *Der Hausfreund*, Aug. 1/14, 250, 1912.

PART SIX—Possibilities and Uncertainties, 1905–1917

Publications

The chief periodical of the German Baptist Union in Russia was *Der Hausfreund*, founded by Julius Herrmann in 1889 in Riga but then transferred to Danzig in Germany upon Herrmann's move to that city in 1893. After the 1905 revolution, *Der Hausfreund* returned to Riga in 1906, edited as a weekly by Baron Üxküll and published by J. A. Frey. Johann Lübeck then began editing the paper in 1907. Because of lack for his full-time support it was necessary to gain in 1909 two other men to share the editorial responsibilities. It appears, however, that Lübeck carried much of the editorial responsibility with also Janis Inke for a time until the paper's demise. The paper continued in Russia until September 1914 soon after the beginning of the First World War.[68]

Der Hausfreund provided devotional and promotional material, news of the Union, associations, churches, and Baptists abroad, as well as promotion of mission and benevolent causes. It also served as a forum for differing viewpoints. It was an important unifying instrument in helping to keep together a very widespread constituency.[69]

On behalf of his association, one reader complained that in comparison to the Mennonite Brethren journal, *Die Friedensstimme*, it lacked information on developments in the State Duma in relation to German affairs and complained it included articles that were "tedious and deficient of understanding." Lübeck admitted that the paper was lacking in a number of areas, but he pointed out that the Mennonite periodicals have a regular editor and strong co-workers. *Der Hausfreund*, however, lacks a person who has the time to read other periodicals to bring in the necessary articles and to correspond with others to gain their help. He declared that *Der Hausfreund* as a Baptist organ must be filled with Baptist reports and not filled with *Lesestoff* (reading matter). He also called for the need of a publishing house for German Baptists in Russia, a plea he had already made several years earlier.[70]

Lübeck also faced the complaint of the unsatisfactory delivery of the paper. He rejected the loud cry of reducing the price of the paper to gain more subscribers and thus make it self-sustaining. In 1913 members of the publication committee were unfavorably comparing *Der Hausfreund* with *Christlicher Botschafter*, the edition of *Der Wahrheitszeuge*, the journal of the Baptist Union of Germany for the Russian market. A. M. Schulz responded defensively by stating that for the most part *Christlicher Botchafter's* workers were so capable because of their training at the Hamburg

---

68. MO, Dec. (1), 1904, 1317. *Der Hausfreund*, Jan. 3/16, 1907, 1, 8; Sep. 23/Oct. 6, 1909, 307; and Nov. 30 /Dec. 13, 1911, 380. Kupsch, 478.

69. MO, Dec. (1), 1904, 1317. *Der Hausfreund*, Nov. 18/Dec. 1, 1909, 368–69. Pritzkau, *Die Geschichte der Baptisten in Süd Russland*, 176–78.

70. *Der Hausfreund*, Sep. 16/30, 1908, 301, and Jan. 19/Feb. 2, 1911, 20.

Seminary. He also maintained that throughout the years most of the critics of *Der Hausfreund* "have never yet put anything into its pocket."[71]

In 1902 *Der Hausfreund* had 1,800 subscribers and in 1909 2,146. *Unseren Lieblingen*, an illustrated weekly for children published since 1906, had 11,146 subscriptions. In the report on publications at the Union conference in Neudorf in 1909, blame was laid on the churches and pastors for the low circulation. In the previous year in 1908, Lübeck wrote that *Der Hausfreund* and other publications were published at a loss. The Union treasury was responsible for the arrears and interest.[72]

Besides *Der Hausfreund*, *Unseren Lieblingen*, and *Jugend-Warte*, the youth magazine produced by the youth association, German Baptists also issued *Die Jahres-Warte*, a Christian calendar. As already noted, Latvian and Estonian Baptists also published their own journals. Baptists in Russia also produced a few books. J. A. Frey published in German and Russian, *Das Land, wo Jesus wandelte* (The Land Where Jesus Walked); Carl Füllbrandt wrote, *Blätter vom Lebensbaum* (Leaves of the Tree of Life), daily mediations on well-known Bible texts; and Johann Pritzkau, *Die Geschichte der Baptisten in Süd-Russland*, his history of the German Baptists in South Russia.[73]

State Relations and Religious Competitors

German Baptists did not participate in the Revolution of 1905 and gave their full allegiance to the Tsar. German Baptists, as the Mennonite Brethren, contributed to the common good in their collections for famine relief in 1907, donating by June a bit over 4,800 rubles. At the Union conference in Neudorf in 1909, Friedrich Brauer read Romans 13:1–7 and prayed fervently for the Tsar, the Empire, and for all subjects. The national hymn was sung. As a religious body with legalization, it was nevertheless necessary to receive authorization for new churches, pastors, and Union conferences. The Union conference for Neudorf in 1909 could not proceed until finally a telegram from the Minister of Internal Affairs sent his approval. As with the Mennonite Brethren and other evangelical groups, officials now attended their conferences. Brauer wrote that he was ashamed of the conference in 1909 in the presence of the officials over the questionable voting on the site for the seminary.[74]

In 1912 German Baptists became alarmed with the decision of the Minister of Religious Affairs that all general conferences must be conducted in Russian. The editor of *Der Hausfreund* wrote that few of their pastors had mastered the Russian language

---

71. Ibid., Jan. 19/Feb. 2, 1911, 20; June 1/14, 1911, 175; and Aug. 21/Sep. 3, 1913, 273.

72. *BMM*, July 1902, 230 (504). Eighth Union Conference, 1909, *Minutes*, 27. *Der Hausfreund*, Sep. 26/Oct. 9, 1907, 309; Sep. 16/30, 1908; and Dec. 3/16, 1908, 389.

73. *Der Hausfreund*, Aug. 29/Sep. 11, 1907, 279; Jan. 2/15, 1908, 8; Mar. 5/17, 1908, 76; and Nov. 30/Dec. 13, 1911, 381.

74. Pritzkau, 171–76. *Der Hausfreund*, June 6/19, 1907, 182, and Sep. 23/Oct. 6, 1909, 306–7. Eighth Union Conference, 1909, *Minutes*, 33.

and thus few of their churches could participate. He hoped for an exemption but at the same time felt the language question will sooner or later confront them.[75]

In his interview in St. Petersburg in 1913 with J. H. Franklin, foreign mission secretary of the American Baptist Foreign Mission Society (ABFMS), F. A. Arndt, pastor of the German Baptist church in the city, reported that eight German Baptist churches had been recently closed in southern Russia. He went on to say, "Without question the thing to do is to work quietly and not to irritate the officials." In writing to the ABFMS in 1913, Friedrich Brauer admitted that missionaries of the Union are not able to preach everywhere and it was difficult to gain permission from the government to preach. He also mentioned the closing of the seminary in Lodz, which failed to gain state authorization. In 1914 he again wrote to the ABFMS stating, "We have been obliged to labor with more care than was the case in the previous year. We have become objects of severe scrutiny."[76]

The regime had always regarded German Baptists with some suspicion concerning their relations with the native Russian population. With the growing strength of reactionary forces in the Empire, the new era that began in 1905 with so much optimism was now turning into a period of serious concern.

In this period Seventh-day Adventism continued to be a threat. It did not gain large numbers of German Baptists but was nevertheless a continuing thorn in the flesh. In an editorial in *Der Hausfreund* in 1912, the editor charged Adventists for using all kinds of tactics to spread their message. In 1914 the editor declared its propaganda was "unevangelical, carnal, and sordid." He charged them in not bringing the gospel to the world but to root up believers.[77]

Friedrich Hörmann, who was serving in Orenburg, noted the spread of Adventism and wrote a refutation of it, which was published in *Der Hausfreund* and also as a tract. In 1902 J. Kessler, then president of the Union, reported to the American Baptist Missionary Union on battling against not only Adventists but also the "Free Church," probably the Mission Covenant, which opposed the need for believer's baptism and observed open communion. In 1914 R. W. Pelzer, working with the German Baptist mission in Saratov, found himself contending against both Adventists and Pentecostals, a new movement that had just appeared.[78]

With legalization German Baptist antagonism with Lutherans abated but still might appear. In 1911 one correspondent from the Volga complained of a Lutheran pastor who with governmental support plotted a large-scale persecution. On the other

75. *Der Hausfreund*, Oct. 3/16, 1912, 324.

76. Interview with Arndt, "Extracts from Notes made by Franklin," ABMU/ABFMS, *Correspondence*, 1900–1919. Letters of Brauer to the ABFMS, Feb. 19, 1913, and Apr. 7, 1914, ABMU/ABFMS, *Correspondence*, 1900–1919.

77. *Der Hausfreund*, July 11/24, 1912, 227, and July 16/29, 1914, 232.

78. Ibid., Oct. 6/19, 1910, 318; Nov. 24/Dec. 7, 1910, 371–73; Dec. 1/14, 1910, 379–81; Dec. 8/21, 1910, 390–91; May 25/June 7, 1911, 166; and 1914, no. 14, beilage. *BMM*, July 1902, 230 (504).

hand, in the Caucasus Carl Füllbrandt found even Lutheran churches open to him, unheard of for him in Russia, evidently in villages with no preaching for a year.[79]

There was, however, some sparring in Lutheran and Baptist publications from both sides. *Der christliche Orient*, the periodical of the Deutsche Orient Mission, a Lutheran competitor in Russia, printed an attack on Baptists by a "Pastor Klein" from Rostov in 1908. He faulted them for their opposition to infant baptism, rejecting religious nurture within the Christian community, and lack of interest in education. Carl Füllbrandt responded with an article in *Der Wahrheitszeuge*. Later In 1913 Füllbrandt attempted to refute in a booklet and in an article in *Der Hausfreund*, "Darfst du Baptist werden?" (Can You Be A Baptist?), that appeared in *Christlicher Volksbote*. The Lutheran author attacked Baptists for rejecting infant baptism and linking Baptists with the sectarian fanatics in Germany and the revolutionary Münsterites in Luther's time.[80]

In 1904 the Deutsche Orient Mission published a booklet, *Die Maljowantzi*, by Andreï I. Stefanovich that included some serious charges against German Baptists in Russia. He alleged that German and Russian Baptists had earlier been united, but under the threat from the regime of punishment and exile during the time of stundist suppression the German Baptists separated from the Russian Baptists. As a consequence the Russian Baptists were now unable to continue in orderly fashion and fell into incompetent hands with even a movement toward mysticism analogous to the Malevantsy, a heretical sect. In 1909 Carl Füllbrandt and Friedrich Brauer, two German Baptists, and Vasiliï Pavlov, the Russian Baptist leader, collaborated in producing a refutation, "Nur Wahrheit!" (Only the Truth!). The Baptist authors maintained German and Russian Baptists never formed a united association and thus a later separation was a "phantasy." Although Russian Baptists were suppressed, German Baptists in Russia were neither punished nor exiled. Except for a quiet witness, German Baptists in Russia had until 1906 no formal mission among Russians. The authors also insisted that the Russian Baptist work with their gifted leaders has been "completely self-sustaining under all the storms and persecution and also through all kinds of severe winds of foreign teaching and abnormal protuberances."[81] It was a remarkable statement from both German and Russian leaders that the Russian work existed apart from the German work.

---

79. *Der Hausfreund*, Dec, 7/20, 1911, 392. *Der Sendbote*, July 26, 1911, 472.

80. *Der christliche Orient*, 1909, 55–56. *WHZ*, May 19, 1909, 172–74. Füllbrandt, *Darfst du Baptist werden?*, and *Der Hausfreund* from July 3/16 to July 24 /Aug. 6, 1913.

81. Stefanovich, *Die Maljowantzi*, 2–6. *Der Hausfreund*, July 8/21, 1909, 214–16.

29

Evangelical Agencies and Other Religious Bodies

IN THE FIRST YEARS of the twentieth century before the First World War, the movement of evangelical dissidents had evolved primarily into a Baptist movement but culturally divided between Russian and other Slavic peoples on the one hand and German and Baltic peoples on the other hand. Most adherents were members of four denominational bodies but essentially one in doctrine and polity. Russians were divided between the Russian Baptist Union and the Evangelical Chrisian Union. The German and Baltic side included the German Baptist Union (or Union of Baptist Churches in Russia) and Mennonite Brethren.

In 1908 the *Missionary Review of the World*, the chief Protestant journal on missions, published an article by James L. Barton, "The Religious Situation in Russia," much of it based on the report in the preceding year of a committee on Russia appointed by the Foreign Mission Boards of North America.[1] Barton stated that the stundists, the major group of Russian dissidents, observe immersion and were essentially Baptist. He declared, "Without question, the Baptist movement in Russia is more pronounced and are better established than any other denomination outside of the Orthodox Church." He noted the changed religious conditions in the country where all may profess their respective faiths but pointed out that the manifestos were only decrees whose provisions have not been enacted into law, causing confusion in their application among local officials.

Barton played up the positive role that the Bible societies and the Young Men's Christian Association were playing and the prospects for the Russian Evangelical Alliance. He declared that "Russia presents an opportunity surpassed by no other country

---

1. Barton, "The Religious Situation in Russia," *MRW*, Oct. 1908, 727–33.

for an immediate Christian advance" but yet the approach must be tailored to "local conditions and present circumstances." From a second report of the committee on Russia, he noted its recommendations to assist existing evangelical organizations in the country financially and with outside expertise. The need was to provide Christian literature and raise up trained Russian leadership, but it was not the right time "for any general denominational advance upon Russia upon the part of mission boards." The leadership needed to be Russian.

Nevertheless, two missions, the Deutsche Orient Missison from Germany and the Committee for Evangelical Mission in Russia, formed in Sweden, both undertook mission work in Russia in the early twentieth century. Both were Lutheran and supported infant baptism thus arousing controversy with Baptists. The Deutsche Orient Mission worked with evangelicals in the country, such as the New Molokans, but its attempt at forming a theological school at Astrakhanka under the leadership of W. L. Jack, a German subject, in the end came to naught. The work of the Committee for Evangelical Mission in Russia attempted to do mission work with Swedish missionaries. In 1908 a comparatively small group of Plymouth Brethren missionaries began a mission in Central Asia among Moslems, and the Mildmay Mission continued its mission to Jews.

From its base in Finland, Methodists strengthened their work in St. Petersburg and other parts of Russia. Although leadership was held by a German-American, its pastors were indigenous. The Salvation Army, already in Finland, was able to enter St. Petersburg just before the First World War. The Disciples of Christ, desiring a Russian field, confined itself almost entirely to financial and moral support of the Evangelical Christian Union. Edmund H. Broadbent, Plymouth Brethren from England, as his predecessor Frederick Baedeker, was only a traveling evangelist. Adventism continued primarily with indigenous support. One new group that appeared in the early twentieth century was Pentecostalism. Although visitors and literature from abroad will further it, it will maintain itself under indigenous leadership. Baptists from abroad sent limited funds to the German Baptist Union but no missionaries.

Evangelical Agencies

British and Foreign Bible Society

The British and Foreign Bible Society (BFBS) continued its extensive distribution of Scripture through its Bible depots and colporteurs, most of whom were of peasant stock and purportedly members of the Orthodox Church. The Holy Synod held a monopoly on the production of Russian Bibles from which the BFBS must buy its Bibles and Testaments. Except for a limited edition in 1907 that was soon sold out, the Holy Synod forbade the distribution of the Bible without the Apocrypha. The Pentateuch, the Psalms, or New Testament, however, circulated without the Apocrypha.

The government provided support by remitting some taxes and steamers and trains provided free travel for colporteurs and carrried Bibles free of charge.[2]

In 1905 the BFBS distributed almost 600,000 Bibles or portions in twenty-one languages. Colporteurs could sell almost anywhere, even on trains and streamers and at fairs and monasteries. The regime forbade colporteurs serving as missionaries or conducting meetings. They must only sell Scripture although they may talk to people to persuade them to buy.[3]

Religious Tract Society

Except for a depot in Warsaw in Russian Poland, the Religious Tract society continued to be shut out of the rest of the Empire since the closing of the Pashkovite society. In 1905, however, it was able to provide a grant to J. A. Frey for electrotype blocks for his new Latvian paper, *Awots*. As reported in 1906, it made another grant to Frey and provided William Fetler, then a resident in London, Russian tracts for distribution in Russia. In 1908 it recorded sending Prokhanov a grant for electrotype blocks for illustrations in *Khristianin* and *Seyatel'*, a weekly tract, and in 1911 money for a tract, "A Great Trial and Its Results." In its report in 1910 it sent to Miss Bechler in Odessa a grant for books and tracts in Hebrew, Yiddish, and Russian, and in 1911 and 1912 grants to Bechler for tracts and to Fetler for publication work.[4]

Young Men's Christian Association (YMCA)

Through the efforts of James Stokes, a philanthropist from New York City, a YMCA was established in St. Petersburg in 1900 with the name "*Mayak*" (Lighthouse). It opened with temporary statutes but two years later received permanent status. Emanuel Nobel, members of the nobility, and even the imperial family also contributed. The press also was supportive, but Pobedonostsev, the procurator, withheld endorsement because it was a Protestant institution.[5]

By 1905 its membership reached 2,000, primarily Orthodox but also Roman Catholics, Protestants, and for a time Jews. Its program included educational classes, lectures, and concerts. The staff was American, increasing to four members, including the general director, Franklin A. Gaylord. Russians provided the secretarial help. Priests of the Orthodox Church directed the religious program, and holy days of the

---

2. *The Bible in the World* (BFBS), 1905, 329–32. Prokhanov, *In the Cauldron*, 163. *MRW*, Mar. 1908, 229; Oct. 1908, 728; and Apr. 1912, 316.

3. *MRW*, Dec. 1906, 886. *The Bible in the World*, 1905, 332.

4. Religious Tract Society, *Report*, 1905, 72–73; 1906, 68–70; 1908, 79–81; 1910, 70; 1911, 68–69; and 1912, 65. In 1911 Miss Bechler was reported as "Mr. Bechler," and in 1912 as "Mr. M. Belcher."

5. Colton, *Forty Years with the Russians*, 90–108. For a bibliography of *Mayak*, see Wardin, *Evangelical Sectarianism*, 44–45, 60, 595–96.

church were observed. It offered sessions for Bible study and prayer. For eight years *Mayak* used the gymnasium of a German school, but then Stokes financed a gymnasium with Nobel equipping it. Stokes also purchased a building for a library. *Mayak* survived the First World War, but under the Communist regime it was terminated.[6]

World's Student Christian Federation

Baron Paul Nicolay continued his student Christian ministry in St. Petersburg, leading Bible studies and translating student literature. He first drew German students but beginning in 1903 Russian students as well. The ministry spread to universities in Moscow, Kiev, Kharkov, Odessa, Dorpat, Riga, and Tomsk but will die out in Odessa and Dorpat for lack of leadership. It published pamphlets with four Russian and four American secretaries serving on its staff. Nikolay prepared the way for successful visits of Ruth Rouse, women's secretary of the Federation, in 1907 and for John R. Mott, general secretary of the Federation, in 1909. Mott visited St. Petersburg and Moscow, speaking to male students in large halls. In 1912 the World Federation accepted the Russian Christian student movement into its membership. Mott returned again in 1913, addressing large meetings.[7]

Nikolay was a Lutheran pietist and ecumenical in his sympathies. In his theology, he insisted only on faith in the deity of Christ with the aim of developing a genuine Christian way of life. As a student organization with Protestant leadership, the authorities and the Orthodox Church regarded it with suspicion, and thus it never attained legal status. Some Orthodox were favorable toward it, but many of the clergy attacked it. In 1911 Rouse could hold public meetings in St. Petersburg and Kiev but not in Moscow. She had to announce ten days in advance her public engagements and provide a text of her address. She wrote that not more than five students could meet at one time. In Moscow the authorities forbade Nicolay to hold a public meeting in the auditorium of the Polytechnic Museum. When in 1913 Nicolay was in New York at the time of the acceptance of the Russian movement into the Federation, he stated that the movement in Russia "hangs by a slender thread but God is holding the thread." It will, however, survive the First World War and the Communist revolution, but the Communist authorities will suppress it in 1927.[8]

---

6. *MRW*, Oct. 1901, 788–89; June 1904, 469; and June 1905, 470. Latimer, *With Christ in Russia*, 43–44.

7. Rouse, *The World's Student Christian Federation*, 161–64. *MRW*, May 1908, 386; May 1912, 388–89; and Feb. 1914, 88–89. *The Student World*, July 1909, 101–4.

8. Simons, "The World's Student Christian Federation in Old Russia," *The European Harvest Field*, Jan. 1930, 27–31. Rouse, 112–63. *MRW*, May 1912, 388–89. Pankratov, *Ishchushchie Boga*, 1:140–44. Day, "The Russian Student Movement," *The Student World*, July 1917, 241–49.

PART SIX—Possibilities and Uncertainties, 1905–1917

Evangelical Alliance

With the change of the religious climate with the manifestos of 1905–1906, the Evangelical Alliance attempted to strengthen its ties with evangelicals in the country. The British Council in London in 1906 sent £250 for the new Alliance School in Berlin and authorized £20 for two evangelists in Odessa. In 1908 it appointed John R. Kilburn as "Organizing Secretary for Russia and Finland." He spent over a month in the country and even acquired a permit to visit the prisons in Moscow. On January 26, 1909, the Russian Evangelical Alliance was organized. Earlier in 1908 the government had approved its constitution. The president was Prince Anatol Lieven, the son of Nathalie Lieven, and Baron Nicolay served as vice-president. In addressing the British Council in April 1909, Anatol Lieven noted that the Russian Alliance, now very small in its beginnings, faced a formidable task in working in a country untouched by the Protestant Reformation, inhabited by people speaking forty to fifty languages, and included evangelical sects whose members have no full understanding of the purposes of the Alliance and are very narrow in their thinking.[9]

I. S. Prokhanov and his Evangelical Christian Union were very supportive of the aims of the Alliance. The first conference of Evangelical Christians in September 1909 in St. Petersburg resolved to hold in the city on Thursday of each Holy Week a prayer meeting for Christian unity, inviting all evangelical believers. It was reported in 1912 that over 500 attended. Besides Prokhanov and an additional Evangelical Christian minister, pastors of the German, Estonian, and Swedish-Finnish Baptist congregations also spoke but no Russian Baptist representatives. The choirs of Prokhanov's church and the German Baptist church sang. In 1914 the meeting was held in Nobel Hall. Prokhanov and Johann Kargel and pastors of the German, Latvian, and Swedish-Finnish Baptist congregations participated. Jakob W. Reimer, Mennonite Brethren from South Russia, also spoke.[10]

One of the most influential conferences in the Evangelical Alliance movement was the annual conference at Blankenburg in Thuringia, Germany, which drew evangelicals from numerous countries, including Russia. Reimer was a frequent visitor. F. P. Balikhin, Russian Baptist pastor and evangelist, and Johann Lübeck, German Baptist pastor and editor, also attended.

In the spring of 1906 at Kegel in Estonia, Baron Woldemar Üxküll with others arranged a "Keswick in Russia," patterned after the Deeper Life conferences in Keswick, England, that drew evangelicals across denominational lines. Johann Kargel participated; William Fetler was also present, who sent the report.[11]

---

9. *EC*, May 1906, 69–70; Nov.–Dec. 1908, 140–42; Jan.–Feb. 1909, 24–27; May–June 1909, 67–68; and Mar. 1910, 47–46.

10. *Bratskii listok*, Apr. 1912, 49–50. *Christian Standard*, July 4, 1914, 46.

11. *Die Friedensstimme*, Dec. 12, 1906, 573.

A Mission To Moslems: Plymouth Brethren in Turkestan

A small band of Plymouth Brethren missionaries undertook a notable but today almost forgotten mission to Turkestan (Central Asia) from 1908 to 1917/1918. In 1906 Edmund H. Broadbent visited the Alliance Bible School in Berlin and reported on his trip to Central Asia that German settlers in the region were feeling a concern for a Christian witness among Moslems. The German settlers included Lutherans and Mennonites. The latter had migrated from 1880 to 1884, motivated in part by economic interests but also imbued with eschatological millennial aspirations.[12]

The two pioneer missionaries, who had been students at the Bible school, were Martin Thielmann (1871–1923), a German-Russian of Mennonite extraction, and Rudolf Bohn, a German subject. Both had gone to England for medical training. The two men arrived in Tashkent in 1908 but soon settled in Nikolaipol, a Mennonite village about 150 miles northeast of Tashkent. Both missionaries ministered among Germans and Thielmann with his knowledge of Russian also preached to Russians, but both began to learn the native language. Their work among Moslems was among nomadic Kirghiz, which in winter forced them to go by horseback in the mountains, and among the Uzbeks (or Sarts) in the towns.

The mission field was a challenge to the new arrivals. Bohn admitted that they entered the field "with trembling." Would the Mohammedans "kill us in their fanatical hatred?" Would the government restrict their activities? Bohn also appealed, "We shall need much grace to work among these Mohammedans, and for this we commend ourselves to your prayers." Thielmann noted that the Kirghiz, living in movable tents, were "simple and stupid," even not knowing anything of the Koran. Wagon or horseback were the means of travel. Eating in Khirghiz homes proved to be a trial; on one occasion Thielmann wrote that upon being offered *kumiss,* mare's milk, the national drink, "It is advisable to drink this with closed eyes, for the Kirghiz do not know much of cleanliness."[13]

Thielmann married in 1909 his wife Auguste, who was of great assistance. As a German subject Bohn could not get residency and had to return to Germany but will return in 1913 with a wife, Pauline. In 1913–1914 Thielmann and his wife went about 200 kilometers across the desert to a German settlement on the Tchu (Chu) River to serve Germans and also to minister here among Kazakhs.[14]

12. For limited accounts of the mission to Turkmenistan, see Stunt, *et. al., Turning the World Upside Down,* 543–45, 633; Tatford, *Red Glow Over Eastern Europe,* 160–68, 279–80; and Warns, "Die Anfänge des Missionswerkes unter Kirgisen und Sarten," *Offene Türen,* Nov.–Dec. 1919, 83–87, and also his short account in *Offene Türen* in May–June, 1917, 50. More important are the accounts and letters of the missionaries in *Offene Türen,* 1909–1917, and *Echoes of Service,* 1908–1917. For a biography of Thielmann, see Reimer, *Seine lezten Worte waren ein Lied.* Also see Wardin, *Evangelical Sectarianism,* 53–54. For the Mennonite migration to Turkestan, see Wardin 275–77.

13. *Echoes of Service,* Mar. 1909, 110–12; Aug. 1909, 287–89; Jan. 1910, 11; and Oct. 1911, 389.

14. Ibid., Aug. 1910, 299; Nov. 1910, 419; June 1913, 238; Feb. 1914, part 1, 69; May, part 1, 1914, 179; and July 1914, part 1, 240.

PART SIX—Possibilities and Uncertainties, 1905–1917

The mission received reinforcements. In 1911 Oswald Herholt and his wife Auguste came from Germany and settled near the Thielmanns. Paul Vollrath and his wife Anna arrived in 1912 from Thuringia, Germany, as well as the wife's sister, Miss Minna Wolf, who settled in Tashkent where they developed a medical ministry. Miss Anna Mohn arrived in 1914 and settled at Nikolaipol. In the summer of 1911, Abraham Friesen, the Mennonite Brethren pioneer missionary from South India, visited the mission.[15]

In 1911 Hermann Jantzen, a German Mennonite born in Turkestan, returned from study in Germany where he attended the Alliance Bible School in 1910–1911. He spoke the local language as a native and was even taken for a Moslem. He began his own ministry to Moslems before and after the First World War but will leave in 1923. His brother Abraham will also serve.[16]

Echoes of Service, the journal in Bath, England, of the Plymouth Brethren mission society also called Echoes of Service, provided information on the work of the mission. In 1909, a periodical, *Central Asien*, printed in Germany was published to further the mission but after one issue was superseded by *Offene Türen*, a German journal patterned after *Echoes of Service*.[17]

As the mission was attempting to convert Moslems and not Orthodox, the Russian authorities did not hinder its efforts except in erecting a hospital. In 1910 bricks and cut wood were ready, but the governor unexpectedly forbade further progress. Thielmann wrote in 1912 that the nominal Christians of the Orthodox faith were a stumbling block to the Moslems. He stated that the field was "very hard ground" and work among the Moslems must be done "very quietly." He claimed the Moslems were very fanatical, more the Uzbeks than the Khirghiz, and Christian converts could lead to political problems. The missionaries read and distributed Scripture to the Moslems and used their medical skills, which often provided the most successful approach. In 1912 Paul Vollrath wrote "we are doing 'pioneering work under water,' and nothing is to be seen at first. Such work is very hard, and may seem lost time; but how shall the millions of Central Asia be reached if no beginning be made?" Some Moslems showed genuine interest but converts were very few.[18]

With the outbreak of the First World War in 1914, the Russian authorities interned in Siberia Bohn, Herholt, and Vollrath, all German subjects, with Vollrath, however, able to continue a medical ministry. In July 1917 Thielmann wrote that he and the interned missionaries, as far as he knew, were well. He was happy that Russia

---

15. Ibid., Oct. 1911, 389; Oct. 1912, 379; and Feb. 1913, 49–50. *Offene Türen*, Feb. 1912, 4–5.

16. For sources for the ministry of Jantzen, see Wardin, *Evangelical Sectarianism*, 54, and his autobiography, Jantzen, *Im wilden Turkestan*. Also see *Offene Türen*, May –June 1917, 50, and Nov.–Dec. 1919, 85–86, and *Echoes of Service*, July 1914, part 2, 270.

17. Wardin, *Evangelical Sectarianism*, no. 409. *Echoes of Service*, Mar. 1909, 220.

18. *Echoes of Service*, Sep. 1910, 349; June 1912, 231; July 1913, 279; and Feb. 1914, part l, 1914, 69–70.

was now a free land where the preaching of the gospel could go unhindered. But with the revolutions in 1917 the mission ended. In his work W. T. Stunt listed the termination of terms of service of the missionaries in 1918. F. A. Tatford listed Bohn and Vollrath ending in 1914 at the time of their internment and their two wives and Miss Wolf in 1916. He listed Mr. and Mrs. Thielmann and Miss Mohn terminating in 1917. Neither author listed Mr. and Mrs. Herhold.[19] Johannes Reimer recorded that the Bohn family left in 1921 and Thielmann died in Chimkent, north of Tashkent, in January 1923.

SMALLER BODIES—INDIGENOUS

Molokans

The Molokans were an indigenous Russian sect that accepted the authority of Scripture and rejected the traditions and sacramental system of the Orthodox Church. Because of their pacifism and opposition to all sacraments, they were often thought in the West to be like Quakers. They generally lived in compact settlements that were widely dispersed with concentrations in Taurida Province, the Volga, Caucasus, and Far East. At the beginning of the twentieth century, some estimated 1,200,000 or as many as 2,000,000 Molokans, but A. I. Klibanov, the Marxist researcher, stated that according to official records Molokans numbered 200,00, although he felt this underestimated their strength but still was much closer to reality than the higher numbers.[20]

As described earlier, Molokans were very traditional in their worship. With a weak Christology they were vulnerable to Baptists who made an appeal for personal salvation and a heart-felt religion. Baptists were particularly successful in gaining Molokan converts in the Caucasus and Taurida and gained many of their most successful leaders from their ranks including Vasiliĭ Pavlov, Vasiliĭ Ivanov, Deĭ and Gavriil Mazaev, F. P. Balikhin, Stepan and Ivan S. Prokhanov, and Il'ya A. Golyaev. Molokans were divided into Old Molokans (separated into various factions), progressive Molokans, and evangelical or New Molokans.

Old Molokans

The greatest number of Molokans were traditional. They strongly resisted the Baptist call of justification by faith and the need for baptism and observance of the Lord's Supper. Confrontations between them and Baptists continued into the twentieth century. At the All-Russian Molokan conference in Vorontsovka in July 1905 that observed the centennial of the legalization of Molokanism by Alexander I, A. I. Platonov, Orthodox

---

19. *Offene Türen*, Mar. 1915, 28–29, and Nov.–Dec., 1917, 91–92. *Echoes of Service*, Jan. 1915, part 2, 24, and June, 1915, part 1, 204. Stunt, 633. Tatford, 279–80. Reimer, 95–100.

20. Kolarz, *Religion in the Soviet Union*, 349. Klibanov, 222.

missionary who attended, later wrote that the growth of Baptists at the expense of the Molokans helped him to realize the need for not postponing reform within his own Orthodox mission. He stated that Baptists threatened to swallow up the Molokans and were doing it by "an excellent and seasoned organization, large financial capital, an extensive publishing enterprise, outstanding preachers and orators, and a large galaxy of devoted and disciplined missionaries, attested to a large extent by their moral style of life." In 1900 the Procurator of the Holy Synod reported that in the last fifteen to twenty years in Taurida Diocese over 3,000 Molokans had defected to Stundo-Baptists because of their similarity of belief, excited preaching, extemporaneous prayers, choirs, and fanaticism in propaganda.[21] In three issues from 1903 to 1906, *Missionerskoe obozrenie* carried an extensive correspondence between Deï Mazaev, president of the Russian Baptist Union, and Maksim I. Kalmykov, president of the Old Molokans. The *Baptist* later printed the correspondence in six issues. The controversy was primarily on church ordinances, particularly baptism but also on the Lord's Supper.[22]

In 1909 Vasiliï Ivanov wrote an article "*Novogodnie prazdniki*" (For a New Year Holiday) in which he recorded his reply to D. V. Zaïtsev, a Molokan, who in December 1908 held two lectures in the vicinity of Baku in defense of Molokanism. Zaïtsev maintained Baptists attracted Molokans through their preaching and beautiful singing with musical notes. He asserted that Baptists preached only on faith and the atonement of Christ and rejected good works. Although he admitted that Molokans and Baptists were close spiritual relatives, yet an "impassable abyss" existed as Molokans establish themselves on works "for faith without works is dead." In his refutation, Ivanov stated that Baptists declare works are necessary and cited Deï Mazaev for including it in his preaching. He also said that the gaining of Molokans to the Baptist movement was more than preaching and music; it was the work of the Holy Spirit.[23]

For the second day of Easter in 1909, Ivanov invited Molokan elders and others to his church in Baku for a discussion of baptism and the Lord's Supper. In a Molokan meeting in April 1910, Ivanov discussed with S. Zhabin the question of when the Old Testament ends and the New Testament begins.[24]

William Fetler wrote an open letter to F. A. Zheltov, a Molokan who had sent him brochures. Fetler stated that Zheltov's writing on spiritual baptism was just beautiful words with no fire in them. Fetler averred the Quakers and members of the Salvation Army in England, who do not practice water baptism, burn in them a holy fire, bringing people from sin and eternal destruction, while charging him deterring the

---

21. Platonov, "Molokanstvo, baptizm i nasha velikaya tserkovnaya nuzhda," *MO*, Sep. (2), 1905, 490–91, 493. Procurator of the Holy Synod, *Report*, 1900, 237.

22. *MO*, June 1903, 1305–19; Apr. 1905, 861–82; and Oct. 1906, 443–54. *Baptist*, June 1 to 29 and July 13, 1911.

23. *Baptist*, 1909, no. 4, 11–13.

24. Ibid., 1909, no. 11, 8, and 1910, no. 12, 90.

saved from water. Fetler also stated it was not necessary to debate about water but to compete spiritually to bring more souls to Christ and for us to appear by the Holy Spirit in the perfect image of Christ.[25]

Progressive Molokans

At the centennial congress of Molokans in Vorontsovka, N. F. Kudinov, a spokesman of a progressive party, spoke for change. He presented a comprehensive program. It included the need for a Molokan catechism, teaching the law of God in the spirit of Molokanism in Molokan schools, introducing spiritual-moral conversations for youth and children, and forming choirs for youth and children and provide for their musical training. He also proposed institutions for preparing teachers, opening schools where none existed, a spiritual-moral journal, a council of elders to execute resolutions of the church, and majority vote of all members of a congregation. The conservatives held the upper hand and were able to postpone the consideration of reform to the next congress comprised of delegates from the churches.[26]

The Society of Educated Molokans, a radical party, arose among Molokans under the leadership of Alexandr S. Prokhanov (1871–1912), the brother of Ivan S. Prokhanov, the Evangelical Christian leader. Alexandr had studied for two years at the Faculty of Protestant Theology in Paris and also medicine in England and Russia. He became both a doctor of theology and doctor of medicine. In 1899 he founded the Society of Educated Molokans and was the editor of its publication, *Dukhovnyï khristianin,* which was begun in 1905, editing it until his death in 1912. He was a rationalist and attempted to reconcile religion with science. The pursuit for truth was not guided by faith in the Bible but by one's own judgments. The periodical included articles on debate and conflict with Baptists.[27]

The *Baptist* under the editorship of Deï Mazaev and Vasiliï Pavlov was very critical of the views of Alexandr. An article in 1907, "*Slovo k molokanam*," stated that *Dukhvonyï khristian* from its very first number breathed poison in relation to Baptists. It declared that all evangelicals in close spiritual kinship believed in the Trinity and the authority of the Bible. In 1910 the *Baptist* claimed in an article, "*Molokanstvo,*" that *Dukhovnyï khristian* was especially antagonistic toward Baptists. The writer declared that A. S. Prokhanov was "a completely unbelieving person" and although he expressed "true freedom of spirit and champion of brotherhood, Christian love, this

---

25. Ibid., 1910, no. 12, 90.
26. Platonov, 473–94. Klibanov, 217–21.
27. *Solnitse,* 1939–1940, nos. 1–12, 1–3, 32–33. Klibanov, 215–17. MO, Oct. 1899, 311. See Wardin, *Sectarian Evangelicals,* 179, on a listing of articles in *Dukhovnyï khristian* on conflict and debate with Baptists.

journal expressed only hatred toward Baptists and in addition obviously in some articles a completely anti-Christian course."[28]

New Molokans

In the 1820s Molokans settled in three villages in Taurida Province near the Mennonite colony of Molochna. In the 1890s they had grown to 10,000 but divided into five sects. Three of them remained fundamentally Molokans but the other two adopted sacraments, including baptizing infants, immersing them three times as the Orthodox. As a result of the missionary work of Yakov Delyakov, then an independent missionary, the so-called Second Don Sect developed with evangelical tenets, which became known as New Molokans. Through the mission activity in the 1870s and 1880s of such men as Johann Wieler and Vasilii Pavlov, Baptists formed three Baptist congregations. Rivalry between Baptists and Molokans was intense.[29]

In 1905 the New Molokans established itself as a separate denomination with the name, "Christians of the Evangelical Faith," under the leadership of Zinovii D. Zakharov, a wealthy landowner and member of the Russian State Duma. Through its mission worker Andreï I. Stefanovich, the Deutsche Orient Mission, a Lutheran agency with special interest in the East, began in 1899 to reach out to Russians. In 1905 Russians began to attend its mission school near Berlin. Under its director, Johannes Lepsius (1858–1926), the Deutsche Orient Mission developed a special relationship with the New Molokans. Both the New Molokans and the mission accepted evangelical principles and practiced infant baptism, and both were concerned about the threat of Baptist competition. After attending the New Molokan congress in 1905, Lepsius reported that Baptists had pushed themselves into the stundist movement and "tried to reap what others had sown." No doubt repeating what he heard at the congress from Zakharov, he wrote that after the New Molokans had allowed Baptists to speak at their meetings and cooperated with them in evangelism the Baptists agitated the question of baptism, threw out the net, founded their own congregation, and excluded those not immersed as believers.[30]

In September 1905 the New Molokans held a conference in Astrakhanka, celebrating as did the All-Molokan conference in July the centennial of receiving confessional freedom in 1805 as well as the opportunity of holding their first conference. The New Molokans erected a tabernacle to hold 2,000 while the Old Molokans on the other side of the village constructed a tabernacle to seat 3,000, holding a conference of their own at the same time. Zakharov led his conference, which attracted a number of

28. *Baptist*, 1907, no. 5, 18, and 1910, no. 37, 290–92.
29. For biographical sources on the New Molokans, see Wardin, *Evangelical Sectarianism*, 337–39.
30. Diedrich, "Johannes Lepsius und die südrussische Stundisten," *Akten des Internationales Dr. Johannes- Lepsius-Symposiums* 1986, 230–35. Lepsius, "Das Evangelium in Russland," *Der christliche Orient*, Dec. 1905, 177–87.

guests, who besides Lepsius included P. Z. Easton, American Presbyterian missionary from Persia, Baron Paul Nikolay, head of the Russian Christian Student Movement, and such Swedish missionaries as N. F. Höijer, William Sarwe, and Johannes Svensson. Also present were N. J. Yakovlev from Moscow, and S. P. Zinov'ev, the brother-in-law of Count Korff, an exile in the Caucasus from 1899 to 1905 but now from Orel. A surprising visitor was V. M. Skvortsov, the head of the anti-sectarian mission of the Orthodox Church, sporting a black beard and golden eyeglasses. In asking to say a word, he congratulated them on the freedom granted by the Tsar's manifesto and said "May God again lead us back to unity." On invitation the governor of Taurida Province arrived on the first day with a small entourage of officials.[31]

Zakharov introduced the meeting by noting the occasion to hold the jubilee as well as to thank the Tsar for his grant of freedom. A son of Zakharov, possibly Grigor, read a lengthy account of relations with the government over the years and noted that the New Molokans, marked as stundists, were persecuted in the closing of their meeting hall for three years from 1896 to 1899. At the close of the message the gathering voiced three cheers for the Tsar and sang the Russian national hymn.

The choir on four long rows of benches sang between speeches and prayers with two and three-voice old Molokan songs from the Old and New Testaments. Lepsius noted not only the use of Old Molokan hymns, noting to what he called their shrill harmonization, but also German chorales and Sankey songs. He felt the Russian evangelicals needed to solve the problem of their style of music, suggesting that they should sparingly use German chorales and especially avoid the American "hurdy-gurdy" melodies.[32]

Lepsius also recorded that Baptists had a large congregation in the neighboring village of Novo-Vasilevka, located in a building built by the Baptist leader Deï Mazaev on family property. Mazaev lived in a home near Astrakhanka, and Lepsius wrote he was recognizable by his top hat. On the fourth day of the conference, Mazaev invited those in attendance to gather at the Baptist church hall for a meeting with a midday meal to consider the issue of baptism. Lepsius also accepted the opportunity to go alone with Stefanovich as interpreter to a Baptist meeting where he spoke on baptism.[33]

Only a little over a year later the Congress of Sectarian Rights in St. Petersburg assembled with attendance of Baptists, Evangelical Christians, and New Molokans. Deï Mazaev took the place of Kargel as presiding officer. The New Molokan delegation led by Zakharov's son, Grigor, will walk out because of the intransigence of Mazaev and the Baptists in refusing to accept baptized infants as church members. Svensson, who had also been at the Astrakhanka congress, and Walter L. Jack, later school director in Astrakhanka, will write very critical accounts of Mazaev and his domination of the

31. Lepsius, "Das Evangelium in Russland," Jan. 1906, 8–16, and Feb. 1906, 29–30.
32. Ibid., Jan. 1906, 10, 13–14.
33. Ibid., 14–15.

proceedings. The question of Baptists and baptism will continue to be a problem for the New Molokans. Ernst-Ferdinand Klein, a German Lutheran, wrote, "I must hear and converse very much about Baptists. It is one of the burning questions in Christian circles." Klein had attended in 1908 the fourth congress of the New Molokans, a gathering that attracted delegates from five provinces—Saratov, Samara, Orenburg, Vladimir, and Tambov—as well as from the Crimea and Caucasus.[34]

The opening in Astrakhanka in 1907 by the Deutsche Orient Mission of a Teacher and Pastor's Seminary under Walter L. Jack was of great benefit to the New Molokans. In 1908 Zakharov gave land for the construction of a two-story building and helped to raise money for it. At the cornerstone laying, Deï Mazaev spoke! The building was opened in 1909. At times the authorities closed the school and reopened it but will prohibit pastoral training. The school never gained legalization and was officially closed in 1910. It continued illegally, still existing in 1913 and possibly to the next year.[35]

The New Molokans will survive until after the First World War. In his work on sectarians, F. M. Putintsev in 1935 will write that the churches of the New Molokans no longer existed. The churches were either burned or were submerged into the Baptists or Evangelical Christians.[36]

Malevantsy

The Malevantsy, the heretical millennial sect that arose out of stundism in the Province of Kiev in the 1880s, had reached its peak by 1905. According to F. M. Putintsev, it began to decline seriously after 1905 and especially after 1917. He wrote in 1935 that in Kiev region only a "pitiful remnant" remained. He claimed they were much like Tolstoyans in the belief that God was within man. They were vegetarians, rejecting drink and tobacco, and opposed military service.[37]

SMALLER BODIES—COLLEGIAL

Methodists

Methodism was an eighteenth century revival movement in England that spread worldwide. It was evangelical and Arminian in theology, evangelistic, and advocated holy living. It was a connectional body with bishops, superintendents, and

---

34. See Wardin, *Evangelical Sectarianism*, 391, for references to the Congress on Sectarian Rights in St. Petersburg. Klein, *Russische Reisetage*, 22. *Bratskiï listok*, 1909, no. 2, 11–12.

35. For the school in Astrakhanka, see the account in the chapter, "Theological Education: The Problems."

36. Putintsev, *Politicheskaya rol' i taktika sekt*, 472–73.

37. Ibid., 456–58.

local preachers, unlike Baptists whose polity rested on the independence of the local church. Its attitude toward other evangelicals was ecumenical and thus a body that was collegial as it sought relationships with them.

As some other bodies it developed first a base in Finland. As a duchy within the Russian Empire with its western culture and own Lutheran state church, Finland proved more hospitable to smaller Protestant movements than was the case in Russia. The Methodist mission commenced in Finland in 1883. Methodists formed in 1892 the Finland and St. Petersburg Mission, which became in 1904 the Finland and St. Petersburg Mission Conference.[38]

Although the Methodist Finnish work grew, St. Petersburg for many years was just a small outpost of the Finnish work. In August 1907 St. Petersburg reported just twenty full members and thirty-two scholars in the Sunday school. When George A. Simons arrived that year as the new superintendent, he claimed in a later report that he found only a small Swedish group, served for fifteen years by a local pastor, composed of "10 aged women and a feeble man, not one of whom belonged to our church." He also admitted "for many years it was thought wise to report some 25 or more Methodists in St. Petersburg to the Board of Foreign Missions."[39]

The Methodist work in Russia took a decided upswing with the decision in 1907 to make St. Petersburg the center of the Finland and St. Petersburg Mission Conference and the sending of George A. Simons (1874–1952), a vigorous young man, thirty-three years of age with command of both English and German, to head the work. He arrived in St. Petersburg in the same year as William Fetler. His father, George Henry Simons, born in Germany on a north Frisian island, immigrated to America where he became a prominent member of the German Methodist Conference. His mother was Ottilie Schulz from Wisconsin. For four years Simons worked as a bank clerk. His first pastoral service was in the First German M. E. Church of Brooklyn, where his father had served. He earned degrees from Baldwin-Wallace College, New York University, and Drew Theological Seminary.[40]

Simons came at a propitious time when there was still wide opportunity for evangelistic work. Just the year before in 1906 Hjalmar Salmi, a native of St. Petersburg but educated in Finland, held a revival among Finns in two villages outside St. Petersburg that resulted in the conversion of over 150. Salmi was appointed pastor for St. Petersburg and preached in Russian, Finnish, and Swedish. Simons also had

---

38. For the commencement of Methodism in Finland, see Carlson, "The Beginnings of Methodism in Finland," *The Gospel in All Lands*, Nov. 1896, 503–8.

39. Methodist Episcopal Church, Board of Foreign Missions, *Report*, 1907, 126–27, 131. Simons, "Report of the Superintendent," World Methodist Council, mns., United Methodist Church. For an excellent review of Methodism in Russia with an analysis of its journal, *Khristianskiĭ pobornik*, see Dunstan, "George A. Simons and the Khristianski Pobornik," *Methodist History*, Oct. 1980, 21–40.

40. "Biographical Sketch of George Albert Simons," mns., United Methodist Church. Simons, "Observations and Experiences in Russia and the Baltic Countries," *The European Harvest Field*, Sep. 1929, 14–15.

the help of another preacher, but with the departure of the earlier local preacher for Swedish services this work had to be started anew. Simons did not look for American missionaries, which he felt would alarm the Russian authorities, but sought to enlist native speakers. Simons gained the services of Anna Eklund of Helsinki (1867–1949), trained in deaconess homes in Germany, who spoke Finnish, Swedish, German, and some Russian. In 1908 she became head of Bethany, a deaconess home in St. Petersburg, which operated in a five-room apartment. Z. D. Zakharov, the New Molokan leader and member of the State Duma, was present at the opening. In 1907 the North German Conference transferred to the Finland and St. Petersburg Conference the Methodist congregation in Wirballen, started in 1893 in what today is Lithuania.[41]

In his report in 1910, Simons reported a significant advance in the work. With the assistance of Salmi, who preached in three languages, and a couple of other preachers, preaching was conducted in Russian, Finnish, Swedish, Estonian, German, and English. The constituency was over 500 with nine nationalities represented. Membership itself was 139 with 59 probationary members. The Sunday school with 278 pupils and 15 officers and teachers was conducted in Russian but with classes for other nationalities. In 1909 the authorities legalized the Methodist society in St. Petersburg. Work continued in Finnish villages near St. Petersburg as well as in Kovno and Wirballen with preaching also in Estonia and Siberia. Simons also listed men in training for service in Russia who will use Russian as their first language but other languages as opportunity arose. A lady was appointed for educational work.[42]

The Methodist work made a significant advance in publication and translation. Almost immediately after his arrival, Simons launched in January 1908 a quarterly in English, *Methodism in Russia*, edited by Simons and printed by the Methodist Press in Rome, to arouse support in Europe and America. As an indication of its ties with other evangelicals, the periodical included an article, "The Students in Russia," by Baron Paul Nicolay. The journal informed readers that the bookstore of J. Grothe in St. Petersburg was a depository of Methodist literature. The most important publication was *Khristianskiĭ pobornik* (Christian Advocate), a monthly in Russian that Simons began in January 1909. The periodical continued until 1917. It was primarily instructional, devotional, and missionary and an advocate of Methodist doctrine, but it avoided trumpeting evangelical goals or criticism of the regime or the Orthodox Church. Simons reported in 1910 that the publication was issued in 1,000 copies with extra issues for Christmas, Easter, and at conferences. He also noted the printing of *The Standard Catechism* and that the translation of the *Doctrines and Discipline of the Methodist Episcopal Church* was nearing completion with the first part in print. Additional literature included a pamphlet in Russian, "The Methodists: Who They Are

41. Copplestone, *History of Methodist Missions*, 4:320, 367–69. Methodist Episcopal Church, Board of Foreign Missions, *Report*, 1907, 126–31 *Khristianskiĭ pobornik*, Jan. 1909, 4–5.

42. Methodist Episcopal Church, Board of Foreign Missions, *Report*, 1910, 476–81. Simons, "Report of the Superintendent," mns.

and What They Want," and some of John Wesley's sermons. In 1909 the Methodist Book Concern for Russia was established with the deaconess home initially serving as depository.[43]

In 1911 the Conference was separated into a Finland Conference and a Russian Mission Conference, which left Simons free of responsibilities in Finland. In 1912 Simons reported that the Russian Conference had around 500 members, thirteen preachers, fifteen charges, and nine Sunday schools with over 700 children. In St. Petersburg Simons spoke an average of eight times a week as well as on frequent trips elsewhere. The deaconess home had three sisters and two probationary sisters. In St. Petersburg itself, however, the Methodist church had only 130 members and probationers. The Conference prepared a Russian hymnal with about 100 selections, mostly translations of hymns from English. The Russian Conference contributed for the year $424 for conference benevolence and $235 for foreign missions, besides supporting a day school in China and one in Korea.[44]

As other evangelical work, the Methodists also faced increasing restrictions, although it evaded the regulation forbidding children's services for children. In 1912 the authorities ordered Methodist services in St. Petersburg suspended. A few weeks later Simons was able to get permission to hold meetings as a Methodist society but forced to rent at another location a large hall that seated over 400 but with no room for a Sunday school. In his report in 1913, Simons noted the failure of the government to enact legislation to carry out the promise of religious liberty in the manifestos of 1905–1906 and officials following their own rules. On the other hand, he claimed the Methodist work "enjoys not only the good will of the authorities, but also the intelligent and sympathetic interest of officials in many places."[45]

Simons noted in his 1913 report that Methodists had dedicated five chapels in Russia and were building a sixth chapel in Siberia. As with other evangelicals, all the chapels but one were designated as "houses of prayer" with the designation of "church" reserved for the Orthodox Church. The one exception was the church building in Kovno, dedicated in 1909 with the title of "church," granted through the "special favor" of the prime minister Peter Stolypin and the "kindly interest" of the Tsar. From a gift of Mrs. Fanny Nast Gamble in America, daughter of the German Methodist patriarch in America, William Nast, Simons opened a prayer house in St. Petersburg that seated up to 200 persons. It was dedicated in 1915.[46]

---

43. Simons, "Report of the Superintendent," mns., 19. Also see Dunstan, "George A. Simons and the Khristianski Pobornik."

44. Methodist Episcopal Church, Board of Foreign Missions, *Report*, 1912, 414–15.

45. Ibid., *Report*, 1912, 415, and 1913, 409–10.

46. Ibid., *Report*, 1913, 410–11. Dunstan, 35, 39.

PART SIX—Possibilities and Uncertainties, 1905–1917

Salvation Army

The Salvation Army arose in England in the nineteenth century under William Booth as an evangelical movement with an evangelistic and social ministry. It was formed like a military organization. In theology it followed Arminian and holiness tenets but did not observe any ordinances such as baptism and the Lord's Supper. As Methodists, the Salvation Army established a base in Finland, working among both Finns and Swedes, before it entered Russia proper. By 1893 it had forty-one officers and twelve corps in addition to four slum corps and outposts. In 1895 it built a Temple in Helsingfors (Helsinki), and two years later in 1897 Booth himself visited Finland. In 1906 it had grown to 74 corps and outposts, 184 officers, and 10 institutions.[47]

A chance meeting in a railway compartment in August 1908 between Bramwell Booth, son of William Booth, and W. T. Stead, editor of *The Review of Reviews,* led Booth to suggest to Stead in his forthcoming visit with Peter Stolypin, prime minister of Russia, to ask entry for the Salvation Army into Russia itself. In answering Stolypin's questions, Stead assured him that the Army did excellent work and did not meddle in politics. Stolypin was impressed, felt there should be no obstacles, and asked for a copy of its statutes. The publication of the Salvation Army, *The War Cry,* ran an article in September with the headlines, "The Opening of Russia" and "At Last the way is Clear." In March 1909 Booth visited St. Petersburg for two days, visiting top officials but not Stolypin who was ill. He also visited with Miss A. I. Peuker and Paul Nicolay.[48]

Booth sent Lieutenant-Commissioner Povlsen and his wife to St. Petersburg where they lived for eighteen months, but as the authorities had not issued as yet permission they could not operate as Salvation Army officers. In September 1911 Stolypin was assassinated, and in the spring of 1912 the British Embassy sent information that the Salvation Army was denied entry. The Povlsens left, and Booth will die later in the year.[49]

In 1913 the Salvation Army opened an exhibit in the Finnish pavilion at a hygienic fair in St. Petersburg, which displayed the work of the Army in Finland. It received first prize for its exhibit. From its booth an illustrated brochure in Russian was distributed. The Salvation Army gained permission to publish a Russian edition of *The War Cry* but with the requirement of changing its name to *Vestnik Spaseniya* (The Messenger of Salvation). Adam Pieschevski, a converted Polish Jew, became editor, while Constantine Boiye of Finland agreed to be the registered owner. William Fetler, a supporter of the work of the Salvation Army, provided his subscription list for the new publication. The first issue was distributed at the pavilion and with

---

47. For the beginnings of the Salvation Army in Finland, see Wiggins, *The History of the Salvation Army,* 4:45–51, 150. Salvation Army *Yearbook,* 1906, 4.

48. *The War Cry,* Sept. 5, 1908, 13, and May 15, 1909. Wiggins, 5:72–75, 303–4.

49. Wiggins, 5:75. Becker, "Ten Years in Russia," *All the World,* Oct.–Dec. 1955, 266. Larsson, "10 Years in Russia," part l, *The War Cry,* Dec. 27, 1975, 13.

the second issue the publication was allowed to be sold on the streets by uniformed Salvationists with the words, "*Vestnik Spanseniya*," on their banners. The attempt to change the name on the banner to "*Armiya Spaseniya*" (The Salvation Army) brought reprimands, and some sellers carried both names on either side of their banners, using the side thought most appropriate at the moment.[50]

A writer to *Tserkovnyĭ vestnik*, the Orthodox periodical, after buying a copy of *Vestnik Spaseniya* expressed alarm at the appearance of the Salvation Army. He said it had begun working on the street. He called it "a new church enemy" with a "strong inner order, wealth, devoted to the ecstasy of the people."[51] The Salvation Army had finally slipped in and will survive the First World War, but the Communist regime will terminate it in 1923.

Evangelical Association

The Evangelical Association, a German body in the USA, closely related to Methodists, began a mission in Riga, supported by its Women's Missionary Society, from the plea of a small group of members for a missionary. The North German Conference appointed Reinhold Barchet, a German subject, who arrived in Riga in 1911. After some effort, Barchet received a permit from the regime in St. Petersburg in 1912. The authorities approved its constitution, and the mission took the name, "Evangelical Association, White Cross."[52]

In September 1912 the mission dedicated a rented hall, located in the center of Riga. A congregation was organized in the same year, and by the following year a mission was opened across the river at Hangensburg (Agenskalns). The two congregations numbered seventy-five in 1913. While Barchet was in Germany, the First World War broke out and he was forced to serve in the German army. He was severely wounded in 1915 in Flanders. Although it lost its leader, the mission survived the war, but its members were scattered, located now in the new state of Latvia. It continued as a German and Latvian work but in 1938 lost over sixty percent of its membership when Germans in Latvia were repatriated to Germany. With the occupation of Latvia by the Soviet Union in 1940, the mission ceased.[53]

Church of Christ (Russian Poland)

As recorded in the chapter on "Theological Education: Its Problems," The Disciples of Christ in America, a restorationist body in the USA, which sought to restore the

---

50. Larsson, "Ten Years in Russia," part 3, *The War Cry*, July 26, 1969, 2.
51. *TsV*, 1913, no, 4, 1449–50.
52. Eller, *History of Evangelical Missions*, 185–86.
53. Ibid., 187–91.

polity and unity of the Apostolic church, provided assistance to I. S. Prokhanov of the Evangelical Christian Union in his establishment of a Bible school in St. Petersburg in 1913. At the time both Prokhanov and the Disciples looked upon each other as brethren, supporters of Christian unity, although Prokhanov rejected the view of the latter that immersion of a candidate was sacramental, necessary to complete one's salvation.

About this time in Warsaw in Russian Poland, Waclaw Zebrowski left the Roman Catholic Church and became a priest of the Mariavites.[54] In a further spiritual quest, he visited Prokhanov in St. Petersburg and other evangelicals elsewhere and came to accept evangelical principles. Several Protestant denominations attempted to gain him for their cause. Although he wished baptism as a believer, he rejected baptism from Russian and German Baptists, which would force him to identify as a Baptist, which his followers would strongly oppose, and would also, as he said, cause him "to bear again the yoke of sectarianism." As patriotic Poles, he and his followers would have considered it treasonous to be baptized by a Russian.

Upon acquaintance with Louis R. Patmont, a member of the Disciples of Christ from America but who had lived in Eastern Europe when his father was a Bible colporteur, Zebrowski and his followers organized themselves on May 1, 1913, as a Church of Christ. On May 5 Patmont, whom Zebrowski considered a "neutral" brother, baptized him in the Vistula River with Zebrowski in turn baptizing the elders of his church. It was not long before about forty others were baptized with others awaiting baptism. On May 19 Patmont with Z. T. Sweeney from America, who had now jointed Patmont, participated in ordaining Zebrowski and his young preachers with the laying on of hands.

In writing in 1945, Patmont wrote that the invasion of the Germans in 1914 brought an end to this ministry. Zebrowski died several years before a second German invasion in 1939. In any case, the Disciples lost contact whatever remained of the movement.[55]

Smaller Bodies—Competitive

Plymouth Brethren

The Plymouth Brethren, who arose in the early nineteenth century in England as a non-sectarian movement, were simlar to Baptists in their views on biblical authority, evangelism, and believer's baptism by immersion. They differed from Baptists in the Lord's Supper, which they called "breaking of bread." It was observed weekly with a time of thanksgiving and prayer. They recognized no order of clergy nor formed

---

54. For the development of the Church of Christ in Warsaw, see Patmont, "The Restoration Movement in Poland," *Christian Standard*, June 21, 1913, 3–4, and Patmont, "Bible Christians in Eastern Europe," *Christian Standard*, Jan. 20, 1945, 6.

55. Patmont, "Bible Christians in Eastern Europe," *Christian Standard*, Jan. 20, 1945, 6.

conferences with centralized authority. The larger group of Plymouth Brethren was called "Open Brethren" for their willingness to relate to other evangelicals. Frederick Baedeker, as has been noted, was able to relate to all evangelical groups in the Russian Empire and was a strong supporter of the Evangelical Alliance, including the Blankenburg Conference. Baptists and Plymouth Brethren cooperated in Germany in establishing the Alliance Bible School. Plymouth Brethren students of the school were pioneers in a mission to Moslems in Turkestan in the early twentieth century. The views of the Plymouth Brethren were attractive to many early evangelicals in Russia, such as Pashkovites and stundists, for their lay ministry, open communion, and freedom from denominational organization. Baptists, however, looked upon the Plymouth Brethren or the "Darbyite" influence, named after J. N. Darby, a leading Plymouth Brethren figure of the "Exclusive Brethren" branch, as a threat to their pastoral leadership, close communion, and denominational organizations. Abraham Kroeker, a Mennonite Brethren, closely allied with Baptists, wrote an article in 1907 entitled, "Die darbystische Gefahr" (The Darbyite Danger).[56]

A successor to Baedeker and his ministry in Russia and elsewhere was Edmund Hamer Broadbent (1861–1945), a Plymouth Brethren from England, who engaged in a fifty-year ministry that covered Europe and Russia with trips in the Baltic, Caucasus, Turkestan, and across Siberia.[57] His attitude was different from Baedeker. Unlike Baedeker he promoted Plymouth Brethren assemblies. His bias against Baptists is seen in his book, *The Pilgrim Church*, in which he charged, contrary to normal organizational developments, that the original evangelical congregations in Russia, "emphasized the priesthood of all believers and liberty of ministry," while German Baptists imposed a system of pastoral control. He also charged that the Russian government "favored the Baptist system," and the "large gifts from American Baptists" were divisive for those who wished to maintain their independence.[58]

Although independent assemblies on the Plymouth Brethren model, nurtured by Broadbent and others, existed, their congregations did not survive as a self-sustaining movement. Their dispersal over a wide territory, lack of strong native leadership, and failure to form a cohesive center within their own polity proved fatal. Under the harsh political realities of the Communist regime, they will be absorbed into the Baptist and Evangelical Christian movements.

---

56. See Jordy, *Die Brüderbewegung in Deutschland*, 2:184–86, for letters from Russian believers in 1913 with expressions of Plymouth Brethren ideals. For the attitude of German Baptists toward Plymouth Brethren, see Wardin, *Evangelical Sectarianism*, 228. Kroeker, "Die darbystische Gefahr," *Die Friedensstimme*, 1907, no. 25, 314–15.

57. For a biography of Broadbent, see Lang, *Edmund Hamer Broadbent*. For Broadbent's travels and ministry, see Wardin, *Evangelical Sectarianism*, 52–53.

58. Broadbent, *The Pilgrim Church*, 341–42.

PART SIX—Possibilities and Uncertainties, 1905–1917

Seventh-day Adventists

Seventh-day Adventists, who arose in America in the nineteenth century, became a world-wide movement with their advocacy of the seventh day and their own special eschatological views. Their preaching highlighted prophetic themes from the books of Daniel and Revelation. They were similar to Baptists in local church autonomy but yet were part of a strong cohesive denominational body. They exhibited mission zeal and upheld a high code of morality for each member, which opposed tobacco, coffee, and pork with many of them vegetarians. As Baptists and Mennonite Brethren, they observed believer's baptism by immersion. They observed the Lord's Supper generally each three months and as Mennonite Brethren with foot washing. In music German Adventists tended to use *Zionslieder*, also used by German Baptists, and Russian Adventists tended to favor *Gusli,* produced by Prokhanov. They condemned other Christians as "false" and part of a "spiritual Babylon." In their evangelism they were considered a special threat, seeking converts from Baptists and other evangelicals.[59]

In 1911 S. D. Bondar, official of the Council of Spiritual Affairs of the Orthodox Church, produced a book on Seventh-day Adventists in Russia. It was so carefully researched and balanced that J. T. Boettcher, then president of the Russian Union of Adventists, gave it his highest praise. Bondar reported that they numbered in 1901 only 1,288 members in thirty-seven churches and thirteen workers, but with the manifesto on religious liberty in 1905 Adventism began to exhibit "special vitality." By 1911 it had grown to almost 4,000 members in 149 congregations and groups. In 1914 the membership was 5,880 members in 240 churches with forty ministers.[60]

In December 1905 the Adventists met in a general meeting in St. Petersburg with Russians, Germans, Estonians, and Latvians in attendance. In 1906 Adventist leaders sent to Nicholas II a memorial, declaring their loyalty to the regime and later in the year the regime issued an edict granting the Adventists freedom to propagate their views. On January 1, 1908, the Adventists in Russia began operating as a separate union from the German Union in three local conferences in the Baltic, Caucasus, and South Russia, which included fields in Siberia and Central Asia. In 1911 the Russian Union divided into two separate unions—a Russian Union and a Siberian Union with five fields, including the Volga, the Urals, Turkestan, Western Siberia, and Eastern Siberia.[61]

In 1907 Adventists formed an Adventist Tract Society. A publishing house near its union headquarters in Riga began in 1908 publishing literature in Russian, German, Latvian, Estonian, and Polish. Also Adventists distributed a monthly publication,

---

59. For a dispassionate account of Seventh-day Adventists in Russia, see Bondar, *Adventism 7-go dnya*. For Bondar's description of their faith and practice, see pp. 65–66. For an account of Seventh-day Adventists from 1905 to 1914 by a Seventh-day official, see Lohne, *Adventists in Russia*, 73–80. For confrontations between German Baptists and Adventists, see Wardin, *Evangelical Sectarianism*, 247.

60. Bondar, 31–33. Lohne, 69, 77–79.

61. Lohne, 74–75, 77. Bondar, 31.

Maslina (The Olive-Tree), printed by the Adventist International Tract Society in Hamburg. For theological education, Adventist ministers went to Friedensau in Germany, which maintained a division for Russian students.[62]

As with other sectarians, the regime began to restrict Adventist operations. The publishing effort was closed, although Adventists found a private company to do its printing. In 1910 government officials began to attend general or local conferences. The government also began prohibiting general meetings, and officers of conferences could meet only locally with churches or committees. With increasing persecution and closing of churches, Adventists in 1912 sent a deputation to the Ministry of the Interior. Also a deputation met with the director of the Department of Spiritual Affairs who told the delegation that the regime did not recognize conferences or unions but only local churches and forbade ministers from traveling and ministering in other localities.[63]

Although comparatively small and widely dispersed, Adventism will survive the First World War and the Communist regime. Unlike so many other smaller bodies that either disappeared or were absorbed, Seventh-day Adventists, in spite of division, have maintained their presence in Russia and adjoining territories to the present day.

Pentecostals

In the early twentieth century, Pentecostalism was a new movement that spread rapidly from its beginnings in America to other parts of the world. It took early root in Scandinavia, and adjoining it, Finland and St. Petersburg, as well as other parts of the Empire. Pentecostalism not only accepted revivalism, the necessity of a spiritual rebirth of the individual, and a life of holiness through an immediate filling of the Holy Spirit, but also the miraculous spiritual gifts of the Holy Spirit as exercised in Apostolic days. They claimed such gifts as glossolalia or speaking in tongues, interpreted as a sign of the baptism of the Holy Spirit, divine healing, and prophetic knowledge. Pentecostalism began as a revival movement among existing denominations and did not seek immediately a separate denominational status, but with opposition to its message soon formed its own congregations and denominational structure. Both Baptists and Evangelical Christians were vulnerable to its advance.[64]

Thomas B. Barratt (1862–1940), a Methodist minister in Oslo, Norway, accepting Pentecostalism while in the USA in 1905–1906, became an apostle for the movement not only in Scandinavia but also in Russia. He began publishing in 1910 *Korsets*

---

62. Bondar, 31, 100.
63. Spicer, *Our Story of Missions for Colleges & Academies*, 25. Lohne, 77–78.
64. For the penetration of the Pentecostal movement into the Russian Empire, see Wardin, "Pentecostal Beginnings among Russians in Finland and Northern Russia, 1911–1921, *Fides et Historia* 26/2 (Summer 1994), 50–61. For a listing of bibliographic sources, see Wardin, *Evangelical Sectarianism*, 348–51.

Seier (The Victory of the Cross), which in 1912 also appeared in Swedish and Finnish and from 1913 to 1915 in Russian. Barratt will not completely break with Methodism until he formed his own church in Oslo in 1916 but in the meantime traveled outside Norway with the new message. He journeyed six times to Finland and also visited St. Petersburg, the first one in 1911 when he wrote that he visited "engineer Prokhanov," staying at his home. He preached for Estonian Baptists as well as Prokhanov's congregation.[65]

Evidence of Pentecostal and holiness manifestations appeared even earlier in Estonia before Barrett's visit to St. Petersburg in 1911. When F. B. Meyer, an English Baptist, preached in Estonia in 1902, he was surprised to find among Estonian Baptists the gift of tongues and even heard of cases of casting out evil spirits. As already noted, Baron Woldemar Üxküll, Baptist leader in Estonia, helped to host a "Keswick in Russia," a Deeper Life Conference in 1906. It also appears that Üxküll invited Barrett as early 1907 to visit Estonia, but Barrett could not come at the time. Even though Üxküll edited for a time *Der Hausfreund*, and raised money in America for a Baptist school in Russia, he will eventually leave the Baptists and become a Pentecostal.[66]

As expected, Prokhanov and other evangelical leaders in Russia learned of the Pentecostal movement before Barrett's appearance. As early as 1908, *Khristianin*, Prokhanov's paper, produced two articles on the movement. The first article, "O dukhovnykh probuzhdeniyakh" (On Spiritual Revivals), criticized believers who dwelt on Pentecost and the miraculous days in the first chapters of the Acts of the Apostles without noting at the end of the book Paul's imprisonment in Rome. The second article, "Ozhidat' li nam' durgoï Pyatidesyatnitsy?" (Do We Await Another Pentecost?), noted that in Paul's writing glassolalia was a very minor gift and only a sign for "unbelievers," not evidence of the filling of the Holy Spirit.[67]

William Fetler, who as a student at Spurgeon's Pastors' College in England experienced first-hand the Welsh Revival of 1905 and a disciple of Charles G. Finney on the filling of the Holy Spirit, was far more open to Pentecostalism. Services in *Dom Evangeliya* exhibited a Pentecostal fervor and his critics accused him of Pentecostalism, which he denied. Andreï E. Leushkin, a critic of Fetler, claimed Fetler acted like a Pentecostal behind his pulpit and in conversation told Leushkin that while abroad he was attracted to it. In 1910 Fetler launched a revival journal, *Gost'* (The Friend), which was designed to be the organ of a new organization, "The Brotherhood of the Acts of the Apostles." Its members, men and women, would receive a biblical name and as the

---

65. For information on Barratt, see Bloch-Hoell, *The Pentecostal Movement*, 75–86. On Barrett's first visit to St. Petersburg, see *Korsets Seir*, Oct. 15, 1911, 159, and Nov. 1, 1911, 164.

66. *The Baptist Quarterly* 45/1 (January 1993), 30. *Korsets Seir*, Oct. 15, 1911, 159. Bebbington, *The Gospel in the World*, 100–103.

67. *Khristianin*, 1908, no. 2, 16–19, and no. 8, 1–15.

first apostles who were baptized by the Holy Spirit to give themselves entirely to the Lord.[68]

Pentecostal Penetration in Finland and St. Petersburg

Probably one of the first, if not the first, Russian preacher to accept Pentecostalism was Aleksandr I. Ivanov, who in 1909 became pastor of the Evangelical Christian Church in Helsinki, Finland. From records A. I. Klibanov found in the archives of the Department of Police, Ivanov claimed he started preaching Pentecostal doctrine in 1910. With the split of his church in 1913, Ivanov developed his own work, renting a building in Helsinki with an appeal to sailors on warships in the harbor and personnel in the Helsinki garrison. With his preaching against militarism, a feature at this time in American Pentecostalism, some sailors on the warship *Slava* refused in 1915 to participate in military drill and were imprisoned. A few months later in November the authorities exiled Ivanov with two members of his congregation to Siberia and attempted to stop the Pentecostal meetings, but the attempt was unsuccessful.[69]

A letter in 1913 from Frank Bartleman (1871–1936), Pentecostal evangelist and writer from America who traveled to Finland and St. Petersburg in 1913 and again in 1914, reported another defection to Pentecostalism among Russian Evangelical Christians in Vyborg, a town in Finland near the Russian border. Bartleman claimed that before his arrival a Russian of the Evangelical Christian faith in Vyborg had received the baptism of the Holy Spirit, and the Evangelical Christian leader in Helsinki who went to correct him also had a similar experience. The leadership of the Evangelical Christians in St. Petersburg sent one of its leading ministers to win back the Pentecostal converts but if unsuccessful to exclude them. But he also underwent a Pentecostal experience, spoke in tongues, and carried the new message with zeal to Helsinki. The Evangelical Christians excluded all three men from fellowship as well as Ivanov and others who accepted Pentecostalism in Helsinki.[70]

Bartleman preached a series of messages in Vyborg, interpreted in both Finnish and Russian, but left the town. He went on to St. Petersburg for four days, probably accompanied by Ivanov, where he ministered in an Estonian-Swedish mission in five meetings and will return in 1914 for six days for eight meetings. In his letter in 1913 Bartleman claimed the three men who had had the Pentecostal experience in Viborg were determined to carry Pentecostalism into Russia proper, and in a 1914 letter noted that the three were already busy at work in the country. Unfortunately Bartleman failed to give their names. An issue in Prokhanov's paper, *Utennyaya zvezda*, in 1914

---

68. *Pis'ma k brat'yam*, 14–15, 95–96. *MO*, Jan. 1911, 190–92. Klibanov, 309.

69. Klibanov, 304–6.

70. For Bartleman's letter, see *The Bridegroom's Messenger*, Jan. 25, 1914, 4, and Aug. 1, 1914, 3. For the exclusion of Pentecostals by Evangelical Christians, see *Pis'ma k brat'yam*, 57.

warned of Pentecostalism that had appeared in Helsinki, Viborg, and St. Petersburg and listed A. I. Ivanov, S. I. Prokhorov, and Pekka Hakkarainen (or Khakkarainen). One of the three who went into Russia was probably Prokhorov, general evangelist for Evangelical Christians who may have been sent from St. Petersburg to Viborg. A second was probably Hakkarainen, an Estonian who could preach in both Finnish and Russian, who had begun work as a Pentecostal preacher in Vyborg in May 1913 and in 1914 participated in a revival among Finns in the city. A third was probably Nicolaï P. Smorodin, who lived in Vyborg and later became pastor of the Pentecostal congregation in St. Petersburg. Place and date indicate that Ivanov was probably not one of the three, but he also joined the others in a mission to Russia.[71]

Pentecostalism Outside St. Petersburg

Pentecostalism was also soon spreading outside St. Petersburg. In his letter of 1914, Bartleman claimed that one of the three he had met in Viborg was now preaching in a large hall in another part of Russia. He also reported that two young Russian brethren had gone to Tiflis to bring Pentecostalism there. Bartleman observed, "so the fire is kindled north and south. I believe it is yet going to meet in the middle and set all Russia afire." In 1914 *Baptist* reported that in absence of the pastor Smorodin began preaching in the Baptist church in Millerovo in Rostov *oblast*. The pastor sent a warning to the Baptist paper, calling Smorodin a wolf in sheep's clothing, and claimed his preaching brought sad results. *Gost'*, Fetler's journal, reported in 1914, issue no. 6, Pentecostalism's appearance among Baptists and described in issue no. 9 the disruptive activity of Smorodin in Millernovo.[72]

The two young Pentecostals who went to Tiflis to the Baptist church, Maslov and Stepanov, were not only noted in Bartleman's letter but *Utrennyaya zvezda* warned that they were on the way. They came from Finland with Evangelical Christian certificates. According to Bartleman, at least 250 of the Tiflis congregation of about 270 accepted the new teaching, and numbers had been healed and baptized in the Holy Spirit.[73]

One of the pastors of the Tiflis church, Andreï E. Leushkin, became alarmed and telegraphed Prokhanov in St. Petersburg as well as Fetler and Ivan Neprash, a leader in Fetler's church. Prokhanov sent a circular letter to all Evangelical Christian congregations. But N. V. Odinstov, a Baptist who visited Tiflis, found no heresy, and Vasiliï Ivanov, now editor of *Baptist,* tended to tolerate it. Prokhanov now took the opportunity to condemn the Baptist leadership for condoning heresy. On its part the

---

71. *Utrennyaya zvezda*, 1914, no. 15, 6. For references to Hakkarainen, see Schmidt, *Die Pfingstbewegung in Finnland*, 109, 205. For references to Smorodin, Prokhorov, and Ivanov, see *Istoriya*, 397, and Poysti, "A Recent Moscow Happening," *The Gospel Call*, June 1946, 3, 5–7.

72. *The Bridegroom's Messenger*, Aug. 1, 1914, 3. *Baptist*, 1914, nos. 13–14, 23. *Gost'*, 1914, no. 6, 55, and no. 9, 226. Klibanov, 306–7.

73. *The Bridegroom's Messenger*, Aug. 1, 1914, 3. *Utrennyaya zvezda*, 1914, no. 15, 6.

Tiflis congregation permitted the Pentecostal missionaries to preach in their own private quarters under the supervision of more experienced brethren. Maslov and Stepanov will leave, and in October N. P. Smorodin and A. I. Ivanov arrived, who in turn were followed by Prokhorov and a certain Gerasimov. Finally the Tiflis church disciplined thirty of its Pentecostal members, sixteen of whom returned to the church while fourteen were excluded with some of them also eventually returning. Nevertheless a separate Pentecostal group remained under the leadership of A. I. Kapranov.[74]

The Visit of Andrew D. Urshan, 1916

Andrew D. Urshan (1884–1967), a Nestorian from Persia, converted in an American Presbyterian school in Urmiah, migrated to Chicago in 1901 where he became a Pentecostal, visited Tiflis in 1916. Two years before in 1914 he had returned to Persia for mission work but because of war he entered Russia. In Tiflis he found, however, only a few Pentecostals but preached in the Baptist church, leaving behind a strengthened Pentecostal group. He now spent a month in a colony of Nestorians and Armenians but then left for St. Petersburg, but now called Petrograd. Because of the loss of his passport and other papers, the U.S. consul gave him a temporary passport to expedite his trip across Russia on his return to America.[75]

In Petrograd Urshan found that the Pentecostals, strongly opposed by both Orthodox and evangelical Protestants, were meeting in secret and in serious decline because of the entrance of heretical doctrine. During his comparatively short stay, Urshan was successful in helping to revive the work. New converts wanted to be immersed, but he was somewhat in a quandary whether he should baptize them in the name of the Trinity or in the name of Jesus only. As early as 1910 Urshan had accepted the formula of Jesus only, based on examples in the book of Acts, but wanted more study on the issue and opposed rebaptism of anyone already immersed with the Trinitarian formula. Upon the request of a convert to be baptized in the name of Jesus only, he then baptized him and many others and even now rebaptized those who had been baptized in the name of the Trinity who requested it. He even allowed an old Russian brother to rebaptize him in the name of Jesus only. Urshan left for Oslo, where he visited Barrett, then to England and in June 1916 sailed to the USA.[76]

74. *Pis'ma k brat'yam*, 57–58. *Baptist*, 1914, nos. 9–10, 17–18, and nos. 17–10, 23. Belousov, "Tryasunstvo," *Baptist*, 1925, no. 2, 15. *Istoriya*, 398. Moskalenko, *Pyatidesyatniki*, 51–53. Klibanov, 306.

75. For Urshan's life, see his two autobiographies—*The Story of My Life*, and a revised and expanded version with an epilogue by his son Nathaniel A. Urshan, *The Life Story of Andrew Bar David Urshan*. The expanded version first appeared in the late 1920s in Urshan's publication in Chicago, *The Witness of God*.

76. *The Weekly Evangel*, Sep. 30, 1916, 9. Urshan, *The Life Story*, 167–72, 179–80. An independent account that corroborates Urshan's account of the introduction of the Jesus only baptism in Russia is Smorodin, "Vospominaniya," mns., 3, SBHLA. On the basis of primary sources, the account of Zhidkov in *BV*, 1957, no. 3, 62, that Urshan introduced Pentecostalism in St. Petersburg in 1911 is clearly in error. Urshan was not in St. Petersburg before 1916.

PART SIX—Possibilities and Uncertainties, 1905–1917

Urshan's short stay in Russia left a continuing impact on Pentecostalism in the country. Pentecostalism in northern Europe now increasingly accepted the Jesus only formula with such early leaders as Ivanov and Smorodin accepting the practice. Smorodin became so important in the movement that its adherents began to be called "Smorodintsy." This body continues in Russia as "Evangelical Christians in the Spirit of the Apostles." They exist apart from the much larger "Voronaevtsy" or "Union of Christians of the Evangelical Faith," introduced by Ivan E. Voronaev in Ukraine in 1921, who observe the Trinitarian formula in baptism.

30

War and Revolution, 1914–1917

THE SUDDEN OUTBREAK OF the First World War in July 1914 came as a surprise. It not only brought havoc to the people of Russia but also will bring again another period of suppression for evangelical sectarians. Because of their origin, it will also put severe pressure on the German Baptist Union as well as the Mennonite Brethren.

In spite of increasing restrictions, evangelicals, however, were still continuing to expand. Shortly before, German Baptists were joyfully celebrating fifty years of history of their first churches in Volhynia. After decades the German Baptist church in St. Petersburg finally in 1912 acquired its own property. In 1915 the Methodists dedicated their own building in the city, while I. S. Prokhanov in 1913, after years of appeal, finally gained permission to open a Bible school.

But war and revolution will play out their devastating effects. The German Baptists and other Germans in Volhynia and other western territories will be exiled from their homes. The German Baptist church in St. Petersburg will cease. After the revolutions, the Methodist work in Russia itself will terminate. The Bible school in St. Petersburg will cease operating and will not reopen until a number of years after the war had ended. The war unleashed on the sectarians reactionary forces, which slandered them and encouraged government action to close churches and exile leaders as experienced during the dark days of suppression in the 1880s and 1890s.

In the long run, the war brought the collapse of the Tsarist regime that had off and on brought so much anxiety and concern to the evangelical cause. It will then lead to the establishment of an atheistic regime that in the end will attempt not only the suppression of evangelicals but all believers of any faith. As under the Tsars, it too will have its shifts in church-state relations.

PART SIX—Possibilities and Uncertainties, 1905–1917

Political Support from Evangelicals

With its rufusal to stop its mobilization in support of Serbia, Germany declared war on Russia on August lst (July 19, o.s.). As he related several years later, William Fetler led a procession with the church's choir after the morning service on Sunday, August 2 (July 20, o.s). They stopped on street corners with a short message, prayer, and the singing of the national anthem. At three in the afternoon, Fetler with the choir and members of his church stood with banners before the Winter Place where a great crowd gathered. Tsar Nicholas and other members of the imperial family with ministers of state appeared and heard the Tsar declare his willingness to fight as long as one last enemy solider remained on Russian soil. As a further sign of loyalty, on September 1 (o.s.) the St. Petersburg *Dom Evangeliya* and Moscow Baptist congregations issued an appeal to gather for prayer for the Tsar, the imperial house, and the commander-in-chief, Duke Nikolaï Nikolaevich, and for God's blessing. The St. Petersburg church also appealed to Baptist churches to contribute to a Good Samaritan Fund to assist the Red Cross.[1] *Dom Evangeliya* opened a hospital of eighty beds in the city. *Gost'* reported in January 1915 twenty-five wounded were already in the infirmary, including Jews and Tartars. The Baptist church in Moscow also opened a hospital, but the authorities demanded the hanging of an ikon on the wall, removing a sign, and staffing the personnel with Orthodox. The Baptists agreed to all demands except their insisting that the manager must be Baptist since he managed the funds Baptists themselves had raised, but the authorities refused granting this concession and the hospital closed. In a report in *Missionary Review of the World*, Baptists also opened medical facilities in Kiev and Odessa. In Baku the Molokans opened an infirmary for wounded soldiers with the Baptist church under Vasilii V. Ivanov contributing to the effort. Women in the churches prepared bed linens, such as in the Baptist churches in Baku and in Balashev in Samara.[2]

The Evangelical Christians under I. S. Prokhanov also gave their support to the war effort. In its first issue after the beginning of the war, *Utrennyaya zvezda* declared that all sectarians were ready to sacrifice their lives for the country. In a gathering of Evangelical Christians on July 20, Prokhanov stated that their first responsibility was to pray to avert war but if impossible then pray to shorten its calamity and to call on God to bless the armed forces and friendly governments. Prayer was raised to bless the Tsar and his house, the government, and friendly states and for wisdom and strength for full victory. The editorial "*Voina*" (The War) in *Utrennyaya Zvezda* on July 25 carried similar sentiments. Evangelical Christian churches held prayer meetings for the war effort.[3]

---

1. Fetler, "Revolution and Religion in Russia," *MRW*, May 1917, 339–40. Klibanov, 332–33.
2. *Utrennyaya zvezda*, Sep. 19, 1914, 7. *Gost'*, 1915, 18. Kandidov, *Sektantstvo i mirovaya voïna*, 15. Curtiss, 385–86. *MRW*, Nov. 1914, 866. *Baptist*, 1914, nos. 15–16, 17–18, and nos. 21–24, 5–6.
3. *Antireligioznik*, 1931, no. 7, 85. *Utrennyaya zvezda*, July 25, 1914, 1. Klibanov, 332.

In writing to his Disciples of Christ supporters in America, Prokhanov stated that his church collected 1,000 rubles for a contribution to the Committee of the Empress for medical needs of the military. He also wrote that every church of the union was assisting in caring for sick and wounded soldiers.[4] Evangelical Christians also contributed to families of reservists now in war, and women prepared bedding.

Mennonites, although exempt from military service, were also quick to show support for the war effort. In Chortitsa on July 22 Mennonites prayed for victory and the health of the Tsar and his house. In the Molochna, Mennonite leadership called on young men to volunteer for the medical corps and young men to transfer from the Forestry Service to the corps. Mennonites contributed money to the government, the Red Cross, sick and wounded, soldiers' families, as well as wagons and horses for transport. They also provided medical facilities, supplies, and beds for wounded soldiers.[5]

The German Baptist periodical, *Der Hausfreund*, made little comment on the war during the few months it still existed. In a review of world events in a segment entitled "*Der Weltkrieg*" in its August 6 issue, it wrote that "War is always a misfortune for the populace, at present it signifies a fearful catastrophe for Europe." It also stated, "Therefore all believers of the earth should continue with prayer and supplication that the Lord make an end of the bloody work of war."[6]

In its last issue in September, it printed, however, a lengthy article, "The Patriotic Manifestation in Landau," that described a large patriotic rally of German-speaking settlers in the German Catholic colony of Landau in the Odessa region. On Sunday August 3 /16, eight to ten thousand came on foot or by wagon. The meeting included speeches, all in Russian, cheers for the Empire and the Russian Army, and the singing of the national hymn. One of the participants was Bernard J. Herb, the German Baptist pastor of Johannestal since 1912 and formerly a missionary to Poles, who began his message from Scripture, "Throw all your cares on Him for He cares for you." The brass choir from his church with other brass choirs provided music.[7]

Anti-Sectarian Attack

Even before the outbreak of the war, Ioann I. Vostorgov in 1913 in his booklet, "*Vrazheskiĭ dukhovnyi avangard*" (The Hostile Spiritual Vanguard) charged Baptists and Adventists, originating in German Lutheranism and receiving funds and literature from Germany, were engaged in a cultural conquest of Russia. In the heated chauvinistic anti-German atmosphere, other authors produced their articles and booklets

---

4. *The Christian-Evangelist*, Dec. 3, 1914, 1571. *Utrennyaya zvezda*, Aug. 29, 1914, 1, and Oct. 24, 1914, 6.

5. *Utrennyaya zvezda*, Aug. 8, 1914, 5. Toews, *Czars, Soviets & Mennonites*, 63–66.

6. *Der Hausfreund*, Aug. 6/19, 1914, 251.

7. Ibid., September, 10/23, 1914, 283. Miller, *In the Midst of Wolves*, 149–50.

on stundists and Baptists for their German ties and alleged German sympathies.[8] In *Missionerskoe obozrenie* in December 1915 and January 1916, F. Kruglov published two articles of attack. One was entitled, "The Moral Side of the Life of the Baptists and Reasons for Their Gravitation toward the Germans," and a second, "Sectarianism in 1914," in which he described Baptists and Evangelical Christians and their alleged German sympathies. In 1915 Andreï M. Rennikov published in Petrograd a work of 395 pages, *Zoloto Reina: O Nemtsakh v Russii* (The Gold of the Rhine: On the Germans in Russia) on the alleged pro-German sentiment and pacifism of stundists and Baptists.[9]

In the State Duma in August 1915, N. B. Shcherbatov, Minister of the Interior, charged that Baptists with many sincere believers are "undoubted instruments of the German government." Father Stanislavskiï, a member of the Duma from the Right charged sectarians for pro-German views and their soldiers surrendering at the first opportunity. M. I. Skobolev of the Left, however, attempted to counteract such allegations, and in 1916 P. N. Miliukov, head of the Constitutional Democratic Party, condemned unsubstantiated charges and the persecution of their pastors and churches. But the allegations and slanders continued along with repressive measures.[10]

On the issue of military support for the war, both Marxist and Orthodox writers attempted to blacken the reputations of evangelicals for their own ideological reasons. Marxists will play up the military participation of evangelicals to prove they were anti-revolutionary supporters of the Tsarist regime, while the Orthodox will play up their avoidance of war service to demonstrate their danger to the regime.

The Orthodox writer, Dmitriï L'vovich in his article, "On War and Military Service" in *Missionerskoe obozrenie*, unfairly lumped evangelicals with other sectarians as Dukhobors, Molokans, and Tolstoyans who opposed military service. As a major source, he quoted from the Baptist work in 1909, *Baptisty, ikh uchenie i zadachie*, which condemned the shedding of blood and admonished Baptists to seek the eradication of the spirit of war and its militaristic spirit. In his work Rennikov charged that *Gost'*, Fetler's journal, kept silent on the war and other journals supported prayer to stop the bloodshed. He also attempted to cite examples of public opposition to the war effort.[11]

Unlike Mennonites, Russian and German Baptists and Evangelical Christians accepted military service, but yet charges of pacifism and lack of military support continued against them. In 1913, the year before the war, William Fetler, on hearing that the Ministry of Internal Affairs intended to label Baptists as a dangerous sect

---

8. Vostorgov, *Vrazheskiï dukhovnyi avangard*. See Blane, 87–88, for a discussion of the work by Vostorgov.

9. See Wardin, *Evangelical Sectarianism*, 400–402, for a bibliographic listing of writers attacking evangelicals for pro-German origins and sentiments and lack of support for the war.

10. *MO*, Jan. 1916, 137. Curtiss, 384–86.

11. *MO*, Jan. 1915, 58–60, 62–63. Rennikov, *Zoloto Reina*, 384–85.

because of the refusal of its members to serve in the army, visited the vice-president of the Department of Spiritual Affairs citing the Baptist confession that accepted the obligation of military service. Fetler said that some Baptists may reject service in objection to the oath the military required.[12]

An official in the Moscow Baptist Church wrote in September 1914 that thousands of Baptists were in the military. In 1916 an official of *Dom Evangeliya* in St. Petersburg (now called Petrograd for a less sounding German name) claimed that many in the congregation had lost their lives or were wounded in battle. I. S Prokhanov stated in 1914 that around fifty men of his Evangelical Christian congregation were in the army.[13]

The chief of the police administration of Kiev Province reported to the governor of Kiev that he could not cite any definite cases of sectarian opposition to the war but it came from rumors based on the belief that sectarians opposed breaking the command, "Thou shalt not kill," and believing war was murder. He pointed to the rural clergy as often using such allegations simply to counteract stundist influence.[14]

On the other hand, there is evidence that not all Baptists and Evangelical Christians were ready for military service as Fetler and Prokhanov attempted in their statements to the authorities. Some Baptists sought alternative service or refused military service altogether. In his visit to Petrograd and other cities near the front, J. G. Kokki, a Baptist from Finland, was told by a solider that many Russian Baptists refused to engage in warfare on the front but were allowed to serve in other capacities such as medical assistant or serving in the wagon train, bakeries, or sanitary department. The chief chaplain of the Armed Services reported in January 1917 that many sectarians, weary of the war and hoping for revolution, were refusing to fight. At this date many other soldiers as well felt the same way. A Tolstoyan journal, *Istinnaya svoboda*, reported that from the beginning of the war to April 1, 1917, military regional courts charged 114 Baptists and stundists, 256 Evangelical Christians, and 249 unspecified for refusing military service, a very small number compared to their numbers as a whole, but probably still others were able to avoid the courts.[15]

SUPPRESSION: RUSSIAN BAPISTS AND EVANGELICAL CHRISTIANS

The regime sought suppression of evangelicals through various measures, such as exile, closure of churches, forbidding conferences, and termination of publications. Leading members of the Russian Baptist Union were exiled or imprisoned. Charges were made

12. *Utennyaya zvezda*, Aug. 2, 1913, 6.
13. Klibanov, 333–34. *The Christian-Evangelist*, Dec. 3, 1914, 1571.
14. Klibanov, 335.
15. ABFMS, *Report*, 1916, 187. Ivanov, "The Making of a Conspiracy: Russian Evangelicals During the First World War," *REE* 22/5 (Oct. 2002), 35. Kandidov, 38.

that German money built William Fetler's *Dom Evangeliya*, and a fire broke out on its premises. The bookstore and the dispatch department of *Gost'* suffered heavy damage. While leading a prayer service in *Dom Evangeliya* on Saturday evening in November, authorities arrested William Fetler and while in custody told him to settle his affairs in three days and then exile to Siberia. Through the appeal of influential friends, he and wife and three-month old son were allowed to go abroad, first to Sweden but then after five months to the United States.[16]

Robert Fetler, William's younger brother, had been studying at Spurgeon's Pastors' College in London but returned in 1914 to Petrograd for military training. In 1916 authorities ordered him to leave Petrograd within seven days to go to Yakutsk in eastern Siberia. The regime charged him with gaining support from England (even though a Russian ally) and the Pioneer Mission in plotting to turn Russia into an English colony. He petitioned to go abroad, as his brother, but was allowed in the meantime to stay in Ufa. After the February revolution he returned to Petrograd, but soon after the Communist revolution in October he left for Siberia, settling in Omsk, and then in Vladivostok in the Far East.[17]

Ivan Neprash, William Fetler's co-pastor and former teacher at Astrakhanka Seminary, was expelled from Petrograd in 1915. He avoided the police by traveling for almost two years in European Russia and even to Irkutsk in Siberia. But he was drafted to serve in the army for four months. After the February Revolution in 1917, he returned to Petrograd, but soon after the Communist revolution in October he and his wife traveled for two months by way of Siberia and Japan to settle in the USA. He became dean of the Russian Bible Institute, founded in late 1917 by William Fetler in Philadelphia.[18]

In Odessa in December 1914, the authorities exiled Mikhail D. Timoshenko, editor of *Slovo istiny,* and seven other sectarian ministers to Narym region in Siberia. After his release in 1917 he wrote of his exile in a work, *V Narymskiĭ kraĭ: Vospominaniya i vpechatleniya ssyl'nago*, published in Moscow in 1917. Beginning in May 1917, it was published in installments in *Slovo istiny.*

Vasiliĭ G. Pavlov, pastor of the Russian Baptist Church in Odessa, was set to be arrested in December 1914 but he was absent and escaped to Tiflis. The Odessa Court, however, sentenced him in 1916 for eight months for publishing a brochure, "Rebirth Through Baptism." He avoided arrest by extended travel. From Tiflis he went to Moscow, where he was elected elder in 1916. He took a trip from Moscow to the Volga, Orenburg, Turkestan and then by way of the Caucasus back to Moscow. After

---

16. Blumit and Smith, *Sentenced to Siberia*, 29–36. Fetler, "A Short History of the 'Dom Evangeliya' in Petrograd," *The Friend of Missions*, Dec. 1933, 165. *WHZ*, Mar. 6, 1915, 77.

17. *Baptist Times and Freeman*, May 8, 1914, supp., xvi. *The Gospel in Russia*, Apr.–June 1917, 1–2. Fetler, "A Short History," *The Friend of Missions*, Dec. 1933, 164–66. Ivanov, 35.

18. *The Friend of Russia*, June 1918, 14. Steeves, "Russian Baptist Union," 107.

the February revolution he remained in Moscow where he and his son, Pavel, with Timoshenko established the publishing house of Slovo istiny.[19]

Another Baptist leader, the outstanding pastor and evangelist, F. P. Balikhin, was exiled in early 1915 to Narym region. The veteran evangelist and pastor in Baku, Vasiliĭ V. Ivanov, wrote in December 1915 that he would be imprisoned for two months. Andreĭ Kostykov, pastor of the Baptist church in Elizabetgrad, was arrested in 1914 and was exiled for two years in Voronezh. But Deĭ Mazaev, president of the Russian Baptist Union, and his brother Gavriil, pastor in Omsk, avoided arrest, as during the suppression of the 1880s and 1890s. Gavriil's church, however, was closed in 1916.[20]

Fortunately for the Evangelical Christians, Prokhanov escaped arrest. In 1916 he was indicted as the founder of the All-Russian Evangelical Union, alleged a revolutionary organization, but because of increasing problems in the declining years of the Tsarist regime he was never tried. Martin Schmidt, a former teacher at the Lodz Seminary but who then taught in Prokhanov's Bible School in St. Petersburg, was exiled in 1914 as a German subject to the far north. His wife returned to Germany, but he was not released until 1918, enabling him to return to his home in Königsberg. Fedora I. Balousov was an Evangelical Christian evangelist whom the Evangelical Christian Union sent to work in Odessa. In 1914 he was arrested with other brethren and sent to Narym region but will be freed at the time of the February revolution.[21]

Both Russian Baptists and Evangelical Christians suffered not only the exile of their pastors but also the closing of many of their churches. While in Sweden, soon after his deportation in 1914, William Fetler reported that eleven more pastors had been deported, ten to Siberia, and six churches closed. Before his own exile in 1916, Robert Fetler wrote: "More than a hundred of our preachers have been exiled; some to the remotest parts of Siberia. The prayer halls have been closed in many places." In his autobiography, Prokhanov wrote that all evangelical meetings were forbidden in Petrograd and congregations in other parts of Russia were closed. Members of his church in Petrograd then met in secret. In December 1914 Ebelov, the Military Governor-General of New Russia, closed six congregations in Odessa, Kherson Province—four Baptist, one Evangelical Christian, and one Adventist. At the same time in Odessa, M. D. Timoshenko, as already noted, and others were exiled. In March 1915, Ebelov closed in Taurida Province five Baptist churches, including Balikhin's church in Astrakhanka, and five Evangelical Christian congregations.[22]

---

19. *Slovo istiny*, Oct. 1917, 160. Füllbrandt, "Wassily Pawloff," WHZ, Mar. 26, 1922, 94–96. *Utrennyaya zvezda*, Mar. 18, 1916, 6.

20. *Slovo istiny*, Oct. 1917, 160. *Pioneer Review*, May 1916, 17. *Istoriya*, 533. *Seyatel'*, July 1916, 10.

21. Prokhanov, *In the Cauldron*, 169–70. WHZ, June 5, 1915, 184, and Sep. 14, 1919, 151. *Istoriya*, 519.

22. ABFMS, *Report*, 1915, 198. *The Friend of Missions*, Dec. 1933, 165. Prokhanov, *In the Cauldron*, 169–70. *Slovo istiny*, Oct. 1917, 160.

PART SIX—Possibilities and Uncertainties, 1905-1917

The large *Dom Evangeliya*, Fetler's church in Petrograd, went through many vicissitudes. The church had been opened on Christmas Sunday in December 1911. With its worship services and publishing, it was a great evangelistic center. In 1913 the authorities closed the church, alleging it was not built according to specifications they had approved, but the church continued holding its services in two theaters, two concert halls, and a public hall throughout the city. On January 12, 1914, the *Dom Evangeliya* reopened. Upon the beginning of the war in July, the church opened a medical facility for wounded soldiers. In November, the authorities will exile Fetler and will also close the hospital, although it will be later reopened. The authorities again closed the church and considered using it as a barracks but instead it was reopened. The building was used two weeks at a time, however, as a mobilization center, which disrupted its services. Robert Fetler was forced to leave in 1916, and the church will be taken over as a hospital and barracks. After the February Revolution, it again reopened. The *Dom Evangeliya* continued under the Communist regime until authorities seized it around 1927 for a club house.[23]

The regime also curtailed publications. *Slovo istiny*, the Baptist paper in Odessa, was stopped and its editor exiled. The regime had suspended *Baptist* in 1913 but allowed it to appear again in 1914 in Baku under the editorship of Vasiliĭ V. Ivanov, but the war will end it. Surprisingly *Gost'*, Fetler's journal, will survive the war but will be terminated in 1919. Both of Prokhanov's publications continued, *Khristianin* to 1917 and *Utrennyaya zvezda* to 1922.[24]

Prokhanov's bookstore "Raduga" in Petrograd will continue, but the Raduga publishing firm in Halbstadt in the Molochna will again come under scrutiny. In 1914 Raduga was closed, but by petitions from Heinrich Braun, the manager of the firm, it reopened in January 1915 but prohibited from publishing uncensored German or Baptist books. In an article in *Missionerskoe obozrenie* in May-June 1915, it was claimed that Raduga was a major means for Germans and Baptists in spreading their literature through desk and wall calendars, booklets, and leaflets but also selling Prokhanov's publications produced in Petrograd by Petrograd Raduga and an independent typography. In July 1915 Peter J. Dyck recorded that the authorities arrested Jakob Braun, but his brother, Heinrich, disappeared at the time. If Raduga in Halbstadt survived, its production was strictly circumscribed.[25]

---

23. Fetler, "A Short History," Dec. 1933, 164–66, and Mar. 1934, 44–45.

24. For the years of publication of various evangelical journals in this period, see Wardin, *Evangelical Sectarianism*, 182 and 330.

25. Prokhanov, *In the Cauldron*, 169–70. Ivanov, 32. *MO*, May–June 1915, 188. Dyck, *Troubles and Triumphs 1914-1924*, 17–18.

Suppression: Mennonite Brethren and German Baptists

During the suppression of evangelicals in the 1880s and 1890s, the Mennonite Brethren and German Baptist Union in Russia, having gained legalization as non-Russian bodies, were protected. The outbreak of the First World War, however, put both organizations in serious jeopardy. As bodies of German origin, ties, and language, the populace regarded them with great suspicion as potential enemies. The failure of Germans to assimilate with Russian culture, the growing animosity toward their land acquisitions and wealth, the fear of the expansion of Germany, and the resentment of the penetration of German culture made all German subjects a target of attack. The regime proscribed German publications, which terminated the German Baptist periodical, *Der Hausfreund*, the Mennonite Brethren *Die Friedensstimme*, and the Old Mennonite *Der Botschafter*. Authorities again directed their attention to the publishing house in Halbstadt in the Mennonite colony of Molochna. German was also prohibited in public discourse. According to entries in Peter J. Dyck's diary, in 1914 the regime forbade preaching in German but allowed it again in early 1915 and then forbade it in 1916. Conferences were also forbidden.[26]

The German population was affected by legislation of forced liquidation that forced Germans to sell their property and move from areas close to the western frontier. Tsar Nicholas signed the first law in February 1915 that particularly affected the German Baptists in Volhynia, one of the strongest areas of German Baptist membership, who were now forced to leave their homes and churches. The Tsar signed a second liquidation law in December that greatly extended the territory to include the original Mennonite colonies to the East, a law that began to be implemented by the fall of 1916 although not fulfilled. A third law, approved in February 1917, would have forced all Germans into Siberia, but the fall of the Tsarist regime stopped its implementation. Mennonites also had the double threat of losing their exemption from military service, but such legislation was never passed.[27]

Mennonites also received harsh criticism in Russian publications. Andreï M. Rennikov not only attacked all Germans in his book, *Zoloto Reina*, but in an article in *Novoe Vremya*, May 23, 1915, wrote: "The danger lies in the spirit of the Mennonites, their attitudes, self-isolation, disdain toward the Russian people, exploitation of Russian peasantry, tendency to support Germanism, and everything that goes against Russian national interests." In 1916 S. D. Bondar from the Ministry of Spiritual Affairs, who had written balanced and scholarly work on Baptists and Adventists, published in Petrograd, *Sekta Mennonitov v Rossii*, a work that stressed the German character of the Mennonites, making them appear dangerous to the country. After the

---

26. Dyck, *Troubles and Triumphs*, 13, 14, and 25. Warns, "Die Drangsale der Mennoniten in Russland während der Kriegs- und Revolutionsjahre 1914–1920," *Offene Türen*, May–June 1922, 37.

27. Abraham Friesen, *In Defense of Privilege*, 217, 232, 237–39.

war Abraham Kroeker wrote a critique of the work, claiming the author, after gaining the confidence of the Mennonites, distorted the evidence to support his thesis.[28]

With their compact settlements, most of which were east of the areas of military operations and because of their location and limited time for implementation of the legislation on liquidation, Mennonite Brethren did not suffer nearly as badly as the German Baptists from the effects of the war. As noted, the closure of churches and deportation of members seriously affected German Baptists in Volhynia. In addition, two of their associations, the Weichsel-Gebiet Association in Russian Poland and the Latvian Association in the Baltic region, were in the military zone that suffered military invasion and occupation. The Latvian Association not only experienced closure of churches and exile of pastors but also the exodus of refugees to St. Petersburg and further into Russia proper. After the war, K. Freywald, a German Baptist from Libau, wrote that with the war and occupation the Baptist work was completely suspended with many ministers and most members of the churches fleeing to other parts of Russia. Although not experiencing occupation, the Estonian Association farther to the north also suffered from the closing of their churches.[29]

A number of Baptist pastors of the German Baptist Union were exiled. In 1914 the authorities exiled F. A. Arndt, pastor of the German Baptist church in St. Petersburg, and his family to the Volga, which will terminate the German Baptist work in the city. Far to the south in Odessa, Johannes Lübeck, pastor in Odessa and an editor of *Der Hausfreund*, was imprisoned in December 1914 with other sectarian pastors and transported to Narym region in 1915. His wife and daughter left for Germany, his youngest son was in Ufa, and his eldest son was a prisoner of war in France. After the war, he wrote a work, *Meine Verbannung nach Siberien*, about his experiences in exile. In late fall 1915, Severin Lehmann, German Baptist leader and pastor of the Zions Church in Riga, age sixty-eight, and J. A. Frey, leading Latvian Baptist leader in Riga, were exiled to Irkutsk in Siberia. Lehmann's health deteriorated. He was moved to Nishniï-Udinsk in Siberia and in 1916 suffered a stroke. In March 1918 he died. Frey, however, was able to return to Riga after a year and a half in exile.[30]

In Russian Poland a number of German Baptist pastors also faced exile. Eugen W. Mohr, pastor of the large First Lodz church and former teacher at the Lodz Seminary, was exiled to the Volga in August 1914. He was able to serve German Baptists at Reinsfeld but died of a stroke in June 1917. Peter P. Brandt of the Second Lodz Church was also exiled in August to the Volga and served in the Reinsfeld area. Others from Russian Poland included Gustav Freutel from Zyardow, who was sent to Vyatka; Emil J. Bonikowski near Chelm, who was deported to Siberia; and Franz Ondra from Zelow

---

28. See Friesen, *In Defense of Privilege*, 446–47, ft. 60, for the quotation from Rennikov's article. For Kroeker's critique, see *Christlicher Familienkalender*, 1918, 59–60.

29. *WHZ*, Nov. 10, 1918, 183, and Jan. 19, 1919, 16. *EC*, Oct.–Dec. 1917, 143.

30. *WHZ*, June 26, 1915; Nov. 10, 1918, 183; and Sep. 14, 1919, 151. Lübeck, *Meine Verbannung nach Siberien*, 21, 35. *Der Familienfreund*. Nov. 15, 1927, 3–4. Miller, *In the Midst of Wolves*, 24–25.

who died in the Province of Tomsk in September 1915. Wilhelm Tuszek in Zezulin went into hiding and then returned when the area was under German occupation, but his congregation was gone. His assistant, Kurt Brechlin, however, was exiled from 1915 to 1918. Frederick Brauer, pastor of the German Baptist church in Warsaw and president of the German Baptist Union, was able to continue at his post during the war. Pastors born outside Russia and as foreigners subject to exile were Mohr, Brandt, Freutel, and Ondra.[31]

A considerable number of German Baptist pastors from Volhynia, also subject to the liquidation decree, were exiled. Gustav A. Spingath from Stawetzkaja-Sloboda, Christopher R. Baier from Toporischtsch, Adolph K. Bandzmer from Novo Rudni, Johann J. Fuchs from Sorotschin, and Heinrich J. Piltz form Horstschick were forced to settle in Siberia. Robert Jacksteit from Rozyszcze was exiled to Astrakhan, Martin Jeske from Lucinow to Tsaritsyn, Bernhard J. Goetze from Ivanowitsch to Crimea, and Eduard A. Wuerch from Neudorf to Outer Mongolia. Robert J. Petasch from Zhitomir was also deported. Johann E. Pritzkau, the pioneer pastor in Alt-Danzig, farther east in Ukraine, however, avoided exile.[32]

Suppression: Smaller Religious Bodies

Because of their German ties in theological education, publication, personnel, and their antimilitary views, the Seventh-day Adventists were also under suspicion. Authorities forbade the dissemination of their literature and closed their churches and missionary conferences. Some Adventists who were inducted into the army served in medical or other noncombatant roles. Others, however, were sentenced to hard labor for objection to military service.[33]

Methodists and the Salvation Army, comparative late comers, fared rather well during the war period. George A. Simons, the superintendent of the Methodist mission and an American citizen, was able to stay in Russia until 1918, a year after the Communist revolution, when he was recalled by the American government. The periodical, *Khristianskii sobornik*, continued until 1917. Although the war dampened the German work it brought to the fore the English work with Sunday evening services and the English classes that had already begun in 1912. Although the services of the deaconesses to care for the wounded were rejected, they nevertheless continued their social work. On the other hand, the German pastor in Riga was exiled and the work there suspended. The Methodist work in Virbalis and Kaunas in Lithuania was

---

31. Kupsch, 120, 144, 167-68, 178-79, 201, 405. WHZ, June 26, 1915, 205. Miller, *In the Midst of Wolves*, 28-29, 44-45, 93, 126-28.

32. Miller, *In the Midst of Wolves*, 30, 44, 72, 90-91, 103-4, 130-33, 156, 194, 224-25, and 236-37.

33. Heinz, "Origin and Growth of the Adventists in Russia," *JAHSGR* 10/4 (Winter 1987), 40. *Seventh-day Adventist Encyclopedia*, 1352.

seriously disrupted with the flight or removal of their congregations, but under the German occupation the work here revived.[34]

Without government approval, the Salvation Army enrolled its first corps of eight members in Petrograd on December 20, 1914, and a second corps of five members in March 1915. It also opened a Slum Post outside the Moscow Gate that provided food and clothing to families of conscripted soldiers. In September it opened a home for refugee women and children. The circulation of *Vestnik Spaseniya* continued on the streets of Petrograd. The Salvationists in Canada equipped five ambulances for the Russian front. In October 1915, however, authorities interrogated members of a house meeting. At a house meeting in November, authorities threatened worshipers with fines or imprisonment for attending illegally, but through the intervention of Queen Mother Olga the charges were dropped. After the February Revolution, the Salvation Army was maintaining by the middle of September seven corps, two homes for children, two slum posts, and a women's hotel.[35]

Suppression: Aftereffects

Even though the suppression was severe with many closed churches and pastors in exile, as during the suppression of the 1880s and 1890s, not all churches were closed or all pastors exiled. The presidents of the Russian and German Baptists and Evangelical Christians were able to keep their positions and the major leader of the Mennonite Brethren, Heinrich Braun, avoided deportation. In spite of the termination of most evangelical publications, the Baptist paper *Gost'* and the Evangelical Christian publications *Khristianin* and *Utrennyaya zvezda* were able to continue. Although closed at one point, the YMCA survived as well as the World's Student Christian Federation. The British and Foreign Bible Society continued its ministry of Bible distribution.

As during the earlier suppression, evangelicals also were able to minister in a substratum. A field of Russian evangelizaation suddenly opened among the Russian prisoners of war in numerous camps in Germany and Austria, reaching a population of possibly two million if not two million and a half. Baptists in Germany almost immediately took the opportunity to evangelize with tracts and scripture. The Christian tract Society of Kassel, a German Baptist organization, distributed by ministers who received permission books, Scripture, and tracts. With repatriation numbers decreased, but a report on German Baptist work as late as 1920 reported the continuing work of evangelists who preached, baptized, and organized churches in the camps. About 1,000 prisoners were converted and baptized from the middle of 1919 to September 1920 with twenty-five churches organized and supporting their own

---

34. Dunstan, 36, 40. Copplestone, 509–12.
35. Coutts, *The History of the Salvation Army*, 6:37, 43–44. *The War Cry*, Aug. 26, 1916, 3.

treasuries. On their return to Russia, converted prisoners strengthened the Baptist and Evangelical Christian work in the country.[36]

German Baptists were not the only group interested in a mission to Russian prisoners. About the same time, leading Baptists in Sweden, K. A. Modén, Jacob Bystrom, and C. Benander, formed a Swedish committee to supply literature. Soon after his arrival in America, William Fetler in February 1916 helped to organize with widespread support from prominent Christian leaders, "The Gospel Committee for Work among Russian War Prisoners," in which he became director. Others will become engaged, such as Licht dem Osten, a mission formed in Germany in 1920 and led by Jakob Kroeker and W. L. Jack in Wernigerode-am-Harz in Germany. The YMCA undertook a religious, educational, and social ministry among Russian prisoners.[37]

The effort of the regime to limit the influence of Baptist pastors by exiling them proved counterproductive in Siberia. J. A. Frey from Latvia recounted in an article, "God's Fire," how Baptists in Siberia, forbidden to meet as congregations, met in small groups in private homes, which set revival fires. Frey claimed that from January to September 1917 over 1,000 individuals were won to the faith with more following. Two and then three evangelists traveled to various localities to baptize the converts.[38]

THE FEBRUARY REVOLUTION

The February Revolution, occurring in March 1917 according to the Western calendar, brought the abdication of Tsar Nicholas and the establishment of a Provisional Government. The restrictions and suppression of the Old Regime were swept away, and a new era of freedom again had dawned. The editor of *Missionary Review of the World* wrote enthusiastically in an editorial, "New Opportunities in Russia," that the spy system was ended, sectarians were no long banned, Jews were emancipated, and people who for so long were bound to an "autocratic and unenlightened Church" were now enjoining religious liberty.[39] On his return to Petrograd, I. V. Neprash found *Dom Evangeliya* "was overflowing with joy and with eagerness for work." He began holding open-air meetings, the first in front of the Winter Palace and then fifteen meetings weekly in eight large halls. Other members held services in other parts of Petrograd and outside the city. Martin Schmidt wrote that "a joyful movement and the hopeful presentiment of a bright future for the work of the Lord" went through the

---

36. *WHZ*, Jan. 12, 1915, 32, and Oct. 12, 1919, 168. *MRW*, Apr. 1916, 260–64. *The Watchman-Examiner*, Sep. 16, 1920, 1142. Blumit and Smith, *Sentenced to Siberia*, 124–29. *The Friend of Russia*, July 1920, 60.

37. For the Swedish committee see *MRW*, Apr. 1916, 263. For Fetler's role, see Fetler, *The Marvellous Results of Work Among Russian War Prisoners*, and Blumit and Smith, *Sentenced to Siberia*, 119–30. Colton, 22–37. For other sources for mission work among Russian war prisoners, see Wardin, *Evangelical Sectarianism*, 54–56, 593.

38. *The Baptist*, Oct. 2, 1920, 1226–27.

39. *MRW*, Aug. 1917, 563–64.

congregations of believers. Exiled preachers were freed from Siberia, church houses were opened, Christian publications were again permitted, and district and general conferences were again held.[40]

Only a couple of months after the February Revolution, both the Russian Baptists and Evangelical Christians held general conferences. The Baptists met first in Vladikavkaz in the Caucasus from April 20 to 27, what they called their "First Free Congress." It was the first since 1911. The Evangelical Christians met in Petrograd from May 17 to 25, their first since 1912. In Siberia Russian Baptists held their "First Free Congress" in November in Omsk, while Evangelical Christians met in April in Novonikolaevsk.[41]

At the Baptist congress in Vladikavkaz around ninety delegates and fifty guests attended. It chose as officers of the congress Gavriil I. Mazev, president; I. V. Neprash, vice-president; and M. D. Timoshenko and S. V. Belousov, secretaries. The first order of business was to receive the three Evangelical Christians who arrived at the conference bringing a letter from the Council of Evangelical Christians to form a "unity committee" and a request to begin cooperative work. A lengthy period of discussion ensued, including questions on the structure and aims of the Evangelical Christians and the autonomy of congregations. Deï Mazaev, president of the Union, reviewed minutes of former congresses that spoke of relations between the Baptists and Evangelical Christians and the agreement in 1912 at Vladikavkaz for congregations in both unions to exclude members who had been accepted improperly. Finally the congress resolved to send a delegation of five that included Pavel V. Pavlov and M. D. Timoshenko with insistence on the fulfillment of the Vladikavkaz Agreement. If the delegation was successful in its mission, the congress authorized a Union Committee of Deï and Gavriil Mazaev, V. G. Pavlov, I. K. Savel'ev, and William Fetler (although still in the USA) and two candidate members to find a path for common work.[42]

In his speech to the congress, Deï Mazaev reported that from the end of 1915 to 1917 the activity of the Union was reduced to nothing because of war, severe persecution, and the timidity of some. With the old saying, "In unity is strength," the congress resolved to unite the resources of the union into one center, annulling separate regions, recognizing only the geographically remote areas of Siberia, the Far East, and Turkestan as operating separately. It set October 1 for a collection of funds for missions and December 25 for a collection for the support of disabled pastors, their widows, and orphans. It also authorized a fund for the establishment of a Bible seminary.

At the congress of Evangelical Christians in Petrograd, the Baptist delegation had the opportunity to express its views. Prokhanov, the president, expressed the view that the problem of accepting excluded members from churches of another union should be based not on judgement but on grace and forgiveness. It would be better to ask

40. *Home and Foreign Fields*, Feb. 1921, 11. WHZ, Sep. 14, 1919, 151.
41. Dolotov, *Tserkov' i sektantstvo v Sibiri*, 80–82.
42. *Slovo istiny*, 1917, no. 1, 14–15.

all congregations to declare forgiveness to all who grieved them by joining another congregation without statement from their previous congregation. He was ready, however, to make some sacrifice to advance the cause of unity. The congress resolved to forgive members whom their churches had excluded and joined Baptist congregations and forgive these congregations, even without their apology for accepting them. For excluded Baptists who joined Evangelical Christian congregations, it counseled these members to apologize to the Baptist congregations that excluded them, and for Evangelical Christian congregations to act according to their judgement toward those who refuse to apologize. The congress elected its own Union Committee, headed by Prokhanov, and looked forward to the convening of a general council of both bodies in Moscow before Christmas.[43]

The Evangelical Christian Congress in Petrograd had no less than 140 participants. It sent a telegram to the Provisional Government expressing thanksgiving to God for the coming of an era of civil and religious freedom. At the end of the congress, the delegates resolved, "Upon hearing a message by Prokhanov on a Christian-democratic party, the congress finds it not desirable for congregations to be captivated by politics, but, on the other hand, the congress welcomes the formation of a Christian-democratic party as a personal undertaking of some members of the union, putting for their goal a worldwide system of state life of the people in conformity with royal Christian ideals. The participation in a party is a personal matter of conscience of each and a fulfillment of a state duty."[44]

As in earlier years, Prokhanov continued to be involved in the political and social life of the country. On August 14 Prokhanov spoke at the State Conference in Moscow before political, industrial, and military leaders. He declared that in the face of Prussian militarism (the war still continued), anarchy, and counter-revolution the country needed a strong regime based on the trust of all organized forces, the improvement of the army and order in the nation, and decisive social, political, and economic measures. He also called for the need of a "psychological factor of faith in the material and spiritual resources of the country and in the great providential destiny of Russia." In a listing of three major goals, he listed first the need for a reformation and democratization of the state church and its separation from the state; secondly, an affirmation of freedom of conscience and full religious liberty; and thirdly, the spreading in society of evangelical and ethical principles and popularizing the commandments of Christ.[45]

Other evangelicals also expressed their political views. Pavel V. Pavlov, the son of Vasilii G. Pavlov, wrote an article in *Slovo istiny*, "The Political Demands of the Baptists." He stated that the Christian church based on God's word laid the basis of democratic government. He claimed the constitution of the USA was a document that copied the democratic structure of Baptist churches with their elective authority

---

43. Ibid., 15.
44. *Otchet 4-go Vserossiiskago S"ezda Evangel'skikh Khristian*, 6, 20–21, 190–91.
45. *Slovo istiny*, 1917, no. 8, 106–7. Klibanov, 346–47.

and equality of all members. Pavel advocated a democratic republic with personal freedoms, religious liberty, and separation of church and state. In April Pavlov's father, Vasiliĭ, gave a lecture on separation of church and state that was also published in *Slovo istiny*. After a review of relations between the state and state churches, he presented a basis for separation.[46]

Abraham Kroeker, the Mennonite Brethren, before the Communist seizure of power in the October revolution, condemned in July the ideals of Lenin on the extreme Left and expressed his concern of anarchy. He said that God gave Kerensky, the war minister (soon president of the Provisional Government), a man who has averted "the worst possibilities."[47] George A. Simons, the Methodist superintendent, joyfully hailed the shift from despotism to freedom and democracy. *Khristianskiĭ pobonik* now reflected the democratic ideals of the new era.[48]

THE OCTOBER REVOLUTION AND ITS AFTERMATH

The evangelical leadership supported the democratic ideals of democratic regimes in the West, stressing personal freedom and religious liberty and a concern for security but no specific program that would meet the fundamental economic and social problems of the Russian populace. For them full religious liberty and the disestablishment of the Orthodox Church were top priorities. In October (in November according to the Western calendar) the Communist Party seized power and the Provisional Government was no more. Although the Communists faced resistance that developed into an extended period of civil war, in the end they consolidated their control of the state. In contrast to the weak leadership of the democratic forces, leadership led by Lenin was a factor in Communist success. Moreover the Communist decrees on peace and land, which brought an end to the war for Russians, and the nationalization of land, which abolished the large estates, met popular demands. The decree on peace met the desires of a war-weary populace, and the decree on land met the desires of a peasantry for an equitable distribution of land.

Although evangelicals and the rest of the nation suffered a period of military conflict, economic dislocation, and famine, the period of the New Economic Policy (NEP) from 1921 to 1928 brought economic stability and growth. Although evangelicals under the first ten years of Communist rule faced some restriction, nevertheless it proved to be a period of impressive evangelical gains. The decree in January 1918 on the separation of church and state and freedom of conscience eliminated the dominant position of the Orthodox Church. The regime also showed certain favoritism toward sectarians who had opposed the old order and might be won over to the

---

46. *Slovo istiny*, 1917, no. 1, 2–4, 10–12, and nos. 2–3, 29.
47. Reĭnmarus, "*Sektantstvo v 1917*," *Antireligioznik*, 1930, no. 5, 16.
48. Dunstan, 39–40. Copplestone, 513.

revolutionary cause. The state constitution in July 1918 guaranteed religious freedom and the right of religious and anti-religious propaganda.

On the other hand, the Union of Soviet Socialist Republics (USSR), as the Russian state came to be called, was entirely secular and under an atheistic regime that sought the eventual elimination of religion. Separation of church and state will be a weapon to eliminate the church and separate religion from the school. The regime nationalized all church property and the juridical rights of religious bodies. It undertook to educate the coming generation with an atheistic view of the world and to this end eliminated Sunday schools and religious youth organizations. Under Stalin from 1928 to the beginning of the Second World War, evangelicals and all other religious bodies will suffer the most intense persecution, not even imagined under the Tsarist regime, that included closure of churches and other religious organizations and the execution of church leaders. Under the Soviet regime, as under the Tsars, evangelicals will suffer alternating periods of greater toleration with greater restriction until the fall of the USSR itself in 1991.

Between 1919 and 1924, a number of the old pioneers of the Russian Baptist movement passed away. F. P. Balikhin died of typhus on January 20, 1919, and eight days later Vasilii V. Ivanov also died. Deï Mazaev followed in 1922 and Vasilii Pavlov and the German Baptist pioneer, Johann E. Pritzkau, in 1924. Other members of the older generation, however, survived many years. Gavriil Mazaev, brother of Deï and pastor of the Baptist church in Omsk, died in 1937 at the age of 79. Johann (Ivan) Kargel died in 1937 in Ukraine at the age of 88, Il'ya A. Golyaev died in exile in Tashkent in 1942 at the age of 83, and Jakob J. Wiens (Vins) died in the USA in 1944 at the age of 69.

In the next generation, William Fetler will die in the USA in 1957 at the age of 74 after fifty years of service in Russian missions. On the other hand, other members did not fare well. Robert Fetler, William's younger brother, after serving in the Far East and China, settled in Latvia in the 1920s where his brother now resided. After the occupation of Latvia by the Soviet Union, he and his family will be deported to Siberia in 1941 where he died almost immediately and was buried in a labor camp. S. V. Belousov, editor of *Baptist,* died in 1925 from tuberculosis at the age of 43. Other Baptist leaders died during the Stalinist purge of the mid-1930s if not later. Pavel V. Pavlov, son of Vasilii Pavlov, who had been exiled in 1929, died in a labor camp. N. V. Odintsov, president of the Russian Baptist Union, was imprisoned for three years in Yaroslav and in 1934 exiled to the village of Makovskoe in Krasnoyarsk *kraï* in Eastern Siberia and in 1939 shot in Moscow. Petr Wiens (Vins), the son of Jakob and pastor in Blagoveshchensk in Siberia, first imprisoned in 1930 will be executed in Siberia. Pavlov Ivanov-Klyshnikov, the son of Vasilii Ivanov, was exiled in 1932 to a camp for ten years but died before his term ended. P. V. Datsko was rearrested in 1939 and will die in a camp in 1941. Vasilii Stepanov was rearrested in 1937 and will die in the Gulag.[49]

---

49. "Margarita (Fetler) Kumyzova's Story," mns. 2–3, 13, SBHLA. Steeves, "Russian Baptist Union," 276–78. *REE* 32/1 (Feb. 2012), 14, ft. 68.

PART SIX—Possibilities and Uncertainties, 1905–1917

Baptists in Poland and the Baltic states did well in their independent countries between the First and Second World Wars. On the other hand, Baltic Baptists suffered loss and restrictions under the Soviet and German occupations from 1940 to 1991. By the early 1930s the German Baptists and Mennonites in the Soviet Union itself suffered closure of churches and loss of their institutional life. Of the fifty-two German Baptist mission workers in 1928, by 1934 twenty-five were exiled within the country with three dying, three escaping, and six released. In addition, sixteen were fugitives, five were exiled to Germany, and one died in prison. On the outbreak of the Second World War, the regime deported their members in European Russia not under German occupation to Siberia and Central Asia. In his work on German Baptist ministers from Volhynia, Donald Miller recorded thirteen of them were sent to the Gulag or imprisoned; eight will be shot, two survived, but the fate of the other three are unknown. No doubt other names could be added if known. Mennonite Brethren suffered a similar fate as the German Baptists.[50] No other Baptists in the world have suffered as much and as long as Baptists in Russia. They lived under six decades of Tsarist rule and seven and a half decades of Soviet rule under alternating periods of suppression and limited toleration. They experienced complete suppression with closure of churches, imprisonment, death camps, exile, and deportation and lived through periods of invasion, revolution, civil war, and famine.

In the former territory of the Soviet Union today are about 293,000 Baptists in 7,000 churches who are members of the Baptist World Alliance. Possibly around another 75,000 live in other independent unions or churches. As the result of the large emigration of German-Russians from Russia in recent years about another 70,000 in 500 churches live in Germany and are in independent Baptist or Mennonite Brethren associations or churches. Another 5,300 are members of the Baptist Union of Germany. In the USA are 16,500 Ukrainian /Russian Baptists in 106 churches, while others live in Canada. In addition, there are as many if not more Pentecostals than Baptists in the territory of the former Soviet Union. Evangelical Christians and small bodies of Methodists and Mennonites are also present. After over a century and a half in Russia and its annexed territories, all free church evangelicals, including Slavic (mainly Baptist and Pentecostal) and German-Russian and Baltic (mainly Baptist and Mennonite Brethren) probably number 900,000 worldwide.[51]

---

50. Wardin, "Baptists (German) in Russia and USSR," MERRSU, 3:199. Miller, *In the Midst of Wolves*, 266. For the fate of the Mennonite Brethren, see Toews, *A History of the Mennonite Brethren Church*, 121–23.

51. For Baptist statistics, see Baptist World Alliance, Congress, *Proceedings*, 2005, 238–241; Wardin, *Baptists Around the World*, 217–35; and Wardin, *The Twelve Baptist Tribes*, 39–40. For statistics of German- Russian Baptists and Mennonites in Germany, see Klassen, *Russlanddeutsche Freikirchen in der Bundesrepublik Deutschland*, 126, 273. Pentecostal statistics may be found in Johnstone and Mandryk, *Operation World*, under the countries of the former Soviet Union, but as estimates may be inflated and should be used with care.

War and Revolution, 1914–1917

Although foreign credentials marked the slavic free church evangelicals, they nevertheless were also indigenous. They suffered both for themselves and for the nation. Their style of worship is unlike fellow evangelicals in the West and embedded in the Russian soul. Although for years they have been on the edge of Russian history, they too have the right to claim Russia as their own.

Images

Gottfried F. Alf

First Row—Vince, Pavlienko, Datzcho, Homiac, Levuchkin, Rudienko.
Second Row—(C. T. Byford), Madame Pavloff, Pavloff, Kuchnireff, S. Stephanoff, Erstratenko, Balichin.
Third Row—Savelieff, Fetler, Golaieff (J. N. Prestridge), B. Stephanoff, Ivanoff, Kostromin.

(Frontispiece)

Ivan S. Prokhanov

William A. Fetler

Maps

Bibliography

Aaltio, Teuvo. "A History of the National Baptists in Finland." B.D. thesis, International Baptist Theological Seminary, Rüschlikon, 1958.

Adams, Arthur E. "Pobedonostsev's Religious Politics." *Church History* 22/4 (Dec. 1953), 314-26.

Amburger, Erik. *Geschichte des Protestantismus in Russland*. Stuttgart: Evangelisches Verlagswerk, 1961.

Anderson, Mrs. M. F. *The Baptists in Sweden*. Philadelphia: American Baptist Publication Society, c. 1860.

Astaf'ev, Nikolaï N. "Opyt istorii biblii v Rossii v svyazi s prosveshcheniem i nravami." Vols. 3-5. SPB, 1892.

Balders, Günther, ed. *Ein Herr, ein Glaube, eine Taufe: 150 Jahre Baptistengemeinden in Deutschland 1834-1984*. 3rd ed. Wuppertal and Kassel: Oncken Verlag, 1989.

———. "Johann Gerhard Oncken—Aspect of His Life and Work." Paper at the General Council of the Baptist World Alliance, Dresden, 1999.

———. *Theure Bruder Oncken*. 2nd ed. Wuppertal and Kassel: Oncken Verlag, 1978, 1984.

Barton, James L. "The Religious Situation in Russia." *Missionary Review of the World*, Oct. 1908, 727-33.

Bawden, C. R. *Shamans, Lamas and Evangelicals: The English Missionaries in Siberia*. London: Routledge and Kegan Paul, 1985.

Bebbington, D. W. *The Gospel in the World*. Carlisle, UK, and Waynesboro, GA: Paternoster Press, 2002.

Bekker, Jacob P. *Origin of the Mennonite Brethren Church*. Hillsboro, KS: The Mennonite Brethren Historical Society of the Midwest, 1973.

Belousov, S. V. "Tryasunstvo." *Baptist* 2 (1925), 15-17.

Benford, Benjamin Lee. "Evangelical Bible Society in the Russian Empire." In *The Modern Encyclopedia of Russian and Soviet History*, 11:8-11.

———. "Hermann Dalton and Protestantism in Russia." Ph.D. diss., Indiana University, 1973.

Birrell, Charles M., ed. *The Life of the Rev. Richard Knill of St. Petersburg*. 6th ed. London: James Nisbet and Co., 1861.

Blackwell, Alice Stone, ed. *The Little Grandmother of the Revolution: Reminiscences and Letters of Catherine Breshkovsky*. Boston: Little, Brown, and Company, 1917, 1919.

Blane, Andrew Quarles. "The Relations between the Russian Protestant Sects and the State, 1900-1921." Ph.D. diss., Duke University, 1964.

Bloch-Hoell, Nils. *The Pentecostal Movement*. Oslo: Universitetsforlaget, 1964.

Blumit, Oswald A., and Oswald J. Smith. *Sentenced to Siberia*. 13th ed. Washington, DC: The Russian Bible Society, 1947.

Bibliography

Bobrishchev-Pushkin, Alexander M. "Shtundisty illi baptisty?" *Russkaya mysl'* 11 (1903), 159–66.

———. *Sud i raskol'niki-sektanty*. SPB, 1902.

Bogolyubov, D. K. "O s"ezde sektantov v S.-Peterburge." *Tserkovnyĭ vestnik,* 1909, no. 38, 1187–88.

Bolshakoff, Serge. *Russian Nonconformity*. Philadelphia: Westminster Press, 1950.

Bonch-Bruevich, Vladimir D. *Materialy k istorii i izucheniyu russkago sektantsva i raskola.* Vol. 1. SPB, 1908.

———. *Presledovanie baptistov evangelicheskoĭ sekty*. Christchurch, Hants, England: Svobodnoe Slovo, 1902.

———. "Presledovanie Bapistov v Rossii." *Vestnik evropy,* June 1910, 160–83.

———. "Serdi sektantov." *Zhizn',* 1902, nos. 2, 5, 6.

Bondar, S. D. *Adventism 7-go dnya*. SPB, 1911.

———. *Sekta Mennonitov v Rossii v svyazi s istorieĭ nemetsko kolonizatsii na yuge Rossii.* Petrograd, 1916.

———. *Sovremennoe sostoyanie russkago baptizma.* SPB, 1911.

———. "Sovremennyĭ baptizm v Rosssii." *Missionserskoe obozrenie,* Oct. 1911, 302–18.

Bonekemper, Karl. "Johannes Bonekemper und seine Famiilie." *Immanuel! Eine Hütte Gottes bei den Menschen*. St. Chrischona: Pilgrim Mission, c. 1868, 15–40. Translated by Theodore Wenzlaff, *Heritage Review,* Sep. 1979, 14–20.

——— "Stundism in Russia." *Missionary Review of the World,* Mar. 1894, 201–204.

Brandenburg, Hans. *The Meek and the Mighty*. New York: Oxford University Press, 1977.

Brauer, F. M. "Unser Besuch in Kijew." *Der Hausfreund,* Feb. 7/20, 1907, 41–43.

Braun, H. J. "Mennoniten oder Baptisten?" *Die Friedensstimme,* May 5, 1910, 3–5. (See Abe J. Dueck, *Moving Beyond Secession,* 117–22, for an English translation.)

Breyfolge, Nicholas V. *Heretics and Colonizers: Forging Russia's Empire in the South Caucasus.* Ithaca and London: Cornell University Press, 2005.

Broadbent, E. H. *The Pilgrim Church*. London: Pickering and Inglis, 1931.

Brooks, Jesse W., ed. *Good News for Russia*. Chicago: The Bible Institute Colportage Association, 1918.

Brown, John. *The Stundists: The Story of a Great Religious Revolt*. London: James Clarke & Co., 1893.

Brüggen, E., von der. "Die evangelisch-religiöse Bewegung in Russland." *Deutsche Rundschau,* Jan. 1883, 115–28.

Busch, E. H. *Ergänzungen der Materialen zur Geschichte und Statistik des Kirchen-und Schulwesens der Evangelisch-Lutherischen Gemeinden in Russland*. SPB and Leipzig: Gustav Haessel and H. Haessel, 1867.

———. *Materialen zur Geschichte und Statistik des Kirchen-und Schulwesens der Evangelisch-Lutherischen Gemeinden in Russland*. SPB: Commissionsverlag von G. Haessel, 1862.

Byford, Charles T. *Peasants and Prophets*. 2nd ed. London: James Clark & Co., 1912.

———. *The Soul of Russia*. London: Kingsgate Press, 1914.

Canton, William. *A History of the British and Foreign Bible Society*. Vol. 5. London: John Murray, 1904–1910.

Carlson, B. A. "The Beginnings of Methodism in Finland." *The Gospel in All Lands,* Nov. 1896, 503–8.

Chepurin, N. *Obzor sektantskoĭ literatury: Relgioznyya razdeleniya v sektantstve*. SPB, 1914. Also in *Missionerkskoe obozrenie,* Apr.–Nov. 1914.

Bibliography

Christophilus. *Ein Blatt aus der Geschichte des Stundismus in Russland.* Berlin: Deutsche Orient Mission, 1904.

Coad, F. Roy. *History of the Brethren Movement.* Grand Rapids: Eerdmans, 1968.

Coleman, Heather J. *Russian Baptists and Spiritual Revolution, 1905-1929.* Bloomington and Indianapolis: Indiana University Press, 2005.

Colton, Ethan T. *Forty Years with the Russians.* New York: Association Press, 1930.

Copplestone, J. Tremaine. *History of Methodist Missions.* Vol. 4. New York: Board of Global Ministries of the United Methodist Church, 1973.

Corrado, Sharyl. "The Philosophy of Ministry of Colonel Vasily Pashkov." M.A. thesis, Wheaton College, 2000.

Coutts, Frederick. *History of the Salvation Army.* Vol. 6. London: Hodder and Stoughton, 1973 (1914-1918).

Cox, Jeffrey. "What I Have Learned about Missions from Writing *The British Missionary Enterprise Since 1700.*" *International Bulletin of Missionary Research* 32/2 (Apr. 2008), 86-87.

Cross, A. G. "Chaplains to the British Factory in St. Petersburg, 1783-1813." *European Studies Review* 2/2 (Apr. 1872), 125-42.

Ĉukers, Fridrichs, et. al., eds. *Dzīvības Celš: Veltījums latviešu baptistu 100 gadu jubilejai.* Latvian Baptist Union of America, 1960.

Curtiss, John Shelton. *Church and State in Russia: The Last Years of the Empire, 1900-1917.* New York: Octagon Books, 1965.

Dalton, Hermann. *Evangelische Strömungen in der Russischen Kirche in der Gegenwart.* Heilbronn: Gebr. Henninger, 1881.

―――. *Lebenserinnerungen.* Vol. 2. Berlin: Martin Warneck, 1906-1908.

―――. *Der Stundismus in Russland.* Gütersloh: C. Bartelmann, 1896.

Day, George M. "The Russian Student Movement." *The Student World*, July 1917, 241-49.

Delyakov, Yakob. "The Autobiography of Jacob Dilakoff, Independent Missionary in Russia." Translated by Benjamin Labaree and Mary Lewis Shedd. *The European Harvest Field* 16 (1935), Mar.-June, Sep.-Dec.

Detzler, Wayne Alan. "Johann Gerhard Oncken's Long Road to Toleration." *Journal of the Evangelical Theological Society* 36/2 (June 1993), 229-40.

Diedrich, Hans-Christian. "Johannes Lepsius und die Südrusischen Stundisten." *Akten des Internationalen Dr. Johannes-Lepsius-Symposiums 1986.* Halle-Wittenberg: Martin-Luther Universität, 1986, 230-36.

―――. *Siedler, Sektierer und Stundisten: Die Entstehung des russischen Freikirchtums.* Berlin: Evangelische Verlagsanstalt, 1985.

―――. *Ursprünge und Anfänge des russischen Freikirchentums.* Erlangen: Oikonomia, 1985.

Dillon, E. J. "The 'Quaker-Spiritualist' Revival in Russia." *Review of Reviews*, Apr. 1893, 317-21.

―――. "A Russian Religious Reformer." *The Sunday Magazine*, Apr. 1902, 330-36.

Doerksen, Victor G. "A Second Menno? Eduard Wüst and Mennonite Brethren Beginnings." *The Mennonite Quarterly Review* 74/2 (Apr. 2000), 311-25.

―――. "Mennonite Templers in Russia." *Journal of Mennonite Studies* 3 (1985), 128-37.

Dolotov, A. *Tserkov' i sektantstvo v Sibiri.* Novosibirsk: Sibkraïizdat, 1930.

Donat, Rudolph. *Das wachsende Werk.* Kassel: Oncken Verlag, 1960.

―――. *Wie das Werk begann.* Kassel: Oncken Verlag, 1958.

Bibliography

Dorodnitsyn, Aleksiï Ya. *Materialy dlya istorii religiozno-ratsionalisticheskago dvizheniya na yuge Rossii vo vtoroï polovine xix-go stoletiya*. Kazan, 1908.

———. "Nemetskie missionery neobapizm (Neo-Baptismus) izvestnago pod imenem shtundy na yuge Rossii." *Chteniya v obshchestve lyubiteleï dukhovnago prosveshcheniya*, 1893, no. 3, 316–52; no. 6, 719–39.

———. *Religiozno-ratsionalisticheskoe dvizhenie na yuge Rossii vo vtorï polovine xix-go stoletiya*. Kazan, 1909.

Dostoyevsky, Fedor M. *Diary of a Writer*. Vol. 1. New York: Charles Scribner's Sons, 1949.

Dubovy (Dubovoï), Andrew. *Pilgrims of the Prairie: Pioneer Ukrainian Baptists in North Dakota*. Translated by Marie Halun Bloch. Dickinson, ND: Ukrainian Cultural Institute, Dickinson State College, 1983.

———. "Vzglyad na russkikh sektantov." *Sobodnoe Slovo*, June 1916, 597–99.

Dueck, Abe J. *Moving Beyond Secession: Defining Russian Mennonite Brethren Mission and Identity 1872 –1922*. Winnipeg, MB, and Hillsboro, KS: Kindred Productions, 1997.

Duin, Edgar C. *Lutheranism under the Tsars and the Soviets*. 2 vols. Ann Arbor: University Microfilms, 1975.

Dunstan, John. "George A. Simons and the Khristianski Pobornik." *Methodist History*, Oct. 1980, 21–40.

Dyck, Harvey L., trans. and ed. *A Mennonite in Russia: The Diaries of Jacob D. Epp, 1851-1880*. Toronto: University of Toronto Press, 1991.

Dyck, Johannes. "Moulding the Brotherhood: Johann Wieler (1839–1889) and the Communities of the Early Evangelicals in Russia." Th.M thesis, International Baptist Theological Seminary, Prague, 2007.

Dyck, John P., ed. *Troubles and Triumphs, 1914-1924: Excerpts from the Diary of Peter J. Dyck*. Springstein, MB, 1981.

Eesti Baptisti koguduste ajaloolik Album: 25 Juubeli aasta mälestusets. Tallinn: J. Felsberg and A .Tetermann, 1911.

Ehrt, Adolph. *Das Mennonitum in Russland*. Berlin-Leipzig: Julius Beltz, 1932.

Ekelmann, Otto. *Gnadenwunder: Geschichte der Ersten Ostpreussischen Baptistesngemeinde in Memel und ihrer Missionsfeld in Ostpreussen und Russland, 1841-1928*. Memel, 1928.

Eller, Paul H. *History of Evangelical Missions*. Harrisburg, PA: Evangelical Press, 1942.

Epp, George K. *Geschichte der Mennoniten in Russland*. 2 vols. Lage: Logos Verlag, 1997-1998.

Epp, Heinrich. *Notizen aus dem Leben und Wirken des verstorbenden Aelesten Abraham Unger, Gruender der "Einlager-Mennoniten-Brüdergemeinde."* Halbstadt: H. J. Braun Verlag, 1907. Translated as "Recollections from the Life and Work of the Late Elder Abraham Unger." *Direction* 19/2 (Fall 1990), 127–39, and 20/1 (Spring 1991), 132–40.

Evans, Stanley. *The Churches in the U.S.S.R*. London: Cobbett Publishing Co., 1943.

Ewing, John W. *The Goodly Fellowship: A Century Tribute to the Life and Work of the World's Evangelical Alliance 1846–1946*. London and Edinburgh: Marshall, Morgan & Scott; Grand Rapids: Zondervan, 1946.

Fast, Hermann. "Nachrichten aus Russland." *Der Sendbote*, Feb. 21, 1906, 122–23.

Fetler, William A. (V. A.). *The Marvellous Results of Work Among Russian War Prisoners and the Greatest Missionary Challenge of the Christian Era*. 2nd ed. Chicago: Russian Missionary Society, c. 1928.

———. "Revolution and Religion in Russia." *Missionary Review of the World*, May 1917, 339–40.

———. *Statistika russkikh baptistov za 1909 god*. SPB, 1910.

———. *Statistika Russkikh Evangel'skikh Khristian Baptistov za 1910 god*. SPB, 1911.

Fetler, Robert. "A Short History of the 'Dom Evangelia' in Petrograd." *The Friend of Missions*, Dec. 1933, 164–66, and Mar. 1934, 44–45.

Florinsky, Michael T. *Russia: A History and an Interpretation*. Vol. 2. New York: The Macmillan Company, 1947, 1953.

Freeman, Aileen. "Bonch-Bruevich and the Development of Bolshevik Policy toward the Sectarians." M.A. thesis, Carleton University, 1979.

Freeze, Gregory L. *The Parish Clergy in Nineteenth-Century Russia: Crisis, Reform, Counter-Reform*. Princeton: Princeton University Press, 1983.

Friedmann, Robert. *Mennonite Piety through the Centuries*. Goshen, IN: The Mennonite Historical Society, 1949.

Friesen, Abraham. *In Defense of Privilege: Russian Mennonites and the State Before and During World War I*. Winnipeg, MB, and Hillsboro, KS: Kindred Productions, 2006.

Friesen, Peter E. *Die Alt-Evangelische Mennonitische Brüderschaft in Russland (1789–1910)*. Halbstadt: "Raduga," 1911. Translated as *The Mennonite Brotherhood in Russia (1789–1910)*. Fresno: Board of Christian Literature, General Conference of Mennonite Brethren Churches, 1978.

———. *Konfession oder Sekte?* Halbstadt: Raduga, 1914. See Dueck, *Moving Beyond Secession*, 142–57 for a translation.

Friesen, Rudy P., and Sergey Shmakin. *Into the Past: Buildings of the Mennonite Commonwealth*. Winnipeg: Raduga Publications, 1996.

Froese, G. P. "Ein Bericht über die Mission unter den Russen." In A. H. Unruh, *Die Geschiche der Mennoniten-Bruedergemeinde*. Hillsboro, KS: General Conference of the Mennonite Brethren Church of North America, 1955, 258–64.

Füllbrandt, Carl, Sr. *Darst du Baptist werden?* Odessa, 1913.

Füllbrandt, Carl, Jr. "Wassily Pawloff." *Der Wahrheitszeuge*, Mar. 16, 1922, 94–96.

Garrard, Mary N. *Mrs. Penn-Lewis, a Memoir*. London: The Overcomer Book Room, c. 1930.

Geldbach, Erich. "The Religious Situation in Germany: Past and Present." *America Baptist Quarterly* 23/3 (Sep. 2004), 238–57.

Gidney, W. T. *The History of the London Society for Promoting Christianity amongst the Jews from 1808 to 1908*. London: London Society for Promoting Christianity amongst the Jews, 1909.

Giesinger, Adam. "The Landau Baptists." *Journal of the American Historical Society of Germans from Russia* 17/4 (Winter 1994), 16–21.

Glaubens-Bekenntniss und Verfassung der gläubiggetauften und vereinigten Mennoniten-Brüdergemeinde in Südlichen Russland. Einlage: A. Unger, 1876.

Godet, Georges. *Persécutions actuelles en Russie*. Neuchatel: Attinger, 1896.

———. "The Russian Stundists: Their Origin, History, and Persecution." *Missionary Review of the World*, Oct. 1896, 740–46, and Nov. 1896, 822–29.

Goertzen, Norma S. "The Influence of Radical Pietism on Russian Mennonites." *The Covenant Quarterly* 38/4 (Nov. 1980), 19–26.

Goncharenko, Evgeni. "Perfect Future in Past Traditions." *Religion in Eastern Europe* 31/4 (Nov. 2011), 15–19.

Good, Jane E. "Sergei Mikhailovich Kravchinskii." *The Modern Encyclopedia of Russian and Soviet History* 18:54–56.

Bibliography

Goosen, H. H. *Adolf Reimer, Ein Treuer Bote Jesus Christi unter Deutschen und Russen.* Yarrow, BC, 1960.

Grachev, Yu. S. *Gerusy—Giryusy (Goris).* Wheaton, IL: Evangelical Word Publishing, 1996.

Gutsche, Waldemar. *Westliche Quellen des russischen Stundismus:* Kassel: J.G. Oncken, 1956.

Harms, J. F. *Geschichte der Mennoniten Brüdergemeinde.* Hillsboro, KS: Mennonite Brethren Publishing House, 1924.

Harsch, Lloyd. "The Multicultural Heritage of North Dakota Baptists." Ph.D. diss., Southwestern Baptist Theological Seminary, 1999.

Hayne, Coe. "The Twenty-fifth Anniversary of Russian Baptists in North America." *Missions*, Nov. 1926, 587–90.

Hebly, J. H. *Protestants in Russia.* Grand Rapids: Eerdmans, 1976.

Heier, Edmund. *Religious Schism in the Russian Aristocracy, 1860-1900: Radstockism and Pashkovism.* The Hague: Martinus Nijhoff, 1970.

Heinz, Daniel. "Origin and Growth of the Adventists in Russia." *Journal of the American Historical Society of Germans from Russia* 10/4 (Winter 1987), 39–43.

Hildebrand, Cornelius. "Aus der Kronsweider Erweckungszeit." *Der Botschafter* 8/6 (1913), 8–19. Translated in *The Mennonite Quarterly Review* 58/2 (Apr. 1984), 83–124.

Hingley, Ronald. *The Russian Mind.* New York: Charles Scribner's Sons, 1977.

Högberg, Lars E. *En missionärs minnen.* Stockholm: Svenska Missions-Förbundets Förlag, 1924.

———. *Skuggor och dagrer frå(set ring over a)n misssionersarbetet i Ryssland.* Stockholm: Svenska Missionsförbundets Förlag, 1914.

Hourwich, Isaac. "Religious Sects in Russia." *The International Quarterly* 8 (1903-1904), 159–74.

Huebert, Heinrich. "Two Letters of Heinrich Huebert—the First Brethren Elder." *Direction* 25/1 (Spring 1996), 55–59.

Hutchinson, Lincoln, ed. *Hidden Springs of the Russian Revolution: Personal Memoirs of Katerina Breshkovskaia.* Stanford: Stanford University Press, 1931.

Istoriya Evangel'skikh Khristian-Baptistov v SSSR. Moscow: All-Union Council of Evangelical Christians-Baptists, 1989.

Ivanov, Andrey. "The Making of a Conspiracy: Russian Evangelicals During the First World War." *Religion in Eastern Europe* 22/5 (Oct. 2002), 22–45.

Ivanov, Vasiliĭ V. "Kniga episkopa Aleksiya." *Baptist*, Sep. 1908, 23–27.

———. "Polozhenie baptistov." *Baptist*, Feb. 23, 1911, 69–71.

———. "Put' V. V. Ivanova [=Klyshnikova] v ssylku." *Seyatel' istiny*, 1925, July, 10–12; Aug., 10–11; Sep–Oct., 8; and Nov., 9–11.

Ivanov, Vasiliĭ V., and Deï Mazaev. *Vsemirnyĭ kongress baptistov v Londone v 1905 godu.* Rostov-on-Don: V. Pavlov & Company, 1907–1909.

Jack, Walter L. "Zwei Konferenzen in Petersburg." *Der christliche Orient.* Mar. 1907, 36–41.

Jantz, Harold. "Pietism's Gift to Russian Mennonites." *Direction* 36/1 (Spring 2007), 58–73.

———. "A Pietist Pastor and the Russian Mennonites: The Legacy of Eduard Wuest." *Direction* 36/2 (Fall 2007), 232–46.

Jantzen, Hermann. *Im wilden Turkestan: Ein Leben unter den Moslems.* Giessen/Basel: Brunnen Verlag, 1988.

Johnstone, Patrick, and Jason Mandryk. *Operation World.* Carlisle, Cambria, UK, 2001.

Jones, Malcolm V. "Destoyevsky, Tolstoy, Leskov and Redstokizm." *Journal of Russian Studies* 13 (1972), 3–20.

———. "A Note on Mr. J. G. Blissmer and the Society for the Encouragement of Spiritual and Ethical Reading." *Slavic and East European Review* 53 (1975), 92–96.

———. "The Sad and Curious Story of Karass, 1802-35." *Oxford Slavonic Papers* 8 (1975), 53–81.

Jordy, Gerhard. *Die Brüderbewegung in Deutschland*. Vol. 2. Wuppertal: R. Brockhaus Verlag, 1979–1981.

Jowers, Clyde. "The Promotion of Religious Liberty by the Baptist World Alliance." Th.D. diss., New Orleans Baptist Theological Seminary, 1964.

Kahle, Wilhelm. "Ein Bericht über Allianz- und Baptistengemeinden des Kaukasus aus dem Jahr 1888." *Kirche im Osten* 25 (1982), 121–28.

———. *Evangelische Christen in Russland und der Sovetunion: Ivan Stepanovič Prokhanov (1869-1935) und der Weg der Evangeliumschristen und Baptisten*. Wuppertal and Kassel: Oncken Verlag, 1978.

———. "Zur Geschichte der freikirchlichen evangelischen Gemeinden in Moskau." *Kirche im Osten* 31 (1988), 23–68.

Kallistov, Nikolaï. "Ruskaya obshchina baptistov v Tiflise." *Tserkovnyï vestnik*, 1879, no. 49, 2–5; 1880, no. 32, 4–7.

Kal'nev, Mikhail A. *Nemtsy i stundobaptizm*. Moscow, 1897.

Kandidov, Boris P. *Sektantstvo i mirovaya voïna*. Moscow: "Atheist," 1930.

Kargel, J. G. *Zwischen den Enden der Erde unter Brüdern in Ketten*. Wernigerode am Harz: Licht im Osten, 1928.

Kaups, Richard. *Viiskümmend aastate apostlite radadel, 1884-1934*. Tallinn: Publishing House of the Estonian Baptist Union, 1934.

Kean, William. *The Bible in Russia*. London: British and Foreign Bible Society, 1904.

Keller, P. Konrad. *Die deutschen Kolonien in Südrussland*. Vol. 2. Odessa: Jakob Zentner, 1914. (Translated by Anthony Becker in 1973.)

Keshe, Martha Sergeevna. "Semeïnoe vospominanie o Martine Karloviche Kal'veït." Mns. Southern Baptist Historical Society and Archives.

Khakhanov. A. "Molokane i baptisty Zakavkaz'ya." *Etnograficheskie obozrenie*, 1901, 45–46.

Kiploks, Edgar. "The Lutheran Church in Russia." *The Lutheran Quarterly* 3/1 (Feb. 1951), 46–59.

Kjaer-Hansen, Kai. *Joseph Rabinowitz and the Messianic Movement*. Edinburgh: The Handsel Press; Grand Rapids: Eerdmans, 1995.

Klassen, John N. *Russlanddeutsche Freikirchen in der Bundesrepublik Deutschland*. Nürnberg and Bonn: VTR/VKW, 2007.

Klein, Ernst F. *Russische Reisetage*. Potsdam: Deutsche Orient-Mission, 1909.

Klibanov, A. I. *History of Religious Sectarianism in Russia (1860s–1917)*. Oxford: Pergamon Press, 1982.

Klimenko, Michael. "Anfänge des Baptismus in Südrussland (Ukraine) nach offiziellen Dokumenten." Th.D. diss., Friedrich-Alexander-Universität, 1957.

Klippenstein, Lawrence. "Johann Wieler (1839–1889) among Russian Evangelicals: A New Source of Mennonites and Evangelicalism in Imperial Russia." *Journal of Mennonite Studies* 5 (1987), 44–60.

———. "Russian Evangelicalism Revisited: Ivan Kargel and the Founding of the Russian Baptist Union." *Baptist History and Heritage* 27/2 (Apr. 1992), 42–48.

Klukas, Herbert. *Geschictliche Quellen der Deutschen Baptistengemeinde Cataloi, bei Tulcea, in der Dobrudscha, Rumaenien*. Delta, BC, 1998.

Bibliography

Kmeta, Ivan A. *With Christ in America: A Story of the Russian-Ukrainian Baptists.* Winnipeg: Christian Press, 1948.

Köbner, Julius. "The Baptist Missionary Society." *Evangelical Christendom*, 1851, 495–96.

Koch, Fred C. *The Volga Germans in Russia and the Americas, from 1763 to the Present.* University Park and London: The Pennsylvania University Press, 1977.

Kolarz, Walter. *Religion in the Soviet Union.* New York: St. Martin's Press, 1961.

Kommittén för Evangelisk Mission i Ryssland. *Den evangeliska rörelsen i Ryssland.* Stockholm, 1909.

Korff, M. M. *Am Zarenhof.* Wernigerode am Harz: Licht im Osten, 1927.

Koval'kov, V. M., and E. I. Sokolov. "I. G. Ryaboshapka." *Bratskiï vestnik*, 1981, no. 6, 57–65.

Kozitskiï, P. "O prichinakh, prepyatstvuyushchikh uspeshnoï bor'be so shtundizmom." *Tserkovnyï vestnik* 21 (1891), 321–26.

———. "O prichinakh, sposobstvuyushchikh bystromu rasprostraneniyu shtundizma v yuzhno- russkikh guberniyakh." Tserkovnyï *vestnik* 7 (1890), 122–23, and no. 8, 137–39.

———. "O prichinakh, sposobstvuyushchikh rasprostraneniyu shtundizma v malorusskikh guberniyakh." *Tserkovnyï vestnik* 50 (1889), 857–60.

Krahn, Cornelius. "Government of Mennonites in Russia." *The Mennonite Encyclopedia* 2:556–57.

———. "Russia." *The Mennonite Encyclopedia* 4:381–93.

Kroeker, Abraham. "Die darbystische Gefahr." *Die Friedensstimme* 25 (1907), 314–15.

———. *Pfarrer Eduard Wüst, der grosse Erweckungsprediger in der deutschen Kolonien Südrusslands.* Spat bei Simferopol, Russia, 1903.

———. "Prediger Johann Wieler." *Christlicher Familienkalender*, 1908, 1–2.

Kroeker, Jakob. *Die Sehnsucht des Ostens.* Wernigerode am Harz: Licht dem Osten, c. 1920.

Kronlins, Janis. *Gaišā celā: Dr. theol. h.c. Jāna Aleksandra Freija dvīze un darbi 1863-1950.* Latvian Baptist Union of America, 1964.

Krusenstjerna, Ada von. *Im Kreuz hoffe und siege ich.* Giessen and Basel: Brunnen-Verlag, 1962.

Kumyzova, Margarita. "Margarita (Fetler) Kumyzova's Story." Translated by Lydia Hartsok. Mns. Southern Baptist Historical Library and Archives.

Kupsch, Eduard. *Geschichte der Baptisten in Poland, 1852-1932.* Lodz, c. 1932.

Kurz gefasste Lebens-Beschreibung des selig vollendeten Bruders in Christo, Karl Ondra. Danzig, 1888.

Kutepov, Nikolaï. *Kratkaya istoriya i verouchenie russkikh ratsionalisticheskikh i misticheskikh ereseï.* 3rd ed. Novocherkassk, 1907.

———. "Sovremennaya baptistskaya, shtundistskaya i molokanskaya propaganda na yuge Rossii. *Pribavleniya k tserkonym vedomostyam* 7 (1888), 171–76; no. 13, 371–72.

Kweetin, John. *A Hidden Jewel: Short Sketch of the Life and Work of Rev. John Alexander Frey as He Is Known to the Writer for Thirty Years.* New York, 1920.

Lang, George H. *Edmund Hamer Broadbent, Saint and Pioneer.* London: Paternoster Press, 1946.

Langenskjold, Margareta. *Baron Paul Nicolay: Christian Statesman and Student Leader in Northern and Slavic Europe.* Translated by Ruth Evelyn Wilder. New York: George H. Doran, 1924.

Lanin, E. B. "The Tsar Persecutor." *Contemporary Review* 61 (Jan. 1892), 1–25.

Larson, Karl. "Ten Years in Russia." *All the World*, Jan.–Mar., 1942 to Oct.–Dec., 1943.

Larsson, A. P. *Tjugufem år Ryssland.* Stockholm: N. J. Schedins Förlag, 1905.

Latimer, Robert Sloan. *Dr. Baedeker and His Apostolic Work in Russia*. London: Morgan and Scott, 1907.

———. *Under Three Tsars: Liberty of Conscience in Russia, 1856–1909*. New York: Fleming H. Revell, c. 1909.

———. *With Christ in Russia*. London: Hodder and Stoughton, 1910.

Lehmann, Joseph. *Geschichte der deutschen Baptisten*. Vol. 2. Casssel: J. G. Oncken, 1896–1900.

———. "The Russian Stundists." *Baptist Missionary Magazine*, April 1877, 84–88.

Leibbrandt, Georg. "The Emigration of the German Mennonites from Russia to the United States and Canada in 1873–1880." *The Mennonite Quarterly Review* 6/4 (1932), 205–26, and 7/1 (1933), 5–41.

Lenker, J. N. *Lutherans in All Lands*. 5th ed. Milwaukee: Lutherans in All Lands Company, 1896.

Lepsius, Johannes. "Das Evangelium in Russland." *Der christliche Orient*, Dec. 1905, 177–87.

Leroy-Beaulieu, Anatole. *The Empire of the Tsars and the Russians*. Vol. 3. New York and London: G. P. Putnam's Sons, 1893–1896.

Leskov, Nikolaï S. *Schism in High Society: Lord Radstock and his Followers*. Translated by James Muckle. Nottingham: Bramcote Press, 1955.

Levindanto, N. A. "Pamyati Deya Ivanovicha Mazaeva." *Bratskiĭ vestnik*, 2–3, 1953, 95–98.

Liebert, Gottfried. *Geschchte der Baptisten in Russisch-Polen*. Hamburg: Oncken Press, c. 1874.

Lieven, Sophie. *Eine Saat, die reiche Frucht brachte*. Basel: Brunnen-Verlag, 1952.

Lion, Solomon E. "Ot propaganda k teroru." *Katorga i ssylka*, 5, 1924, 19–20.

Loewen, Harry. "Echoes of Drumbeats: The Movement of Exuberance Among the Mennonite Brethren." *Journal of Mennonite Studies* 3 (1985), 118–27.

Loewen, John Howard. *One Lord, One Church, One Hope and One God: Mennonite Confessions of Faith in America:* Elkhart, IN: Institute of Mennonite Studies, 1985.

Lohne, Alf. *Adventists in Russia*. Hagerstown, MD: Review and Herald Publishing Association, 1987.

Lohrenz, John H. *The Mennonite Brethren Church*. Hillsboro, KS: Board of Foreign Missions, Conference of the Mennonite Brethren Church of North America, 1950.

Longenecker, Stephen L., and Ronald C. Arnett. *The Dilemma of Anabaptist Piety*. Camden, ME: Penobscot Press, 1997.

Löwen, Heinrich. *In Vergessenheit geratene Beziehungen*. Bielefeld: Logos, 1989.

Lübeck, Johannes. *Meine Verbannung nach Siberien*. Winnipeg: Deutsche Buchhandlung, n.d.

Luckey, Hans. *Johann Gerhard Oncken und die Anfänge des deutschen Baptismus*. 3rd ed. Kassel: Oncken Verlag, 1934, 1958.

Lyalina, G. S. *Baptizm: Illyuzii i real'nost'*. Moscow: Politizdat, 1977.

———. "Liberal'no-buzhuaznoe techenie v baptisme (1905–1917 gg.)." *Voprosy nauchnogo ateizma*, 1 (1966), 312–40.

Lyasotskiĭ, I. "Kak ya otpal ot pravoslaviya." *Baptist* 1, 1908, 20–24.

McCaig, Archibald. *Grace Astounding in Bolshevik Russia*. London: The Russian Missionary Society, 1929.

———. *Wonders of Grace in Russia*. Riga: Revival Press, 1926.

McGlashan, Ann, and William H. Brackney. "German Baptists and the Manifesto of 1848." *American Baptist Quarterly* 33/3 (Sep. 2004), 258–80.

Bibliography

McGlothlin, W. J. *Baptist Confessions of Faith*. Philadelphia: American Baptist Publication Society, 1911.

Maevskiï, Vladimir. *Vnutrennyaya missiya i ee osnovopolozhnik*. Buenos Aires, 1954.

Martens, Cornelius. *Unter dem Kreuz: Erinnerungen aus dem alten und neuen Russland*. Wernigerode am Harz: Licht im Osten, 1929,

———. *Taten Gottes im Osten*. 2nd ed. Leonberg, Württenberg: Philadelphia-Verlag, n.d.

Martens, Helena (Wieler). "Grandmother's Letter." Translation of "Grossmutters Brief." Typed mns. Mennonite Heritage Centre, Winnipeg.

Mazaev, Deï. "Ne ta doroga." *Baptist* 34, 1911, 268.

Mazaev, Gavriil. *Obrashchenie na istinnyï put' i vospominaniya baptista G. I. M.* Omsk: Board of the Siberian Department of the Baptist Union, 1919.

Melgunov, Sergeï. *Tserkov i gosudarstvo v Rossii*. Vol. 1. Moscow, 1907–1909.

Meshcherskiï, Vladimir. *Lettre au Lord Redstock/Pisma k Lordu Redstoku*. SPB, 1876.

Miller, Donald. *In the Midst of Wolves: A History of German Baptists in Volhynia, 1863-1943*. Hillsboro, OR, 2000.

Miliukov, Paul. *Outlines of Russian Culture*. Translated by Michael Karpovich. Vol. 1, *Religion and the Church*. New York: A. S. Barnes, 1960.

Mitrokin, L. N. *Baptizm*. Moscow: Politizdat, 1966.

Modén. L. A. *Vittnen och Troshjältar*. Stockholm: Baptistmissionens Böksförlags, 1930.

Moskalenko, A. T. *Pyatidesyatniki*. Moscow: Politizdat, 1966.

Muckle, James. "Charlotte Elliott and the Beginnings of Russian Evangelical Hymnody." *Bulletin* of the Hymn Society of Great Britain and Ireland 10/2 (May 1982), 33–38.

———. "Henry Lansdell, Leskov and Tolstoy." *Neue Zeitschrift für Missionswissenschaft* 4, 1978, 291–308.

Müller, George. *The Life of Trust*. New York and Boston: Thomas Y. Crowell and Co., 1898.

Nagirnyak, A. P. "Deï Ivanovich Mazaev." *Materialy nauchno-bogoslovskoï konferentsii Rossiïskogo Soyuza evangel'skikh khristian-baptistov*. Moscow: Russian Union EkhB, 2007, 152–71.

Nesdoly, Samuel J. "Evangelical Sectarianism in Russia: A Study of Stundists, Baptists, Pashkovites, and Evangelical Christians, 1855-1917." Ph.D. diss., Queen's University, 1971.

Neufeld, Abram H., ed. and trans. *Herman and Katharina: Their Story*. Winnipeg: Center for Mennonite Studies in Canada, 1984.

Newman, A. H., ed. *A Century of Baptist Achievement*. Philadelphia: American Baptist Publication Society, 1901.

Nichols, Gregory L. "Paskovism: Nineteenth Century Piety." M.A. thesis, Wheaton College, 1991.

———. *The Development of Russian Evangelical Spirituality: A Study of Ivan Kargel (1849-1937)*. Eugene, OR: Pickwick Publications, 2011.

Novikoff, Olga. "A Cask of Honey with a Spoonful of Tar." *Contemporary Review*, Feb. 1889, 207–15.

Olsson, Karl A. *By One Spirit: A History of the Evangelical Covenant Church of America*. Chicago: Covenant Press, 1961.

Orlow, Damon L. *Red Wedding*. Chicago: Henry Regnery Company, 1952.

Orr, J. Edwin. *The Second Evangelical Awakening in Britain*. London and Edinburgh: Marshall, Morgan and Scott, 1949.

Packer, J. A. *Among the Heretics in Europe*. London: Cassell and Company, 1912.

Pankratov, A. S. *Ishchushchie Boga*. Vol. 1. Moscow, 1911.
Parker. W. H. *An Historical Geography of Russia*. Chicago: Aldine Press, 1969.
Patmont, Louis R. "Bible Christians in Eastern Europe." *Christian Standard*, Jan. 20, 1945, 6.
———. "The Restoration Movement in Poland." *Christian Standard*, June 21, 1913, 3–4.
Pavlov, Vasiliĭ. "Pravda o baptistakh." *Baptist* 42–47, 1911.
———. "The Christianizing of the World—Russia." BWA, Congress, *Proceedings*, 1911, 23–31.
———. "Vospominaniya ssyl'nago." Vladimir D. Bonch-Bruevich, *Materialy k istorii i izucheniyu rosskago sektantstva*. Vol. 1. SPB, 1908, 1–24.
Penner, Peter. *Russians, North Americans and Telugus*. Winnipeg, MB, and Hillsboro, KS: Kindred Productions, 1997.
Peters, G. W. *Foundations of Mennonite Brethren Missions*. Hillsboro, KS, and Winnipeg, MB: Kindred Press, 1984.
———. *The Growth of Foreign Missions in The Mennonite Brethren Church*. Hillsboro, KS: Board of Foreign Missions, The Conference of the Mennonite Brethren Church of North America, 1947.
Petrov, N. I. "Novyya svedeniya o stundisme." *Trudy Kievskoĭ dukhovnoĭ akademii*, 1887, no. 3, 377–403, and no. 4, 600–620.
———. "Svedeniya o divizhenii yuzhno-russkago sektantstva v poslednie gody." *Trudy KievskoI dukhovnoĭ akademii*, 1886, no. 22, 537–40.
Pierard, Richard V., ed. *Baptists Together in Christ, 1905-2005*. Falls Church, VA: Baptist World Alliance, 2005.
Pike, G. Holden. "The Bible in Russia." *The Sunday Magazine* 28 (n.s.), 1889, 634–36.
Pis'mo vsem baptistskim obshchinam i otdel'nym brat'yam baptistam v Rossii. Tiflis, 1916.
Pius, N. H. *An Outline of Baptist History*. Nashville: Nashville Baptist Publishing Board, 1911.
Platonov, A. I. "Molokanstvo, baptizm' i nasha velikaya tserkovnaya nuzhda." *Missionerskoe obozrenie*, Sept. 2, 1905, 473–94.
Plett, Delbert F. *The Golden Years: The Mennonite Kleine Gemeinde in Russia (1812-1849)*: Steinbach, MB: D.F.P. Publications, 1985.
Plett, I. P. *Zdes' terpenie i vera svyatykh*. Vol. 2. N.p.: "Khrstianin" MSTs EkhB, 2010.
Pobedonostsev, Konstantin P. *Reflections of a Russian Statesman*. Translated by Robert Crozier Long. Ann Arbor: The University of Michigan Press, 1965.
Pokrovskiĭ, M.N., ed. *Pis'ma Pobedonostseva k Aleksandru III*. Vols. 1–2. Moscow: Novaya Moskva, 1925.
———. *Pobedonostsev i ego korrespondenty: Pis'ma i zapiski*. Vols. 1–2. Petrograd and Moscow: Gosudarstvennoe izdatelstvo, 1923.
Poysti, N. J. "A Recent Moscow Happening." *The Gospel Call*, June 1946, 3, 5–7.
Prestridge, J. N. *Modern Baptist Heroes and Martyrs*. Louisville: World Press, 1911.
Prokhanov, Ivan S. *In the Cauldron of Russia*. New York: All-Russian Evangelical Christian Union, 1933.
———. *O sluzhenii zhenshchin v tserkvakh*. SPB, 1911.
———. *O vozlozhenii ruk i rukopolozhenii*. SPB, 1911. Also in *Khristianin* 6, 1924, 75–87.
Prugavin, Alexandr S. *Religioznye otshchepensty: Ocherki sovremennago sektantsva*. Vol. 2. SPB, 1904.
Putinstsev, F. M. *Politicheskaya rol' sektantsva*. Moscow: Bezbozhnik, 1928.
———. *Politicheskaya rol' i taktika sekt*. Moscow: Gosudarstvennoe antireligioznoe izdatel'stvo, 1935.

Bibliography

Puzynin, Andrey P. *The Tradition of the Gospel Christians.* Eugene, OR: Pickwick Publications, 2011.

Radcliffe, Jane. *Recollections of Reginald Radcliffe.* London: Morgan and Scott, 1896.

Reddig, Ken. "Mennonite Publishing in Russia: The Raduga Press of Halbstadt." *Mennonite Historian* 13/1 (Mar. 1987), 1–2.

Reimer, Johannes. *Seine letzten Worte waren ein Lied: Martin Thielmann, Leben und Wirken des Kirgisen Missionars.* Lage: Logos Verlag, 1997.

Reïnmarus, A. "Sektantstvo v 1917." *Antireligioznik* 5, 1930, 14–18.

Religious Freedom in Russia, Consisting of an Argument in Behalf of Russian Baptists Held Amenable to the Russian Penal Statute Against Change of Religion. Philadelphia: Bible and Publication Society, 1874.

Rennikov, A. M. *Zoloto Reina: O Nemtsakh v Rossii.* Petrograd, 1915.

Report of the Alliance Deputation of the American Branch of the Evangelical Alliance, Appointed to Memorialize the Emperor in Russia on Behalf of Religious Liberty. New York: Evangelical Alliance, 1871.

"Rev. J. G. Oncken." *American Baptist Memorial*, May 1854, 129–36.

Riasnovsksy, Nicholas V. *A History of Russia.* New York: Oxford University Press, 1963.

Riediger, Peter. "Mission der Mennoniten in Russland unter den Russen." Translated as "Mennonite Missions Among the Russians." Mns. B. B. Janz Papers, Centre for Mennonite Brethren Studies, Winnipeg.

Riss, Ya. M. "Brat. Ya. A. Freï." *Bratskiï vestnik* 7, 1947, 39–42.

Roemmich, Heinrich. "Der Ursprung des ukrainischen Stundism." *Heimat der Deutschen aus Russland*, 1967/1968, 65–74.

Roi, Johannes F. A. de le. *Geschichte der evangelischen Juden-Mission seit Entstehung des neueren Judentums.* 2 vols. 2nd ed. Leipzig: J. C. Hinrichs, 1899.

Roland, Richard H. "The Population of Volga-German Settlements in Late Nineteenth Century Russia: A Source Based on Religious and Settlement Data from the 1897 Census of the Russia Empire. *Journal of the American Historical Society of Germans from Russia* 13/4 (Winter 1990), 10–24.

Ronis, Osvaldo. *Uma Epopéia de Fé: História des Baptistas Letos no Brasil.* Rio de Janeiro: Committee of Religious Education and Publication of the Brazilian Baptist Convention, 1974.

Rouse, Ruth. *The World's Student Christian Federation.* New York: S.C.M. Press, 1938.

Rozhdestvenskiï, Arseniï. *Yuzhnorusskiï shtundizm.* SPB, 1889.

Rushbrooke, J. H. "Vasili Pavlov: A Russian Baptist Pioneer." *The Baptist Quarterly* 6/8 (Oct. 1933), 361–67.

Sawatzky, Heinrich. *Mennonite Templers.* Translated by Victor G. Doerksen. Winnipeg: CMBC Publications and Manitoba Mennonite Historical Society, 1990.

Schäfer, Richard. *Geschichte der Deutschen Orient-Mission.* Potsdam: Lepsius, Fleisch-mann & Grauer, 1932.

Scharpff, Paulus. *A History of Evangelism.* Grand Rapids: Eerdmans, 1986.

Schmidt, Wolfgang. *Die Pfingstbewegung in Finnland.* Helsingfors: Kirchengeschichtliche Gesellschaft Finnlands, 1935.

Schoenfield, Hugh J. *The History of Jewish Christianity from the First to the Twentieth Century.* London: Duckworth, 1936.

Shanafelt, T. M. *The Baptist History of South Dakota.* Sioux Falls: South Dakota Baptist Convention, 1899.

Shcherbina, F. A. "Malorusskaya shtunda." *Nedelya*, 1877, no. 1, 22–32, and no. 2, 54–61.

Sikorskii, I. A. *"Psikhopaticheskaya epidemiya 1892 goda v Kievskoï Gubernii."* St. Vladimir Imperial University, *Universitetskiya izvestiya* 33 (1893), 1–46.

Simons, George Albert. "Biographical Sketch." Mns. The United Methodist Church, General Commission on Archives and History.

———. "Observations and Experiences in Russia and the Baltic Countries." *The European Harvest Field,* Sept., 14–15; Oct., 17–19, 1929.

———. "Report of the Superintendent." Mns. World Methodist Council. The United Methodist Church, General Commission on Archives and History.

———. "The World's Student Christian Federation in Old Russia." *The European Harvest Field,* Jan. 1930, 27–31.

Skvortsov, Dimitrii I. *Sovremennoe russkoe sektantstvo.* Moscow, 1905.

Skvortsov, Vasilii M. *Missionerskoe posokh.* SPB, 1912.

———. "Organizatsiya shtundistkoï propagandy." *Moskovskiya vedomosti,* Aug. 10, 1894, 1–2.

———. "Ratsionalisticheskoe sektantstvo." *Missionerskoe obozrenie,* Jan. 1911, 186–89.

Smith, C. Henry. *Smith's Story of the Mennonites.* Revised and enlarged by Cornelius Krahn. 5th ed. Newton, KS: Faith and Life Press, 1981.

Smith, Eli, and H. G. W. O. Dwight. *Missionary Researches in Armenia.* London: George Whitman, 1834.

Smorodin, Maria Aleksandrovna. "Vospominaniya." Mns. Southern Baptist Historical Library and Archives.

Sokolov, E. I. "M. T. Ratushnyï." *Bratskii vestnik* 6, 1980, 41–45.

———. "V. V. Ivanov." *Bratskii vestnik* 1, 1982, 47–52.

Solberg, C. K. *A Brief History of the Zion Society for Israel.* Minneapolis: The Zion Society for Israel, 1928.

Spicer, William A. *Our Story of Missions for Colleges and Academies.* Mountain View, CA: Pacific Press Publishing Association, 1921.

Stanyukovich, Konstantin. *Polnoe sobranie sochinenii.* Vols. 3, 7. 2nd ed. SPB: A. F. Marks, 1906–1907.

Stead. William T. *Truth about Russia.* London: Cassell and Company, 1888.

Steeves, Paul D. "Ivan Stepanovich Prokhanov." *The Modern Encyclopedia of Russian and Soviet History* 30, 8–14.

———. "The Russian Baptist Union, 1917–1935: Evangelical Awakening in Russia." Ph.D. diss., University of Kansas, 1976.

Stefanovich, Andreï I. *Die Maljowantzi.* Berlin: Verlag Deutsche Orient Mission, 1904.

Stepniak, pseud. *The Russian Peasantry: Their Agrarian Condition, Social Life and Religion.* New York: Harper & Brothers, 1888.

Stevenson, Lilian. *Mathilda Wrede of Finland, Friend of Prisoners.* London: G. Allen and Unwin, 1925.

Strel'bitskii, I. *Kratkii ocherk shtundizma i svod tekstov, napravlennykh k ego oblicheniyu.* 4th ed. Odessa, 1899.

Stroelin, Karl. *Die Schwaben in Russland.* Stuttgart: W. Kohlhammer, 1925.

Stumpp, Karl. *German-Russians: Two Centuries of Pioneering.* Translated by Joseph S. Height. Bonn, Brussels, and New York: Edition Atlantic-Forum, 1967.

Stunt, W. T., et. al. *Turning the World Upside Down.* Eastbourne, Sussex: Upperton Press, and Bath, Somerset, UK: Echoes of Service, 1972.

Bibliography

Sudermann, David. "*Allianz* in Ukraine: More Pieces of the Puzzle." *Mennonite Historian* 23/1 (Mar. 1997), 1–2, and 23/2 (June 1997), 6–7.

Sundell, Alwar, ed. *De Började—Vi Fortsätter: Baptismen i Finland 100 År, 1856–1956*. Vasa: Facklans Förlag, 1956.

Svensson, Johannes. *De ewangeliska kristnas konferens i St. Petersburg den 28 jan.–5 febr. 1907*. Ekenäs, Sweden, 1907.

Tatford, Frederick A. *Red Glow over Eastern Europe*. Bath: Echoes of Service, 1986.

Terletskiĭ, G. I. *Sekta pashkovtsev*. SPB, 1891.

Thompson, Albert W. *A Century of Jewish Missions*. New York: Fleming H. Revell, 1902.

Toews, Jacob John. "Cultural Background of the Mennonite Brethren Church." M.A. thesis, University of Toronto, 1951.

Toews, John A. *A History of the Mennonite Brethren Church*. Fresno: Board of Christian Literature, General Conference of Mennonite Brethren Churches, 1975.

Toews, John B. *Czars, Soviets & Mennonites*. Newton, KS: Faith and Life Press, 1982.

———. *Perilous Journey: The Mennonite Brethren in Russia, 1860–1910*. Winnipeg, MB, and Hillsboro, KS: Kindred Press, 1988.

———. "The Calm Before the Storm: Mennonite Brethren in Russia, 1900–1914." *Direction* 31/1 (Spring 2002), 74–95.

———, ed. and tr. "The Early Mennonite Brethren: Some Outside Views." *The Mennonite Quarterly Review* 58/2 (Apr. 1984), 83–124.

———, ed. *The Story of the Early Mennonite Brethren (1860–1869): Reflections of a Lutheran Churchman*. Winnipeg, MB, and Hillsboro, KS: Kindred Publications, 2002.

Tolstoĭ, M. "Samozvannyĭ missioner v pravoslavnoĭ Moskve." *Dushepoleznoe chtenie* 2, 1877, 78–87.

Töws, Aron A. *Mennonitische Märtyrer*. Vols. 1–2. Winnipeg, MB: 1949, 1954.

Trotter, Mrs. Edward. *Lord Radstock, an Interpretation and a Record*. London: Hodder and Stoughton, c. 1914.

Unruh, A. H. *Die Geschichte der Mennoniten Bruedergemeinde*. Hillsboro, KS: General Conference of the Mennonite Brethren Church of North America, 1955.

Urry, James. "A Religious or a Social Elite? The Mennonite Brethren in Imperial Russia." Symposium, "Dynamics of Faith and Culture in Mennonite Brethren History," Winnipeg, November 14–15, 1986, 24–29.

———. "John Melville and the Mennonites: A British Evangelist in South Russia, 1837–ca. 1875." *The Mennonite Quarterly Review* 54/4 (1980), 305–22.

———. *None but Saints: The Transformation of Mennonite Life in Russia 1789–1889*. Winnipeg: Hyperion Press, 1989.

———. "The Closed and the Open: Social and Religious Change amongst the Mennonites in Russia, 1789–1889." Ph.D. diss., Oxford University, 1978.

———. "The Cost of Community: The Funding and Economic Management of the Russian Mennonite Commonwealth Before 1914." *Journal of Mennonite Studies* 10 (1992), 22–55.

———. "Through the Eye of a Needle: Wealth and the Mennonite Experience in Russia." Conference, "Images of Imperial Russia," Conrad Grebel College, University of Waterloo, May 9–10, 1984.

Urshan, Andrew D. *The Life Story of Andrew Bar David Urshan*. Portland, OR: Apostolic Book Publishers, 1978.

———. *The Story of My Life*. St. Louis: Gospel Publishing House, c. 1917.

Ushinskiĭ, A. D. *Verouchnie malorusskikh shtundistov.* 3rd ed. Kiev, 1886.
Uspenskiĭ, G. I. *Polnoe sobranie sochenii.* Moscow, 1949, 8, 189-211.
V. V. "Stundisty na yuge Rossii." *Tserkovnyĭ vestnik* 48, 1882, 6-8.
Val'kevich, Victor L. *Zapiska o propagande protestantskikh sekt v Rossii i, v osobennosti, na Kavkaz.* Tiflis, 1900.
Veltistov, K. I. "Nemetskiĭ baptizm v Rossii." *Missionerskoe obozrenie,* 1902, Jan., 64-78; Mar., 462-70; June, 1019-1036; 1904, Dec. (1): 1317-1333.
Vostorvov, Ioann I. *Kak lgali russkie baptisty, vo glave s Fetlerom, v Amerike na Tserkov' Pravoslavnuyu i na russkoe pravitel'stvo?* Moscow, 1911.
———. "Vrazheskiĭ dukovnyĭ avangard." Moscow, 1913.
Vvedenskiĭ, Aleksandr I. *Deĭstvuyushchiya zakonopolozheniya kasatel'no staroobryadtsev i sektantov.* Odessa, 1912.
Wagner, William L. *New Move Forward in Europe: Growth Patterns of German Speaking Baptists in Europe.* South Pasadena, CA: William Carey Library, 1978.
Wallace, D. Mackenzie. *Russia.* New York: Henry Holt, 1877.
Wardin, Albert W., Jr. "August G. A. Liebig: German Baptist Missionary and Friend to the Mennonite Brethren." *Journal of Mennonite Studies* 28 (2010), 167-86.
———. "Baptist Immersions in the Russian Empire: Difficult Beginnings." *Journal of European Baptist Studies* 10/3 (May 2010), 37-44.
———. "Baptist Influences on Mennonite Brethren with an Emphasis on the Practice of Immersion." *Direction* 8/4 (Oct. 1979), 33-38.
———. ed. *Baptists around the World: A Comprehensive Handbook.* Nashville: Broadman and Holman, 1995.
———. "Baptists (German) in Russia and USSR." *The Modern Encyclopedia of Religions in Russia and the Soviet Union,* 3:192-202.
———. *Evangelical Sectarianism in the Russian Empire and the USSR: A Bibliographic Guide.* Lanham, MD, and London: The American Theological Library Association and The Scarecrow Press, 1995.
———. *Gottfried F. Alf: Pioneer of the Baptist Movement in Poland.* Brentwood, TN: Baptist History and Heritage Society, 2003.
———. "How Indigenous Was the Baptist Movement in the Russian Empire?" *Journal of European Baptist Studies* 9/2 (Jan. 2009), 29-37.
———. "Jacob J. Wiens: Mission Champion in Freedom and Repression." *Journal of Church and State* 28/3 (1986), 495-514.
———. "Mennonite Brethren and German Baptists in Russia: Affinities and Dissimilarities." Paul Toews, ed., *Mennonites and Baptists: A Continuing Conversation.* Winnipeg, MB, and Hillsboro, KS: Kindred Press, 1993, 97-112.
———. "Pentecostal Beginnings among Russians in Finland and Northern Russia, 1911-1921." *Fides et Historia* 26/2 (Summer 1994), 50-61.
———. "The Baptists in Bulgaria." *The Baptist Quarterly* 34/4 (Oct. 1991), 148-50.
———. "The Disciples of Christ and Ties with Russia." *Discipliana* 52/3 (1991), 33, 35-41.
———. "The Oncken Movement: Baptist Penetration in Northern and Eastern Europe." *Amercan Baptist Quarterly* 28/4 (Winter 2009), 396-406.
———. *The Twelve Baptist Tribes in the USA.* Atlanta: Baptist History and Heritage Society, 2007.
———. "William Fetler: The Thundering Evangelist." *American Baptist Quarterly* 25/3 (Fall 2006), 235-46.

Bibliography

Warns, Johannes. "Die Anfänge des Misssionswerken unter Kirgisen und Sarten." *Offene Türen*, Nov.–Dec. 1919, 83–87.

———. "Die drangsale der Mennoniten in Russland während der Kriegs- und Revolutionsjahre 1914–1920." *Offene Türen*, May–June, 1922, 35–40.

———. *Russland und das Evangelium*. Cassel: J. G. Oncken, 1920.

Warth, Robert D. "Konstantin Petrovich Pobedonostsev." *The Modern Encyclopedia of Russian and Soviet History*, 38:139–42.

Wieler, Johann. "Erweckungen und Verfolgungen in Süd-Russland." *Der Sendbote*, 1874, Apr. 1, 51; Apr. 8, 55; Apr. 15, 58.

Wiens, J. J. "Essay on the Baptist Movement in the Far East of Siberia." Mns. Archives of the International Mission Board of the Southern Baptist Convention.

Wiggins, Arch R. *The History of the Salvation Army*. Vols. 4–5. London: Thomas Nelson and Sons, 1964, 1968.

Wilkinson, Samuel Hinds. *In the Land of the North: The Evangelization of the Jews in Russia*. London: Marshall Brothers, 1905.

Windholz, George. "Psychiatric Commitments of Religious Dissenters in Tsarist and Soviet Russia: Two Case Studies." *Psychiatry* 48 (1985), 329–40.

Wright, W. "The Training of a Translator; or, Amirkhanianz and His Work." *Monthly Reporter of the British and Foreign Bible Society*, 1889, Feb., 21–22, and Mar., 42–43.

Yasevich-Borodaevskaya, V. I. *Bor'ba za veru*. SPB, 1912.

Yushenko, A. "Kondratiĭ Malevannyĭ." *Istoricheskiĭ vestnik*, 1913, 132; no. 4, 237–42.

Zavitnevich, V. "Svedeniya o dvizhenii yuzhno-russkago sektantstva v polednie gody." *Trudy Kievskoĭ dukhovnoĭ akademii* 11, 1886, 506–41.

Zaozerskiĭ, N. "Chem silen' shtundism?" *Bogoslavskiĭ vestnik* 10, 1893, 179–95.

Zhabko-Potapovich, Lev. *Khrystove svitlo v Ukraïni*. Winnipeg, MB, and Chester, PA: Ukrainian Evangelical-Baptist Alliance, 1952.

Periodcals

All the World (Salvation Army)
American Baptist Magazine
American Baptist Memorial
American Baptist Quarterly (ABQ)
Antireligioznik
Aquila
Baptist (Russia)
Baptist and Reflector
Baptist History and Heritage
Baptist Missionary Magazine (BMM)
Baptist Quarterly, The
Baptist, The
Baptist Times and Freeman
Baptist Ukrainy
Baptist World
Beseda
Bible in the Word, The (BFBS)
Bogoslavskiï vestnik
Botschafter, Der
Bratskiï listok
Bratskiï vestnik (BV)
Bridegroom's Messenger, The
Bulletin of the Hymn Society of Great Britain and Ireland
BWA News (Baptist World Alliance)
Catholic Presbyterian
Christian-Evangelist, The
Christian Standard
Christian Week
Christlicher Familienkalender
Chronik
Chteniya v obshchestve lyubiteleï dukhovnago prosveshcheniya (ChOLDP)
Church History
Contemporary Review
Covenant Quarterly, The

Periodcals

Dein Reich Komme
Delo
Der christliche Orient
Deutsche Rundschau
Die christliche Welt
Direction
Dukhovnyï khristianin
Dushepoleznoe chtenie
Echoes of Service
Elisabetgradskiï vestnik
Etnograficheskie obozrenie
European Harvest Field, The
European Studies Review (ESR)
Evangelical Alliance Quarterly
Evangelical Christendom (EC)
Evangelist (Bulgaria)
Evangel'skaya vera
Familienfreund, Der
Fides et Historia
Free Russia
Friedensstimme, Die
Friend of Missions, The
Friend of Russia, The
Gemeinde, Die
Golos
Gospel Call, The
Gospel in All Lands, The
Gospel in Russia, The
Gost'
Grazhdanin
Hausfreund, Der
Heritage Review (Germans from Russia Heritage Society)
Home and Foreign Fields (Southern Baptist)
International Bulletin of Missionary Research
International Quarterly
Istoricheskiï vestnik
Journal of European Baptist Studies
Journal of Mennonite Studies (JMS)
Journal of Russian Studies
Journal of the American Historical Society of Germans from Russia (JAHSGR)
Journal of the Evangelical Theological Society (JETS)

Katorga i ssylka
Khristianin
Khristianskiï pobornik
Kievskaya starina
Kirche im Osten
Korsets Seir
Leisure Hour
Lutheran Church Review
Lutheran Quarterly, The (LQ)
Mennonite Historian
Mennonite Quarterly Review, The (MQR)
Mennonitische Blätter
Mennonitisches Jahrbuch
Methodist History
Mission World, The
Missionary Echo
Missionary Herald
Missionary Magazine (MM)
Missionary Review of the World (MRW)
Missionerskiï sbornik
Missionerskoe obozrenie
Missions
Missions of the World, The
Missionsblatt
Mitteilungen und Nachrichten für die evangelische Kirche in Russia
Monthly Extracts of the Correspondence of the British and Foreign Bible Society (BFBS)
Monthly Reporter of the British and Foreign Bible Society (BFBS)
Moskovskiya vedomosti
Nauka i religiya
Nedelya
Neue Zeitschrift für Missionswissenschaft
Novosti
Odessaer Zeitung
Odesskiï vestnik
Offene Türen
Oxford Slavonic Papers (OSP)
Pacific Baptist
Pioneer Review
Pravoslavnoe obozrenie
Pribavlenie k Tserkovnym vedomostyam
Psychiatry

Periodcals

Quarterly Reporter of the German Baptist Mission (QR)
Razsvet'
Reich Christi, Das
Religion in Eastern Europe ((REE)
Religious Tract Society Record
Review of Reviews
Rukovodstvo dlya sel'skikh pastyreï
Russian Life
Russkaya mysl'
Russkoe obozrenie
St. Vladimir Imperial University, *Universitetskiy izvestiya.*
Sankt-Peterburgskie vedomosti
St. Petersburger Zeitung
St. Petersburgisches evangelisches Sonntagsblatt (SPES)
Sendbote, Der
Seyatel'
Seyatel' istiny
Slavic and East European Review
Solnitse
Student World, The
Sunday Magazine, The
Strannik
Svobodnaya mysl'
Svobodnoe Slovo
Texas Baptist
Trudy Kievskoï dukhovnoï akademii (TrKDA)
Tserkovnyï vestnik (TsV)
Unitarian Review
Utrennyaya zvezda
Vera i razum
Vestnik evropy
Voprosy nauchnogo ateizma
Wahrheitszeuge, Der (WHZ)
Wandering Wolhynians
War Cry, The (The Salvation Army)
Watchman-Examiner, The
Weekly Evangel, The
Zhizn'
Zionsbote

Index

Adam, Bertha, 442
Åland Islands, 32–33
Albrecht, Johann, 318
Alcohol, 138, 160, 435–36
Alexander II, 39, 93–94, 95, 106, 125, 160, 189, 205, 274
Alexander III, 188–89, 197, 205
Alf, Gottfried, 47–52, 84, 86, 296, 301, 311, 318, 428, 495
    baptism, 48
    imprisonments, 49
    type of immersion, 68, 137
Althausen, Adolf, 247
Altmann, Immanuel, 439–40
American Baptist Home Mission Society, 265, 273
American Baptist Missionary Union, 292–93, 296, 300, 313, 328, 410, 443
American Bible Society, 235
Amirkhanianz (Amirchanjanz), Abraham F., 160, 163, 194, 196, 216–17, 223, 233, 241, 245–46
Andreev, Ivan, 119, 130, 192
Anticlericalism, 206
Antoschewski, Josef, 428
Archipov, Radion, 122, 128
Armenians
    evangelical, 245–46
    missions among, 14
Arndt, Friedrich A., 302–3, 349, 352, 375, 425–26, 443, 446, 484
Arnold, A. J., 264
Assmann, Heinrich, 48

Babienko, Trofim (Theofil), 216, 225–26, 274, 282–83
Baedeker, Frederick W., 179, 189, 191, 194–96, 217–18, 221, 225, 227, 233, 243–44, 245, 259, 260–62, 263, 265, 273, 278–79, 290, 298, 301, 390

Bagdasarjanz, Sembat, 160, 217, 245–46, 258, 274
Baier, Christopher, 485
Balaban, Gerasim (Vitenko), 106, 107, 109–10, 115–16, 118–19, 121, 123–24, 125, 128, 129, 133, 135, 143
Balikhin, Fedor P., 161, 194, 230, 253, 258, 260, 330, 343, 347, 349, 352, 354, 360, 413, 418, 452, 481, 491
Balikhin, Maksim, 251
Baltic
    Baptists in, 29–46, 303–5, 306–10, 426–27
    statistics, 165, 321
Baltic Baptist Association (Latvian), 307
Balzer, Heinrich, 56
Bandzmer, 485
Baptist, 331, 336, 345, 347
Baptist Missionary Society (Russian), 331, 345
Baptist World Alliance, 258, 327, 340, 346, 348–52
    black delegates, 327–28
    proposal of Russian seminary, 397–402
Baptists, hostility toward, 18, 29–46, 32–33, 35–38
Barchet, Reinhold, 465
Barratt, Thomas B., 469–70, 473
Bartel, Heinrich, 63, 65, 68–69
Bartleman, Frank, 471–72
Barton, James L., 448–49
Bechler, Miss, 450
Bekker, Benjamin, 66, 69
Bekker, Jacob P., 57, 62, 66, 68–69
Beklemisheva, Elena V., 346
Bellyustin, Ivan S., 176
Belogorskiĭ, N., 319
Belousov, Fedora I., 481
Belousov, S. P., 360, 382, 488
Benander, C., 487
Benford, Benjamin, 265

Index

Berg, Peter, 64, 98, 100
Bergeman, F. V., 164
Bergmann, Hermann A., 417
Berneike, H., 84, 303
Benzien, Karl, 74, 76
Beseda, 253, 267–68, 275
Bezzubov, P. S., 278
Bible
   coarses.389–90
   colporteurs, 161
   distribution of, 180, 183–85, 232–35
   influence of, 94–96
Bible societies, 17, 95
Bier, Philipp, 419
Biryukov, Pavel, 270
Bismarck, Otto, 39, 208
Blackwood, Arthur, 170–71
Blankenburg Conference, 410, 434–35, 452
Blücher, Toni von, 390
Bobrinskiĭ, Alekseiĭ, 173, 175, 178, 179, 184, 189, 192, 197–98, 236, 237–38, 243
Boettcher, J. T., 468
Bogdanov, Egor M., 146, 162–63, 194, 225
Bogolyubov, D. I., 377
Bohn, Rudolf and Pauline, 453–55
Boiye, Constantine, 464
Bonch-Bruevich, Vladimir D., 219, 227, 270, 273, 276, 355
Bondar, S. P., 336, 357–58, 418–20, 468, 483–84
Bonekemper, Johannes, 101–2
Bonekemper, Karl, 71, 101
Bonikowski, Emil, 484
Book peddlers/sellers, 236
Booth, Bramwell, 464
Booth, William, 464
Bortovskiĭ, N., 393
Brandt, Peter P., 484
Brandtmann, Johann, 34–36, 39
Brauer, Friedrich, 343, 349, 374, 386, 395–96, 424, 428, 429, 431, 433, 434, 437, 438, 443, 445–46, 447, 485
Braun, Abraham, 409–10, 412
Braun, G. J., 380
Braun, Heinrich J., 290, 365, 409, 411, 412, 415–16, 417–19, 436, 482
Braun, Jacob, 482
Brechlin, Franz, 485
Brennwalder, Marie, 441

Breshkovsky, Catherine, 243
Brethren (Plymouth Brethren), 278–79, 320, 453–55, 466–67
British and Foreign Bible Society, 17, 95, 183, 185, 233–34, 449–50
Broadbent, Edmund H., 279, 320, 409, 467
Bronshtein, 347
Brotherhood of the Acts of the Apostles, 470–71
Brown, John, 119, 218–19, 221, 271
Brune, Alexander K., 57
Burgardt, Johannes, 83
Burmistrov Y. M., 236
Busch, E. H., 66
Byford, C. T., 338, 340, 344–45, 348, 350
Bystrom, Jacob, 487

Chapels, 50, 120, 136
Chechetkin, M. D., 230, 253
Chepurin, N., 377
Chertkov, Vladimir G., 175, 270
Chertkova, Elizaveta Ivanova, 171, 175, 180, 182, 197, 228, 235, 242, 375
Christians of the Evangelical Faith, 280
Church Brethren, 320
Church of Christ, Poland, 465–66
Churzin, N. V., 376
Claassen, Johann 61, 62–63, 64, 65, 66–67, 98–99
Claassen, Katharina, 66.
Clifford, John, 333, 348, 352, 387, 439
Committee for Evangelical Mission in Russia, 241, 449
Congregational Church (English and American Chapel), 16, 17, 171, 228
Congregationalists, 437
Congress on Sectarian Rights
   consultative, 328
   St. Petersburg, 329
Conradi, Louis Richard, 282–83
Conwell, Russell, 349–50
Courland, 34–35
   Baptist petitions, 38–39
   Lutheran opposition, 35–38
Craig, J. 182–83
Crimea, German Baptists, 313
Czech Baptists (Polish), 427–48

Dadianov, T. F., 387

Dalton, Hermann, 13, 18, 40, 95, 102–3, 119, 140–41, 182–83, 196, 265–66, 298
Darby, J. N., 467
Darbyite Danger, 467
Datsko, P. V., 491
Deeper Life, 435, 452
Delyakov, Jakob (Yakov) D., 96, 146, 152–53, 156, 162–64, 185, 194–95, 233, 235, 238–39, 253, 280, 458
Delyakov, Joseph, 239
Demikhovich, Ya., 379
Deutsche Orient Mission, 391, 393, 449
Dick, David J., 410
Dietrich, Heinrich, 14
Dimitriï, Archbishop, 104, 107
Dirks, Heinrich, 408
Disciples of Christ, 403–5, 465–66
Dissenters, 7
Dobrudja, 70, 73, 76, 77, 273
Dom Evangeliya, 346, 367, 369, 476, 479–80, 482, 487
Dondukov-Korskov, A. M., 209
Dorodnitsyn, Aleksiï, 208, 211
Dostoevsky, Fedor M., 174
Drahomonov, Mykhaïlo, 270
Dubovy, Andrew, 136, 274
Dück, Isaak, 409, 416
Dück, Wilhelm, 409
Durasoff, Steve, 378
Dyck, Abram, 98
Dyck, Peter J., 482, 483

Easton, P. Z., 158, 160, 161, 164–65, 194, 459
Ebelov, governor-general, 481
Edict of Toleration, 1905, 325–26
Edinger, Karl, 70
Ekelmann, Otto, 36–37
Eklund, Anna, 462
Embassy Churches, 16
Engel, Friedrich, 69–70, 71, 73
Engel, Martin, 70, 73
Epp, David, 57
Epp, David, H., 417, 421–22, 423
Epp, Jacob D., 57
Estonian Baptists, 308–10, 426–27, 470
statistics, 310, 426
European Baptist Congresses, 330, 332–33, 352–53

Evangelical Alliance, 24, 38, 70, 128–29, 263–65, 275, 434, 452
Evangelical Association, 465
Evangelical Bible Society, 17
Evangelical Christians, 352, 364–67, 371–84, 386–88, 488–89
 Baptist division, 371–79
 Baptist relations, 327, 346, 347
 confession of faith, 380–81
 congresses, 379–82, 488–89
 efforts at reconciliation, 382–84, 386–88, 488–89
 objection to Baptist name, 373–75
 statistics, 388
 Vladikavkaz Agreement, 387
Evstratenko, Andreï, 218, 219, 259, 272, 333, 348

Fägerström, Gustav, 33
Faltin, Rudolph, 247
Fast, Hermann, I., 243, 262, 266, 267, 268, 301–2
February Revolution, 487–90
Fedorov, V., 363
Fetler, Andrew (Andreis), 307
Fetler, Melanie, 344, 349–50, 361
Fetler, Robert, 480–382, 491
Fetler William A., 328, 33–32, 335, 338, 340, 341, 342–44, 346, 349–53, 354, 361, 362, 375, 380, 382, 383–84 , 386, 387, 390, 397–98, 400–401, 450, 452, 456–57, 464, 470–71, 472, 476, 478–79, 480–81 487, 488, 491, 498
Fetzer, J. G. 313, 317, 318
Finland, 33–34, 239
 Finnish Baptists, 33–34
 Methodists, 461–63
 Pentecostals, 470–72
 Salvation Army, 464
 Swedish Baptists, 33
First World War, 475–77
 anti-sectarian attacks, 477–87
 evangelical support, 476–79
 pacifism, 479
 Russian war prisoners, 486–87
Fischer, Christian, 79, 83, 146, 313
Fisk Jubilee Singers, 262
Flocken, Frederick W., 73, 116
Forchhammer. Otto, 64, 69, 95, 291, 301, 305, 344, 356, 379, 406, 408, 415, 422–23

Index

Forssell, David, 32
Franklin, James H., 351, 378, 400–401
Franko, Ivan Ya., 270–71
Free church evangelicals, statistics, 492
Freutel, Gustav, 484
Frey, John A. (Janis), 304, 307, 314, 341, 352, 386, 425, 427, 444–45, 450, 484, 487
Freywald, K., 484
Freze (Froese), Peter, 100
Friedensstimme, 294
Friesen, Abraham, 292–93, 369, 411
Friesen, Peter Martin, 80, 121, 145, 147, 163, 287–90
Froese (Fröse), Gerhard P., and Anna, 413, 416, 417
Fuchs, Johann J., 485
Fudel', I., 272
Füllbrandt, Karl (Carl) G., 305, 313, 338, 339–40, 349, 425, 427, 431, 434, 436, 438, 445, 447

Gaertner (Gertners), Adam, 35–37, 39
Gagarina, Vera, von der Pahlen, 171, 178, 180, 182, 194–95, 197, 228, 242
Galitsin, Katherine, 173
Galling, W. E., 301
Gamble, Fanny Nast, 463
Gaponchuk (Haponchuk), 221
Gargulla, J. G., 89
Gaylord, Franklin A., 450
Gerasimov, 473
German Baptists in Germany, 19–25
    confession of faith, 21–22
    denominaional characteristics, 21–23
    expansion in Europe, 24–25
    opposition, 23–24
    support from abroad, 24
German Baptists in Russia, 42–54, 69–77, 81–90
    associations, 77, 84, 295
    beginnings, 42–54, 69–73, 81–82
    benevolence, 441–42
    Bible courses, 85
    Caucasus, 313
    chapels, 430
    church edifices, 430–31
    Crimea, 313
    criticism of Pashkovites, 298
    deportations, 87–89, 483–85
    Don region, 313–14
    emigration, 429–30
    First World War, 477
    foreign missions, 440–41
    geographical distribution, 435–30
    governmental relations, 84, 86–90, 330–31, 337–42, 352–53, 445–46
    holy kiss, the, 434
    home missions, 439–40
    mission to Russians, 437–38
    Moscow, 301
    pastors, 431
    Persia, 441
    personal morality, 435–36
    publications, 314–15, 444–45
    recognition of 1879, 89–90
    relations with Mennonite Brethren, 73–77, 85, 419, 421
    relations with Russian Baptist Union, 439
    relations with Seventh-day Adventists 282
    relations with Ukrainian stundists and Russian Baptists, 84, 107–8, 318–19
    St. Petersburg, 42–46, 297–303, 426, 438
    Siberia, 314, 436–37
    statistics, 86, 163, 297, 320–21, 363, 424, 426–30
    Sunday schools and youth societies, 432
    support from abroad, 85, 296–97, 299, 303, 442–43
    suppressions, 483–85, 492
    tobacco, use of, 85
    Union of Baptist Churches of Russia, 295–96
    Volga, 310–13
Germanophobia, 208, 478
Germans, influence of, 4–5, 141
Gerusy, 226–27, 261–62, 272, 283
Godet, Georges, 120. 221, 263, 271
Goetze, Bernard J., 321, 485
Golovchenko, Ivan, 225
Golyaev, Il'ya A., 161, 346, 348, 362, 386, 387, 491
Gorbachev, Gerasim U., 154
Gorchakov, Alexander, 128–29
Gordon, A. J., 239
Görz, Abraham, 409, 416–17
Goshchapov, 225
Grimm, Eduard Wilhelm, 29–30

Gritton, John, 264
Griva, Petr, 114, 132, 146
Grothe, J., 236, 239, 462
Gruenfeldt, 380
Guiness, Fanny, 242
Guiness, Henry Grattan, 185–86, 242

H. v. K, 271
Haak, Johannes, 413
Hakkarainen, Pekka, 472
Hamburg Baptist Theological Seminary, 315, 396, 412, 425
Hammer, Friedrich, 312–13, 317
Hartwich, M., 51
Haupt, W., 304
Hausfreund, Der, 304, 314, 444–45
Heier, Edmund, 181, 228
Heikel, Anna, 33
Heikel, Henrik, 33
Heikel Victor, 33
Heinrichs, Jacob, 410–11, 413, 417–18, 421, 440–41
Heiter, Ernst, 429
Henriksson, J., 33
Herasimenko, E., 273
Herb, Alfons, 429
Herb, Bernard J., 428, 428, 477
Herholt, Oswald and Augusta, 454
Heringer, Martin, 76
Herrmann, Julius, 303–4, 306, 309, 314, 316
Hiebert, N. N., 293
Hiebert, Nickel, 146
Hilton, Edward, 198
Hilton, Henry, 198
Högberg, Lars E., 190–91, 240, 244
Höijer, N. F., 194, 223, 240–41, 255–57, 459
Hörmann, Friedrich, 438–39, 446
Horn, L., 421
Hottmann, Joseph, 59, 60–66
Huebert, Abraham, 293
Huebert, Heinrich, 62, 66, 98
Husmann, Harm, 311–13, 317, 320, 443
Hymander, John, 33–34

Inkis (Inke), Janis, 304, 307, 349, 379, 427
Inkis, K. G., 403
Intelligentsia, 269–72
Isaak, David P., 365, 416
Isaak, Johann, 413

Isaak, Peter, 413
Ivanenko, Grigor P., 267
Ivanov, Aleksandr I., 471–74
Ivanov, Egor N., 220
Ivanov, N., 341
Ivanov, Vasiliĭ N., 233, 284
Ivanov, Vasiliĭ V., 154–56, 158, 164, 221, 225, 231, 233, 251, 253, 256–57, 260, 266, 280, 291, 327–28, 346, 347, 349, 357, 360, 374, 375, 379, 386, 456, 472, 481, 482, 491
Ivanov-Klyshnikov, Pavel V., 360, 491
Izaak, I. F., 328, 379

Jack, Walter L., 329, 392–93, 459–60, 487
Jacksteit, Robert, 485
Jacobson (Estonian), 44, 115
Jacobson (Jekabsons), Friedrch (Frizis), 34
Jankowski, Andreas, 37–38, 64
Jankowski, J., 39, 43
Jannson, Eric, 349
Jantz, Jakob, 79
Jantzen, Hermann, 454
Janzen, Cornelius, 415
Janzen, Jacob, 64
Jeske, Martin, 485
Jewish missions, 246–48, 439–40
Jews
    converts, 83
    resistance to Christianity, 49
Johannson, H., 432
Johnson, John, 403
Joseph, Ruben, 441
Junker, Fritz, 439
Juraschka, Daniel, 34, 36, 37–8

Kahle, William, 376, 384, 393
Kallistov, Nikolaĭ, 154, 160
Kalmykov, Maksim I., 456
Kal'nev, Mikhail A., 214, 289, 319, 342–43, 438
Kalweit, Karl, 151, 152, 157
Kalweit, Martin K., 43, 115, 151–54, 157, 158, 165, 217, 226–27, 332–33, 414
Kalweit, Ottiliya (Ottilie), 160
Kalweit, Otto, 160
Kappes, 59
Kapranov, A. I., 473
Kapranova, sister, 381

Index

Kapustinskiĭ, Sazont E., 220–21, 226, 227, 233
Kapustyan, Alexandr, 106, 107, 115, 116, 120–22, 128, 143, 146
Kargel, Johann G. (Ivan V.), 43–45, 79, 84, 120–21, 152, 158, 194–95, 230, 238, 242, 251–52, 295, 296, 299, 327, 329, 346, 368, 369, 376, 379, 381, 389, 426, 435, 452, 491
Kean, William, 362
Keevil, Joseph, 403
Kelm, Mathias, 51
Kerensky, Alexander, 490
Keriakov, 105, 106
Kessler, Johann, 85, 313, 315, 320, 425
Kharusin, A., 417–18
Khilkov, D. H., 268
Khlystun, Trifon, 146, 220, 223, 226
Khristianskiĭ pobornik, 462
Kiefer, F., 298–300, 318–19
Kielblock, T. F., 152, 157, 259
Kilburn, J. B., 330, 339, 452
Kilius, 233
Kirchner, Elena V., 236, 267–68
Kirsch, E. F., 233
Kiselev, 194
Klein, Ernst-Ferdinand, 354, 460
Kleine Gemeinde, 55, 61
Klemm, Martin, 430
Klempel, Hermann, 314, 437
Klibanov, A. I., 143, 281, 354, 384, 455
Kliewer, G. G., 319
Klimenko, Michael, 105, 113
Kludt, 320
Klundt, Jakob, 76, 84, 116
Klyshnikov, Efim T. (Vasiliĭ S. Ivanov), 155
Köbner, Julius, 20–21, 23, 24, 25, 30–31
Köhler, Christopher, 390
Kokki, J. G., 479
Kolesnikov, Ivan, 273, 274
Kolodin, Vasiliĭ R., 163, 194, 251, 255
Kondratskiĭ, Daniel, 117–18
König, Karl, 83
Korff, Modes M., 173, 178–80, 181–82, 183–84, 192, 193–95, 197, 199–200, 228, 242, 495
Kostromin, Teodor, 226, 231, 273
Kostykov, Andreĭ, 481
Kotzebu, P. E., governor-general, 74, 89, 106–7

Koval, Yakov, 119, 123–24, 130, 140, 192
Kovno German Baptist Church, 305
Kowalsky, J., 71, 73
Kozakevich, Michael, 126, 139–40
Kozitskiĭ, Pavel, 127, 128, 138, 139, 206, 250, 271–72
Kravchenko, K. I., 343
Kravchenko, Maxim, 108, 109, 132
Kravchinskiĭ, Sergeĭ M. (S. Stepniak), 270
Kroeker, Abraham, 293–94, 365, 408, 412, 416, 418–19, 422, 467, 484, 490
Kroeker, Jakob, 293–94, 410, 412, 426, 434, 487
Krüger, M. A., 436–37
Kruglov, F., 478
Kruse, Nathalie von, 173
Kudinov, N. F., 457
Kursit, Ya.. A., 344
Kushnerenko, Grigoriĭ, 115, 144, 146
Kushnerov, Ivan P., 231, 276–77, 328, 330, 339, 344, 349, 374
Kutepov, N., 255–56

Langhans, Wilhelm, 87–88
Lansdell, Henry, 185
Larsson, A. P., 194–96
Lasch, Martin, 310–11
Latimer, R. S., 281, 351, 359
Latvian Baptists, 34–38, 41–42, 306–8, 426–27
  migration to Brazil, 308
  relations with Germans, 303–4, 306–7
  statistics, 307–8
Law of 1883 for dissenters, 190, 204–5
Lehmann, Gottfried Wilhelm, 21, 24, 30–31
Lehmann, Joseph, 130, 288
Lehmann, Severin W., 89, 296–97, 301, 304, 310–13, 396, 425, 426, 431, 436, 441, 484
Lepp, Aron, 72, 76, 80
Leppke, Edward, 80
Lepsius, Johann, 391, 410, 458–59
Leroy-Beaulieu, Anatole, 271
Leskov, Nikolaĭ, 171, 175, 181, 198
Leushkin, Andreĭ E., 220, 259, 353, 372–73, 375–76, 386, 470, 472
Liebig, August, 45, 73–75, 76–77, 116, 130, 149, 158, 192, 194–95, 305–6, 315

Liebig, August (*cont.*)
    relations with Mennonite Brethren,, 73–75, 76–77, 80, 82, 84, 289
Liebig, Ludwig, 77, 84
Lieven, Anatol, 452
Lieven, Karl, 17
Lieven, Nathalie, 170, 171, 173, 178–79, 193–97, 198, 228, 238, 240, 243, 267, 325, 368
Lieven, Paul, 182, 410
Lieven, Sophie, 173, 182, 242, 277
Lindblom, August, 33
Lindl, Ignaz, 12
Linowski, Franz, 70
Lion, Solomon E., 143
Liprandi, A. P., 209
Lodz German Baptist Church, 305–6, 427, 430
Loebsack, Heinrich, 282
Lorenz, Just, 312
Losev, I. T., 356
Lübeck, Johannes, 424, 435, 444, 452, 484
Luther, L., 352
Lutherans, 10–13, 437, 446–47
    Jewish missions, 246–47
    opposition to Baptists, 23, 34–38, 47–49, 53, 82, 90, 298, 320–21
    pietism, 12
    separatists, 12–13, 58
    Volhynia, 51, 52, 85
L'vovich, Dmitrii, 478
Lyalina, G. S., 354
Lyasotskii, Gavriil, 118, 124
Lyasotskii, Ivan, 87, 118, 124, 226
Lydell, Adolph, 241
Lysenko, Peter I., 131

MacArthur, Robert S., 349, 398, 400
McCaig, Archibald, 338
McCash, I. N., 403
Macalpine, George, 398–99
Maier (Meyer), Heinrich, 81
Malevannyï, Kondratiï A., 280–81
Malevantsy, 280–81, 460
Margaritov, S., 419–20
Marks, Johann, 305, 311
Martens, Cornelius, 413–14
Martschoff, Vasil, 315, 436
Mascher, Karl, 390, 410–11, 413, 440
Maslov, 472–73

Matveev, G. M., 385
Mayer, Karl von, 180
Mazaev, Andreï M., 146, 158, 252, 259, 331
Mazaev, Deï I., 161, 229, 252–54, 258–59, 272, 291, 326–28, 329, 331, 340, 344, 346, 348, 353–54, 355–56, 361, 367, 372–74, 384, 386, 387, 392, 396, 439, 456, 437–60, 481, 488, 491
Mazaev, Gavriil I., 161, 229, 252–57, 272, 333, 343, 354, 481, 488, 491
Mazaev, Gavriil V., 328
Mazaev, Ivan G., 163, 244–45
Mazaev, Margaret M., 344
Mazaev, Timofeï, 255
Melville, John, 16, 17, 56–57, 76, 95
Memel German Baptist Church, 29–30, 41
Mennonite Brethren, 55–67, 78–81, 286–94
    Alliance movement, 410
    Blankenburg Conference, 290, 410
    close/open communion, 290
    conferences, 77, 78
    congregations, 409–10
    Dorodnitsyn attack, 211, 291–92
    emigration, 79
    exuberance movement, 65–67
    foreign missions, 292–93, 410–12
    German Baptist relations, 68–69, 73–77, 287–89, 291, 311–14, 419, 421–22
    identity, 79–81, 287–88, 421–23
    immersion, 62–63
    June reforms, 66–67
    Kuban, 65
    military exemption, 79
    mission to Russians, 412–15, 420
    Old Mennonite relations, 289–90 406–7, 421–23
    opposition, 63–64
    political challenges, 407–9
    publications, 293–94
    Raduga, 365, 415–16, 418–20
    recognition, 65
    secession, 60–65
    Seventh-day Adventists, 290
    Siberia, 409
    state relations, 291–92, 416–21
    statistics, 67, 78, 286
    Ukrainian baptisms, 98–100, 131
    Ukrainian stundist relations, 97–100, 144–47
    Volga, 68–9, 311

Index

Mennonites, 15–16
   church life 18, 56–57
   Communist suppression, 492
   First World War, 477, 483–88
   institutions, 406–7
   migration into Ukraine, 15
   outside influences, 55–56
   Russian Poland, 48
Meshcherskiĭ, Sophia, 17
Meshcherskiĭ, Vladimir P., 174
Methodists, 460–63, 485
Meyer, August, 34, 37, 304
Meyer, F. B., 385, 397, 470
Meyerson, Theodor Carl, 247
Migration, 272–74
Miliukov, P. N., 337, 478
Miller, Donald, 492
Mission support from abroad, 44, 50, 130, 312–13
Missionerskoe obozrenie, 212
Mladostundism, 116–20, 133
Modén, K. A., 487
Mohn, Anna, 454–55
Mohr, Eugen W., 317, 349, 352, 394–96, 436, 442, 484
Möllersvärd, Carl, 32
Molokans, 8, 135, 146, 150, 152–53, 156, 161–64, 239, 279–80, 435
   New Molokans (Christians of the Evangelical Faith), 147, 163, 280, 329, 391, 458–60
   Old Molokans, 455–57
   Progressive Molokans, 457–58
   Water Molokans, 153, 156
Moravians, 13
Morozov, Grigoriĭ N., 220, 226, 233
Morozova, Efrosiniya (Priska), 98
Morrison, M. A., 234
Moslem Missions, 453–55
Mott, John R., 240, 451
Müller, Friedrich, 208
Müller, Friedrich A., 317
Müller, George, 189–90, 198, 298
Music/hymnals, 116, 135–36, 157, 158–59, 179, 236, 269, 359–60, 365, 427, 428, 432–33, 459
Musokovia, Agafia, 124

Nagirnyak, A. P., 256–57
Nasgowitz, Ludwig, 87–88
Nassipaiko, Ivan 438
Nekrasova, Zinaida, 268
Neprah, Ivan V., 393, 472, 480, 487, 488
Nesdoly, Samuel J., 378
Neudorf German Baptist Church, 52–53, 84, 430
Neufeld, Aganetha, 411
Neufeld, Elise, 293
Neufeld, Heinrich, 63, 64, 66, 98, 100
Neufeld, Hermann A., 290
Neufeld, Peter J., 415
Neuman, 380
Neumann, Adolf, 87–88
Nicholas II, 229, 231, 265, 325–26, 476
Nicolson, William, 182
Niemetz, Ferdinand, 30, 35–36, 38–39, 40–41
Nikolay, Paul, 228, 238, 240–41, 376, 389, 390–91, 451, 452, 459, 462, 464
Nobel, Emanuel, 450–51
North Dakota, 274
Novikov, Olga, 187
Novosil'tseve, 225
Nürnberg, W., 42–44

Oaths, 249, 316
October Revolution, 490
   Communist regime, 490–91
Odintsov, N. V., 408, 472, 491
Odnoi'ko, P. D., 259
Old Believers, 206
Omsk Russian Baptist Church, 333
Oncken, Johann Gerhard, 19–21, 23–25, 29, 72, 73, 80, 88, 94, 154
   trip to St. Petersburg, 39–41
   trip to Ukraine and Dobrudja, 75–76
Oncken, William Sears, 265, 442
Ondra, Franz, 484–85
Ondra, Karl, 43, 52–54, 63, 79, 81, 83–85, 87–88, 113, 137, 194, 305, 315
Onishchenko, Teodor, 103, 104–5
Oryenskiĭ, general, 193
Ossadchiĭ, Ilya, 106
Östling, Eric, 32–33

Packer, J. A., 344–45
Pashkov, Alexandra, 177, 179, 180
Pashkov, Vasiliĭ A., 45, 130, 145–47, 164, 177–82, 184, 192–97, 198, 199–200, 228, 235, 239, 241–42

Pashkov, Vasiliĭ A. (*cont.*)
   conversion, 177–78, 495
   exile, 196
   opposition, 188–90
   preaching, 179
Pashkovite Movement, 135, 177–200, 241–45, 277–78
   immersion, 245, 284
   publications, 182–85
   problems with, 184, 191, 235
   relations with Baptists, 278, 327
   relations with Molokans, 192–93
   relations with sectarians, 192–95
   relations with stundists, 192, 244
   restrictions, 227–29
   social service, 179–82
   spread, 244, 284
   statistics, 327
Patashenko (Pedasenko), Andreĭ, 99
Patmont, Louis R., 406
Pavlik, Mikhaĭlo, 270–71
Pavlov, N. I., 417–19
Pavlov, Pavel, 359, 481, 489–90, 491
Pavlov, Vasiliĭ, 146, 154–60, 162–64, 165, 173, 193–96, 204, 205, 216–17, 220, 222, 224, 229–30, 236, 251–52, 255, 259, 260, 289, 319, 326, 327–28, 330–33, 338–39, 340–41, 342–44, 345–47, 349, 350, 353–54, 355–57, 359, 360–61, 362, 382, 383, 385–86, 395, 397, 424, 433, 447, 457, 458, 480–81, 488, 489, 491
Pelzer, R. W., 446
Penn-Lewis, Jessie, 228–29
Penner, Bernard, 66, 67
Penner, Johann and Anna, 411
Penner, Peter J., 422
Penski, August, 43, 52, 85
Pentecostals, 446, 469–74
   "Jesus Only," 473–4
   Smorodintsy, 474
   Voronaevtsy, 474
Perk, Gerhard, 282
Perk, Peter P., 233, 331–32, 343–44, 359, 365, 416
Permian, M., 441
Persia, 96, 411, 441, 493
Persianov, Aleksandr A., 352, 371, 404, 438
Petasch, Robert, 485
Peters, Hermann, 67

Petitions, 38–39, 128–29, 263–64, 342
Petrick, E., 302, 316
Petrov, N. I., 208
Peuker, Alexandra I., 179, 184, 243, 464
Peuker, Maria G., 182, 184
Pieschevski, Adam, 464
Pietism, 12
Piltz, Heinrich J., 485
Pinkov, 219
Platonov, A. I., 455–56
Plonus, Ch., 39, 42–43, 44, 62
Pobedonostsev, Konstantin, 119–20, 178, 182, 184–85, 188–90, 193, 196, 197, 205–9, 213, 214, 218, 229, 234, 242, 244, 257–58, 264, 265–66, 269, 272–73, 279, 281, 283–85, 326
Podin, Adam K., 302, 349
Political views, 354–57
   anti-revolutionary, 354–55
Popov, Ivan I., 163
Popov, M. F., 375–76
Povlsen, 464
Pravdin, B., 355
Prestridge, J. N., 400
Primachenko, Leon D., 216, 231, 272
Prison ministry, 180, 237, 239
Pritzkau, Ephraim, 107, 112
Pritzkau, Johann, 71–73, 75, 81, 84, 89, 94, 107–8, 112–14, 130, 425, 434, 437–38, 445, 485, 491
Prokhanov, Aleksandr S., 457–58
Prokhanov, Ivan S., 161, 162, 207, 210, 231, 243, 263, 264, 266–69, 272, 326, 335, 337, 339, 341, 346, 348–49, 352, 359, 364–70, 384, 386, 389, 399–401, 403–5, 408, 416, 426, 450, 452, 470, 472, 476–77, 479, 481, 488–89, 497
   publications, 364–66
   relations with Disciples of Christ, 403–5, 466
   relations with Fetler, 367–70
   St. Petersburg Bible Institute, 399–401, 403–5
   vice-president of the Baptist World Alliance, 384–86
Prokhanov, Stepan, 226, 266, 268
Prokhorov, S. I., 472–73
Protestantism, 9–18
   missions in Russia, 14–16
Prugavin, Alexander S., 185, 271

Index

Putintsev, F. M., 355, 460
Puzynin, Andrew, 376

Quakers, 243, 262, 456

Rabinovitz, Joseph, 235, 247–48
Radcliffe, Reginald, 171, 194–95
Radstock, Lord (Granville Augustus William Waldegrave), 169–76, 177–78, 184, 263, 264, 298, 495
   preaching style, 172, 174, 189, 278
Radstock Movement
   critics, 174
   defenders, 175–76
   evangelistic ministry, 171–72
   personal morality, 173
   social ministry, 173
Raduga, 416, 482
Railton, 326
Ratushnyĭ, Mikhail T., 103–7, 115–17, 119, 120–22, 126, 128, 130, 133, 138, 143, 144, 146, 159, 192, 194, 203, 204, 216, 219, 224, 242, 251, 259, 381
Rauschenbusch, August, 86–87, 122, 124–25, 129, 130–31, 203, 312, 320
Rauschenbusch, Walter, 352
Reformed Church, 13–14, 101–2
Regier, Abraham, 339
Regier, Isaak P., 365, 416
Reimer, Adolf A., 403, 413–15, 426, 434
Reimer, C., 413
Reimer, Heinrich, 440
Reimer, Jacob, 61, 66
Reimer, Jakob W., 290, 315, 410, 413, 414, 452
Reimer, Johann, 290
Reimer, Johannes, 45
Reiswig, Phillip, 282
Religious Tract Society, 17–18, 182–85, 190, 235, 450
Rempel, Johannes, 415, 439
Rennikov, Andreĭ M., 478, 483
Riediger, Peter, 412, 41
Riga
   German Baptists, 303–4
   Latvian Baptists, 303–4
Riss, Martins, 42
Rochester Baptist Theological Seminary (German Department), 315
Rockefeller, John D., 443

Rodionov, Semen G., 154–55, 158
Roman Catholics,
   mission activity among, 82–83
   opposition to Baptists, 82, 83
Romanenko, Arkhip, 146
Romania, 272–74, 283
Romanov, Queen Mother Olga, 486
Roosevelt, Theodore, 394, 398
Rosenau, F., 314, 317
Rosenberg, Leon L., 331, 344, 347, 413, 440
Rotaryuk, Josef, 438
Rouse, Ruth, 451
Rozhdestvenskiĭ, Arseniĭ, 127, 140, 194
Rumbergs, Jekabs (Jacob Rumberg), 42, 297, 303, 306–7
Russian Baptist "martyrs," 351
Russsian Baptist Union, 251–54, 325–63
   All-Russian Youth and Sunday School Congress, 332, 344
   confession of faith, 346
   congresses, 251–54, 326–27, 328, 331–32, 342–48, 488
   evangelism, 259
   internal organization, 357–58
   Mazaev leadership, 254–57
   mutual assistance, 260–62
   pastors, 360–61
   regional congresses, 333
   statistics, 327, 362–63
   worship, 257–59, 358–60
Russian Baptists from the Caucasus, 151–65
   church life, 159–61
   expansion, 161–64
   Molokan penetration, 152–56, 161–63
   statistics, 165
Russian Bible Society, 17
Russian Empire
   economy, 5–6
   government, 5–6
   legal system, 274–7
   people, 4–5
   religions, 6–8
Russian Evangelical Alliance, 376
Russian Orthodox Church, 6–7
   All-Russian missionary conferences, 210–11, 336–37
   brotherhoods, 126–7, 211–12, 342
   church weaknesses, 127
   clergy, 6–7

Russian Orthodox Church (*cont.*)
  hostility toward evangelical sectarians, 335–36, 347
  Inner Mission, 209–13, 284
  opposition to Protestantism, 18
  spiritual measures against stundists, 126–27
Russian Poland
  church life, 49–50
  Germans in, 47–51, 427–28
Russkiĭ rabochiĭ, 175, 184, 197
Ryaboshapka, Ivan, 84, 108–9, 114–17, 121–22, 131–33, 135, 137, 138, 139–40, 143, 144, 146, 192, 194–95, 203–4, 216, 223–24, 242, 246, 251

Salberg, Mia, 180
St. Petersburg
  Baltic Baptists, 302
  German Baptists, 42–46, 297–303, 426, 438
  Swedish Baptists, 301, 302
St. Petersburg congress (1884), 192
St. Petersburg Evangelical City Mission, 183
Salmi, Hjalmar, 461–62
Salvation Army, 456, 464–65, 486
Samson, George W., 129, 130
Sarwe, William, 459
Savel'ev, I. K., 331, 347, 349, 372, 386, 488
Savel'ev, Teodor S., 284, 376
Sazontovna, Palageya, 233
Schaff, Philip, 128
Schellenberg, David, 291
Schiek, John, 273–74
Schiewe, Adam Reinhold, 45–46, 243
  banishment (1877), 87–88
  banishment (1895), 302
  Estonia, 308–10
  St. Petersburg, 45–46, 296, 298–302
Schirrmann, Gottlieb, 87–88
Schismatics, 7–8
Schleuning, A., 312
Schmidt, Martin, 349, 352–53, 394, 396, 400–401, 403, 404, 481, 487–88
Schmidt, Nicolaï, 410
Schmidt, Peter P., 410
Schulz, A. M., 444–45
Schulz, William, 81–82, 121
Schwan, F., 40, 43, 299

Schweiger, F., 431
Sears, Bernas, 20
Sectarian rights, publications on, 341
Seibel, W. K., 438
Selenius, Alexander, 33
Semerenko, Josef A., 218–19
Sendbote, Der, 314–15
Serbulsky, Mathew, 99
Seventh-day Adventists, 274, 282–83, 309, 313, 320, 438, 446, 468–69, 485
Shakespeare, J. H., 348, 350, 351, 385, 400, 439
Shcherbatov, N. R., 478
Shcherbina, F. A., 105, 143
Sherer, I. I., 233
Shuvalova, Helena I., 243
Siemens, Johann, 80
Sievers, Count, 40–41, 67, 129
Signeul, Oscar E., 301
Simoleit, Friedrich W., 390
Simons, George A., 340, 380, 461, 463, 485, 490
Simons, George Henry, 461
Sinieck, 37–38
Skaldin, W., 438
Skobolev, M. I., 478
Skvortsov, Dmitriĭ, I., 228
Skvortsov, Vasiliĭ M., 126, 208–10, 212, 275, 289, 377–78, 380, 459
Smorodin, Nikolaĭ, 472–74
Society for the Distribution of the Holy Scripture in Russia, 95, 234–35
Society for the Encouragement of Spiritual and Ethical Reading (Pashkovite), 182–83, 190, 197
Society for the Spread of Religious Enlightenment (Russian Orthodox), 212
Soloveĭ, Alekseĭ, 120
Sorokhodov, Ivan N., 146, 162
Spingath, A., 485
Spurgeon, Charles Haddon, 161, 184, 236, 386
Stadling, Jonas, 267, 309
Stanislavskiĭ, Father, 478
Stead, William T., 182, 193–94, 196, 271, 464
Steane, Edward J., 129
Steeves, Paul, 367, 378, 384
Stefanovich, Andreĭ, 447

Index

Stepanov, 472-73
Stepanov, Semen P., 349, 352, 360, 362-63, 376, 383-84
Stepanov, Vasilii P., 346-47, 348, 372, 375, 386, 491
Stepanovich, Andreï I., 391, 458
Stokes, James, 450-51
Stoltenhoff, August H., 305
Stolypin, Peter A., 337, 340, 347, 350, 418, 420, 463, 464
Stoyalov, Alexeï A., 163
Stoyalov, Andreï A., 146
Stoyanov, A., 225
Strel'bitskii, I., 206, 208-9
Stretton, Hesba, 271
Strigun, Anton, 192
Ströter, Ernst, 410
Ströter, professor, 315
Strzelez, Karl, 428
Stundism-German, 12
Stundism-Ukrainian, 93-110, 132-50
    anti-stundist poems, 212
    Baptist claims, 276
    beginnings, 103-10
    charge of socialism, 142
    cult of suffering, 127
    economic and social factors, 93-94
    faith and order, 132-34
    immersions, 98-99
    indigenous factors, 147-50
    morality, 138-40
    ordinances, 137-38
    relations to *Narodniks*, 132-43
    relations with Mennonite Brethren, 96-100, 145-47
    repression, 120-31, 144
    social and economic life, 140-43
    statistics, 165, 283-84
    worship, 127, 134-38
Stundo-Baptism, 111-20, 132-50, 277
    growth of hostility, 205-9
    immersions, 111-14, 116
    legal measures, 213-14
    legal system, 274-77
    Orthodox counter measures, 209-13
    suppression, 204-5, 213-14, 215-31
    survival, 249-77
Stunt, W. T., 455
Sukkau, Heinrich P., 414
Svennson, Johannes, 329, 459

Swedish Mission Covenant, 240-41, 308
Sweeney, Z. T., 404, 466

Taft, William Howard, 348, 351, 398
Tarajan, Patvakan, 245, 260, 262, 274
Taran, Yakov, 114
Tatford, F. A., 455
Templer (The Friends of Jerusalem), 60
Ter-Asaturon, K. A., 246, 260
Tereshchuk, 123
Terletskii, G. I., 169, 185, 191, 192, 194, 198
Terletskii, Vladimir, 126
Tettermann (Tetermann), Andrew, 310, 426-27
Theological education
    Alliance Bible School, The, 390-91, 409-10
    Astrakhanka Seminary and Teacher's Training School, 391-93, 418-20
    German Baptist Seminary, Lodz, 393-96
    Moscow Baptist Theological Seminary (1993), 402
    Russian Baptist Theological Seminary (proposed), 390-402
    St. Petersburg Bible Institute, 399-400
Thielmann, Martin and Augusta, 453-55
Thielmann, Peter, 409
Tiedtke, J., 317
Tiflis Russian Baptist Church, 154, 157-59, 259
Timoshenko, Daniel, 338
Timoshenko, Mikhail D., 338, 341, 353, 382, 480, 481, 488
Tobacco, use of, 85, 138, 160, 435-36
Tolstoy, Leo, 175, 181, 237, 267, 281
Tolstoy, M., 174
Tract societies, 17-18
Tracts, 96, 180, 183, 185
Treskovskii, V. N., 158-59, 160
Truderung, Oskar G., 344, 394, 428, 432, 440
Tsimbal, Efim, 108, 113
Turkestan (Turkmenistan), 409, 453-55
Tuszek, Wihelm, 485

Udarov, Dimitrii, 193
Ukrainian peasants, 141
Underground publications, 266-69
Unger, Abraham, 63, 64, 66, 69, 72, 76, 79, 80, 84, 98, 100, 113-14, 287

Unger, Cornelius, 63
Unruh, Abraham, 417
Unruh, Heinrich, 290, 293, 411
Unruh, Kornelius, 411
Unruh, Peter, 410, 413
Urlaub, Johann, 352, 399, 402
Urshan, Andrew D., 473–74
Ushinskiĭ, A. D., 119, 250
Uspenskiĭ, Gleb I., 162
Üxküll, Woldemar, 310, 314, 327–28, 330, 355, 390, 393–95, 437, 452, 470

Val'kevich, Viktor L., 206–8, 237, 239, 250, 266
Velitsyn, A. A., 208–9
Veltistov, K. I., 81, 87–88
Vertograd, 243
Viebann, George von, 390
Vining, A. J., 350–51, 397
Vins (Wiens), Jakob, 349, 360, 380, 382, 391–92, 413–15, 491
Vins, Peter, 491
Vogel, Julius K., 89
Volga
    German Baptists, 310–13
    Mennonite Brethren mission, 68–69
Volhynia
    German Baptists in, 51–54
    Migration to, 51–52
Vollrath, Paul and Anna, 454–55
Voronaev, Ivan E., 474
Voronin, N. I., 135, 146, 152–54, 155, 156, 157–58, 159, 163, 165, 223, 260, 326–27
Vostorgov, Ioann I., 347, 351, 477
Vvedenskiĭ, Alexander I., 377
Vyasovskiĭ, 360

Wagner, Georg, 274
Ward de Charrière, Elizabeth. 175–76
Warns, Johannes, 338, 390
Weiss, Konrad, 99
Weist, Wilhelm, 48
Wenske, Eduard, 432
Wieler, Franz, 66
Wieler, Gerhard, 63–67, 69, 97–99
Wieler, Johann, 43, 66, 76, 80, 81, 106, 108, 114–16, 120, 124, 130, 134, 135, 144–47, 148–49, 153, 163, 216, 224–25, 242, 251–52, 287, 301, 412, 458
    relations with Ukrainian stundists, 114–16, 134, 144–47
Wieler, Johann, Sr., 66
Wiens, Franz, 411
Wiens, Jakob, 409
Wiens, Johann, 411
Wilkin, Martin H., 125
Willms, August, 99
Wolf, Minna, 454–55
Women, 133–34, 161, 242–43, 361–62, 381–82
World's Student Christian Federation, 451
Wrede, Henrik, 239
Wrede, Mathilda, 237, 239
Wuerch, Eduard A., 485
Wüst, Eduard, 57–60
    mission festivals, 58
    opposition, 59–60
    preaching 58

Yakovlev, N. J., 459
Yanyshev, Ioann, 178
Yasevich-Borodaevskaya, V. I., 271
Yasnovsky (Yasnovskiĭ), Maria N., 173, 244, 344, 349, 352, 361, 362
YMCA, 450–51
Young, Edward, 129

Zaïtsev, D. V., 456
Zakharov, Grigor, 392, 459
Zakharov, Zinoviĭ D., 163, 194, 251, 252, 280, 330, 337, 355–56, 380, 384, 392, 458–60, 452
Zaozerskiĭ, N., 206, 213
Zaremba, Felician, 14
Zasetskaya, Julia (Yuliya), 171, 175, 180, 198
Zavitnevich, V., 155, 160
Zebrowski, Waclaw, 466
Zhabin, S., 456
Zhapko-Potapovich, Lev, 195
Zheltov, F. A., 456
Zhidkov, Ivan I., 185, 233–34
Zhidkov, Jacob, 234
Zhidkov, Mikhail, 234
Zimmerman, Israel, 83
Zin'kivs'kyĭ, Trokhym, 270
Zinov'ev, S. P., 459
Znachko-Yavorskiĭ, Aleksandr, 103, 142

www.ingramcontent.com/pod-product-compliance
Lightning Source LLC
Chambersburg PA
CBHW080530300426
44111CB00017B/2667